INDUSTRIAL ORGANIZATION

INDUSTRIAL ORGANIZATION

THEORY, EVIDENCE, AND PUBLIC POLICY

Kenneth W. Clarkson

Professor of Economics
and
Director, Law and Economics Center
University of Miami

Roger LeRoy Miller

Professor of Economics
and
Associate Director, Law and Economics Center
University of Miami

McGRAW-HILL BOOK COMPANY

New York   St. Louis   San Francisco   Auckland   Bogotá
Hamburg   Johannesburg   London   Madrid   Mexico   Montreal   New Delhi
Panama   Paris   São Paulo   Singapore   Sydney   Tokyo   Toronto

This book was set in Times Roman by Better Graphics.
The editors were Bonnie E. Lieberman and Jonathan Palace;
the production supervisor was John Mancia.
The drawings were done by VIP Graphics.
The cover was designed by Miriam Reccio.
R. R. Donnelley & Sons Company was printer and binder.

INDUSTRIAL ORGANIZATION

Theory, Evidence, and Public Policy

1 2 3 4 5 6 7 8 9 0 DODO 8 9 8 7 6 5 4 3 2 1

ISBN 0-07-042036-X

Library of Congress Cataloging in Publication Data

Clarkson, Kenneth W.
    Industrial organization.

    Includes indexes.
      1. Industrial organization (Economic theory)
2. Microeconomics. 3. Industry and state.
I. Miller, Roger LeRoy. II. Title.
HD2326.C52   338.6   81-17200
ISBN 0-07-042036-X   AACR2

CONTENTS

PREFACE

The relevant market for industrial organization texts has a concentration ratio of somewhere between 60 and 80 percent. According to the standard industrial organization theory, a concentration ratio in this range creates a significant barrier to entry. More recent developments in industrial organization theory, however, deemphasize concentration and its relationships to entry, profitability, and other performance outcomes. Both new and old approaches to industrial organization focus on the importance of product characteristics in determining a firm's share in the market and its ultimate performance. That is where this book comes in. We believe there are five characteristics that make this book a viable competitor in the highly concentrated industrial organization textbook market.

INTEGRATION OF TRADITIONAL AND RECENT THEORIES

First, our text has interwoven both the standard industrial organization theory and hundreds of accompanying empirical studies with recent developments in the theory of firm behavior and market outcomes. Because these empirical studies draw heavily on microeconomic theory, we have added a small number of appendixes and sections focusing on the relevant tools of price theory. This permits the book to be used with a minimum of one semester of microeconomics. We have reviewed industrial organization studies for the past four decades and have incorporated those that are particularly important for understanding industrial organization today.

EMPHASIS ON PUBLIC POLICY

Second, we have fully integrated the economics of industrial organization with current questions involving public policy, particularly as they relate to judicial decisions and administrative regulations. In that regard we have included a separate chapter discussing the development of legal views of competition and monopoly; an appendix explains how to do legal research in the industrial organization field. Another chapter focuses on current antitrust and trade regulation decisions. A chapter on administrative and regulatory agencies is also included. Each chapter focuses on the interaction of industrial organization and public policy.

MARKET ORIENTATION

Third, to enter such a highly concentrated market, we know that our product must meet consumer demands. To that end we have relied heavily on suggestions and comments from a number of professors who teach and conduct research in the field of industrial organization. The McGraw-Hill Book Company's external reviewers and several other individuals on earlier drafts of the manuscript, rigorously provided comments, and we have attempted to include all of them in one form or another in the text that follows. We have also incorporated comments from those directly involved in the public policy process, including input from the staff of the Department of Justice and the U.S. Senate. In addition, portions of the book have been used extensively in undergraduate and graduate economics of industry classes at the University of Virginia, as well as in economic analysis courses at the University of Miami School of Law.

UNIQUE CHAPTERS

While we have mainly organized the chapters in response to colleagues' comments and suggestions, there are some chapters that we feel are unique. They are as follows:

Chapter 11—Price Discrimination: Methods and Applications The entire chapter is devoted to the types of price discrimination and resulting applications.

Chapter 19—Antitrust and the Courts Today Current antitrust and trade regulation policies are treated concisely.

Chapter 20—Regulatory Agencies Extensive coverage of administrative agencies and their regulations are included.

SPECIAL APPENDIXES

In addition to the unique chapters, we have included a number of special appendixes that provide further insights into understanding industrial organization. These include:

Appendix B to Chapter 2—The Present Value Criterion Provides fundamentals for understanding intertemporal industrial organization problems.

Appendix to Chapter 4—Measurement Problems Focuses on the difficulties of obtaining accurate measures of market structure and performance.

Appendix to Chapter 18—Legal Research Provides basic background in legal research for public policy industrial organization analysis.

ACKNOWLEDGMENTS

To thank all who have contributed to this volume would turn a short preface into a long chapter. However, we must extend our special thanks to those who painfully reviewed various drafts, including William P. Albrecht, University of Iowa; Roger Beck, University of Alberta; Thomas Borcherding, Simon Fraser University; Andrew Caverly, Department of Justice; Louis De Alessi, University of Miami; John Diehl from the law firm of Nixon, Hargrave, Devans & Doyle, Rochester, N.Y.; Robert Feinberg, Pennsylvania State University; Thomas D. Hall, University of Hawaii; William Hosek, University of Nebraska; Robin Kaperst, University of Miami School of Law; James MacDonald, U.S. Department of Agriculture; William MacLeod from the law firm of McDermott, Will & Emery, Chicago, Ill.; Sharon Oster, Yale University; Richard Rosenberg, Pennsylvania State University; T. Y. Shen, University of California; Henry Steele, University of Houston; Philip Ward, legislative aide in the U.S. Senate; and Steve Wiggins, Texas A&M University.

We also extend our appreciation to Judith Miley at the University of Miami Law and Economics Center, who often improved the presentation of ideas, and to Jonathan Palace and others at McGraw-Hill for their numerous editorial and technical contributions. Finally, we especially thank Linda Craig and Sharon Marsh for their valuable administrative and secretarial contributions.

The first edition of any book is only the beginning, and we encourage those who use our text to share with us their thoughts as well as their individual contributions to the field.

Kenneth W. Clarkson
Roger LeRoy Miller

CHAPTER 1

INTRODUCTION

Traditionally, the study of industrial organization investigates the structure of firm sizes, the causes of this structure, and the effects of the structure upon markets. It also places relatively more emphasis on empirical studies of the factors that influence the structure and performance of firms than do other areas of economic inquiry. Equally important, industrial organization focuses largely on public policy questions posed by antitrust laws and regulation. In this sense the field of industrial organization is an extension and application of basic price theory.[1]

THE SCOPE OF INDUSTRIAL ORGANIZATION

Over 12 million business firms exist or operate in the United States, ranging in size from the smallest corner newsstand with a few hundred dollars' worth of assets a year to American Telephone and Telegraph with $113.8 billion in assets in 1979.[2] Of the three basic forms of business organization—proprietorship, partnership, and corporation—the bulk of firms are proprietorships and partnerships, in which one or more individuals own all the resources of the firm and are fully responsible for the operation of the firm. There are over 10 million such small proprietorships and partnerships in the United States. More than a million and a half firms have taken on the corporate form of business organization. Those approximately 1.6 million corporations generate more than twice as much **accounting profit** as the 10 million small proprietorships and partnerships.

---

[1] Some even maintain that there is no separate field of industrial organization. See, for example, George Stigler, *The Organization of Industry* (Homewood, Ill.: Irwin, 1968), p. 1.

[2] *Fortune*, July 14, 1980, p. 158.

Basically, corporations generate the bulk of manufacturing activity in the United States. Of the 1.6 million corporations in existence, the largest 200 manufacturing corporations generate more than half of all manufacturing sales. Clearly, we will have to study in detail the corporate form of ownership in the United States if we are to understand the economics of U.S. manufacturing and related industries.

ORIGINS OF THE PUBLIC CONCERN OVER INDUSTRY

A significant portion of industrial study focuses on large industrial firms. Large firms are generally believed to develop and behave in a manner that restricts entry into the industry, thus limiting their competition. The ultimate result may be the formation of a **monopoly**. Fear of this sort of development has fostered a large degree of legislation and regulation.

As far back as the fourth century B.C., monarchs realized that political power controls markets and that controlling entry into a market could lead to higher profits for those given that privilege. Salt, tea, and other goods with relatively inelastic demands have often been the subject of royal monopoly. The Ptolemaics in Egypt established royal monopolies between the fourth and first centuries B.C. Later the Roman emperors acted similarly between the first and third centuries B.C. Monopoly privileges were dispensed to nobles by rulers during the Middle Ages and later were given to trading companies and guilds. The granting of legal monopolies to private parties continues to this day.

Legal monopolies may be granted by all levels of government, and they may be taken away. For example, at the federal level the Civil Aeronautics Board (CAB) granted air routes to a select few companies. Furthermore, until recently the CAB regulated prices and dimensions of service quality of the airlines who had been given these routes. The new deregulation programs of the CAB reversed this trend, eroding its power to regulate prices and to prohibit new entrants from serving existing routes.

Monopolies also occur at the local level. In the smallest towns, business regulations in the form of special licenses to operate a business or provide a service are granted and revoked. In other cases, zoning laws effectively prohibit entry of new gas stations, restaurants, or other specific types of business establishments.

Unjust Monopoly Prices

Aristotle wrote often about the unjust prices charged by a monopolist. In a now-famous quote, Adam Smith wrote in 1776 that "[p]eople of the same trade seldom meet together, even for merriment and diversion, but the conversation ends in a conspiracy against the public, or in some contrivance to raise prices."[3] In an attempt to counter monopolies, laws against private monopolies

[3] Adam Smith, *The Wealth of Nations* (New York: Random House, 1937), p. 128.

started in ancient Babylonia and India. In England, the Parliament even started to limit the right of kings to grant royal monopolies when it passed the Statute of Monopolies in 1624.

Natural Monopolies and Their Regulation

A **natural monopoly** is said to exist if long-run average total costs decline throughout the relevant range of outputs. If total costs of producing any given output are to be minimized, production should be carried out by a single firm. In part, this natural monopoly argument has been used to rationalize public regulation of transportation through the Interstate Commerce Commission and the CAB. In addition, we have seen other government regulatory agencies formed for the purpose of regulating natural gas distribution, telephone service, and the generation of electric power.

Other Forms of Monopoly and Their Control

We have discussed legally granted monopolies and natural monopolies. The third kind of monopoly is the simple, private, so-called artificial monopoly formed by collusion, merger, or a host of other methods designed to restrict production and raise prices to the monopoly level. Economists in the United States have not been unanimously in favor of regulating or even attempting to regulate artificial monopolies. One group felt that combinations in trusts in the nineteenth century were the result of vigorous competition or cost savings. It was thought that if monopoly power obtained by trusts was exercised too much, entry would cause prices to fall. Earlier in this century, a growing number of economists began to doubt this line of reasoning. Today it appears that the majority opinion is one of severe doubt or incredulity over this initial line of reasoning. It is now a minority view that entry outside of the colluding parties will regulate artificial monopolies.

By the late 1800s, both Republicans and Democrats were against trusts and combinations and sought new legislation to constrain them. This resulted in passage of the Sherman Act in 1890 and the Clayton and Federal Trade Commission Acts in 1914. It was not until a number of years later, particularly in the 1930s, that many economists started to side with legislators and laypersons in their distrust of artificial monopolies. It was also in the 1930s that new theories of market structure began to appear. Some economists believed that the polar extremes of pure competition and pure monopoly did not describe the U.S. economy very well. In 1933, for example, both Joan Robinson of Cambridge, England, and Edward Chamberlin of Cambridge, Massachusetts, published books putting forth theories of imperfect, or monopolistic, competition. These theories placed themselves squarely between the two polar extreme models just mentioned. While many questions were answered by their works, others were not, particularly one question regarding behavior and performance of firms in an industry that has a large number of firms, but that cannot be properly analyzed by the competitive model. When economists tried to analyze this problem, the field of industrial organization began to take shape.

INDUSTRIAL ORGANIZATION AS A FIELD

Industrial organization as a separate economic field, or specialty, is a relatively recent phenomenon. The label "industrial organization" and the initial impetus to study it came from Harvard University in the late 1930s. Prior to that time, there were descriptive institutional courses in the fields of corporations, agriculture, marketing, utilities, financial organizations, and trusts. These courses were generally not integrated with economic theory. According to Grether,[4] it was the Great Depression coupled with the publication of Berle and Means' *The Modern Corporation and Private Property* in 1932 that led to a demand for a more basic theoretical/empirical approach to the use of economics in understanding business institutions. Additionally, the hearings, studies, and final report of the Temporary National Economic Committee on the concentration of economic power in the late 1930s provided further impetus and apparently welcomed empirical materials for such an approach.

At Harvard, Professors Chamberlin and Mason began the first truly *industrial organization* course. As an introduction to a collection of essays he started writing in 1936, Mason characterized the study of business organizations as "eclectic methodology" and as a "muddy, but not uninteresting, field."[5] Empirical studies started to come out of Harvard at an increasing rate. They included Wallace's study on market control in the aluminum industry[6] and numerous others surveyed by Bain in 1948.[7]

In the late 1930s and early 1940s, the primary interest of investigators in industrial organization was pricing policy or, according to Mason in a 1938 position paper, "the deliberative action of buyers and sellers to influence price" and, in particular, the policies of large industrial firms.[8] All these case studies and empirical work generally focused on theoretical structures associated with pure monopoly. In this context, markets and market structures "must be defined with reference to the position of a single seller or buyer."[9] By 1948 Bain, one of the earliest of Mason's Ph.D.s in the field, had become dissatisfied. He concluded that empirical research until then had made "little definite progress in establishing an objective classification of markets, with subcategories

---

[4] Ewald T. Grether, "Industrial Organization: Past History and Future Problems," *American Economic Review*, vol. 60 (May 1970), pp. 83–89.

[5] Edward S. Mason, *Economic Concentration and the Monopoly Problem* (Cambridge, Mass.: Harvard University Press, 1957), pp. 4, 8.

[6] Donald H. Wallace, *Market Control in the Aluminum Industry* (Cambridge, Mass.: Harvard University Press, 1937).

[7] Joe S. Bain, "Price and Production Policies," in H. S. Ellis, ed., *A Survey of Contemporary Economics* (Homewood, Ill.: Irwin, 1948), pp. 129–173.

[8] Edward S. Mason, "Price and Production Policies of Large-Scale Enterprise," *American Economic Review*, Supplement (March 1939), p. 55.

[9] Ibid., p. 65.

which would contain industries with uniform and distinctive types of competitive behavior."[10]

Approach to Industrial Organization

One of the major concerns in the development of industrial organization has been the quality of performance, including efficiency, in a particular industry. Indeed, some have said that examining quality of performance is the goal of industrial organization. Industrial organization, then, should be able to help us understand what makes for good or bad performance in an industry. This understanding can assist public policy formation by indicating those ways that will make the economy perform "better." The common framework of analysis in industrial organization has thus become the so-called market structure-conduct-performance approach in which one studies the interrelationships between structure, conduct, and performance, often assuming that structure determines conduct, which in turn determines performance. In most analyses causal relationship goes directly from structure to performance results or from structure to combined conduct-performance results in which business conduct is, in essence, inferred from performance results. To quote Richard Caves, "Market structure is important because the structure determines the behavior of firms in the industry and that behavior in turn determines the quality of industries' performance."[11] Recently the joint interrelationships and dynamics among structure variables, conduct, actions, and performance outcomes have been recognized. In other words, if firms adaptively respond or react, they will alter conduct and/or structure.[12]

In Figure 1-1 we put in schematic form the structure-conduct-performance framework for industrial organization analysis, adding the basic demand and supply conditions.

Market Structure   Market or industry structure refers to those attributes of the market that influence the nature of the competitive process. Market structure thus includes size and size distribution of firms, barriers and conditions of entry, and product differentiation, as well as firm cost structure and the degree of government regulation.

Certain types of antitrust laws deal directly with market structure. For example, Section 7 of the Clayton Act (amended) deals directly with market structure by focusing on the number of firms in the industry. It prohibits the

---

[10] Bain, op. cit., p. 158.

[11] Richard Caves, *American Industry: Structure, Conduct, and Performance*, 2d ed. (Englewood Cliffs, N.J.: Prentice-Hall, 1967), p. 16.

[12] See Almarin Phillips, "Structure, Conduct, and Performance—and Performance, Conduct, and Structure?" in Jesse W. Markham and Gustav F. Papanek, eds., *Industrial Organization and Economic Development: In Honor of E. S. Mason* (Boston: Houghton Mifflin, 1970), pp. 26–37. See also William L. Baldwin, "The Feedback Effect of Business Conduct on Industry Structure," *Journal of Law and Economics*, vol. 12 (April 1969), pp. 123–153.

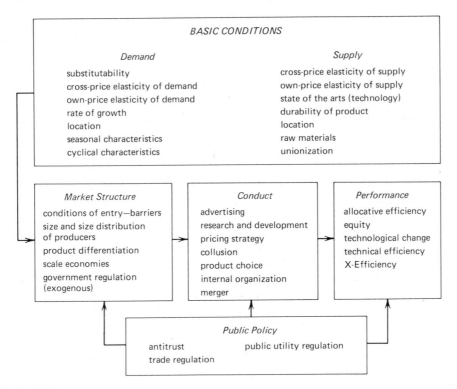

FIGURE 1-1
Traditional industrial organization framework.

development of market structure via the merger route that might discourage competition or encourage a monopoly. Here it is clear that the structure-conduct-performance link is firmly accepted as fact by legislators. Market structure is important because such structure determines the behavior of firms, which then determines the quality of the industry's performance.

However, encompassing the activities of large, diversified corporations within the framework of the structure-conduct-performance analysis creates a serious problem. In particular, how does one apply the market structure framework to such corporations? Some allege that large corporations are free of market competitive forces.[13] But if large corporations are indeed free of market pressures, isn't it futile to analyze their behavior and performance results in the market structure framework just outlined?

There is also difficulty in actually measuring the elements of structure, with the exception of the number of firms and the measures of concentration. Measurement of market structure has not seriously progressed in recent years.

[13] See, for example, John K. Galbraith, *American Capitalism: The Concept of Countervailing Power*, rev. ed. (Boston: Houghton Mifflin, 1956).

Conduct   Market structure affects the actual operation and conduct of individual firms. Market structure may, for example, influence internal organization of the firm, including some employment policies, working conditions, and other factors that directly or indirectly affect the allocation of resources within the firm and the products provided by it. Determining the conduct of firms in a market involves studying their product designs and differentiation, the way they establish prices, and the advertising and sales promotion activities they engage in. At this point we ask questions about the degree to which they collude, whether collusion is open or implicit, the degree to which they engage in research and development, and how responsive they are to changes in their economic and legal environment. When we look at certain market conduct phenomena, such as cartelization and collusion, we ask the question, "Are collusive agreements, when existent, durable?"

Performance   Market performance is the appraisal of how the economy satisfies specified goals, including, but not limited to, efficiency, growth, equity, and employment. In order to make performance judgments, normative economics must be utilized. The only way we can assess the "goodness" or "badness" of an industry's or an economy's performance is by first postulating normative goals or by placing values implicitly or explicitly on the costs and benefits of different outcomes of industry structure and conduct.

Recent work, however, has weakened the determinacy conditions of the structure-conduct-performance approach. In addition, the dynamic properties of the market have been more heavily emphasized. Thus past performance may be linked with current structure, which in turn determines current conduct and performance.

Recent Trends in Industrial Organization

A number of variations and expansions in the field of industrial organization have occurred since the initial Harvard approach. While Harvard concentrated on industry studies that can be classified as descriptive in nature, varying schools of thought have approached industrial organization in a different manner. The Harvard studies led primarily to the structure-conduct-performance approach that was developed by Bain, Caves, and others. In contrast, the Chicago school relied more on applied price theory in the context of a logical deductive system. In this approach Stigler and others at Chicago treated industrial organization as a logical extension of price theory with a heavy emphasis on empirical testing. This approach relied less on institutional frameworks.

In addition to these methodological differences, industrial organization has become more quantitative over time. In recent years studies have focused more on statistical examinations of interfirm and interindustry differences in explaining behavior and performance.

Industrial organization has also expanded the types of topics studied. For example, in recent years extensive investigations have been conducted of the internal structure and organization of firms and how that organization affects behavior. Oliver Williamson, Armen Alchian, and others are associated with this line of inquiry.

Despite the differences in approaches, each method seeks to answer common questions. What determines differences in the market organization? What factors cause differences in profitability among firms and across industries? To what extent can the structure of the firms themselves determine their product choices, their methods of marketing, their pricing policies, and other dimensions of firm behavior? Different approaches have focused on benefits from and costs of diversification, mergers, and differences in plant sizes, as well as on the factors that determine investment and technological innovation.[14]

DEFINING INDUSTRIAL ORGANIZATION

We have made reference to industrial organization as a concept. It is appropriate for us to be more specific in our definition before we go on. Clearly, "industrial organization" really does not tell anybody outside of economics what the subject means or is all about. Industrial organization as a subject does not tell one how to organize a firm. It clearly is not a course in the form of organization and management of industrial enterprises. The formal definition here will be limited to the following:

> **Industrial organization** is a specialty in economics that helps to explain why markets are organized as they are and how their organization affects the way these markets work.

Thus, the study of industrial organization attracts those individuals interested in the way in which industries are organized, what factors influence a firm's behavior, and how these factors affect society in general. The focus of interest in the past, in the present, and probably in the future centers on national economic problems caused by different types of market organization. Industrial organization is intricately tied up with serious public policy questions concerning the desirability of mergers between large firms, antitrust action against existing firms, the possibility of unlawful price fixing, and so on.

Boundaries of the Field

It is interesting to see what has happened to the field since it started in the 1930s. Today the American Economic Association uses a form of classification given in Table 1-1. Here we see that industrial organization is broken into four major subheadings:

1 Industrial organization and public policy
2 The economics of technological change

---

[14] Values play an important role in answering questions raised by such analyses and in ensuing policy determinations. See Herbert H. Liebhafsky, *American Government & Business* (New York: Wiley, 1971) and Duncan MacRae, Jr., *The Social Function of Social Sciences* (New Haven: Yale University Press, 1976).

3 Industry studies
4 Economic capacity

Within those four broad categories, there are a large number of subheadings that are further divided into sub-subheadings. Thus, the field of industrial organization today covers everything from monopolistic theory to public enterprises, location theory to the effects of taxes and subsidies on research and development, and industry studies in every major industry in the country.

Industrial organization as it is studied today is primarily concerned with those decentralized free enterprise markets characteristic of much of the United States economy. To be sure, many of the principles derived from an industrial organization study can be applied to other types of economic systems, such as socialist and centrally planned economies. But that application would require the field of industrial organization to become even larger than it is today. Furthermore, in order to keep a book of this size manageable, our applications must be concerned primarily with product markets in the manufacturing sector of the economy rather than with agricultural, service, and labor markets.

OUR APPROACH TO INDUSTRIAL ORGANIZATION

Much of the industrial organization literature has explained firm and industry or market outcomes using a partial equilibrium approach, with explanations of how firms interact to produce outcomes based on explicit assumptions about the structure of the industry. As we have seen, this approach has given rise to the structure-conduct-performance paradigm where structure implies conduct, which in turn determines performance. More recent developments in industrial organization focus more on the simultaneous determination of structure and performance using economic theory. Here emphasis is placed on those factors that determine a firm's behavior and how industry structure results from that behavior. In the subsequent chapters, we depart somewhat from the traditional focus on the standard models of competition—monopoly and oligopoly—as the major explanation of firm and market outcomes. We recognize that these models are useful, but they are often incomplete in that they leave unexplained a considerable amount of firm behavior and market outcomes. In this volume we will include a traditional price-theory approach to provide additional insights into industrial organization concerns. At the same time, we will cover the traditional models and representative empirical studies based on these models.

Remember, then, that we will be attempting ultimately to determine how *market* processes (as opposed to political, sociological, or psychological processes) direct the activities of producers in meeting consumer demands. In particular, we will be examining the conditions under which these processes might break down and what governmental policies might be called for to "modify" them in order to improve the performance of an industry (assuming we know what "improve" means).

In Unit I, we will focus on firm and market structure. The chapters in this

TABLE 1-1
INDUSTRIAL ORGANIZATION

I. **Industrial Organization and Public Policy**
   A. Industrial Organization and Market Structure
      1. General
      2. Monopolistic theory
      3. Government policy
      4. Monopolistic aspects of commercial banking
      5. Monopolistic aspects in transport
   B. Public Policy toward Monopoly and Competition
      1. General
      2. Public utility regulation
      3. Policy toward agriculture
      4. Policy toward transportation
      5. Policy toward commercial banks
   C. Public Utilities and Government Regulation of Other Industries in the Private Sector
   D. Public Enterprises
   E. Economics of Transportation
      1. General
      2. Urban transportation
      3. Port aspects of shipping
      4. Airports other than purely transport aspect
      5. Subsidies
      6. Location theory
II. **Economics of Technological Change**
   A. Technological Change; Innovation; Research and Development
      1. General
      2. Relationship to growth models
      3. Technological unemployment theory
   B. Technological Change and Innovation
   C. Research and Development
      1. General
      2. Effects of taxes and subsidies
      3. Depreciation allowances

unit examine the theory of the firm (Chapter 2), various measures of market structure (Chapter 3), and the relationship between market structure and performance (Chapter 4). Unit II describes models of industries and markets. Primary emphasis is given to competition and monopoly (Chapter 5), oligopoly (Chapter 6), and monopolistic competition (Chapter 7). In Unit III, we focus on specific aspects—firm behavior and pricing rules (Chapter 8), advertising, product differentiation, and trademarks (Chapter 9), price discrimination (Chapters 10 and 11), delivered price systems, exclusive dealing, and reciprocal buying (Chapter 12), and administered prices, price rigidity, and fair trade laws (Chapter 13). Next, we analyze forms of collusion (Chapter 14) before turning to questions of vertical integration and mergers (Chapter 15). Barriers to entry (Chapter 16) and technological innovation, copyrights, and patents (Chapter 17) conclude this unit. The final unit, Unit IV, looks at public policy and is organized into chapters on law (Chapter 18), the courts and antitrust (Chapter 19),

TABLE 1-1 *(continued)*
INDUSTRIAL ORGANIZATION

III. Industry Studies
   A. General: Articles Relating to All Industrial Sectors
   B. Industry Studies: Manufacturing
      1. General
      2. Metals (iron, steel, and other)
      3. Machinery (tools, electrical equipment, and appliances)
      4. Transportation and communication equipment
      5. Chemicals, drugs, plastics, ceramics, glass, and rubber
      6. Textiles, leather, and clothing
      7. Forest products, building materials, and paper
      8. Food processing (excluding agribusiness), tobacco, and beverages
      9. Other industries
   C. Industry Studies: Extractive Industries
      1. General
      2. Mining (metal, coal, and other nonmetallic minerals)
      3. Oil, gas, and other fuels
   D. Industry Studies: Distributive Trades
      1. General
      2. Wholesale trade
      3. Retail trade
   E. Industry Studies: Services and Related Industries
      1. General
      2. Electrical, communication, and information services
      3. Personal services
      4. Business and legal services
      5. Repair services
      6. Insurance
      7. Real estate
      8. Entertainment, recreation, tourism
IV. Economic Capacity

---

and regulatory agencies (Chapter 20). Appendixes appear in Chapters 1, 2, 3, 4, 7, and 18 to clarify terms and concepts.

APPENDIX: Methodology and the Nature of the Concern

Industrial organization is a part of economics, which is considered a social science. Economics is an empirical science that focuses on both positive theory and normative judgments.

POSITIVE VS. NORMATIVE ECONOMICS

Positive economics concerns itself with questions of facts, which can be refuted. It relates to the value-free nature of the analysis; no subjective or ''gut'' feelings enter into the analysis. Positive analysis relates to basic statements, such as ''if A, then B.'' This is an example: "If the price of gasoline goes up relative to all other prices, other conditions remaining the same, then the amount of gas that people will buy will fall." It is a statement of *what is*. It is not a statement of anyone's value judgment or subjective feelings. Other sciences, particularly the hard sciences, such as physics and chemistry, are considered to be virtually value-free. After all, how can someone's values enter into a theory of molecular behavior? But economists face a different problem. They deal with behavior of individuals, not molecules. Thus, it is more difficult to stick to what we consider to be value-free or positive economics without reference to our feelings.

When our values are interjected explicitly or implicitly into the analysis, we enter the realm of normative economics, or normative analysis. A positive economic statement is this: "If the price of gas goes up, people will buy less." If we add to that analysis the words "and therefore we *should* not allow the price to go up," we have entered the realm of normative economics; we have told everyone what ought to be. In fact, any time you see the word *should*, you will know that values are entering into the discussion.[15]

In this book we will examine models and empirical investigations based on both positive and normative economics. However, we will also look at public policy, a world often containing oughts and shoulds. In other words, when we look at policy, we are often talking about welfare judgments—normative economics.

Both positive and normative economics have their pitfalls. In positive economics problems may arise from the inclusion of various terms or concepts in the theory that do not have corresponding counterparts in the real world. If the concepts depart significantly from the real world, even a logically consistent derivation of implications may contain unreliable comparative, static, or predictive outcomes. Furthermore, positive economics relies on empirical verification of the model's implications. Incorrect hypothesis testing and interpretation clutter empirical findings.[16]

In normative economics, certain positive relationships are usually asserted. These assertions often carry both an assumption of truthfulness and an assumption that each of the outcomes is properly weighted.[17] In some cases an examination of public policy is limited to descriptions of the effects of alternative government programs. This is part of the positive economic science. Public policy becomes normative only when we establish criteria for evaluating policy alternatives (implicitly or explicitly) and proceed to make recommendations.

Models and Realism

At the outset, it must be emphasized that no model in any science, and therefore no microeconomic model, is completely realistic in the sense that it captures every detail and interrelationship that exists. Such a model would be impossible to build and impossible to work with. For example, no model of the solar system could possibly take account of all aspects of the entire system. The nature of scientific model building is such that the model should capture the essential relationships that are sufficient to analyze or answer the particular question at hand. For example, when we attempt to

---

[15] Except in predictions when you may find "the effect of A should be B."

[16] For example, data from a noncontinuous distribution may be tested by using statistical methods for continuous population variables. In other cases endogenous variables may be included in reduced-form econometric testing procedures.

[17] One cannot, however, independently test the truth of welfare judgments outside a rule of unanimity. Furthermore, any outcome short of unanimity carries the possibility of inconsistent and conflicting outcomes of the same rule of choice.

construct a model of consumer behavior in the face of changing prices for a particular commodity, there are at the very least a million determinants of how each consumer will respond to such changes in prices. However, most of those determinants are left out of our model. It is not that they are meaningless; rather, the model that we usually use, which includes the price of the particular commodity, the income of the consumer, and the price of substitutes for the commodity in question, seems to be adequate. That is, just taking into account the magnitude of these four determinants of consumer demand, the model works "well," even though the model is "unrealistic" because it does not capture *all* the various determinants of consumer demand. In sum, then, a micro-economic model cannot be faulted merely by stating that it is unrealistic vis-à-vis the real world, for that same model may be very realistic in terms of elucidating the *central* issue at hand or forces at work.

Assumptions

Every model is based on a set of assumptions or axioms. In one sense, we do not directly or explicitly test the assumptions or axioms on which we base our models. To be fruitful, assumptions are indeed indirectly tested by comparing their implications with facts in the real world. When facts in the real world refute theories that are based on a certain set of assumptions, then the real-world facts, or empirical findings, are often indirectly refuting those assumptions.

When students undertake the study of chemistry or physics, they often do not question the unrealistic nature of the assumptions used in physical or chemical models. In physics, for example, there is a model of a "perfect gas." Of course, no actual gas in the world meets the requirements of the assumption of a perfect gas, and yet the model that is based on this assumption of a perfect gas—called Boyle's law—is well known and accepted. Why? Because it seems to work well. Now, you might ask, what does work "well" mean? Part of the reason the perfect gas model works well is the existence of rules of correspondence that allow one to go from perfect to imperfect gases.[18]

Deciding on the Usefulness of a Model   We generally do not attempt to determine the usefulness or "goodness" of a model merely by discussing the credibleness or the realism of its assumptions. Rather, if we use scientific methodology, we prefer and consider good the models that yield usable predictions and implications for the real world. The more implications, the better; the more implications not falsified by empirical, real-world facts, the better yet. The scientific approach to analysis of the world around us requires that we have a willingness to consider evidence. Evidence is used to test the usefulness of a model. Consider, for example, two competing models that concern themselves with the following phenomenon. Every time paper currency is left on a table in the student union, it disappears. One model is based on several assumptions, including that of wealth maximization—making oneself as well off as possible. This model predicts that if the cost of taking possession of the paper currency (which represents general purchasing power over all commodities) is low relative to the benefits, individuals will engage in this activity. A competing model uses some theory of magnetic attraction—paper currency emits a magnetic force which causes people's hands to pick it up.

A testable, that is, refutable, implication for the first model is that money will disappear faster the larger the denomination of the bills left. This is not an implication of the

---

[18] See Ernest Nagel, "Assumption in Economic Theory," *American Economic Review*, vol. 53 (May 1963), pp. 211–219, for a discussion of the role of assumptions in economic theory.

other competing model. We can run an experiment now to test the predictive capacity of these two models. On some days we randomly leave a dollar bill on a table at different time intervals. Then we keep increasing the possible take, leaving next $5 each time, then $10, then $50, then $100. If we see that more individuals hang around the student union as the denomination of the bill gets larger (the wealth effect is greater), we have an observed fact that does not refute the implication or prediction of the first model. However, it does refute the second model, which would predict that the number of students that hang around would be the same no matter what the denomination of the bill was because denomination does not determine magnetic force. In this case, we would choose the first model and tend to reject the second. Note here that we can never *prove* theories, only disprove them.

We also generally use the Principle of Occam's Razor: If two models are competing with one another and each predicts equally well, the least-complicated model will generally be chosen. It was William of Occam[19] who once said, *"Essentia non sunt multiplicanda praeter necessitatem."* In other words, essences shouldn't be multiplied beyond what we need for what we are studying. This is also known as the principle of parsimony. The notion of simplicity in model building is worth one further comment. Often the goal of constructing a theory is to have a general model. The more simple the model, the more generalized it is. The more realistic model explains only a more specialized case and is therefore less interesting.

The Broad Class of Rational Models

Many microtheoretic models are classified under the general heading of rational behavior models. We define rational behavior very simply: Alternatives are ranked systematically and consistently, and choices are made accordingly, all within real-world limitations. A rational behavior model is simply one that uses the assumption of rationality. The reason that economists have continued to use this type of model is because the assumption of rationality works in providing refutable implications which frequently appear to be consistent with real-world social phenomena.

When queried, individuals may demonstrate thought processes that do not correspond to the systematic behavior depicted in a model. Nonetheless, a rational behavior model is not necessarily worthless because of this lack of correspondence. Our economic models are models of behavior rather than thought processes. (Our definition of rational behavior is that behavior which is predictable and systematic.) More important, even if specific individuals behave in an unsystematic manner, large groups of individuals taken together may demonstrate collective rationality, which dominates the unsystematic elements of individual behavior within the group.

Rational Individuals and Rational Analysis

It is useful here to make the distinction between rational individuals and rational analysis. We define rational analysis as a logically consistent theory that enables us to derive empirically testable or refutable implications or predictions about the behavior of groups of people. If these predictions or implications are not refuted by experience, then the rational theory has proved to be consistent with the real-world data, or at least it has

---

[19] A fourteenth-century English scholastic philosopher.

not been disproved. We make no statements about whether or not individuals really are rational; nothing in a rational theory is dependent upon the premise that individuals are logically consistent in their thought processes. A good example has been given by several researchers doing experiments in mental institutions. Presumably individuals with severe mental illness do not think "rationally." Nonetheless, psychologists Allyon and Azrin found that the number of hours that psychotics in a study group were willing to work was a positive function of how much they were paid in the form of tokens which could be exchanged for clothing, toiletries, candy, cigarettes, and such additional hospital privileges as privacy. During one 20-day period, patients were rewarded with tokens when they completed their chosen jobs. In the following 20-day period, they were given tokens whether or not they completed their tasks. After about five days of the second 20-day period, the number of hours worked by the experimental group dropped to zero. When again they were paid only if their tasks were completed, the total number of hours worked per day increased immediately.[20]

The Unit of Analysis: The Individual

All the theories developed in microeconomic analysis are based on propositions about individual behavior in response to changes in environment. Although the point may seem self-evident, many of us are rather loose in our discussions of "society" or "the public." If you were to say that the public has decided to clean up the nation's water because that's what is best for society, such a statement would sound somewhat unscientific. There is no such thing as an organized group called "the public" capable of making that decision. Moreover, a reference to "society" is a reference to some sort of entity that presumably is capable of deciding what is good for itself. Individuals can determine whether or not they like the outcome of a particular economic change, and individuals can determine whether they are happy or sad. Society, however, cannot.

Perhaps a more appropriate way of making the same statement would be as follows. Politicians who expressed an interest in passing legislation to clean up the nation's waterways got voters to respond to them because of the increasing level of pollution in those waterways, which caused harm to many individual voters. When a sufficiently large percentage of the electorate became sufficiently concerned, those individuals in positions of political power made the decision to pass legislation to reduce the level of pollution.

Notice that the analysis here has been in terms of individual behavior. When we look at it this way, we see that the terms "public" and "society" are a bit too broad and vague to have much scientific meaning in rational discourse. One of the reasons that the terms "public" and "society" are seldom useful for economic analysis is that both terms are often simultaneously and interchangeably used when referring to an outcome chosen by the electorate. In our society, however, most election outcomes are governed by a majority rule, so that only 50-plus percent of the voting population may choose a particular outcome. These outcomes are sometimes simultaneously interchanged or associated with the notion of what is good and just. But if that is the interpretation, goodness and justice may have slightly less than 50 percent of the voting population in disagreement. For this reason we will avoid the use of loose statements such as the public interest or society's interest.

[20] T. Allyon and N. H. Azrin, "The Measurement and Reinforcement of Behavior of Psychotics," *Journal of the Experimental Analysis of Behavior*, vol. 8 (November 1965), pp. 357–383.

It should not seem particularly unusual that the basic unit of analysis in the science of economics is the individual. The physicist, for example, in the course of scientific investigation, may wish to describe the response of a "typical" molecule of gas when there is an increase in the temperature—even though the behavior of one particular molecule is unpredictable for all practical purposes. The economist may wish to predict the response of consumers in New York to a rise in the relative price of their food even though a particular individual living in a particular condominium near Central Park, perhaps in response to other stimuli, may actually buy more food when the price goes up.

Although we treat the individual as the basic unit of analysis, we normally apply price theory to the behavior of individuals in groups. From a methodological point of view, we talk in terms of individualism because we obtain better predictions about group behavior by identifying and taking into account the diverse and often conflicting objectives of the individuals who make up the group. Thus, our understanding of the behavior of groups is not dissimilar to the physicist's understanding of the behavior of a gas by considering the behavior of the molecules involved. In other words, we assert that more accurate predictions about group behavior are derivable than predictions about individual behavior.

THE FIRM AND MARKET STRUCTURE: THEORY AND MEASUREMENT

CHAPTER 2

THEORY OF THE FIRM

We want to analyze business behavior to see how firms choose inputs and outputs, set prices, and perform other activities that determine industry structure. First we will look at what production is, then we will try to answer the question, Why do firms exist? Next we will analyze limits to firm size and then try to understand the costs facing each firm. The model of profit maximization will be given considerable space, after which we will present alternative theories of the motivation of the firm.

DEFINING PRODUCTION

We can define **production** as any use of resources that converts or transforms a commodity into a different commodity over time and/or space. Production, in this fairly broad sense, therefore includes not only manufacturing but also storing, wholesaling, transporting, retailing, repackaging, and even attempting to alter regulatory agency rulings, using lawyers and accountants to find tax loopholes, and so on.

Production includes both goods and services because the term "commodity" refers to both. However, we will simplify the analysis in the following pages by considering only the production of goods. Services, such as cleaning, repairing, and so on, could be handled in a similar manner.

Production is a flow concept. It is an activity that is measured as a *rate of output per unit time period*, where output is expressed in constant-quality units. Thus, when we talk of increasing production, we mean increasing the rate of output, with all other dimensions of production held constant.[1]

---

[1] Increasing the rate of output will also increase volume of output for the same period of time. Unless otherwise specified we will assume a constant rate-volume ratio of output.

WHY DO FIRMS EXIST?

Commodities are produced by firms. Initially we will limit our definition of a firm (the unit that produces) to any organization in which there is a legally defined employer and one or more employees.[2] The employees are paid a contractual wage that they receive per unit of time independent of the rate of output and the rate of sales. On the other hand, the owner, who is also defined as an entrepreneur—the organizer and undertaker of business risks—does not receive a contractual wage rate. Rather, the owner receives what revenue is left over, if any, after all contractual payments are made. In accounting, "what is left over" from each year's revenues is called profit, or net income. It is also called the residual, or net revenues, by economists.

Why do firms exist? In principle, an individual could, for example, make automobiles, but automobile *firms* in fact produce most automobiles. Many of the production activities that go into the final product called an automobile are carried out within an automobile manufacturing firm.

Firms will exist whenever cooperative or joint group effort results in a larger product than the sum of the products of individual isolated efforts.[3] The difference, of course, must be at least as great as the costs of organizing, monitoring, metering,[4] and enforcing contracts with employees less the transaction costs associated with each independent residual claimant contracting with one another.

Much can be learned about the reasons firms exist merely by recognizing that economic transactions are not costless. Exchange between two parties has its costs of offers, negotiations, acceptance, delivery, inspections, warranty, and other activities associated with the exchange of goods or services, generally called **transaction costs**. Given the existence of transaction costs, it may be cheaper to organize production in such a way that some market transactions are eliminated and instead replaced by transactions within the organization that are governed by an entrepreneur who both monitors and directs the production process.[5]

However, such an organization does have its drawbacks. Production by a group of individuals who are not the residual claimants of any profits increases the costs of monitoring, metering, directing, and renegotiating contracts. If 10 Haitian basket weavers operate separately as individual entities in which each one is an entrepreneur, each one will feel the full brunt of "not doing his or her

---

[2] More generally, we could define a firm as an organization that buys and hires resources and sells goods and services. A single-person proprietorship would fall under this broader definition.

[3] The existence of a firm may also depend on whether there is great utility or disutility from team effort.

[4] A detailed discussion of the notion of monitoring and metering and of the existence of firms can be found in Armen A. Alchian and Harold Demsetz, "Production, Information Costs, and Economic Organization," *American Economic Review,* vol. 62 (December 1972), pp. 777–795. See also Ronald H. Coase, "The Nature of the Firm," *Economica,* vol. 4 (November 1937), pp. 386–405. The article is also reprinted in George Stigler and Kenneth Boulding, eds., *Readings in Price Theory* (Homewood, Ill.: Irwin, 1952), pp. 332–335. Also see Oliver E. Williamson, *Economics of Discretionary Behavior* (Englewood Cliffs, N. J.: Prentice-Hall, 1964), pp. 21–24.

[5] See Ronald H. Coase, "The Nature of the Firm."

job.'' Income and profits will fall for each individual who slacks off in proportion to how much the individual slows down. However, if all 10 are put into one firm in which they work together as a coordinated group, each specializing, say, in one aspect of production, the cost of any one individual member's not doing the job will be spread out equally among all members. Hence, if a firm is used to organize production, the cost to an individual of slacking off on the job is less than in a situation where the worker is also the residual claimant to any profits. Moreover, in a firm, it is more difficult to meter the output of each individual in the group because they are all working together. Thus, it is more difficult to work out a proper incentive system to reward a worker who generates a higher output by way of a greater work effort. These are all factors working *against* organizing firms.

In order for firms to be successful, some device must be found to offset this disadvantage. Most firms hire individuals who specialize in monitoring others. These monitors make sure that workers perform. Monitors also attempt to meter the output of workers. The ultimate monitor in a firm is the entrepreneur, or employer. If the entrepreneur, or employer, doesn't monitor effectively, his or her net wealth position is reduced. Employees, in choosing to work for a firm, implicitly agree to being monitored by the entrepreneur.

Sometimes the acceptance of monitoring by the entrepreneur is explicit. In China, for example, employees sometimes hire individuals to directly monitor their own effort.

> On the Yangtze River in China, there is a section of fast water over which boats are pulled upstream by a team of coolies prodded by an overseer using a whip. On one such passage an American lady, horrified at the sight of the overseer whipping the men as they strained at their harnesses, demanded that something be done about the brutality. She was quickly informed by the captain that nothing could be done: Those men own the right to draw boats over this stretch of water and they have hired the overseer and given him his duties.[6]

In addition to the technological advantages in team production and the avoidance of certain transaction costs, other factors contribute to the viability of the firm as an economic organization. First, a firm may capture the rewards from creating an identifiable brand name that can be attached to all of the firm's products. The existence of an available brand name permits the firm to introduce new products at relatively lower costs. Furthermore, warranty repairs, sales adjustments, and other related activities often cost less if provided by a single organization. Second, a firm permits avoidance of certain government-imposed constraints, including taxes and price controls. For example, a firm may transfer resources from one division to another at any internal price, thus avoiding resource inefficiencies that would exist if the transaction were subject to price controls.[7] Finally, the existence of a firm often permits for better

---

[6] Anecdote told by Steve Cheung in John C. McManus, ''The Cost of Alternative Economic Organizations,'' *Canadian Journal of Economics,* vol. 8 (August 1975), pp. 334–350.

[7] For a rigorous analysis of how transfer prices should be set so as to obtain efficiency within the firm, see Jack Hirshleifer, ''On the Economics of Transfer Pricing,'' *Journal of Business,* vol. 29 (July 1956), pp. 172–184.

relationships among the producing parties. Instituting set rules for all participants in the production process has its advantages. In fact, it is hypothesized that the decline of the inside contracting system where independent contractors all operated at one plant was largely attributable to its particular form of organization and consequent effects on individual participants. In the inside contracting system, the management of the firm provided floor space, machinery, raw materials, and working capital, and also arranged for the marketing of the finished product. Actual production, however, was carried out not by employees but by a contract system usually based on piece-rate compensation. The Winchester Repeating Rifle Company was a firm that employed this system during its most productive years. Apparently Winchester, after discovering the monopsony (buyer's monopoly) power by individual contractors and the differences in earned incomes that created certain social problems and other difficulties, abandoned this form of organization.[8] The actual choice among the different organizational forms largely depends on the differences in the costs of enforcing behavioral constraints, in addition to the reduction of the various costs of contracting and transacting the advantages of team production. A firm also permits the combination of risk taking with management of the firm, because the costs of enforcing constraints that would provide the incentive for the manager to maximize the wealth of the risk taker are lower when combined with tasks of management.[9]

LIMITS TO FIRM SIZE AND OUTPUT

Three factors contribute to the limitation of firm size and rate of output:

1 Production capabilities
2 Transaction costs
3 External supply effects

Production Capabilities

Physical or economic factors may limit a firm's output. For example, given current technology, it may be physically impossible for a firm to build a four-bedroom home in one minute or 5,000,000 houses in one year. It may also be physically impossible to build machinery capable of extracting 1,000 tons of pure gold per minute from unrefined ore. Production capabilities are directly related to economies of scale. In general, production capabilities are limited by economic factors, not by physical characteristics of society.

The economies of scale of managerial control underlie production capability limitations. Because of larger operations and more extensive hierarchical levels of bureaucracy, losses occur in the reproduction of information and/or distortion of the information, even when no conflicting objectives arise among the

[8] John Buttrick, "The Inside Contract System," *Journal of Economic History,* vol. 12 (Summer 1952), pp. 205–221.
[9] Frank H. Knight, *Risk, Uncertainty and Profit* (Boston: Houghton Mifflin, 1921), p. 260.

firms' agents.[10] The capacity of a central coordinator to assimilate all the information necessary for decision making is also limited. This results in increased uncertainty, which in turn creates further coordinating problems for the central coordinator and subsequent hierarchical levels.[11]

Transaction Costs

One tends to think of the firm as an organization brought together to enjoy technological economies associated with a joint production. But as we have seen above, substitution of internal organizations for market exchange allows for the internalization of transaction costs and their subsequent reduction in contracting and monitoring. As Williamson has pointed out, one of the most distinctive advantages of the firm is the wider variety and greater sensitivity of control instruments that are available for enforcing intrafirm, as opposed to interfirm, activities.[12] The firm can carry out more precise performance evaluations than a buyer can, and the firm's reward and penalty instruments are more refined than those in the external marketplace.[13] The firm also has a comparatively more efficient conflict-resolution machinery than that found in the external marketplace.[14] At some point, however, increased marginal costs of coordination outweigh the gains from additional evaluation of performance and resolution of conflicts, a condition that limits firm size.

External Supply Effects

The same forces that permit an expansion of an individual firm within the industry may also contribute to external diseconomies of scale. In the simplest case where each firm's expansion is proportional to the industry growth, limitations with respect to expansion of total industry output translate into rising supply prices for the individual firm. An industry's difficulties may arise from using less superior inputs at higher output ranges, from paying increased costs of transportation and materials, from the exhaustion of available labor supply at the prevailing wage rate, or from other factors. Although one firm may not be

[10] Oliver E. Williamson, "Hierarchical Control and Optimal Firm Size," *Journal of Political Economy*, vol. 75 (April 1967), pp. 123–138.

[11] David Schwartzman, "Uncertainty and the Size of the Firm," *Economica*, vol. 30 (August 1963), pp. 287–291.

[12] Oliver E. Williamson, *Corporate Control and Business Behavior: An Inquiry into the Effects of Organizations Form on Enterprise Behavior* (Englewood Cliffs, N.J.: Prentice-Hall, 1970).

[13] One scholar who has studied the choice between contractual and noncontractual (that is, informal and mostly extralegal) relationships among transactors in a business setting from a sociological point of view has pointed out this phenomenon and has argued persuasively why it is efficient. See Stewart Macaulay, "Non-Contractual Relations in Business: A Preliminary Study," *American Sociological Review*, vol. 28 (February 1963), pp. 55–67, esp. p. 63. That is to say, Macaulay argues that contracting is not always the best manner in which to transact business. It follows that a firm which acts as a substitute for specific cross-market contracting can be viewed as efficient.

[14] Intraorganizational settlements of conflicts are common. See Andrew Whinston, "Price Guidelines in Decentralized Organizations," in William W. Cooper et al., eds., *New Prospectives in Organization Research* (New York: Wiley, 1964), pp. 405–443.

large enough to influence prices of factors of production, all firms acting together may have external diseconomies. These external diseconomies translate
directly into increased prices to the individual firm for its factors of production
and place limits on the size of any single firm.

In Figure 2-1 we reproduce quantities that would be supplied by an individual firm subject to external diseconomies of scale. The supply curve for the
individual firm given one set of alternative prices is shown as MC. With higher
input prices, the marginal cost for the firm is shown as $\overline{MC}$. If all firms expand
together, input prices may rise so that the marginal cost curve shifts to $\overline{MC}$.
Consequently, the amount that the firm would supply at alternative prices is Q
for price P and $\overline{Q}$ for price $\overline{P}$. S then represents the supply curve for the firm
when it is subject to external supply effects.

PROFIT MAXIMIZATION

When we discussed why firms exist, we made an implicit assumption about the
motivations or goals of the firm. It was stated that the buck stopped at the
ultimate monitor—the owner-entrepreneur, or employer, who had a residual
claim on whatever funds remained after all expenses were paid. This residual
claim is called profit. The entrepreneur who is monitoring will slack off less in
his or her duties when the monitoring can be linked to the immediate impact on
net worth. This is the basis for the assumption of profit maximization or, better
stated, **net worth maximization** (in the present value sense discussed in the
Appendix). In consumer theory, utility or satisfaction maximization provides a
basis for the analysis. In the theory of the firm in production, profit or wealth
maximization is the usual underlying hypothesis.

The question arises whether this assumption of the net worth maximization
is realistic and can accurately predict firm behavior. If we are trying to explain
business behavior, we do not actually have to assume that entrepreneurs con-

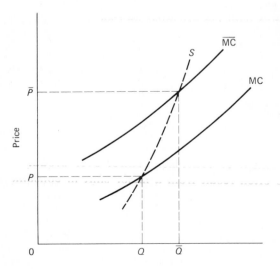

FIGURE 2-1
Firm supply function with external
diseconomies.

sciously try to maximize profits. We hypothesize that their behavior is consistent with the maximization of profits—they behave *as if* profit maximization is the goal. Several analogies help here. If a physicist wants to predict where a billiard player will hit the cue ball in order to cause a particular ball to go into a pocket on the billiard table, the physicist predicts the billiard player's behavior by hypothesizing that the player knows the laws of physics, even though this may be an unrealistic assumption.[15] But remember from our discussion of methodology in Chapter 1 that it is not necessary for assumptions to be directly testable. Indeed, normally they are indirectly tested by the refutable predictions of the model. If the real world consistently refutes a model's prediction, then the assumption of the model may be inappropriate. Another analogy has been given to us by Fritz Machlup.[16] The example of assumption used in model building concerns an automobile driver. The driver is on a two-lane highway. He must consider the speed, position, and acceleration of his own car, in addition to the same variables for the car he is trying to pass as well as for those cars in the oncoming lane. Furthermore, he must consider weather and road conditions. After all these considerations are taken into account, an optimal decision is made. Clearly, any rigorous solution to the driver's problem would require at least a modicum of higher mathematics, but that is not what is done. The problem is solved intuitively by experience. So, too, is the problem of what to charge in order to make a profit. The profit-maximizing model may assume perfect knowledge without uncertainty, but such perfect knowledge and absence of uncertainty on the part of the firm's managers clearly do not need to exist, just as knowledge of higher mathematics does not need to exist for the driver on the two-lane highway. Just as the driver intuitively reaches a decision, the entrepreneur can seek profit maximization as his or her intuition suggests.

Properties of Profits

We define **profits** as the difference between revenues and costs. In the short run, to maximize profits, the firm will set short-run marginal costs equal to marginal revenue. In the competitive long run, average unit costs will equal marginal costs, which will equal price, so that firms will earn zero economic profits. As we mentioned before, profits can be considered the residual claim given to entrepreneurs for risk taking.

The Function of Profits

Profits provide the major instrument of consumer control over producers. Temporary variations in profits often result from a major shift in consumer

---

[15] Example attributed to Milton Friedman.

[16] Fritz Machlup, "Marginal Analysis and Empirical Research," *American Economic Review,* vol. 36 (September 1946), pp. 519–554, and "Theories of the Firm: Marginalist, Behavioral, Managerial," *American Economic Review,* vol. 57 (March 1967), pp. 1–33.

demand for one product relative to others. Suppose a change in preferences leads to an increase in the demand for a commodity. Until existing production can be expanded, individual consumers will bid for the existing products and inventories, thus creating higher prices and, in most cases, higher profits. These profits, in turn, provide the signal for individual manufacturers to expand production and for new enterprises to enter and begin producing the now more highly valued good. Subsequently, resources move to those industries with brisk sales and higher profits. This shift results in greater production, lower prices, and improved resource allocation.

TRADITIONAL THEORIES OF PROFITS

When goods and services are sold, the owners of labor, land, and capital receive wages, rents, and interest. The question now remains, Why doesn't the summation of payments to the owners of labor, land, and capital equal the revenues received from the sale of products? In other words, why should there ever be anything left over? Why should there ever be profits, which are the residual left after all costs are taken into account? In order to answer these questions, we must devise a theory of why profits exist. Unfortunately, there is no single accepted (or acceptable) theory that we can offer. Instead, we present three possible reasons why profits exist. These theories have to do with risk taking, disequilibrium, and monopoly power. They are not mutually exclusive.

Risk Taking

One theory of profit contends that profits are the reward for bearing risk. Every person who undertakes a new business opportunity is subjecting himself or herself to the risk of failure, or to the risk of earning less in that venture than in another. Individuals who engage in contractual labor avoid, to a large extent, such a risk. They can sign long-term contracts that guarantee a specified wage rate. Owners of land (or natural resources) can do the same thing. But the owner of a business does not have a contract with some "higher power" that guarantees that revenues will exceed cost. If the business fails, it is the owner who explicitly suffers a reduction in wealth, or net worth. And businesses do fail. Some estimates show that two out of three new small businesses eventually fail. Clearly, in order to get an entrepreneur to take a risk, something beyond his or her normal compensation must be expected. That is to say, the potential for economic profits must be lurking in the future in order for the entrepreneur to accept the risks.

The reason that individuals must be rewarded or compensated for undertaking risk is that most people seem to dislike risk. Consider an example. You are offered a business proposition. You must invest $1,000. The chance of losing the whole $1,000 is 50 percent. On the other hand, the chance of earning an additional $1,000 ($2,000 gross returns) is 50 percent. The expected value of this proposition is zero: $-\$1,000 + (\$0)(.5) + (\$2,000)(.50)$. Would you go into this business? Probably not. You have to be better rewarded for taking the risk of losing all your money.

Some businesses fail and others don't. When we average out the losses and the profits, we find that, on average, positive economic profits are made. The reason they are made, according to the risk theory of profit, is to compensate entrepreneurs who dislike risk for undertaking the risk of failure. If entrepreneurs were risk seeking, they might accept options with zero or sometimes negative expected values.

Disequilibrium

Another theory of profits concerns the possibility of markets being out of **equilibrium**. A market is in **disequilibrium** when higher- or lower-than-normal rates of return are being earned. Remember that the long-run equilibrium of a perfectly competitive situation is one in which zero economic profits are earned. We are constantly moving *toward* long-run equilibrium; thus, in the short run we are normally in disequilibrium. Consider an example where there is an abrupt increase in demand for a particular product. The first entrepreneurs to perceive this increase in demand will be able to enter the market. Their production and sales plans can be adjusted before others catch on. They will be rewarded for recognizing this momentary disequilibrium by higher-than-normal returns. That is, they will receive economic profits.

The same analysis may hold with respect to the supply side. Certain entrepreneurs who realize that a newly available method of production could earn them higher profits may attempt to take advantage of that knowledge. They put the new production technique into effect and do indeed temporarily earn economic profits.

Notice here the economic profits are temporary. In the long run, under this disequilibrium theory of profits, all economic profits would be competed away if there were no unexpected events modifying supply or demand. Only a normal (accounting) rate of return can be earned.

Temporary profits may also be negative. A sudden unexpected decrease in the demand for a product will lower rates of return to the industry. Until production has been curtailed and/or firms leave the industry, revenues fall short of the amounts necessary to compensate entrepreneurs. Similarly, an increase in the costs of production will temporarily lower profits on the supply side, again resulting in decreased production and exit from the industry.

Imperfect Competition

A third theory of profits concerns monopoly power. We have already shown that a profit-maximizing monopolist will reduce output and raise prices. The monopolist *may* then earn monopoly profits. So long as the monopolist can prevent entry into the industry, monopoly profits can prevail even in the long run. Thus, this is not a disequilibrium theory of profits.

Critics of the monopoly theory of profits contend that such profits can exist only in the short run (although this may be many years). After all, it is difficult to permanently prevent entry into an industry, even by legislative means. Monopolists must, by their very position in the market, expend resources to protect their monopoly position. Those resources may eventually eat away at the monopoly profits. Thus, to the critics of the monopoly theory of profits, such profits are akin to disequilibrium economic profits because they are only temporary.[17]

The Theories Are Not Rivals

We have just given three theories of economic profit. Rather than being rivals, they each help explain why economic profits exist.

ALTERNATIVE THEORIES OF THE FIRM

For more than two decades, the theory of the firm, or the theory of managerial behavior, has been extensively debated because of dissatisfaction with the traditional profit-maximizing axiom in predicting behavior in the firm. Some say that managers or administrators incur expenditures beyond those necessary to maximize the wealth of the firm, and claim that administrators behave as if the firm's objective were to maximize either assets or the number of employees.[18] A consequence of this dissatisfaction has been the introduction of many new and competing models of firm behavior. These explanations seem to rely on differences in the specific motives a manager may possess and can be divided into three major classes—maximization of the single-variable utility function, maximization of a multiple-variable utility function, and nonmaximization models.

The first class consists of both single-period models, such as profit rate or sales rate maximization models, and intertemporal models, which replace the single-period profit or sales maximization objective with a multiple-period capital value or growth maximization criterion. The second class is composed of models that identify numerous goods which can be included in the manager's utility function, as well as the relevant trade-offs between these goods. Such

---

[17] Gordon Tullock, "The Welfare Costs of Tariffs, Monopolies, and Theft," *Western Economic Journal,* vol. 5 (June 1967), pp. 224–232, and Richard A. Posner, "The Social Costs of Monopoly and Regulation," *Journal of Political Economy,* vol. 83 (August 1975), pp. 807–827.

[18] A number of studies have directly tested the relevance of a profit-maximization view by comparing the profitability of large, so-called manager-controlled firms with the profitability of smaller, owner-controlled firms. The results are ambivalent. Compare David R. Kamerschen, "The Influence of Ownership and Control of Profit Rates," *American Economic Review,* vol. 58 (June 1968), pp. 432–447, who found no statistically significant difference in profitability, with John Palmer, "The Profit-Performance Effects of the Separation of Ownership from Control in Large U.S. Industrial Corporations," *Bell Journal of Economics,* vol. 4 (Spring 1973), pp. 293–303, who found statistically significant differences in profitability, and James Bothwell, "Profitability, Risk, and the Separation of Ownership and Control," forthcoming in the *Journal of Industrial Economics,* who showed statistically significant differences when the possibility of systematic differences in the risk was assumed by the two types of firms.

goods can be divided into those involving pecuniary gains to managers and those involving nonpecuniary gains that managers can capture, including the gains available to administrators from distributing rewards to individuals inside and outside the firm.

In corporations where ownership is widely held, the most commonly used model of managerial behavior focuses on managerial trade-offs between pecuniary wealth (profits) and additional sources of utility to managers, such as leisure, security, social responsibility, and power (however defined). The survival of so many competing theories of managerial behavior rests partly on the difficulty of testing the numerous explanations and partly on the differences in social and institutional arrangements of existing organizations. Most of the predicted differences among these competing models can be explained, apparently, as a consequence of different forms of property rights and the associated penalties and rewards that guide individual behavior. That is, one could design an incentive system that would predict the same behavior that these models predict. Table 2-1, shows a classification of major theories of the firm.[19] We will now examine some of them in more detail.

Staff Maximization

Whenever there is a separation of the ownership of a business from its control, the possibility arises that the managers will not act in the best interests of the owners.[20] Since monitoring is itself a costly activity, owners would not be motivated to completely eliminate managerial activities that benefit the managers at the expense of owners. Given the separation of ownership and control, managers are able to seek to satisfy their own utility by choosing some utility-producing resource combination other than that necessary to achieve maximum profit or wealth for the owners. The manager may, for example, be willing to trade off some of the owners' profit for increased staff size, particularly if it is difficult for the managers to "get caught" when not acting 100 percent in the owners' interest. We can represent the trade-off in terms of indifference curves, three of which we show in Figure 2-2.

We see in Figure 2-2 that the horizontal axis measures staff hours per unit time period and the vertical axis measures profit per unit time period. Assume that the indifference curves for a manager are convex to the origin. A profit curve shows the relationship between profit and staff size. As more staff mem-

[19] For additional discussion of alternative objectives for firms' decision makers, see Robert F. Lanzillotti, "Pricing Objectives in Large Companies," *American Economic Review*, vol. 48 (December 1958), pp. 921–940; Richard M. Cyert and J. G. March, *A Behavioral Theory of the Firm* (Englewood Cliffs, N.J.: Prentice-Hall, 1963); William J. Baumol and Maco Stewart, "On the Relevant Theory of the Firm," in *The Corporate Economy: Growth, Competition and Innovation Potential* (New York: Macmillan, 1971), chap. 5; and Lawrence B. Mohr, "The Concept of Organizational Goal," *American Political Science Review*, vol. 67 (June 1973), pp. 470–481.

[20] See, for example, Adolf A. Berle and Gardiner C. Means, *The Modern Corporation and Private Property*, rev. ed. (New York: Harcourt Brace Jovanovich, 1968). Also see Louis DeAlessi, "Private Property and Dispersion of Ownership in Larger Corporations," *Journal of Finance*, vol. 28 (September 1973), pp. 839–851.

TABLE 2-1
CLASSIFICATION OF THE MAJOR MAXIMIZING THEORIES OF THE FIRM

Classification of theory	Theory
Univariate criterion models	
Single period	1 Profit maximization 2 Sales or assets maximization (subject to a profit constraint) 3 Organizational slack maximization
Multiple period	1 Wealth maximization 2 Rate of growth of sales or output 3 Present value of sales maximization 4 Target rate of return
Multivariate utility models	
Trade-offs between	1 Profits and leisure 2 Profits and congeniality in the firm 3 Profits for managers and owners 4 Profits and control 5 Profits and security 6 Profits and social responsibility 7 Profits and product perfection 8 Profits and congeniality outside as well as inside the firm 9 Profits and managerial discretion 10 Profits, output, and emoluments 11 Profits and other nonpecuniary rewards 12 Profits and certain asset portfolios 13 Profits and professional excellence 14 Profits, status, power, and prestige 15 Profits and size of staff

Source: Kenneth W. Clarkson, "Managerial Behavior in Nonproprietary Organizations," in K. W. Clarkson and D. L. Martin, eds., *The Economics of Nonproprietary Organizations* (Greenwich, Conn.: JAI Press, 1980), p. 5.

bers are added, profit rises to a maximum of B associated with a staff size of S_2 and then falls, reaching zero with a staff size of S_0. If a manager's utility is to be maximized, the staff size would be set at S_1, for that is where indifference curve II is tangent to the "budget constraint" or trade-off line between profit and staff size (point E). If there were no separation of ownership and control, or if monitoring by owners were costless, the size of the staff would be set at S_2 and profits would be at their maximum of B unless the owners themselves preferred a large staff. In other words, managers would represent the owners in setting the optimal staff size.

This is a utility-maximizing theory of managerial behavior. It requires the existence of expensive information among the owners-stockholders. It also requires that the firm have some degree of market power.[21] If the firm were in a

[21] Oliver E. Williamson, *The Economics of Discretionary Behavior: Managerial Objectives in a Theory of the Firm* (Englewood Cliffs, N.J.: Prentice-Hall, 1964).

FIGURE 2-2
Staff maximization. Staff hours per unit time period are measured on the horizontal axis. Profit is expressed as dollars per unit time period on the vertical axis. Up to S_2, as staff is added, profits increase. After that point, profits decrease. Thus, the profit-maximizing size of staff is at S_2; however, the managers are assumed to obtain utility from a larger staff size. Thus, they hire staff up to the point where they can reach their highest indifference curve, II, or at point E. Staff hired will be equal to S_1, which is greater than S_2. The corresponding profit A will be less than the maximum profit B.

completely competitive market, it would have to maximize profits merely to survive, unless owners decided to spend some of their income on staff or unless all firms exhibited the same behavior.

Sales Maximization

Another model of the firm is based on a theory of **sales maximization**.[22] Managers may pursue sales maximization if they think that their own compensation and/or their professional prestige depends more on sales volume than on profits. We must insert the constraint here that stockholders do require a minimum rate of return on investment. Note that we are referring now to the *rate* of profit—or profits/investment per year—rather than to absolute profits.

We present the model of sales maximization in Figure 2-3. Profit, expressed as a rate of return on investment, is represented on the vertical axis, and unit sales per unit time period is shown on the horizontal axis. The relationship between the profit rate and unit sales is given by the curve; the profit rate reaches a maximum at a rate of sales Q_1. However, assume that the point of maximum revenues (price times quantity) occurs at a quantity of sales Q_3. Even if management wishes to maximize sales revenues, it will not be able to produce at the quantity Q_3, because a constraint is imposed upon it. That constraint is the minimum profit rate which we have drawn in arbitrarily at 10 percent per year. Thus, the managers will set sales at Q_2 rather than at the profit-maximizing rate of Q_1.

You will notice that we have drawn indifference curves I, II, and III vertically in Figure 2-3, because we assume that management obtains no utility

[22] William J. Baumol, *Business Behavior, Value, and Growth*, rev. ed. (New York: Harcourt Brace Jovanovich, 1967).

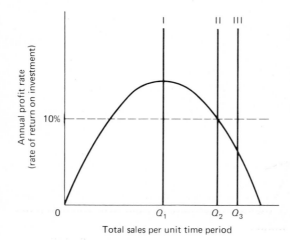

FIGURE 2-3
Sales maximization. Assume that
profitability, expressed as a rate of
return on investment, is an increasing
function of total sales up to rate of
sales Q_1; after that, profitability
diminishes. Assume, also, that there
is a minimum annual rate of return
that managers must meet and that it
is 10 percent. The indifference curves
for the managers are I, II, and III.
They are vertical, indicating that
managers receive no utility from
profitability per se. The highest
indifference curve that managers can
reach is not III, with the rate of sales
at Q_3, because that rate of sales
yields a rate of profitability below 10
percent per year. Therefore, the rate
of sales that managers will strive for is
Q_2, which puts them on indifference
curve II. Note that this rate exceeds
the profit-maximizing rate of sales Q_1.

whatsoever from profitability. Thus, a higher utility curve is merely a vertical line that is farther to the right. How can managers increase unit sales and hence revenues? Provided they are operating in the elastic portion of their demand curve, managers can lower the price of the product and increase total revenues. Further, managers can engage in more advertising to increase sales by shifting the demand curve outward to the right. Some empirical work on the sales maximization hypothesis uses a method of testing suggested by William J. Baumol, who claimed, "Executive salaries appear to be far more closely correlated with the scale of operations of the firm than with the profitability."[23] In his revised edition (1967), Baumol modified this hypothesis from that of sales maximization to maximization of the rate of growth of sales. Thus, he has replaced a single-period sales maximization hypothesis with a multiperiod sales maximization hypothesis. McGuire, Chiu, and Elbing tested this hypothesis and found that executive incomes and sales (scale of operations) correlate more highly than executive incomes and profits.[24] From these results, they concluded that Baumol's hypothesis was supported. Mabry and Siders further tested Baumol's hypothesis and obtained much weaker results.[25] Their results gave evidence that neither supports nor rejects the sales maximization

   [23] William J. Baumol, *Business Behavior, Value, and Growth* (New York: Macmillan, 1959), p. 46.
   [24] Joseph W. McGuire, John S. Chiu, and Alvar O. Elbing, "Executive Incomes, Sales, and Profits," *American Economic Review,* vol. 52 (September 1962), pp. 753–761. Note that using linear correlation coefficients to test the sales maximization hypothesis may not be valid, because one implication of profit maximization is that salaries of top management will be highly associated with the scale of operations. See Armen A. Alchian and William R. Allen, *Exchange and Production: Theory in Use* (Belmont, Calif.: Wadsworth, 1969), pp. 478–479.
   [25] Bevars D. Mabry and David L. Siders, "An Empirical Test of the Sales Maximization Hypothesis," *Southern Economic Journal,* vol. 33 (January 1967), pp. 367–377.

hypothesis. In further tests, Marshall Hall finds no support for the sales maximization hypothesis.[26] One implication in Hall's model is that increments in current sales can be partly explained by past profits that are greater than the implicit profit constraint. This implication, however, was not supported by Hall's empirical tests. Baker has used new data to test the relationship between sales and profits. He concludes that neither profits nor sales have a separate influence on top management compensation.[27]

Growth Maximization

A similar model of the firm involves **growth maximization**, that is, a manager's efforts to maximize the rate of growth of sales revenues. Presumably this would explain why managers are so amenable to mergers with other firms.[28] If they see that their salaries are related to the rate of growth of their firm and to having larger organizations under their influence, they will engage in activities to enlarge the firm. However, they are still constrained by some profitability requirement. In principle, this profitability requirement exists because if profitability becomes too low, some group of stockholders might be able to take over the firm (and fire some or all of the current managers).[29]

[26] Marshall Hall, "Sales Revenue Maximization: An Empirical Examination," *Journal of Industrial Economics*, vol. 15 (April 1967), pp. 143–156.

[27] Samuel Baker, "Executive Incomes, Profits, and Revenues: A Comment on Functional Specification," *Southern Economic Journal*, vol. 35 (April 1969), pp. 379–383. Compare Gregory J. Werden and Mark J. Hirschey, "An Empirical Analysis of Managerial Incentives," *Industrial Organization Review*, vol. 8 (1980), 66–78, which shows that compensation for management is related to *both* profits and sales. Also see Hayne E. Leland, "The Dynamics of a Revenue-Maximizing Firm," *International Economic Review*, vol. 13 (June 1972), pp. 376–385; Conway L. Lackman and Joseph L. Craycraft, "Sales Maximization and Oligopoly: A Case Study," *Journal of Industrial Economics*, vol. 23 (December 1974), pp. 81–95; Richard Schramm, "Profit Risk Management and the Theory of the Firm," *Southern Economic Journal*, vol. 40 (January 1974), pp. 353–363; George K. Yarrow, "Growth Maximization and the Firm's Investment Function," *Southern Economic Journal*, vol. 41 (April 1975), pp. 580–592; and Robert E. Wong, "Profit Maximization and Alternative Theories: A Dynamic Reconciliation," *American Economic Review*, vol. 65 (September 1975), pp. 689–694.

[28] For a rigorous theoretical treatment of the implications of risk-averse management on firm behavior see Louis N. Christofides and Francis Tapon, "Discretionary Expenditures and Profit Risk Management: The Galbraith-Caves Hypothesis," *Quarterly Journal of Economics*, vol. 93 (May 1979), pp. 303–319.

[29] This growth maximization hypothesis has been subjected to some empirical tests. For example, in Mark J. Hirschey and Gregory J. Werden, "Managerial Incentives in the Financial Sector," *Economics Letters*, vol. 2 (1979), pp. 269–274, the authors demonstrate indirect support for such a hypothesis by showing a significant positive correlation of growth in sales to management compensation in both industrial and financial firms.
Frequently the hypothesis has been tested more directly by examining the investment efficiency of retained earnings. The most recent empirical work in this area has been influenced by Mueller's so-called life-cycle theory, in which he argues that only "mature" firms suffer adverse effects of a growth maximization objective by management. See Dennis Mueller, "A Life Cycle Theory of the Firm," *Journal of Industrial Economics*, vol. 20 (July 1972), pp. 199–219. The results of empirical investigations taking account of the life-cycle theory are mixed. Compare Henry Grabowski and Dennis Mueller, "Life-Cycle Effects on Corporate Returns on Retentions," *Review of Economics and Statistics*, vol. 57 (November 1975), pp. 400–409, supporting the growth maximization/life-cycle hypothesis, with David Kamerschen and Robert D. Kerchner, "Market Share Valuation of Control," forthcoming in *Industrial Organization Review*, in which the authors find no substantial statistical support for Mueller's growth maximization/life-cycle hypothesis.

Galbraith's View   A combination of managerial utility maximization, sales maximization, and growth-rate maximization is inherent in the view of the firm presented in John Kenneth Galbraith's *New Industrial State* and *Economics and the Public Purpose*. Galbraith points to the managerial drive for prestige and technical virtuosity. He further suggests that the managers can carry out their plans because they are able to influence the behavior of consumers, primarily by advertising. Because the corporation is run by managers who wish to have an easy life for themselves, Galbraith emphasizes that large corporations will try to avoid risks and will engage in extensive planning to produce stability.[30] This so-called planning sector of the economy is run by corporate technocrats—*technically* skilled individuals who, in Galbraith's view, make all the important business-planning decisions.

Multivariate Models

Rather than replace the profit entity in the objective function with another single variable, some authors have expanded the number of arguments in the function.[31] For example, Armen Alchian and Reuben Kessel introduced a utility maximization hypothesis of managerial behavior by adding nonpecuniary motives to the objective (utility) function.[32] Some empirical confirmation of the implications was found in firms possessing higher degrees of monopoly (*closed market*) power. Thus, these firms were found to place less emphasis on pecuniary productivity differences between employees and more emphasis on an individual's personal characteristics (appearance, personality, religion, race, and so forth). In some cases these characteristics are used as signals for both desirable and undesirable attributes of employees. An additional and independent test has been provided by Ross Eckert for the behavior of regulatory commissioners.[33] The evidence presented confirms that regulatory commissioners do act in predictable fashions when facing certain institutional constraints that make an activity more or less rewarding than the incentives facing managers in profit-seeking organizations. For example, commissioners have shown little interest in expanding regulatory activities when they can capture few of the gains from further regulation. A somewhat different approach has

---

[30] This thesis for explaining mergers, especially those that are conglomerate in nature, was apparently first discussed and tested in Dennis Mueller, "A Theory of Conglomerate Mergers," *Quarterly Journal of Economics,* vol. 83 (November 1969), pp. 643–659.

[31] Several empirical studies support the existence of multivariable objective functions, since they show significant correlation between compensation and several explanatory variables such as profit, sales, sales growth, etc. See, for example, Hirschey and Werden, "Managerial Incentives in the Financial Sector" and "An Empirical Analysis of Managerial Incentives."

[32] Armen A. Alchian and Reuben A. Kessel, "Competition, Monopoly, and the Pursuit of Pecuniary Gain," National Bureau of Economic Research, *Aspects of Labor Economics* (Princeton: Princeton University Press, 1962), pp. 157–175.

[33] Ross D. Eckert, "Regulatory Commission Behavior: Taxi Franchising in Los Angeles and Other Cities" (Ph.D. diss., University of California, Los Angeles, 1968).

been proposed by Oliver Williamson.[34] He also extends the number of entities included in the objective function of the manager. In this extension, however, Williamson exactly specifies the entities in the utility function. According to his hypothesis, managers can increase their utility in one of three definite ways:

1 Increase their salaries by obtaining higher levels of wealth for the owners.

2 Increase their salaries by expanding sales and assets at the expense of greater returns for the owners.

3 Trade off owner's wealth for nonpecuniary sources of utility (larger offices, thicker carpets, more gifts to charity, less strict personnel policies, and so on).

Williamson, unlike Baumol, uses both a minimum or acceptable level of profits and a capital market constraint. Evidence presented by Williamson suggests that in certain applications, such as responses to a profit tax or a lump sum tax, his utility maximization explanation is a better predictor of managerial behavior than the classical theory. In other situations (for example, shifts in demand and responses to a sales tax), his model is just as reliable as the classical theory of profit maximization.

The choice of a theory for managerial behavior is not easy, nor does it appear to be eased by the empirical findings. For example, Williamson claims that the Alchian-Kessel hypothesis is a special case of his model:

> Subject to loose performance constraints imposed by the capital market (both the stockholders and the firm's creditors), the management is largely free to exercise the monopoly power that the firm possesses at its own discretion. Thus, while we fully agree with the Alchian-Kessel discussion on nonpecuniary motives and their suggestion that profits be replaced by a general preference function, we would suggest that regulated industries are merely a special case of the general case where competition in the product market—for reasons of concentration, conglomerate bigness, or barriers to entry—is weak.[35]

However, one could say that the Alchian-Kessel theory is the more general hypothesis. Williamson looks at narrowly defined trade-offs between salary and "expense preference." Alchian and Kessel specify a general preference function and analyze behavior under alternative constraints in various conditions, including lack of competition in the product and capital markets:[36]

> What is important is not a matter of differences in tastes between monopolists and competitive firms, but differences in the terms of trade of pecuniary for nonpecuniary

---

[34] Oliver E. Williamson, "Managerial Discretion and Business Behavior," *American Economic Review,* vol. 53 (December 1963), pp. 1032–1057. Also see Louis DeAlessi, "Managerial Tenure under Private and Government Ownership in the Electric Power Industry," *Journal of Political Economy,* vol. 82 (May/June 1974), pp. 645–653.

[35] Williamson, "Managerial Discretion and Business Behavior." p. 1054.

[36] Actually, Alchian and Kessel used a special case—regulated utilities—as an example of a situation where the relevant exchange ratio between pecuniary and nonpecuniary entities in the general preference function would be different from the exchange ratio found in competitive markets.

income. And given this difference in the relevant price or exchange ratios, the difference in the mix purchased should not be surprising.[37]

A review of Table 2-1 reveals a considerable variety of different multivariate functions. During the 1960s and 1970s there seemed to be a race by various researchers to find new variables to place in the utility functions. Merging from these alternative specifications, profits remain an important explanatory variable although firm size also has been found to be important.[38] In addition, researchers such as McEachern have postulated and verified that the structure of ownership itself is determinant of compensation of top managers in companies controlled by owners that are not participating actively in the management tasks. McEachern found that compensation was more positively linked to profitability than to sales revenue.[39]

Satisficing Behavior[40]

According to the **satisficing behavior** theory of firm behavior, the firm sets for itself a minimum standard of performance. It aims at a satisfactory rate of profit; presumably, once this rate of profit is obtained, the firm will slack off. An implication of the satisficing theory of firm behavior is that within the firm no consistent attempt is made to minimize costs for any given level of output, provided, of course, that a satisfactory rate of return is being earned. In other words, there is internal slack.

Criticisms of Non-Profit-Maximizing Assumptions

Aside from the question of the role of assumption in economic theory, criticisms have been leveled against the alternative models presented above. One criticism is that there is indeed a market in managers. Every management team of every firm faces the possibility that some other management team may

---

[37] Alchian and Kessel, op. cit., p. 163.

[38] Murray Brown and Nagesh S. Revankar, "A Generalized Theory of the Firm: An Integration of the Sales and Profit Maximization Hypotheses," *Kyklos,* vol. 24 (1971), pp. 427–443; Charles E. Ferguson, "The Theory of Multidimensional Utility Analysis in Relation to Multiple-Goal Business Behavior: A Synthesis," *Southern Economic Journal,* vol. 32 (October 1965), pp. 169–175; John Williamson, "Profit, Growth, and Sales Maximization," *Economica,* vol. 33 (February 1966), pp. 1–16; Robert T. Masson, "Executive Motivations, Earnings, and Consequent Equity Performance," *Journal of Political Economy,* vol. 79 (November/December 1971), pp. 1278–1292; George K. Yarrow, "Executive Compensation and the Objectives of the Firm," in Keith Cowling, ed., *Market Structure and Corporate Behavior: Theory and Empirical Analysis of the Firm* (London: Gray-Mills, 1974), pp. 149–173; Geoffrey Meeks and Geoffrey Whittington, "Directors' Pay, Growth, and Profitability," *Journal of Industrial Economics,* vol. 24 (September 1975), pp. 1–14; and William A. McEachern, *Managerial Control and Performance* (Lexington, Mass.: Heath, 1975). Yarrow and McEachern provide good critical surveys of previous literature. See also David J. Smyth, W. J. Boyes, and D. E. Peseau, *Size, Growth, Profits, and Executive Compensation in the Large Corporation: A Study of the 500 Largest United Kingdom and United States Industrial Corporations* (New York: Holmes and Meier, 1975), pp. 71–79.

[39] McEachern, *Managerial Control and Performance,* op. cit., pp. 77–78.

[40] Herbert A. Simon, "Theories of Decision Making in Economics and Behavioral Science," *American Economic Review,* vol. 49 (June 1959), pp. 253–283.

convince the stockholders that they will increase the profitability of the firm if allowed to take control. Given the existence of a market for corporate management, managerial behavior that deviates dramatically from profit maximization presumably will not be allowed to continue indefinitely. Clearly, however, the more impediments there are to controlling corporate management, the more likely is the firm to operate in a non-profit-maximizing dimension.

Additionally, critics of non-profit-maximizing models of the firm point out that not only existing stockholders but also *potential* stockholders must be considered.[41] Remember, the price of an asset is the discounted stream of its anticipated future net income. If the asset in question is the common stock of a firm, then its value or price in the marketplace will be the present value of the expected stream of future net profits. Thus, to the extent that current management decisions fail to maximize long-run profits, the current market price of the firm's stock will be less than it otherwise would be. Some outsiders might note this, and the corporation will become a sitting duck for a takeover bid. A group of investors could attempt to take over the corporation by buying a large block of its stock at its current low price, firing the current managers, and installing new managers, thereby increasing anticipated future profitability. The market value of the stock would then rise. Those who took over would receive an increase in their net worth—a capital gain—because the stock they owned in the company could now be sold for more than they paid for it. Thus, to the extent that a market exists for corporate takeovers, non-profit-maximizing behavior has some limits set on it.

The extent to which the managers depart from profit-maximizing behavior depends heavily on the transaction costs of new managers taking over the firm. Smiley estimates that the market value of a firm's stock may fall by roughly 13 percent below its potential value before takeover becomes likely.[42] In addition he estimated that a 1968 amendment to the Securities and Exchange Act of 1934 (Williams Amendment) severely restricted the use of cash tender offers and takeovers, increasing the cost of tender offers by as much as 27 percent.[43]

Reconciliation One of the most appealing aspects of the non-profit-maximization hypothesis to managers of large firms is the fact that they can often serve themselves at the apparent expense of the shareholders. Fortunately, Professors Jensen and Meckling have developed a rigorous theoretical analysis[44] that

---

[41] Henry G. Manne, "Mergers and the Market for Corporate Control," *Journal of Political Economy,* vol. 73 (April 1965), pp. 110–120; Robin Marris, *The Economic Theory of Managerial Capitalism* (New York: Macmillan, 1964), esp. chap. 1.

[42] Robert Smiley, "Tender Offers, Transactions Costs, and the Theory of the Firm," *Review of Economics and Statistics,* vol. 58 (February 1976), pp. 22–32, and A. R. Appleyard and George K. Yarrow, "The Relationship between Takeover Activity and Share Evaluation," *Journal of Finance,* vol. 30 (December 1975), pp. 1239–1249.

[43] See Robert Smiley, "The Effect of the Williams Amendment and Other Factors on the Transaction Costs and Tender Offers," *Industrial Organization Review,* vol. 3 (1975), pp. 138–145.

[44] See Michael Jensen and William Meckling, "Theory of the Firm: Managerial Behavior, Agency Costs, and Ownership Structure," *Journal of Financial Economics,* vol. 3 (1976), pp. 305–360.

explains the presence and extent of management perquisite consumption consistent with firm value maximization. The authors argue that "agency costs" prevent the existence of purely profit-maximizing, hired management, but that the value of the firm is nonetheless maximized after deducting these costs, which are real and no less of a cost than wages, materials, and so on. The Jensen-Meckling hypothesis represents a promising beginning toward reconciling the major and often conflicting analyses of non-profit-maximizing behavior.[45]

APPENDIX A: Pricing and Output Decisions

INDUSTRY PRICING IN THE IMMEDIATE RUN

Initially let us consider price in the immediate run (market period, or very short run), when there is no time allowed for adjustment on the part of suppliers of a product. The supply curve is perfectly inelastic. Assume the industry is any group of firms that produces a homogeneous product. See Figure A2-1.

The market demand curve is derived by horizontally summing all the individual demand curves. In the immediate run (market period), the supply curve is vertical. The equilibrium quantity Q_0 is uniquely determined by supply. The market-clearing, or equilibrium, price is determined by the intersection of market demand curve DD with SS (at price P_e). If demand increases to $D'D'$, the market-clearing price will increase to P'_e, but the equilibrium quantity will remain at Q_0.

[45] Also see Kenneth W. Clarkson and Donald L. Martin, eds., *The Economics of Nonproprietary Organizations* (Greenwich, Conn.: JAI Press, 1980).

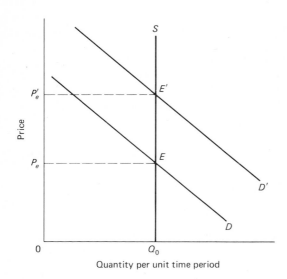

FIGURE A2-1
Rationing a fixed supply in the immediate period.

THE DEMAND CURVE FACING THE PERFECTLY COMPETITIVE FIRM

A firm in a perfectly competitive industry does not influence the price of the commodity sold and must take price as given. The market-clearing, or equilibrium, price is determined by the interaction of market demand and market supply.

Since price is given, the demand curve facing an individual firm will look like *dd* in Figure A2-2, where $9 is the "going price" (equilibrium price determined by the intersection of the market demand curve and the market supply curve). It has a price elasticity $\eta = \infty$; that is, it is perfectly elastic.

MARGINAL REVENUE FOR THE PERFECT COMPETITOR

Marginal revenue is the change in total revenue due to an increase in sales of one unit. It can be related to the price elasticity of demand:

$$MR = P\left(1 + \frac{1}{\eta}\right)$$

In a perfectly competitive industry, price elasticity of demand equals $-\infty$. Thus, this equation becomes

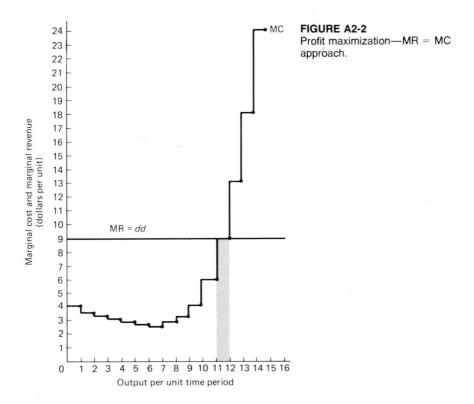

FIGURE A2-2
Profit maximization—MR = MC approach.

$$MR = P\left(1 + \frac{1}{-\infty}\right) = P(1 + 0) = P$$

Hence, for a perfectly competitive firm, marginal revenue is equal to price.

Profit Maximization

Profits are maximized when marginal revenue equals marginal cost. For the perfectly competitive firm, marginal revenue is the same as its demand curve, dd. It is the horizontal line at \$9 per unit.

Short-Run Break-Even and Shutdown Prices

Any price line represents a marginal revenue curve for the perfect competitor, and the profit-maximizing rate of output is always the output at which the price line intersects the marginal cost curve. In Figure A2-3 the short-run break-even point is at E; the short-run break-even price is P_1, the price that just covers average total costs. The short-run shutdown point is at E'; the short-run shutdown price is P_2 and is equal to the minimum average variable cost. It does not pay the firm to continue production if it cannot at least cover variable costs.

Market Equilibrium and Firm Optimization

Market equilibrium and firm optimization are shown in Figure A2-4. In panel (a), we show the market demand as DD and the market supply as SS. Their intersection is at point E. The market-clearing price is P_e, and the market-clearing quantity is Q_e. Then P_e gives the demand curve dd facing the perfect competitor in panel (b). That firm's marginal cost curve intersects dd at point e. The profit-maximizing quantity produced by the perfect competitor is q_e.

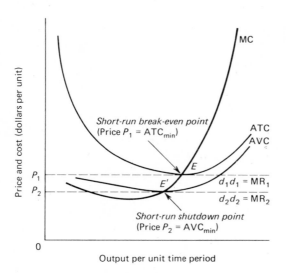

FIGURE A2-3
The firm's short-run break-even and shutdown points.

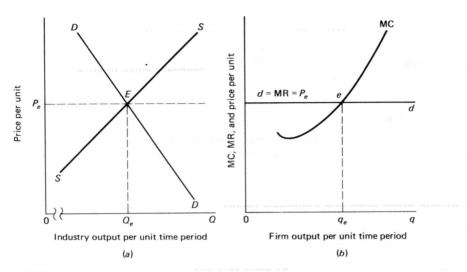

FIGURE A2-4
Market equilibrium and firm optimization.

Long-Run Equilibrium Plant Adjustments

In the long run the firm can change the scale of its plant. In Figure A2-5, if the long-run equilibrium price is P_1, the optimal plant is not given by the cost curves SAC_1 and SMC_1, for, at the profit-maximizing rate of output with that plant, q_1, the firm is not operating on the long-run average cost curve LAC. The firm would want to expand its plant until its cost curves were given by SAC_2 and SMC_2. The profit-maximizing rate of output is q_2; the firm is operating on LAC. Profits per unit have increased from the vertical distance between P_1 and C_1 to the vertical distance between P_1 and C_2.

FIGURE A2-5
Long-run equilibrium for a competitive firm.

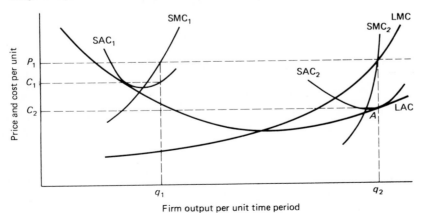

Firm output per unit time period

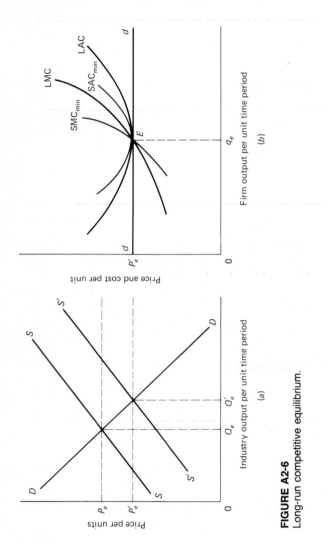

FIGURE A2-6
Long-run competitive equilibrium.

42

Long-Run Competitive Equilibrium

Economic profits will increase entry of other firms into the industry. In Figure A2-6, if economic profits are being made, there will be entry into the industry. The supply curve will shift rightward in panel (*a*) from SS to $S'S'$. The industry output will increase from Q_e to Q'_e; the market-clearing price will fall from P_e to P'_e. The firm eventually will find itself in the situation depicted in panel (*b*) where, at the profit-maximizing rate of output Q_e, LAC = LMC = P'_e = SMC = SAC. No economic profits or losses are being made.

Long-Run Supply Adjustments

As with the demand curve, long-run supply curves will be more price-elastic than short-run supply curves, other things being equal. In Figure A2-7, the immediate-run (market period) supply curve S_1S_1 is vertical. Its price elasticity is equal to zero. As more time is allowed for adjustment, it becomes more elastic, moving from S_1S_1 to S_2S_2 and so on.

MONOPOLY PRICING AND OUTPUT

The demand curve facing a single-seller monopoly is the industry demand curve, and it is downward-sloping. As the curve forms, we will assume that the monopolist is charging the same price to all purchasers, that is, it is a nondiscriminatory monopoly.

In panel (*a*) of Figure A2-8, we show a linear demand curve along which the price elasticity of demand decreases as we increase quantity. At the midpoint on the demand curve, price elasticity of demand is equal to -1 and marginal revenue is equal to 0. In panel (*b*) we can see that total revenues start at 0, reach a peak of output rate Q_1, and then fall to 0 when price reaches 0 at output Q_2. Total revenues are maximized at the output rate at which $\eta = -1$.

Therefore, it is clear from Figure A2-8 that the monopolist would never operate at a rate of output larger than Q_1 because marginal revenue is negative. This is equivalent to saying that the monopolist will never operate in the inelastic region of the demand curve DD.

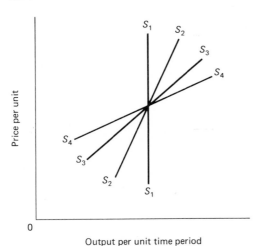

FIGURE A2-7
Allowing for the time of adjustment.

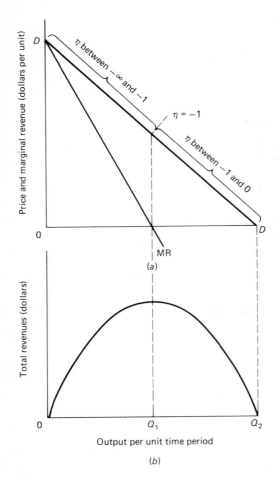

FIGURE A2-8
Elasticity and total revenue.

Monopoly Marginal Revenue

A monopolist would never willingly operate where marginal revenue is less than 0, because even if there were zero costs of production, monopolists could always reduce output and thereby increase revenue and profit.

Profit Maximization

In a perfect monopoly, profit maximization occurs where marginal revenue equals marginal cost. In Figure A2-9 this is at an output rate of approximately 10. (Also, the MC curve must be cutting the MR curve from below.)

Remember that a perfect competitor always operates at the minimum point on the average cost curve. A monopolist can operate so as to minimize average total costs if its long-run average total cost is a constant. Then that monopolist will be operating at the minimum point on the short-run average total cost curve. Thus, the only distinction necessary and forcibly implied by the pure theory of competition and monopoly is that the monopolist's price exceeds marginal cost, while the competitor's price is equal to marginal cost.

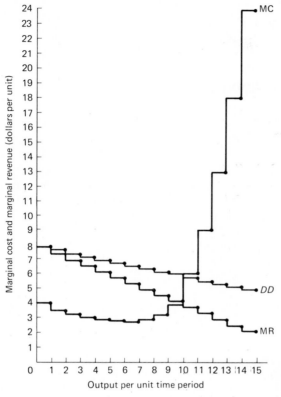

FIGURE A2-9
Profit maximization—MR = MC
approach.

No Supply Curve for a Monopolist

Since a supply curve is defined as the locus of points showing the minimum prices at which given quantities will be forthcoming, a monopolist does not have a supply curve. In Figure A2-10 we show two different demand curves D_1D_1 and D_2D_2 that yield exactly

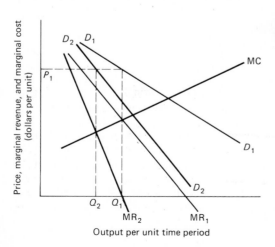

FIGURE A2-10
No supply curve for a monopolist.

the same profit-maximizing price but two different quantities supplied by the monopolist. Hence, there is no unique relationship between price and quantity supplied by a monopoly.

APPENDIX B: The Present Value Criterion

Profit maximization over time means net worth maximization, which is equivalent to maximizing the present value of the expected stream of all future profits. In order to understand what present value means, we examine discounting and present value calculations.

What is the present value of $110 to be received one year from now? That depends on the market rate of interest. If the market rate of interest is 5 percent, we can figure out the present value by answering the question, "How much money must I put aside today in a bank, at a market rate of interest that will give me $110 one year from now?" Or

$$(1 + 0.05)P_1 = \$110 \tag{B2-1}$$

where P_1 is the sum that must be set aside now.

In solving this equation, we get

$$P_1 = \frac{\$110}{1.05} = \$104.76 \tag{B2-2}$$

That is to say, $104.76 will accumulate to $110 at the end of one year with a market rate of interest of 5 percent. Thus, the present value of $110 one year from now, using a rate of interest of 5 percent, is $104.76. The formula for present value thus becomes

$$P_1 = \frac{A}{1 + r} \tag{B2-3}$$

where P_1 = present value for a sum one year hence
A = future sum of money paid or received one year hence
r = market rate of interest

Present Values for More Distant Periods

The present value formula for figuring out today's worth of dollars to be received at a future date can now be easily seen.[46] How much would have to be put in a savings account today, if the account pays a rate of 5 percent per year, compounded annually, to have $110 two years from now? After one year, the sum that would have to be set aside, P_2, would have grown to P_2 ($1.05). This amount during the *second* year would increase to P_2 ($1.05) ($1.05) or to P_2 ($1.05)^2. To find the P_2 that would grow to $110 over two years, set

---

[46] For a discussion of present value criterion, see Ezra Solomon, "The Arithmetic of Capital-Budgeting Decisions," *Journal of Business,* vol. 29 (April 1956), pp. 124–129; Ralph Turvey, "Present Value versus Internal Rate of Return: An Essay in the Theory of the Third Best," *Economic Journal,* vol. 73 (March 1963), pp. 93–98; and James B. Ramsey, "The Marginal Efficiency of Capital, the Internal Rate of Return, and Net Present Value: An Analysis of Investment Criteria," *Journal of Political Economy,* vol. 78 (September–October 1970), pp. 1017–1027.

$$P_2 \, (\$1.05)^2 = \$110 \tag{B2-4}$$

and solve for P_2:

$$P_2 = \frac{\$110}{(1.05)^2} = \$99.77 \tag{B2-5}$$

Thus, the present value of $110 to be paid or received two years hence, discounted at an interest rate of 5 percent per year compounded annually, is equal to $99.77. In other words, $99.77 put into a savings account yielding 5 percent per annum compound interest would accumulate to $110 in two years.

The general formula for discounting becomes

$$P_t = \frac{A}{(1 + r)^t} \tag{B2-6}$$

where the exponent t refers to the number of years in the future the money is to be paid or received. Table B2-1 gives the present value of $1 to be received t years hence for

TABLE B2-1
PRESENT VALUES OF A FUTURE DOLLAR

Year	3%	4%	5%	6%	8%	10%	20%	Year
1	.971	.962	.952	.943	.926	.909	.833	1
2	.943	.925	.907	.890	.857	.826	.694	2
3	.915	.890	.864	.839	.794	.751	.578	3
4	.889	.855	.823	.792	.735	.683	.482	4
5	.863	.823	.784	.747	.681	.620	.402	5
6	.838	.790	.746	.705	.630	.564	.335	6
7	.813	.760	.711	.665	.583	.513	.279	7
8	.789	.731	.677	.627	.540	.466	.233	8
9	.766	.703	.645	.591	.500	.424	.194	9
10	.744	.676	.614	.558	.463	.385	.162	10
11	.722	.650	.585	.526	.429	.350	.134	11
12	.701	.625	.557	.497	.397	.318	.112	12
13	.681	.601	.530	.468	.368	.289	.0935	13
14	.661	.577	.505	.442	.340	.263	.0779	14
15	.642	.555	.481	.417	.315	.239	.0649	15
16	.623	.534	.458	.393	.292	.217	.0541	16
17	.605	.513	.436	.371	.270	.197	.0451	17
18	.587	.494	.416	.350	.250	.179	.0376	18
19	.570	.475	.396	.330	.232	.163	.0313	19
20	.554	.456	.377	.311	.215	.148	.0261	20
25	.478	.375	.295	.232	.146	.0923	.0105	25
30	.412	.308	.231	.174	.0994	.0573	.00421	30
40	.307	.208	.142	.0972	.0460	.0221	.000680	40
50	.228	.141	.087	.0543	.0213	.00852	.000109	50

Each column shows how much a dollar received at the end of a certain number of years in the future (identified on the extreme left-hand or right-hand column) is worth today. For example, at 5 percent a year, a dollar to be received 20 years in the future is worth only 37.7¢. At the end of 50 years, it isn't worth even a dime today. To find out how much $10,000 a certain number of years from now would be worth, just multiply the figures in the columns by 10,000. For example, $10,000 received at the end of 10 years discounted at a 5 percent rate of interest would have a present value of $6,140.

various interest rates. The interest rates that were used to derive the present value are sometimes called the rates of discount, or the discount rates. We have specified the rate of discount in our examples as the market rate of interest available on savings. (That particular rate may not always be appropriate.) We note two important conclusions:

1 The farther in the future a sum of money is to be paid or received, the lower is its present value for any given discount rate.
2 The higher the interest rate used, the lower is the present value of any given sum of money to be paid or received at a particular future time.

The Present Value of an Annuity (A Sequence of Periodic Future Amounts)   We can use the above formula for present value to derive the present value (also called capitalized value and discounted value) of an expected future stream of income. For example, in the simplest case, we might want to know the present or capitalized value of an annuity of $1 per year for 20 years. We are looking at a stream of payments in the future. What we want to obtain is that amount of money which must be set aside today at a specified interest rate so that the payments will flow at the intervals and for the period required, exhausting the original account with the last payment. To find this amount, that is, the present value, we have to discount each dollar for each year it is to be received in the future. This would be done using the following formula, where A_1 would be a dollar to be received at the end of year 1, A_2 a dollar to be received at the end of year 2, and A_{20} a dollar to be received at the end of year 20:

$$P_{20} = \frac{A_1}{(1 + r)} + \frac{A_2}{(1 + r)^2} + \frac{A_3}{(1 + r)^3} + \qquad \text{(B2-7)}$$
$$\cdots + \frac{A_{20}}{(1 + r)^{20}}$$

The formula in Eq. (B2-7) is usually called a capital value formula rather than a present value formula to indicate the computation of the current price of the rights to a series of receipts (or obligation of a series of costs) in the future.

When the stream of receipts or costs is to last forever, or to infinity, Eq. (B2-7) becomes simplified to[47]

[47] The proof goes as follows:
Let $S = 1 + R + R^2 + \cdots + R^t$, where R is any number. Multiply by R to obtain

$$R \cdot S = R + R^2 + R^3 + \cdots + R^t + R^{t+1} \qquad \text{(a)}$$

Now subtract this last equation from the first equation:

$$S - RS = 1 - R^{t+1} \qquad \text{(b)}$$

which becomes

$$S(1 - R) = 1 - R^{t+1} \qquad \text{(c)}$$

or

$$S = \frac{1}{1 - R} - \frac{R^{t+1}}{1 - R} \qquad \text{(d)}$$

$$P = \frac{A}{r} \qquad \text{(B2-8)}$$

where A represents the sum to be received or spent once per year, in perpetuity. For the formula to be correct, that annual sum must be a fixed one. This formula is a good approximation of present value at higher interest rates for periods greater than 20 years. Look at Table B2-2. Here we show the present capitalized value of an annuity of $1 that is received at the *end* of each year. Take a relatively high rate of interest, say, 20 percent. The present value becomes indistinguishably close in 40 years to what it is at infinity, $5. Thus Eq. (B2-8) is a good approximation, even though the series of $1 payments stops well short of infinity.

Present Value of a Profit Stream

Now we are able to see that if cost in year t equals C_t, revenues in year t equal R_t, and profit equals II, the present value of a stream of profits from year 1 to year n equals

$$\pi = \sum_{t=1}^{n} \frac{R_t - C_t}{(1 + r)_t} \qquad \text{(B2-9)}$$

If R is less than 1, as t approaches infinity (∞) the numerator in the last term approaches 0 and so does the entire term; and $S = 1/(1 - R)$.

Now let $R = 1/(1 + r)$, where r is less than 1. Assume A_1 to A_t are all equal and $t = \infty$. Then

$$P = \frac{A}{1 + r} + \frac{A}{(1 + r)^2} + \cdots + \frac{A}{(1 + r)^\infty} \qquad \text{(e)}$$

If we add and subtract A on the right-hand side, Eq. (e) becomes

$$P = -A + A + \frac{A}{1 + r} + \frac{A}{(1 + r)^2} + \cdots + \frac{A}{(1 + r)^\infty} \qquad \text{(f)}$$

Factoring out an A,

$$P = -A + A\left[1 + \frac{1}{1 + r} + \left(\frac{1}{1 + r}\right)^2 + \cdots \right.$$
$$\left. + \left(\frac{1}{1 + r}\right)^\infty\right] \qquad \text{(g)}$$

But the expression in brackets is equal to

$$\frac{1}{1 - R} = \frac{1}{1 - \{[1/(1 + r)]\}} \qquad \text{(h)}$$

so that

$$P = -A + A\left\{\frac{1}{1 - [1/(1 + r)]}\right\} \qquad \text{(i)}$$
$$= -A + \frac{A}{r/(1 + r)}$$
$$= -A + \frac{A}{r} + \frac{Ar}{r} = -A + \frac{A}{r} + A = \frac{A}{r}$$

TABLE B2-2
PRESENT VALUE OF $1 PER YEAR FOR VARIOUS PERIODS AT DIFFERENT DISCOUNT
RATES

Year	3%	4%	5%	6%	8%	10%	20%	Year
1	0.971	0.960	0.952	0.943	0.926	0.909	0.833	1
2	1.91	1.89	1.86	1.83	1.78	1.73	1.53	2
3	2.83	2.78	2.72	2.67	2.58	2.48	2.11	3
4	3.72	3.63	3.55	3.46	3.31	31.6	2.59	4
5	4.58	4.45	4.33	4.21	3.99	3.79	2.99	5
6	5.42	5.24	5.08	4.91	4.62	4.35	3.33	6
7	6.23	6.00	5.79	5.58	5.21	4.86	3.60	7
8	7.02	6.73	6.46	6.20	5.75	5.33	3.84	8
9	7.79	7.44	7.11	6.80	6.25	5.75	4.03	9
10	8.53	8.11	7.72	7.36	6.71	6.14	4.19	10
11	9.25	8.76	8.31	7.88	7.14	6.49	4.33	11
12	9.95	9.39	8.86	8.38	7.54	6.81	4.44	12
13	10.6	9.99	9.39	8.85	7.90	7.10	4.53	13
14	11.3	10.6	9.90	9.29	8.24	7.36	4.61	14
15	11.9	11.1	10.4	9.71	8.56	7.60	4.68	15
16	12.6	11.6	10.8	10.1	8.85	7.82	4.73	16
17	13.2	12.2	11.3	10.4	9.12	8.02	4.77	17
18	13.8	12.7	11.7	10.8	9.37	8.20	4.81	18
19	14.3	13.1	12.1	11.1	9.60	8.36	4.84	19
20	14.9	13.6	12.5	11.4	9.82	8.51	4.87	20
25	17.4	15.6	14.1	12.8	10.7	9.08	4.95	25
30	19.6	17.3	15.4	13.8	11.3	9.43	4.98	30
40	23.1	19.8	17.2	15.0	11.9	9.78	5.00	40
50	25.7	21.5	18.3	15.8	12.2	9.91	5.00	50
∞	33.3	25.0	20.0	16.7	12.5	10.00	5.00	∞

Here we show the present value of $1 received at the end of each year for a specified number of years. For example, the present value of a dollar received at the end of each year for 10 years at an interest rate of 5 percent would be $7.72. If it were received for 50 years, it would have a present value of $18.30.

CHAPTER 3

THE MEASUREMENT OF MARKET STRUCTURE

Market structure plays an important role in testing economic hypotheses and in creating or enforcing public policy actions. Sometimes we wish to know a market's structure because this information may be useful in deciding which models can be applied to which firms in various circumstances. We often wish to assess the structure of the market in order to predict what will happen when, say, a new law is passed that adds a per-unit tax to the industry. Or we may wish to analyze the degree to which competition exists in the industry to know whether antitrust laws should be applied to change the current situations. In virtually all situations in which an industry assessment is to be made concerning the degree of competition and monopoly, we have to be able to describe and measure the degree of competitiveness, and to do so, we have to decide the criteria for measuring competition and monopoly. We have two sets of problems here:

1 How do we describe competition or monopoly?
2 How do we determine the industry to which the definition may be applied?

WHAT DO WE MEAN BY MONOPOLY?

One way to describe monopoly is to identify the opposite of competitive characteristics. A competitive industry, for example, is characterized by situations in which:[1]

---

[1] These conditions are necessary but not sufficient for competition.

1 No firm controls the terms at which it supplies the market. Rather, each firm is a price taker.

2 There are no long-run economic profits, and production in long-run equilibrium occurs at minimum average costs, with price equaling marginal cost.

3 There are a large number of firms with product homogeneity and no barriers to entry.

Certainly we could describe a competitive industry in other ways, but the above list leads us to at least three possible ways of measuring monopoly by the monopolists:

1 Ability to engage in independent conduct
2 Performance
3 Structure

Three Ways to Approach the Problem

Independent Conduct Measurements   We first approach our definition of a perfectly competitive industry by examining the firm's ability to control price —to be a price searcher. Measuring a firm's market power accurately is often difficult, as it typically requires defining the firm's demand curve.

Market Performance   Our second definition of a perfectly competitive industry involves producing at minimum average costs, with price equal to marginal cost. We must compare price with marginal cost and determine the long-run average cost function. Even if we were able to do so easily, we would still face the not insignificant task of interpreting what each particular measure of market power really means.[2]

Market Structure   We can measure the number of firms and look at the barriers to entry to better understand the market structure of an industry. As we will see, although indexes of monopoly structure in a market may be relatively easy to compute, we do not always know which measure is appropriate or how to interpret it when we find it. Moreover, as we shall also see, predictions based on market structure indexes often prove to be quite inaccurate.

PRODUCT DEFINITION: AN ALTERNATIVE?

One method of measuring markets is to focus on products. If we choose to define a market in terms of products, however, we must realize that goods and services can be closely related either because they are substitutable by consumers or because there is substitutability on the producer's side of the market.

---

[2] See pp. 59–62.

When the products are substitutable for both consumers and producers, they may seem to belong obviously in the same market classification, but this is not always the case. Consider some examples where the degree of substitutability on behalf of the buyers and sellers is quite different.

1 A consumer looking for items on which to spend recreational funds may consider as substitutes books, concert tickets, and the rental of a fishing boat. Clearly, there is little substitutability of factors of production techniques on the producer's side of the market here.

2 To take another example, women's footwear is usually a poor substitute for men's footwear for most buyers. Yet, on the producer's side, there is quite a bit of substitutability between the factors and techniques of production.

A Compromise   One way to take account of both producer and consumer substitutability is to consider a market as consisting of consumer substitutes, considering producers' substitutability only when it has implications for conditions of entry by nonproducing firms. This compromise does not always provide a satisfactory result, for it sometimes allows a market definition that includes commodities which are not close substitutes. This is seen particularly in the Bureau of Census grouping for pharmaceutical preparations (S.I.C. 2834). Different types of vitamin tablets are usually not substitutes, nor is penicillin a substitute for aspirin.

Elasticity Measures

In analyzing the substitutability among products, we must develop further the concept of cross-price elasticity of demand as a means to define an economic industry. First we must again define **price elasticity.**

Definition of Price Elasticity   Price elasticity of demand is a measure of the relative responsiveness of quantity demanded to a change in price. When we assume that the changes both in the quantity demanded and in the price are quite small, then we can define the coefficient of price elasticity of demand (denoting elasticity with the Greek letter η, or *eta*) as

$$\eta = \frac{\dfrac{\Delta q}{q}}{\dfrac{\Delta P}{P}} = \frac{\Delta q}{\Delta P} \cdot \frac{P}{q} \tag{3-1}$$

where the Greek letter *delta* (Δ) signifies small change, P is price, and q is quantity.

This definition of price elasticity leads to a measure that is completely independent of the units in which quantities and prices are measured. This makes it easy for us to compare the price elasticities of various commodities. Consider a purely hypothetical example for wheat

where $P = \$5/\text{bushel}$
$q = 100$ bushels
$\Delta P = \$1/\text{bushel}$
$\Delta q = 5$ bushels

Then Eq. (3-1) becomes

$$\frac{\dfrac{5 \text{ bushels}}{100 \text{ bushels}}}{\dfrac{\$1/\text{bushel}}{-\$5/\text{bushel}}} = \frac{0.05}{-0.20} = -0.25$$

This result has no dimensions; they all were canceled out.

Individual and Market Elasticities of Demand   The derivation of market demand curves incorporates information from individual demand curves. As might be expected, a definite relationship exists between the individual price elasticities of demand and the market price elasticity of demand. The market price elasticity of demand is equal to the weighted average of all the individual price elasticities of demand. The weights are equal to the relative quantities purchased by each individual buyer at any given price, as can be seen in the following exercise. Let

$$X = x_1 + x_2 \tag{3-2}$$

where X is the market quantity demanded and x_1 and x_2 are the individual quantities demanded. Then with a small change, Δ, Eq. (3-2) becomes

$$\Delta X = \Delta x_1 + \Delta x_2 \tag{3-3}$$

Divide both sides of Eq. (3-3) by ΔP, the small change in market price, and multiply both sides by P/X:

$$\frac{\Delta X}{\Delta P} \cdot \frac{P}{X} = \left(\frac{\Delta x_1}{\Delta P} \cdot \frac{P}{X}\right) + \left(\frac{\Delta x_2}{\Delta P} \cdot \frac{P}{X}\right) \tag{3-4}$$

Then multiply each term on the right-hand side of Eq. (3-4) by x_1/x_1 and x_2/x_2, respectively.

$$\begin{aligned}
\frac{\Delta X}{\Delta P} \cdot \frac{P}{X} &= \left(\frac{\Delta x_1}{\Delta P} \cdot \frac{P}{X} \cdot \frac{x_1}{x_1}\right) + \left(\frac{\Delta x_2}{\Delta P} \cdot \frac{P}{X} \cdot \frac{x_2}{x_2}\right) \\
&= \left(\frac{\Delta x_1}{\Delta P} \cdot \frac{P}{x_1} \cdot \frac{x_1}{X}\right) + \left(\frac{\Delta x_2}{\Delta P} \cdot \frac{P}{x_2} \cdot \frac{x_2}{X}\right)
\end{aligned} \tag{3-5}$$

We can now rearrange Eq. (3-5) into some recognizable terms:

$$\frac{\Delta X/X}{\Delta P/P} = \left(\frac{\Delta x_1/x_1}{\Delta P/P} \cdot \frac{x_1}{X}\right) + \left(\frac{\Delta x_2/x_2}{\Delta P/P} \cdot \frac{x_2}{X}\right) \tag{3-6}$$

In Eq. (3-6), we recognize three terms representing price elasticity of demand, and we can also recognize that the terms x_1/X and x_2/X merely represent the proportion of the total market demand that is accounted for by individuals 1 and 2, respectively. If we let each share be denoted by g_1 and g_2, respectively, we get

$$\eta_{\text{total market}} = g_1 \cdot \eta_{\text{individual 1}} + g_2 \cdot \eta_{\text{individual 2}} \tag{3-7}$$

Cross Elasticity of Demand: Substitutes and Complements Revisited

Now we can also use a definition of elasticity to define **substitutability** and **complementarity**. Up to this point, we have discussed what happens to the quantity demanded of a good when its *own* price changes; we have been referring to the own price elasticity of demand. Now we examine the **cross-price elasticity of demand**, which is defined as

$$\eta_{xy} = \frac{\Delta q_x/q_x}{\Delta P_y/P_y} \tag{3-8}$$

The subscripts refer to two commodities, x and y. Whenever η_{xy} or η_{yx} is positive, we classify the two commodities as substitutes. When η_{xy} or η_{yx} is negative, we classify them as complements.[3] See Figure 3-1.

The Relationship between Absolute Own Price Elasticity and the Sum of the Cross Elasticities We can develop an important rule which states that the absolute value of the own price elasticity of demand is equal to the sum of the cross elasticities, or

$$\eta_{xx} = -(\eta_{xy} + \eta_{xz} + \cdots + \eta_{xN}) \tag{3-9}$$

Looking at a couple of cross elasticities of demand, therefore, doesn't tell you very much about the own price elasticity of demand.

Justice Reed in *United States v. E. I. du Pont de Nemours and Company*[4]

---

[3] The definition of complementarity or substitutability as implied in Eq. (3-8) is a gross definition that includes all income or wealth effects. We are referring to gross substitutes and gross complements, because there is no way to take account of compensating changes in the level of real income. In other words, we might want to relabel the cross elasticity of demand, as defined in Eq. (3-8), as the *total* cross-price elasticity of demand.

[4] 351 U.S. 377 (1956).

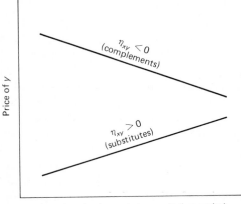

FIGURE 3-1
Complementarity and substitutability. Here we show the relationship between the quantity of x demanded per unit time period and the price of y. If that relationship is positive, the commodities are substitutes; if it is negative, they are complements.

implicitly recognized that an effective monopoly was related to the total sum of cross elasticities for substitute products. In this case the government produced evidence that du Pont produced approximately three-fourths of the cellophane sold in the United States and argued that this constituted monopolization within the meaning of Section 2 of the Sherman Act.

> But where there are market alternatives that buyers may readily use for their purposes, illegal monopoly does not exist merely because the product said to be monopolized differs from others. If it were not so, only physically identical products would be a part of the market. To accept the Government's argument, we would have to conclude that the manufacturers of plain as well as moistureproof cellophane were monopolists, and so with films such as Pliofilm, foil, glassine, polyethylene, and Saran, for each of these wrapping materials is distinguishable. These were all exhibits in the case. New wrappings appear, generally similar to cellophane: is each a monopoly? What is called for is an appraisal of the "cross-elasticity" of demand in the trade. . . . In considering what is the relevant market for determining the control of price and competition, no more definite rule can be declared than that commodities reasonably interchangeable by consumers for the same purposes make up that "part of the trade or commerce," monopolization of which may be illegal.

Income and Substitution Effects—Gross Substitutes and Complements It is possible to examine both price elasticity and income elasticity. When this is done, the substitution effect and the income effect for the price elasticity of demand become apparent.[5] We can look at the effect of a change in the price of

[5] This is the famous Slutzky equation, which is equal to

$$\left| \frac{\Delta q_t/q}{\Delta P/P} = \frac{\Delta q_s/q}{\Delta P/P} - \left(\frac{Pq}{R}\right)\left(\frac{\Delta q_i/q}{\Delta R/R}\right) \right|$$

This equation indicates that the price elasticity of demand $(\Delta q_t/q)/(\Delta P/P)$, as normally measured, is a combination of two things: the price elasticity of demand only with respect to a relative price change $(\Delta q_s/q)/(\Delta P/P)$, plus some fraction of the income elasticity of demand. That fraction (Pq/R) is the share of total expenditures taken up by the good in question.

y on the quantity of x demanded holding money income and other variables constant and divide that effect into an income effect and a substitution effect. The numerator in Eq. (3-8) for the cross-price elasticity of demand is the sum of these two effects. Thus, we are really looking at the gross cross elasticity of demand, and we see that our definitions above were the gross substitutes and complements. On the other hand, if the numerator in Eq. (3-8) consists only of the substitution effect of the change in price of y on the quantity of x demanded, then we are looking at the *net* cross elasticity of demand, and our definitions give us net substitutes and net complements. This may seem an unimportant distinction, but in actual measurement, when we shift from gross to net cross elasticity of demand, we find that two goods might be gross complements and net substitutes simultaneously. This would occur if the substitution effect of a rise in the price of y increases the quantity of x demanded, while at the same time the income effect tends to reduce the quantity of x demanded to more than offset the substitution effect.

Goods x and y may be gross substitutes and net complements simultaneously, a condition that would occur if an increase in the price of y reduced the quantity of x demanded. However, if x were such an inferior good, its income effect would increase the quantity of x demanded, more than offsetting the substitution effect. In empirical work, the choice of whether one looks at gross or net cross elasticities may well change one's definition of the products that should be included in a market.

Cross-Price Elasticity of Supply We have already mentioned that substitutability in inputs and techniques may be an important aspect in defining a market. Perhaps firms should be grouped together, depending on whether one producer can easily switch resources over to the production of the other firm's product in the event of a change in the price charged by the latter firm. To measure this grouping empirically, we must look at the cross-price elasticity of supply, which is defined as equal to

$$\frac{\text{percentage change in the amount of } x \text{ supplied by producers of } x}{\text{percentage change in the price of } y} \qquad (3\text{-}10)$$

This equation looks very similar to Eq. (3-8), but it is not. Equation (3-8) refers to the response of potential buyers; Eq. (3-10) refers to the potential response of sellers to a change in the price of y. Neither of these measures necessarily reflects the changes in the quantity of x actually bought and sold, for this depends on the price of x, which is assumed constant when we calculate the cross elasticity measures given in Eqs. (3-8) and (3-10).

Where to Draw the Line Let us suppose that all of the measurement problems in holding other things constant and getting exact price and quantity changes have been solved. We now draw up a list of very well calculated, let us even say exact, cross elasticities of demand between product x and all other products. We rank all positive cross elasticities and list the largest ones first. Clearly, the larger the cross-price elasticity of demand is, the closer the substitute relationship between y and other products will be. One question remains: Where do we draw the line? Where is the cutoff point at which we say that products below that point are no longer in the same market? Economic theory provides no precise answer. Without a definite dividing line between close and distant substitutes, any cutoff becomes a matter of opinion, judgment, or even normative economics. Even if there appears to be a big gap between, say, the sixth and seventh goods looked at, drawing the dividing line between these two goods would be just as arbitrary as drawing it between the fourth and the fifth goods would be.

An Empirical Question   The decision as to which products are close substitutes poses an empirical question. We may make reasonable guesses, but many possible substitutes will still be left in doubt. Is it really true that beer is a substitute for wine? It might seem reasonable, but don't we now have to know the cross-price elasticity of demand before we can be sure?

Should We Abandon Cross-Price Elasticity as a Criterion?   Any cutoff point has been shown to be arbitrary in deciding which products should be grouped into a market classification. Does that necessarily mean that we should abandon the measure of cross-price elasticity of demand? Perhaps not, for both the theoretical and empirical measures of cross-price elasticity of demand may correspond to actual firms' policymaking.[6] All firms are affected by other firms' activities, but only those activities which significantly influence a particular firm will be taken into account. If we are interested in the behavior of a set of firms, we might wish to group the firms according to how they individually decide which other firms affect their policies. Using cross-price elasticity of demand is a method of discovering the degree to which firms are affected by each other's pricing behavior. Using this measure thus allows us to *infer* which firms are likely to take each other into account when they decide on their individual policies. (Note, however, that knowledge of high cross-price elasticities of demand does not tell us anything about what type of reaction a firm is likely to have when another firm changes price, quality, or advertising.)[7]

---

[6] For a contrary view see Klaus Stegemann, "Cross Elasticity and the Relevant Market," *Zeitschrift für Wirtschaftsund Sozialwissenschaften,* vol. 2 (1974), pp. 151–165; and Kenneth Boyer, "Industry Boundaries," in Terry Calvani and John Siegfried (eds.), *Economic Analysis of Antitrust Law* (Boston: Little, Brown, 1979), pp. 88–106. In particular, Boyer suggests that "market share elasticities" are superior measures to cross elasticity of demand.

[7] Robert L. Bishop, "Market Classification Again," *Southern Economic Journal,* vol. 28, (July 1961), pp. 83–90; Kenneth G. Elzinga and Thomas F. Hogarty, "The Problem of Geographic Market Delineation in Antimerger Suits," *Antitrust Bulletin,* vol. 18 (Spring 1973), pp. 45–81; David Schwartzman, "The Cross-Elasticity of Demand and Industry Boundaries: Coal, Oil, Gas, and Uranium," *Antitrust Bulletin,* vol. 18 (Fall 1973), pp. 483–507; Jack Z. Sissors, "What Is a Market?" *Journal of Marketing,* vol. 30 (July 1966), pp. 17–21.

PERFORMANCE MEASURES

Alternatively we may wish to measure market structure more directly by focusing on performance measures. The degree of monopoly power is an important variable in industrial organization research. In this section, we will look at three indexes of market structure based on monopoly power: the **Lerner index**, the **Bain index**, and the **Papandreou index**.

The Lerner Index

Abba Lerner has given us a measure of market structure based on monopoly power that skirts the necessity of inferring the degree of monopoly power from sales data. This index is

$$\text{Lerner index of monopoly power} = \frac{P - MC}{P} \tag{3-11}$$

where P is the price of the product and MC is marginal cost of production of the product. The Lerner index varies between 0 and 1, with higher numbers representing greater monopoly power. In essence, this index looks at the performance of a monopolist. This index measures the degree to which price deviates from marginal cost. For example, if MC = \$5 and monopoly price = \$10, the Lerner index equals

$$\frac{\$10 - \$5}{\$10} = 0.5$$

or 50 percent.

The Lerner index of monopoly power requires the ability to measure marginal cost. This is not an easy task, to say the least. Moreover, price must refer to a constant-quality unit since differences in quality imply real change in price. Thus the researcher attempting to compute the Lerner index of monopoly power in order to compare firms in an industry has to be sure that he or she has quantified all qualitative aspects of the product.

Some Further Considerations of the Lerner Index

The Lerner index attempts to measure the actual monopoly power exercised by a single firm in a market, whereas a concentration ratio is a measure of the potential for monopoly power evident in an entire market.

Note that the Lerner index is a measure of actual conduct because it does not measure the potential for monopoly behavior of the firm. It is based on comparative static price theory and thus is incapable of telling us whether a current divergence between price and marginal cost is a justifiable result of past behavior or actually constitutes a cost to society.

Problems with the Lerner Index

The Lerner index is not a reliable index of the severity of the monopoly effects, as we will show in Figure 3-2. Consider two single-firm monopolies, I and II. Assume that the demand curve facing firm II is equal to one-half the demand curve facing firm I. They are selling in different markets, but they are both monopolies. The demand curve for the first monopolist is $D_I D_I$. The demand curve for the second monopolist is $D_{II} D_{II}$, which, it turns out, is also the marginal revenue curve for the first monopolist because it is one-half of $D_I D_I$. The marginal revenue curve for the second monopolist is MR_{II}. Both monopolists face demand curves that have the same price elasticity at any given price. Why?

Each firm will produce at MR equals MC. We assume a common and constant MC. The first firm will produce quantity Q_1 at the intersection of MR_I and MC, or at point E. The second firm will produce quantity Q_{II}, where the marginal revenue curve MR_{II} intersects MC at point E'. Both firms will charge the identical price P_m. Their Lerner monopoly power indexes will be equal because $(P_I - MC_I)/P_I = (P_{II} - MC_{II})/P_{II}$. However the respective welfare costs, as represented by the shaded triangles I and II, are quite different. The welfare loss or cost (sometimes referred to as deadweight loss), is much greater from monopoly I than from monopoly II.

The Bain Index

One of the pioneers in modern industrial organization, Joe S. Bain, has suggested looking at profits to determine the degree of monopoly power. He reasons that persistent excess in profits in a market generally reflects monopolistic elements. Measured profit data are readily available, in contrast to esti-

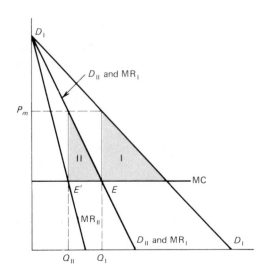

FIGURE 3-2
The welfare cost of two monopolies with equal Lerner Indexes. The two monopolists have the same marginal cost curves MC. One has one-half the demand of the other. They both sell at the same price P_m. The welfare cost of monopoly in the first case is the shaded triangle I; in the second case, it is the shaded triangle II. The former has a larger welfare cost than the latter, but they both have the same Lerner Index of monopoly power because the marginal cost and the price are the same.

mates of price elasticity of demand or marginal costs. One problem, of course, is that the economist's view of pure economic profits is not the same thing as the accountant's view. Thus, to obtain the measure of excess profit, one must correct accounting profits for, at a minimum, the opportunity cost of capital or normal rate of return.[8] Bain defines accounting profits as

$$\pi_A = R - C - D \tag{3-12}$$

where R = total receipts
C = current costs
D = depreciation

Thus, the definition of excess profit, or pure economic profit, is equal to

$$\pi_e = R - C - D - iV \tag{3-13}$$

where V = the value of owners' investment
i = rate of return that could have been earned on the investment

and the profit rate would be π_e/V.

Relationship between Bain and Lerner Indexes

The profit rate appears to be related to the difference of price from average costs. Remember that the Lerner index looked at the deviation of price from marginal cost. Thus, the two indexes appear to be similar (if MC = AC), but there is one fundamental difference between them. A pure or otherwise monopolist may earn persistent economic profits, but such profits are not inevitable. Additionally, even a pure monopolist cannot earn economic profits if there is insufficient demand for his or her product. Thus, the Bain index is uncertain because, while persistent high rates of economic profits may indicate monopoly, the absence of such economic profits does not mean that monopoly power is absent. It tells us about the likelihood of monopoly power, but it is not a direct measure.

The Papandreou Index

Andreas G. Papandreou has come up with a couple of measures describing monopoly power. These measures are based on the cross-price elasticity of demand.[9]

---

[8] Joe S. Bain, "The Profit Rate as a Measure of Monopoly Power," *Quarterly Journal of Economics,* vol. 55 (February 1941), pp. 271–293.
[9] Andreas G. Papandreou, "Market Structure and Monopoly Power," *American Economic Review*, vol. 39 (September 1949), pp. 883–897.

Papandreou does not accept, however, the cross-price elasticity of demand measure presented in Eq. (3-8). He points out that such a measure would be the same for the pure monopolist as for the perfect competitive firm, since in pure competition the i firm does not affect the sales of the j firm, for the i firm is too small to have any price effect on anyone else. The cross-price elasticity of demand between two competitors is thus zero. But by definition, because the pure monopolist has no rivals selling a close substitute, his or her cross-price elasticity of demand with respect to other commodities is also zero. Hence, the cross-price elasticity of demand gives the same result for two polar market structure extremes.

Additionally, Papandreou points out that the simple cross-price elasticity of demand measure cannot account for the constraint imposed on a firm by its own productive capacity. In other words, there is a limit to how much business one firm can take away from one or more other firms, simply because in the short run there is a production limit. Simple cross-price elasticity of demand measures potential ability to attract demand from other firms by lowering price, but it tells us nothing about potential supply, because one needs to know productive capacity to measure supply.

Coefficient of Penetration   Papandreou proposed that we estimate the coefficient of penetration which will describe the realizable change in sales of a firm that results from price changes made by other firms.[10] This index is a firm's ability to penetrate a rival's market.

Coefficient of Insulation   The other side of the coin is a firm's ability to withstand similar attacks by other firms.[11] When Papandreou uses these two coefficients together, he is able to describe combinations that would imply different degrees of market power. Few researchers, however, have been able to find a way to apply the indexes to actual industries and firms.

MEASURES OF CONCENTRATION—GROUPING FIRMS IN AN INDUSTRY

The difficulties of defining the market by product or performance measures have led economists, policymakers, and others to find an alternative form of measurement. Over time there has been a movement toward measures that

[10] The coefficient of penetration index is equal to

$$C_{Q_i P_j} = \lambda_j \left[\frac{P_j}{Q_i} \times \frac{\delta(M)}{\delta P_i} \right]$$

where $C_{q_i P_j}$ is the coefficient of penetration
  $M = f_i(P_i, P_j, P_n)$ and P_n is a composite price of all other firms in the industry
  λ_j = firm's output limitation

[11] The coefficient of insulation can be found in Theodore Morgan, "A Measure of Monopoly in Selling," *Quarterly Journal of Economics*, vol. 60 (May 1946), pp. 461-463.

focus on the size distribution of firms in the industry. In turn the size distribution of firms in the industry has been condensed into a single measure of **industry concentration**.

In industrial organization, we often see the terms "market concentration," "business concentration," and "economic concentration." The term or concept "concentration" appears to be one of the most important descriptions of the degree to which a segment or segments of our economy are competitive. There are a number of ways to measure industry concentration. The most popular is the percentage of total sales or employment accounted for by, say, the top four or top eight firms. Thus, a four-firm **concentration ratio**, as it is called, of 80 percent implies more monopoly power by this measure than a four-firm concentration ratio of 50 percent. By their very nature, higher concentration ratios tell us that more sales or other measures of economic activity are under the control of only a small number of firms. This relationship in turn has been linked to the notion that both the incentive and the opportunity exist to collude or otherwise engage in cartel policies that increase revenues to the industry. An example of an industry with 25 firms is given below.

Sales

Firm 1	$150,000,000
Firm 2	100,000,000
Firm 3	80,000,000
Firm 4	70,000,000
Firms 5–25	150,000,000
Total	$550,000,000

Firm 1 through Firm 4 $= \$400,000,000$

$$\text{4-firm concentration ratio} = \frac{\$400,000,000}{\$550,000,000} = 81.8\%$$

Although at first glance the concentration ratio seems to be a useful measure of monopoly power, it has a serious shortcoming. Monopoly power is a function not only of a firm's market share, but also of potential supply from either existing firms or firms that could enter the industry. As Paul Samuelson pointed out,[12] an industry one-firm concentration ratio could be 100 percent, and yet the monopoly power of that one firm could be zero if the potential supply elasticity were great enough. In other words, a price that yields monopoly profits in this situation will cause the existing monopoly to be deluged by new entrants or expansion by existing marginal firms in the industry.

Concentration in Larger Segments

We have examined above the four-firm concentration ratio, but it is possible to look at the share held or controlled by the largest eight firms, twenty firms, or

---

[12] Paul A. Samuelson, *Foundations of Economic Analysis* (New York: Atheneum, 1965), p. 79. In essence, concentration reflects the number of actual market rivals of a firm, whereas the conditions of entry tell us about potential rivals.

fifty firms. Data are available which show these concentration ratios for all manufacturing industries in 1947, 1954, 1958, 1963, 1966, 1967, 1970, and 1972.[13] One can look at concentration in all of manufacturing, for example. We could obtain the shares of the larger number of firms for the 20, 50, 100, or 200 largest firms out of all those half million that are in manufacturing. This type of gross measure would, of course, compound all the problems that we considered earlier. What would it mean, for example, if the share for the largest firms went up? Has the rest of the manufacturing economy become larger? Have some larger firms merged with other firms? Furthermore, as we will see, such a measure would give little indication or basis for prediction with respect to policies engaged in or performance of the industry. Intertemporal comparisons would also be questionable because of turnover in the relative rankings of the largest firms.

Concentration ratios for single industries may also be questionable. For example, it is possible for the relative ranking of concentration ratios by industries to change when we go from four- to eight-firm concentration ratios. In Table 3-1, we give an example showing how this change has occurred in the construction machinery and petroleum industries. Nonetheless, a simple ranking of concentration ratios for the four or eight largest firms in each industry will usually give a relative concentration ranking which will be roughly similar to the ranking that results from any other absolute number of control units used to calculate the concentration ratio.[14]

Measuring the Size: Assets, Income, and Labor Force

The concentration of control for an industry or for the whole economy can be measured with respect to business assets, business income, and the number of workers employed. We can then come up with three corresponding concentration measures. Often the concentration ratio used is determined by which statistics are most available. For example, when looking at the concentration of control of all business activity, we generally look at the control of total business assets rather than business income or labor force, mainly because of the greater accessibility of data on business assets.

The choice of the variable to be used to calculate concentration illustrates another dimension of the industry ranking problem. Thus one may find a different result in ranking when assets are used as the key measure from the ranking that results from the use of employment measures.

Illustrating the Problem of Market Definition   As we pointed out above, a serious problem arises in defining and measuring the market. This problem

---

[13] See U.S. Bureau of the Census, *Census of Manufacturers*, 1972, Subject and Special Statistics, Concentration Ratios in Manufacturing, vol. I, pp. SR2-6–SRZ-49 (U.S.G.P.O. 1976) and Table 3-1.

[14] For a comprehensive study showing the similarity in results from using a variety of concentration measures, see Gideon Rosenbluth, "Measures of Concentration," in George J. Stigler, ed., *Business Concentration and Price Policy* (Princeton, N.J.: Princeton University Press, 1955), pp. 57–95.

TABLE 3-1

CONCENTRATION RATIOS FOR VARIOUS INDUSTRIES
(in percent)

	Share of value of shipments accounted for by the:			
	Largest four companies		Largest eight companies	
	1967	1972	1967	1972
Motor vehicles	92	93	98	99
Primary copper	77	72	98	*
Aircraft	69	66	89	86
Synthetic rubber	61	62	82	81
Blast furnaces and steel mills	48	45	66	65
Industrial trucks and tractors	48	50	62	66
Construction machinery	41	43	53	54
Petroleum	33	31	57	56
Papermills	26	24	43	40
Meatpacking	26	22	38	37
Newspapers	16	17	25	28
Fluid milk	22	18	30	26

*Withheld by Commerce Department to avoid disclosing figures for individual companies.
  Source: U.S. Department of Commerce.

becomes particularly bothersome when we deal with concentration. The method we use to define the market may or may not yield an accurate (more useful for explaining or predicting firm behavior) concentration ratio calculation. Most of the time the more narrowly we define the market, the higher measured concentration ratios we will find. Most companies specialize to some degree, even if they pursue diverse activities. For example, if we are looking at the market for alcoholic beverages, we may find that some firms specialize in wine, some in beer, and some in so-called hard liquor. If we used a broadly defined market as alcoholic beverages, we would probably arrive at a low concentration ratio. If we examined wine, or beer, or hard liquor markets separately, the concentration ratio would undoubtedly increase. If we define the market even more narrowly, studying the white wine versus red wine markets or bourbon versus gin markets, the concentration ratios typically will get even higher.

Spatial Isolation

A high concentration ratio may result from structural monopoly power because of spatial isolation. Consider an obvious example in the cement industry. The four leading firms account for about 30 percent of all nationwide sales. On a factory basis, however, 90 percent of all cement is shipped 160 miles or less. Yet, when the nation is divided into 51 regions, only three of the regions are served by the leading four producers, and the four producers account for less than 50 percent of all sales in those regions.

Choosing the Correct Market With significant differences in national and regional concentration ratios, the choice of the relevant market becomes important. Consider regional markets, such as east, midwest, and northwest, each with a concentration ratio of 85 percent, as shown in Table 3-2. Combining the sales of the four largest firms in the national market (firms 1, 2, 3, and 6), however, gives an aggregate output of 205 units or a concentration ratio of only 68 percent. With a larger number of similarly sized regional markets, the difference between measured concentration in the national market and each of the submarkets is more pronounced. Consider, for example, a monopolized market of roughly similar size operating in each of the 50 states. Each state's market would have a concentration index of 100 percent. A four-firm concentration ratio for the nation as a whole, however, would be only slightly greater than 8 percent.

A Way Out of the Dilemma In order to avoid understating concentration in a broad market, we can look at the weighted average of the ratios of the various submarkets. Rather than adding up the submarkets individually, we attribute to the broad market the average concentration level of its component parts. This procedure may, nonetheless, overstate the degree of concentration in a broadly defined market. Basically, we are trying to solve a theoretical problem by improving our arithmetic methods. The way we should look for the appropriate definition of a market is through our theory, not by seeking an arithmetic sleight of hand.

Commonly Overlooked Suppliers Another problem with concentration ratios is that they almost always ignore two very important alternative sources of supply: foreign imports and used or scrap materials. The profound significance of the omission of foreign competitors has been demonstrated empirically by Sichel and Marfels.[15] Both of their studies indicate that substantial overstatement of concentration levels occurs when foreign competition is omitted.

Similarly, omission of competition from sellers of used products or scrap could overstate concentration. But this analysis is complicated by the fact that suppliers of the new product are not unmindful of the consequences of scrap

---

[15] Werner Sichel, "The Foreign Competition Omission in Census Concentration Ratios: An Empirical Evaluation," *Antitrust Bulletin,* vol. 20 (Spring 1975), pp. 89–105; and Christian Marfels, "The Impact of Foreign Trade on Concentration Levels: Empirical Findings for Canadian Manufacturing Industries and for the Steel Industries of Four Countries," *Antitrust Bulletin,* vol. 24 (Spring 1979), pp. 129–147.

TABLE 3-2
CONCENTRATION IN REGIONAL AND NATIONAL MARKETS

Firm	Regional market			National market
	East	Midwest	Northwest	
1	40	20	5	65
2	20	20	10	50
3	15	20	15	50
4	10	0	35	45
5	10	15	15	40
6	5	25	20	50
Four largest	85	85	85	205
Total	100	100	100	300
Concentration ratio (4)	85%	85%	85%	68%

materials as a competitive source of supply for later production, nor are purchasers unmindful of the scrap value of the product they purchase new.[16]

OTHER CONCENTRATION INDEXES

We have already discussed the most commonly used business concentration indexes that relate directly to the percentage of employers' assets or value of sales accounted for by the top four or top eight firms in an industry. There are a host of various other concentration indexes called *summary measures*, which examine the evenness or unevenness of the size distribution of firms in a given market, given any level of concentration. They cover the distribution of all firms in an industry and are related to various statistical concepts of dispersion. Numerous researchers have gone so far as to argue that concentration is synonomous with unevenness in the dispersion of firm sizes.[17] Of course, not all researchers agree.[18] In particular, Adelman argues strongly that dispersion

---

[16] For a rigorous theoretical analysis of the issue and an empirical investigation applied to the aluminum industry, see Peter Swan, "Alcoa: The Influence of Recycling on Monopoly Power," *Journal of Political Economy*, vol. 88 (February 1980), pp. 76–99.

[17] See, for example, P. E. Hart and S. J. Prais, "The Analysis of Business Concentration: A Statistical Approach," *Journal of the Royal Statistical Society*, vol. 119 (1956), pp. 150–181.

[18] There are *several* dispersion measures, with the choice among them itself a matter of some debate. See, for example, P. E. Hart, "Entropy and Other Measures of Concentration," *Journal of the Royal Statistical Society*, vol. 134 (1971), pp. 73–85. Hart argues that two of the more popular dispersion-based measures (redundancy and entropy) are generally inappropriate. A numbers-equivalent measure also accompanies both the entropy measure and the Herfindahl index (pp. 80–81). In an empirical evaluation of an entropy measure, a numbers-equivalent measure, and a four-firm concentration ratio, one investigator has found that while the other two measures *are* correlated with price-cost margins, the numbers-equivalent measure is *not* correlated. See Richard A. Miller, "Numbers Equivalents, Relative Entropy, and Concentration Ratios: A Comparison Using Market Performance," *Southern Economic Journal*, vol. 39 (July 1972), pp. 107–112. For an argument in favor of an entropy-based measure, see Christian Marfels, "On Testing Concentration Measures," *Zeitschrift für Nationalökonomie*, vol. 32 (1972), pp. 461–486.

has no real economic consequences.[19] Rather, he argues that it is the actual number of firms in the industry that counts. Conventional models of monopoly and oligopoly emphasize the fewness of firms and, hence, reinforce Adelman's view.

Nonetheless, various studies purportedly show that asymmetry among the sizes of firms in an industry critically determines conduct and performance of all firms in that market.[20]

The Concentration Curve

If we measure the cumulative percentage of total industry assets that are held by the leading firms in an industry, for example, we come up with what is defined as a **concentration curve**. We see in Figure 3-3 a hypothetical concentration curve for industry XYZ. It is composed of four firms that have assets of $40, $25, $20, and $15 million, respectively. The horizontal axis represents the number of firms cumulative from the largest to the smallest. The vertical axis measures the percentage of industry assets accounted for by these firms. We could just as easily have drawn the concentration curve with respect to number of employees or total sales.

A steeply rising concentration curve is indicative of a higher degree or *absolute* concentration relative to a gradually rising curve. When comparing two industries on the same graph, an industry whose concentration curve always lies above another industry's has a higher degree of absolute concentration. (When the two curves cross, an ambiguity exists, however.) Clearly, we have to use the percentage of total assets rather than dollar values to be able to compare two different industries or even a concentration at two different points of time for the same industry. One drawback to using percentage of total assets when comparing two industries is that we do not know the relative economic importance of the industries being compared. Is it meaningful to put concentration curves for the steel industry and the horseshoe industry on the same graph?[21]

The Lorenz Curve

Most beginning economics students are exposed to the **Lorenz curve** when they study the distribution of income and wealth.[22] The Lorenz curve relates the

[19] Morris A. Adelman, "The Measurement of Industrial Concentration," *Review of Economics and Statistics*, vol. 33 (November 1951), pp. 269–296.

[20] See, for example, Dean A. Worcester, Jr., *Monopoly, Big Business, and Welfare in the Postwar United States* (Seattle: University of Washington Press, 1967).

[21] See United States Federal Trade Commission, *Concentration of Productive Facilities, 1947* (Washington, D.C.: U.S. Government Printing Office, 1949). Nelson uses the area under the concentration curve as an index of concentration. See Ralph L. Nelson, *Concentration in Manufacturing Industries of the United States, A Mid-Century Report* (New Haven, Conn.: Yale University Press, 1963), pp. 20–21, Table 5:A.

[22] Max O. Lorenz, "Methods of Measuring the Concentration of Wealth," *Journal of American Statistical Association*, vol. 9 (1905), pp. 209–219.

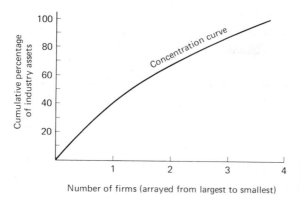

FIGURE 3-3
Concentration curve for industry assets.

percentage of total market value of shipments to the percentage of firms in the market accumulated from the smallest firm to the largest.

We now apply the Lorenz curve idea to a hypothetical market in Figure 3-4. We have labeled the horizontal axis the percentage of firms cumulated from the smallest-sized firm. Contrast this with the horizontal axis in Figure 3-3, which showed the concentration curve. There we looked at the *number* of firms cumulated from the *largest* firm. The vertical axis in Figure 3-3 is exactly the same as the vertical axis in Figure 3-4.

The diagonal line in Figure 3-4 represents an industry that has equal distribution of firms measured by asset size. In other words, all firms are of identical size if the Lorenz curve coincides with the diagonal line. To the extent that the curve is bowed outward toward the southeast, inequality in firm size will appear in any particular market. Conceivably, however, a high degree of concentration could exist in an industry which has only a few firms of equal size. That

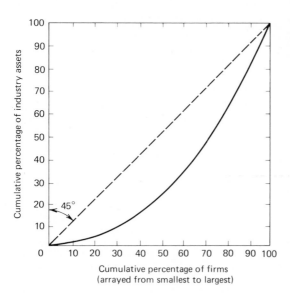

FIGURE 3-4
Lorenz concentration curve.

is why the Lorenz curve, which indicates the percentage of the cumulated number of firms in the industry, is often called a measure of inequality, or relative concentration. In other words, *the Lorenz curve measures relative concentration* rather than the absolute measure provided by either a concentration ratio or the concentration curve discussed in the previous section.

The Lorenz curve as a summary index clearly suffers from an inability to indicate any growth of monopoly and concentration. A statistician looking at the Lorenz curve can demonstrate that a decline in the number of sellers could bring about a *decrease* in relative concentration, even though most economists would believe that a decline in the number of sellers increases concentration. Here the difference between relative and absolute concentration becomes clear. The decline in the number of firms in the industry that allows the remaining firms to become closer in size reduces relative concentration or inequality while increasing absolute concentration.[23] Furthermore, some economists believe that in some industries, there are a large number of "insignificant" firms compared to industry giants. These economists contend that any measure of concentration which changes the numbers of these insignificant firms is not meaningful.[24]

Truncated Indexes   One way out of this problem is to use a truncated index. One might examine, for example, the number of largest companies required to produce 75 percent of the industry's output. This approach eliminates the so-called marginal firms from the index. Presumably, industry-to-industry variation of firm numbers will be minimized.

The Gini Coefficient

The **Gini coefficient** is a statistical measure based on the Lorenz curve.[25] We can use Figure 3-4 showing the Lorenz curve to demonstrate the concept of the Gini coefficient. We compare the area between the 45° straight line and the Lorenz curve of actual firm asset distribution to the entire area under the diagonal—that is, to the triangle that represents one-half of the box in Figure 3-4. In other words,

$$\frac{\text{Gini coefficient}}{\text{of inequality}} = \frac{\begin{array}{c}\text{area between diagonal and}\\ \text{Lorenz curve of actual}\\ \text{income distribution}\end{array}}{\begin{array}{c}\text{triangular area under}\\ \text{diagonal line}\end{array}}$$

[23] See John M. Blair, "Statistical Measures of Concentration in Business: Problems of Compiling and Interpretation," *Bulletin of the Oxford University Institute of Statistics*, vol. 18 (November 1956), p. 356.

[24] Ibid., p. 352.

[25] It was originally developed by Corrado Gini, *The Variabilità e Mutabilità* (Bologna's Tipogr. dip. Cuppini, 1912).

What does this mean? It means that the Gini coefficient will range from 0 to 1. If we had perfect equality of firm size distribution, the Gini coefficient would be 0, because there would be no area between the diagonal line, or curve of absolute equality, and the curve of actual distribution of firm assets. The greater that area becomes, however, the greater becomes the Gini coefficient and, hence, the measure of inequality. As an index of inequality, the Gini coefficient suggests one plausible inference when there are small numbers of evenly matched firms. A duopoly or a triopoly with equal market shares has a Gini coefficient of 0, yet the firms certainly could not be considered competitive industries. Additionally, the shape of the Lorenz curve and, hence, the value of the Gini coefficient is quite sensitive to errors in defining the number of firms in the industry. As the borderline firms one includes become smaller or larger, the indicated degree of inequality tends to become higher. Note, further, that two firms that each produce one-half of the industry's output will yield the same value Gini coefficient (0) as 100 firms that each supply 1 percent of the industry output. We would surmise, however, that industry behavior will be quite different in the two cases.

Applications of the Gini Coefficient   The Gini coefficient has been used in a considerable amount of applied work, including studies by Horowitz and Horowitz, Woytinsky, and Kemp.[26]

Problems with the Gini Coefficient   The Gini coefficient suffers from the same problem that confronts virtually all summary concentration indexes: Accurate information about market share of *every firm* in the market is needed. Since the Bureau of the Census is not allowed to publish any statistics that could contain information about individual companies, it is often impossible to get accurate information. Moreover, two different Lorenz curves are capable of generating equal Gini coefficients because they enclose the same relative areas. Hence, the Gini coefficient, like other one-parameter measures, does not represent a unique distribution of firm sizes in a given market.

Herfindahl Index

Another popular measure of dispersion of firm size is the Herfindahl index originally suggested by O. C. Herfindahl in his 1950 Columbia University Ph.D. dissertation entitled "Concentration in the Steel Industry."[27] The Herfindahl

---

[26] Ann R. Horowitz and Ira Horowitz, "Firms in a Declining Market: The Brewing Case," *Journal of Industrial Economics,* vol. 13 (March 1965), pp. 129–153; W. Woytinsky, *Earnings and Social Security in the United States,* Social Security Research Council (Washington, D.C.: U.S. Government Printing Office, 1943); and Bernard A. Kemp, "More on Measures of Market Structure," *Systems Evaluation Group Research Contribution,* no. 6, Center for Naval Analysis (Washington, D.C.: The Franklin Institute, 1966).

[27] The Herfindahl index can be shown to be equal to $v^2 = 1/N$, where V is the coefficient of variation and N is the number of firms in the market.

summary index is defined as the sum of squares of the sizes of firms in an industry where size is the percentage of total industry assets. In other words, it is equal to

$$\text{Herfindahl index} = \sum_{i=1}^{N} \left(\frac{x_i}{T}\right)^2 \tag{3-14}$$

where N is the number of firms

x_i is the absolute size of individual firm i

T is the total size of the market

Thus, we see that the fraction x_i/T is simply the percentage of total industry assets, sales, or other variables accounted for by the ith firm.

Let us take an example. In a given market, the total assets are equal to 1,000. There are four firms. They have absolute sizes of 500, 350, 100, and 50. The Herfindahl index for this market is equal to $.5^2 + .35^2 + .1^2 + .05^2$, or .385.

When all firms are of equal size, the index becomes $1/N$. If there is only one firm in the industry, the Herfindahl index is equal to 1.

Measure of Changes in Market Shares   Stigler has demonstrated that the Herfindahl index may be used to measure changes in market shares.[28] This index takes account of all firms in the market and seems to bear a similarity to other measures of monopoly power. Although popular, it is difficult to construct empirically because of the data necessary.[29] One can, of course, calculate a minimum Herfindahl index with limited data on the largest firms.

The Herfindahl index tends to have a distribution strongly skewed toward low values. Unless monopoly power is dissimilarly distributed, differences are easily detected when using this index.[30]

Other Indexes

A host of other indexes attempts to describe the degree of dispersion of firm size within an industry. We will look briefly at several of them.

Relative Mean Deviation Intercept   The distribution of industry assets (or sales or employment) can be regarded as a statistical dispersion measuring the extent to which assets (or sales or employment) of each firm in the industry differ from the assets of the average-sized firm. Statistically, the sum of the

[28] George J. Stigler, "The Measurement of Concentration," in *The Organization of Industry* (Homewood, Ill.: Irwin, 1968), pp. 29–38.

[29] See, nonetheless, Ralph L. Nelson, *Concentration in the Manufacturing Industries in the United States* (New Haven, Conn.: Yale University Press, 1963) for a series of Herfindahl indexes for American industry.

[30] This problem may be eliminated by taking a log or other monotonically increasing transformation of the index.

differences from the mean is always equal to zero. Therefore, we must average the *absolute* values (ignoring plus or minus sign) of these differences in order to get a dispersion measure, usually called the mean deviation. The relative mean deviation is then obtained by dividing the mean deviation by the mean.

Pietra Ratio, Prais Disparity, and Stochastic Indexes   An index of inequality related to the relative mean duration intercept has been named the Pietra ratio. Another index, the Prais Disparity, shows that the greater the disparity is between sizes of the largest and smallest firms, the greater the degree of concentration will be.

The Yule, Pareto, and lognormal indexes calculate concentration when the distribution of firms in the industry is determined by a stochastic growth process.[31]

HOW DO WE DEFINE THE INDUSTRY?

Now we can tackle the serious problem of defining the market and making a distinction between the market and the industry.

The Standard Industrial Classification System

Most studies of hypotheses concerning industrial organization use data collected through the Census of Manufacturers. The U.S. government, through a task force under the direction of the Office of Management and Budget (OMB), has developed an elaborate system of **Standard Industrial Classification** (S.I.C.) codes. With this system, a single code is assigned to the output of every business enterprise.[32] Once firms have been given a S.I.C. code, data such as sales, assets, or value of shipments may be collected and aggregated to form industry statistics and measures of industrial structure. Other countries and certain international organizations such as the United Nations have their own standard industrial classifications that they use for their official statistics. For example, the 1968 United Kingdom Standard Industrial Classification consists of 27 major industrial groups, which are in turn divided into 181 subgroups. In the United States the S.I.C. system is organized around a series of seven numbers. The first digit of any classification indicates the sector of the economy, for example, 5 for trade, 0 for agriculture and forestry, 2 and 3 for manufacturing. For manufacturing establishments the first two digits together tell which prod-

---

[31] For a further discussion and comparison of concentration indexes, see David R. Kamerschen and N. Lam in "A Survey of Measures of Market Power," *Rivista Internazionale di Scienze Economiche e Commerciali,* vol. 22 (1975), pp. 1131–1156; and Christian Marfels, "A Bird's Eye View to Measures of Concentration," *Antitrust Bulletin,* vol. 20 (Fall 1975), pp. 485–503. Also see Leslie Hannah and J. A. Kay, *Concentration in Modern Industry: Theory, Measurement and the U. K. Experience* (London, England: Macmillan, 1975).

[32] See M. R. Conklin and H. T. Goldstein, "Census Principles and Product Classification, Manufacturing Industries," in George J. Stigler, ed., *Business Concentration and Price Policy* (Princeton, N. J.: Princeton University Press, 1955), pp. 15–36.

uct group is in a manufacturing group, of which there are 20 such groups, 20–39. In total, 99 major groups are designated by a two-digit code. The first three digits together further subclassify the establishment. Then we go to five digits and all the way up to seven digits, which is a classification of some 7,500 different products. In Table 3-3, we show the S.I.C. two-digit manufacturing industry group. In Table 3-4, we show the further breakdown of a typical two-digit S.I.C. code and its component three-digit and four-digit subclassifications. Component industries for the four-digit Motor Vehicle Parts and Accessories (S.I.C. No. 3714) are given in Table 3-5.

The purpose of the S.I.C. system is to place data concerning industries and products into a meaningful system that will be constant over time. Current data can be compared with past data. One must remember that the classification of industries and products is not the result of economic theory or mechanical rules. Rather, conferences between industry representatives and government agencies generally have been used to decide which products and firms go into which classifications. Also remember that the S.I.C. system was not organized for studying industrial concentration, but for the purposes of recording census and other governmental statistics.

The primary emphasis in defining an industry is on the supply side. Most industries are defined in terms of firms' engaging in producing a product or

TABLE 3-3
S.I.C. TWO-DIGIT MANUFACTURING INDUSTRY GROUP

Manufacturing

Major Group 20. Food and kindred products
Major Group 21. Tobacco manufactures
Major Group 22. Textile mill products
Major Group 23. Apparel and other finished products made from fabrics and similar materials
Major Group 24. Lumber and wood products, except furniture
Major Group 25. Furniture and fixtures
Major Group 26. Paper and allied products
Major Group 27. Printing, publishing, and allied industries
Major Group 28. Chemicals and allied products
Major Group 29. Petroleum refining and related industries
Major Group 30. Rubber and miscellaneous plastics products
Major Group 31. Leather and leather products
Major Group 32. Stone, clay, glass, and concrete products
Major Group 33. Primary metal industries
Major Group 34. Fabricated metal products, except machinery and transportation equipment
Major Group 35. Machinery, except electrical
Major Group 36. Electrical and electronic machinery, equipment, and supplies
Major Group 37. Transportation equipment
Major Group 38. Measuring, analyzing, and controlling instruments; photographic, medical, and optical goods; watches and clocks
Major Group 39. Miscellaneous manufacturing industries

Source: Office of Management and Budget, *Standard Industrial Classification Manual* (Washington, D.C.: U.S.G.P.O., 1972), p. 5.

TABLE 3-4
S.I.C. TWO-DIGIT CODE AND THREE- AND FOUR-DIGIT SUBCLASSIFICATIONS

37 Transportation Equipment

371 Motor Vehicles and Motor Vehicle Equipment
3711 Motor vehicles and passenger car bodies
3713 Truck and bus bodies
3714 Motor vehicle parts and accessories
3715 Truck trailers

372 Aircraft and Parts
3721 Aircraft
3724 Aircraft engines and engine parts
3728 Aircraft parts and auxiliary equipment, not elsewhere classified

373 Ship and Boat Building and Repairing
3731 Ship building and repairing
3732 Boat building and repairing

374 Railroad Equipment
3743 Railroad equipment

375 Motorcycles, Bicycles, and Parts
3751 Motorcycles, bicycles, and parts

376 Guided Missiles and Space Vehicles and Parts
3761 Guided missiles and space vehicles
3764 Guided missile and space vehicle propulsion units and propulsion unit parts
3769 Guided missile and space vehicle parts and auxiliary equipment, not elsewhere classified

379 Miscellaneous Transportation Equipment
3792 Travel trailers and campers
3795 Tanks and tank components
3799 Transportation equipment, not elsewhere classified

Source: Office of Management and Budget, *Standard Industrial Classification Manual* (Washington, D.C.: U.S.G.P.O., 1972), p. 441.

group of products that are related by technological processes or raw materials used in their production. Thus, the definition of a market has been looked at from substitutability on the supply side. In many cases (if not all), substitutability on the consumption side seems to be ignored completely. The Senate subcommittee "Report on Concentration in American Industry" takes to task concentration ratios based on S.I.C. classifications.

> No attempt is made in this report to fit the Census classification to the actual competitive structure of industrial markets. The result is in some cases a fairly accurate reflection of the degree of market concentration, in others an overstatement, and in others, an understatement of such concentration. . . . For some categories, the measure of concentration may be extremely significant and indicate relative market powers; for others it may not be significant at all for this purpose.[33]

---

[33] United States Senate Subcommittee on Antitrust and Monopoly of the Committee of the Judiciary, *Concentration in American Industry,* 85th Cong., 1st Sess. (Washington, D.C.: U.S. Government Printing Office, 1957), p. 5.

TABLE 3-5
S.I.C. FOUR-DIGIT MOTOR VEHICLE PARTS AND ACCESSORIES

3714 Motor Vehicle Parts and Accessories

Establishments primarily engaged in manufacturing motor vehicle parts and accessories, but not engaged in manufacturing complete motor vehicles or passenger car bodies. Establishments primarily engaged in manufacturing or assembling complete automobiles and trucks are classified in Industry 3711, tires and tubes in Industry 3011, automobile glass in Major Group 32, automobile stampings in Industry 3465, vehicular lighting equipment in Industry 3647, ignition systems in Industry 3694, storage batteries in Industry 3691, and carburetors, pistons, rings, and valves in Industry 3592.

Acceleration equipment, motor vehicle
Air brakes, motor vehicle
Automotive wiring harness sets, other than ignition
Axle housings and shafts, motor vehicle
Axles, motor vehicle
Bearings, motor vehicle: except ball and roller
Brake drums, motor vehicle
Brakes and brake parts, motor vehicle
Bumpers and bumperettes, motor vehicle
Camshafts, motor vehicle
Choker rods, motor vehicle
Cleaners, air: motor vehicle
Connecting rods, motor vehicle engine
Control equipment, motor vehicle: acceleration mechanisms, governors, etc.
Crankshaft assemblies, motor vehicle
Cylinder heads, motor vehicle
Defrosters, motor vehicle
Differentials and parts, motor vehicle
Directional signals, motor vehicle
Drive shafts, motor vehicle
Engines and parts, except diesel: motor vehicle
Exhaust systems and parts, motor vehicle
Fifth wheels, motor vehicle
Filters: oil, fuel, and air—motor vehicle
Frames, motor vehicle
Fuel pumps, motor vehicle
Fuel systems and parts, motor vehicle: gas tanks, fuel pipes and manifold
Gas tanks, motor vehicle
Gears, motor vehicle
Governors, motor vehicle
Heaters, motor vehicle
Hoods, motor vehicle
Horns, motor vehicle

Hydraulic fluid power pumps, for automotive steering mechanisms
Instrument board assemblies, motor vehicle
Lubrication systems and parts, motor vehicle
Manifolds, motor vehicle
Motor vehicle engine rebuilding, on a factory basis
Motor vehicle parts and accessories (except motor vehicle stampings)
Mufflers, exhaust: motor vehicle
Oil strainers, motor vehicle
Pipes, fuel: motor vehicle
Power transmission equipment, motor vehicle
Radiators and radiator shells and cores, motor vehicle
Rear axle housings, motor vehicle
Rebuilding motor vehicle engines and transmissions, on a factory basis
Rims, wheel: motor vehicle
Sanders, motor vehicle safety
Shock absorbers, motor vehicle
Steering mechanisms, motor vehicle
Third axle attachments or six-wheel units for motor vehicles
Tie rods, motor vehicle
Tire valve cores, motor vehicle
Tops, motor vehicle: except stamped metal
Transmission housings and parts, motor vehicle
Transmissions, motor vehicle
Universal joints, motor vehicle
Vacuum brakes, motor vehicle
Wheels, motor vehicle
Windshield frames, motor vehicle
Windshield wiper systems, all types
Winterfronts, motor vehicle
Wiring harness sets (other than ignition), automotive

Source: Office of Management and Budget, *Standard Industrial Classification Manual* (Washington, D.C.: U.S.G.P.O., 1972), p. 172.

Industry and Commodity Approach to Classification

In determining market classification, the government utilizes the industry approach and the commodity approach. With the former, each plant for which data are obtained is assigned to one of 43 four-digit industry groups. The plant is assigned to an industry according to its primary product or activity. Then its entire output is included in that classification. Using the commodity approach, output of specific products is assigned to a total product group without respect to the primary activity of the plant from which the product comes. In other words, the output of any plant is divided among appropriate commodity groups, even though the plant itself has to be classified within only one primary industrial group.

Two discrepancies arise between commodity and industry categories when these classification procedures are utilized. With the industry approach, there will clearly be some output assigned to an industry group that doesn't belong there. With the commodity approach, on the other hand, product output totals may include output that is not primary to the plant in which it originated. That tells us that the four-digit industry classification as defined by the government is not comparable with summation of the five-digit product classes underlying it. In order to determine how important such discrepancies may be, the Bureau of the Census provides two "discrepancy" measures called the *coverage ratio* and the *specialization ratio*.

The Coverage Ratio   The **coverage ratio** is defined as the extent to which the primary market of an industry originates in plants that are classified specifically in that industry. It is defined as

$$\text{Coverage ratio} = \frac{\text{shipments of product } x \text{ that come from plants classified in industry } x}{\text{total shipments of product } x}$$

Thus, in 1972 a coverage ratio of, say, .70 in commercial laundry equipment, for example, indicates that 70 percent of the commercial laundry equipment output originates in plants classified in this industry.

Specialization Ratio   The **specialization ratio**, otherwise called the primary-product specialization ratio, tells us the degree to which plants classified in the industry actually specialize in making the products primary to that industry. It is defined as

$$\text{Specialization ratio} = \frac{\text{shipments of product } x \text{ coming from plants classified in industry } x}{\text{total shipments of plants classified in } x}$$

In 1972 the same industry had a specialization ratio of .91. That means that 91 percent of the output of plants classified in that industry actually consists of commercial laundry equipment, or otherwise stated, 9 percent of the output of that industry consists of something else. These ratios may change over time. In 1947, for example, both the coverage and specialization ratios were .94 for commercial laundry equipment.

The lower the specialization ratio, the more diversified the plants are in an industry. The paint and allied products industry, for example, has a specialization ratio of 60 percent, meaning that 40 percent of the output of plants in that industry consists of something other than paints and allied products.

Problems with the Data

The product dimension of a market usually tends to predominate when economists discuss the concept of market. Every market has geographic and time dimensions as well. We can define a market as a collection of firms, each of which is supplying products that have some degree of substitutability to the same potential buyers.

Market Does Not Equal Industry   The term "market" or what an economist would define as an industry is not necessarily the same thing as an OMB task force or S.I.C.-defined industry. After all, firms in the same industry may not supply substitutable products. In fact, they may sell their products to quite different sets of consumers. Additionally, as we have seen, firms in the same S.I.C.-coded industry may produce other products besides the one under study or besides the one for which they are classified by the federal government. Westinghouse, for example, is classified as a supplier of electrical goods and equipment as its main product line. It also produces gas-fired incinerators and plywood, but the S.I.C. system allocates all of Westinghouse's assets to electrical goods and equipment. Since industry data are often used to test implications about market behavior, there are obvious difficulties in doing empirical research.[34] In short, the economic market or industry for a product may not be the same thing as the statistically defined industry producing that product.

Exports and Imports   All empirical research faces data problems. In many instances the relevant data are simply unavailable, in other instances the available data measure a variable that is not exactly the variable desired. This is often the case when using S.I.C. data to measure industrial structure. Consider the problem of exports. The more the leading companies export relative to the industry average, the more industry measurements, such as the value of shipments that focus on the relative output of leading firms will be biased upward. Conversely, the more industry leaders import relative to the industry average, the more such measurements will be biased downward. Another problem arises

---

[34] The reason market and industry have been interchanged is because of the widely available industry data provided by the U.S. Bureau of the Census.

when large companies own a number of plants and make shipments from one plant to another in the same industry. Large companies usually own more plants than smaller companies, which often possess only a single plant. In such a situation, the leading companies appear to have a larger share of the industry because of the double-counting of shipments.[35]

We have discussed coverage and specialization ratios above. Taken together, these ratios give a relatively accurate appraisal of the adequacy of the data compiled for different industries. Unfortunately, separate specialization and coverage ratios are not published for all sets of leading companies and industries. Thus, we cannot determine if the shipments of these companies are representative of their actual shipments of those products classified in the industry under study. For example, if the product specialization ratio for the leading companies is lower than the average for the industry as a whole, the concentration ratio will be biased upward. The same will be true if the coverage ratio for the leading companies is higher than for the industry as a whole.

CONCENTRATION RATIOS—A SUMMARY OF THEIR INADEQUACIES

Before going on to the actual measurement of concentration ratios, it is important to summarize the inadequacies mentioned in the previous discussion. We list them below, although not necessarily in order of their importance.

1 Because they are based on national figures, they ignore regional market power and concentration.

2 They ignore imports and exports.

3 They do not consider the ability of potential entrants to compete.

4 The S.I.C. system may not accurately reflect economic markets under study.

5 They do not reflect turnover.

6 They give no information about the relative size and position of the group of firms included in the ratio.

7 They describe only a part of the number and size distribution of firms.

8 They do not imply types of conduct specifically by firms in the market under study.

9 The cutoff point for computing the index is arbitrary in terms of the number of firms.

APPENDIX: Concentration Ratios and Trends

There are numerous actual measures of concentration. Most of these measures are collected and published by the Bureau of the Census. In Table A3-1 we show the change

---

[35] For an additional discussion, see Morris A. Adelman, "A Current Appraisal of Concentration Statistics," *American Statistical Association, Business and Economics Statistics Section, Proceedings* (1957), pp. 227-231.

TABLE A3-1
SHARE OF TOTAL VALUE ADDED BY MANUFACTURE ACCOUNTED FOR BY THE 50 AND
100 LARGEST IDENTICAL MANUFACTURING COMPANIES: 1972 AND EARLIER YEARS

Year of company ranking, and company rank group (a)	Year of company ranking, and company rank group								
	1972 (b)	1970 (c)	1967 (d)	1966 (e)	1963 (f)	1962 (g)	1958 (h)	1954 (i)	1947 (j)
1972									
Largest 50 companies	25	23	23	23	22	22	20	19	12
Largest 100 companies	33	31	30	30	29	28	26	25	17
1970									
Largest 50 companies	23	24	23	24	23	22	20	19	12
Largest 100 companies	32	33	31	31	29	29	26	25	18
1967									
Largest 50 companies	22	24	25	25	24	24	22	21	19
Largest 100 companies	30	32	33	33	32	31*	29	28	20
1966									
Largest 50 companies	22	23	24	25	24	24	22	21	14
Largest 100 companies	30	31	32	33	32	31	29	28	24
1963									
Largest 50 companies	21	23	24	24	25	24	23	22	15
Largest 100 companies	29	31	32	33	33	32	30	29	22
1962									
Largest 50 companies	22	23	24	25	25	24	23	22	15
Largest 100 companies	29	31	33	33	32	32	30	29	21
1958									
Largest 50 companies	20	22	23	24	24	24	23	23	19
Largest 100 companies	27	29	31	31	32	31	30	29	22
1954									
Largest 50 companies	20	21	23	23	24	23	23	23	19
Largest 100 companies	27	28	31	31	31	30	30	30	21
1947									
Largest 50 companies	17	19	20	21	21	21	20	21	17
Largest 100 companies	24	26	27	27	28	27	27	27	23

Note: The 100 largest companies in each specified year were selected, and their proportion of total value added by manufacture in each of the other years was computed. Thus this table measures the changes in concentration ratios for a fixed group of companies from one year to another. In case of mergers, the larger of the two at the time of merger was considered to be the predecessor company.
Source: Bureau of the Census, *Census of Manufacturers,* Subject and Special Statistics, vol. 5 (Washington, D.C.: U.S.G.P.O., 1976), pp. SR2-4.

in the share of total value added for the largest 50 and 100 companies between 1947 and 1972. The Federal Trade Commission publishes data on the distribution of industry measures of concentration. For example, the distribution of assets for various firm sizes in manufacturing, mining, retail trade, and wholesale trade are given in Table A3-2. Table A3-3 gives the value of shipments for a number of industries by 4, 8, 20, and 50 firm ratios for 1972 and selected earlier years. In addition, the specialization and coverage ratios are also given in this table.

TABLE A3-2
COMPOSITION OF THE SAMPLE, BY TOTAL ASSETS, FOURTH QUARTER 1978

	Manufacturing			Mining		
	Total assets*		Number of corporations in sample†	Total assets*		Number of corporations in sample‡
Asset sizes	Million dollars	Percent		Million dollars	Percent	
All asset sizes	1,086,350	100	8,977	52,659	100	649
$1,000 million and over	632,866	58	199	23,424	44	40
$250 million to $1,000 million	165,924	15	199			
$100 million to $250 million	66,796	6	434	7,548	14	48
$50 million to $100 million	37,522	3	540	3,759	7	52
$25 million to $50 million	30,813	3	874	3,277	6	68
$10 million to $25 million	38,358	4	1,852	3,521	7	76
$10 million and over	972,280	89	4,243	41,529	79	284
Under $10 million	114,071	11	4,734	11,130	21	365

	Retail trade			Wholesale trade		
	Total assets*		Number of corporations in sample§	Total assets*		Number of corporations in sample¶
Asset sizes	Million dollars	Percent		Million dollars	Percent	
All asset sizes	224,928	100	2,046	215,335	100	2,727
$1,000 million and over	48,939	22	18	20,851	10	11
$250 million to $1,000 million	22,707	10	48	22,968	11	49
$100 million to $250 million	12,005	5	76	16,080	7	107
$50 million to $100 million	8,079	4	116	15,355	7	212
$25 million to $50 million	5,979	3	144	13,082	6	295
$10 million to $25 million	7,185	3	128	22,914	11	350
$10 million and over	104,895	47	530	111,249	52	1,024
Under $10 million	120,033	53	1,516	104,087	48	1,703

*Estimated universe total; figures are rounded and will not necessarily add to totals.
†Drawn from a universe of approximately 260,000.
‡Drawn from a universe of approximately 24,000.
§Drawn from a universe of approximately 525,000.
¶Drawn from a universe of approximately 185,000.
Source: Federal Trade Commission, *Quarterly Financial Report, Fourth Quarter* (Washington, D.C.: U.S.G.P.O., 1979).

TABLE A3-3
SHARE OF VALUE OF SHIPMENTS ACCOUNTED FOR BY THE 4, 8, 20, AND 50 LARGEST COMPANIES IN EACH MANUFACTURING INDUSTRY: 1972 AND EARLIER YEARS

1972 code	Industry	Year	Companies (number)	Total (million dollars)	Value of industry shipments				Primary product specialization ratio (percent)	Coverage ratio (percent)
					Percent accounted for by					
					4 largest companies	8 largest companies	20 largest companies	50 largest companies		
2082	Malt beverages	1972	108	4,054.4	52	70	91	99	100	100
		1967	125	2,929.7	40	59	86	98	100	100
		1963	171	2,315.1	34	52	78	94	100	100
		1947	404	1,316.0	21	30	44	(NA)	100	99
2599	Furniture and fixtures, n.e.c.	1972	477	372.0	13	23	39	59	87	79
		1967	317	179.0	18	28	43	65	87	75
		1963	354	121.6	16	27	42	64	86	70
2731	Book publishing	1972	1,120	2,856.9	19	31	56	77	93	86
		1967	963	2,060.2	20	32	57	77	94	85
		1963	936	1,534.6	20	33	56	76	93	88
		1947	635	463.9	18	29	48	(NA)	92	93
2834	Pharmaceutical preparations	1972	680	7,149.5	26	44	75	91	87	97
		1967	791	4,696.4	24	40	73	90	87	97
		1963	944	3,314.3	22	38	72	89	87	94
		1947	1,123	941.3	28	44	64	(NA)	91	98

1972 code	Industry	Year	Companies (number)	Value of industry shipments						Primary product specialization ratio (percent)	Coverage ratio (percent)
				Total (million dollars)	Percent accounted for by						
					4 largest companies	8 largest companies	20 largest companies	50 largest companies			
2911	Petroleum refining	1972	154	25,921.1	31	56	84	95		99	97
		1967	276	20,293.9	33	57	84	96		98	97
		1963	266	16,496.9	34	56	82	95		98	97
		1947	277	6,623.7	37	59	83	(NA)		99	97
3021	Rubber and plastics footwear	1972	82	600.0	59	70	89	99		94	99
		1967	51	427.0	59	75	92	(D)		(NA)	(NA)
		1963	44	354.2	62	77	94	100		93	90
		1947	20	198.7	81	93	100	(X)		80	99
3612	Transformers	1972	168	1,461.9	59	75	90	97		96	97
		1967	150	1,188.4	65	78	92	97		95	98
		1963	144	722.9	68	79	93	98		92	94
		1947	134	357.0	73	84	93	(NA)		85	91
3662	Radio and TV communication equipment	1972	1,524	9,140.2	19	33	58	77		91	91
		1967	1,111	8,555.8	22	37	61	81		89	92
		1963	1,001	7,145.6	29	45	69	84		88	90

NA: not available. D: withheld to avoid disclosing figures for individual companies. X: not applicable.
Source: Bureau of the Census, *Census of Manufacturers,* Subject and Special Statistics, vol. 5 (Washington, D.C.: U.S.G.P.O., 1976), pp. SR2–9, 18, 20, 22, 24, 37, 39.

CHAPTER 4

MARKET STRUCTURE AND PERFORMANCE

In our discussion in Chapter 1 of the structure-conduct-performance relationship, we hypothesized a link between market structure and performance. In the previous chapter we identified measures of market structure, and we now turn our attention to the empirical relationship of those measures to industrial organization performance.

Our theories of competition and monopoly predict that firms with substantial monopoly power will charge higher prices, producing less and selling less output. They will also typically earn higher rates of profit and use their "entrenched" positions to resist competitive pressures. Many researchers have looked at concentration ratios as an appropriate proxy for monopoly power. They have then looked at the relationship between measured monopoly power and such important performance variables as profits, prices, market and firm growth, firm turnover, and technological change.

ECONOMY-WIDE CONCENTRATION AND PROFITABILITY

Before we look at concentration of particular industries, we will investigate the amount of concentration prevailing in the economy as a whole. Most of the work in this area has concerned two areas of empirical dispute:

1 Whether there is a trend toward increasing concentration

2 Whether there is greater concentration in the United States when compared with other countries[1]

The first major study of the level of economy-wide concentration over time was performed by Nutter.[2] Nutter's basic conclusion was that no clear trend toward increasing concentration was to be found. Later studies have confirmed this result, using more recent data.[3] An investigation of overall profits during the past three decades, whether expressed in real or percentage terms, appears to show an upward trend that probably peaked in the mid-1960s. Further, as Table 4-1 reveals, real aftertax profits as a percentage of receipts have been relatively stable for some time. When expressed as a percent of GNP, they have actually declined in recent years.

THE STRUCTURE-CONDUCT-PERFORMANCE PARADIGM

In Bain's original specification of the structure-conduct-performance paradigm, an explicit link existed between market structure and performance through conduct. As we have previously indicated, market structure formed the basis for conduct that included actual policies employed by firms. Many of these forms of conduct, such as price leadership, will be investigated in the chapters that follow. Conduct, in turn, affects firms' revenues and costs, hence also affecting profitability and other measures of performance. It is hard to argue against the notion that conduct is a cause of a firm's performance. It is quite another thing to accept the further notion that particular conduct is the only explanation of performance or even an indication of the competitiveness of a market. Moreover, market conduct is often unobservable. We cannot find out,

---

[1] Although it is difficult to compare economy-wide measures of concentration between nations, those who have attempted to make the comparison have generally concluded that concentration is lower in the U.S. as compared to other industrialized nations. See, for example, David K. Round, "Concentration in Australian Markets," *Management Forum,* vol. 2 (June 1976), pp. 93–105; Christian Marfels, *Concentration Levels and Trends in the Canadian Economy, 1965–1973: A Technical Report* (Ottawa: Ministry of Supply and Services Canada, 1977); Masao Baba, "Industrial Concentration in Japan: The Economic Background to the Revision of the Antimonopoly Law," *Internationales Asien Forum,* vol. 7 (April 1976), pp. 54–74; Max D. Stewart, *Concentration in Canadian Manufacturing and Mining Industries* (Economic Council of Canada, August 1970), chap. 5.

[2] G. Warren Nutter, *The Extent of Enterprise Monopoly in the United States: 1899–1939* (Chicago: University of Chicago Press, 1951).

[3] See David R. Kamerschen, "Changes in Concentration Among American Manufacturing Industries," *Zeitschrift für die Gesamte Staatswissenschaft,* vol. 127 (October 1971), pp. 621–639; Henry A. Einhorn, "Competition in American Industry, 1939–58," *Journal of Political Economy,* vol. 74 (October 1966), pp. 506–511; and B. T. Allen, "Average Concentration in Manufacturing, 1947–1972," *Journal of Economic Issues,* vol. 10 (September 1976), pp. 664–673. See also David R. Kamerschen, "An Empirical Test of Oligopoly Theories," *Journal of Political Economy,* vol. 76 (July/August 1968), pp. 615–634; J. Lawrence Hexter and John W. Snow, "An Entropy Measure of Relative Aggregate Concentration," *Southern Economic Journal,* vol. 36 (January 1970), pp. 239–243. For a contrary view, see Leonard Weiss, "Mergers, Industrial Concentration, and Antitrust Policy," *Journal of Economic Issues,* vol. 10 (June 1976), pp. 354–381.

TABLE 4-1
NOMINAL AND REAL AFTERTAX PROFITS, 1950–1976

Year	Nominal aftertax profits (billions of dollars)	Real aftertax profits (billions of dollars)*	Aftertax profits as a percentage of receipts†	Aftertax profits as a percentage of GNP
1950	15.7	35.1	7.1	5.5
1951	15.5	32.1	4.8	4.7
1952	16.0	32.5	4.3	4.6
1953	15.2	30.6	4.3	4.2
1954	17.0	34.1	4.5	4.6
1955	22.6	45.4	5.4	5.7
1956	20.9	41.4	5.3	5.0
1957	20.6	39.4	4.8	4.7
1958	18.5	34.5	4.2	4.1
1959	24.6	45.4	4.8	5.1
1960	23.9	43.5	4.4	4.7
1961	24.1	43.3	4.3	4.6
1962	30.9	55.0	4.5	5.5
1963	33.4	58.7	4.7	5.6
1964	39.0	67.7	5.2	6.1
1965	46.2	78.8	5.6	6.2
1966	48.9	81.1	5.6	6.5
1967	46.8	75.5	5.0	5.9
1968	46.4	71.8	5.1	5.3
1969	41.8	61.4	4.8	4.5
1970	33.4	46.3	4.0	3.4
1971	39.5	52.5	4.1	3.7
1972	50.5	65.0	4.3	4.3
1973	50.4	61.0	4.7	3.9
1974	32.4	35.4	5.5	2.3
1975	42.4	42.4	4.6	2.8
1976	53.9	50.9	5.5	3.2

*Based on CPI index where 1975 = 100.0.
†Manufacturing corporations only.
Source: Economic Report of the President, 1977.

for example, if firms in a particular market are acting independently as they respond to market conditions or are acting in unison through some type of conscious policy incorporating the actions of all the firms in the industry. In other words, we have no objective means of measuring market conduct.

Nonetheless, market conduct, as we shall see, plays a crucial role in antitrust enforcement. Many antitrust resources are employed to restrict so-called anticompetitive practices. These, too, will be examined in later chapters. We will restrict ourselves here to an investigation of the findings that link structure with performance.

IMPORTANCE OF PROFITABILITY STUDIES IN PUBLIC POLICY

When the 1968 White House Task Force on Antitrust Policy recommended new legislation to supplement the antitrust statutes, its members based their case on a number of rate-of-return studies. They proposed to limit concentration and to control other factors that, they believed, contribute to high rates of return on capital.

> The adverse effects of persistent concentration on output and price find some confirmation in various studies that have been made of return on capital in major industries. . . . It is the persistence of high profits over extended time periods and over whole industries rather than in individual firms that suggests artificial restraints on output and the absence of fully effective competition.[4]

Later proposals, such as the Antitrust Pre-Merger Notification Act (to amend the Clayton Act, 15 U.S.C. 12 ff.) and the Antitrust Civil Process Act (to amend 15 U.S.C. 1311), also were concerned with potential corporate actions that "may substantially lessen competition" or that "tend to create a monopoly" and result in higher rates of return.

CONCENTRATION AND PROFITS

Implicit in these recommendations is the view that there is an identifiable, determinate relationship between the loose indicators of monopoly power (concentration, entry barriers, advertising) and the rate of return.[5] Monopoly power, in this context, is measured by the deviation of the average rate of return in an industry above some competitive norm.[6] The rate of return, in most cases, is defined as the ratio of accounting profits (obtained from the income statement) to net worth or assets (obtained from the balance sheet).

Many studies, including those of Joe Bain, H. Michael Mann, and George Stigler, investigate the statistical relationships among rates of return, levels of concentration, and other indicators of monopoly power.[7] Bain's original study,

---

[4] White House Task Force on Antitrust Policy, reprinted in Yale Brozen, "The Antitrust Task Force Deconcentration Recommendation," *Journal of Law and Economics,* vol. 13 (October 1970), pp. 279–280.

[5] Curiously, there has been very little rigorous theoretical analysis of the possible link between concentration and monopoly power. One such demonstration has been given in Thomas R. Saving, "Concentration Ratios and the Degree of Monopoly," *International Economic Review,* vol. 11 (February 1970), pp. 139–146. Saving demonstrates that a theoretical relation does exist, under certain special assumptions, between concentration ratios and some popular indexes of monopoly power, including the Lerner index.

[6] United States Congress, Senate Committee on Banking and Currency, *Stock Exchange Practices,* 73d Cong., 2d Sess., 1934; Sen. Rept. 1455, United States Congress, Senate Committee on the Judiciary, *Improvement Act of 1976, Part II—Minority Views,* to accompany S. 1284, 94th Cong., 2d Sess., 20 May 1976.

[7] Joe S. Bain, "Relationship of Profit Rate to Industry Concentration: American Manufacturing, 1936–1940," *Quarterly Journal of Economics,* vol. 65 (August 1951), pp. 293–324; H. Michael Mann, "Seller Concentration, Barriers to Entry, and Rates of Return in Thirty Industries, 1950–1960," *Review of Economics and Statistics,* vol. 48 (August 1966), pp. 296–307; George J. Stigler, *Capital and Rates of Return in Manufacturing Industries* (Princeton: Princeton University Press, 1963).

made some 30 years ago and using data from the late 1930s, finds a small correlation (28 percent) between rates of return and concentration and reveals that the average rate of return among the most-concentrated industries is higher than that among the least-concentrated industries. Leonard Weiss used Mann's data in a multiple-regression and found a significant positive relationship between profits, and the product of high concentration and high-entry barriers.[8] When certain industries are excluded to improve the statistical confidence of the final results, however, the relationship is reversed: Highly concentrated industries have lower average rates of return than less concentrated industries![9]

The Federal Trade Commission has also conducted its own test of the relationship between concentration and profitability, using data for 1949 through 1953 for 125 food manufacturing firms. The commission found that the rate of profit was significantly and positively related to a weighted average of the four-firm concentration ratio when it was corrected for local markets.[10] The test also included variables measuring advertising-sales ratio, growth of output, firm diversification, and size in its estimation.

Another study by Gale investigated the relationship of concentration measured by a dummy variable, sales, industry shipments, and other variables to the profit rate.[11] He found a positive relationship between the rate of profit and concentration when the market share is at least 4 percent. His tests included data for 106 manufacturing firms between 1963 and 1967.

In 1973 Jones, Laudadio, and Percy estimated the rate of profit with respect to a Herfindahl index and a number of additional variables reflecting advertising-sales ratios, capital requirements, and dummy variables for regional markets and imports.[12] They found a positive relationship between concentration and profits with the overall significance of the data dependent on the exclusion of scale and import variables.

At least 50 other studies have appeared, as well as numerous critiques of the entire literature. The underlying assumption of such studies is that in markets where firms, particularly the top four to eight, are able to maintain higher than normal rates of return, some amount of monopoly power must exist. Most

[8] Leonard Weiss, "Quantitative Studies of Industrial Organization," in Michael D. Intriligator, ed., *Frontiers of Quantitative Economics* (Amsterdam: North Holland, 1969), pp. 362–411. Also see Stephen A. Rhoades, "Concentration, Barriers, and Rates of Return: A Note," *Journal of Industrial Economics,* vol. 19 (November 1970), pp. 82–88; the reply by H. Michael Mann in *Journal of Industrial Economics,* vol. 19 (July 1971), pp. 291–293; a rejoinder by Rhoades in the *Journal of Industrial Economics,* vol. 20 (April 1972), pp. 193–195; and see P. David Qualls, "Concentration, Barriers to Entry, and Long-Run Economic Profit Margins," *Journal of Industrial Economics,* vol. 20 (April 1972), pp. 146–158.

[9] Leonard Weiss, "The Concentration-Profits Relationship and Antitrust," in Harvey J. Goldschmid, H. Michael Mann, and J. Fred Weston, eds., *Industrial Concentration: The New Learning* (Boston: Little, Brown, 1974), pp. 184–231.

[10] The Federal Trade Commission, *Economic Report on the Influence of Market Share on the Profit Performance of Food Manufacturing Industries* (Washington, D.C.: U.S. Government Printing Office, September 1969).

[11] Bradley T. Gale, "Market Share and Rate of Return," *Review of Economics and Statistics,* vol. 54 (November 1972), pp. 412–423.

[12] J. C. H. Jones, Leonard Laudadio, and M. Percy, "Market Structure and Profitability in Canadian Manufacturing Industry: Some Cross Section Results," *Canadian Journal of Economics,* vol. 6 (1973), pp. 356–368.

studies have concluded that higher concentration ratios are representative of market structures permitting firms to obtain higher-than-normal rates of return when compared to market structures with lower concentration ratios. Some more sophisticated studies have controlled for other aspects of market structure besides concentration, such as advertising.[13]

A Look at Consolidations

Another possible test of the concentration rate of return, or profitability relationship, is to investigate the returns to consolidations. Dewing looked at a random selection of 35 industry combinations that met several conditions regarding existence and national significance, number of plants involved, and availability and accuracy of data.[14] He tested the hypothesis that a merger or combination involving a major share of industry capacity would increase concentration and subsequently increase the earnings of those firms involved in the consolidation. Professor Dewing's results revealed that the average combination was less profitable than the profits of predecessor firms before they had merged. The decrease in returns was attributed to competitive pressures resulting from entry and other competitive forces.

PROBLEMS WITH PROFIT RATE STUDIES

The sought-after relationship between concentration and **profit rates** is marred by a number of weaknesses, the least of which being that concentration ratios are not precise or unambiguous. After all, we do not have a very scientific method of deciding which firms should be counted in the industry. Additionally, profit rates and profit rate analyses are saddled with difficulties, not the least of which is the fact that they are based on accounting concepts. There are differing valuations of a firm's invested capital, particularly relating to research and development and advertising (but more on this later and in the Appendix to this chapter). Finally, most profit rate studies rely on cross-sectional data rather than looking at what happens to rates of return over time.

A more careful examination of concentration studies with respect to their individual robustness, however, points to a different conclusion. The relationship between concentration and rate of return has not been satisfactorily proved or disproved, although more studies have found *some* positive relation-

---

[13] See, for example, William S. Comanor and Thomas A. Wilson, "Advertising, Market Structure, and Performance," *Review of Economics and Statistics,* vol. 49 (November 1967), pp. 423–440; William Shepherd, "The Elements of Market Structure," *Review of Economics and Statistics,* vol. 54 (February 1972), pp. 25–37; David R. Kamerschen, "The Determination of Profit Rates in 'Oligopolistic Industries,'" *Journal of Business,* vol. 42 (July 1969), pp. 293–301; J. C. H. Jones, Leonard Laudadio, and M. Percy, "Profitablity and Market Structure: A Cross-Section Comparison of Canadian and American Manufacturing Industry," *Journal of Industrial Economics,* vol. 25 (March 1977), pp. 195–211; Richard A. Miller, "Market Structure and Industrial Performance: Relation of Profit Rates to Concentration, Advertising, Intensity, and Diversity," *Journal of Industrial Economics,* vol. 17 (April 1969), pp. 104–118.

[14] Arthur S. Dewing, "A Statistical Test of the Success of Consolidations," *Quarterly Journal of Economics,* vol. 36 (November 1921), pp. 84–101.

ship. Much of the debate centers on poor statistical techniques, differences between static and dynamic profit rates, disequilibrium forces, the instability of results with respect to the inclusion or exclusion of certain industries with poor data or statistical characteristics, and weighted versus unweighted concentration rates.

Brozen, for example, shows that the rates of return for each period in the original Bain study are subject to substantial variation over time.[15] Such variation confirms an alternative hypothesis that rates of return tend toward equality in the long run but are subject to temporary disequilibrium forces that may cause substantial temporary increases (or decreases) in *observed* rates of return. Brozen tests this hypothesis using Mann's study, which shows high rates of return.[16] Table 4-2 reveals that higher rates of return do tend toward equilibrium over time.[17]

Nearly every study reveals difficulties with the actual data base used to test the relationships between rates of return and market power. Attempts to use different variables (such as those found in the Kilpatrick study and in studies based on firm rather than industry data) also fail to show significant relationships.[18] Finally, the overall predictive ability of empirical rate-of-return studies is very poor in the sense that large proportions of the observed differences in rates of return are not explained.

It is equally important (as the Appendix to this chapter demonstrates) that the accounting profit rate these studies use, whether computed on a base of net worth or on a base of assets, *does not correspond to the underlying economic decision variables.* Accounting variables, in general, are rarely economic decision variables. Solomon identifies these difficulties, and Bloch, Ayanian, and Clarkson estimate the associated biases.[19] When unrealized income and increased capitalization of expenditures from intangible capital (such as advertising and research, whose returns begin at some future period) are properly accounted for, profit measurements in industries with higher-than-average rates of return are altered substantially.

[15] Yale Brozen, "The Antitrust Task Force Deconcentration Recommendation," *Journal of Law and Economics,* vol. 13 (October 1970), pp. 279–292, and "Bain's Concentration and Rates of Return Revisited," *Journal of Law and Economics,* vol. 14 (October 1971), pp. 351–370.

[16] Yale Brozen, "Barriers Facilitate Entry," *The Antitrust Bulletin,* vol. 14 (Winter 1969), pp. 851–854.

[17] But see Dennis C. Mueller, "The Persistence of Profits Above the Norm," *Economica,* vol. 44 (November 1977), pp. 369–380, which gives evidence that supernormal profits *do* intend to persist over time.

[18] Robert W. Kilpatrick, "The Choice among Alternative Measures of Industrial Concentration," *Review of Economics and Statistics,* vol. 49 (May 1967), pp. 258–260.

[19] Robert Ayanian, "The Profit Rates and Economic Performance of Drug Firms," in Robert B. Helm, ed., *Drug Development and Marketing* (Washington, D.C.: American Enterprise Institute, 1975); Harry Bloch, "Advertising and Profitability: A Reappraisal," *Journal of Political Economy,* vol. 82 (March/April 1974), pp. 267–286; Kenneth W. Clarkson, *Intangible Capital and Rates of Return: Effects of Research and Promotion on Profitability* (Washington, D.C.: American Enterprise Institute, 1977); Ezra Solomon, "Alternative Rate of Return Concepts and Their Implications for Utility Regulation," *Bell Journal of Economics and Management Science,* vol. 1 (Spring 1970), pp. 65–81.

TABLE 4-2

MOVEMENT OF AVERAGE ACCOUNTING RATE OF RETURN ON
NET WORTH FOR NINETEEN CONCENTRATED INDUSTRIES
CLASSIFIED BY BARRIERS TO ENTRY, 1950–1960 TO 1961–1966

	1950–1960*	1961–1966†
High barriers		
Class mean	16.1%	13.1%
(Eight industries)		
Substantial barriers		
Class mean	11.3%	8.9%
(Seven industries)		
Moderate-to-low barriers		
Class mean	12.7%	10.0%
(Four industries)		
All manufacturing corporations	11.1%‡	11.2%‡

*H. Michael Mann. "Seller Concentration, Barriers to Entry, and Rates of Return in Thirty Industries, 1950–1960." *Review of Economics and Statistics,* vol. 48 (August 1966), pp. 296–307.

†Computed from data in H. Michael Mann. "A Note on Barriers to Entry and Long-Run Profitability," *Antitrust Bulletin,* and from his 1950–1960 data in "Seller Concentration, Barriers to Entry, and Rates of Return in Thirty Industries, 1950–1960."

‡*Economic Report of the President,* 1969, p. 310.

Source: Yale Brozen. "Barriers Facilitate Entry," *The Antitrust Bulletin,* vol. 14 (Winter 1969). Reprinted by permission. Copyright © 1969 by Federal Legal Publications.

Bain's earlier analysis of the profit rate as a measure of monopoly power should have provided a warning.

The unadjusted accounting rate of profit, as computed by the usual methods from balance sheets and income statements, is prima facie an absolutely unreliable indicator of the presence or absence either of monopoly power or of excessive profits. . . . The relationship between price and accounting average cost tells us nothing about the degree of monopoly power and little about the extent of excess profit.[20]

Economic theory, of course, predicts that there will be differences between firms' and industries' economic rates of return, both in the short run and in the long run, even after making the appropriate corrections for advertising and for research and development.[21]

---

[20] Joe S. Bain, "The Profit Rate as a Measure of Monopoly Power," *Quarterly Journal of Economics,* vol. 55 (February 1941), pp. 271–293.

[21] Another problem of the concentration studies relates to the *specification* of the relationship expected to be observed. Is it smooth, linear, continuous, and monotonic, as many studies suggest? For studies that suggest that nonlinear or discontinuous specifications may be more appropriate, see Lawrence J. White, "Searching for the Critical Industrial Concentration Ratio," in S. Goldfeld and R. Quandt, eds., *Studies in Non-Linear Estimation* (Cambridge, Mass.: Ballinger 1976), pp. 61–75; and James W. Meehan and Thomas D. Duchesneau, "The Critical Level of Concentration: An Empirical Analysis," *Journal of Industrial Economics,* vol. 22 (September 1973), pp. 21–36.

Accounting for Differences in Rates of Return

Perhaps we should not be surprised by the mixed results of empirical findings on the relationship of concentration and profitability. High rates of profit in concentrated industries merely indicate that something is inhibiting the inflow of new resources. But the profitability does not reveal causation that could influence public policy, potential predatory actions, recognition of natural economies of scale, distribution of holdings of particular raw materials, or other factors.[22]

Differences in average rates of return in various industries are the result of many factors. First, the rates observed in any one period may be transitory, the result of disequilibrium in one or more markets.[23] Second, there may be differences in fringe benefits and other nonpecuniary payments, which would cause observed pecuniary rates of return to differ under competitive market conditions.[24] Third, the greater the risk associated with an industry is, the greater the expected rate of return must be to attract capital in the financial markets.[25] Fourth, there are differences in resource use efficiency, and those differences may cause variations in rates of return if superior resources are distributed unequally and earn rents that are not completely capitalized on the books of firms owning them. Fifth, some industries will be subject to, or will lobby for, specific legislation that creates entry barriers which, in turn, cause higher rates of return than are observed in other unregulated industries. Moreover, firms with patent protection may show, over short periods of time, rates of return in excess of those achieved by firms without patents. Sixth, at any particular moment in time the positive costs of acquiring information and adjusting to new relative prices and demand conditions will contribute to differences in rates of return in industries as well as in individual firms. Disequilibrating forces will

[22] See, for example, Donald Dewey, "Industrial Concentration and the Rate of Profit: Some Neglected Theory," *Journal of Law and Economics,* vol. 19 (April 1976), pp. 67–78.

[23] See, for example, the discussion of this bias in George J. Stigler, "A Note on Profitability, Competition, and Concentration," in *The Organization of Industry* (Homewood, Ill.: Irwin, 1968), pp. 142–146.

[24] In *Capital and Rates of Return in Manufacturing Industries* (New York: Arno Press, 1975), pp. 59–61, Stigler argues that small corporations tend to understate profitability because they pay out "profits" as "salaries" for tax purposes. It therefore appears that large firms earn greater profits than smaller ones, even though this is not true in fact. After adjusting for this discrepancy, Stigler found no significant relation between rate of return and concentration. Stigler's method of adjustment, however, has been challenged by Kilpatrick, who reaches the opposite conclusion under his own method of adjustment. See Robert W. Kilpatrick, "Stigler on the Relationship between Industry Profit Rates and Market Concentration," *Journal of Political Economy,* vol. 76 (May–June 1968), pp. 479–488.

[25] For a rigorous analysis of how to incorporate risk into studies on market structure and profitability, see James L. Bothwell and Theodore E. Keeler, "Profits, Market Structure, and Portfolio Risk," in R. Masson and P. D. Qualls, eds., *Essays on Industrial Organization in Honor of Joe S. Bain* (Cambridge, Mass.: Ballinger, 1976), pp. 71–88, in which the authors explain the use of the β-coefficient, the commonly used measure of risk developed in the corporate finance literature.

become less important over longer time periods, but other autonomous shocks come into play.[26]

Considering these qualifications, it is highly unlikely that observed rates of return would be equal for firms in a particular industry or for firms across all industries. Also, one cannot conclude that a high observed rate of return is sufficient evidence of monopoly power.

CONCENTRATION AND PRICE-COST MARGINS

The mixed outcomes of the various studies focusing on concentration and profitability have caused some researchers to focus more on prices and their relationship to costs. In fact, Stigler and Chamberlin argued that the effectiveness of collusion, which can be measured by the **price-cost margins**, will rise with concentration.[27]

The difference between price and cost for the average product would seem to be higher in a monopolized industry than in a competitive one.[28] A number of researchers have looked at the relationship between concentration ratios and the average price-cost margin in the market. Many studies show that price-cost margins are higher in concentrated than in unconcentrated industries.[29]

In a study of supermarkets prepared for the Joint Economic Committee of the U.S. Congress, concentration was found to have had a significant and positive effect on the profit-sales ratio of grocery chains.[30] In addition, studies by Marvel reveal a significant relationship between the Herfindahl index and the price of regular gasoline, although premium gasoline had an insignificant relationship between the index and its price.[31]

A more recent study by John Kwoka looks at the relationship between

[26] Thus we cannot conclude that greater concentration causes higher profitability. It is possible that the factors contributing to high profit rates are not uniformly distributed across concentration classes. If such distortions were randomly distributed across some classes, the correlation between concentration and profits would be more meaningful.

[27] See George J. Stigler, "A Theory of Oligopoly," *Journal of Political Economy*, vol. 72 (1964), pp. 44–61, and Edward H. Chamberlin, *Theory of Monopolistic Competition: A Reorientation of the Theory of Value*, 8th ed. (Cambridge, Mass: Harvard University Press, 1962), pp. 46–51.

[28] The price-cost margin is defined as the difference between price and the average variable costs.

[29] See, for example, three studies by Norman R. Collins and Lee E. Preston, *Concentration and Price-Cost Margins in Manufacturing Industries* (Berkeley, Calif.: University of California Press, 1968); "Price-Cost Margins and Industry Structure," *Review of Economics and Statistics*, vol. 51 (August 1969), pp. 271–286; and "Concentration and Price-Cost Margins in Food Manufacturing Industries," *Journal of Industrial Economics*, vol. 14 (July 1966), pp. 226–242.

[30] Bruce W. Marion, et al., *The Profit and Price Performance of Leading Food Chains, 1970–1974*, Committee Print, Joint Economic Committee, 95th Cong., 1st Sess., 1977.

[31] See Howard P. Marvel, "Competition and Price Levels in the Retail Gasoline Market," *Review of Economics and Statistics*, vol. 60 (May 1978), pp. 252–258, and "The Economics of Information and Retail Gasoline Behavior: An Empirical Analysis," *Journal of Political Economy*, vol. 84 (October 1976), pp. 1033–1060.

market shares and price-cost margins for 314 manufacturing industries. Kwoka concludes that increasing the market shares of the top two firms increases price-cost margins, while an increase in the share of the third firm actually decreases them, and additional shares have no depreciable effect.[32]

A number of other researchers have contended that high concentration ratios may be acting as a surrogate for other factors which are actually causing the higher average price-cost margins. A study including the rate of technological change in product differentiation found that concentration was not a significant determinant of price-cost margins.[33]

Rate of Return on Sales Rather than Investment

It is important to remember that price-cost margins tell us nothing about the rate of return on investment; they tell us only what the rate of return is on sales. Firms can be making a 300 percent rate of return on sales and yet have a below-normal rate of return on investment. Grocery stores typically make a very low rate of return on sales, such as 1 or 2 percent, but sometimes they may be making a 5, 10, 15, or 25 percent rate of return on investment. However, if we are interested in the allocation of resources, rates of return on sales may be of interest.[34]

CONCENTRATION AND TURNOVER

Turnover is a change in the size ranking of the largest firms in a given industry. Some economists believe that the degree of market turnover is an indicator of the intensity of competition.

Lack of turnover may give evidence of lack of competition or tacit collusion among supposed competitors. In other words, even with relatively high concentration ratios, if the leading firms change all the time, that may indicate competition and counter any notion of monopoly due to the high concentration ratio. A simple four-firm concentration ratio can hide the fact that the identity of the four largest firms has changed or that there has been a change in their ranking.[35]

---

[32] See John E. Kwoka, "The Effect of Market Share Distribution on Industry Performance," *Review of Economics and Statistics*, vol. 61 (February 1979), pp. 101–109. See also Stephen A. Rhoades and Joe M. Cleaver, "The Nature of the Concentration—Price/Cost Margin Relationship for 352 Manufacturing Industries: 1967," *Southern Economic Journal*, vol. 40 (July 1973), pp. 90–102.

[33] James V. Koch and Robert N. Fenili, "The Influence of Industry Market Structure upon Industry Price-Cost Margins," *Rivista Internazionale di Scienze Economiche e Commerciali*, vol. 18 (November 1971), pp. 1037–1045.

[34] Rates of return on sales are a close proxy for the Lerner index.

[35] See Herbert A. Simon and C. P. Bonini, "The Size Distribution of Business Firms," *American Economic Review*, vol. 48 (September 1958), pp. 607–617, and Seymour Friedland, "Turnover and Growth of the Largest Industrial Firms, 1906–1950," *Review of Economics and Statistics*, vol. 39 (February 1957), pp. 79–83.

Problems of Definition

One of the major problems of the turnover concept is how to define it. Of the two possible definitions, one stresses the change in the size ranking of the largest four or eight firms, and the other stresses the change in the identity of the group of firms (perhaps in addition to the change in size ranking). Which definition one decides on may determine the outcome of one's study.

Additionally, whatever turnover index is used may be subject to the criticism that it ignores the existence of conglomerate power or vertical integration. For example, progressive monopolization of an industry may lead to a high turnover index.[36]

Turnover over Time

A number of studies have been done to determine the change in turnover over time, if any. Many studies show that the number of identity changes among the top 100 firms in manufacturing and mining has declined from the beginning of the century to recently.[37] In a study published in 1963 by Michael Gort, the researcher correlated the 1947 market share of the 15 largest firms in each market with the 1954 market share of the same firms. In over 50 percent of the markets, there was virtually no disturbance in market shares.[38]

CONCENTRATION AND TECHNOLOGICAL CHANGE

While most studies purporting to show the relationship between technological change and concentration really show the relationship between technological change and firm size, there are several studies that are of importance, particularly those done by Stigler and by Phillips.[39] These two researchers looked at the same industries in the same time period and reached opposite conclusions. Stigler showed an inverse relationship between concentration and productivity increases; Phillips found a positive relationship. One possible reason for this

---

[36] See the criticism made by George J. Stigler, "The Statistics of Monopoly and Merger," *Journal of Political Economy*, vol. 64 (February 1956), pp. 33–40, and Morris A. Adelman, "A Note on Corporate Concentration and Turnover," *American Economic Review*, vol. 44 (June 1954), p. 392.

[37] See Stanley E. Boyle and Robert L. Sorensen, "Concentration and Mobility: Alternative Measures of Industry Structure," *Journal of Industrial Economics*, vol. 19 (April 1971), pp. 118–132. But compare Robert J. Stonebraker, "Turnover and Mobility Among the 100 Largest Firms: An Update," *American Economic Review*, vol. 69 (December 1979), pp. 968–973, in which the author concludes that there has been *no* trend toward decreasing turnover during the course of the last several decades.

[38] Michael Gort, "Analysis of Stability and Change in Market Shares," *Journal of Political Economy*, vol. 71 (February 1963), pp. 51–61.

[39] See, for example, Edwin Mansfield, "Size of Firm, Market Structure, and Innovation," *Journal of Political Economy*, vol. 71 (December 1963), pp. 556–576. Also compare George J. Stigler, "Industrial Organization and Economic Progress," in L. D. White, ed., *The State of the Social Sciences* (Chicago: University of Chicago Press, 1956), and Almarin Phillips, "Concentration, Scale, and Technological Change in Selected Manufacturing Industries, 1899–1939," *Journal of Industrial Economics*, vol. 4 (June 1956), pp. 179–193.

difference in conclusion is that Stigler used firm concentration ratios, whereas Phillips used plant concentration ratios. There might now be a preference for the former method, because many firms have multiple plants. Plant concentration ratios are statistically more accurate for most markets than firm concentration ratios, but in any market where the largest plants belong to the same firm, the plant concentration ratio would not provide much improvement. Studies by Williamson and Comanor seem to agree with the results of Phillips' study.[40]

Concentration and Growth

The theory of monopoly pricing and output predicts that firms with monopoly power restrict output. Nonetheless, the same theory does not tell us about the effects of monopoly on the growth in an entire market. All we can say is that the monopolist maximizes its net present value. Thus, there will be a more or less constant evaluation of various possible time spans of profit associated with different courses of action. The monopolist knows that setting a short-run, profit-maximizing price and thus restricting output will increase the probability of entry by other firms because of the increased attractiveness. Nonetheless, the monopolist will still restrict output because of the higher discounted value of short-run profits relative to long-run profits.[41]

Under the above circumstances, a monopoly firm can be shown to profit by stimulating industry growth even though that firm will eventually have to accept a declining share of the growing market. The prediction is a moderate pricing policy, somewhere between the static theoretic prediction for the price and output of a monopoly maximizing only short-run profits and a perfectly competitive price.[42]

Empirical Studies   A number of studies that have looked at the relationship between concentration and market growth seem to suggest different conclusions. Phillips, Hymer, and Pashigian believe there is no relationship between market concentration and subsequent market growth.[43] Studies by Kamerschen, Nelson, and Marcus, however, conclude that an inverse relationship

---

[40] Oliver E. Williamson, "Innovation and Market Structure," *Journal of Political Economy,* vol. 73 (February 1965), pp. 67-73; and William S. Comanor, "Market Structure, Product Differentiation, and Industrial Research," *Quarterly Journal of Economics,* vol. 81 (November 1967), pp. 639-657. Also see Douglas F. Greer and Stephen A. Rhoades, "Concentration and Productivity Changes in the Long and Short Run," *Southern Economic Journal,* vol. 43 (October 1976), pp. 1031-1044. They find a small *positive* relationship between concentration and productivity increases.

[41] There is a problem with the production of durable goods. See pages 228-230.

[42] See George J. Stigler, *The Theory of Price,* rev. ed. (New York: Macmillan, 1952), pp. 231-234. Also see Darius W. Gaskins, Jr., "Dynamic Limit: Optimal Pricing under Threat of Entry," *Journal of Economic Theory,* vol. 3 (September 1971), pp. 306-322.

[43] Almarin Phillips, "Concentration, Scale, and Technological Change in Selected Manufacturing Industries, 1899-1939," *Journal of Industrial Economics,* vol. 4 (June 1956), pp. 179-193; and Stephen Hymer and Peter Pashigian, "Turnover of Firms as a Measure of Market Behavior," *Review of Economics and Statistics,* vol. 44 (February 1962), pp. 82-87.

exists between initial market concentration and later market growth.[44] Unfortunately, the researchers just mentioned were not using the same time period nor the same sample of industries; further, the units of measurement that determine market size differed among the studies.

APPENDIX: Measurement Problems

In this appendix, we will investigate certain problems of market measurement in more detail. There are numerous measurement problems involved in assessing the profitability of a business venture. We will examine the effect of opportunity cost of capital and then turn to the effects of inflation on reported profits. Next, the consequences of capitalizing advertising outlays, research and development (R & D) expenditures, and other intangible capital on profits will be examined. Finally, we will take a more detailed look at problems in choosing the correct variable for measurement.

CONCENTRATION AND PROFITS—A CLOSER LOOK

We have already pointed out the difficulty of trying to establish a relationship between profitability and concentration. We will briefly recap the discussion here.

Profit

Most people, business people included, think of profit as the difference between the amount of money the business takes in and the amount it spends for wages, materials, and so on. In a bookkeeping sense, the following formula could be used:

$$\text{Accounting profits} = \text{total revenues} - \text{total costs}$$

The accounting definition of profits is appropriate when used by accountants, for example, to determine taxable income for a firm. Economists face a different problem; therefore, we use another concept of profit derived from the opportunity cost of capital.

Opportunity Cost of Capital

Firms enter or remain in an industry only if they earn, at a minimum, a *normal rate of return.* By this term we mean that people will not invest their wealth in a business unless they obtain a positive competitive rate of return—that is, unless their invested wealth pays off. Any business wishing to attract capital must expect to pay at least the same rate of return on that capital that all other businesses in a similar situation are willing to pay. For example, if individuals can invest their wealth in almost any publishing firm and

---

[44] David R. Kamerschen, "Market Growth and Industry Concentration," *Journal of the American Statistical Association,* vol. 63 (March 1968), pp. 228-241; Ralph L. Nelson, "Market Growth, Company Diversification and Product Concentration, 1947-1954," *Journal of the American Statistical Association,* vol. 55 (December 1960), pp. 640-649; and Matityahu Marcus, "Advertising and Changes in Concentration," *Southern Economic Journal,* vol. 36 (October 1969), pp. 117-121.

get a rate of return of 10 percent per year, then every firm in the publishing business must *expect* to pay 10 percent as the normal rate of return. *This is a cost to the firm.* It is called the **opportunity cost of capital**. Capital will not stay in industries where the expected rate of return falls below its opportunity cost.

Forgetting the Opportunity Cost of Certain Other Inputs

Often, single-owner proprietorships grossly exaggerate their profit rates because they forget about the opportunity cost of the time that the proprietor spends in the business. We are now referring to the opportunity cost of labor. For example, you may know people who run small grocery stores. These people, at the end of the year, will sit down and figure out what their profits were. They will add up all their sales and subtract what they had to pay to other workers, what they had to pay to their suppliers, what they had to pay in taxes, and so on. They call the end result "profit." However, they will not have figured into their costs the salary that they could have made if they had worked for somebody else in a similar type of job. For somebody operating a grocery store, that salary might be equal to $6 an hour. If so, then $6 an hour is the opportunity cost of the grocery store owner's time. In many cases, people who run their own businesses lose money in an economic sense. That is, their profits, as they calculate them, may be less than the amount of labor income they *could* have earned had they spent the same amount of time working for someone else. Take a numerical example. If an entrepreneur can earn $6 per hour, it follows that the opportunity cost of his or her time is $6 × 40 hours × 52 weeks, or $12,480 per year. If this entrepreneur is making less than $12,480 per year in accounting profits, he or she is actually losing money. (This does not mean that such entrepreneurs are stupid. Rather, they are willing to pay for the benefits of being the boss.)

We have spoken only of the opportunity cost of capital and the opportunity cost of labor, but we could have spoken in general of the opportunity cost of all inputs. Whatever the input may be, its opportunity cost must be taken into account in order to figure out true economic profits.

Accounting Profits Are Not Economic Profits

The term *profits* in economics means the money that entrepreneurs make, over and above their own opportunity cost plus the opportunity cost of the capital they have invested in their business. Profits, which can be regarded as total revenues minus total costs, must now include *all* costs. Our definition, then, of economic profits will be the following:

Economic profits = total revenues − total opportunity cost of all inputs used

We can picture this relationship in Figure A4-1. We are assuming that the accountants' bookkeeping costs for all factors of production except capital are correct.

PRICE LEVEL ADJUSTMENTS AND PROFITABILITY

During periods of inflation a number of factors influence the level of profitability, including underestimation of the costs of goods sold, underdepreciation of fixed assets, and underamortization of assets.

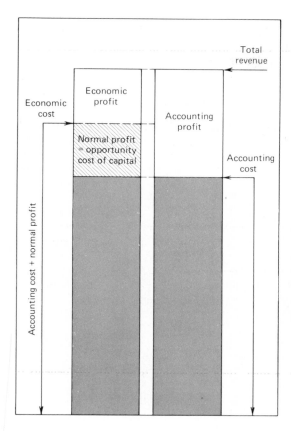

FIGURE A4-1
Simplified view of economic and accounting profit. Here we see that on the right-hand side, total revenues are equal to accounting costs plus accounting profit. That is, accounting profit is the difference between total revenues and total accounting costs. On the other hand, we see in the left-hand column that economic profit is equal to total revenues minus economic cost. Economic cost is equal to accounting costs plus a normal rate of return or normal profit, which is the opportunity cost of capital.

Underestimation of Costs of Goods Sold

During inflation the selling price of goods and services rises to reflect the new price levels. Under the tax laws the cost of goods sold must be represented by the actual amount paid. Thus, the gain in reported profits may be purely illusory, because the full amount of the difference between selling price and reported costs may be allocated to replenishing the physical level of inventories. The use of last-in, first-out (LIFO) inventory valuation mitigates some of these problems, because inventory is valued at recent prices, but eventually the profits will be illusory when the firm reduces its levels of inventories and must use old prices in its computations.

In Table A4-1, we show the underestimation of cost of goods sold for the three major automobile producers for the years 1976 and 1977.

Underdepreciation and Underamortization of Assets

Depreciation and amortization methods acknowledge that assets have a useful life beyond the normal accounting period. Depreciation represents that portion of the useful life of the asset that is consumed during each year's production. During periods of inflation the amounts allocated to depreciation or amortization of assets by conventional accounting methods understate actual costs because, like inventories, asset values are based on the historical acquisition costs of fixed assets. To avoid the problem of under-

TABLE A4-1
ADJUSTMENTS FOR PRICE-LEVEL CHANGES FOR COST OF GOODS SOLD,
DEPRECIATION, AND AMORTIZATION (millions of dollars)

	Chrysler		Ford		GM	
	1976	1977	1976	1977	1976	1977
Undercosting of goods sold	$125.2	$123.9	$ 60	$ 250	$ 80	$ 146.5
Underdepreciation of fixed assets	169.2	184.6	290	311	635.7	646.3
Underamortization of special tools	118.7	107.4	129	112	33.1	112.1
Total underdepreciation and underamortization	287.9	292	419	423	668.8	758.4
Total estimated under-reporting of expenses	$413.1	$415.9	$ 479	$ 673	$ 748.8	$ 904.9
Reported aftertax profits	$448.6	$163.2	$1,043.6	$1,672.8	$3,081.5	$3,337.5

Source: Form 10-K Annual Report, for year ended December 31, 1977.

statement, depreciation and amortization should be made on a replacement cost basis to more accurately reflect the actual consumption of fixed assets in real dollars.

Table A4-1 gives the underdepreciation of fixed assets and underamortization of special tools for the three full-line automobile producers. The table also shows that in total, these adjustments are significant, and in some years they turn accounting profits to economic losses. For example, in 1977 Chrysler had a reported aftertax profit of $163,200,000, but the total estimated underreporting of expenses was $415,900,000, resulting in a loss of $252,700,000.

Toward the beginning of this chapter, we discussed the different costs associated with production. One of the costs that was discussed was the opportunity cost of continued possession of assets such as machines, equipment, and buildings. An accurate measure of total costs and, hence, the rate of return on an investment, requires careful consideration of the opportunity cost of the continued possession of all assets that the firm owns.

INTANGIBLE CAPITAL AND PROFITABILITY

Many of the assets that the firm owns are intangible and are called ''intangible capital.'' Examples of intangible capital include, but are not limited to, goodwill established in the market, trademarks, patents, and trade secrets. Intangible capital also includes the creation of future returns from advertising and research and development.

If we wish to determine the profitability or rate of return earned by a firm, we have to examine the relationship between net revenues and *the investment that would be required to currently replicate the existing firm's total assets.* That investment would most certainly include intangible capital. If a firm had spent an amount of money in the past on a nationwide advertising campaign to make the community aware of its existence and the quality of its products, the intangible capital, for example, brand recognition, resulting from that advertising outlay forms part of the investment that someone else would have to make to replicate the existing firm's capacity.

Research and Development

Clearly, then, to understand any profit that a company is earning requires us to have a complete accounting of all the costs involved in selling the firm's product. The costs include the opportunity cost of continued possession not only of tangible capital such as machines and buildings, but also of intangible capital such as the results of past research and development expenditures (R&D) that have not yet been applied to actual production. For example, if a pharmaceutical company has spent $10 million this year in R&D on a drug that will not be marketed for another three years, that drug company is implicitly forgoing the return on $10 million over the three-year period. In other words, it is incurring a cost of continued possession of R&D. After all, it could have taken that $10 million and invested it in, say, government bonds yielding 8 percent. For the three years in question, then, the pharmaceutical company could receive 8 percent of $10 million, or $800,000, per year. This $800,000 per year is an opportunity cost of continued possession of $10 million worth of R&D.

Depreciation of Advertising Outlays

Not only must we take account of the cost of continued possession of R&D, for example, but we should also take account of the fact that an expenditure on advertising is not really the same as an expenditure on labor. Wages paid to workers represent a current expense related to the current use of an input that yields its output immediately; however, advertising does not yield its output immediately. Rather, it has a longer-run effect. Companies typically do not consider 100 percent of their outlay on a machine as a current expense in the year that the machine is purchased. Tax law prevents this; but also, from an economic point of view, if the machine lasts for, say, five years, the true cost of the services from the machine are, in the most simple example, equal to one-fifth of its purchase price each year.[45] From an accounting point of view, the firm depreciates the machine each year by an amount based on its expected service life and the rules that the Internal Revenue Service has set up for depreciation. However, the IRS allows firms to deduct as a current expense all costs associated with advertising in the year that they are made. From an economic point of view (not to be confused with sound *tax* accounting), these costs should be treated similarly to those associated with the purchase of tangible capital. Just because advertising represents intangible capital does not mean its cost is appropriately charged to the year in which it is spent.[46]

---

[45] This is called straight-line depreciation.

[46] From a firm's point of view, however, it is usually best to expense any costs in the year in which they are incurred and to depreciate capital expenditures as fast as the law allows. The reason has to do with present-value calculations. Any expenses that the IRS allows to be deducted from revenues reduce current operating profit and, therefore, income taxes owed. Thus, the present value of any tax savings is greater the sooner that savings is obtained if future tax rates do not significantly increase to offset the savings. This conclusion assumes that the firm continues to show an accounting profit.

TABLE A4-2
ADVERTISING, RESEARCH AND DEVELOPMENT (R&D) AS PERCENTAGE OF
NET SALES, BASIC RESEARCH AS A PERCENTAGE OF R&D EXPENDITURES
BY INDUSTRY

Industry	Advertising as percentage of net sales (1949–1971)	R&D as a percentage of sales (1961–1971)[a]	Basic research as a percentage of R&D expenditure (1960–1971)[a]
Pharmaceuticals	3.7	5.3	16.0
Chemicals	3.7	3.1	11.5
Foods	2.3	0.4[b]	8.4[c]
Electrical machinery	1.6	3.6	3.6
Rubber products	1.5	1.7	4.1[d]
Office machinery	1.0	3.1	2.0
Motor vehicles	0.8	2.5	2.4[e]
Paper products	0.7	0.9	2.5[f]
Petroleum	0.5	0.9	8.6
Ferrous metals	0.3	0.7	7.3
Aerospace	0.3	3.5	1.3

Source: Kenneth W. Clarkson, *Intangible Capital and Rates of Return* (Washington, D.C.: American Enterprise Institute, 1977), pp. 61–62.
[a] Computed using 1973 dollars.
[b] Data not available for 1963.
[c] Data not available for 1962.
[d] Data not available for 1964, 1965, and 1971.
[e] Data not available for 1966–1971.
[f] Data not available for 1960.

Correcting Accounting Rates of Profit

In order to correct standard accounting rates of profit for a firm that engages in advertising and research and development, we have to do two things:

1 depreciate intangible assets resulting from expenditures on advertising and research and development over their expected lifetimes rather than expensing them in the year in which they are incurred; and

2 take account of the opportunity cost (that is, forgone interest) of such intangible capital as that embodied in research and development before these investment expenditures become an asset.

A study taking account of these corrections has been completed by K. W. Clarkson.[47] We present here some of the results of Clarkson's study. In Table A4-2, we show advertising and promotion expenditures expressed as a percentage of net sales for different industries. We note a dramatic difference in those industries in terms of their promotional expenditures. Pharmaceuticals and chemicals spend approximately ten times more on advertising and promotion than do ferrous metals and aerospace industries. This table also shows research and development (R&D) expenditures as a percent-

[47] Kenneth W. Clarkson, *Intangible Capital and Rates of Return: Effects of Research and Promotion* (Washington, D.C.: American Enterprise Institute for Public Policy Research, 1977).

age of sales. Again, there is a marked difference among industries. The pharmaceutical industry spends almost eight times more on R&D than does the ferrous metals industry.

Moreover, there is a different average expenditure of R&D funds for basic research among the different industries. Again, pharmaceutical enterprises head the list, allocating more than 12 times as much of each R&D dollar to basic research as the aerospace industry does.

Clarkson takes account of the necessity of depreciating intangible capital—advertising and R&D—and also of adding the opportunity cost of continued possession to that intangible capital. Table A4-3 shows the average rate of return on net worth for different industries with and without these corrections on the cost side. There are some remarkable differences. The pharmaceuticals industry, which is the most intangible capital-intensive of the industries studied, and the one that has the longest expected payout period for investment in R&D, has a dramatic drop in its rate of return from 18 percent to a little less than 13 percent. As would be expected, where there is little advertising and promotion, little R&D, and a fast payout period for investment in R&D, there is almost no change in the computed rate of return. Ferrous metals have an uncorrected rate of return of 7.55 percent and a corrected rate of return of 7.28 percent.

THE CORRECT SELECTION OF VARIABLES

Any time a measure of industry structure such as a concentration ratio or firm dispersion index is used, a decision on which variables to pick must be made.

When constructing a concentration index or other measure of market structure, one could use sales, net output, assets, number of employees, and so on. There will often be

TABLE A4-3
AVERAGE RATE OF RETURN, 1959–1973

Industry	No depreciation of intangible or capital accumulation	With advertising and research capitalization and depreciation
Pharmaceuticals	18.29	12.89
Electrical machinery	13.33	10.10
Foods	11.81	10.64
Petroleum	11.23	10.77
Chemicals	10.59	9.14
Motor vehicles	10.46	9.22
Paper	10.49	10.12
Rubber products	10.11	8.69
Office machinery	10.48	9.90
Aerospace	9.23	7.38
Ferrous metals	7.55	7.28
All above:		
Average	11.2	9.6
Variance	7.5	2.5

Source: K. W. Clarkson, *Intangible Capital and Rates of Return: Effects of Research and Promotion on Profitability,* American Enterprise Institute for Public Policy Research, Washington, D.C., 1977, Table 16.

differences, however, in the index when different variables are chosen. For example, absolute concentration measured by fixed capital assets tends to be higher than absolute concentration measured by sales. This result occurs because firms with larger sales tend to have a greater ratio of capital assets to sales than firms with smaller sales do. Additionally, larger firms may use more capital and less labor per unit of output than do smaller firms. We might conclude, then, that a relatively higher absolute concentration ratio when measuring assets is a reflection of a difference in the optimal capital-labor combination at higher levels of output. For this reason, a number of researchers shy away from using asset size as a variable on which to construct absolute concentration ratios. They also point out that the use of assets or total employment introduces an additional element of arbitrariness: A decision must be made on what proportion of the firm's assets or total employment is actually included in the industry under study. The researcher must then arbitrarily allocate unspecialized inputs between different outputs and therefore different industries. Using sales or value added as a measure of size avoids this problem, provided that product-line components of total sales are known.

Relationship among Results Using Major Variables

Is there a general relationship among the research results using the different variables discussed above? Mueller did a study using all major variables.[48] He believes that a general relationship exists between the relative level of concentration and the various variables that are used. He analyzed 4-firm and 20-firm concentration ratios for 28 industry groups as measured by assets, net capital assets, sales, and net income after taxes and found the following relationships:

 1 Net capital assets usually show higher concentration ratios than either total assets or sales.
 2 Net income after taxes is the highest level of measured concentration.
 3 Sales data show the lowest levels of concentration.
 4 Total assets rarely exhibit the highest or lowest concentration ratios.

Essentially Mueller demonstrated that a researcher could judiciously pick the variable used in constructing concentration ratios to obtain either a higher or a lower ratio.

Regional and Local Industrial Concentration

We have just observed that choice of variable may bias measured concentration ratios or at least alter them. Measuring industrial concentration on a regional or a local level, rather than merely on a national level, can also give dramatically different results. One study showed that "the average regional concentration ratio for every regional industry exceeds the corresponding national ratio" and "the average local concentration ratio in every industry exceeds the national concentration ratio."[49] For the industry studied by these researchers, the weighted national concentration figure was 19 percent, whereas the weighted average local concentration figure ratio was 61 percent. This difference suggests that transportation costs may dictate what type of index should be used.

[48] W. F. Mueller, "Statement, Economic Concentration—Overall and Conglomerate Aspects," Hearings before the Senate Subcommittee on Antitrust and Monopoly, July 1964, pp. 109–129.
[49] David Schwartzmann and Joan Bodoff, "Concentration in Regional and Local Industries," *Southern Economic Journal,* vol. 37 (January 1971), p. 344.

MODELS OF INDUSTRIES
AND MARKETS

CHAPTER 5

COMPETITION AND MONOPOLY

In the industrial structure of the United States, some firms are closer to the competitive model and some are closer to monopoly. Policymakers often place great emphasis on the degree of competition in a particular industry. In this chapter, we will examine both the meaning of competition and the meaning of monopoly. We will then evaluate the loss which the economy suffers from monopoly.

THE MEANING OF COMPETITION

At the outset, we must distinguish between a fairly relaxed notion of competition and a formal model of perfect competition.[1] The more relaxed view of the competitive process focuses on the concept of rivalry among economic transactors.

Perfect Competition

Basically, in a market characterized by **perfect competition** no individual buyer or seller influences the price by his or her purchases or sales. Five conditions are necessary before a perfectly competitive market can arise, and the presence of all five is essential in the formal world of perfect competition. We list these assumptions here.

---

[1] See Paul J. McNulty, "Economic Theory and the Meaning of Competition," *Quarterly Journal of Economics,* vol. 82 (November 1968), pp. 639–656.

Homogeneity of Product   Unless we are dealing with a homogeneous product, it is meaningless to talk about a large number of sellers, because each product is different from the others. Buyers must be able to choose among many sellers of a product that they believe to be the same.

Costless Resource Mobility   Firms must be able to enter any industry freely; resources must be able to move without friction among alternative uses; and goods and services must be salable wherever the price is highest.

Large Number of Buyers or Sellers[2]   In order that each economic agent have no influence upon price, a large number of them must act independently. In addition, the largest buyer or the largest seller must provide only a small fraction of the total quantities bought and sold.[3]

Product Divisibility   The product must be divisible to the extent that small quantities of it can either be purchased or at least be rented. This assumption eliminates potential entry barrier problems in competitive markets.

Perfect Information   All buyers and sellers must have perfect information about their demand curves and their cost curves. Thus complete information is available about the prices at which commodities can be bought and sold. This condition guarantees that the price per constant-quality unit, corrected for transportation charges, will be uniform. Further, it assures proper resource allocation.

Sometimes a distinction is made between pure and perfect competition, particularly as shown in work by Edward Chamberlin.[4] According to Chamberlin, the sufficient conditions for the existence of *pure competition* are (1) homogeneity of product and (2) insignificant size of individual sellers relative to their total market. In order to obtain *perfect competition*, we must add several additional characteristics, the most important being the absence of barriers to entry by new firms, coupled with resource mobility. As we have just seen, additional conditions associated with perfect competition include continuous divisibility of inputs and outputs and perfect knowledge of both present and future market conditions.

---

[2] It is correct to state that in a perfectly competitive market, under certain reasonable conditions in a general equilibrium model, no producer has any effect on market price. See Eugene F. Fama and Arthur B. Laffer, "The Number of Firms and Competition," *American Economic Review,* vol. 6 (September 1972), pp. 670–674.

[3] Strictly speaking, perfect competition does not require large numbers of sellers if there is free entry into the industry and all actual or potential firms face constant costs (no economies or diseconomies of scale).

[4] See Edward H. Chamberlin, *Theory of Monopolistic Competition: A Re-Orientation of the Theory of Value* (Cambridge, Mass.: Harvard University Press, 1939), chap. 1.

Rivalry

In a world of scarce resources, conscious interdependence or **rivalry** will perforce arise among sellers and among buyers. Rivalry among sellers is shown in many ways: advertising, improvement in the quality of the product, sales promotion, development of new products, and other conduct. Rivalry among buyers also stimulates specific activities: finding better deals, figuring out ways to take advantage of quantity discounts, offering a higher price to obtain a product that is in fixed supply, and so on.

Vigorous rivalry may exist among sellers and among buyers that cannot, nonetheless, be called perfect competition. For example, jockeying for position in the car market among the Big Three is an example of vigorous rivalry, but the market structure is not one of perfect competition. On the other hand, perfect competition between producers may exist without conscious rivalry. Two Nebraska wheat farmers on adjacent farms are perfect competitors, but certainly are not conscious rivals.

Competition and Survivorship

Rivalry does not require an understanding of microeconomic theory. Although a typical course in microeconomics requires the student to examine total, average, and marginal product curves, business people may not be aware of such curves. That is to say, rivalry may exist without exact knowledge of these curves and demand curves.

In a world of scarce resources, consumers will opt for the lower-priced product, other things held constant. It is immaterial that the firm has exact information on its costs and demands. The firm that chooses the best combination of output, qualities, quantities, and price will ultimately survive, forcing other firms at least to imitate it if they also wish to survive. This is sometimes called the **survivor principle.**[5] It helps us to understand the nature of real-world rivalry.

However, the more commonsense notion of rivalry outlined here will not be particularly evident in the analysis of a competitive market. We now specify the model of perfect competition.

Perfect Competition and Rivalry

The definition of perfect competition might have added the additional attribute of a complete lack of *conscious* rivalry. Once we assume perfect information, no real market rivalry can exist, and therefore no market process is present for analysis. Indeed, in a perfectly competitive market, all the signs of conscious

---

[5] See George J. Stigler, "The Economies of Scale," *Journal of Law and Economics,* vol. 1 (October 1958), pp. 54–71, and Harry E. Frech, III, and Paul B. Ginsberg, "Optimal Scale of Medical Practice: Survival Analysis," *Journal of Business,* vol. 47 (January 1974), pp. 23–36.

rivalry will be absent and there will be no motivation to advertise, no need for market research, and certainly no differentiation because the product is homogeneous. On the buyer's side, no buyer will ever need search for a more favorable deal, no buyer will ever regret having made a purchase, and certainly no buyer will ever bother to look at brand names. In short, no activity on the part of individuals can be classified as conscious rivalry in a perfectly competitive market.[6]

In some ways, however, this lack of conscious rivalry contradicts the analytical usefulness of the model that will follow. For example, we can analyze situations in which surpluses or shortages might exist. We might see that an equilibrium will occur at some price different from that currently existing in the market.[7] However, the only way the equilibrium can come about is by means of a dynamic process that works through rivalry among economic transactors.[8] In the case of excess supply, for example, sellers may accept a lower price for their product in order to get rid of unwanted inventories. Thus, the perfectly competitive market can really have meaning only at an equilibrium price (or in a world with instantaneous movements from one equilibrium to another).

The point to be made here is not that the perfectly competitive model has no value. Indeed, we will find that this model allows us to understand the consequences of a number of common restrictions on economic behavior. We must, however, realize that in dealing with a perfectly competitive model, we will have to modify it by changing the assumptions to some extent in order to apply the model to real-world phenomena. The analysis of static equilibria that follows is useful in understanding perfect competition. Because one or more of the assumptions do not accurately describe actual conditions in the market, the model's usefulness is not reduced any more than such criticisms lessen the assumption of a vacuum in physics.

COMPETITION AND EFFICIENCY

The perfectly competitive world can be described as follows. The demand for the perfect competitor's product is perfectly elastic. All can be sold that is desired to be sold at the market price, and none can be sold at any higher prices. Thus, the perfect competitor has only two choices: Should production occur and, if so, how much? The profit-maximizing perfect competitor chooses an output rate for which marginal revenue is equal to marginal cost. We know

[6] There is much confusion between the concept of rivalry and competition. The distinction between the two concepts may be analogized to the distinction between conduct and market structure, which we discussed in Chapter 1. In the modern sense, the term "rivalry" refers to actual conduct or behavior; on the other hand, the term "competition" refers to a structurally determinable model used to predict conduct in the marketplace.

[7] See Kenneth J. Arrow, "Toward a Theory of Price Adjustment," in Moses Abramowitz, et al., *The Allocation of Economic Resources* (Stanford, Calif.: Stanford University Press, 1959).

[8] Actually, given enough time to adjust, virtually any two firms that are potential competitors can affect the equilibrium price.

that the perfect competitor faces a perfectly elastic demand curve; thus, profit maximizing dictates that price be set equal to marginal cost, or $P = MC$.

An implication of the perfect competition model is that output in the industry is consistent with economic efficiency. It is fashionable to say that for any given distribution of income, the imaginary world of perfect competition maximizes so-called economic welfare. This is a situation in which it is impossible to improve any one person's position without worsening that of anyone else. For this reason, improving competition has often been a policy goal.

Perfect Competition Is Not a Reality

Methodologically, the construct of a perfectly competitive world has been used for model-building purposes. Nonetheless, policymakers often describe the state of perfect competition as a goal, perhaps to be attained asymptotically. But we can think of numerous objections to any general policy of improving competition. In other words, a perfectly competitive world is not necessarily the ultimate policy goal. First of all, we know that perfect competition is impossible because knowledge is never perfect.

Second, only a few farmers out of millions of producers actually face real-world, perfectly elastic demand curves. Additionally, demand is often insufficient in many industries to support *numerous* efficient-sized firms. How can one imagine having hundreds of competing telephone systems and electric companies? Thus, perfect competition may be an unrealistic goal. To attain perfect competition presumably means remaking the whole world.

Chamberlin has indicated that pure competition cannot be regarded as ideal from the point of view of welfare economics, because of differences in abilities, tastes, income, location of buyers, desires, and so on. In other words, according to Chamberlin, consumers are willing to sacrifice a certain amount of allocative efficiency for variety. Chamberlin contends that the social welfare ideal can therefore not be pure competition but some combination of pure and monopolistic competition.[9] However, if variety produces utility to consumers, then allocative efficiency may still be achieved.

The Political Aspects of Competition

Economists often deal in abstract models about the economy. The abstract model of perfect competition is a clear case in point. As we have pointed out, perfect competition can lead to economic efficiency, but the political repercussions of a perfectly competitive world may have been and continue to be much more powerful in forming the general social consensus in favor of, if not perfect competition, at least more competition. A market with numerous buyers and

---

[9] Edward H. Chamberlin, *The Theory of Monopolistic Competition: A Re-Orientation of the Theory of Value,* 6th ed. (Cambridge, Mass.: Harvard University Press, 1948), pp. 214–215.

sellers—at least a large enough number required for competition—results in decentralization and dispersion of power. The economic problem of satisfying human wants is solved through a rather mechanical interaction of demand and supply forces in the marketplace as opposed to the conscious exercise of power that might be held in private hands when monopoly prevails or in government hands when government regulation and state enterprise prevail. The limitation upon the power of government and monopoly is a major part of classical liberal ideology. This in turn has provided some of the foundation of the design of the American government system.

Additionally, the competitive market process solves the economic problem impersonally; so-called big business people and government bureaucrats are not personally involved. When no one is involved in overall decision making or policy, economic agents in the society cannot direct their frustration onto the decision of an identifiable individual. Lastly, a political argument that favors a competitive market involves the apparent freedom of opportunity that results. Perfect competition, you will remember, requires no barriers to entry. Under such a condition, individuals may enter the profession or calling they prefer, limited only by their own ability, skill, and talent (and sometimes capital).

Workable Competition

A perfectly competitive world is politically appealing to many, but as we have discussed above, does not and never did exist. Thus, as a policy guide, a competitive model suffers certain defects. In response to this problem, a search occurred in the 1940s and 1950s for more operational norms of what John M. Clark termed "workable competition."[10] Having observed that perfect competition never did, can, or will exist, Clark argued that deviations from the perfectly competitive model in the long run do not necessarily harm society. Thus, he set out to formulate a set of minimal criteria for judging the workability of a competitive economy. His formula has been modified by a number of economists.

Structure, Conduct, and Performance   After Clark's seminal work appeared, numerous economists wrote their own versions of minimal criteria for workable competition. Stephen Sosnick has reviewed this literature completely up to the late 1950s.[11] Here we summarize 15 criteria of workable competition, using the standard structure-conduct-performance trichotomy that Sosnick used.

---

[10] John M. Clark, "Toward a Concept of Workable Competition," *American Economic Review,* vol. 30 (June 1940), pp. 241–256; "Competition: Static Models and Dynamic Aspects," *American Economic Review* vol. 45 (May 1955), pp. 450–462; *Competition as a Dynamic Process* (Washington, D.C.: Brookings Institution, 1961).

[11] See Stephen H. Sosnick, "A Critique of Concepts of Workable Competition," *Quarterly Journal of Economics,* vol. 72 (August 1958), pp. 380–423. Also see Charles E. Ferguson, *A Macroeconomic Theory of Workable Competition* (Durham, N.C.: Duke University Press, 1964).

Structural norms:

 1 Artificial inhibitions on entry and mobility do not exist.
 2 Price-sensitive quality-differentials exist in the products offered for sale.
 3 The number of traders is as large as scale economies allow.

Conduct criteria:

 4 Firms do not collude.
 5 No exclusionary, predatory, or coercive tactics are used by firms.
 6 No fraud is used in sales promotion.
 7 Price discrimination, which is "harmful," does not exist.
 8 Rivals cannot have perfect information about whether others will follow their price changes.

Performance criteria:

 9 Profits are at levels *just* sufficient to reward innovation, efficiency, and investment.
 10 Qualities and outputs respond to changes in consumer demand.
 11 Firms exploit their ability to introduce technologically superior new products and processes.
 12 Marketing expenses are not "excessive."
 13 The production operations of each firm are efficient.
 14 Sellers who best serve customer wants are most rewarded.
 15 Cyclical instability is not intensified by price changes.

These criteria can be treated as signals that something like competition is occurring. In this sense they act as policy guidelines.

The Critics of Workable Competition   Clark and his followers have encountered their share of criticism. Basically, the critics question whether the approach of workable competition is operationally meaningful.[12] What does "enough" mean? What does "excessive" mean when referring to promotional expenses? What does "harmful" price discrimination mean? The list can go on and on. Such questions raise important value judgments that certainly are not part of positive economic analysis. Even when dealing with the notion of the efficiency of production operations, one can decide on efficiency only by having a yardstick; but to have a yardstick, one must know both what is possible and what is desired. The latter requires subjective rather than objective analysis. Also, what if some of the criteria are satisfied, but others are not? How do we then decide on the workability of competition?

Jesse Markham has come up with an alternative method of evaluating industry structure and performance against some of the norms and criteria mentioned above. He has proposed that

---

[12] Carl Kaysen and Donald F. Turner, *Antitrust Policy* (Cambridge, Mass.: Harvard University Press, 1959), pp. 53–56.

> [a]n industry may be judged to be workably competitive when, after the structural characteristics of its market and the dynamic forces that shaped them have been thoroughly examined, there is no clearly indicated change that can be effected through public policy measures that would result in greater social gains than social losses.[13]

Problems arise even with this alternative. Well-informed individuals may arrive at different conclusions about how to measure the social gains and the social losses of a public policy measure. To cite an example, it has often been suggested that oil companies be broken up into smaller entities. Consumerist Ralph Nader and his followers believe that such divestiture will produce clear-cut positive differences between social gains and social costs. Others, who believe strongly that oil companies might lose the efficiency benefits of scale economies, see social costs exceeding social gains with such a public policy measure. In addition, Markham's definition does not specify an admissible set of public policy measures to be used in his criteria. Finally, we cannot always calibrate the gains and losses of alternative options in the same denomination, nor do they always accrue to the same people.

Perfect Competition as a Goal

The difficulties in using the perfect competition model lead us to reject it as a scientifically suitable goal or objective of political or public policy analysis. Perfect competition is a model to be used as a tool rather than as an objective or an end toward which to strive. Those who use perfect competition as a bench-mark for social policy may make the mistake of trying to fit the real world into a model rather than build a model to describe the outcomes.

THE MEANING OF MONOPOLY

Economics textbooks commonly define a monopolist as any firm facing a downward-sloping demand curve. Otherwise stated, a monopolist is a seller who must reduce price in order to sell a larger output. The current most widely accepted definition of monopoly was not, however, one that classical economists would agree with.

Earlier Notions of Monopoly

It would be an understatement to say that classical economists applied the word *monopoly* to a large variety of situations.[14] For most classical economists, a monopolist was anyone who received payment beyond that needed to induce

---

[13] Jesse W. Markham, "An Alternative Approach to the Concept of Workable Competition," *American Economic Review*, vol. 40 (June 1950), pp. 349–361.

[14] See Lewis A. Kochin, "Monopoly Profits and Social Losses," *Research in Law and Economics*, vol. 2 (Greenwich, Conn.: JAI Press, 1980), pp. 201–212.

that person to supply his or her product. Land was a premier example, often used by the classical economist John Stuart Mill, who stated "It is at once evident, that (economic) rent is the effect of a monopoly. . . ."[15] Mill further stated that

> a thing which is limited in quantity, though its possessors do not act in concert, is still a monopolized article.[16]

In addition to the above notion of monopoly, classical economists often applied the term *monopolist* to any seller who sold in a closed market. Adam Smith called the market for colonial trade by English merchants a monopoly, even though no collusion occurred and the number of merchants was large. Clearly, classical economists believed that monopoly led to higher prices. In fact, Adam Smith wrote that "the price of monopoly is upon every occasion the highest which can be got."[17] According to a well-known economist in the nineteenth century, "The power of the purchasers to offer a high price forms the only limit to the rapacity of monopolists."[18] That writer, J. M. McCulloch, expressed part of the universal opinion that whatever else monopoly is, it is bad.

Is Monopoly Bad?   Adam Smith gave three reasons why monopoly was bad (that is, it did not maximize the wealth of nations). He first cited the reduction in output. In other words, the monopolist's output would be inappropriate, or, as he said, "monopolies derange . . . the natural distribution of the stock of society."[19] The second reason Smith gave was that resources would be used to obtain, maintain, and expand monopolies and would therefore be essentially wasted; that is, they could have been used otherwise to the advantage of society. Finally, his third reason was that monopolies were technically inefficient and would produce less from the same amount of inputs than competitors could produce.

Smith clearly felt that a reduction in output was the most serious problem with monopoly. Modern economists have attempted to measure the welfare losses attributable to those output restrictions by monopolists. Perhaps a more unique feature of his reasoning involves how monopolies are obtained and maintained. Can we treat monopoly profits merely as a transfer from other members of society? Many modern economists do not believe so, nor did Smith. Because competition for monopoly profits will arise, resources will be used to capture those profits, and those resources are often labeled a welfare loss to society. Further, if transfers from consumers to monopolists can be prevented, then customers of a potential monopoly will have an incentive to

---

[15] John S. Mill, *Principles of Political Economy* (Toronto: University of Toronto Press, 1965), p. 416.

[16] Ibid., p. 417.

[17] Adam Smith, *The Wealth of Nations* (New York: Random House, 1937), p. 610.

[18] John M. McCulloch, *The Principles of Political Economy*, 2d ed. (London: William Tait, 1830), p. 313.

[19] Adam Smith, op. cit., p. 596.

organize and prevent the formation of the monopoly. Thus, customers may also incur costs for the prevention of monopoly formation at the same time that the potential monopolists are spending resources to obtain the monopoly. Symmetrically then, the resources used in these consumer efforts could have been used for other purposes. Thus, the total welfare loss from monopolies may indeed be great. In the next two sections, we examine these propositions fully.

Price and Output Losses—Comparing Pure Monopoly with Perfect Competition

We can compare competition and monopoly from two perspectives—costs and output rates. Strictly speaking, in order to compare monopoly with competition, we must first obtain the long-run equilibrium of the pure monopolist. We know that, in the long run, the monopolist who can find no plant size that at least results in a competitive rate of return will go out of business. If, on the other hand, the monopolist is making a profit in the short run with one plant size, that monopolist must determine if an even greater profit can be obtained with a larger or a smaller plant size. As with the long-run equilibrium of a competitive firm, the monopolist will adjust plant size in order to operate on the long-run average cost curve. The long-run profit-maximizing rate of output will be such that long-run marginal cost equals marginal revenue. The only difference will be in the long-run equilibrium price and output.

Comparing Costs Conceptually, in the long run, a perfectly competitive firm operates with an optimal plant size such that short-run average cost (SAC) = long-run average cost (LAC) = marginal revenue (MR) = price (P) = average revenue (AR) = long-run marginal cost (LMC) = short-run marginal cost (SMC). This optimal situation is shown in Figure 5-1(a). However, compare this situation with the long-run equilibrium for the single-plant monopolist depicted in panel (b) of Figure 5-1. The profit-maximizing rate of output is Q_m. It is the output at which long-run marginal cost = marginal revenue = short-run marginal cost. But at that rate of output, neither SAC nor LAC is at a minimum. The minimum SAC occurs at point A, where SMC intersects SAC. The scale of the plant will not be such that either short-run or long-run average costs are a minimum at the rate of output chosen to maximize profits. Thus, in comparing monopoly with competition, some observers infer from a comparison of panels (a) and (b) that monopoly is inefficient because average costs are not at a minimum. Note that the only way this statement could have any possible meaning is if the cost conditions for a monopoly and for the entire set of pure competitors would be exactly the same if we switched from one market structure to the other market structure. This is a heroic assumption. Let us keep the assumption for the moment and compare the long-run price and output combinations in the two extreme market structures.

Comparing Price and Output under the Two Market Structures In Figure 5-2, we have drawn an industry demand schedule DD. Assume now that the

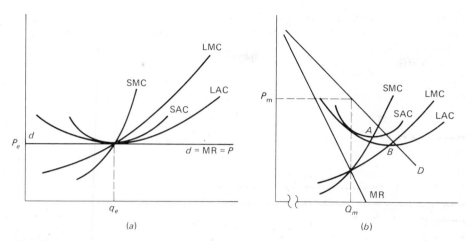

FIGURE 5-1
Comparing monopoly and competitive costs. In panel (a) we show long-run equilibrium for a perfectly competitive firm. Its rate of output q_e is such that SMC = SAC = LAC = LMC = MR = P. Moreover, average total cost is at a minimum. In panel (b) we show the situation for a monopolist. At the profit-maximizing rate of output Q_m, the monopolist is not operating at the minimum point A on its short-run average cost curve SAC, nor at the minimum point B on its LAC curve.

industry is perfectly competitive and that each competitor has a horizontal long-run marginal cost curve depicted by the horizontal line MC. Thus the horizontal summation of each firm's marginal cost curve is going to be the horizontal line at price P_c. The intersection, then, of the industry supply curve, which is MC, will be at E; the market-clearing price will be P_c and an equilibrium quantity will be Q_c. Now we assume that overnight the industry is fully

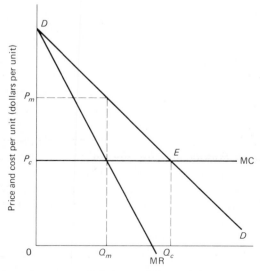

FIGURE 5-2
Comparing price and output for monopoly in competition. Assume constant marginal cost for the industry. Given an industry demand curve DD, and assuming that the industry supply curve is MC, the competitive industry output would be Q_c; the industry price would be P_c. Now consider the possibility that all firms become a single-monopoly firm overnight and that there are no changes in costs. The profit-maximizing rate of output will now fall to Q_m; the price will go up to P_m. The conclusion is that monopolization of a perfectly competitive industry restricts production and increases price, *ceteris paribus*.

monopolized—say, by government fiat—and owned by one person or firm, and further that all cost curves remain exactly the same. The monopolist sets the rate of output where marginal cost = marginal revenue. (Perfect competitors do this also, but for them MR = P.) The monopolist, then, sets the rate of output at Q_m. The monopolist can sell this rate of output at a price of P_m. Thus, under the assumption that the cost curves remain the same when the industry goes from competition to monopoly, we can state that the monopolist restricts production and raises price.

Competition and Monopoly with Strong Cost Advantages   If there are extensive economies in scale at the firm level, then it is conceivable that a monopoly could be selling more output at a lower price than could a group of numerous competitors selling the same product. Consider this possibility in Figure 5-3. Here we show that the market supply curve under competition is, for numerous firms, Σ MC. It is the horizontal summation of all individual firms' marginal cost curves above the minimum point of their average variable cost curves. Equilibrium occurs at price P_c; quantity, at Q_c. Now assume that the firms are monopolized. If there are really substantial cost advantages, the new marginal cost curve will everywhere be below the old industry supply curve. This new marginal cost curve is labeled MC for a monopolist. The monopolist will set the rate of output where marginal revenue = marginal cost. This rate of output will be Q_m. The monopolist will be able to sell that rate of output at a price of P_m. In this case, monopoly leads to an increase in the rate of output sold at a lower price.

MEASURING MONOPOLY WELFARE LOSS—CONSUMER AND PRODUCER SURPLUS

In order to understand the meaning of the welfare loss due to the output restriction of monopoly, we must examine the concepts of consumer and producer surplus.

The Meaning of Consumer Surplus

Often when you purchase a quantity of a commodity at a particular market price, you may say to yourself that you really received a bargain. Since you were willing to pay more for the item, we call the difference between what you were willing to pay and what you actually paid **consumer surplus**. Formally, the definition we choose is the following:

> Consumer surplus is the difference between the price a consumer actually pays for some given amount of a good and the price that the consumer would have been willing to pay rather than do without it.

In order to estimate consumer surplus for your total purchases of any commodity, all you need do is carry out this "all or none" experiment. Say that you

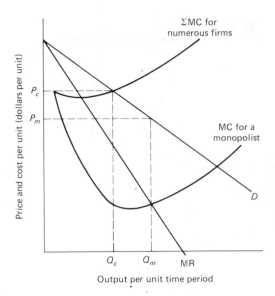

FIGURE 5-3   *(ie large eco of scale)*
Monopoly with strong cost advantage.
Assume that the horizontally summed
marginal cost curve ΣMC for a
competitive situation is given as drawn.
Now the firm is monopolized, and it
experiences tremendous cost
advantages such that the marginal cost
curve for the monopolist falls
dramatically as drawn. Profit-maximizing
rate of output goes from Q_c out to Q_m
and, price falls from P_c to P_m.

buy about 40 gallons of gas a month for your car. Ask yourself how much you
would be willing to pay for that quantity of gas rather than do without it
completely. Because an individual's marginal evaluation of additional units
falls, consumer surplus will also fall at the margin (assuming the price you pay
remains constant). That gives your *total valuation* for that quantity of the
commodity. Then compare your total valuation with the actual total price that
you must pay for 40 gallons per month (price per unit times quantity purchased). The difference is the consumer surplus that you derive from the purchase of 40 gallons of gas each month.

   Diminishing Marginal Valuation   Consumer surplus exists because the prevailing price of a product is an indication of the marginal valuation of or the
marginal use value received from the commodity in question. **Marginal valuation** is the marginal rate of substitution between x and y expressed in money
terms, where y represents all other goods. In other words, marginal valuation is
MRS_{xy} in money terms. Marginal valuation can also be called **marginal use
value**. If we assume diminishing marginal valuation, we know that the marginal
valuation placed on the last unit of a commodity purchased will be less than the
marginal valuation placed on prior units purchased. This can be seen in Figure
5-4.

   In this situation, if the individual is asked for the maximum he or she would
pay for one Coke per day, it might be $1. The marginal use value of the first
Coke is therefore $1 times 1, or the first shaded rectangle. Next, after the
individual has already purchased and consumed one Coke, the following question is asked: "How much would he or she be willing to pay for a second Coke
per day?" In this experiment, the amount is 75¢. Thus the marginal use value of

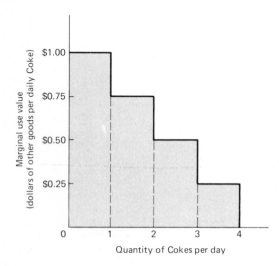

FIGURE 5-4
Declining marginal use value. On the horizontal axis, we measure quantity of Cokes per day. On the vertical axis, we measure marginal use value expressed in terms of dollars of other goods given up in order to purchase Cokes. We run an experiment in which an individual is offered one Coke. The individual is willing to give up $1 of all other goods to purchase this Coke and, therefore, that is a monetary measure of his or her marginal use value of one Coke. Now, after one Coke has been consumed, the individual is offered a second. Assume that he or she is willing to give up 75¢ of all other goods; thus, the marginal valuation, or marginal use value, of the second Coke is 75¢.

the second Coke, given that the first Coke has been purchased and consumed, is 75¢ per Coke times one Coke, or the second shaded rectangle. We also determine marginal use values for the purchase of three or four Cokes per day. Now we know that adding up the rectangles gives us the total valuation derived from the consumption of a particular number of Cokes per day. In other words, if four Cokes per day were purchased, the total marginal use value would be $1 (for the first Coke), plus 75¢ (for the second), plus 50¢ (for the third), plus 25¢ (for the fourth), or $2.50; this amount is equal to the entire shaded area in Figure 5-4.

What would happen if this individual were offered Cokes at 25¢ apiece for as many Cokes as he or she wanted to buy? The individual would continue purchasing Cokes until the marginal valuation was equal to that price of 25¢ each. Thus, this individual would purchase four Cokes per day. The *total* valuation or use value derived from the purchase of four Cokes has just been calculated as $2.50. However, the total price that had to be paid for the four Cokes was 25¢ times 4, or $1.00. Thus, the difference between the total valuation of four Cokes and the total price paid was $2.50 minus $1.00, or $1.50 per day. This figure, $1.50 per day, represents the consumer surplus from purchasing four Cokes per day at a constant price of 25¢ apiece.

Using a Demand Curve to Measure Consumer Surplus   We can generalize this discussion by assuming infinite divisibility of Cokes, that is, that one can also buy *fractions* of a Coke. We come up, therefore, with the demand curve *dd* in Figure 5-5. At any point along that demand curve, we can find the individual's marginal valuation of a daily Coke. For a quantity of two Cokes per day, the marginal valuation is found at E, or P_1. That is the marginal use value received from purchasing and consuming two Cokes per day. When viewed in

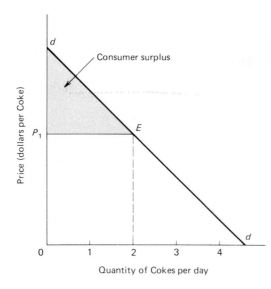

Price (dollars per Coke)

Quantity of Cokes per day

FIGURE 5-5
The demand curve and consumer surplus. If we assume that the demand curve represents the individual's marginal valuation or marginal use value, then we can derive a graphical interpretation of consumer surplus. Assume that the price in the market is given as P_1. Two Cokes per day will be chosen. The marginal valuation of the last Coke is equal to P_1, expressed as dollars of other goods given up. The total amount paid for the Cokes is therefore equal to price times quantity, or $0P_1E2$. However, the total valuation is the entire area under the demand curve to E or quantity 2 ($0dE2$). The difference is the shaded triangle, which represents consumer surplus—the excess of total valuation over what was actually paid for the particular quantity purchased.

this manner, the area under the demand curve out to the vertical line at the quantity of Cokes purchased per day is the total valuation received from the consumption of that quantity.[20]

Now assume a particular fixed price P_1 per Coke. The quantity demanded will be two. The total use value derived from the consumption of two Cokes would be the area under the demand curve down to E, or $0dE2$. However, the price that had to be paid for two Cokes is P_1 times 2, or the rectangular area $0P_1E2$. The difference, then, between the dollar measure of total valuation and what had to be paid for the Cokes is the shaded triangle, P_1dE. That is labeled consumer surplus; it is a geometric presentation of the amount of money income that a consumer would pay in addition to what he or she already paid rather than go without the two Cokes per day.

The Producer's Side

A similar analysis can be made on the producer's side. In Figure 5-6 we show an upward-sloping supply curve SS. We assume an equilibrium price of P_e. The quantity produced will be Q_e. Remember that the supply curve represents the

[20] The above argument is strictly correct only in the situation where the consumer's demand price for any quantity of the good in question is independent of income. For normal or superior goods this is clearly not the case, and the area under the demand curve exaggerates the aggregate willingness to pay. (The converse occurs for inferior goods.) Only when the income elasticity is zero is our argument strictly valid. Alternatively, if we were dealing with what is called an income-compensated demand curve (a demand curve that shows only substitution effects), we need not worry about the income effects on the demand for the good in question. In our discussion we will abstract from the income effects by making, as a first approximation, the assumption that the summation of marginal valuation equals total valuation.

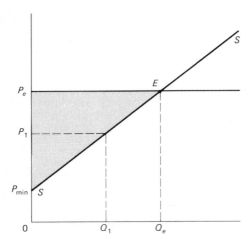

FIGURE 5-6
Producers' surplus or quasi-rents. The supply curve SS shows the minimum price at which a given quantity will be forthcoming; and, therefore, the amount of resources necessary to obtain a given quantity. However, if price is P_e, the market value of quantity Q_e is equal to the entire rectangle $0P_eEQ_e$. The difference is the triangle $P_{min}P_eE$. The shaded triangle is producers' surplus; it equals the revenues received in excess of what is necessary to keep resources producing the quantity Q_e per unit time period.

locus of minimum prices at which different quantities will be forthcoming. Thus, for example, for quantity Q_1, producers would be willing to supply that quantity at price P_1. However, the market-clearing price is P_e, which is higher than P_1. *Economic rent* is the sum of the difference between the prices at which producers would be willing to sell their products and the prices they actually receive. This particular economic rent is also called producers' surplus (to be symmetric with the terminology for consumers).

The shaded area in Figure 5-6 is our measure of economic rent. It is the quantity of money income over and above what is necessary to keep resources in the industry sufficient to produce quantity Q_e. Thus, the triangle, $P_{min}P_eE$ is similar in nature to the shaded area in Figure 5-5.

Putting Producers and Consumers Together

When we put the supply and demand curves together, we can see that at any market-clearing price there is a consumer surplus enjoyed by consumers and a quasi-rent enjoyed by producers. The surplus and quasi-rent are the two shaded triangles in Figure 5-7.

Welfare Costs We can obtain a geometric measure of the magnitude of the reduction in welfare that results from a market imperfection—taxes, subsidies, monopoly, and so forth—by comparing the diagram in Figure 5-7 with a situation in which there is such imperfection. We look at the reductions in consumer surplus and in quasi-rents caused by the imperfection. In Figure 5-8, we do this for a hypothetical output restriction. In competitive equilibrium, the intersection of DD and SS is at E. The market-clearing price is P_e. The market-clearing quantity is Q_e. The consumers' surplus is the triangle $P_eP_{max}E$. The quasi-rent is represented by the triangle $P_eP_{min}E$. Now a government authority imposes an output restriction that limits firms to producing no more than Q_R. Assume for

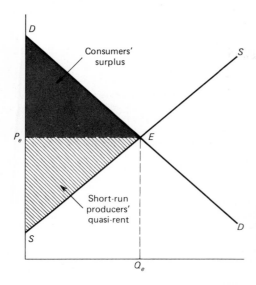

FIGURE 5-7
Putting consumers' and producers' surpluses together. At any given market-clearing price P_e, consumers' and producers' surpluses are the shaded triangles.

simplicity that the output quota is passed out to the most efficient firms so that the original supply schedule up to the restricted quantity is a part of the new supply schedule. The new supply schedule now becomes S up to point A and is then vertical to S'. The intersection of the new supply curve with the old demand curve is at point E'. The price at which Q_R will be sold is P'_e. Note that reductions occur in consumer surplus and in quasi-rent. Revenues first used to produce $Q_e - Q_r$ now go to other uses. The reduction in consumer surplus is equal to $P_e P'_e E' E$. The change in producer surplus, or quasi-rents, is equal to the reduction given by the triangle ABE.

Producers, however, may not be worse off since there is a transfer from consumers to producers equal to the rectangle $P_e P'_e E' B$. Thus, not all the reduction in consumer surplus was lost. Consumer surplus that was lost completely

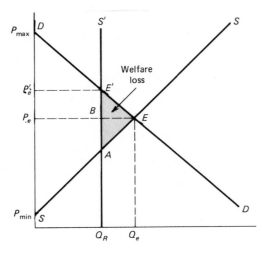

FIGURE 5-8
The welfare cost of output restriction. If output is restricted to a maximum of Q_R, the supply curve becomes SAS'. (We assume that output allotments are given to the most efficient producers, so that we keep the same supply curve through the portion S to A.) The new equilibrium is at point E'; the new market-clearing price is P'_e. The welfare loss will be the triangle $AE'E$.

was the triangle left over, or $BE'E$. When we add this to the producer surplus loss, or ABE, we obtain the welfare loss triangle, or $AE'E$, due to an output restriction at Q_R. This welfare loss (estimated in a partial equilibrium framework) is also called *deadweight loss*.

MEASUREMENT OF MONOPOLY LOSSES

We have already shown in previous sections, using consumer surplus and producer surplus, the welfare cost of output restriction. We now wish to look explicitly at the welfare cost of monopoly.

The Welfare Cost of Monopoly

We are now in a position to estimate the social welfare cost of monopoly. Consider a hypothetical situation. We have a choice of either pure monopoly or pure competition. The cost curves are exactly the same in both cases (see Figure 5-9).

Assume for simplicity that marginal cost is constant. In a perfectly competitive situation, the curve labeled MC is also the supply curve and is the horizontal summation of all the individual firms' marginal cost curves. The competitive solution is at the intersection of MC and DD, at point E. The competitive quantity would be Q_c and the competitive price would be P_c, because we assumed constant marginal costs. The amount of quasi-rent is zero. However, the amount of consumer surplus at price P_c is the triangle $P_c P_{max} E$.

Now assume that the industry is monopolized and the cost curve remains exactly the same. The monopoly firm looks at the marginal revenue curve MR. It chooses the profit-maximizing quantity at the intersection of MR and MC at

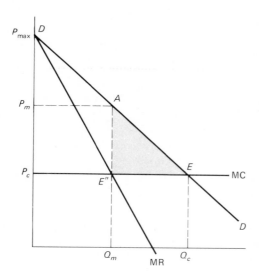

FIGURE 5-9
The welfare cost of monopoly. Assume a constant marginal cost MC. Perfectly competitive equilibrium is found where the industry supply curve MC intersects the industry demand curve DD. Output would be Q_c; the price would be P_c. Assume now that a monopolist takes over and that there is no change in marginal costs. The monopolist sets output where marginal revenue equals marginal cost at point E''. The quantity sold will be Q_m. Price will be P_m. The reduction in consumer surplus is equal to $P_c P_m AE$. However, part of that reduction in consumer surplus is transferred to producers. This transfer or increase in producer surplus is equal to $P_c P_m AE''$. What is left is the shaded triangle $E''AE$, which is our measure of the welfare loss of monopoly.

point E''. It then finds the price at which it can sell this quantity Q_m by consulting the demand curve DD. The product is sold at price P_m. Monopolization of the industry results in a higher price and a lower quantity produced and consumed. It also results in a reduction in consumer surplus equal to P_cP_mAE. But the rectangle P_cP_mAE'' is transferred from consumers (a wealth transfer) to the monopolist, leaving a deadweight loss equal to the triangle $E''AE$. Note that the resources released from the monopolized industry go into other industries where they are fully employed and where they generate benefits just equal to their total cost of $Q_mE''EQ_c$. The welfare loss is then the triangle $E''AE$.

Estimating Monopoly Efficiency Loss

In order to estimate the welfare efficiency loss, we have to know the dimensions of the triangle in Figure 5-9. We make several assumptions to simplify the calculations. First, every industry has a perfectly horizontal supply curve; second, every industry has an average demand elasticity of 1 with no income effects over the relevant range; and third, there are no distortions outside of the manufacturing sector.

The area $E''AE$ is equal to one-half of the difference between the monopoly price less the competitive price times the difference between the competitive output less the monopoly output [that is, $\frac{1}{2}(P_m - P_c)(Q_c - Q_m)$]. The total monopoly profits will be equal to the difference between the monopoly price less the competitive price times the monopoly output or area $P_mAE''P_c$. If we assume the elasticity of demand is close to unity, then monopoly revenues, P_mQ_m, are roughly equivalent to competitive revenues, P_cQ_c, and it can be shown that the welfare loss is approximately

$$E''AE = \frac{[(P_m - P_c)(Q_m)]^2}{2[P_mQ_m - (P_m - P_c)(Q_m)]}$$

where $(P_m - P_c)(Q_m)$ is excess profits.

In 1977, a big year for automobile sales, the Big Three domestic automobile producers sold 9,054,000 cars. Total sales for the companies in those years were $109.5 billion, with a reported aftertax accounting profit of $5.2 billion. Net worth for the Big Three was $27.1 billion in 1977. To obtain an estimate of monopoly profits, we must make at least two adjustments. First we will assume that the capital representing net worth could have earned at least 10 percent real rate of return elsewhere, so that $2.7 billion of reported $5.2 billion would represent the opportunity cost of the investment. If this industry is riskier than the average, then the rate of interest should be greater than 10 percent. Second, reported tax profits do not include adjustments for inventory replacement costs, long-term returns from advertising and from research and development, or historical acquisition costs used in computing profits (see Chapter 4 for a discussion of these factors). These adjustments would lower profits by approximately $2 billion. Consequently, monopoly profits would be accounting profits of $5.2 billion minus opportunity cost of capital $2.7 billion minus $2 billion for the overstatement of profits during inflation. Thus, monopoly profits for the three big automobile producers during 1977 were approximately $500 million. Using this result, along with the assumptions of a long-run horizontal average-cost curve and industry elasticity of demand of -1, yields a deadweight loss of approximately 12 cents per car. The transfer to producers, on the other hand, P_cP_mAE'', is approximately $52.45 per automobile. We have, of course, used some simplified assumptions, but the magnitudes are representative of those that would occur with slightly declining or increasing long-run marginal costs and elasticities approximately equal to -1.

Empirical Estimates of Monopoly Efficiency Loss

One of the first studies undertaken to estimate the actual welfare loss associated with monopoly in the United States was done by Professor Arnold C. Harberger.[21] In examining the period from 1924 to 1928, he made heroic assumptions: Marginal cost was assumed constant, and the price elasticity of demand was assumed to be -1 in all industries. He identified monopolized industries by their relatively high average rates of return on assets. As can be seen from Table 5-1, he estimated the welfare loss to be 0.1 percent of national income.

Criticisms of Harberger's assumptions and analysis have been numerous. George J. Stigler[22] pointed out that the rational monopolist would operate only

---

[21] Arnold C. Harberger, "Monopoly and Resource Allocation," *American Economic Review,* vol. 54 (May 1954), pp. 77–87.

[22] George J. Stigler, "The Statistics of Monopoly and Merger," *Journal of Political Economy,* vol. 64 (February 1956), pp. 33–40.

TABLE 5-1
WELFARE LOSS ASSOCIATED WITH MONOPOLY IN THE
UNITED STATES

Investigator	Demand elasticity	Estimated welfare loss as a percentage of national income
Harberger*	-1.1	0.1
Kamerschen†	Various, averaging -2 to -3	6.0
Worcester‡	-2	0.5

*A. C. Harberger, "Monopoly and Resource Allocation," *American Economic Review,* vol. 54 (May 1954).

†D. R. Kamerschen, "An Estimation of the Welfare Losses for Monopoly in the American Economy," *Western Economic Journal,* vol. 4 (December 1966).

‡D. A. Worcester, Jr., "New Estimates of the Welfare Loss to Monopoly, United States, 1956–1969," *Southern Economic Journal,* vol. 40 (October 1973).

in the range where elasticity is equal to -1 if marginal cost were 0. Moreover, monopolists reported profit rates that included economic rents to specific resources such as patent royalties. Further, intangible items including goodwill are often not counted as assets by monopoly firms so that their reported profit is shown to be a relatively larger percent of total assets.

Stigler's suggestions were taken into account by other researchers. We find in Table 5-1 the results obtained by Kamerschen and Worcester. The former's estimate is a relatively high 6 percent of national income. The latter's estimate, however, based on firm rather than industry data, is 0.5 percent of national income and not much greater than Harberger's original estimate.[23]

Even if these figures are accurate estimates of the welfare triangles or deadweight losses, they do not take account of the welfare losses associated with the dissipation of monopoly rents when resources are used to obtain, maintain, and protect those monopoly positions.

RENT SEEKING—AN ADDITIONAL COST OF MONOPOLY

We have already mentioned that Adam Smith pointed out that the lure of monopoly profits leads to the use of resources to capture those profits.[24] Consider the desire to obtain monopoly profits by either an import restriction or a tariff. Presumably, domestic producers will invest resources in lobbying for such a restriction or tariff until the marginal return on the last dollar is equal to its expected return in producing the increased profits or transfer from consumers to protected producers. As pointed out above, those who will be hurt by such a measure may attempt to prevent such a transfer by putting resources into influencing the government in the other direction. These two expenditures, which offset each other to some extent, are wasteful from the standpoint of society, because they are attempts to transfer or resist transfers of wealth

---

[23] Similar studies have been performed using Australian and Canadian data, with similar results. See C. B. Hefford and David K. Round, "The Welfare Cost of Monopoly in Australia," *Southern Economic Journal,* vol. 44 (April 1978), pp. 846–860, in which the authors estimated loss at approximately one-tenth of 1 percent of "gross domestic product"; and John C. Jones and Leonard Laudadio, "The Empirical Basis of Canadian Antitrust Policy: Resource Allocation and Welfare Losses in Canadian Industry," *Industrial Organization Review*, vol. 6 (1978), pp. 49–59, who estimated the loss at 3.7 percent of national income.

But compare this with Keith Cowling and Dennis Muller, "The Social Costs of Monopoly Power," *Economic Journal,* vol. 88 (December 1978), pp. 727–748, which uses firm-level data for both the United States and the United Kingdom and estimates several alternative definitions of losses over several years for both countries. The estimates range from approximately two-tenths of 1 percent to over 13 percent, with the bulk coming in the 4 to 9 percent range.

For a study of the loss associated with only one industry, see Russell C. Parker and John M. Connor, "Estimates of Consumer Loss Due to Monopoly in the U.S. Food Manufacturing Industries," *American Journal of Agricultural Economics,* vol. 61 (November 1979), pp. 626–639.

[24] For a more recent and more extensive specification of rent seeking see George J. Stigler, "The Theory of Economic Regulation," *Bell Journal of Economics and Management Science,* vol. 2 (Spring 1971), pp. 3–21, and Anne O. Krueger, "The Political Economy of the Rent-Seeking Society," *American Economic Review,* vol. 64 (June 1974), pp. 291–303, and Richard A. Posner, *Antitrust Law: An Economic Perspective* (Chicago: University of Chicago Press, 1976). For an earlier treatment, see Gordon Tullock, "The Welfare Costs of Tariffs, Monopolies, and Theft," *Western Economic Journal,* vol. 5 (June 1967), pp. 224–232.

rather than to increase wealth. Realizing that this waste occurs requires us to alter our theoretical estimate of the welfare loss due to monopoly presented in Figure 5-8. The welfare loss in that diagram represents a transfer, not a reduction in national product.

We could say the same thing about theft: it merely involves a transfer. But, of course, that is not the case. Theft is extremely costly to society because of the resources—armed guards, police, new door locks, breakproof windows, window grating—that are involved in protection against theft. Basically, transfers in themselves cost society nothing; but for those individuals who undertake such transfers, they *are* costly. Therefore, many resources may be invested in making these transfers or in attempting to prevent them. This offsetting commitment of resources is wasted from the standpoint of society as a whole. The amount of transfer that the successful monopolist can obtain from consumers is just as appealing as loot that a successful thief can obtain. Entrepreneurs may be expected to invest resources to form a monopoly. They may predictably continue investing resources until the marginal cost equals the properly discounted return. On the other hand, potential customers who do not want the transfer to take place may be willing to make investments to prevent such a transfer. If they are unsuccessful, they may still continue their efforts to break up the monopoly. The monopoly owners, on the other hand, will use resources to defend their monopoly and to continue to receive transfers from consumers. The more successful the monopoly is, the more it will use of its resources in attempts to retain its monopoly position. It is difficult to identify and measure these resources, in part because open attempts to attain monopolization are illegal. Clearly, though, the staffs of the Antitrust Division of the U. S. Department of Justice, and the Bureau of Competition of the Federal Trade Commission, as well as the attorneys retained by companies in danger of prosecution, constitute at least part of the social cost of monopoly—probably only a very small part. Management at higher levels would be expected to use considerable resources to build up or break down monopolies. We also have to include in the total cost of monopoly the efforts made to obtain monopoly by those who did not succeed, in addition to those who were successful.

We can apply this analysis along the lines of Posner to the dissipation of monopoly rents accruing from regulation.[25] Posner uses the example of rate regulation by the CAB when it had the authority to place a floor on airline prices that exceeded the marginal cost of providing air transportation under competitive conditions. Price is originally equal to marginal cost in a competitive situation. When minimum price was increased by the CAB, profits increased. This result was short-lived, however, because nonprice competition was not constrained. The airlines expended resources on such competition until marginal cost of air transportation rose to the CAB-established price. The

---

[25] Richard A. Posner, "The Social Costs of Monopoly and Regulation," *Journal of Political Economy,* vol. 83, no. 4 (August 1975), pp. 807–827. But see Oliver E. Williamson, "Economics as an Antitrust Defense Revisited," *University of Pennsylvania Law Review,* vol. 125 (1977), pp. 699–737.

industry was soon earning only a normal rate of return. The monopoly profits initially generated by the regulatory price floor were simply transformed into higher costs for the industry. Although the demand curve may have been shifted to the right because of increased expenditures on service, the higher costs were not completely offset by any increase in consumer surplus. Had this been the case prior to regulation, the higher level of service would have been provided without the regulatory price floor. The expenditures on monopolizing had a socially valuable by-product that we label "improved service," but the value of that by-product was clearly less than its cost. Generally, economists have ignored in their analyses any socially valuable by-product of monopolization. This seems appropriate because, except under regulation, efforts at monopolization, such as forming an oil cartel or merging firms in order to produce a monopoly, yield little or no social value.

Posner goes on to estimate, in the manner of Harberger and others, the social cost of regulation in agriculture, transportation, electrical power, banking, insurance, medical services, and communications. While pointing out that the estimates are very crude, Posner concludes that "they do suggest that the total costs of regulation may be extremely high given that about 17 percent of GNP originates in industries . . . that contain the sorts of controls over competition that might be expected to lead to supercompetitive prices." Indeed, the costs of regulation probably exceed the costs of private monopoly. Posner estimates, for example, that the costs of the regulation of airlines used to be, on a yearly basis, about 20 percent of industry sales.[26]

X-INEFFICIENCY

Adam Smith felt that monopolies were technically inefficient. He was referring here to costs other than the allocative and rent-seeking losses mentioned earlier. We shall now focus on internal firm efficiency or the lack thereof. Much of this concept originates from the supposedly intuitive idea that many firms have inefficient internal resource allocation rules or inefficient managers and employees. Any firm that maintains inefficient resource allocation is in a suboptimal equilibrium. That firm, by changing its management techniques or rules governing the allocation of its internal resources, can increase output without any increase in input, or so it is argued.

The suboptimal inefficient firm equilibria have been labeled X-Inefficiency by Harvey Leibenstein.[27] Indeed, Leibenstein attempted to show that the welfare loss due to monopoly or tariffs was small in many instances relative to the social losses due to X-Inefficiency. Leibenstein ascribes X-Inefficiency to a lack of motivational efficiency and an inefficient market for knowledge.

---

[26] Posner, op. cit., pp. 818, 819, esp. Table 2.

[27] Harvey Leibenstein, "Allocative Efficiency Vs. 'X-Inefficency,'" *American Economic Review*, vol. 56 (June 1966), pp. 392–415; "Competition and X-Inefficiency: Reply," *Journal of Political Economy*, vol. 81 (May/June 1973), pp. 765–777; and "A Branch of Economics Is Missing: Micro-Micro Theory," *Journal of Economic Literature*, vol. 17 (June 1979), pp. 477–502.

Motivational Deficiency of Resource Owners

According to Leibenstein, X-Inefficiency arises largely from losses of output due to motivational deficiency of resource owners:

> [With a given] . . . set of human inputs purchased and . . . knowledge of production techniques available to the firm, a variety of outputs are possible. If individuals can choose, to some degree the APQT bundles (Activity, Pace, Quality of work, Time spent) they like, they are unlikely to choose a set of bundles that will maximize the value of output.[28]

One of Leibenstein's favorite examples from the field of economic development involves two identical inefficient petroleum refineries in Egypt. The introduction of a new manager at one of the refineries (the one that produced less) apparently brought about an immediate improvement in output. After some time passed, there was a *spectacular* improvement in output. The increase in output was attributed to the new manager.

X-Inefficiency Is Greater in Monopoly than in Competition

X-Inefficiency can affect both monopolists and competitors. However, presumably the monopolist will suffer from it more because he or she is not disciplined by competition. Hence, the more competitive the industry is, the fewer will be the number of firms suffering from X-Inefficiency. Clearly, the welfare loss due to monopoly would have to include the additional loss in output due to X-Inefficiency when such X-Inefficiency exists because of the part of the monopoly not subject to competitive pressures. Hence, the welfare loss becomes the summation of the conventional allocative deadweight loss (and any additional allocative loss due to X-Inefficiency), plus the purely nonallocative loss due entirely to X-Inefficiency.[29]

Further Explanation of Monopoly X-Inefficiency

There may be a relationship between the rent-seeking activities of monopolists and potential monopolists and the increased X-Inefficiency due to monopoly. It may be that monopoly X-Inefficiency is simply part of the continuing price paid by the monopolist for his or her monopoly, a layer of management that a competitor does not need. In such a situation the monopolist is inefficient in production not because of poor management, lazy workers, or improper motivation, but rather because a monopolist's enterprise is larger than the size that minimizes average costs. This is particularly evident in a cartel where each firm has a cartelizing agent (or agents) to monitor the cartel's activity. The cartel does not undertake to unify management of production; thus, the cartel remains

---

[28] Leibenstein, "Competition and X-Inefficiency: Reply," pp. 765–777.

[29] William S. Comanor and Harvey Leibenstein, "Allocative Efficiency, X-Efficiency, and the Measurement of Welfare Losses," *Economica,* vol. 36 (August 1969), pp. 304–309.

decentralized and perhaps forgoes any possible economies of scale. This cartel is almost certain to waste resources in the way Leibenstein calls X-Inefficiency.[30]

Criticisms of X-Inefficiency

Stigler has criticized Leibenstein's notion of X-Inefficiency, particularly when such inefficiency is attributed to motivational factors.[31] Stigler points out that all contracts between people in whom there is a mutual desire for fulfillment of reciprocal contractual promises require resources to enforce those agreements. (There is no such thing as a free lunch.) Clearly output and utility would be larger if no resources were necessary for such enforcement. But "output and utility would also be larger if water boiled at 180° F."[32] Stigler criticizes Leibenstein's Egyptian oil refinery example. Leibenstein tells us, "It is quite possible that had the motivation existed in sufficient strength, this change (new manager) would have taken place earlier."[33] But, as Stigler points out, "Potential motivation can indeed rewrite all history. If only the Romans had tried hard enough, surely they could have discovered America. (Thus motivation can be invoked to explain every unperformed task that is physically possible, no matter how rewarding.)"[34]

Further, Stigler does not believe that Leibenstein's theoretical apparatus can show that monopoly is less efficient than competition. Leibenstein assumes that (1) monopolists do not maximize profits, and (2) competitors are driven closer to minimum costs by entry of new rivals, some of whom are efficient. In order to reach Leibenstein's conclusion, we must accept the first assumption, which is an abandonment of formal theory. In so doing, we solve the question of the effect of monopoly on efficiency without argument or evidence. The difficulty in the second required assumption regarding competitive selection is understood by focusing on general equilibrium. After all, where did driven-out entrepreneurs go, and where did the efficient entrepreneurs come from? Such an assumption does not demonstrate or even argue convincingly that the going and coming of entrepreneurs of various qualities somehow (at least asymptotically) converge on a high-efficiency equilibrium in each competitive industry.

If Leibenstein's notion of X-Inefficiency is not tautological—that is, if we did not have to allocate resources to increase monitoring and identify internal efficiencies and other related tasks—then a likely interpretation of X-Inefficiency would relate the overall structure of the chosen organizational form. In particular, nonproprietary organizations have been shown to adopt

---

[30] Ibid., p. 504.

[31] George J. Stigler, "The Existence of X-Efficiency," *American Economic Review*, vol. 66, (March 1976), pp. 213–216.

[32] Ibid., p. 214.

[33] Leibenstein, "Allocative Efficiency Versus X-Inefficiency," p. 398.

[34] Stigler, "The Existence of X-Efficiency," p. 214.

inefficient resource allocation rules more often than profit-seeking firms do.[35] In fact, most of the evidence supporting the X-Inefficiency hypothesis can be directly linked to the nonproprietary form of organization or to compensation schemes that weaken the link between the participant's rewards and the efficiency of the firm.

THE THEORY OF SECOND BEST

One can easily conclude from the preceding discussion that the monopolization of an industry results in a misallocation of resources. This conclusion appears to be generally, but not always, correct. Consider one industry, Y, that is the only noncompetitive one in an economy whose other industries Z_1, Z_2, Z_3, and so forth are all perfectly competitive. We know that since Y is monopolized, overall output will be reduced compared to a perfectly competitive situation. Thus, while too little is produced in Y industry, too much is produced in Z_1, Z_2, and Z_3.

Now let's change the scenario. Let's make all other industries (Z_1, Z_2, Z_3, and so on) pure monopolies. If Y is perfectly competitive, there is too little produced in Z_1, Z_2, and Z_3, and too much produced in Y. What might happen if industry Y is monopolized? It would reduce its output and be brought back in line with other industries. It may be that the allocation of the nation's resources could actually be improved by the monopolization of industry Y under the assumptions given here.[36] A **second-best solution**, re-equating the marginal rate of substitution between x and y (MRS_{xy}) with the marginal rate of transformation between x and y (MRT_{xy}) to optimize the allocations of the nation's resources, may involve monopolization.

The best economy, according to standard welfare theory, is one in which all industries are perfectly competitive or all monopolists perfectly discriminating. Any monopolization of an industry will make the economy less efficient. In a second-best world, however, some industries are already monopolized, and distortions are already present. In such a world, it is not clear whether monopoly in yet another industry will make the economy less efficient or more efficient. There is no simple answer to this question. The theory of second best is a theory of how to get the best results in the remaining markets when one or more markets already contain imperfections, such as monopoly, about which nothing can be done. This second-best argument is sometimes used to support the monopolization of an agricultural industry. It is a typical argument used by supporters of milk-marketing organizations that allow their competitors to act like monopolists. The argument goes as follows: The rest of the economy is

---

[35] See Kenneth W. Clarkson, "Managerial Behavior and Nonproprietary Organizations" in K. W. Clarkson and D. J. Martin, eds., *Economics of Nonproprietary Organizations*, (Greenwich, Conn.: JAI Press, 1980) pp. 3–26; and Louis De Alessi, "Property Rights: A Review of the Evidence," in R. Zerbe, ed. *Research in Law and Economics* (Greenwich, Conn.: JAI Press, 1980), pp. 1–47.

[36] Assume that the labor-leisure choice is not altered.

pervaded by monopoly; hence, monopolizing agriculture may improve the nation's allocation of resources.

A Simple Example

We want to show a simple example in which two sectors interact: manufacturing and agriculture. The manufacturing sector is assumed to be fully monopolized; hence, there is the resultant misallocation of resources. The farm sector is perfectly competitive. We assume that there is no feasible way of getting rid of the monopoly in manufacturing. We can work only with the agricultural sector. We thus organize the farmers into a monopoly; farm prices will rise. This increase in farm prices causes the demand curve for manufacturing goods to shift outward to the right. Resources flow out of farming into manufacturing. A host of other changes may result, such as an increase in monopoly profits, disuse of some productive inputs, or a decrease in some prices. Let's assume all these changes have taken place and the economy has settled down into an equilibrium illustrated in panels (*a*) and (*b*) of Figure 5-10. Manufacturing goods sell for $40 with 2.1 billion units supplied at a cost of $20 per unit. Agricultural goods sell at $3 with 7 billion bushels supplied at $1.50 cost per unit. Are we in a situation where total national output can be increased by a further change in the pattern of resource allocation? Let's see.

We attempt to transfer resources that have a market value of $1.5 million from the farm monopoly into manufacturing. This requires a sacrifice of 1 million bushels of agricultural output, given the marginal cost of $1.50, and a gain of 75,000 manufactured-good units. The manufactured goods can be sold to consumers at a cost of slightly less than $40, so the value gain has to be a little less than $3 million. However—and here is the hitch—forgone agricultural goods have a value of slightly more than $3 per unit to consumers, mean-

FIGURE 5-10
Resource allocation with all monopolies.

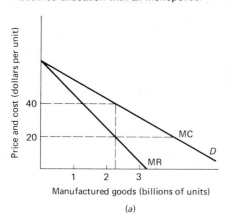

(a)

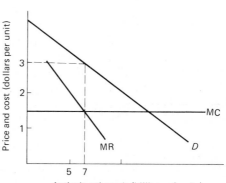

(b)

ing that the values consumers have sacrificed exceed $3 million. Similar reasoning can demonstrate that a change of one unit of resources from manufacturing into agriculture will also reduce the total value of economic output. Thus, it follows that the aggregate value of national output has to be at a maximum in the equilibrium attained by monopolizing both sectors. Since we couldn't make the manufacturing sector perfectly competitive by monopolizing the agricultural sector, we have secured an apparent equilibrium that maximizes the aggregate value of the economy's product.

What we have shown is a special case of using the theory of second best, where monopolization is "good." Actually, the only reason that this happened to turn out so favorably is that we constructed the curves in panel (a) and (b) of Figure 5-10 so that the ratio of the equilibrium price to marginal cost in the manufacturing good sector (40 ÷ 20 = 2) equals the ratio of price to marginal cost in the agricultural sector (3 ÷ 1.5 = 2).

Proof of Second-Best Theorem

The formal proof of the second-best theorem is rather complicated.[37] We can demonstrate it on a much less technical level by using Figure 5-11. Here we show a product transformation curve TT. We know that a welfare maximum occurs when the social welfare function W_3 is tangent to the product transformation curve. This occurs at point E. Assume for the moment that E is unattainable. Some institutional restraint or some natural impediment occurs, leaving only combinations along the line CC attainable. If we wanted to satisfy the

[37] See Kelvin Lancaster and Richard G. Lipsey, "The General Theory of Second Best," *Review of Economic Studies*, vol. 24 (1956), pp. 11–32. Also see M. Boiteux, "Sur la gestion des monopoles publiques astreints à l'equilibre budgetaire," *Econometrica*, vol. 24 (January 1956), pp. 22–40. English translation "On the Management of Public Monopolies Subject to Budgetary Constraints," in *Journal of Economic Theory*, vol. 3 (September 1971), pp. 219–240.

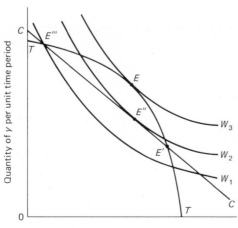

FIGURE 5-11
Theory of second best. TT is a product transformation curve. W_1, W_2, and W_3 are social welfare functions. The welfare maximum occurs at point E. Assume, however, that only points on the line CC are attainable. The Pareto condition would require that we move to E' or E''' because that would put us back on the transformation curve TT. However, a move to point E'' would put us on a higher social welfare curve W_2 than we would be on if we were either at E''' or at E'.

Quantity of y per unit time period

Quantity of x per unit time period

Pareto criterion ($\text{MRT}_{xy} = \text{MRS}_{xy}$), we would not say that a movement from the curve CC to point E''' or E' was called for because that move would merely put us on the product transformation curve. That movement to E''', for example, would put us on social welfare function W_1. If, instead, we were to move to point E'', we could attain a higher social welfare function, W_2. Thus, in accordance with the theory of second best, when one of the marginal conditions for Pareto maximum is unattainable, it may be better to violate some of the other marginal conditions in order to attain welfare maximum.

The theory of second best has been used to question the desirability of economic policies that attempt to attain Pareto conditions by considering an isolated situation. Proponents of such piecemeal policies, striving to achieve the Pareto conditions in one market, contend that so long as the markets in question are relatively unrelated, it does not matter that some of the conditions for the attainment of Pareto maximum are unsatisfied in the other markets. Economic policy for the steel industry, for example, should not be influenced by imperfect competition in the toothpick industry.

Limitations on the Theory of Second Best

Although the theory of second best has been used to justify allowing or even increasing the number of distortions in the economy, its limitations would appear to make one think twice about using it for such purposes.

The Economy Is Not So Simple   In our modern economy, where there are elaborate horizontal and vertical interrelationships, final consumers do not buy all products. Many products are used as intermediate parts by other firms before a final product is made, and the theory of second best fails to deal adequately with intermediate firms. Thus, no simple statement about how much a nonmonopolized industry should be allowed to monopolize can be made in attempting to reach maximum welfare. In general, the simple numerical example presented in panels (a) and (b) of Figure 5-10 cannot be applied to the whole economy. Indeed, the Lancaster-Lipsey second-best solutions are not general. Further, we have no way of knowing how representative they are for more complex cases that involve complementarity and substitutability in production and consumption or for intermediate goods.[38]

INADEQUACIES OF THE BASIC MODELS

Failure to adequately validate the pure forms of the monopoly and competitive models caused early researchers to modify the conditions and assumptions

[38] Criticisms and interpretations of the second-best theory can be found in numerous articles, including Otto A. Davis and Andrew B. Whinston, "Welfare Economics and the Theory of Second Best," *Review of Economic Studies,* vol. 32 (January 1965), pp. 1–14; Collected papers by Takashi Negishi, et al, in the *Review of Economic Studies,* vol. 34 (July 1967), pp. 301–331; Edward J. Mishan, "Second Thoughts on Second Best," *Oxford Economic Papers,* vol. 14 (October 1962), pp. 205–217; and Clarence C. Morrison, "The Nature of Second Best," *Southern Economic Journal,* vol. 32 (July 1965), pp. 49–52.

underlying these models. The X-Inefficiency hypothesis is a recent example of one possible change in these models. Earlier attempts to modify the conditions of the monopoly and competitive models focused more on the demand conditions facing individual firms. In the next two chapters we look at oligopoly models, which are an extension of the pure monopoly model, and monopolistic competition models, which are an extension of the competitive model.

CHAPTER 6

OLIGOPOLY

The strict conditions of pure competition or monopoly are seldom, if ever, met in industry. Even farmers, often given as examples of the pure form of competitive firms, hold inventories. Furthermore, prices for identical commodities in different localities sometimes vary by more than transportation costs. On the other hand, even the single seller of a product or service must face competition from substitute products. Thus, pure forms of both monopoly and competition are best viewed as endpoints on a spectrum.

Monopolistic competition (discussed in the following chapter), for example, can be classified as a model with many of the characteristics of the competitive model. At the other end of the spectrum we find models that fall into the category of oligopoly, distinguished primarily by the number of firms in an industry. While there is no general theory of oligopoly, each oligopoly model focuses on the underlying concept of interdependence. The term **oligopoly** means that there is more than one firm in the industry; it is generally understood that the range is somewhere between two and a dozen or more firms. After this point, the oligopoly models differ. Some models contain a larger number of market characteristics that are closer to competition, while other models with only a few firms have characteristics resembling a shared monopoly.

THE COURNOT MODEL

One of the main differences among oligopoly theories is the characterization of firm interdependence. The way one firm reacts to another is called its "reaction function." The Cournot theory, our starting point, has a particularly simple reaction function.

Well over a century ago, Antoine Augustin Cournot published a theory of duopoly.[1] Unfortunately for Cournot, this theory did not become widely known or discussed until the 1930s. Cournot's model is intrinsically interesting and is often used as a basis of departure for further analysis.

Assumptions in the Cournot Model

The assumptions employed by Cournot's basic model are as follows:

1 The product is homogeneous.
2 There are two sellers, later generalized as n sellers.
3 Each seller has identical marginal costs.
4 Each seller has perfect information about every point on the market demand curve.
5 Market changes are made through output rather than through price.
6 Finally, Cournot's crucial assumption concerns the behavioral rule that each duopolist, in selecting his or her own rate of output, assumes that the other duopolist's output will remain constant.

This last assumption about rival's reaction functions is what makes Cournot's theory classical in persuasion and similar to most other oligopoly theories in their treatment of rivals' responses.[2] After all, rivalry action is the essence of oligopoly; it is absent from theories of perfect competition and pure monopoly. The classical theories simply *postulate* some kind of conscious rival behavior, usually based on *assumptions* about a rival's behavior. Contrast this with some modern theories which assume a goal such as joint profit maximization and then predict the type and success of behavior of each economic agent that is sensibly directed to reach the specified goal. Cournot's model assumes self-delusory behavior, with each duopolist behaving as if he or she can act without provoking an output reaction from the other duopolist. This is, in essence, a no-learning-by-doing model. In any event, Cournot was able to show that given his assumptions, duopolists will approach an equilibrium rate of output and price.

The Cournot Approach toward Equilibrium

In order to understand how the model works, we start with an industry demand function for the commodity. To keep the flavor of Cournot's original publication (he used artesian wells as the commodity), we will use mineral water as the commodity. We assume for simplicity that the demand curve is linear and marginal cost is equal to zero.

Look at Figure 6-1. The industry demand curve is DD, and the marginal revenue curve is MR. The two firms are I and II. Firm I starts the ball rolling, while firm II is temporarily inactive. Hence, DD is the demand curve facing

---

[1] Antoine Augustin Cournot, *Récherches sur les principes mathématiques de la théorie des richesses* (Paris, 1838). English translation by Nathaniel T. Bacon, *Researches into the Mathematical Principles of the Theory of Wealth* (New York: Macmillan, 1897, reprinted 1927).
[2] The main exception is game theory, as explained later in this chapter.

firm I; it sets the rate of output where marginal revenue equals marginal cost. In this case, this is the output at which the marginal revenue curve intersects the horizontal axis. It sets a rate of output of Q_1^I. The superscript refers to the firm and the subscript refers to the period, or "round." Thus, Q_1^I indicates the output produced by duopolist I in the first round, or first period. It does this under the assumption that the second duopolist will maintain its rate of output at 0.

Now firm II enters the market. It takes as given firm I's output rate of Q_1^I. Firm II believes that its demand curve is DD minus the rate of output Q_1^I. Its demand curve is $D'D'$, which is derived by subtracting firm I's rate of output Q_1^I from DD. Firm II will maximize profit by setting its rate of output where its new marginal revenue curve MR' intersects the horizontal axis, which is its marginal cost curve. Firm II will produce at rate Q_1^{II}. Firm I has the next move. It assumes that firm II will keep its rate of output at Q_1^{II}. Firm I perceives its new demand curve as the market demand curve minus the rate of output of firm II. This new demand curve is $D''D''$ in Figure 6-1. The marginal revenue curve for this demand curve is labeled MR''. Firm I will change its rate of output so that marginal revenue MR'' equals marginal cost $= 0$. This is where MR'' intersects the horizontal axis, or where the rate of output is Q_2^I.

Each firm takes the other firm's output as given and then maximizes its profits by choosing the appropriate profit-maximizing rate of output. The new

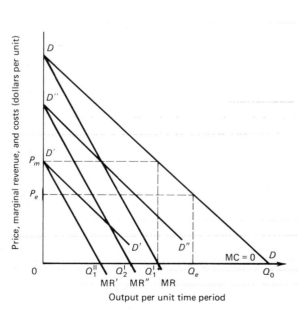

FIGURE 6-1
The Cournot duopoly model. Marginal cost is equal to zero and, therefore, coincides with the horizontal axis. We start with demand curve DD. Duopolist I maximizes profit by setting output rate at Q_1^I because this is where MR = MC. Firm II now believes that its demand curve is $D'D'$, which is derived by subtracting the rate of output Q_1^I from demand curve DD. Duopolist II therefore maximizes profit by setting output at Q_1^{II}. Now firm I has the next move. It assumes that firm II will keep its rate of output at Q_1^{II}. It therefore perceives demand curve $D''D''$, which is drawn by subtracting output rate Q_1^{II} from demand curve DD. Duopolist I now sets its profit-maximizing rate of output at the new intersection of MR'' with MC, or at rate Q_2^I. This process continues. A determinate equilibrium will be reached where price is P_e, total output is Q_e, and each firm's profit-maximizing rate of output is $\frac{1}{2}Q_e$. If there were only one firm, the profit-maximizing output would be at Q_1^I sold at price P_m.

output prompts a successive change in the rival's demand curve, and a new lower price is chosen. This process, however, will not go on indefinitely. Ultimately, in the case of the two firms in Figure 6-1, the rate of output for each firm will tend toward an equilibrium amount equal to $\frac{1}{3}Q_0$. The price at which each firm sells its output is P_e. Notice that this differs from the perfectly competitive solution, which would require that price be equal to marginal cost which, in this case, would be zero. Thus, in the Cournot duopoly model, price exceeds marginal cost, and the rate of output is less than it would be under perfect competition. However, in the Cournot model, the rate of output is greater than it would be in a pure monopoly. In a pure monopoly, the rate of output would be set at Q_1^I,[3] since there MR = MC. The monopoly price would be P_m in Figure 6-1.[4]

Reaction Functions

For any level of output offered by duopolist II, there exists an output for duopolist I that will maximize firm I's profits. In Figure 6-2 the locus of these output points gives the output reaction curve $R^I R^I$ for duopolist I. Similarly, the output reaction curve for duopolist II, $R^{II} R^{II}$, is given in Figure 6-2.

If duopolist I produces output Q_1^I, duopolist II will move to point a on its output reaction curve and produce Q_1^{II}. While duopolist II's output, Q_1^{II}, maximizes its output, duopolist I will now want to expand output to Q_2^I (point b). Duopolist II will seek a lower output, Q_2^{II}, given firm I's expansion (point c). The process continues until the two duopolists reach output E, where an equilibrium is achieved. This equilibrium is often referred to as the Cournot point.

THE BERTRAND MODEL

A variant of the Cournot duopoly analysis was given by Joseph Bertrand in what turned out to be a confused and perhaps mistaken criticism of Cournot.[5] Bertrand's duopoly model is similar to Cournot's. The difference is that Bertrand postulates price adjustment rather than output adjustment by rivals. In the Bertrand adjustment process, each rival cuts his or her own price by a small

---

[3] The Cournot solution applies to more than two sellers. Mathematically, if we assume a linear demand curve given by $P = a - bQ$, then the equilibrium rate of output for each firm is equal to $a/[2b + b(n - 1)]$ or $a/b(n + 1)$, where a/b is the quantity intercept of the demand curve and n is the number of firms in the industry. In our simple duopoly model, $n = 2$; in a monopoly solution, $n = 1$; and in a perfectly competitive solution, n approaches ∞. See Roy J. Ruffin, "Cournot Oligopoly and Competitive Behavior," *Review of Economics Studies*, vol. 38 (October 1971), pp. 493–502.

[4] The Cournot model is equivalent to the monopoly model as applied to individual firms, with an added market demand constraint. Cournot generalized his solution for more than two firms and found that total industry output would always equal $[(n/n + 1)(T)]$, where n = the number of firms and T is equal to the zero cost output in competitive equilibrium. He also found that the equilibrium price is equal to $D/(n + 1)$, where D = the vertical intercept of the demand curve. Given this result, Cournot predicts that as the number of firms increases, industry output rises and price falls. Not surprisingly, the larger the number of firms in the industry, the closer the Cournot solution is to a perfectly competitive equilibrium.

[5] Joseph Bertrand, "Théorie mathématique de la richesse sociale," *Journal des Savants*, Paris (September 1883), pp. 499–508. See also Harold G. Lewis, "Some Observations on Duopoly Theory," *American Economic Review*, vol. 38 (May 1948), pp. 1–9; and Fritz Machlup, *The Economics of Seller's Competition*, vol. 2 (Baltimore: Johns Hopkins Press, 1952), pp. 377–380.

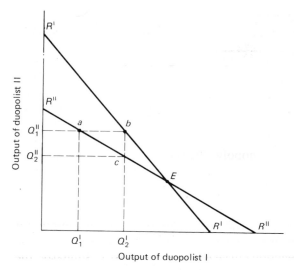

FIGURE 6-2
The Cournot equilibrium.

amount to capture the entire market under the assumption that the other rival will maintain his or her present price. The products are assumed to be homogeneous so that the lower-priced seller takes the entire market. But, of course, each time a seller cuts a price, the other seller will lower his or her price just enough to capture the entire market. This price-cutting process continues, ending only when the price is reduced to marginal cost or a competitive solution. Thus, even though we have merely changed the adjustment variable from output to price, the Bertrand solution is the competitive market outcome, whereas the Cournot solution is not. The Cournot duopolist who supplies some given quantity for any period is necessarily limiting the portion of the market that he or she can capture. The Bertrand monopolist offers a price at which he or she can capture the entire market because all consumers will want to switch suppliers at that lower price.

The Bertrand solution may seem less strange when we realize that once there is more than one firm in a market, the attainment of joint maximum profits requires some form of collusion. In the Bertrand model, there is no collusion.

The Bertrand and Cournot models illustrate the importance of differing assumptions in the firm's belief about its rival's reaction to its own behavior. The assumptions in these models imply major differences in the perceived demand conditions facing the duopolist, which produce radically different outcomes.

THE EDGEWORTH MODEL

Edgeworth's model proposes two changes from Cournot's assumptions.[6] The first is that the two suppliers of mineral water have a limited productive capac-

[6] Francis Y. Edgeworth, *Papers Relating to Political Economy*, vol. I (London: Macmillan, 1925), pp. 111–142, and *Mathematical Psychics* (London: Routledge & Kegan Paul, Ltd., 1881). Also see Archibald J. Nichol, "Edgeworth's Theory of Duopoly Price," *Economic Journal*, vol. 45 (March 1935), pp. 51–66.

ity. The quantity demanded at zero price exceeds what one single producer can supply. The second change is that in the very short run, two different prices for mineral water may be quoted in the market.

Most important is the assumption made by Edgeworth not only that each duopolist selects the price that will maximize profit, but also that this price is selected on the assumption that the other duopolist will not alter its price.

Moving toward Equilibrium in the Edgeworth Model

In the long run, Edgeworth's model implies that the duopolists will charge the same price for the product and that they will divide the market equally. Thus, we can use Figure 6-3 to show that the rate of output for duopolist I is shown on the right-hand side, and the rate of output for duopolist II is shown on the left-hand side. The common vertical axis measures the price per unit. The demand curve for duopolist I is d_I, and the demand curve facing duopolist II is d_{II}. *Both of these demand curves are constructed on the assumption that in the long run both sellers charge the same price.* These proportionate demand curves each equal one-half the market demand.

The maximum productive capacity for duopolists I and II are q_{max}^I and q_{max}^{II}, respectively. As in the Cournot model, the sellers persistently attempt to profit-maximize and are incapable of learning from experience. The Edgeworth model is also a no-learning-by-doing model.

We start with duopolist I (who is temporarily a monopolist), who sets a profit-maximizing price P_1. This is profit maximizing because the corresponding rate of output q_1^I occurs where the marginal revenue curve intersects the horizontal axis, which is also the marginal cost curve in this example. For simplicity we have not drawn in the marginal revenue curve. (To check the accuracy of the figure, see if q_1^I lies equidistant between point 0 and the point where the demand curve hits the horizontal axis.)

Duopolist II, however, sees price P_1 charged by duopolist I and believes that by setting his or her price just below P_1, customers can be taken away from duopolist I, who will continue to charge P_1.

However, when this price setting has been done, duopolist I sees that customers can be taken away from duopolist II if an even smaller price is charged. This price war continues until price P_n is reached. At this price, neither firm can increase its output, because its output is equal to its capacity production. At price P_n, both duopolist I and duopolist II are producing at their respective maximum, q_{max}^I and q_{max}^{II}. Now what will happen? Clearly, if P_1 is a profit-maximizing price, then one duopolist will see that by raising the price above P_n, he or she can increase total profits. The other duopolist will follow suit and price will rise. Thus, the Edgeworth model does not yield a solution at all. It merely gives the limits on the price and rate of output that will be seen in the duopoly market. The maximum price to be charged will be P_1, and the minimum price will be P_n. There is no unique equilibrium price; there is no unique equilibrium output. But there is a range of possible prices and outputs.

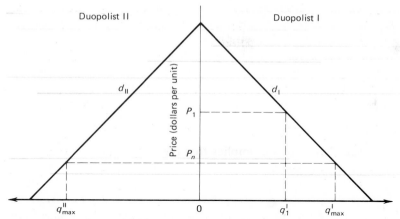

FIGURE 6-3
The Edgeworth duopoly model. The proportionate demand curves are marked as d_1d_1 and $d_{11}d_{11}$. The assumed maximum rate of output for each firm is q^1_{max} and q^{11}_{max}, respectively. Duopolist I sets a profit-maximizing price of P_1. (Remember that the horizontal axis in these models is equal to marginal cost because MC = 0.) However, duopolist II will set price below P_1 and attempt to take customers away from duopolist I. This process will continue until price P_n is reached. At this price, each firm will start increasing price toward the profit-maximizing P_1. There is no unique equilibrium output or equilibrium price. (Without an effective output constraint, price would fall to zero—the competitive solution.)

Before going on to other oligopoly models, we note here that the Cournot and Edgeworth models are not presented because of their relevance or realism. Rather, we show them to demonstrate the difficulties inherent in theorizing about oligopoly. The difficult problems in obtaining the demand curve facing the firm when there is mutual dependence between the oligopolists are at the crux of all problems with oligopoly theory.

HOTELLING MODEL

The Edgeworth model was shown to suggest an element of instability in markets in which there were only two sellers. Hotelling challenged this idea in 1929; he did not believe that price or output instability was a general characteristic of duopoly.[7]

Assumptions

The assumptions employed by Hotelling are as follows:

 1 Homogeneous products are sold in two separate geographical locations.

[7] Harold Hotelling, "Stability in Competition," *Economic Journal*, vol. 39 (March 1929), pp. 41–57.

2 Two sellers, Smith and Jones, are located along a linear market length represented in Figure 6-4. With four segments in the market—one segment on either side of each seller—each consumer must pay his or her own transportation cost, which is assumed to be C per unit distance.

3 Buyers are distributed uniformly along the market; each buyer makes a given purchase per unit time period, making demand perfectly inelastic.

Implications

Given the above assumptions, the Hotelling duopolist has discretion over price. Jones cannot, however, arrive at a price that exceeds Smith's price by more than the cost of transportation (C) from Smith's place of business to Jones's $(x + y)$. In other words, Jones's price, P_j, cannot exceed Smith's price, P_s, by more than $C(x + y)$. We know, therefore, that Jones will always service the market area labeled J in Figure 6-4 and that Smith will always service the market area labeled S. The area between Jones's and Smith's areas will be serviced by both of them; Jones will service area X and Smith will service area Y. The actual lengths of X and Y depend on prices P_j and P_s. At the dividing point, the delivered price to the buyer of the homogeneous good is equal for Jones and Smith at that point and that buyer is therefore indifferent between the two sellers. In other words, Jones's price plus transportation costs must equal Smith's price plus transportation costs at the point of demarcation, or $P_j + CX = P_s + CY$.

When Hotelling added the identity:

$$\text{Length of market} = J + X + Y + S$$

he was able to show that these two equations determined an equilibrium price and quantity.[8]

Hotelling's Criticism of Edgeworth and Bertrand Hotelling's model apparently was used as a criticism of Edgeworth and Bertrand. Hotelling did not believe that sudden switches of consumers from one seller to another were

[8] For more recent views of dynamic entry deterrence, see D. A. Hay, "Sequential Entry and Entry-Deterring Strategies in Spatial Competition," *Oxford Economic Papers*, vol. 28 (July 1976), pp. 240–257; Edward C. Prescott and Michael Visscher, "Sequential Location among Firms with Foresight," *Bell Journal of Economics*, vol. 8 (Autumn 1977), pp. 378–393; and B. Curtis Eaton and Richard G. Lipsey, "The Theory of Market Pre-Emption: The Persistence of Excess Capacity in Growing Spatial Markets" *Economica*, vol. 46 (May 1979), pp. 149–158.

FIGURE 6-4
Hotelling's linear market model.

characteristic of markets. Indeed, he expected that a price cut would attract few customers. Consequently, he contended that as long as consumers gradually switched to rivals, the market would remain stable.

Criticisms of Duopoly Models

We have already pointed out that the Cournot and Bertrand models implied self-delusion on the part of each duopolist. This self-delusion has troubled numerous observers, including Hurwicz:

> There is no adequate solution of the problem of defining "rational economic behavior" on the part of an individual when the very rationality of his actions depends on the probable behavior of other individuals . . . [When discussing oligopoly] the individual's "rational behavior" is determinate *if* the pattern of behavior of "others" can be assumed *a priori* known. But the behavior of "others" cannot be known *a priori* if the "others," too, are to behave rationally! Thus, a logical *impasse* is reached.[9]

In the Cournot model, for example, each seller has assumptions about his or her rival's behavior. Each duopolist knows the present situation but, except in equilibrium, is seriously wrong about the future. Further, if the duopolist does not learn accurately about the future, his or her position will not improve.

Entry versus Dissolution The Cournot model predicted that as more firms enter the market, the total output would be larger and the market would be closer to the price-quantity competitive solution. But if we are to believe Cournot's model, we must distinguish between an increase in the number of firms due to the entry of new firms as opposed to the dissolution of existing firms. Cournot says virtually nothing about either type of entry;[10] he simply gives the number of firms without explaining their type. But if we look at the cost functions that he assumes, duopoly, triopoly, or even oligopoly cannot endure because costs do not change with the size or number of firms. Any price higher than long-run marginal cost attracts entry. Permanent oligopoly cannot exist unless there are institutional restrictions on entry or the ownership by established firms of an essential resource (such as the artesian wells chosen by Cournot).

No Collusion Possible Both the Cournot and the Bertrand models ignore the possibility of collusion which, if it occurs, always increases the joint profits. As we shall see later, collusion usually increases net wealth, but unfortunately for

---

[9] Leonid Hurwicz, "The Theory of Economic Behavior," *American Economic Review,* vol. 35 (December 1945), pp. 909, 910.

[10] For an expanded version of the Cournot theory, in which it is assumed that firms take into account the varying probabilities that new firms will enter in response to their own output adjustments, see Morton J. Kamien and Nancy L. Schwartz, "Cournot Oligopoly with Uncertain Entry," *Review of Economics and Statistics,* vol. 42 (January 1975), pp. 125–131.

the colluders, there is always an incentive for each firm to cheat. Such action tends to lead to the deterioration of any collusive agreement made.

A Rebuttal to the Criticisms The simple duopoly model given above has been criticized basically on the unrealistic nature of the assumptions, but there certainly is a methodological debate about the relevancy of "realistic" assumptions. Taking a very strict view of scientific methodology similar to that presented on pages 11-16, the predictive or, at the very minimum, explanatory power of the methodology is the test of the validity of a theory, not the realism of its assumptions. Thus, the question to be answered is, "Do sellers in the real world act as if they had adopted the Cournot or the Bertrand decision rules?" This is, of course, an empirical question. Some researchers have found casual evidence that supports such a proposition.[11] Although little empirical testing has been done, Gollop and Roberts have resoundingly rejected the Cournot duopoly theory. They were unable to reject the hypothesis of interdependent behavior using a translog production function for the coffee-roasting industry.[12]

LARGER-NUMBER MODELS

We now move on to models of oligopoly that include more than two firms. We will begin by examining a simple model and then proceed to look at models presented by Stigler, Sweezy, Chamberlin, Fellner, Nutter and Moore, and others.

A Simple Oligopoly Model

Assumptions To begin this discussion of oligopoly on its most general level, we make five assumptions:

1 The position and shape of the LAC curve relative to the industry demand curve is such that the industry can support only a small number of efficient plants and firms.

2 The firm (and plant) LAC is upward-sloping over the relevant range of outputs (no natural monopolies). The total cost curve of each firm is continuous and normal in the sense that marginal costs will always be positive and above LAC.

3 Single-plant firms are the only possibility because of large diseconomies at the firm level, the possibility of antitrust action, and so forth. In other words, the cost of combining plants under common ownership and control is prohibitive.

4 There are no barriers to entry into or exit from the industry; they are free.

5 The firms produce homogeneous (similar) products.

---

[11] William J. Baumol, *Business Behavior, Value, and Growth* (New York: Harcourt, Brace & World, 1967), p. 27.

[12] Frank M. Gollop and Mark J. Roberts, "Firm Interdependence in Oligopolistic Markets," *Journal of Econometrics,* vol. 10 (1979), pp. 313-331.

The Oligopolist's Demand Curve   Now we are faced with the difficult task of drawing the demand curve for an oligopolist. We cannot use the industry demand curve because the oligopolist is not a monopolist. We cannot use a horizontal demand curve at the market-clearing price because the oligopolist is not a perfect competitor. We can say nothing about the demand curve of an oligopolist until we make an assumption about the interaction among oligopolists. We have to know something about the *reaction function* that we are looking at. Does each oligopolist believe that others will not react to changes in his or her price and/or output? If the typical oligopolist believes that they will react, then we must specify the manner in which the oligopolist expects them to react. In a perfectly competitive model, each firm ignores the reactions of other firms because each firm can sell all that it wants at the going market price. In the pure monopoly model, the monopolist does not have to worry about the reaction of rivals, since by definition there are none. This interdependence lies at the heart of every single oligopoly model and, as you might imagine, every time a new assumption about interaction among oligopolists is made, a new oligopoly model is born. For this simplest of oligopoly models, we will assume the following:

> Each firm expects and indeed knows that any change in price will be matched by all other firms in the industry.

We can see in Figure 6-5 the result of this assumption. The industry demand curve is D. If the industry has only two firms, then each firm will believe that its demand curve is equal to one labeled $1/2D$. This follows from our assumption that whatever price the industry chooses will be matched by its rivals. If we go to three firms in the industry, then each individual demand curve, as perceived by the individual oligopolist, will be $1/3D$.

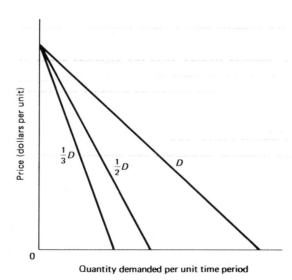

FIGURE 6-5
Proportionate demand curves. If each firm expects that any change in price will be matched by all other firms in the industry, and if there are two firms in the industry, each will face a demand curve that is $\frac{1}{2}D$. If there are three firms in the industry, each will face a demand curve that is $\frac{1}{3}D$.

each firm faces $1/n$ of industry demand.

Price (dollars per unit)

$\frac{1}{3}D$ $\frac{1}{2}D$ D

0

Quantity demanded per unit time period

The Equilibrium Number of Firms Since we have assumed unrestricted entry and exit, and since we assume that all firms have identical cost curves, we can determine the number of firms that will be in the industry by examining the long-run average cost curve. This curve is shown in Figure 6-6. If there were one firm in the industry, other firms would be attracted because the long-run cost curve lies below the industry demand curve D for a large range of outputs. If there were two firms in the industry, there would still be an incentive to enter. Finally, if three firms were in the industry, a fourth firm would not desire to enter because the LAC curve is always above the proportionate demand curve $1/4D$. By our assumptions, if four firms were in the industry, none could cover long-run average costs. They would all suffer economic losses.

In this simple model, it is possible that in the long run, economic profits will be obtained.[13] This can be seen by transferring the proportionate demand curve for an individual oligopolist when there are three firms (Figure 6-7). The demand curve facing each of the three individual firms is $1/3D$. The long-run average cost curve is given as LAC, and the long-run marginal cost curve is LMC. The profit-maximizing rate of output for each individual oligopolist is at the intersection of marginal revenue and long-run marginal cost, or at a rate of output q_1. The price that the product will sell for is identical for each firm at P_1. Unit cost, given LAC, is C_1. Economic profits per unit time period are equal to the shaded area in Figure 6-7.

Given the assumptions in this model, this is the long-run equilibrium.

[13] See Donald Dewey, "Industrial Concentration and the Rate of Profit: Some Neglected Theory," *Journal of Law and Economics,* vol. 19 (April 1976), pp. 67–78.

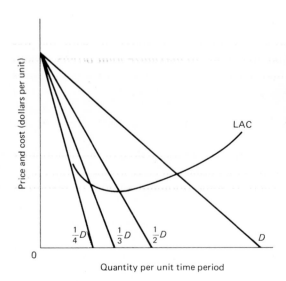

FIGURE 6-6
Establishing the equilibrium number of firms. If the long-run average cost curve for the industry is LAC, then only three firms can be supported in this industry. If a fourth firm enters, each will face a demand curve equal to ¼D. The LAC curve is everywhere above that proportionate demand curve.

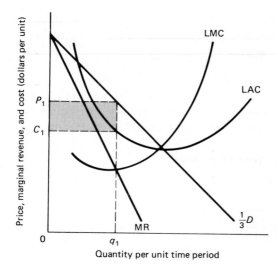

FIGURE 6-7
<u>Long-run economic profits.</u> We have
assumed that three firms will exist in
this industry. Each faces a proportionate demand curve ⅓D. The marginal revenue curve facing each firm is
MR, the output for each firm is q_1, and
the price is P_1. Costs are equal to C_1,
and, thus, profit is the shaded area.

Interdependence and Uncertainty

Let's change our assumptions. Firms now recognize their interdependence, but
they are still not completely certain how interdependent they are. In other
words, pricing and output decisions are made on the basis of inaccurate or
incomplete information about rivals' reactions. Again, it is difficult to proceed
with model building unless we make specific assumptions about how decision
makers in firms *think* other firm's decision makers will react.

The Stigler Oligopoly Model of Implicit Collusion

Stigler's model eliminates reaction functions.[14] He starts off with the hypothesis that oligopolists would like to collude to maximize joint profits. Collusion, however, is costly to undertake and even more costly to police. If all firms
in an industry acted together, they could set output and price to maximize total
profits in the industry. Monopoly profits would therefore exist. Oligopoly,
however, occurs in a world that is imperfect, because transactions costs are not
zero.

In the Stigler approach to oligopoly, the agreed-upon goal of the oligopolists
is to collude; however, each recognizes that none can be restrained from cheating on any collusive agreement. There is some optimum amount of resources
that will be used to detect trickery and cheating, but these resources are certainly not sufficient to allow the oligopolists to collude as if they were one firm.

[14] George J. Stigler, "A Theory of Oligopoly," *Journal of Political Economy,* vol. 72 (February
1964), pp. 44–46.

There will be some equilibrium deviation from any collusive solution that would represent a monopoly maximum for the oligopolists. Stigler treats oligopoly as an implicit or explicit cartel that is formed with full knowledge that the policing scheme used will be imperfectly, although tolerably, effective.

Open Oligopoly What Stigler has given us is essentially the basis for an open oligopoly model that predicts that oligopolists can maximize the present discounted value of their profit stream by giving up part of the market to new entrants on a gradual basis. Thus, this open oligopoly model predicts that existing firms will not price in order to deter entry. Rather, they will set a higher price that will maximize the present value of their profit stream.[15] We can see the two options facing existing oligopoly firms in Figure 6-8. Basically, the present value of a series of the declining profits may exceed the present value of a perpetually steady profit rate if the initial level of profits is high enough in the former situation. Thus, the existing oligopolists have the choice of two time profiles of profit rate, labeled A and B. Profit time-profile A represents very high profits in the near future because of high prices, followed by declining profits because of entries causing lower prices. Profit time-profile B shows a profit rate that in fact grows slightly over time. Depending on the rate of discount used, A or B will have the highest present value. If the rate of discount is relatively high, the present value of profits earned in the future will be small, and the present value of profit time-profile A will be higher than that for B.[16] If the discount rate is low, then profits far into the future will have a higher value, and time profile B will be preferable because it will have a higher net present value.

Fog has suggested that large oligopolistic firms have a long time horizon, which implies a low rate of discount. Thus the prediction would be that oligopolistic industries will be stable in terms of the number of firms or their

[15] See pp. 45–50 for an explanation of present value.
[16] See page 48.

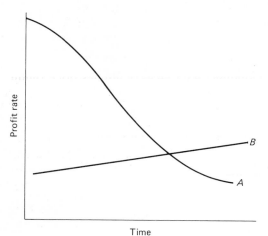

FIGURE 6-8
The options facing an open oligopolist.

concentration ratios.[17] Basically, then, we have a testable implication of the Stigler open oligopoly model. Stigler's model would predict a reduction in concentration ratios over time for oligopolies, whereas Fog's model would predict stability. Kamerschen attempted to test these two competing models.[18]

In brief, Kamerschen looked at two separate samples of oligopolistic markets from 1947 to 1963 and found a gradual reduction in the number of oligopolies using a four-firm concentration ratio of 75 as the cutoff point. Moreover, using another set of markets, the four-firm concentration ratio decreased during the time period under question for 12 out of 26, increased for 10, and was constant for 4 industries. Kamerschen's results give some encouragement to Stigler's open oligopoly hypothesis, although his results are subject to qualifications. After all, declining concentration ratios could be due to other influences over the same time period, such as antitrust pressures or diversification by firms.

Other Testable Implications of the Stigler Model   The testable implications of the Stigler collusive oligopolist model are as follows:

1 The fewer the number of firms involved is, the more effective the cartel will be.[19] A smaller number of firms means lower costs of policing a cartel arrangement.

2 Secret price cuts will be offered relatively more often to large than to small buyers, because the payoff from getting more business from the large buyer for any given price reduction is greater than that from a small buyer, given equal probabilities of detection.

3 The more homogeneous the product is, the easier it is to enforce a collusive pricing agreement. When the product is heterogeneous, price cuts can take the form of quality improvements and are difficult to eliminate.

4 The more unstable the industry demand and/or cost conditions are, the less likely it is that collusion will be successful. It is more difficult to enforce an agreement in an industry that has to adapt to constantly changing circumstances of demand and supply.

Kinked Demand Curve

An oligopoly model presented by economist Paul Sweezy implies price rigidity without collusion.[20]

---

[17] Bjarke Fog, "How Are Cartel Prices Determined?" *Journal of Industrial Economics,* vol. 5 (November 1956), pp. 16–23.

[18] David R. Kamerschen, "An Empirical Test of Oligopoly Theories," *Journal of Political Economy,* vol. 76 (July/August 1968), pp. 615–634.

[19] Chapter 14 further examines collusive or cartel arrangements.

[20] Paul M. Sweezy, "Demand under Conditions of Oligopoly," *Journal of Political Economy,* vol. 47 (August 1939), pp. 568–573. This model was advanced almost simultaneously by Robert L. Hall and Charles J. Hitch, "Price Theory and Business Behavior," *Oxford Economic Papers,* vol. 2 (May 1939), pp. 12–45.

Assumptions   In the Sweezy model, the assumption is made that the market consists of rivals who will quickly match price reductions but only incompletely and hesitantly follow price increases. This assumption allows us to postulate a demand curve facing an individual oligopolist.

The Nature of the Kinked Demand Curve

In Figure 6-9, we draw the kinked demand curve implicit in the Sweezy model. We start off at a given price of P_0 and assume that the quantity demanded at that price for this individual oligopolist is q_0. The oligopolist assumes that if his or her price is lowered, rivals will react by matching that reduction to avoid losing their respective shares of the market. Thus the quantity demanded at the oligopolist's lowered price will not increase greatly. This portion of the demand curve is relatively more inelastic, shown by the demand curve to the right of point E in Figure 6-9. On the other hand, if the oligopolist increases price, no rivals will follow suit. (If they do follow, they will follow incompletely.) Thus, the quantity demanded at a higher price for this oligopolist will fall off dramatically. The demand schedule to the left of point E will be the relatively elastic, flatter part of the curve to the left of point E. Consequently, the total demand curve facing the oligopolist is dd, which has a kink at E.

The Marginal Revenue Curve

For the kinked demand curve in Figure 6-9, we first draw a marginal revenue curve out from the vertical axis for the elastic portion of the demand curve (from the upper d to point E on the demand curve dd). At quantity q_0, however, the demand curve abruptly changes slope and becomes steeper. The marginal revenue curve there is discontinuous at the kink, or at quantity q_0. We see,

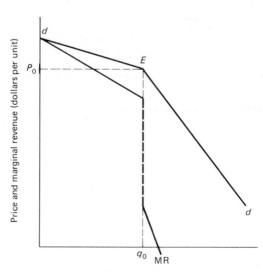

FIGURE 6-9
The kinked curve demand. Start with the price of P_0. The firm assumes that if it raises prices, no firm (or at least only a few firms) will follow. Its demand is relatively elastic; however, if it lowers price, other oligopolists will follow. Its demand is relatively inelastic; thus, there is a kink at E. The kinked demand curve is dd; the marginal revenue curve is discontinuous at the output rate q_0 and is labeled MR.

therefore, that the discontinuous part is represented by the dashed line at quantity q_0. The length of the discontinuity is proportional to the difference between the slopes of the upper and lower segments of the demand curve at the kink. Remember that the MR curve always bisects any horizontal line (perpendicular to the vertical axis) drawn from the vertical axis to the demand curve, except when there is a gap.

Reactions to Fluctuations in Marginal Cost

The oligopolist does not react to relatively small changes in marginal cost over the discontinuous portion of the marginal revenue curve. For example, in Figure 6-10, assume that marginal cost is represented by mc. The profit-maximizing rate of output is q_0, which can be sold at a price of p_0. Now assume that the marginal cost curve rises to mc′. What will happen to the profit-maximizing rate of output? Nothing. Both quantity and output will remain the same for this oligopolist. What will happen when marginal cost falls to mc″? Nothing. This oligopolist will continue to produce at a rate of output q_0 and will charge a price of p_0. Thus, whenever the marginal cost curve cuts the discontinuous portion of the marginal revenue curve, fluctuations (within limits) in marginal cost will not affect output or price because the profit-maximizing condition MR = MC will hold.

Reactions to Changes in Demand

It is also possible to show situations in which a shift in demand will not affect the price charged by the oligopolist. It will, however, change the quantity produced.

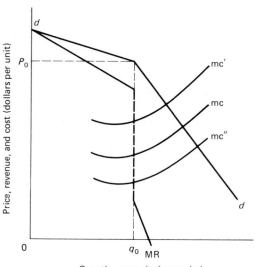

FIGURE 6-10
Changes in cost may not alter the profit-maximizing price and output. So long as the marginal cost curve "intersects" the marginal revenue curve in the latter's discontinuous portion, the profit-maximizing rate of output q_0 and the profit-maximizing price P_0 will remain unchanged.

Consider panel (a) in Figure 6-11. The profit-maximizing rate of output for this oligopolist is q_0. The profit-maximizing price is p_0. The marginal cost curve intersects the marginal revenue curve in its discontinuous part.

Now there is a change in demand from dd in panel (a) to $d'd'$ in panel (b) in Figure 6-11. However, the kink stays at the same price, P_0. We are assuming, therefore, that the shift in the demand curve dd to $d'd'$ is an exact outward shift with the slopes of the two different parts of the curve remaining the same. The cost curve does not change either. The marginal cost curve, mc, in panel (b) is the same as the marginal cost curve in panel (a). Clearly, the marginal cost curve intersects the new marginal revenue curve at a higher rate of output, and the profit-maximizing rate of output therefore increases from q_0 to q_1. So long as the increase in demand is such that the marginal cost curve continues to "intersect" the discontinuous portion of the marginal revenue curve, the price will remain at P_0 even though output has changed. This example could be altered so that there would be a decrease in demand. The results would be the

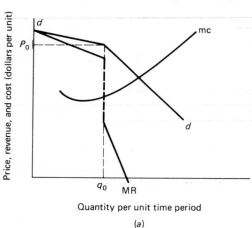

Quantity per unit time period

(a)

Quantity per unit time period

(b)

FIGURE 6-11
Changes in demand may not change profit-maximizing price. In panel (a) we show demand curve dd with a kink at output rate q_0. The price that is charged is P_0. In panel (b) we show a shift or increase in demand to d' d'. However, if the kink remains at price P_0, that price will be maintained in the market, but output will increase for the oligopolist to q_1.

same as long as the decrease in demand were sufficiently small to allow the marginal cost curve to continue "intersecting" the marginal revenue curve in its discontinuous portion. The price would remain the same with a decrease in demand, but the quantity provided by each oligopolist would fall.

The Inverted Kinked Demand Curve

Look at Figure 6-12, where we show a kinked demand curve with the kink at point E. However, the upper portion is relatively steeper than the lower portion. This is the reverse of the kinked demand curves we have been looking at. This reverse kink would be based on the individual oligopolist's expectation that all of its competitors will match any price increase that he or she initiates, but none will match a price cut. Presumably, such expectations would occur during an inflationary period.

In Figure 6-12 we find that the inverted kinked demand curve produces multiple equilibria. Marginal revenue equals marginal cost at outputs q' and q''. This indeterminancy of output with the inverted kinked demand curve severely weakens the usefulness of this theory.

Criticisms of the Sweezy Model

Sweezy's article was at first regarded by many economists as a definitive new general theory of oligopoly. Subsequent research and theoretical questioning have, however, cast some doubt on its general usefulness.

Theoretical Problems   The model has many theoretical problems, not the least of which concerns how the initial price P_0 was determined (we start off the model with P_0 given). If we do not know how P_0 was reached, we do not have a general theory of oligopoly pricing and output decision making.

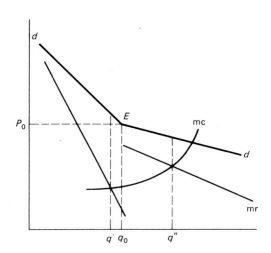

FIGURE 6–12
Inverted kinked demand curve. If firms follow price increases but do not follow price decreases, the kinked demand is inverted. Presumably this applies to an inflationary situation.

While it may be true that the kinked demand curve is accurate when interim knowledge about rivals' reactions is low, it is difficult to imagine that it is a long-run stable situation. Some economists contend that the kinked demand curve applies to a new industry in its early stages or to an industry in which new and previously unknown rivals enter the market.

Of course, the problem is that we still have a no-learning-by-doing model. The kink mentality is a barrier to changes in price that will increase profits, and this barrier is wholly the oligopolist's cerebral fabrication. It would seem that there are many ways in which the barrier could be circumvented. After all, that's what business is all about—a collection of devices for circumventing barriers to higher profits.

Empirical Evidence   The empirical evidence is not strong enough to support the existence of a kink. A study by George Stigler showed that in seven oligopolistic industries, price rises in one firm were met by price rises in other firms. Thus there seemed to be no asymmetry in the reaction of rivals to changes in price inherent in the kinked demand curve.[21] These empirical studies do not disprove a theory, but they do cast doubt on the completeness of the Sweezy solution to the oligopoly pricing and output problem.

THE CHAMBERLIN MODEL

Chamberlin also recognized that rivalry is expensive to participants. He states that, given perfect knowledge and the knowledge that each seller can have an impact upon the market, in the case of duopoly,

> [if] sellers have regard to their total influence upon price, the price will be the monopoly one. . . . If the sellers are three or more, the results are the same, so long as each of them looks to his ultimate interest. There is no gradual descent to a purely competitive price with increase in numbers, as in Cournot's solution.[22]

Chamberlin's Simple Duopoly Model   The best way to understand Chamberlin's multifirm oligopoly model is to look at his simple duopoly model. Chamberlin assumes that after the initial round, firm I recognizes that firm II will react to firm I's actions. After this recognition takes place within firm I, it also takes place within firm II. In other words, the two firms jointly recognize that the best thing they can do is to share the monopoly profits. Chamberlin's solution is presented in Figure 6-13. The combined profit-maximizing rate of

[21] George J. Stigler, "The Kinky Oligopoly Demand Curve and Rigid Prices," *Journal of Political Economy,* vol. 55 (October 1947), pp. 432–449. Also see Julian Simon, "A Further Test of the Kinky Oligopoly Demand Curve," *American Economic Review,* vol. 59 (December 1969), pp. 971–975; Walter J. Primeaux, Jr., and Mark R. Bomball, "A Reexamination of the Kinky Oligopoly Demand Curve," *Journal of Political Economy,* vol. 82 (July/August 1974), pp. 851–862; and Walter J. Primeaux, Jr., and Mickey C. Smith, "Pricing Patterns and the Kinky Oligopoly Demand Curve," *Journal of Law and Economics,* vol. 19 (April 1976), pp. 189–199.

[22] Edward H. Chamberlin, *The Theory of Monopolistic Competition: A Re-Orientation of the Theory of Value,* 6th ed. (Cambridge, Mass.: Harvard University Press, 1948), pp. 48, 54.

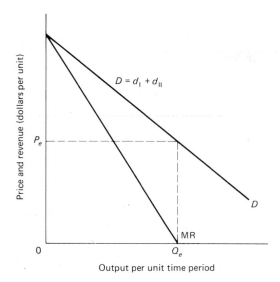

FIGURE 6-13
The Chamberlin model. Chamberlin's model of duopoly assumes that the two firms jointly recognize that they want to share full monopoly profits; thus, total output is equal to Q_e and is sold at price P_e. Each firm produces one-half of that output. The demand curve is the summation of two proportionate demand curves.

output for the two firms is the output at which marginal revenue intersects the horizontal axis where marginal cost equals zero. This is at output rate Q_e. The profit-maximizing price for the shared monopoly would be P_e. Thus, each firm would produce exactly one-half Q_e and sell at price P_e. This is a stable duopoly solution, in contrast to the unstable Edgeworth solution.

Implicit in the Chamberlin model is a system of stable prices charged by all firms without explicit collusion. No written or even verbal agreement is in evidence. This is a form of noncollusive behavior that leads to the same results that a perfectly operated cartel would have. The problem with such a model is that it implies joint profit splitting with zero enforcement costs. If such a model could be used to describe a situation with two firms, why couldn't it be used to describe a situation with three, four, or five firms? In other words, at what point does the number of firms become so large that the incentive to cut price is so great that the implicit cartel breaks down? This model does not tell us the answer.

When Chamberlin's Model Yields a Competitive Price Chamberlin did not seem very specific in stating when his model would break down into a competitive solution. He said, "The break comes when the individual's influence upon the price becomes so small that he neglects it."[23] In other words, the only situation that will produce competitive outcomes, even when there is perfect knowledge and no uncertainty, is when a large number of firms exist in an industry. In Chamberlin's world, with a large number of firms each will cut price because its individual actions have little effect. This is hard to reconcile with perfect knowledge and instantaneous reactions, coupled with profit-

[23] Ibid., p. 48.

maximizing desires. Chamberlin gets himself out of this inconsistency by stating that no seller looks upon himself or herself as the cause of the disturbance, because he or she secures whatever gains obtained by cutting price with "comparatively little disturbance to any of his rivals. Under these circumstances, there is no reason for him to withhold a shading of his price which is to his advantage, and which has no repercussions."[24]

Actually, Chamberlin is implying that any number of firms short of the number necessary to make the individual firm demand curve perfectly elastic will be insufficient to guarantee a competitive price-output outcome.

THE FELLNER MODEL

Fellner offers us a noncollusive, partially achieved joint profit-maximization model.[25] Basically Fellner discusses the activities of oligopolists who do not explicitly collude. The barriers to joint maximization that Fellner discusses are, nonetheless, common to both collusive cartels and noncollusive oligopolies. They include

1 Mistakes and uncertainties
2 Individual firm maneuvering with respect to profit division, thus preventing joint profit maximization
3 Differential risk aversion and appraisal by participants
4 Difficulty in coordination of nonprice variables, such as the rate of innovation, cost, and irreconcilable product differences

Although Fellner acknowledges the fact that the larger the number of participants is, the more difficult joint maximization becomes, he does not analyze the problem of number of firms.[26] In spite of this lack of analysis, Fellner says that the number of sellers in all concentrated markets would be likely to increase, and that competition and technological progress would also increase over time.

THE NUTTER-MOORE MODEL

G. Warren Nutter and John Moore developed a tentative oligopoly theory that is more complex and "more realistic" than those already outlined. In the Nutter-Moore model,[27] each seller posts prices openly. Nonetheless, information costs or pricing friction exist for both buyers and sellers, who must pay for time and other resources to find out each seller's prices. The model is one that carries through over time; thus, both buyers and sellers look at gains and losses in the future and properly discount them back to the present. Both buyers and

[24] Ibid., p. 49.
[25] William J. Fellner, *Competition among the Few* (New York: Knopf, 1949).
[26] Ibid., pp. 185, 189.
[27] G. Warren Nutter and John H. Moore, "A Theory of Competition," *Journal of Law and Economics,* vol. 19 (April 1976), pp. 39–65.

sellers monitor market prices. Given the industry demand curve, the cost of monitoring, and the discount rate, sellers can formulate rules telling them how much rivals are cutting prices. Then, primarily on the basis of how many sales sellers have lost over time, Nutter and Moore seek to predict how much prices will be cut during any time period. Without detailing their complicated model further, we can cite one of their basic conclusions. They point out that in a world without friction, firms would respond instantaneously to any price cut initiated by rivals and would therefore nullify prospective gains from price cutting.

Thus, we may conclude that friction is necessary to generate competition and that without friction in the price system, there cannot be competitive behavior.

In a world of friction, the more firms there are in an industry, the less control any of them believes it has over the future prices of the industry. Thus when there are many firms, any one firm will consider it more likely that a rival will cut price if it does not.

> Hence, other relevant things the same, the permanent loss from price cutting, as perceived by a potential price maker, will diminish as the number of firms increases. As long as price is above the conventionally defined competitive level, there will be some number of firms—not necessarily "large"—that will make it profitable for one of them to cut price. Under the proper circumstances, price might settle at the competitive level, where it is equal to marginal cost. It is not difficult even to imagine a long-run conjecture in which price would be at that level while the few firms in the industry were earning profits.[28]

A further conclusion is that a seller's **search intensity** falls rather steadily when another firm's search intensity increases.

The Nutter-Moore theory seems to be an extension of the Stigler open oligopoly theory. When we look at those two models together, it can be seen that oligopoly is not just a form of monopoly. Further, it is evident that the amount of price cutting tends to increase with the number of firms.

Other Oligopoly Models—Day and Demsetz

A model presented by Day assumes that no firm has knowledge of either the industry demand curve or of rivals' responses. That is, each seller takes prices as given and adjusts his or her output to these prices. Further, there is a one-period time lapse between input and output. Day's model reaches the following conclusion: Competitive equilibrium obtains even with a sole surviving low-cost producer.[29] His competitive result does not depend on the numbers of sellers in the market at any time. Clearly, Day is considering potential as well as actual entry.

---

[28] Ibid., p. 60.
[29] Richard H. Day, "A Note on the Dynamics of Cost Competition within an Industry," *Oxford Economics Papers*, vol. 20 (November 1968), pp. 369–373.

In another model, Demsetz distinguishes between rivalry and competition, contending that even with only one efficient producer there can be rivalry.[30] Demsetz uses the example of firms' bidding to become the monopoly supplier of electricity. These firms bid the price down until it just covers average cost including a normal rate of return. Thus, the price will approach a competitive level.

GAME THEORETICAL MODELS

Approximately four decades ago Von Neumann and Morgenstern published a book that was hailed by economists as a breakthrough in the study of market models for oligopoly, particularly duopoly theory.[31] The theory of games can be applied to a number of possible motivations that might hold true for the decision maker. Consider, for example, two alternative strategies for increasing the profits of the firm. In Figure 6-14 we specify two possible strategies of lowering prices and increasing advertising expenditures that will divide industry profits of $10,000. On the vertical axis we show strategies for Firm A and on the horizontal axis strategies for Firm B. In this game each firm may lower prices or increase advertising expenditures to increase profits. The figure shows only the change in profits to Firm A from alternative strategies. Because the total change in profits to both firms is specified as $10,000 for this payoff matrix, the change in profits to Firm B is $10,000—A's payoff. It is assumed that each party is aware of the relative payoffs from each alternative action, and that there is no interdependence in the selection of the chosen option. In this example, if A chooses to lower prices, the optimal strategy for Firm B is to also lower prices since B would earn $5,000 ($10,000 − $5,000 = $5,000) by lowering

[30] Harold Demsetz, "Why Regulate Utilities?" *Journal of Law and Economics,* vol. 11 (April 1968), pp. 55–65.

[31] John Von Neumann and Oskar Morgenstern, *Theory of Games and Economic Behavior,* 3d ed. (Princeton: Princeton University Press, 1953). The Von Neumann–Morgenstern theoretical structure can be applied to any rival behavioral situation, but it fits nicely into the theory of oligopoly, particularly duopoly. For a more recent application of game theory to oligopoly, see James W. Friedman, *Oligopoly and the Theory of Games* (Amsterdam: North-Holland, 1977).

	Strategies for Firm B	
	Lower prices	Increasing advertising
Lower prices	$5,000	$5,500
Increasing advertising	$4,000	$4,500

Strategies for Firm A

FIGURE 6-14
A two-strategy matrix.

prices and \$4,500 (\$10,000 − \$5,500 = \$4,500) by increasing advertising. It is also assumed that A and B will both either lower prices or increase advertising, because either action will increase total profitability for each firm. Note that the minimum gain to Firm A from lowering prices is \$5,000 and from increasing advertising is \$4,000. Consequently, A will choose to lower prices since this move will maximize the minimum gain for the firm. This option is often referred to as a "maxmin" strategy or maximizing the "minima" from the available rows depicting alternative strategies.

The strategy for Firm B is to choose from the various options shown in each column the option that minimizes payment for Firm A. In this case B would choose to lower prices since the minimum greatest payoff (or maximum referred to as "minmax") to A is \$5,000. In this situation both firms choose to lower prices and each earns \$5,000. This equilibrium is often referred to as a "saddle point" since neither Firm A nor Firm B will alter its final decision given the action of the other. Saddle points do not exist in every payoff matrix, which allows for the possibility of alternative or mixed strategies in which probabilities are assigned to the various alternatives available to the decision maker.

Game theory can be applied to a number of firms, and coalitions may be formed with the possibility of cartelization. Martin Shubik has shown that approximately 40 different solutions have been identified in the theory of games.[32] In each solution alternative forms of rational behavior can be derived from various motivations to explain decision makers' actions.

One popular formulation of a game theory solution has been proposed by Nash. In Nash's equilibrium each bargainer is assigned cardinal utilities at the status quo point. In a thorough and rigorous solution Nash shows that the best solution for each decision maker is the one that maximizes the combined product of the utilities at that point.[33]

Game theory is also useful in identifying certain general characteristics of complex situations where there are incentives for cooperation. In many cases these games become extensions of the classic paradoxical solution of the prisoners' dilemma games.[34] In these games, two individuals suspected of involvement in a crime are interrogated separately and confronted with alternative potential imprisonments. If neither prisoner confesses, each will be given a 6-months sentence on a minor charge. If one prisoner confesses and the other does not, the suspect that turns state's evidence will not be prosecuted while the other will receive a 10-year sentence. If both confess, each suspect will

[32] Martin Shubik, "A Curmudgeon's Guide to Microeconomics," *Journal of Economic Literature,* vol. 8 (June 1970), p. 425.

[33] John F. Nash, "The Bargaining Problem," *Econometrica,* vol. 18 (April 1950), pp. 155–162. Also see Frederik Zeuthen, *Problems of Monopoly and Economic Warfare* (London: G. Rutledge & Sons, Ltd., 1930), for earlier attempts to model game theoretic behavior; and Alan Coddington, *Theories of the Bargaining Process* (Chicago: Aldine, 1968), esp. pp. 24–48, for a more recent review of bargaining theories.

[34] See, for example, Robert D. Luce and Howard Raiffa, *Games and Decisions* (New York: Wiley, 1957).

receive a 5-year sentence. Assuming that both suspects dislike prison and that no outside costs would be imposed by confessing, each suspect will find that confessing is the dominant strategy. Yet each suspect could be made better off by not confessing if they do so jointly. Thus, the best outcome from the viewpoint of the suspects requires information and communication. This could be obtained, for example, by an informal rule that an individual who confesses will later meet sufficient private costs from doing so. Lave found that in repetitious prisoners' dilemma games, isolated subjects were able to cooperate with one another without communication.[35]

FORGETTING POTENTIAL EXPANSION BY OTHER FIRMS

Potential supply by other firms is often overlooked in examining oligopoly power. Below we give an example to show how a firm with apparent oligopoly power may have that power attenuated by the supply elasticity of other firms. We will use the case of General Motors.

Deriving the Relationship between One Firm's Demand and All Firms' Supply

The automobile industry has been used as an example of an oligopoly for many years. What we would like to show in this application is that even though General Motors (GM) may appear to have a significant amount of oligopoly power, that power is attenuated by the supply elasticity of the other automobile firms.

Let General Motors produce q_i. Then

$$Q_s = q_i + q_0 \tag{6-1}$$

where Q_s = industry supply
q_0 = supply of all other firms

Both supply and demand are a function of price, and in equilibrium

$$Q_D(P) = Q_s(P) = q_i + q_0 \tag{6-2}$$

where Q_D = market demand for autos. Then

$$q_d = Q_D - q_0 \tag{6-3}$$

where q_d = demand for GM's cars. In other words, what's left over is the demand for GM cars.

[35] Lester B. Lave, "An Empirical Approach to the Prisoners' Dilemma Game," *Quarterly Journal of Economics*, vol. 76 (August 1962), pp. 424–436.

The complete notation is then

$$Q_s = \text{industry supply}$$
$$q_i = \text{GM supply}$$
$$q_0 = \text{all other supply}$$
$$Q_D = \text{industry demand}$$
$$q_d = \text{GM demand}$$

Each of the variables in Eq. (6-3) may be changed by the same small amount to get

$$\Delta q_d = \Delta Q_d - \Delta q_0 \tag{6-4}$$

Divide Eq. (6-4) by $q_d \Delta P$ to get

$$\frac{\Delta q_d}{q_d \Delta P} = \frac{\Delta Q_D}{q_d \Delta P} - \frac{\Delta q_0}{q_d \Delta P} \tag{6-5}$$

Now multiply Eq. (6-5) by P to get

$$\frac{\Delta q_d}{q_d} \cdot \frac{P}{\Delta P} = \left(\frac{\Delta Q_D}{q_d} \cdot \frac{P}{\Delta p} \right) - \left(\frac{\Delta q_0}{q_d} \cdot \frac{P}{\Delta P} \right) \tag{6-6}$$

Rearrange Eq. (6-5). Multiply the first right-hand term by Q_D/Q_D and the second term by q_0/q_0.

$$\frac{\Delta q_d}{\Delta P} \cdot \frac{P}{q_d} = \left(\frac{Q_D}{q_d} \right) \frac{\Delta Q_D}{Q_D} \cdot \frac{P}{\Delta P} - \left(\frac{q_0}{q_d} \right) \frac{\Delta q_0}{q_0} \cdot \frac{P}{\Delta P} \tag{6-7}$$

But this equals

$$\eta_d = \left(\frac{Q_d}{q_d} \right) \eta_D - \left(\frac{q_0}{q_d} \right) \epsilon_o \tag{6-8}$$

where ϵ_o = the supply elasticity of the other auto manufacturers
η = price elasticity of demand

From Eq. (6-8), we see that the price elasticity of demand for General Motors products, η_d, is a function of the market price elasticity of demand, η_D, the price elasticity of supply of other firms, and the (inverse of the) relative share of industry output accounted for by the firm under study, Q_D/q_d. What is clear from Eq. (6-8) is the importance of ϵ_o. Since η is always negative, when we subtract ϵ_o, we always increase absolutely the price elasticity of demand facing the individual firm. In the short run, a demand curve for General Motors products might be inelastic. However, in the long run, if ϵ_o is sufficiently large, that is no longer true. This analysis explains why a firm such as General Motors will set a price lower than expected in a market in which the demand is relatively inelastic in the short run.

Some Hypothetical Numbers

Various estimates have been made of the price elasticity of demand for new automobiles. A rough average is $\eta_D = -2$.

Remember that when the firm maximizes profits

$$MR = P\left(1 + \frac{1}{\eta_D}\right) = MC \tag{6-9}$$

Thus, if we rearrange Eq. (6-9), we get

$$\frac{P - MC}{P} = \frac{-1}{\eta_D} \tag{6-10}$$

Now, if we make the assumption that marginal cost is approximately equal to average cost (not an unreasonable assumption for firms' selling millions of cars), then Eq. (6-10) becomes

$$\frac{P - AC}{P} = \frac{-1}{\eta_D} \tag{6-11}$$

Then, if the industry price elasticity of demand is approximately equal to -2, we would expect that

$$\frac{P - AC}{p} = -\frac{1}{-2} = \frac{1}{2} \tag{6-12}$$

This would indicate that 50¢ of each dollar would be a profit margin. However, if we look at the data relating to General Motors and other automobile companies, we do not find anything near a 50 percent profit margin on sales. What we find are figures much closer to 6 to 10 percent as the rate of return on sales. A 10 percent rate of return on sales is consistent with a price elasticity of demand facing an individual firm of about -10 when we use Eq. (6-12).

We can approximate, then, the price elasticity of supply facing General Motors by using this information. Let us substitute for $\eta_d = -10$ and for $\eta_D = -2$ in Eq. (6-8). The share of industry output accounted for by General Motors is about 50 percent, so that $Q_D/q_d = 2$, and $q_0/q_d = -1$. Thus, Eq. (6-8) becomes

$$-10 = (2)(-2) - (1)\epsilon_0 \tag{6-13}$$

The price elasticity of supply of other firms, ϵ_0, is approximately equal to 6.

A 1 percent increase in the price that General Motors charges for its cars will elicit a 6 percent increase in the quantity supplied by other companies. Thus, the monopoly or oligopoly power that General Motors has is limited by the supply of the other firms in the industry.

CONCLUSION

Of the competing oligopoly models, none stands out as being either more theoretically correct or more empirically valid. In their own way, each model contributes something toward an understanding of the behavior of decision makers in industries characterized by a small number of firms. For the most part, these theories have identified critical elements necessary for identifying decision makers' behavior, particularly the roles of information and rival behavior. While most theories exhibit similar properties, such as firms that tend toward the maximization of collective profits, it is clear that the coordination of pricing policies to maximize these profits is extremely difficult and requires interfirm communication, knowledge of transactions, and responses by firms.

CHAPTER 7

MONOPOLISTIC COMPETITION

The models of perfect competition and pure monopoly represent two extreme forms of price determination. In the perfectly competitive model, we assume that there are numerous firms which produce a homogeneous product and which have no influence over price; they are price takers. In the pure monopoly model, we assume that the firm is a single seller of a good; the firm is a price maker. There are, however, market situations that seem to fall in between these two extremes (oligopoly having been discussed already). After all, although many firms have some control over price and do not face a perfectly elastic demand curve, they are not really oligopolists or pure monopolists. In the 1930s, economists searched for a model that somehow bridged the gap between perfect competition and pure monopoly. It was, therefore, with great expectations that the economic world received models that had the qualities of both perfect competition and pure monopoly. These were the models of monopolistic competition, developed by Harvard's Edward Chamberlin and Cambridge's Joan Robinson. Chamberlin wrote *The Theory of Monopolistic Competition*, and Robinson wrote *The Economics of Imperfect Competition*; both books were published in 1933. The theory that we outline will be taken mainly from Chamberlin's work. He presented some of the key characteristics of monopolistically competitive industries; they are outlined below.

PRODUCT DIFFERENTIATION

Perhaps the most important feature of the monopolistically competitive market is **product differentiation**. The products, though similar, are not identical. Remember that in a perfectly competitive market products are homogeneous, whereas in a monopoly there is only a single product. We also refer to a homogeneous product as one that the firm sells. We are now in a situation where each individual manufacturer of a product has an absolute monopoly over a product that is slightly differentiated from other similar products. There are numerous examples of such product differentiation—cigarettes, toothpaste, soap, and so on. Indeed, it appears that product differentiation characterizes most, if not all, American markets. We do not have the single option to buy just one particular type of television set, just one type of pantsuit, or just one type of automobile. A number of similar but differentiated products are usually available in each product classification.[1]

Actually, monopolistic competition is only one instance of this differentiation, which is sometimes called "variation of production." Each firm has to decide on an optimal product assortment; each firm has to decide on the appropriate level of quality for each product. Product variation can be found in market structures other than monopolistic competition and is a factor that should be explained by our models.

Some economists like to differentiate between product differentiation that is "real" and that which is "artificial." Real product differentiation involves variations in physical characteristics, such as an actual chemical difference between two brands of clothes detergent. Artificial product differentiation involves different packaging materials, brand names, and advertising outlays for what is inherently the same product. The above types of product differentiation, of course, represent only the tip of the iceberg. For example, firms can also differentiate their products on the basis of location and on service provided with the product sold.

The point to be made here is that in a monopolistically competitive market, each individual producer realistically has an absolute monopoly in the production and sale of a differentiated product, although many close substitutes for that product are available.

Whatever might be the source or sources of product differentiation, the ultimate fact is that consumers believe that a considerable range of differences exist between individual products in any class of products. Additionally, consumers are willing to pay higher prices for some products than for others, believing that those prices reflect the perceived quality differentials. If consumers pay 15¢ more for half a gallon of Clorox than they pay for any other brand of hyperchlorite solution liquid bleach, the fact that the bleaches are chemically identical does not matter. Analytically, they are different products.

A Summary of Sources of Product Differentiation

We now realize that product differentiation includes any differential in attitude toward similar products by buyers. Thus, the sources of product differentiation

---

[1] Some of the difficulties of defining product markets, especially for potential empirical testing as discussed in chap. 5, are apparent here as well.

encompass all considerations that cause buyers to prefer one competing good over another. We briefly summarize the sources of product differentiation here:

1 Differences in quality or design
2 Differences in consumer ignorance regarding essential characteristics and qualities of the goods purchased (for example, durable goods that are infrequently purchased and are complex in design)
3 Brand names, trademarks, or company names derived from sales promotion activities of sellers, particularly advertising and service
4 Differences in the location of sellers of similar goods

We will discuss product differentiation in more detail in Chapter 9. Now let us look at sales promotion and advertising although they, too, will be discussed in more detail in Chapter 9.

Demand Increasing Cost—Advertising and Sales Promotion Monopolistic competition differs with respect to perfect competition in that there is no need for sales promotion in perfect competition. No individual firm in a perfectly competitive market will advertise. After all, if the firm can sell all that it wants at the going market price, it has no incentive to incur advertising costs because the gains would be distributed across *all* firms in the industry. But such is not the case for the monopolistic competitor. Since the monopolistic competitor has only some monopoly power, advertising may result in increased profits. How much advertising will be undertaken? As much as is profitable. It will be carried to the point where the marginal revenue from one more dollar of advertising equals one dollar of marginal cost.

The often-stated view that the goal of the advertiser is to make the demand curve more inelastic for his or her product is an incorrect assessment of the goal of advertising.

Consider Figure 7-1. We have drawn two demand curves, DD and $D'D'$. Using the vertical axis formula for price elasticity of demand, it is clear that $D'D'$ is more elastic than DD at point A. Does this necessarily mean that a firm would like to have advertising cause the demand curve to rotate around point A from $D'D'$ to the more inelastic DD? That depends on the profit-maximizing rate of output. At rates of output in excess of Q_1, sales for the demand curve $D'D'$ are higher, because any given quantity greater than Q_1 can be sold for a higher price than the same quantity sold by the firm on the inelastic demand curve DD.

The goal of advertising is to shift the demand curve to the right. A monopolistic competitor who advertises will always prefer a demand curve shift to the right over a demand curve shift to the left, whether or not the former is more or less elastic.

In the strictest model of monopolistic competition, advertising by one monopolistic competitor does not induce retaliatory action by others. That is to say, advertising is not undertaken as a reaction to encroachments of other

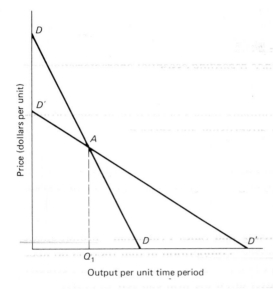

FIGURE 7-1
Advertising and the price elasticity of demand. It is often asserted that advertising is undertaken in an attempt to make demand more inelastic. However, consider demand curves *DD* and *D'D'*. The latter is more elastic than the former; however, *D'D'* would be preferable at output rates in excess of *Q₁*, because it is to the right of *DD*, even though *DD* is relatively less elastic.

forms on the particular market in question.[2] Nonetheless, it is not unusual for all the firms in a monopolistically competitive industry to advertise their products. Sometimes this advertising is called "competitive" or "defensive" in the sense that, although it has no effect on *increasing* sales, it is necessary for *keeping* sales where they are and preventing other firms from taking business away. Competitive advertising is sometimes contrasted with informative advertising, which actually imparts information that can be used by the consumer in deciding which product to buy. The distinction between competitive and informative advertising is a murky one; no operationally meaningful *modus operandi* has been offered to make that distinction.

Brand Name Advertising

Some 50 years ago, Stocking observed that "the primary economic function of advertising is to stimulate or control consumption."[3] We must also understand that advertising does make buyers aware of the availability of products and certain characteristics of products. Such advertising clearly results in both

---

[2] This initially seems to be a strange assumption, because shifting one's own demand curve outward means shifting someone else's demand curve inward. However, if many firms exist, a perceptible shift in one firm's demand curve will be matched by imperceptible shifts in the demand curves of all other firms. Actually, in the purest model of monopolistic competition, a large number of firms exist; this model conforms to the competitive one in terms of the nonreaction by other firms. It is only when we move toward a situation where there are *not* a large number of monopolistically competitive firms that the assumption appears "strange."

[3] Collis A. Stocking, "Modern Advertising and Economic Theory," *American Economic Review*, vol. 21 (March 1931), p. 50.

private and social gains. Some observers contend that brand advertising has some but not all of these positive characteristics. Brand promotion attempts to convince the buyer that products of a given seller are usually of uniform and superior quality compared to products of competitors. It is not surprising that most brand name advertising associates the name with quality and also associates that quality with a higher price.

One problem with advertising is that the sales promotion done by one company may cancel out the sales activities of another company. The consumer is left with little net gain. If all bleaches are the same, advertising appeals for different brands may not help all consumers. Nonetheless, if advertising seems to succeed, each individual firm has an incentive to advertise. We have described this advertising as competitive or defensive. If other firms advertise, the firm that doesn't advertise will find its demand curve shifting inward. Thus, it must advertise to offset other firms' advertising. Advertising by all firms, however, may increase the market demand for the products of all firms, hence increasing individual firm demand curves as well.

Product Groups

In this chapter we no longer assume that the industry is composed of a collection of firms producing a homogeneous commodity. It is impossible to maintain the homogeneity assumption when we talk in terms of an industry with differentiated products. Of course, we could treat each firm as producing a distinct product and thus being an industry by itself. Chamberlin sought to solve this problem by lumping together firms producing very closely related products, called **product groups.** Some product groups that come to mind are breakfast cereals, automobiles, toilet paper, and hand soap. The departure from the homogeneity assumption creates some theoretical problems but may reduce some empirical problems.[4] Product group definitions are more likely to correspond to the government's S.I.C. definitions than to homogeneity definitions. Thus, testing propositions about product groups may be relatively easy for firms involved in monopolistic competition.

DEMAND CURVE FOR MONOPOLISTICALLY COMPETITIVE FIRM

The monopolistically competitive firm perceives that it has some small amount of monopoly power. Hence, it does not consider that its demand curve is perfectly horizontal at the going market price for the product.

We can best analyze the individual firm in a monopolistically competitive industry (product group) as if each firm faces the same proportional demand curve. This is, in fact, Chamberlin's definition of the demand curve facing the individual monopolistic competitor. "Such a curve will, in fact, be a fractional part of the demand curve for the general class of product and will be of the same

---

[4] For the problems in identifying products with industries, see chap. 4 and its appendix.

elasticity.''[5] If there are 50 sellers, the demand curve for the individual seller will show at each price one-fiftieth of the total quantity demanded at that price. We are implicitly assuming, then, that all firms are of equal size. We will make the further assumption that all firms have identical costs.

Look at Figure 7-2. Here we show the *proportional* demand curve $d_p d_p$, which represents the amount of demand for a typical firm when all firms are charging the same price. In other words, it is constructed by taking one-fiftieth of total market quantity demanded at each price for 50 equal-sized firms. In general, when there are n equal-sized firms, the proportional demand curve is constructed by taking $1/n$ of the total market quantity demanded at each price.

Let's start out at a price of P_1. Each firm would therefore sell q_1 units of output per unit time period. However, according to Chamberlin's assumption, the individual firm will act as if all other firms are keeping their price at P_1. Thus we assume with Chamberlin that the individual firm *perceives* a firm demand curve of $d_f d_f$ at price P_1. Notice that this firm demand curve has more elasticity at price P_1. At every price it has more elasticity than the proportional demand curve $d_p d_p$, because the individual firm in this model does not think that other firms will react to changes in its price. Therefore, if the individual firm lowers its price in order to capture a larger share of the market, it perceives that it will be able to take business away from other firms that retain the higher price on their products. If this were a perfectly competitive case (and indeed we can analyze perfect competition in this way also), then $d_f d_f$ would be perfectly horizontal at price P_1. The present case is not perfectly competitive, however; therefore, $d_f d_f$ has a marginal revenue curve everywhere below it. This marginal revenue curve is labeled mr_f. To repeat, the individual monopolistic com-

[5] Edward H. Chamberlin, *The Theory of Monopolistic Competition,* 5th ed. (Cambridge, Mass.: Harvard University Press, 1948), p. 90.

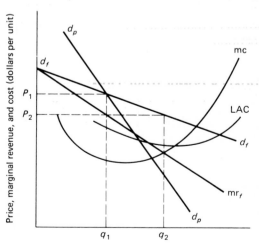

Price, marginal revenue, and cost (dollars per unit)

Individual firm's output per unit time period

FIGURE 7-2
Monopolistic competition—the firm and the industry. The proportional demand curve $d_p d_p$ is drawn by assuming that all firms charge the same price and that all firms are of equal size. At a price of P_1, the firm will be producing at q_1. It perceives a firm demand curve of $d_f d_f$, which is drawn by assuming that all other firms will keep their prices at P_1. At price P_1, however, marginal revenue does not equal marginal cost. This occurs at output rate q_2. The individual firm believes that it can sell this quantity at price P_2. Such an output rate is not attainable at that price, however, because all firms acting together will individually face $d_p d_p$.

petitor perceives its demand curve to be $d_f d_f$, the one that it obtains if it changes its price while all other firms leave their prices unchanged.

Under the above assumptions, P_1 is not a price that an individual monopolistically competitive firm will charge. The firm will increase output until marginal revenue equals marginal cost, or to output q_2. It perceives that it can sell this quantity at price P_2.

However, q_2 is unattainable for the industry at price P_2. Figure 7-2 is drawn for a typical firm. All firms acting together in their attempt to increase output *cannot* move along an individual demand curve $d_f d_f$. Rather, they must move along their respective proportional demand curve $d_p d_p$. Thus, $d_f d_f$ slides along $d_p d_p$ until the short-run equilibrium is reached. Price P_2 and quantity q_2 are not an equilibrium combination. Each firm must find itself not only on its own firm demand curve $d_f d_f$, but also on the proportional demand curve $d_p d_p$.

EQUILIBRIUM IN MONOPOLISTIC COMPETITION

Short-run equilibrium is defined as a situation in which the going market price is such that no firm has an incentive to change its own price or output. This situation can occur only where marginal revenue, mr_f, equals marginal cost, mc. In Figure 7-3, the proportional demand curve $d_p d_p$ intersects the firm demand curve $d_f d_f$. Only at this intersection point is the firm not frustrated in its attempts to set price and quantity. At price p_e, the individual firm demand curve $d_f d_f$ intersects the proportional demand curve $d_p d_p$. The firm is operating simultaneously on its own perceived demand curve and on the proportional demand curve. Moreover, this is a profit-maximizing rate of output because it occurs where the marginal cost curve intersects the firm's perceived marginal revenue curve mr_f.

Notice that in this short-run example of equilibrium, positive economic profits are being made by each individual firm, as can be seen by the position of

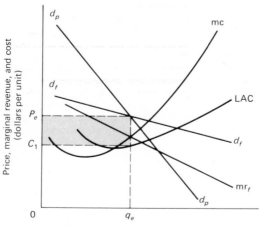

Individual firm's output per unit time period

FIGURE 7-3
Short-run equilibrium in a monopolistic competition. Eventually an output rate q_e will be found where mr_f = mc and where the firm's perceived demand curve $d_f d_f$ intersects its proportional demand curve $d_p d_p$. It will sell its output at price P_e; its average total costs are C_1; and its profits are the shaded area.

the long-run average cost curve LAC. It intersects the quantity line below the price line. Economic profits are shown in Figure 7-3 by the shaded rectangle, $(P_e \cdot q_e) - (C_1 \cdot q_e)$.

LONG-RUN EQUILIBRIUM

Figure 7-3 could also represent the long-run equilibrium for the individual firm in a monopolistically competitive industry if entry into the industry were blocked. If entry is not blocked, the existence of positive economic profits will attract new firms into that industry, competing these positive economic profits away.

The long-run equilibrium will be defined in exactly the same way as the short-run equilibrium, but economic profits will be zero. They will be competed away by entry of new firms into the industry where they exist, just as they are competed away in the perfectly competitive industry in the long run. In other words, the long-run average cost curve must be tangent to the firm's demand curve at the short-run equilibrium price. *for LReqil.*

This tangency can be seen in Figure 7-4. The profit-maximizing quantity produced per unit time period is perceived by the individual firm as q_e, for this is where marginal revenue equals marginal cost. The price that can be obtained for that quantity is P_e; that is the price where the perceived firm demand curve intersects the proportional firm demand curve. With a stable market demand curve, the proportional demand curve $d_p d_p$ will shift toward the origin, as n increases with new firm entry, until economic profits are driven to zero. That is what competition is all about.

The long-run average cost curve is also tangent to the perceived firm demand curve $d_f d_f$ at the rate of output q_e and price P_e, or at point E. Thus at price P_e no economic profits are being received by any individual firm in the monopolistically competitive industry. This occurs because positive economic profits, as

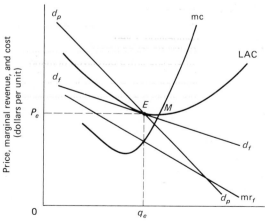

FIGURE 7-4
Long-run equilibrium of firm, monopolistic competition. Positive economic profits will cause entry into the industry. The proportional demand curve $d_p d_p$ will eventually shift leftward until, at the equilibrium price, each individual monopolistic competitor will be earning zero economic profits. At point E, price P_e is just equal to long-run average costs.

Individual firm's output per unit time period

represented in Figure 7-3, create a situation in which other firms want to enter the industry to reap those profits.

We note here that the long-run equilibrium rate of profit is zero; this result relies explicitly on open entry and competition by actual and potential members of the industry.

The LAC Tangency Point and "Excess" Capacity

We have shown that in a perfectly competitive industry, each firm produces at the minimum point on its long-run average cost curve and on its short-run average cost curve. This is because the horizontal demand curve facing any individual firm shifts until the price line or individual demand curve just touches or is tangent to the bottom of the long-run average cost curve. Then entry or exit will cease in the perfectly competive industry. This same kind of analysis applies to monopolistic competition. However, since the demand curve perceived by the firm is downward-sloping because of the monopoly situation developed through product differentiation, the tangency point must be to the left of the minimum point on the long-run average cost curve. This can be seen in Figure 7-4, and it is exaggerated for the purpose of illustration in Figure 7-5. The minimum point M, where marginal cost intersects LAC, is to the right of rate of output q_e.

Productive efficiency of resources occurs where long-run average costs are minimized. In Figure 7-5, the productive efficient rate of output q_c occurs at the minimum point on LAC, or at point M, where the marginal cost curve intersects LAC. The long-run equilibrium rate of output for the monopolistically competitive firm is q_e. The distance between these two outputs, q_c and q_e, has been labeled "excess" capacity. Note that **excess capacity** exists when the demand curve is downward-sloping. Each firm is too small to maximize efficient utilization of resources.

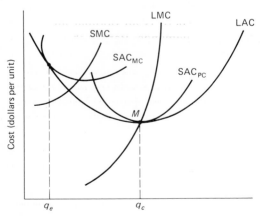

FIGURE 7-5

"Excess" capacity. In perfect competition, LAC = LMC = SAC at the minimum point M. However, given the downward slope of the demand curve facing a monopolistic competitor, the long-run equilibrium occurs at an output to the left of M and at a price above M. The equilibrium rate of output for a monopolistic competitor might be q_e, where short-run average costs equal long-run average costs, but neither is at a minimum. The horizontal difference between q_e and q_c is one measure of excess capacity.

Why "Excess" Capacity?

There are two reasons why excess capacity or a rate of output that is not "ideal" may exist in the monopolistically competitive firm. One is attributed to an inefficient utilization of resources; it occurs whenever $P > \text{MC}$. The other may be attributed to the fact that the monopolistically competitive firm does not produce enough and does not employ enough resources to attain minimum average costs. We noted above that excess profits are driven away by entry when competition prevails in an industry. It appears that excess capacity results when monopoly prevails.

Why Is "Excess" Capacity Not a Reality?

Note that whenever any slope whatsoever (greater than 0) appears on the individual demand curve $d_f d_f$, there is no way for the individual firm to operate at the *minimum* point on a long-run average cost curve or a short-run average cost curve and still cover average costs. Chamberlin contended that the difference between the actual long-run average cost of production for a monopolistically competitive firm in an open market and the minimum long-run average cost represented the "cost" of producing "differentiation." In other words, Chamberlin did not label this difference in unit cost a measure of excess capacity; that was an idea of economists who took up the model after him.[6]

Indeed, Chamberlin argued that it is rational for consumers to prefer differentiation and to willingly accept the resultant increased production cost in return for choice and variety of output. We know that the so-called excess capacity situation is a result of heterogeneity in the product; if there were no heterogeneity and all other assumptions in the model were retained, the firm would operate at the minimum point on its long-run average cost curve and its short-run average cost curve. Output would be ideal.

Proponents of the excess capacity argument cite casual evidence such as the proliferation of gasoline stations. Technologically speaking, each of those stations pumps fewer gallons than it "could." Is this an indication of excess capacity? The answer is not at all obvious. There is an optimal amount of unused (or unemployed) capacity to meet peak demands. Barber chairs are not always filled. Neither are bathrooms in a home. Individuals add guest rooms to their houses that are unused most of the time. In what sense can we call these inventories of unused capacity "excess"? We would somehow have to come up with an argument that product differentiation, and hence excess capacity, was unwanted by the consumer and that its additional costs were in some way "forced" on him or her.

The monopolistic competition tangency solution just outlined at output rate q_e has serious defects. For example, assuming economies of scale, any two

[6] John M. Cassels, "Excess Capacity and Monopolistic Competition," *Quarterly Journal of Economics,* vol. 51 (May 1937), pp. 426–443; Roy F. Harrod, "Doctrines of Imperfect Competition," *Quarterly Journal of Economics,* vol. 48 (May 1934), pp. 442–470; and Richard F. Kahn, "Some Notes on Ideal Output," *Economic Journal,* vol. 45 (March 1935), pp. 1–35.

firms would seem to have an incentive to merge and thus produce more cheaply and more profitably the combined output suitably differentiated. They could share much of the production equipment, which would therefore be used a larger percentage of the time. Presumably, the product differentiation is relatively slight so that only a small percentage of the production facilities have to be altered to produce the differentiated products. It would thus appear that the pressure toward combination, or merger, would destroy the tangency solution. Further, the conclusion that firms in monopolistic competition necessarily produce on the decreasing sections—to the left of "ideal" output q_e—of their long-run average cost curves would also be put in serious doubt.

OTHER DIFFICULTIES WITH THE ANALYSIS

In the preceding analysis, we let the firm demand curve $d_f d_f$ and the industry demand curve $d_p d_p$ represent the relative demand curves facing any firm. We also allowed the average cost curve to represent the average cost curve for any firm. The implication here is that each firm in the group faces identical demand and cost curves, meaning that every firm is the same size, producing similar amounts at similar prices. Further, the demand for the product group is somehow evenly distributed among the differentiated producers. Stigler has raised the following objection regarding the uniformity assumptions:

> How can different products have uniform costs and demands? The quantity axes of the various product diagrams are simply not the same: one measures three-room apartments, another four-room houses, and perhaps still another restaurant meals (an excellent substitute for a kitchen).[7]

The question then, is, How can the costs and demands for different products be the same? Using Stigler's example, the demand for seven units (7-months' use) of a three-room house is not the same as the demand for seven units of a four-room house, even if an identical number of units of each house is demanded at exactly the same price. Stigler is telling us that the uniformity is not *operationally meaningful* when we apply it to a group of heterogenous products.

In addition, Chamberlin's analysis of individual firm demand curves, $d_f d_f$, and the industry demand curve, $d_p d_p$, implicitly assumes homogeneous products. But monopolistic firms sell differentiated products, and individual demand curves would not be identical. This internal inconsistency has generated several criticisms.[8]

---

[7] George J. Stigler, "Monopolistic Competition in Retrospect," in *Five Lectures on Economic Problems* (New York: Macmillan, 1950), pp. 12–24.

[8] See, for example, Harold Demsetz, "The Nature of Equilibrium in Monopolistic Competition," *Journal of Political Economy*, vol. 67 (February 1959), pp. 21–30; "The Welfare and Empirical Implication of Monopolistic Competition," *Economic Journal*, vol. 74 (September 1964), pp. 623–641; and "Do Competition and Monopolistic Competition Differ?" *Journal of Political Economy*, vol. 76 (January–February 1968), pp. 146–148. Also see Robert E. Kuenne, ed., *Monopolistic Competition Theory: Studies in Impact; Essays in Honor of Edward H. Chamberlin* (New York: Wiley, 1967); and Lester G. Telser "Monopolistic Competition: Any Impact Yet?" *Journal of Political Economy*, vol. 76 (March–April 1968), pp. 312–315.

Further, differences in the demand curves yield ambiguous implications regarding whether or not product differentiation eventually leads to output increases and whether such increases lower effective prices to consumers.[9] In addition, implications regarding average production costs are also ambiguous, since higher volumes of output may lower average production costs.

The Meaning of the Chamberlin Group

We have already pointed out that Chamberlin talked of product groups. Surely we can engage in our analysis without carefully defining such product groups. When we do attempt, however, to come up with an operationally meaningful definition of the product group, we run into a number of problems. How do we determine where the cutoff point is between substitutes and nonsubstitutes? For example, there may be products not included in the defined product group that are, in fact, substitutes for the good.

CONTRIBUTIONS OF MONOPOLISTIC COMPETITION MODELS

Despite numerous problems, monopolistic competition models have given us some insights into the nature of certain forms of nonprice competition for certain goods, such as paper products and gasoline, where the perceived differences in the vector of product characteristics are greater than actual differences. These models have also revealed the inadequacies of existing explanations of excess capacity in production.

APPENDIX: Monopsony Power

Whenever a firm cannot purchase all the inputs it desires at the going market price, it buys inputs from firms with market power in the resource. This behavior occurs whenever a firm faces a less than perfectly elastic supply curve for the input in question. We start off our discussion assuming that the purchaser of the input is a producer selling in a perfectly competitive market. Hence, we are looking at imperfect competition in the input market, but perfect competition in the output market. We will alter the latter assumption later.

In the most extreme case, the situation just described is one of **monopsony**, which means a single buyer. Several buyers are called an **oligopsony**. In the following sections, we consider a monopsonist. That is, we are talking about a pure monopoly in the purchase of an input.

---

[9] Yoram Barzel, "Excess Capacity in Monopolistic Competition," *Journal of Political Economy,* vol. 78 (September–October 1970), pp. 1142–1149; Richard Schmalensee, "A Note on Monopolistic Competition and Excess Capacity," *Journal of Political Economy,* vol. 80 (May–June 1972), pp. 586–591; and Harold Demsetz, "The Inconsistencies in Monopolistic Competition: A Reply," *Journal of Political Economy,* vol. 80 (May–June 1972), pp. 592–597.

MARGINAL AND AVERAGE FACTOR COST CURVES

The monopsonist faces an upward-sloping supply curve for inputs because, as the only buyer, he or she faces the entire SS curve. Therefore, the monopsonist must pay higher prices for additional units. However, in the case where no price discrimination in purchasing is possible, the monopsonist must also pay a higher price on all previous units purchased.

The supply curve of an input can be called the average factor cost curve, just as the demand curve for an output is often called the average revenue curve. We derived a curve marginal to the average revenue curve to represent the marginal revenue obtained by a monopolist from an extra unit of sales. Now we look at a curve marginal to the total factor cost curve; we will call it the marginal factor cost curve. It will give the increase in total factor cost that results from a one-unit increase in the purchase of the input under study.[10]

The Relationship between MFC and Elasticity of Supply

We will now attempt to derive the relationship between marginal factor cost and the price elasticity of supply of the variable factor.

If we ignore fixed costs, total costs will be $TC = w \cdot L$, where w is the wage rate and L is the quantity of labor. The increase in TC caused by an increase in the labor input will be

$$TC + \Delta TC = (w + \Delta w)(L + \Delta L) \tag{A7-1}$$

because the wage rate must change. Equation (A7-1) becomes, after carrying out the right-hand side multiplication,

$$TC + \Delta TC = wL + w\Delta L + \Delta wL + \Delta w\Delta L \tag{A7-2}$$

Let ΔL get smaller and smaller; as ΔL approaches 0 ($\Delta L \to 0$), the $\Delta w\Delta L$ also approaches 0. Realizing that $TC = wL$, Eq. (A7-2) becomes

$$\Delta TC = w\Delta L + \Delta wL \tag{A7-3}$$

Dividing through the ΔL, we get

$$\frac{\Delta TC}{\Delta L} = w + \frac{\Delta w}{\Delta L} L \tag{A7-4}$$

But $\Delta TC / \Delta L$ is the change in total costs due to a change in the variable input labor. This is our definition of marginal factor cost, or MFC. Then

$$MFC = w + \frac{\Delta w}{\Delta L} \cdot L \tag{A7-5}$$

---

[10] Marginal factor cost has been called marginal expense of input, marginal expenditure for input, and marginal resource (input) cost.

Now we multiply the last term on the right-hand side of Eq. (A7-5) by w/w:

$$\text{MFC} = w + \frac{\Delta w}{\Delta L} \cdot L \left(\frac{w}{w} \right)$$

or

$$\text{MFC} = w + w \left(\frac{\Delta w}{\Delta L} \cdot \frac{L}{w} \right) \tag{A7-6}$$

We can now factor out w:

$$\text{MFC} = w \left(1 + \frac{\Delta w}{\Delta L} \cdot \frac{L}{w} \right) \tag{A7-7}$$

But the price elasticity of supply of labor, L, is defined as

$$L = \frac{\Delta L}{\Delta w} \cdot \frac{w}{L} \tag{A7-8}$$

Therefore, our expression for marginal factor cost becomes

$$\text{MFC} = w \left(1 + \frac{1}{\epsilon_L} \right) \tag{A7-9}$$

Since ϵ_L is positive for all upward-sloping supply curves, marginal factor cost will be greater than the wage rate. If the elasticity of supply of labor is 2.0 and the wage rate is $100 per week, then Eq. (A7-9) tells us that MFC $= 100(1 + \frac{1}{2}) = 100 \times 1.5 = \$150$. In the case where the firm buys its inputs in a perfectly competitive input market, ϵ_L is equal to $+ \infty$. The second term in parentheses on the right-hand side of Eq. (A7-9) becomes 0; marginal factor cost is therefore equal to the wage rate.

Pricing and Employment of a Single Variable Input

The pure monopsonist is hypothesized to maximize profit.

$$\frac{\text{MFC}_i}{\text{MPP}_i} = \text{MC} = \text{MR} = P \, [\text{for all } i \text{ (inputs)}] \tag{A7-10}$$

Equation (A7-10) represents the profit-maximizing combination of inputs for a firm that is a perfect competitor in the output market, and a pure monopsonist in the input market, where MPP_i is the marginal physical product of resource i and $\text{MPP}_i \cdot P \equiv \text{VMP}_i$. Rearranging Eq. (A7-10), we get

$$\text{MPP}_i \cdot P = \text{MFC}_i \tag{A7-11}$$

or

$$\text{VMP}_i = \text{MFC}_i \tag{A7-12}$$

The output competitor who is a monopsonist in the input market will hire a resource up to the point where the value of marginal product (VMP) equals the marginal factor cost. We can see the pricing and employment of such an input by the profit-maximizing monopolist in Figure A7-1.

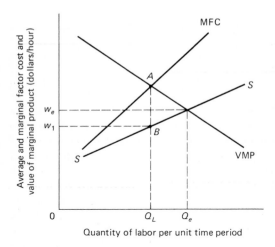

FIGURE A7-1
Price and employment of an input purchased by a pure monopolist. When we consider only a single variable input, the pure monopsonist will hire the input up to the point where MFC = VMP. This is point A. In order to obtain that quantity of labor Q_L, the pure monopsonist will have to pay only the wage rate w_1, which is read off the supply curve SS, where it intersects the quantity line at point B. The competitive wage W_e and output Q_e are also shown.

If labor is the only variable factor of production, we are looking at a VMP curve for labor. The profit-maximizing monopsonist will hire labor up to the point where MFC = VMP. This occurs at the intersection of the MFC and VMP curves, or at point A. That gives the profit-maximizing rate of employment of labor, Q_L. How much does the monopsonist have to pay per unit for that amount of labor? The amount is given by the supply curve SS. The intersection of the quantity desired, Q_L, with the supply curve SS is at point B. The wage rate that must be paid is w_1. We have, then, the wage and employment optimum for a monopsonist input user selling his or her output in a purely competitive market when there is only one variable factor of production purchased in an imperfectly competitive market.

MONOPSONIST PRICING AND EMPLOYMENT WITH SEVERAL VARIABLE INPUTS

With several variable inputs, we have the same analysis that we had in the last section. Taking into account that there are many variable factors of production, Eq. (A7-6) becomes

$$\frac{\text{MFC}_x}{\text{MPP}_x} = \frac{\text{MFC}_y}{\text{MPP}_y} = \cdots = \frac{\text{MFC}_R}{\text{MPP}_R} \tag{A7-13}$$

for all η factors of production.

As the sole user of several variable productive inputs, a monopsonist will adjust the ratios of the inputs until the ratio of the marginal factor cost to the marginal physical product for each input is the same.[11]

NO DEMAND CURVE FOR A MONOPSONIST

Studying the theory of monopoly, we find that we cannot derive a supply curve for a monopolist because no one schedule gives a unique quantity of output forthcoming at any particular price. Output depends on the interaction of MC and MR.

[11] Hence, the least-cost combination of inputs is obtained when the marginal rate of technical substitution equals the marginal factor cost ratio for any pair of inputs.

The same analysis applies to a theory of monopsony, which offers no demand curve for a monopsonist. It is certainly not the VMP curve. The monopsonist has no demand curve for the variable input in the sense of a simple functional relation in which the quantity of the variable input depends on its price per unit. For example, the number of workers demanded depends not only on the supply schedule of workers, but also on elasticity.

This analysis is illustrated in Figure A7-2. We have drawn in a downward-sloping value of marginal product curve VMP. We start off with a supply curve of labor (SS) facing a monopsonist. The change in total costs of labor is MFC. The intersection of MFC with VMP is at point E. The quantity of labor demanded by the monopsonist will be Q_L. The monopsonist will pay wage rate w_1. Assume, however, that there is a rotation in the supply curve to $S'S'$, with an associated marginal curve labeled MFC'. If MFC' intersects the VMP curve at point E (as we have drawn it), the monopsonist will still demand the same quantity of labor, Q_L, but will pay only the wage rate w_2. Since a demand curve is defined as the maximum price for which a given quantity is demanded, VMP cannot be labeled a demand curve for labor by the monopsonist. We have just shown a situation in which the same quantity of labor will be demanded at two different wage rates.

MONOPOLY AND MONOPSONY COMBINED

We can alter the analysis above to take account of the monopsonist input buyer who is also a monopolist in the output market. Instead of looking at the price of the product, we focus on its marginal revenue. Thus, instead of using the value of the marginal product curve (price times marginal physical product) we use the marginal revenue product curve (marginal revenue times marginal physical product), which lies below the VMP. After all, marginal revenue is less than price. The entire analysis above can be redone by utilizing the MRP curve rather than the VMP curve. The profit-maximizing quantity of employment is obtained where the marginal factor cost curve intersects the marginal

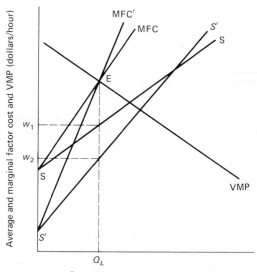

FIGURE A7-2
The monopsonist has no demand curve. A demand curve is defined as a locus of points showing maximum prices at which given quantities will be demanded; however, we can show that the monopsonist will demand the same quantity of labor, Q_L, at two different wage rates, w_1 and w_2, if the supply curve shifts so that the marginal factor cost curves intersect the VMP line at the same point E.

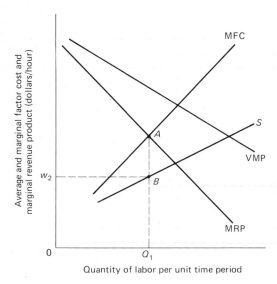

FIGURE A7-3
Pricing and employment of an input hired by the monopsonist—monopolist. If the monopolist is also a monopsonist, it will hire the input up to the point where MFC = MRP at point A. This gives the wealth maximizing employment of Q_1. The wage rate that will have to be paid is given by the intersection of Q_1 with the supply curve SS at point B. It is wage rate w_2.

revenue product curve. This is at point Q in Figure A7-3. The optimum quantity of input is therefore Q_1. This quantity can be obtained by paying a wage rate—if we are considering labor only—of w_2.

Notice that because marginal revenue is always less than the price of the output, the quantity of labor demanded, Q_1 (shown in Figure A7-3), will be smaller than the amount chosen by the competitive firm that purchases from a monopolist.

A SUMMARY OF MONOPSONY AND MONOPOLY SITUATIONS

We have studied input factor pricing and employment with pure competition in the output market and monopsony in the input market and with monopoly in both the input and output markets. In Table A7-1 we present a summary of the various conditions under which output will be produced and the variable input, labor, will be demanded. Table A7-1 is presented graphically in panels (a) through (d) in Figure A7-4.

TABLE A7-1
A SUMMARY OF MONOPSONY AND MONOPOLY SITUATIONS
Optimal output and input employment.

Structure on sellers' side	Structure on suppliers' side	
	Many buyers	**One buyer**
Many sellers	(a) Competition VMP = MRP = MFC = W	(c) Monopsony VMP = MRP = MFC > W
One seller	(b) Monopoly VMP > MRP = MFC = W	(d) Bilateral monopoly VMP > MRP = MFC > W

EXPLOITATION

Exploitation is defined as paying a resource less than the value of its marginal product.

We consider the amount of exploitation that exists in a situation where a firm is both a monopolist and a monopsonist. This duality is depicted in Figure A7-5. The profit-maximizing monopolist/monopsonist will determine the quantity of labor demanded at

FIGURE A7-4
Summary of pricing and employment under various market conditions. The panels in this diagram correspond to the sections marked (a), (b), (c), and (d) in Table A7. In panel (a) the firm operates in perfect competition in both input and output markets. It purchases labor up to the point where the going wage rate w_e is equal to VMP. It hires quantity Q_c. In panel (b) the firm purchases the variable input labor in a perfectly competitive market, but has a monopoly in the output market. It purchases labor up to the point where the wage rate w_e is equal to MRP. It hires a smaller quantity Q_m than in panel (a). In panel (c) and (d), the firm is a monopsonist in the input market. In panel (c) it is a perfect competitor in the output market. It hires resources up to the point where MFC = VMP. It will hire quantity Q_1 and pay a wage rate w_c. In panel (d) the monopsonist is also a monopolist. It hires labor up to the point where MFC = MRP, which is quantity Q_2. It pays wage rate w_m.

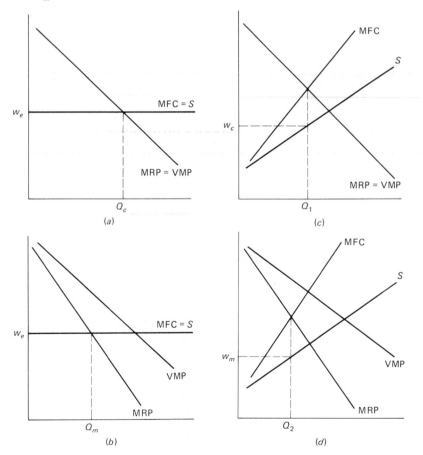

the intersection of MFC and MRP, which is labeled E in Figure A7-5. It will pay a wage rate w_m for the quantity Q_m of labor. Monopolistic exploitation occurs because the monopolist looks at the MRP curve rather than the VMP curve, which would be relevant for a perfect competitor. Monopsonistic exploitation occurs because the monopsonist looks at the MFC curve rather than the supply curve, as does the buyer of labor in a perfectly competitive market.

In a situation of both monopoly and monopsony, exploitation can be summarized as follows:

$$VMP_L - MRP_L = \text{monopolistic exploitation}$$
$$MRP_L - w_m = \text{monopsonistic exploitation}$$
$$VMP_L - w_m = \text{total exploitation}$$

THE PRICE-DISCRIMINATING MONOPSONIST

We have considered only the situation in which the monopsonist was paying the same price for all units of the factor of production under study. In the situation shown in Figure A7-6, the monopsonist purchases a quantity of labor input Q_1 and pays a wage rate of w_1. In other words, at point A marginal factor cost would equal VMP if we assume that the monopsonist is a pure competitor in the product market.

We know that a competitive equilibrium would prevail at the intersection of SS and VMP. The quantity of labor demanded and supplied would be Q_e, and the wage rate would be w_e.

If there were perfect wage discrimination, the monopsonist would also end up at rate of input demand Q_e. This rate would occur because the perfectly discriminating monopsonist would move up the supply curve of labor and pay each individual worker exactly what was necessary to get that person to work. Only the marginal worker would be paid w_e; all other workers would be paid less. It is possible, then, that a perfectly discriminating monopsonist will hire the same amount of workers as a perfect competitor in the

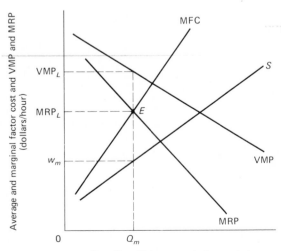

FIGURE A7-5

Exploitation. Exploitation is defined as paying an input less than the value of its marginal product. In the situation depicted here, we have both monopoly and monopsony. The monopolist finds the profit-maximizing rate of employment of labor at the intersection of MFC and MRP, or point E. The profit-maximizing quantity of labor demanded will be Q_m, which will be paid a wage rate w_m. Monopoly exploitation equals ($VMP_L - MRP_L$). Monopsony exploitation equals ($MRP_L - w_m$). Total exploitation equals ($VMP_L - w_m$).

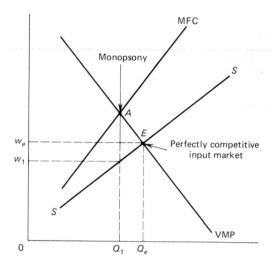

FIGURE A7-6
The price-discriminating monopsonist. A nonprice-discriminating monopsonist will hire where MFC = VMP, which is at point A. Thus, the quantity demanded will be Q_1, and the wage rate paid will be w_1. In a perfectly competitive situation, the wage rate will be w_e, and the quantity of labor demanded will be Q_e. The perfectly price-discriminating monopsonist can, however, move up the supply curve by paying exactly the wage rate needed to get each additional worker without having to pay the previous workers a higher wage rate. The perfectly price-discriminating monopsonist will increase quantity demanded to the competitive solution Q_e. However, only the last worker will receive a wage rate of w_e. All previous workers will receive progressively lower wages.

input market. The only difference will be that the workers will not all get the same wage rate and indeed, all but one of the workers will receive a lower wage.

Given the heterogeneity of both the labor force and the job qualifications, we would expect that there would be some price discrimination for any given amount of monopsony power.

CONDITIONS GIVING RISE TO MONOPSONY POWER

Although it is difficult to imagine a situation in which monopsony power could be very great, it is certainly not difficult to imagine situations in which a firm faces an upward-sloping supply curve for labor. We discuss some of those situations now.

Specialized Factors of Production

The supply curve of highly specialized factors of production is probably upward-sloping to any individual firm. Some workers and professionals have highly specialized skills that cannot be obtained in large quantities at a constant wage rate, at least not in the short run. In order to employ more of these people, the individual firm has to raise its wages. This is necessary to bid employees away from other firms. Note, however, that the longer the time allowed for adjustment is, the more elastic will be the supply curve of any highly specialized factor of production. Thus we can come up with the notion that *monopsony power is less in the long run than in the short run.*

The Company Town

The most commonly cited case of monopsony is the so-called company town which has only one employer. This situation was rather common in the past in the American textile and mining industries. The importance of such cases today is certainly diminishing if not already negligible. Because it is now common for American workers to commute up to

TABLE A7-2
MONOPSONY POWER IN RESOURCE MARKETS:
1978

Resource	Concentration ratio: top five firms
Aluminum	84%
Cement: clinker	26
Chlorine	64
Coal: bituminous and lignite	23
Copper	71
Crude oil (refining capacity)	38
Gypsum	74
Molybdenum	94
Petroleum-based resins: PCV	49
Phosphoric acid	45
Soda ash	91

Source: Standard & Poor's Corporation, *Industry Surveys,* various months, 1979, 1980, and U.S. Department of the Interior, Bureau of Mines, *Mineral Commodity Profiles,* 1978, 1979.

50 miles to work, the amount of monopsony power available to isolated employers is quite small. Moreover, people do relocate. Very little empirical work has been done on the amount of "labor market concentration" on the *hiring* side. But what has been done shows little concentration in large cities. For the United States as a whole, the fraction of counties where the 30 largest firms employed 50 percent of the labor force or more is quite small. In Table A7-2 we show the four-firm concentration ratio which is often equated with monopsony power for several U.S. resource markets.

Collusive Agreements

Just as there was an incentive for oligopolists to collude in order to form, in effect, a monopoly, there is an incentive for monopsonists to collude. A collusive monopsony might result from an agreement among employers not to raise wages individually or not to hire away each other's employees. In some accounting firms, for example, it is considered unethical for large firms to recruit other firms' employees. One study shows that agreements against such recruiting have existed.[12] Separate units of many state university systems, such as those in California and New York, have elaborate agreements that significantly increase the cost of moving a faculty member from one campus to another.[13]

[12] Richard A. Lester, *Adjustments to Labor Shortages: Management Practices and Constitutional Controls in an Area of Expanding Employment* (Princeton, N.J.: Princeton University Press, 1955), pp. 46–49.
[13] See, for example, J. A. Barron, "Restrictive Hiring Practices in Institutions of Higher Learning in California," *Journal of Law and Economics,* vol. 4 (October 1961), pp. 186–192.

FIRM BEHAVIOR AND
MARKET OUTCOMES

CHAPTER 8

PRICING RULES

In this chapter, we wish to examine various pricing techniques utilized by firms with some form of market power, that is, firms that do not face price-taking conditions. We will look at three broad types of pricing: price leadership models, rule-of-thumb models, and other general pricing tactics, leaving more explicit forms of pricing for later chapters.

PRICE LEADERSHIP

Collusive agreements between firms in an oligopolistic market need not be of a formal nature, but can be implicit or tacit, such as agreements based on custom and habit. The notion of **price leadership** follows from the idea of long-standing custom and habit. We will examine four types of price leadership: (1) the dominant firm, (2) the low-cost firm, (3) the barometric firm, and (4) market shares.

Price Leadership by the Dominant Firm

It is sometimes alleged that pricing in oligopolistic industries is controlled by the dominant firm, that is, the largest firm in the industry. The basic assumption in this model is that the dominant firm sets the price and allows other firms to sell all they want at that price. The dominant firm then sells the remainder of the market quantity demanded at that price.[1]

---

[1] Archibald J. Nichol, *Partial Monopoly and Price Leadership* (Philadelphia: Smith Edwards, 1930); William J. Fellner, *Competition among the Few,* op. cit., p. 138; and George J. Stigler, "Notes on the Theory of Duopoly," *Journal of Political Economy,* vol. 48 (August 1940), pp. 521–541.

Given this assumption, a determinant solution for price and quantity can be derived.

Implicit Assumptions

The implicit assumptions of the model of dominant firm price leadership are:

1 The largest producer has virtually complete control over market price.

2 All other firms act like perfect competitors, regarding their own demand function as perfectly elastic at the dominant firm's set price.

3 The dominant firm is able to estimate the market demand curve.

4 Only the dominant firm takes account of any effects it might have on market output and price.

5 The dominant firm is able to predict the supplies of other sellers at each price.

6 The dominant firm behaves passively, fixing the price and allowing other firms to sell all they wish at that price.

Price and Quantity Determination

First we must derive the demand schedule for the dominant firm; this is done in Figure 8-1. We draw the market supply schedule of the smaller firms, shown as Σmc_{small}. It is the horizontal summation of all the marginal cost curves of the smaller firms above their respective minimum average variable cost curves. To

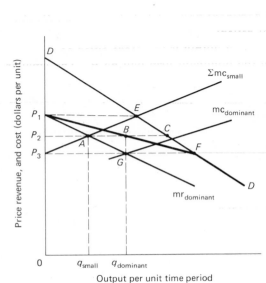

FIGURE 8-1

Price leadership by the dominant firm. The market demand curve is DD. Assume that at price P_1 all the small firms taken together will provide the entire output; that is, the horizontal distance from P_1 to point E. At price P_2, the small firms will provide a quantity P_2A. The dominant firm would therefore provide the rest. Thus, we derive point B on the dominant firm's demand curve by subtracting the horizontal distance from P_2 to point A from the demand curve DD. In other words, $BC = P_2A$. At price P_3, the small firms will provide none of the output, for marginal cost exceeds that price. The dominant firm's demand curve becomes coincident with the industry demand curve. The dominant firm's demand curve is the heavy line P_1BFD. When we draw in the marginal revenue curve up to its discontinuous point, we find the profit-maximizing rate of output for the dominant firm at $q_{dominant}$ or at point G, where $mr_{dominant} = mc_{dominant}$. The profit-maximizing price is found on demand curve P_1FD. It is P_2.

find the demand curve of the dominant firm, we need to find: (1) a point at which all the smaller firms supply the entire market demand and the dominant firm supplies zero demand, and (2) a point where the dominant firm supplies the entire market and the small firms supply zero. In what follows, we add a point between points (1) and (2).

Look at price P_1. At this price the small firms would want to supply the total quantity that the market would purchase at that price, or the quantity from the vertical axis to point E on the demand curve DD. Remember that by assumption, the dominant firm sets the price and *allows* other firms to sell all they can at that price. If the dominant firm set the price P_1 and followed this assumption, the small firms could supply everything; nothing would be supplied by the dominant firm at price P_1. Therefore P_1 is the vertical intercept of the dominant firm's demand curve. Now pick a price P_2 less than P_1. The smaller firms will provide output P_2A—the horizontal distance from the vertical axis to point A on the summed marginal cost curve. At price P_2, total quantity demanded is equal to P_2C, or the horizontal distance from the vertical axis to point C on the demand curve. We measure back from point C an amount equal to P_2A to find out how much is left over for the dominant firm. This takes us up to point B. Thus, the dominant firm will supply output equal to the horizontal distance from P_2 to point B. Now we go to price P_3. At this price the small firms will provide nothing. Their costs are too high. The dominant firm will provide the entire market, or the horizontal distance from the vertical axis to point F on the market demand schedule. The dominant firm demand curve is the thick, kinked demand curve that runs from the vertical axis at price P_1 through B to point F and then along the industry demand curve.

Given this demand curve, the dominant firm acts as a monopolist. We must now draw in a marginal revenue curve that is marginal to P_1FD. It is labeled $mr_{dominant}$. (For simplicity, on the diagram we have not drawn in the marginal revenue curve past the "kink" price F.)

The marginal cost curve for the dominant firm is labeled $mc_{dominant}$. It intersects the dominant firm's marginal revenue curve $mr_{dominant}$ at point G. The dominant firm's profit-maximizing rate of output is therefore given as $q_{dominant}$. The profit-maximizing price set by the dominant firm will be P_2. The smaller firms, in the aggregate, will produce q_{small}.[2] At price P_2, total market demand is satisfied by the combined outputs $q_{dominant}$ and q_{small}. A price-quantity solution is obtained. It is stable because of our assumption that the small firms behaved passively as price takers. In other words, small firms are eliminated from consideration as rivals in the usual sense of the term.

When the Model Disintegrates

The dominant firm price leadership model certainly disintegrates once the other firms in the industry cease to follow the leader. According to one critic of this

---

[2] In order to simplify the diagram, $mc_{dominant}$ was drawn to intersect $mr_{dominant}$ at the quantity $q_{dominant}$ so that a new price line would not have to be drawn in.

model, "The erratic behavior of the competitive fringe around the oligopoly core directly contradicts the implicit assumption of the models that fringe firms will accept the leader's prices in a manner similar to the pure competitor."[3] Additionally, given that different-sized firms may face different cost curves, the same price probably will not maximize short-run profits for all sizes of firms. In periods of slack demand, the fringe firms will attempt to stimulate sales by lowering prices, thus cutting into the dominant firm's sales more than predicted and clearly negating the notion that the dominant firm sets the price. Even smaller firms believing in the possibility of retaliation may take a chance if they think that the dominant firm will not want to upset the entire market just to punish trivial-sized violators.

Additionally, one can surmise that the dominant firm may wish to set a lower price than predicted by our model simply to protect its own market share from being nibbled away by the other firms that are cutting prices. It has also been suggested that the price leader can lower price to retaliate, hoping that this lowering will cause greater price discipline throughout the industry.

Price Leadership by the Low-Cost Firm

An alternative price leadership model involves leadership that is not by the dominant firm, but by the low-cost firm.[4] We will simplify the analysis greatly by considering a duopoly situation in which there is a tacit agreement to share the market. This situation is merely an extension of the market-sharing cartel model we have talked about before. The two firms produce a homogeneous commodity. The market demand curve for this commodity is given in Figure 8-2 by the demand curve DD. Each firm faces a demand curve of dd, which is equal to one-half DD. This is a proportionate demand curve. The marginal revenue curve that is marginal to dd is labeled mr.

The costs of the two firms are different; firm 2 has higher cost curves than firm 1. Firm 2's average and marginal cost curves are given by AC_2 and MC_2, and firm 1's curves are given by AC_1 and MC_1. The lower-cost firm, firm 1, if given a choice, would charge a price of P_1. The higher-cost firm, if given a choice, would charge a higher price, P_2.

In this model, firm 2 has no choice but to follow firm 1. If firm 2 does not follow and sets a price of P_2, its sales will be zero. All customers will go to firm 1, which is selling the product at price P_1. (We assume it can supply that larger quantity demanded.) The lower-cost firm becomes the price leader, and the price is set at P_1. In our diagram firm 2, even though it is the higher-cost firm, will still receive some profit. Firm 1, because of its lower costs, will make a much greater profit.

[3] Robert F. Lanzillotti, "Competitive Price Leadership; A Critique of Price Leadership Models," *Review of Economics and Statistics,* vol. 39 (February 1957), p. 61.
[4] Kenneth Boulding, *Economic Analysis,* 3rd ed. (New York: Harper & Row, 1955), pp. 581–587.

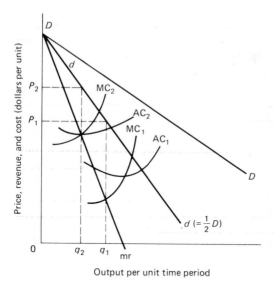

Output per unit time period

FIGURE 8-2
Price leadership by the low-cost firm. Assume that two firms share the market such that each faces a proportionate demand curve $dd = \frac{1}{2}DD$. The marginal revenue curve is mr. The lower-cost firm is represented by AC_1 and MC_1. It will produce at output rate q_1 and will charge price P_1. However, the higher-cost firm would like to produce at output rate q_2 and sell at price P_2. In this model, though, it has no choice but to follow the lower-cost firm. It will still receive profits because P_1 is higher than AC_2 at output rate q_1.

The Unlikely Nature of Price Leadership by a Low-Cost Firm   The price leadership model presented in Figure 8-2 seems unlikely. Why would the lower-cost firm tacitly agree to share the market equally with the higher-cost firm? Assume for the moment that antitrust laws prevent the lower-cost firm from driving the higher-cost firm completely out of business. It would still seem reasonable that the lower-cost firm would not be willing to share the market equally, but rather would set a price so that the higher-cost firm makes lower economic profits and gives up part of its share of the market to the lower-cost firm.

Note that if there are great differences between high-cost firms and low-cost firms, the high-cost firms will not recover full costs and will gradually be eliminated from the industry.[5]

The Barometric Firm Model

Barometric price leadership is another supposed form of noncollusive oligopoly behavior. With this model, the price leader is not necessarily the dominant firm or the low-cost firm, but the leader's price adjustment elicits adherence by other firms in the market.[6] According to some researchers, barometric price leadership leads to the competitive price. According to Lanzillotti,

---

[5] Jesse W. Markham, "The Nature and Significance of Price Leadership," *American Economic Review*, vol. 41 (December 1951), p. 187. For critical comments, see Alfred R. Oxenfeldt, "Professor Markham on Price Leadership: Some Unanswered Questions," *American Economic Review*, vol. 42 (June 1952), pp. 380–384.

[6] Markham, "The Nature and Significance of Price Leadership," p. 181.

Barometric price leadership . . . appears to be essentially a special situation where the conjectures of the barometric price leader turn out to be correct, which only rarely would be the case in a dynamic economy under the assumptions postulated. In effect, the special case is very special indeed; it amounts to essentially a competitive model of price behavior.[7]

Lanzillotti, along with Kaplan and Dirlam, studied pricing policies of larger corporations. They observed an attitude toward price leadership similar to the barometric firm model.[8]

Unfortunately for empirical research, the identity of the so-called barometric price leader changes. In copper, the price leader may be Kennecot, Phelps Dodge, or Anaconda. In rayon yarn, Du Pont and American Viscose were price leaders at different times.

An additional problem is that barometric price leaders are not always followed since they have no power to coerce other firms. Additionally, firms may delay long periods before following the barometric firm's lead. Finally, it has been found that barometric price leaders frequently change published prices after pervasive nonpublished price changes have occurred in the industry. As a matter of fact, the barometric price leader may simply be the first to announce a change that has already occurred and cannot therefore be called the firm responsible for the price change in the rest of the industry. One critic of the model put it succinctly, stating that the barometric firm "commands adherence of rivals to his price only because, and to the extent that, his price reflects market conditions with tolerable promptness."[9]

A Theory of Information

Information is not free, whether it concerns existing and future demands for commodities, alternative sources of supply, production costs, or changes in technology. It is a scarce resource; available means are required to obtain information. This costly information is necessary for a firm to make a decision as to where to set output and price in order to maximize profits. Thus, we might predict that in certain instances some firms would prefer to allow other firms to generate that information. Firms would, if they could, like to be free riders on the information paid for by other firms that would help each firm to set its profit-maximizing prices.

What better way to be a free rider than to allow the dominant, "richest" firm in the industry to do all of the market research and to determine the profit-maximizing price? It is possible that price leadership by a dominant firm has nothing to do with collusion or shared markets, but rather with the fact that smaller firms are allowing the larger firm to spend the resources necessary to

[7] Lanzillotti, op. cit., p. 61.

[8] A. D. H. Kaplan, Joel B. Dirlan, and Robert F. Lanzillotti, *Pricing in Big Business: A Case Approach* (Washington, D.C.: Brookings Institution, 1958), pp. 270-271.

[9] George J. Stigler, "The Kinky Oligopoly Demand Curve and Rigid Prices," *Journal of Political Economy,* vol. 55 (October 1947), pp. 445-446.

obtain the information for setting a profit-maximizing price. Price leadership by a dominant firm can be couched in terms of the theory of information and the problem of the free rider.

RULES OF THUMB

The maintenance of industry discipline can frequently be furthered by rule-of-thumb pricing as a coordinating device. Rules of thumb typically involve cost-plus or **full-cost pricing**, as well as target rate-of-return pricing. For example, if all firms in an industry adhere to full-cost pricing formulas and have similar costs, the behavior of rivals becomes predictable. Efficient producers are assured of realizing normal profits at a minimum cost.

Decision makers in business have been using pricing rules of thumb for a long time, even though the concept did not enter economic analysis until the late 1930s. Cost-plus pricing techniques may be found in the largest corporations. General Motors, U.S. Steel, Du Pont, General Electric, Alcoa, International Harvester, and Union Carbide have all been found to use such techniques.[10] However, cost-plus pricing is by no means limited to large corporations.[11] Hall and Hitch (who are also associated with the kinked demand curve) did an interview survey of pricing practices in 38 British firms.[12] In this study, 30 firms indicated that they adhered to the full-cost principle of pricing, although only 12 firms indicated that it was a rigid policy. It is interesting to note that these 12 firms also differed in the way they estimated output for the purposes of calculating overhead costs. Some used a concept of full output while others took actual or forecasted output. The other 18 firms indicated that they adhered to full-cost pricing in principle, but that they would lower prices if business (or demand) was depressed. A great deal has been written on the subject since that study was published in 1939.[13]

These studies have been carried out in rayon, cotton, hosiery, wool, soap, and other industries. Based on these studies, full-cost pricing is acknowledged as valid by Silberston, although that opinion is qualified by many marginalist and behavioral exceptions. He concludes that although the initial procedure of

---

[10] Abraham D. H. Kaplan, Joel B. Dirlam, and Robert F. Lanzillotti, "Pricing Objectives of Large Companies," *American Economic Review,* vol. 48 (December 1958), pp. 921–940. See also Marshall R. Colberg, Pascomb R. Forbush, and Gilbert R. Whitaker, Jr., *Business Economics: Principles and Cases,* 4th ed. (Homewood, Ill.: Irwin, 1975), pp. 462–467, for a discussion on the cost-plus pricing techniques utilized by GM.

[11] See William W. Haynes, "Pricing Practices in Small Firms," *Southern Economic Journal,* vol. 30 (April 1964), pp. 315–324.

[12] Sir Robert L. Hall and Charles J. Hitch, "Price Theory and Business Behavior," *Oxford Economic Papers,* vol. 2 (May 1939), pp. 12–45.

[13] A survey of the literature can be found in Richard B. Heflebower, "Full Cost, Cost Changes, and Prices," in *Business Concentration and Price Policy* (Princeton, N.J.: Princeton University Press, 1955), pp. 361–396. Some recent developments are reviewed in Harvey Leibenstein, "A Branch of Economics Is Missing: Micro-Micro Theory," *Journal of Economics Literature,* vol. 17 (June 1979), pp. 477–502. Also see Aubrey Silberston, "Surveys of Applied Economics: Price Behaviour of Firms," *Economic Journal,* vol. 80 (September 1970), pp. 511–582.

calculating prices may start with an average cost calculation, this may quickly be modified to reflect market conditions.[14]

Cost-Plus Markups

Cost-plus markup pricing assumes that the firm looks only at average costs plus some profit markup in order to set price. Thus, one typically hears that price is set equal to average costs (however defined) plus some reasonable profit mark-up. One also hears cost-plus markup pricing being called average-cost pricing and full-cost pricing. The theory behind the latter term is that business decision makers arrive at their prices as a sum of "full cost" plus an allowance for profit at some assumed volume of output.

Distinguishing between Fixed and Variable Costs So-called full costs are made up in part of fixed costs. Average fixed costs vary inversely with volume. Thus, the derivation of a full-cost price requires using some normal or standard volume of production. Variable costs are assumed to remain constant per unit of output. When both average fixed costs and average variable costs are held constant, we need only add a profit margin. The result has been referred to as a "benchmark" price.

Problems with Markup, or Full-Cost, Pricing Even though markup pricing appears to be descriptively accurate and businesspeople say they use it,[15] it suffers from at least two theoretical problems specifically pointed out in Heflebower's survey article.

> The theory is a direct challenge to two tenets of generally accepted economic theory, i.e. (1) that demand as well as supply conditions, or costs, enter into price determination . . .; and (2) that the rational solution of all price problems requires the equating of *marginal* revenue and *marginal* cost.[16]

Furthermore, full-cost pricing has become an explanation for price rigidity since price is seldom varied because of changes in demand. According to Heflebower, "Once the price exists, all proponents of the cost-plus price theories agree that price will not be changed because volume rises or falls moderately, except when a rival decreases a price first."[17]

The Relationship between Price Elasticity of Demand and Markup Pricing Profit maximization requires that marginal cost equal marginal revenue in every

---

[14] Silberston, "Surveys of Applied Economics: Price Behaviour of Firms," p. 545.
[15] But see James S. Earley, "Marginal Policies of 'Excellently Managed' Companies," *American Economic Review*, vol. 46 (March 1956), pp. 44–70. Professor Earley finds that the more successful firms tend to behave marginally.
[16] Richard B. Heflebower, "Full Cost, Cost Changes, and Prices," in *Business Concentration and Price Policy*, 1955, p. 363.
[17] Ibid., p. 366.

instance. Using the formula for marginal revenue $MR = P(1 + 1/\eta)$, and if $MC = MR$ to maximize profits, it is necessary that

$$MC = P\left(1 + \frac{1}{\eta}\right) \tag{8-1}$$

Dividing both sides of Eq. (8-1) by $(1 + 1/\eta)$, we find that price equals

$$P = MC\left(\frac{1}{1 + 1/\eta}\right) \tag{8-2}$$

which becomes

$$P = MC\left(\frac{1}{\eta/\eta + 1/\eta}\right) = MC \frac{1}{([\eta + 1]/\eta)} \tag{8-3}$$

which becomes

$$P = MC\left(\frac{\eta}{\eta + 1}\right) \tag{8-4}$$

Now consider the case where there are constant returns to scale over a very wide range of output. With constant returns to scale, long-run average cost equals long-run marginal cost. We also know that LAC is the same as long-run variable cost (in the long run all costs are variable). Thus, Eq. (8-4) becomes

$$P = AVC\left(\frac{\eta}{\eta + 1}\right) \tag{8-5}$$

Assume, as an example, that $\eta = -4$. Using Eq. (8-5), we obtain

$$\text{Price} = AVC\left(\frac{-4}{-3}\right) = AVC(1.33\frac{1}{3}) \tag{8-6}$$

Hence, if $\eta = -4$, then price should be set equal to average costs plus a one-third markup. In other words, markup pricing, based on average costs, may be an attempt by a business to guess at the coefficient of price elasticity of demand.[18]

Table 8-1 shows the relationship of pricing by marginal methods and by rule of thumb. In most cases the difference between the two pricing systems is insignificant. The markup pricing model, therefore, can be a representation of the firm's "feel for the market." Cost-plus markup pricing empirically appears to be consistently directed toward long-run profit maximization. The problem with a study like the one undertaken by Hall and Hitch is that it presumes that

---

[18] See Lorie Tarshis, "Rule of Thumb Pricing Can Be Rational," in D. S. Watson, ed., *Price Theory in Action: A Book of Readings* (Boston: Houghton Mifflin, 1973).

TABLE 8-1
COMPARATIVE RESULTS OF PRICE DETERMINATION BY MARGINAL METHOD AND BY
RULE OF THUMB

When output is	Results of using marginal method if elasticity is 5		Results of using rule of thumb		
	Marginal cost is	Most profit-able price is	Variable cost is	Percentage allowance for over-head and profit is	Computed price is
10	100	125	100	25%	125
15	100	125	100	25%	125
20	100	125	100	25%	125
25	100	125	100	25%	125
30	100	125	100	25%	125
35	100	125	100	25%	125
40	100	125	100	25%	125
45	100	125	100	25%	125
50	110	137.50	105	30%	136.50
55	125	156.25	115	35%	155.25
60	150	187.50	130	45%	188.50

Source: Lorie Tarshis, *The Elements of Economics: An Introduction to the Theory of Price and Employment*
(Boston: Houghton Mifflin, 1947).

what firm decision makers say they are doing about pricing and what they are
actually doing are synonomous. At least one researcher has found that "what
businessmen formally say about their pricing and what they do about it are
often very different."[19]

Target Rate of Return

Target return pricing is a variant of full-cost or markup pricing. Under such a
system, price is set in relation to cost so as to provide a profit margin on the
product that yields a predetermined or "target" rate of return on the investment. In other words, the rate of return to sales is set to yield a specified or
desired rate of return on investment. The classic study on target return pricing
was carried out by Kaplan, Dirlam, and Lanzillotti.[20] The researchers found
that "target return on investment was probably the most commonly stressed
company pricing goal."[21] Lanzillotti indicated that the principal pricing goal of

[19] See article by Gilbert Burck, "The Myths and Realities of Corporate Pricing," *Fortune,* vol.
85 (April 1972), p. 88.
[20] Kaplan, Dirlam, and Lanzillotti, *Pricing in Big Business: A Case Approach*; and John M.
Blair, *Economic Concentration: Structure, Behavior and Public Policy* (New York: Harcourt
Brace Jovanovich, 1972). For an attack on the empirical support for target pricing in these studies,
see David Kamerschen, "The Return of Target Pricing?" *Journal of Business,* vol. 48 (April 1975),
pp. 242–252.
[21] Kaplan, Dirlam, and Lanzillotti, *Pricing in Big Business: A Case Approach*, p. 130.

TABLE 8-2
PRICING GOALS OF LARGE INDUSTRIAL CORPORATIONS

Company	Pricing goal (return on investment after taxes)	Actual rate of return 1953–1958	Collateral pricing goals
General Motors	20%	20.7%	Maintaining market share
U.S. Steel	8	8.4	Target market share Stable price Stable margin
Alcoa	10	9.5	"Promotive" policy on new products Price stabilization
Standard Oil	12	12.6	Maintaining market share Price stabilization
Du Pont	20	22.2	Charging what traffic will bear over long run
Average	14.6	15.1	

Source: R. F. Lanzillotti, "Pricing Objectives in Large Companies," *American Economic Review,* vol. 48 (December 1958), pp. 921–940. J. M. Blair, *Economic Concentration: Structure, Behavior, and Public Policy* (New York: Harcourt Brace Jovanovich, 1972), pp. 476, 483.

dominant oligopolists was that of securing a target return on investment. The average of the target returns mentioned was between 10 and 15 percent after taxes. We give some sample target rates of return on investment in Table 8-2, taken from a study by Lanzillotti.

Attainment of Target Returns   Table 8-2 also shows the target rates of return along with the actual rates of return for the period 1953 to 1968. Over the 16-year period studied, five firms met their profit objectives within less than 1 percentage point, except for Du Pont, which was 2.2 percentage points above its target rate of return.

Demand and Cost Approximation

One tactic considered by some economists[22] as a rule of thumb is used when

> . . . simple demand and cost curves are crudely fitted by quick and inexpensive methods to recently obtained data and, from these simple curves, an approximate profit function is derived and used to determine the price formula (rule of thumb) which maximizes the value of that approximative function.[23]

After running a series of simulations using this type of rule, Baumol and Quandt

[22] William J. Baumol and Richard E. Quandt, "Rules of Thumb and Optimally Imperfect Decisions," *American Economic Review,* vol. 54 (March 1964), pp. 23–46.

[23] Ibid., p. 27.

concluded that several versions of such rules work quite well in producing a price near the actual profit-maximizing price.

OTHER TACTICS

In the following sections, we will consider several tactics that oligopolists can undertake, either as part of their pricing structure or otherwise. We consider nonprice competition, conscious parallelism, focal point pricing, backlogs, and inventory changes.

Nonprice Competition

By their very nature, oligopolistic markets do not exhibit active price competition. Price wars do erupt occasionally, but these wars are seen to be an implicit indication that communication channels among firms in oligopolistic markets are temporarily disrupted. With the exception of the Edgeworth model, the usual prediction for an oligopolistic market is stable prices. Competition for an increased market share, therefore, must take on some other form. The alternative form is what is generally called nonprice competition. Nonprice competition cannot be neatly subdivided into only a few categories because it can encompass a large number of aspects. Nonprice competition is an attempt by one oligopolistic firm to attract customers by some means other than a price differential. Product differentiation takes on many forms, but we will consider only advertising and quality differentials.

Advertising   As we will see in the next chapter, the primary purpose of advertising is to shift the demand curve to the right. This shift allows the seller to sell more at each and every price. Advertising may also have the effect of differentiating the product and of making the product's availability better known. To go into a complete theory of advertising here would involve an analysis of the theory of information dissemination; we will not take this approach. Whatever can be said about advertising, its effects on the firm are certainly not completely predictable. Whether or not advertising in oligopolistic industries is beneficial to society as a whole is a question we cannot answer. Because advertising does exist, by assumption it is perceived to be beneficial by each of the firms engaging in it.

Quality Variations   Quality differentiation results in a division of one market into a number of submarkets. We mentioned product differentiation by quality differentials when we discussed monopolistic competition. A prime example of product differentiation is the automobile industry. There are specific, physically discernible differences between various automobile models within each firm. A General Motors Chevette and a General Motors Seville are certainly not identical. If we were to examine automobiles, we would see that competition among firms creates a continuous redefinition of the different models that are sold by any one company. There is competition among firms to create new-quality classes and thereby gain a competitive edge. Being the first in the market in a new-quality class has often meant higher profits, as illustrated by the phenomenal success of the original Mustang.

Conscious Parallelism

Section 1 of the Sherman Antitrust Act states, "Every contract, combination in the form of trust or otherwise, or conspiracy, in restraint of trade or commerce among the several states, or with foreign nations, is hereby declared to be illegal." The Sherman Act, therefore, does not expressly prohibit oligopolies, because there is no explicit contract or combination in restraint of trade. When there is collusion, as occurred among the big electrical companies in 1960, then a violation of the law is clear.

When a few sellers in an oligopoly appear to be acting in concert but no evidence of overt collusion exists, the resulting pricing practice is termed **conscious parallelism**. Such pricing policies are the result of the recognized interdependence of oligopolists. Each oligopolist knows that other oligopolists will react to a change in his or her price. The result presumably is a tendency to avoid vigorous price competition. The question that has come before the courts is whether or not such "conscious parallelism," a result of oligopolistic interdependence, can properly be viewed as a form of agreement to fix prices in violation of section 1 of the Sherman Antitrust Act. In a famous case argued before the Supreme Court, *Theater Enterprises, Inc. v. Paramount Film Distributing Corporation*,[24] Justice Clark, speaking for the Court, noted,

> . . . this court has never held that proof of parallel business behavior conclusively established agreement or, phrased differently, that such behavior itself constitutes a Sherman Act offense. Circumstantial evidence of consciously parallel behavior may have made heavy in-roads into the traditional judicial attitude toward conspiracy; but "conscious parallelism" has not yet read conspiracy out of the Sherman Act entirely.

In an important article, former Assistant U.S. Attorney General Donald F. Turner contended that, although oligopolistic pricing behavior was similar in nature to competitive pricing behavior, rivals' responses had to be taken into account.[25] Moreover, Turner pointed out that no remedy is effective for oligopolistic interdependence. A court injunction prohibiting each defendant "from taking into account the probable price decisions of his competitors in determining his own price or output would demand such irrational behavior that full compliance would be virtually impossible." Turner further pointed out that a court injunction would have to require the defendants to reduce price to marginal cost and that the enforcement of such a decree would involve the

---

[24] 346 U.S. 537, 74 Sup. Ct. 257, 98 L. Ed. 273 (1954).
[25] Donald F. Turner, "The Definition of Agreement under the Sherman Act: Conscious Parallelism and Refusals to Deal," *Harvard Law Review*, vol. 75 (1962), pp. 655ff.

courts in public utility types of rate regulation for all oligopolists in the United States.

Turner, therefore, would eliminate the use of section 1 of the Sherman Act to prosecute oligopolists. Rather, he suggested as an appropriate remedy breaking oligopolistic firms into smaller units either by special legislation or under section 2 of the Sherman Act, which prohibits monopolization or attempts to monopolize. Turner thought it was appropriate to charge oligopolists with jointly monopolizing their market.

Not all legal scholars agree with Turner's conclusions. Richard Posner, for example, points out that oligopoly is a necessary condition of successful price fixing, but not a sufficient condition. He contends that there is no vital difference between formal cartels and tacit collusive agreements; the latter are simply easier to conceal. According to Posner, if section 1 of the Sherman Act is to deter collusion by increasing the cost of colluding, then the tacit, as well as the overt, colluder should be punished equally.

Posner does point out that the most serious problem with his suggestion to apply section 1 against tacit collusion is proving that the collusion exists.[26]

Inventories, Backlogs, and Oligopolistic Coordination

Oligopolists attempting to make rational decisions face uncertainties in predicting future costs and demand conditions. They must guess about the future, particularly about market demand and about their rivals' reactions, as described in Chapter 6. Inaccurate estimates of both rival reactions and demand curves (positions and elasticity) are bound to be made by individual firms and by the industry taken as a whole. Presume for a moment that all firms in an industry are overoptimistic. Will they have to reduce prices dramatically? Not necessarily, if we take into account that firms are not required to sell all they produce at the end of any given time period. They can build up inventories when they are overoptimistic. This is their compensating mechanism for production-scheduling errors. When they underestimate future demand, they can draw down inventories. Alternatively, they can allow fluctuations in their unfilled order backlogs. In fact, by monitoring the change in finished goods inventories and in order backlogs, business decision makers can use the information to update constantly their estimate of the location and elasticity of the demand curve. One researcher even believes that "the additional degrees of freedom provided by inventories and order backlogs rescue the kinked demand curve theory from oblivion in the real world of uncertainty."[27] But even without looking at the kinked demand curve that predicts price stability, we can state that order backlogs and finished-good inventories allow us to reconcile the implications of standard textbook static-price-theory predictions with reality.

[26] Richard A. Posner, "Oligopoly and the Antitrust Laws: A Suggested Approach," *Stanford Law Review,* vol. 21 (1969), pp. 1562–1576, 1591–1592.
[27] Frederic M. Scherer, *Industrial Market Structure and Economic Performance* (Chicago: Rand McNally, 1971), p. 150.

Assume for the moment that all oligopolists independently equate marginal costs with estimated marginal revenue. There is a high probability that the total quantity of output supplied in the industry will not be equal to the quantity demanded during the time period under study, mainly because future demand conditions are uncertain. The consequence according to static price theory would be disequilibrium leading to unstable prices and perhaps price warfare. We do not observe this happening in most oligopolistic industries, perhaps because standard textbook theory leaves out the important variables of inventory and order backlogs.

Backlogs and Inventories Contribute to Orderly Oligopoly Pricing   Assuming no conflict between industry members over output pricing policies, individual firms will make their output decisions for the next period by equating marginal cost and estimated marginal revenue. If a mistake occurs, the first reaction will be to change inventories or order backlogs, as opposed to cutting price to clear the market when there is an oversupply or to raising price when there is an undersupply. The changes in backlogs and inventories, in addition to new orders, will be used by the oligopolist to project future demand and to adjust future output and pricing decisions. Thus, we say that backlogs and inventories are both a buffer to compensate for incorrect production decisions and a feedback signal to allow for future appropriate adjustments in production to meet actual demand.

We do not mean to say that oligopolists will never change price. Assume for a moment that they have overestimated demand. At some point, their inventory becomes nonoptimal, for too large an inventory creates excessive storage deterioration and opportunity cost.[28] On the other hand, if they underestimated demand, they will not necessarily draw their inventories down completely, for too little an inventory results in the loss of sales when items are out of stock. The same can be said for backlogs.[29] Hence, we expect to see some cuts in prices by oligopolists when inventory levels climb sharply or backlogs fall sharply. Conversely, we expect to see some price increases when inventory levels drop sharply or backlogs increase dramatically. Basically, all we can say is that oligopolists attempting to cooperate tacitly or explicitly with one another to maximize joint profits will allow changes in inventories and backlogs to reduce the amount and frequency of price adjustments. Note that this incentive to avoid price adjustments is absent in a purely competitive industry with numerous firms. Hence, one prediction of this model is that oligopolistic industries will rely more heavily than atomistic industries on backlog and inventory variations to adjust to demand fluctuations and less heavily on price changes. A

[28] Theoretically an optimal level of inventory relative to sales should exist. See George A. Hay, "Production, Price, and Inventory Theory," *American Economic Review,* vol. 60 (September 1970), pp. 531–545; and "The Dynamics of Firm Behavior under Alternative Cost Structures," *American Economic Review,* vol. 62 (June 1972), pp. 403–413.

[29] M. D. Steuer, R. J. Ball, and J. R. Eaton, "The Effect of Waiting Times on Foreign Orders for Machine Tools," *Economica,* vol. 33 (November 1966), pp. 387–403.

limited amount of empirical testing has been done on this subject. Scherer claims that the more concentrated the industries in his study were, the more variable over time their inventories were relative to sales.[30]

A more recent model has been developed to explain variation in buffer stocks based on excess production capacity, finished good and other inventories, and liquid financial assets, as well as nonprice competition in oligopolistic industries. Caves, Jarrett, and Loucks have tested for the effects of these variables among 35 U.S. manufacturing industries and have found partial verification for the complementarity and substitutability properties of buffer stocks.[31]

The Inverse Relationship between Variability of Backlogs and Price Variability

An implication of the above hypothesis is that the greater the variability in order backlogs is, the less the variability in prices will be. This seems to be particularly true in the durable goods industry. A study by Zarnowitz showed that the more variable the ratio of order backlogs to sales were, the less variable prices were.[32] His results, as well as those of Scherer, lend support to the hypothesis that oligopolists use order backlog variations rather than price adjustments to adapt to demand changes, particularly in the short run.

Inverse Relationship between Inventory Variability and Price Variability

Numerous studies have been undertaken to show the relationship between inventory variability and price variability. Our hypothesis predicts that the greater the variability of inventories is, the less the variability of prices will be. A number of studies have attempted to support this hypothesis. Markham found that short-run fluctuations in demand in the rayon industry before 1950 were usually absorbed through inventory variations rather than through price variations or production rate adjustments.[33] Sales declined for several months before production rates were reduced and continued to decline for months before prices were changed.

In the gasoline industry, price wars continue despite large inventories of

---

[30] Scherer, *Industrial Market Structure and Economic Performance*, p. 154.

[31] Richard E. Caves, Joffrey P. Jarrett, and M. K. Loucks, "Competitive Conditions and the Firm's Buffer Stocks: An Exploratory Analysis," *Review of Economics and Statistics,* vol. 61 (November 1979), pp. 485–496.

[32] Victor Zarnowitz, "Unfilled Orders, Price Changes, and Business Fluctuations," *Review of Economics and Statistics,* vol. 44 (November 1962), pp. 367–394.

[33] Jesse W. Markham, *Competition in the Rayon Industry* (Cambridge, Mass.: Harvard University Press, 1952).

gasoline in local markets.[34] In large retail department stores, price variations are used in order to keep inventories from rising too rapidly.[35]

Cost Minimization and Inventory Adjustment

The ability of an oligopolistic industry to maintain a stable price structure that maximizes joint profits seems to depend upon backlog and inventory policies. Variations in backlogs and inventories allow producers to adjust to demand shifts in the short run, thereby minimizing any threat to presumed industry-pricing discipline. Backlog and inventory changes also provide informational feedback.

CONCLUSIONS

In this chapter we have found that decision makers in profit-maximizing firms employ a number of rules for pricing their products. In general, we found that these pricing policies are roughly equivalent to the traditional marginal revenue equals marginal cost condition for profit maximization. Thus, although the rules of thumb that are used by business decision makers often appear to be irrational, they may actually yield the highest level of profits, given information and other transaction costs.

[34] See Richard H. Holton, "Antitrust Policy and Small Business," in A. Phillips, ed., *Perspectives on Antitrust Policy* (Princeton, N.J.: Princeton University Press, 1965), pp. 189–224.
[35] Richard M. Cyert and James G. March, *A Behavioral Theory of the Firm* (Englewood Cliffs, N.J.: Prentice-Hall, 1963), p. 140.

CHAPTER 9

ADVERTISING, PRODUCT DIFFERENTIATION, AND TRADEMARKS

We have already referred to advertising and product differentiation when discussing specific market structures such as oligopoly and monopolistic competition. In this chapter, we will look into these topics in detail. In addition, we will discuss the role of trademarks in industrial organization.

THE SCOPE OF ADVERTISING

In 1985, advertising expenditures are expected to be $92.5 billion. Given an estimated gross national product (GNP) of $4.0 trillion, advertising costs amount to 2.3 percent of the total value of output in the United States. It is interesting to compare 1985's estimate with expenditures of selected years in the past. For example, in 1929, GNP was $103.1 billion and advertising was $2.6 billion; thus, advertising represented 2.52 percent of GNP. Four years later, during the depth of the Great Depression, GNP was $55.6 billion and advertising $1.4 billion; again constituting 2.52 percent. In nominal dollar terms, this seems a tremendous amount of resources to spend on advertising. Today, the percent of GNP spent on advertising appears actually to have declined or at least not to have risen significantly. In Table 9-1 we present advertising outlays in different media, both on the national and the local level. In Table 9-2 we show advertising estimates for separate industries.

TABLE 9-1

ADVERTISING—ESTIMATED EXPENDITURES BY MEDIUM: 1965 TO 1977

Medium	1965		1970		1975		1978, prel.	
	Ex-pend-itures	Per-cent of total	Ex-pend-itures	Per-cent of total	Ex-pend-itures	Per-cent of total	Ex-pend-itures	Per-cent of total
Total	**15,250**	**100.0**	**19,550**	**100.0**	**28,230**	**100.0**	**43,740**	**100.0**
National	9,340	61.2	11,350	58.1	15,410	54.6	24,045	55.0
Local	5,910	38.8	8,200	41.9	12,820	45.4	19,695	45.0
Newspapers	4,426	29.0	5,704	29.2	8,442	29.9	12,690	29.0
National	784	5.1	891	4.6	1,221	4.3	1,810	4.1
Local	3,642	23.9	4,813	24.6	7,221	25.6	10,880	24.9
Magazines	1,161	7.6	1,292	6.6	1,465	5.2	2,595	5.9
Weeklies	610	4.0	617	3.2	612	2.2	1,165	2.7
Women's	269	1.8	301	1.5	368	1.3	670	1.5
Monthlies	282	1.8	374	1.9	485	1.7	760	1.7
Farm publications	71	.5	62	.3	74	.3	105	.2
Television	2,515	16.5	3,596	18.4	5,263	18.6	8,850	20.2
Network	1,237	8.1	1,658	8.5	2,306	8.2	3,910	8.9
Spot	892	5.9	1,234	6.3	1,623	5.7	2,600	5.9
Local	386	2.5	704	3.6	1,334	4.7	2,340	5.4
Radio	917	6.0	1,308	6.7	1,980	7.0	2,955	6.8
Network	60	.4	56	.3	83	.3	160	.4
Spot	275	1.8	371	1.9	436	1.5	610	1.4
Local	582	3.8	881	4.5	1,461	5.2	2,185	5.0
Direct mail	2,324	15.2	2,766	14.1	4,181	14.8	6,030	13.8
Business papers	671	4.4	740	3.8	919	3.3	1,420	3.3
Outdoor	180	1.2	234	1.2	335	1.2	465	1.1
National	120	.8	154	.8	220	.8	310	.7
Local	60	.4	80	.4	115	.4	155	.4
Miscellaneous	2,985	19.6	3,848	19.7	5,571	19.7	8,630	19.7
National	1,745	11.5	2,126	10.9	2,882	10.2	4,495	10.3
Local	1,240	8.1	1,722	8.8	2,689	9.5	4,135	9.4

Source: McCann-Erickson Advertising Agency, Inc., New York, N.Y. Compiled for Crain Communications, Inc. In *Advertising Age* (copyright). Percentages derived by U.S. Bureau of the Census. Reprinted from *Statistical Abstract of the U.S., 1979,* p. 595.

Media Support

Advertising has been a boon to the media. Revenues from the sale of advertising space have accounted for a majority of the gross revenues of newspaper and general periodicals. Furthermore, excluding public educational stations, nearly all the revenues of television and radio stations are derived from advertising sales.[1]

---

[1] U.S. Bureau of the Census, *Statistical Abstract of the United States: 1979* (Washington, D.C.: Government Printing Office, 1979), p. 586.

TABLE 9-2
ACTIVE CORPORATION EXPENDITURES FOR ADVERTISING, COMPARED WITH
RECEIPTS, BY INDUSTRY: 1974

Industry	Total receipts (bil. dol.)	Advertising expenditures		Industry	Total receipts (bil. dol.)	Advertising expenditures	
		Total (mil. dol.)	Percent of receipts			Total (mil. dol.)	Percent of receipts
Total	3,089.7	24,640	.8	Manufacturing Motor veh. and			
Agriculture, forestry[a]	25.5	67	.3	equipment	105.7	627	.6
Mining	64.8	33	.1	Transportation			
Construction	137.0	292	.2	equipment[d]	41.8	132	.3
Manufacturing[b]	1,297.3	11,649	.9	Instruments and			
Food and kindred				products[e]	21.1	420	2.0
products	158.1	2,909	1.8	Transportation and			
Tobacco				public utilities[f]	222.1	799	.4
manufacturers	13.5	495	3.7	Transportation	97.1	459	.5
Textile mill prod.	31.1	212	.7	Wholesale and retail			
Apparel, textile				trade	923.4	8,040	.9
products	30.6	212	.7	Wholesale trade	499.3	1,643	.3
Lumber and wood				Retail trade[b]	423.9	6,396	1.5
products	31.4	113	.4	Food stores	97.8	853	.9
Furniture and fixtures	10.3	94	.9	General merch.			
Paper and allied				stores	83.1	2,112	2.5
products	35.7	200	.6	Apparel, acces			
Printing, publishing	37.4	302	.8	sory stores	20.8	444	2.1
Chemicals, allied				Auto dealers[g]	96.9	776	.8
products	96.7	2,802	2.9	Finance, insurance,			
Petroleum, coal				and real estate[b]	303.2	2,242	.7
products	274.6	274	.1	Banking	90.5	728	.8
Rubber, plastics				Insurance	120.8	397	.3
products	25.1	255	1.0	Real estate	25.7	454	1.8
Leather, leather				Services[b]	115.6	1,496	1.3
products	7.7	83	1.1	Hotels, other lodging	9.1	186	2.0
Stone, clay, glass				Personal services	8.3	124	1.5
products	27.1	147	.5	Business services	35.1	429	1.2
Primary metal				Auto., other repair			
industries	92.5	168	.2	services	12.2	111	.9
Fabricated metal				Motion pictures	7.8	261	3.3
products[c]	60.2	354	.6	Amusement, recre			
Machinery, exc.				ation services[h]	7.7	157	2.0
electric	94.7	632	.7	Not allocable	1.0	21	2.3
Electric, electronic							
equipment	83.6	848	1.0				

[a]Includes fishing. [b]Includes other industries, not shown separately. [c]Includes ordnance; excludes machinery and transportation equipment. [d]Excludes motor vehicles. [e]Includes watches and clocks. [f]Comprises transportation, communications, and electric, gas, and sanitary services. [g]Includes gasoline service stations. [h]Excludes motion pictures.

Source: U.S. Internal Revenue Service, Statistics of Income, 1974, Corporation Income Tax Returns. Reprinted from Statistical Abstract of the U.S., 1978, p. 857.

THE OPTIMAL RATE OF ADVERTISING

Advertising may be considered a form of nonprice competition or behavior by firms other than a perfect competitor. We have talked about advertising expenditures, assuming, of course, that any level of expenditures is optimally allocated. In what follows, we present the Dorfman-Steiner rule for the optimal rate of advertising by the firm.[2]

Diminishing Marginal Returns

Let's start off our discussion by assuming that advertising expenditures have diminishing marginal returns.[3] This would seem to make sense. The firm would exploit its best potential markets first, and would find its attempts to exploit successive markets less productive. Within any particular market, successive increments of advertising should at some point be less productive, since some of the advertising messages will fall on those who have already seen the advertising and have either accepted or rejected the notion of purchasing the advertised product or service.

The Optimal Level to Maximize Profits

As always, we will invoke our familiar marginal benefits equals marginal cost rule to find the profit-maximizing rate of advertising. When the firm increases its expenditures on advertising, that increment will be marginal cost. The benefit will be the increase (if any) in profit. We assume for the moment that neither the price of the final product nor the marginal production cost of the good changes as we increase advertising expenditures by a small amount. The increase in profit resulting from a small increase in advertising expenditures will be equal to the increase in quantity sold times the per-unit profits. Algebraically, then, the profit-maximizing firm should increase advertising expenditures to the point where

$$\Delta A = \Delta q(P - \text{MC}_{\text{production}}) \tag{9-1}$$

The left-hand side of Eq. (9-1) is the marginal cost of increasing advertising expenditures; the right-hand side is equal to the per-unit profit $(P - \text{MC}_{\text{production}})$ times the increased quantity Δq sold as a result of ΔA additional advertising. If we divide both sides of Eq. (9-1) by Δq, we obtain

$$\frac{\Delta A}{\Delta q} = P - \text{MC}_{\text{production}} \tag{9-2}$$

---

[2] This analysis is based on Robert Dorfman and Peter O. Steiner, "Optimal Advertising and Optimal Quality," *American Economic Review*, vol. 44 (December 1954), pp. 826–836.

[3] Robert O. Buzzell et al., *Marketing: A Contemporary Analysis* (New York: McGraw-Hill, 1972), pp. 533–534, and Ambarb G. Rao and Peter B. Miller, "Advertising/Sales Response Functions," *Journal of Advertising Research*, vol. 15 (April 1975), pp. 7–15. Initially the absence of setup costs for subsequent advertising and the value of repetitive exposure may yield increasing returns over some range of activity.

If we take the reciprocal of this equation and multiply through by P, we obtain

$$\frac{P\Delta q}{\Delta A} = \frac{P}{P - MC_{production}} \tag{9-3}$$

The numerator of the left-hand side of Eq. (9-3) is equal to the revenues obtained from additional sales when advertising expenditures are increased. Therefore, the left-hand side of Eq. (9-3) is equal to the marginal revenue resulting from an additional dollar spent on advertising. The right-hand side of Eq. (9-3) is equal to the numerical value (absolute value) of the price elasticity of demand. This follows from the relationship between marginal revenue, price, and price elasticity of demand.

$$MR = P\left(1 + \frac{1}{\eta}\right) \tag{9-4}$$

Now we wish to deal with the absolute value of the price elasticity of demand so that this becomes

$$MR = P\left(1 - \frac{1}{|\eta|}\right) \tag{9-5}$$

Finally, after rearranging Eq. (9-5), we obtain

$$|\eta| = \frac{P}{P - MR} \tag{9-6}$$

Substituting $MC_{production}$ for MR (the profit-maximizing condition) we obtain

$$MC = P - \frac{P}{|\eta|}$$

$$\frac{P}{|\eta|} = P - MC$$

$$\frac{|\eta|}{P} = \frac{1}{P - MC} \tag{9-7}$$

$$|\eta| = \frac{P}{P - MC}$$

Thus, we have the profit-maximizing optimum for the individual firm, which is

$$\frac{\text{MR from last dollar}}{\text{spent on advertising}} = \frac{P}{P - MC} = |\eta| \tag{9-8}$$

The marginal revenue due to an additional dollar spent on advertising is declining; thus, the firm will increase advertising expenditures more when the ratio $P/(P - MC)$ and the absolute price elasticity of demand are both smaller.[4] We can interpret this rule as follows: Numerically low price elasticities of demand invite higher advertising outlays; numerically high price elasticities of demand invite smaller amounts of advertising. This is true because we are operating in the region of diminishing marginal returns from advertising.

The Effects of Advertising on Demand and Cost Curves

The Dorfman-Steiner condition presented above shows that the optimal advertising-sales ratio is dependent upon the amount of advertising and upon price elasticities of demand for the firm's product, thus demonstrating the interdependence between price and nonprice decisions. The optimal level of a firm's advertising also depends on the advertising and price reactions of rival sellers. Each firm must take into account, particularly in oligopoly situations, what other firms will do. What we will try to demonstrate here is the interdependence between a firm's advertising levels and price and the necessity of the joint determination of the optimal levels of these variables. In Figure 9-1 we attempt to show the simultaneous determination of output price and advertising level. Three demand curves are shown, d_1d_1, d_2d_2, and d_3d_3. With each of these demand curves is shown an average total cost curve labeled ATC_1, ATC_2, and ATC_3. The assumption here is that the expenditure on advertising leads to an outward shift in the demand curve. There is no advertising with d_1d_1, but there is an increasing amount of advertising that generates the cost curves ATC_2 and ATC_3, resulting in a shift in the demand curve to d_2d_2 and then d_3d_3.

[4] Rao and Miller, "Advertising/Sales Response Functions."

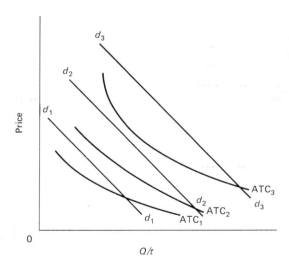

FIGURE 9-1
Interdependence of advertising outlays and demand. Each demand curve d_id_i is drawn with an associated level of advertising. The curve d_id_i has no advertising, and ATC_1 represents production costs. Demand curves d_2d_2 and d_3d_3 have increasing amounts of advertising and costs (ATC_2 and ATC_3).

Note that there is a definite relationship between the different average total cost curves. ATC_2 is obtained by adding a fixed amount of advertising. To do so, one needs essentially to add the rectangular hyperbola derived from dividing different quantities of output into this fixed amount of advertising. In other words, the curve of average advertising costs is considered to be a rectangular hyperbola because we are assuming a fixed dollar amount of advertising in each of the two separate cases that generate ATC_2 and ATC_3.

Determining Maximum Profits.   In order for the firm to determine the optimal level of advertising and price, it must compare the maximum profits associated with each pair of demand and cost curves. This search process requires looking at total revenue = total cost, including advertising costs for each of the three possibilities given in Figure 9-1. We have not drawn in marginal revenue and marginal cost curves in that diagram, but clearly the firm must set hypothetical output rates at each of the intersections for marginal revenue and marginal cost, estimate what price could be charged in each case, and then decide which price and advertising outlay combination generated maximum profits.[5]

THE FUNCTION OF ADVERTISING

Advertising serves many functions, some of which we have already discussed. It may be informative, giving information on prices, quality, availability of products, service warranties, and so on. Advertising may merely provide information to consumers about the existence of a product or of an individual firm in a certain geographical area. However, advertising is also sometimes seen as a barrier to entry that leads to higher concentration ratios, a topic which we discuss below. Many critics of advertising point out a vast amount of advertising that they consider noninformative. Indeed, a significant portion of all advertising consists simply of catchy statements about products. No one will contend that "Pepsi hits the spot" offers any useful information to the consumer. We have already mentioned that some advertising merely informs consumers about the existence of a product or service. For example, outdoor advertising in the form of billboards and signs on buildings may indicate no more than the existence of a firm that offers a particular product or service. Nonetheless, such information is not necessarily useless, even though it may appear so at first glance. Consider the "usefulness" of signs that merely indicate that one can purchase banking services from a particular bank at a particular location. The advertising may consist of the bank's name in large letters on the bank building itself or the bank's name and address on a large billboard. To those consumers who have lived for some time in the geographical area, this information may appear trivial, but to the newcomer it is not trivial. This low-cost information on the mere existence and geographical location of the bank may at some time be useful to some people.

[5] Norman S. Buchanan, "Advertising Expenditures: A Suggested Treatment," *Journal of Political Economy,* vol. 50 (August 1942), pp. 537–557, reprinted in W. Breit and H. Hochman, eds., *Readings in Microeconomics* (New York: Holt, Rinehart, and Winston, 1968).

To make the point more obvious, consider an experiment in which all new-comers to a city would not be permitted to see any forms of outdoor advertising, including signs on buildings. Clearly, the search cost involved in discovering what services and products are available and where they are located would be much greater.

Search versus Experience Goods

Nelson has argued that there are two types of goods: search goods and experience goods.[6] **Search goods** are those whose qualities can be checked out before purchase. A consumer who wants to buy a suit or a dress can, if desired, go to the store advertising the product and check out its qualities before purchasing it. In such cases, an advertiser would be foolish to include inaccurate information in advertising the product. It is too easy for the consumer to detect the fraudulent advertisement.

Experience goods are those about which it is quite difficult to ascertain the quality before purchase. If a new soft drink comes on the market, it is difficult for the consumer to know how it will taste before buying it. One can usually not tell about the quality of experience goods, like soap, deodorant, toothpaste, and alcoholic beverages, by reading a label, or by looking at the shape of the can or tube, or by looking at its contents.

We find that virtually no direct information is given in the advertisement for so-called experience goods. "Drink the Uncola" does indicate that Seven-Up is not cola, but few consumers believe that it is anyway. Nevertheless, consumers obtain *indirect* information from such ads. The information obtained concerns the fact that the product is on the market. The seller who is advertising an experience good is indicating that he or she believes the good is of high quality and worth the consumer's dollar. The argument according to Nelson goes as follows: It would be financially disastrous for a firm to heavily advertise an inferior "experience" good. In the advertising on television and billboards, a visual image is presented that creates the desired strong association between a function and a brand name. One associates washing clothing with Tide or drinking soft drinks with Pepsi-Cola. What would happen if the advertised product actually turned out to be grossly inferior to other products? The consumer would be reminded over and over again on billboards and on television of the name of the inferior product. After the initial purchase, that particular brand would never be purchased again. Thus, heavily advertised experience goods must, by necessity, be higher-quality, according to Nelson, for otherwise the advertising would insure a rapid death in the product market. Firms live or die by repeat sales (sometimes called the law of continuous dealing), and by sales expansion. Noninformative billboard and television ads are a way to get

---

[6] Philip Nelson, "Information and Consumer Behavior," *Journal of Political Economy,* vol. 78 (March/April 1970), pp. 311–329. Also see Richard H. Holton, "Consumer Behavior, Market Imperfections, and Public Policy," in Jesse W. Markham and Gustav F. Papanek, eds., *Industrial Organization and Economic Development: Essays in Honor of E. S. Mason* (Boston: Houghton Mifflin, 1970), pp. 102–115.

consumers to try the advertisers' goods. They are also a way to indicate that the heavily advertised brand *does* yield a higher quality per dollar spent as compared to a nonadvertised brand. Empirically, it does appear that within any one product category, the more heavily advertised brands are of higher average quality and are more uniform than less-advertised brands are.[7] Basically, firms advertise winners rather than losers. Nelson's conclusion is that consumers are better off staying with highly advertised experience goods than changing to unadvertised ones. Nelson also finds that search goods are less heavily advertised than experience goods.[8]

Comanor and Wilson, however, present additional reasons for advertising that are inconsistent with Nelson's conclusion that higher-valued products will be more heavily advertised. Their argument rests on the difference among products that depend on individual taste rankings. No nonarbitrary way of judging experience goods exists to prove that one product is higher in quality than another. In such situations, advertising may accentuate the difference in preferences for particular brands, while the service characteristics remain relatively similar. Comanor and Wilson also argue that firms with lower quality goods may find it advantageous to advertise more to offset quality differences.[9]

Quality and Advertising Exceptions

A number of firms with high-quality products spend little on advertising. The Hershey Company, for example, did not advertise its products in the media for an extended period of time. Other firms, such as IBM, have created a high-quality image for their products without spending significant sums on advertising.[10]

Credence Qualities

Darby and Karni refer to credence qualities as those that are worthwhile but cannot be evaluated in normal use.[11] Any assessment of the value of credence qualities would require additional costly information. The authors use the rather unpleasant example of the claimed advantages of an appendix removal. The claimed advantages will be correct only if the organ is diseased. Discovering the existence and extent of disease, however, often requires costly tests or surgery.

---

[7] Federal Trade Commission, *Chain Stores: Quality of Canned Fruits and Vegetables,* 1933. See also Sharon Oster, "The Determinants of Consumer Complaints," *Review of Economics and Statistics,* vol. 62 (November 1980), pp. 603-609.

[8] Phillip Nelson, "Advertising as Information," *Journal of Political Economy,* vol. 82 (July/August 1974), pp. 729-754.

[9] William S. Comanor and Thomas A. Wilson, "The Effect of Advertising on Competition: A Survey," *Journal of Economic Literature,* vol. 17 (June 1979), pp. 453-476.

[10] Brian T. Ratchford and Gary T. Ford, "A Study of Prices and Market Shares in the Computer Mainframe Industry," *Journal of Business,* vol. 49 (April 1976), pp. 194-218.

[11] Michael R. Darby and Edi Karni, "Free Competition and the Optimal Amount of Fraud," *Journal of Law and Economics,* vol. 16 (April 1973), pp. 67-88.

The trichotomy these authors wish to use is (1) search qualities that are known before purchase, (2) experience qualities that are known without much cost only after purchase, and (3) credence qualities that are very costly to judge even after purchase. They use as their prime example repair services for such diverse subjects as television sets, electronic equipment, and, as above, the human body. The consumer who purchases services from a repair person is purchasing not only repair services, but also information. It is cheaper for the producer to provide information and service jointly rather than separately. Clearly, if the consumer were able to check the information without cost, the opportunity for a repair person to engage in fraud would be eliminated. However, as Darby and Karni point out, even when the consumer is totally ignorant and has no way to verify the information provided by the repair person, the maximum extent of fraud is limited to the price differential between the used durable good and a new good (except in the case of the human body).

MISLEADING ADVERTISING

We will use the term "misleading advertising" to include advertising which is deliberately false or which causes the consumer to form a mistaken interpretation about the nature of the product. It will not apply to advertising that attempts to persuade the consumer to prefer one product over others that are similar or that offer little or no product differentiation.[12]

Thus, misleading advertising would include the misrepresentation of facts including a claim of superior characteristics when none exist or failure to disclose important facts. Informed consumers are aware, of course, that misleading advertising exists, and some have definite opinions about trends in the degree of misleading advertising. A 1971 poll of 2,700 subscribers to the *Harvard Business Review* revealed that 32 percent of the respondents believed that a larger proportion of ads contained "invalid or misleading claims" when compared to ads 10 years earlier. Approximately 38 percent felt that the proportion of misleading ads was smaller in modern advertising than it had been 10 years earlier.[13]

Another form of misleading or false advertising involves a practice called "bait and switch." A bait-and-switch situation occurs when a sale-priced advertised good is unavailable at the store and when the available substitutes are lower in quality or higher in price. The Federal Trade Commission places bait-and-switch tactics at the top of its list of common fraudulent advertising practices. Attempts to deal with misleading advertising have produced a number of laws and statutes that govern the content and substantiation of advertising claims. Under common law, proof that an advertiser had actual knowledge or should reasonably have had knowledge of the falsity of an ad was

[12] See Charles E. Mueller, "Sources of Monopoly Power: A Phenomenon Called Product Differentiation," *Antitrust Law and Economics Review*, vol. 2 (Summer 1969), pp. 59–96.

[13] Stephen A. Greyser and Bonnie B. Reece, "Businessmen Look Hard at Advertising," *Harvard Business Review*, vol. 49 (May/June 1971), pp. 18–26.

required in a misleading advertisement suit. The 1938 Wheeler-Lea Amendment to the Federal Trade Commission Act gave the commission the right to institute suits against false advertising. Since then the FTC has instituted advertising substantiation programs and corrective advertising requirements. One of the first cases involved Profile bread advertisements that promoted its product's weight-reducing qualities, when in fact the bread was simply sliced thinner than other breads and therefore provided fewer calories in each slice.

Comanor and Wilson have argued that there should be more objective information from sources other than the sellers.[14] Explicitly they recommend that information evaluating the qualities of competing products should be encouraged. They also argue that government regulations should be imposed to require standardization of consumer information, limits on the volume of advertising expenditures, and increased postal rates for second- and third-class mail, which are used primarily for advertisements.

THE EFFECTS OF ADVERTISING ON PRICES

A large number of studies have shown a strong positional relationship between higher volumes of advertising and higher prices. For example, the National Committee on Food Marketing issued a report stating that food prices are 4 to 35 percent higher on nationally advertised goods than on local or private-brand goods.[15] Numerous studies have also shown that advertised prescription drugs sell at a premium relative to their unadvertised generic equivalents.[16]

The Relationship of Advertising to Price

The relationship between advertising and price depends on both demand and cost conditions. If advertising is successful, quantity sold increases. With scale economies, average total cost may fall with increased quantity, resulting in outputs that are sold at lower prices.[17] We show the possibility of price being reduced through advertising and lower average total costs in Figure 9-2. Assume in the first instance that there is no advertising. The firm faces demand curve DD and average total cost curve ATC. Assume that the long-run monopolistically competitive solution is attained; zero economic profits are being made. Therefore, the quantity sold will be q_1 and the price will equal P_1. Now advertising is utilized. It is successful, shifting the demand curve to $D'D'$. Average total costs shift to ATC'. The tangency of ATC' to $D'D'$ is such that quantity now produced in q_2 is sold at a price of P_2, which is less than P_1. In this

---

[14] William S. Comanor and Thomas A. Wilson, *Advertising and Market Power* (Cambridge, Mass.: Harvard University Press, 1974).

[15] U.S. National Commission on Food Marketing, *Special Studies in Food Marketing*, Special Study #10 (Washington, D.C.: U.S. Government Printing Office, 1966), p. 65.

[16] See, for example, Subcommittee on Monopoly, Select Committee on Small Business, U.S. Senate, 92nd Cong., 1st Sess., *Advertising and Proprietary Medicines* (Washington, D.C.: U.S. Government Printing Office, 1971). The generic substitutes are active chemical equivalents, not therapeutic equivalents.

[17] Better information may also reduce the variance of prices to consumers.

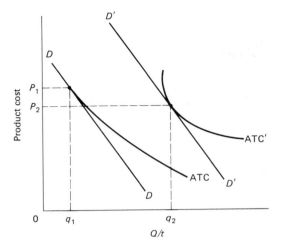

FIGURE 9-2
Relationships of advertising to price.
Advertising increases total costs to
ATC', but increases demand to DD' by
an amount sufficient to realize
economies of scale at higher rates of
output. Thus at q_2 with lower costs,
prices can be lower.

hypothetical example, increased advertising has led to increased sales and to sufficiently lower unit production costs to allow for a lower price.

The above argument is valid only if the total industry demand for the advertised product has increased or if some firms exit from the industry. If advertising merely increases the demand for one firm's product at the expense of another firm's product, then the argument is no longer valid, for as unit production costs decline in one firm, other firms will experience a reduction in demand. It is conceivable, though, that even when demand increases, average prices may fall in the industry. This would occur if some firms were forced out of the industry, allowing the surviving firms to benefit from economies of scale.

Empirical Evidence that Advertising Leads to Reduction in Prices

We have already cited a number of studies which demonstrate that advertising leads to higher prices. We have, however, also just shown that advertising *can* lead to lower prices if production is increased and average total costs are reduced, or if competition (measured by reduced mean and variance of prices) is increased. Some studies purport to show that when one or both of these conditions are satisfied, the results are lower prices. We examine several studies here.

Eyeglasses   Benham has studied the effects of advertising on the price of eyeglasses by comparing prices in states which restrict advertising to those in states which do not.[18] Benham found in 1963 that in states where advertising

[18] Lee Benham, "The Effect of Advertising on the Price of Eyeglasses," *Journal of Law and Economics*, vol. 15 (October 1972), pp. 337–352, and Lee Benham and Alexander Benham, "Regulating through the Professions: A Perspective on Information Control," *Journal of Law and Economics*, vol. 18 (October 1975), pp. 421–447.

was completely banned, the price of eyeglasses averaged \$37.48; in states where there was no restriction on advertising, the average price was \$17.98.[19] Benham's explanation was:

> In general, large-volume, low-priced sellers are dependent upon drawing customers from a wide area and consequently need to inform their potential customers of the advantages of coming to them. If advertising is prohibited, they may not be able to generate the necessary sales to maintain the low price . . . at the same time, the likelihood that small-volume, high-priced retailers survive in the market will increase.[20]

Benham suggests that advertising allows for more competition among existing producers, reducing profit margins. He also suggests that advertising facilitates entry and therefore prohibition of advertising is a barrier to entry.

Perhaps surprisingly, Benham found that the inclusion of price in the ads was not an important factor in leading to reduced prices of eyeglasses. He separated the states which prohibited the appearance of prices in the advertisements from those which allowed unrestricted advertising and found that in states where the prices could not be included in the ads, average prices were only slightly higher than in states with no restrictions.[21] In other words, information on the existence, location, and product assortment seems to generate sufficient consumer interest in competing firms; this interest leads to more competition.

Toy Manufacturers Steiner looked at the toy manufacturing industry before and after the introduction of toy manufacturers' television advertising.[22] He found that markups or profit margins on sales prior to the mid-1950s were statistically much higher than after the 1950s. Prior to the inclusion of retailers' and manufacturers' ads on network television, a typical toy with a \$5 retail price was usually retailed at \$5 or perhaps \$4.95. After the advent of television advertising of nationally retailed toys, the typical retail price of a toy that would have sold for \$5 prior to the advertising was found to average \$3.49. In cities where no television advertising of the toy occurred during the same post-mid-1950s, however, the price continued to average around \$4.98.[23]

Steiner explained that the reduction in average prices was due almost exclusively to a reduction in profit margins or markups. In areas where toys were heavily advertised on television, certain retailers found that their rate of return on investment was higher after reducing markups rather dramatically on those toys. Their volume increased sufficiently to justify the reductions (that is, the demand was elastic at that point). Small-volume, high-priced retailers could no

---

[19] Ibid., "The Effects of Advertising on the Price of Eyeglasses," p. 342.
[20] Ibid., p. 339.
[21] Ibid., p. 349.
[22] Robert L. Steiner, "Does Advertising Lower Consumer Prices?" *Journal of Marketing*, vol. 37 (October 1973), pp. 19–26.
[23] Ibid., p. 24.

longer keep their mark-ups as high as they had in the past, due to the existence of the higher-volume, lower-priced establishments.

Retail Gasoline   Maurizi has attempted to study the impact of local laws prohibiting price advertising of retail gasoline.[24] His results indicate a significantly greater variance in dealer markups in cities that prohibit price advertising, which is consistent with the hypothesis that advertising promotes market efficiency. But Maurizi's results also indicate significantly *lower* average prices in those cities. Maurizi indicates that this result is unreliable due to systematic biases in reported wholesale price charges, and therefore he asserts that "no firm conclusion can be reached regarding the effect of the law on average prices."

Attorneys' Fees   Muris and McChesney recently conducted a case study to determine the impact of attorneys' advertising upon the price and quality of services provided.[25] They compared the price and quality of a legal clinic (a new form of delivering legal services that specializes in services that can be produced on a mass basis, such as simple divorces), with traditional (that is, nonclinical) methods of providing the services. As with other studies of advertising and prices, they found that advertising allows clinics to reduce price. For example, they found that in Maryland in 1975 the average cost of an uncontested divorce exceeded $300, while a legal clinic that began operation in 1976 was able to settle such divorces profitably for $150.

A difference between their study and other studies of advertising is that Muris and McChesney emphasized the relationship between advertising and quality. The importance of studying this relationship stems from the claim that advertising bans, particularly in the professions, are necessary to assure "minimal" quality. Although most economists would argue that consumers should be free to make their own price-quality trade-offs for these services, just as they do for other purchases, many in occupations such as law and medicine disagree. Those who assert that quality must drop often implicitly assume that they themselves could charge reduced prices only by decreasing quality. If lower costs (for example, from increased volume) are the source of the lower prices, however, then lower prices need not sacrifice quality.

Muris and McChesney conducted both subjective and objective tests for quality. Their subjective test consisted of a questionnaire to consumers of both the legal clinic and traditional law firms. They asked seven questions about quality, such as whether the lawyer had been prompt in getting back to the consumer and whether the consumer thought that the lawyer was honest. The overall mean of the clinic scores revealed that consumers preferred the clinic to

[24] Alex R. Maurizi, "The Effect of Laws Against Price Advertising: The Case of Retail Gasoline," *Western Economic Journal*, vol. 10 (September 1972), pp. 321–329.
[25] Timothy J. Muris and Fred S. McChesney, "Advertising and the Price and Quality of Legal Services: The Case for Legal Clinics," *American Bar Foundation Research Journal*, vol. 1979 (Winter 1979), pp. 179–207.

traditional firms.[26] The difference was significant at the 10-percent level. Further, consumers preferred the clinic to the traditional firms on all seven questions asked.[27] This result was statistically significant at the 1 percent level.

For an objective test, Muris and McChesney compared child support awards in divorce cases involving the clinic with cases where the clinic was not involved. In all cases, the wife received the award. When the clinic represented the wife, her award increased, with the finding statistically significant at less than .025. When the clinic represented the husband, the amount he had to pay decreased, although the figure was not statistically significant at generally accepted levels.

Thus, rather than finding that advertising led to lower quality, the case study revealed that quality was not worse on any of the measurements used and was, indeed, better on some measurements. The authors concluded that the clinic studied was able to reduce price and raise quality because advertising allowed specialized production techniques that lowered costs and may have allowed better quality control.

ADVERTISING AND PROFITABILITY

If advertising is considered simply as an investment, then we would expect the rate of return on advertising to be equal on the margin to the rate of return on any other type of investment. When one considers advertising as a possible barrier to entry, however, then the prediction would be for higher levels of advertising expenditures. Indeed, one researcher flatly states that the highest profit rates are associated with industries that advertise heavily.[28] Relating advertising budgets to profitability is surely not a simple matter. As an empirical problem, it requires holding many other variables constant while assessing the relationship between advertising and profitability. Additionally, just identifying other potential sources of market power that could lead to higher rates of profitability is a difficult task. Also, even though advertising is clearly an investment, tax laws allow firms either to account for it or to deduct it as an expense in the year in which it is undertaken.

The first major study attempting to take account of all the above objections and problems was carried out by Comanor and Wilson.[29] In their multiple-regression analysis they included a variable measuring average market advertising to sales ratio. This variable was statistically significant in their regression results. They found that in heavily advertised markets, the average market profit rate was 12 percent, whereas for all markets together, the average market profit rate was only 8 percent. Their conclusion was that this difference was

---

[26] Ibid., p. 199.

[27] Ibid., p. 200.

[28] Leonard Weiss, "Advertising, Profits, and Corporate Taxes," *Review of Economics and Statistics,* vol. 51 (November 1969), pp. 426–430.

[29] William S. Comanor and Thomas A. Wilson, "Advertising, Market Structure and Performance," *Review of Economics and Statistics,* vol. 49 (November 1967), pp. 423–440.

derived from product differentiation barriers that advertising expenses not only created but also maintained.

More recent theoretical arguments provide conflicting implications on the relationship of advertising to competition. The early empirical tests were effectively tests of Bain's hypothesis that advertising outlays resulted in lower cross elasticities of demand between products of established enterprises and new entrants. This result permitted higher prices and higher returns for advertisers.[30] Schmalensee's model of advertising focuses on the relationship between existing firms and new entrants.[31] He argues that in the presence of dynamic effects advertising will not necessarily lead to restrictions on entry. He contends that without asymmetrics in the demand functions for the two types of firms, if "existing firms and the entrant can produce equally effective advertising and equally desirable products," restrictions to entry will not likely exist. Schmalensee does, however, recognize that established firms may have an advantage attributable to their early position in the market. Nelson's model, on the other hand, focuses on the relationship between information and products' demand elasticities—the greater the consumer's knowledge is, the higher the individual elasticity of demand function will be.[32] Nelson then argues that if production costs per unit of utility are lower for some firms than for others, the lower cost firms will find they can profitably expand output by simultaneously increasing advertising expenditures and decreasing price.

In a 1979 article, Comanor and Wilson found that both models have serious limitations.[33] In Schmalensee's model a constant price cost margin is assumed, eliminating the possibility that the reward for past advertising can be obtained by setting higher prices. The limitation in Nelson's model rests on alternative reasons for advertising effectiveness which in turn affect firm behavior. When individual quality rankings depend on tastes, there is no nonarbitrary manner to judge one product superior to another. If the gains from advertising depend on the extent and strength of preferences for the individual products, then Nelson's model is weakened. Additional researchers have carried out similar studies and have come up with similar conclusions.[34]

Critics of the Comanor and Wilson-type results point out that all of the studies have used cross-sectional profit rates, thus exaggerating profit rates in

[30] See Joe S. Bain, *Barriers to New Competition: Their Character and Consequences in Manufacturing Industries* (Cambridge, Mass.: Harvard University Press, 1956).

[31] Richard L. Schmalensee, "Brand Loyalty and Barriers to Entry," *Southern Economic Journal,* vol. 40 (April 1974), pp. 579–588. Also see Schmalensee, "Entry Deterrence in the Ready-To-Eat Breakfast Cereal Industry," *Bell Journal of Economics,* vol. 9 (Autumn 1978), pp. 305–327.

[32] Phillip Nelson, "Information and Consumer Behavior," *Journal of Political Economy,* vol. 78 (March/April 1970), pp. 311–329, and "Advertising as Information," *Journal of Political Economy,* vol. 82 (July/August 1974), pp. 729–754.

[33] William Comanor and Thomas A. Wilson, "The Effect of Advertising on Competition: A Survey," *Journal of Economic Literature,* vol. 17 (June 1979), pp. 453–476.

[34] See, for example, William Shepherd, "The Elements of Market Structure," *Review of Economics and Statistics,* vol. 54 (February 1972), pp. 25–37, and Roger Sherman and Robert D. Tollison, "Advertising and Profitability," *Review of Economics and Statistics,* vol. 53 (November 1971), pp. 397–407.

markets where advertising expenditures are relatively greater as a response to the tax laws.

The Debate Continues

In sum, there is no consensus on the effects of advertising on profitability. Some, like Bloch, find no overall economic rents from advertising, while others, such as Siegfried and Weiss, do find economic rents from advertising.[35]

By focusing on particular goods or industries, researchers have not clearly established a definite relationship between advertising and profitability. Nelson, for example, has demonstrated a statistically significant *negative* correlation between experience durable goods advertising and profit rates.[36] He finds this result more meaningful than a positive correlation between advertising and profitability, which he does find for nondurables, because the latter has a significant "advertising as investment" bias.[37]. Boyer also found *negative* correlation between advertising intensity and profitability in the retailing-service industries relative to manufacturing, where the correlation is positive.[38] Other studies show the *lack* of a statistically significant *positive* correlation.[39] Additional insights into the advertising-profitability relationship emerge from a more detailed look at particular advertising phenomena. An empirical study by Hirschey is of interest in this respect. It shows that *television* advertising has a significantly greater positive impact on profitability than does advertising in general.[40]

ADVERTISING AND CONCENTRATION

Donald F. Turner, former Assistant Attorney General in charge of the Antitrust Division, often stated that extensive advertising promotes industry concentration and is thus harmful to competition. To the extent that advertising represents a barrier to entry, one could predict that the greater the amount of advertising is, the greater the average concentration ratio will be.[41]

---

[35] Harry Bloch, "Advertising and Profitability: A Reappraisal," *Journal of Political Economy,* vol. 82 (March/April, 1974), pp. 267–286, and John J. Siegfried and Leonard W. Weiss, "Advertising, Profits, and Corporate Taxes Revisited," *Review of Economics and Statistics,* vol. 56 (May 1974), pp. 195–200.

[36] Phillip Nelson, "The Economic Consequences of Advertising," *Journal of Business,* vol. 48 (April 1975), pp. 213–241.

[37] Ibid., p. 237.

[38] Kenneth D. Boyer, "Informative and Goodwill Advertising," *Review of Economics and Statistics,* vol. 56 (November 1974), pp. 541–548.

[39] See D. L. Weiss, "An Analysis of the Demand Structure of Branded Consumer Products," *Applied Economics,* vol. 1 (1969), pp. 37–49.

[40] See Mark J. Hirschey, "Television Advertising and Profitability," *Economics Letters,* vol. 1 (1978), pp. 259–264.

[41] Willard F. Mueller and Larry G. Hamm, "Trends in Industrial Market Concentration, 1947 to 1970," *Review of Economics and Statistics,* vol. 56 (November 1974), pp. 511–520, and Neil R. Wright, "Product Differentiation, Concentration, and Charges in Concentration," *Review of Economics and Statistics,* vol. 60 (November 1978), pp. 628–631.

Economies of Scale One of the principal determinants of the relationship between advertising and concentration is economies of scale.[42] In fact, Bain estimated that advertising is the single most important factor in explaining price and cost differentials of established firms relative to new entrants. Economies of scale in advertising arise from several factors, including a minimum saturation level, cumulative effects, quantity discounts, and geographic combinations. Advertising campaigns often must reach a certain minimum expense level before they are cost-effective; many of these campaigns have high common or fixed costs. Automobile manufacturers with large volumes, for example, face lower average per unit costs of advertising. Leonard Weiss reported that General Motors and Ford spent approximately $27 per car sold between 1954 and 1957.[43] During the same period, Chrysler spent approximately $48 per car, American Motors $58, and Studebaker-Packard $64.

A closely related advantage results from the cumulative effect of certain advertising campaigns over time. Perpetual reinforcement is necessary because continuous large advertising budgets facilitate the acquisition of the potential gains from repeated advertisements. This condition is also consistent with a buyer loyalty hypothesis and does not always imply economies of scale, although characteristic of some distribution processes, it may favor large firms.[44]

Another closely related advantage stems from economies of scale of advertising sellers. Here the selling firm can offer quantity and price discounts because the seller itself experiences economies of scale. For example, advertisements for full pages in newspapers are sold at lower rates per square inch than smaller advertisements.

Finally, in many cases the distribution of the potential customers offered by the seller of advertising services does not precisely match the characteristics of the firm's potential clientele. Larger advertising campaigns are likely to reduce the overlap from separate campaigns, hence fewer dollars will be spent on ads that reach nonpotential customers.

Perhaps the most famous litigation involving the scale affects of advertising is the Clorox case.[45] Procter & Gamble was prohibited from acquiring Clorox because the court believed that Procter & Gamble, as a national advertiser,

---

[42] Jules Backman, *Advertising and Competition* (New York: New York University Press, 1967). Note that this hypothesis raises a potentially difficult problem of simultaneity with respect to empirical testing of both the advertising-profitability and the advertising-concentration theories. Two studies have attempted to account for the problem by performing two-stage least squares regressions on a system of simultaneous equations. See Douglas F. Greer, "Advertising and Market Concentration," *Southern Economic Journal,* vol. 38 (July 1971), pp. 19–32; and Allyn D. Strickland and Leonard W. Weiss, "Advertising, Concentration, and Price-Cost Margins," *Journal of Political Economy,* vol. 84 (October 1976), pp. 1109–1121. Both studies conclude that the results obtained with the more elaborate methodology are generally consistent with those obtained from single-equation models, so apparently the problem is not great.

[43] Leonard W. Weiss, *Economics and American Industry* (New York: Wiley, 1961), p. 342.

[44] See Michael E. Porter, "Interbrand Choice, Media Mix, and Market Performance," *American Economic Review,* vol. 66 (May 1976), pp. 398–406.

[45] *Federal Trade Commission v. Procter & Gamble, et al.,* 386 U.S. 568 (1967).

would be able to obtain reduced rates through advertising, ultimately leading to unfair competition.

Empirical Tests

Two tests have been used to demonstrate the relationship between concentration and advertising. The first is simply a direct test for any positive correlation between concentration ratios and advertising intensity. The second is a test for economies of scale in advertising and the capital barriers to entry.

Direct Tests of Advertising and Concentration　The first test for a relationship between concentration ratios and advertising intensity was performed by Kaldor and Silverman using 1938 data.[46] They found that advertising intensity and concentration ratios were positively related up to some intermediate concentration level and inversely related thereafter.

Schnabel reexamined the Kaldor-Silverman data.[47] He found that the average advertising-to-sales ratios used to measure advertising intensity varied considerably. Further, he pointed out that Kaldor and Silverman imputed such ratios to *individual* commodities using the ratios obtained for *groups* of commodities. After correcting for such biases, Schnabel found little relationship between advertising intensity and concentration.

Telser was the first to use regression analysis to establish empirical relationships between concentration and advertising intensity for 42 consumer goods industries during 1947, 1954, and 1958.[48] The correlation, however, was not statistically significant. When Telser looked at *changes* in concentration and advertising intensity, he found virtually no correlation. Telser concluded that there was "little empirical support for an inverse association between advertising and competition. . . ."

Telser's study has been severely criticized by a number of researchers. Kamerschen pointed out that Telser hypothesized and imposed on his data a straight-line, or linear, relationship. If, however, the relationship between advertising intensity and concentration is nonlinear, that relationship could exist in spite of Telser's findings to the contrary. Kamerschen used a different form of Telser's relationship and did find that advertising intensity was a statistically significant variable.[49]

---

[46] Nicholas Kaldor and Richard Silverman, *A Statistical Analysis of Advertising Expenditure and of the Revenue of the Press* (Cambridge, Mass.: Cambridge University Press, 1948).

[47] Morton Schnabel, "A Note on Advertising and Industrial Concentration," *Journal of Political Economy,* vol. 78 (September/October 1970), pp. 1191–1194.

[48] Lester G. Telser, "Advertising and Competition," *Journal of Political Economy,* vol. 72 (December 1964), pp. 537–562.

[49] David R. Kamerschen, "The Statistics of Advertising," *Rivista Internazionale di Scienze Economiche e Commerciali,* vol. 19 (January 1972), pp. 1–25.

Note that even though advertising intensity was a statistically significant variable in the estimated equations, the equations had virtually no explanatory power. All we can say is that Kamerschen found that advertising intensity is weakly related to concentration.

Mann, Henning, and Meehan further criticized Telser's results because of measurement error. They pointed out that the data from the industry sampled did not correspond to the economic markets under study. Telser had used Internal Revenue Service industry data; Mann and his associates used Department of Commerce S.I.C. four-digit industry data. When they recreated Telser's study, they found that advertising intensity was significantly associated with concentration, that is, it had appreciable explanatory power.[50]

The research in this area did not stop with the Mann study. Later studies attempted to show that both I.R.S. data and Department of Commerce S.I.C. data imposed serious biases on the empirical results.[51] Within the past few years, a number of important studies using census data were conducted by Ornstein.[52] These studies show a statistically significant but weak linear relationship and have been confirmed in their general results using modified data.[53]

Several researchers have painstakingly reviewed the extensive literature on studies purporting to show increasing returns to continuous advertising. In particular, Schmalensee, Simon, and Ferguson have concluded that there is little, if any, evidence of scale economies in advertising.[54] They found that no researcher had discovered evidence of quantity discounts or price discrimination in favor of large-scale advertisers.[55] Blank contends that advertising discounts for television simply equalize cost-per-message-delivered rather than offer economies to large advertisers. Also, no one has shown that *increasing* advertising effectiveness is associated with increasing frequency of advertising messages.[56]

No researcher has yet presented overwhelming evidence to demonstrate the relationship between advertising and brand loyalty. In a summary of over 20 years of research, Engel, Kollat, and Blackwell found no evidence that brand

[50] H. Michael Mann, John A. Henning, and James W. Meehan, Jr., "Advertising and Concentration: An Empirical Investigation," *Journal of Industrial Economics,* vol. 16 (November 1967), pp. 34–45. See also Brian C. Brush, "The Influence of Market Structure on Industry Advertising Intensity," *Journal of Industrial Economics,* vol. 25 (September 1976), pp. 55–67, in which the regression is reversed, with concentration used as an explanatory variable in advertising intensity. A significant coefficient was found in linear form.

[51] See Richard A. Miller, "Advertising and Competition: Some Neglected Aspects," *Antitrust Bulletin,* vol. 17 (Summer 1972), pp. 467–478, and also "Symposium on Advertising and Concentration," *Journal of Industrial Economics,* vol. 18 (November 1969), pp. 76–101.

[52] Stanley I. Ornstein, "The Advertising-Concentration Controversy," *Southern Economic Journal,* vol. 43 (July 1976), pp. 892–902, and *Industrial Concentration and Advertising Intensity* (Washington, D.C.: American Enterprise Institute for Public Policy Research, 1977).

[53] Brian C. Brush, "Errors in the Measurement of Concentration and the Advertising-Concentration Controversy," *Southern Economic Journal,* vol. 44 (April 1978), pp. 978–986.

[54] Richard Schmalensee, *The Economics of Advertising* (New York: Humanities Press, 1973); Julian L. Simon, *Issues in the Economics of Advertising* (Urbana, Ill.: University of Illinois Press, 1970); and James M. Ferguson, *Advertising and Competition: Theory, Measurement, Fact* (Cambridge, Mass.: Ballinger, 1975).

[55] David M. Blank, "Television Advertising: The Great Discount Illusion, or Tonypandy Revisited," *Journal of Business,* vol. 41 (January 1968), pp. 10–38.

[56] See Jean-Jacques Lambin, "What Is the Real Impact of Advertising?" *Harvard Business Review,* vol. 53 (May/June 1975), pp. 139–147.

loyalty is directly related to advertising.[57] In fact, Lambin determined empirically that brand loyalty is more strongly influenced by quality and product performance than by advertising.[58]

PRODUCT DIFFERENTIATION

In many ways, it is hard to imagine a significant amount of product advertising without product differentiation. Some researchers take a definitely negative view of product differentiation. Consider Bain's analysis and definition:

> Product differentiation within industries is based generally on the opportunity of producing significantly different designs and qualities of the good in question, the comparative ignorance of buyers with respect to the merits of various alternative products, and the susceptibility of buyers to persuasive appeals concerning the alleged superiority of the outputs of individual sellers.[59]

Going from this analysis, Bain states that the first general rule about product differentiation is that it tends to be more important in consumer goods than in producer goods industries. Buyers in the latter industry are relatively better informed about the qualities and technical aspects of the goods they buy. Moreover, numerous producer goods are standardized, thus leaving little room for physical product differentiation. Bain cites as examples agriculture, fisheries, forestries, and mining, all industries where negligible product differentiation exists. On the other hand, there appears to be widespread product differentiation in manufacturing and processing industries. Bain believes that consumers are poorly informed and are susceptible to persuasive advertising appeals.[60] Advertising, of course, plays an important role in generating product differentiation; for example, soap, cigarettes, and liquor are often strongly differentiated through use of persuasive advertising appeals. On the other hand, electrical appliances and automobiles are differentiated mainly by product design. With gasoline and tires, the differentiation comes about because of the manufacturers' distributive and service capacities.

There are, nonetheless, consumer good industries in which product differentiation has not had much of an impact. According to Bain, this is true with "necessity" goods, such as food, clothing, and household supplies. Table 9-3 lists industries with varying degrees of product differentiation and the principal basis for that differentiation.

[57] James F. Engel, D. Kollat, and R. Blackwell, eds., *Consumer Behavior: Selected Readings,* 2d ed. (Hillsdale, Ill.: Dryden Press, 1973), chap. 23.

[58] Jean-Jacques Lambin, *Advertising, Competition, and Market Conduct in Oligopoly Over Time: An Econometric Investigation in Western European Countries* (Amsterdam: North-Holland, 1976), pp. 117–118.

[59] Joe S. Bain, *Industrial Organization,* 2d ed. (New York: Wiley, 1968), p. 235. Also see Michael Spence, "Product Differentiation and Welfare," *American Economic Review,* vol. 66 (May 1976), pp. 407–414. Spence maintains that monopolistic competition creates an excessive number of product variants except for products with low cross elasticity of demand (few substitutes) and products requiring high initial fixed costs.

[60] Bain, *Barriers to New Competition,* p. 236.

TABLE 9-3
DIFFERENCES IN PRODUCT DIFFERENTIATION

Degree of product differentiation in industries	Basis of product differentiation
Negligible	
Rayon, yarn, and fiber	
Canned fruits, canned vegetables, flour, fresh meats	
Copper	
Cement	
Slight	
Low-priced fountain pens	Product design and advertising
Processed meats, meat packing	Quality and advertising
Steel	Customer service
Low-priced men's shoes	Advertising
Moderate	
Tires	Advertising, product design, and customer service
Higher-quality men's shoes	Advertising and control of distribution outlets
Consumer flower sales	Consumer service and advertising
Refined petroleum products	Advertising and customer service through controlled distribution outlets
Tin cans	Customer service and product design
Great	
Typewriters	Product design, advertising, and customer service
Farm machinery and tractors	Customer service with controlled distribution outlets and product design
Cars	Advertising, product design and reputation, customer service with controlled distribution outlets
Cigarettes	Advertising
Liquor	Product quality and advertising
Higher-priced fountain pens	Product design and advertising

Adapted from Joe S. Bain, *Industrial Organization*, 2d ed. (New York: Wiley, 1968), Tables I, II, III, and IV, pp. 239–240.

Further Thoughts on Forms of Product Differentiation

Basically sellers differentiate the products they buy in four ways.

1 The store or plant is selected on the basis of geographical convenience, thus giving locational and transportational advantages. Examples are the corner drug store and the closest cement plant.

2 <u>Physical differences in the products are altered.</u> Shirts may be made with high- or low-quality polished cotton. Cars can have 12 coats of paint or only 3. Jeans can be prewashed or not. A bicycle can have 1, 3, 10, or 12 speeds.

3 <u>The product is differentiated in terms of its preferential or subjective image on consumers</u>—by advertising, sales promotion, package attractiveness, and brand labeling.

4 <u>Firms offer relatively good service through well-trained staffs, shorter checkout lines, and so on.</u>

At least three of the four above methods of differentiating a product can be considered a "legitimate" response to acceptable demands of consumers. First, the higher the opportunity cost of time is, the more willingly a consumer will pay a higher price for a geographically convenient supplier of a product. Second, some bicycle enthusiasts want the most elaborate 12-speed bike, while some are satisfied with 1 speed. The former are willing to pay more than the latter. Third, some consumers prefer to be waited on by a well-trained staff and are willing to pay the price for the information and training inherent in that aspect of the product. We may even question subjective differentiation, because different consumers have different preferences for the suggestive image accompanying products they buy.

QUALITY DIFFERENCES

<u>One of the major ways to differentiate products is by quality.</u> Here we must distinguish between situations in which buyers can make exact appraisals of the differences and situations in which they cannot make exact appraisals. Consider the example of fuel oil that is sold in different regions and is of different qualities, specifically its sulphur and energy content. Major users of fuel oil, such as electric utilities, can certainly measure the difference. Here we are not talking about a differentiated product such as that in Bain's model. The market equilibrium result is the same that it would be if the product were totally undifferentiated—of exactly equal qualities. The price per constant quality unit is the same to everyone. This analysis holds even for more complicated raw materials and for pieces of industrial machinery. The buyers are able to differentiate the product exactly, and they make the same appraisal in our quality analysis.

It is when a product fills no specific simple technical function that we tend to see a different type of differentiation. When a product can satisfy various uses and different needs, whether they be subjective or physical (for example, consumer durables and cosmetics), we will see product differentiation. Let's look now at one specific aspect of quality—durability.

Durability

Any good that has the possibility of generating a service flow over time is purchased for that service flow. Producers can vary the expected service life of their goods by changing their production techniques. Light bulbs can be made to last 10 or 1,000 hours. Tires can be made to last 10,000 or 40,000 miles. Cotton shirts can be made to last 6 months or 6 years.

The Demand for Durable Goods Using the tools of discounting for present values presented on pages 46–50, we can properly analyze the demand for durable goods. We treat the demand for a durable good not as a demand for the good itself, but rather for the net stream of services that the good yields. "Net" means after taking account of all costs associated with the use of the durable good. Hence, the demand for an automobile is not treated as the demand for the car *per se*, but rather as the demand for the right to use the car every day over a specified period of time. We are dealing with an *expected* flow of services to which the consumer will attach some monetary valuation.

Again, take an automobile for example. Let A equal the monetary valuation of the stream of future services (net of operating costs) expected from the automobile each year; as usual, the interest rate is r. Thus, the present value of the stream of services from the automobile will equal

$$P_t = \frac{A_1}{1+r} + \frac{A_2}{(1+r)^2} + \cdots + \frac{R_t}{(1+r)^t} \qquad (9\text{-}9)$$

where R_t is the resale value or the scrap value of the automobile when it is no longer desired. The denominator of the last term on the right-hand side of Eq. (9-9) is $1+r$ taken to the power t, where t is the expected number of years that the individual will keep the automobile.

Clearly, the larger the expected flow of services per year is, the greater the present value is. Moreover, the larger the expected scrap value is, the larger the present value is. Finally, the lower the rate of interest used in discounting is, the greater the present value of the durable asset is.

The Optimal Durability of a Firm's Product A serious debate has been waged concerning the optimum durability of goods under competition and monopoly. The majority of writers on the subject have concluded that a monopolist tends to produce a good of lesser durability than would be the case under competition.[61] Decreases in durability are one form of increasing price. Further, less durable goods permit a crude form of metering demand.[62] Coase has shown that when a less durable good is produced, the price can be higher

[61] A. J. Douglas and Steven M. Goldman, "Monopolistic Behavior in a Market for Durable Goods," *Journal of Political Economy*, vol. 77 (January/February 1969), pp. 49–59; E. Kleiman and T. Ophir, "The Durability of Durable Goods," *Review of Economic Studies*, vol. 33 (April 1966), pp. 165–178; David Levhari and Yoram Peles, "Market Structure, Quality, and Durability," *Bell Journal of Economics and Management Science*, vol. 4 (Spring 1973), pp. 235–248; and David D. Martin, "Monopoly Power and the Durability of Durable Goods," *Southern Economic Journal*, vol. 28 (January 1962), pp. 271–277.

[62] See Chapter 10 on price discrimination.

because consumers will not face an increase in supply if they buy at the monopoly prices.[63]

Swan, however, has argued that the majority of researchers have been wrong. He believes that firms select the same degree of durability irrespective of the degree of monopoly. His argument is that for any volume of service the product yields, the firm will attempt to minimize total cost. Thus, the optimal degree of durability depends only on the form of the firm's total cost function (which can, of course, be affected by the degree of monopoly).[64]

The decision as to the optimal length of serviceable life of a product is also related to the degree to which a used market for the durable good exists. An interesting example concerns the used textbook market. Some publishing firms and authors believe that they would be better off if the used-book market were abolished.

Eliminating the Used-Book Market

Superficially, it would appear that the elimination of the used-book market would benefit the sale of new books by eliminating a substitute. Thus, if the publisher of this book wants to maximize revenues from the sale of this edition, presumably it should not aid in any way the smooth functioning of a used-book market for this text. After all, used Clarkson and Miller industrial organization books are substitutes for new ones. When someone purchases a used text from a college bookstore, that person does not purchase a new text. No new revenue is made, because the publisher (and the author) get paid only when a new book is sold.

Present Value Falls This analysis is incomplete, however. If you as a student purchased a text new and cannot resell it because a used-book market does not exist, then the present value of the book is lower. At any given nominal price for the textbook, the *price per constant-quality unit* would therefore be higher. Assume that a textbook costs $21. If you are able to resell the textbook at the end of the term for 50 percent of its new-book price, then you anticipate that the cost for one term's use of the book will be $10.50, ignoring interest; however, if the bookstore absolutely refuses to buy the book back, then the cost for one term's use of that same book has doubled to $21. A lower quantity would be demanded.

If one continues this analysis to its ultimate extreme, one would expect

---

[63] Ronald H. Coase, "Durability and Monopoly," *Journal of Law and Economics,* vol. 15 (April 1972), pp. 143–149.

[64] Peter L. Swan, "Durability of Consumption Goods," *American Economic Review,* vol. 60 (December 1970), pp. 884–894; "The Durability of Goods and Regulation of Monopoly," *Bell Journal of Economics and Management Science,* vol. 2 (Spring 1971), pp. 347–357; "Optimum Durability, Second-Hand Markets, and Planned Obsolescence," *Journal of Political Economy,* vol. 80 (May/June 1972), pp. 575–585; and "Alcoa: The Influence of Recycling on Monopoly Power," *Journal of Political Economy,* vol. 88 (February 1980), pp. 76–99.

under certain conditions that individual textbook manufacturers will *aid* in increasing the efficacy of used-book markets so long as their aid is relatively cheaper than the costs of producing and distributing new textbooks. Increasing the efficacy of used-book markets would increase the present value of their textbooks. At the same time, a higher price could be charged for the textbook to reflect increased textbook services from possible resales. This is what has actually happened in the market for used-IBM typewriters. IBM acts as the intermediary in this market, first buying the used typewriters, then reconditioning them, then reselling them. Some textbook publishers also engage in this type of behavior. But other publishing houses instruct their sales staff to dissuade bookstores from acting as intermediaries for used versions of the textbooks sold. Presumably these publishers believe that they will have higher profits by reducing the availability of substitutes for new books.

Other Effects Need To Be Considered   The above analyses are not so simple as outlined; they focus only on increasing the benefits stream from the ownership of a durable good. However, there is a substitution effect at work. Used versions of durable goods are indeed substitutes for newly produced durable goods. The elimination of part or all of the available supply of substitute used durables leads to a shift outward to the right in the demand curve for the new durable good.

A case for the elimination of used versions of the durable good can be seen in Figure 9-3. The demand curve for new books with a used market is *DD*. *DD* is drawn by assuming a given availability of substitutes. Assume that the market price per constant-quality unit is P_1. It is the nominal price, let's say, for each unit of the durable good. Now consider the elimination of the used-version market of the durable good. The demand curve for the new durable shifts from

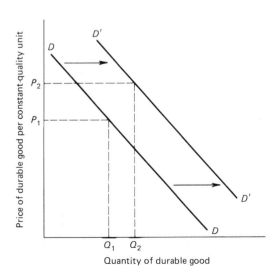

FIGURE 9-3
The case for eliminating the used-durable-good market. The demand curve *DD* is drawn by assuming the existence of a market for the used durable good. The price expressed in present value constant-quality units is, we assume, P_1. Now, the used market is eliminated. This leads to a substitution effect in which the demand curve for the new version of the durable good shifts to the right, outward to *D'D'*, since a substitute has been eliminated. However, the elimination of the used-durable-good market reduces the present value of the good, thus raising its price per present value constant-quality unit from P_1 to P_2. Nonetheless, even at this higher price, the quantity demanded increases from Q_1 to Q_2 because of the shift outward in the demand schedule that resulted from the elimination of the substitute.

Quantity of durable good

DD to *D'D'*. However, the present value of the durable good has fallen because its resale value is no longer as great as it was when the market for the used version of the durable good existed. In other words, we have cut off a part of the future expected stream from owning this durable good. We have cut off the possibility of selling the asset after it has been used. If this is the case, at a constant nominal price per unit sold, P_1, the effective price per constant-quality unit must rise. After all, the purchaser of the durable good is purchasing fewer present-value units with the same amount of dollars. In our example in Figure 9-3, the price rises from P_1 to P_2. However, even at the higher price, P_2, the quantity demanded along the new demand curve *D'D'* increases from Q_1 to Q_2. In this case, the substitution effect outweighed the present-value reduction effect.

A case against the elimination of the used version of the durable good can be seen in Figure 9-4. Everything is the same as in Figure 9-3 except that the shift in the demand curve for the new durable good is not as great. At the higher implicit price per constant-quality unit of the durable good P_2, the quantity demanded, Q_2, is less than the original quantity demanded, Q_1, when the market for the used version of the durable good was in existence.

What one has to compare in these situations is the price elasticity of demand and the cross-price elasticity of demand.[65] This, of course, is an empirical

---

[65] Students interested in a more elaborate examination of this problem are referred to Daniel K. Benjamin and Roger C. Kormendi, "The Interrelationship between Markets for New and Used Durable Goods," *Journal of Law and Economics*, vol. 17 (October 1974), pp. 381–401. Also see H. Laurence Miller, "On Killing Off the Market for Used Textbooks and the Relationship between Markets for New and Secondhand Goods," *Journal of Political Economy*, vol. 82 (May/June 1974), pp. 612–619.

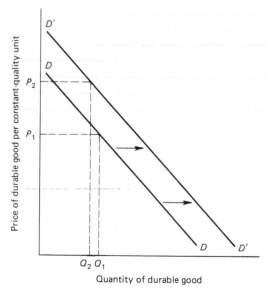

FIGURE 9-4
The case against eliminating the used-durable-good market. This diagram is similar to Figure 9-3, but the shift outward in the demand curve from *DD* to *D'D'* was not sufficient to overcome the implicit increase in the price per present value constant-quality unit of the durable good when the used market was eliminated. Thus, the quantity demanded falls from Q_1 to Q_2.

comparison. From casual observation, however, we can surmise that the IBM Corporation believes that it is better to encourage a used market for its equipment. Specifically, IBM operates an extensive used-IBM-typewriter market, where one can purchase a reconditioned IBM electric typewriter. Clearly, there is no attempt on the part of IBM to destroy ''competition'' for new IBM electric typewriters with used-IBM-electric typewriters.

STYLE CHANGES

Now we consider changes in the style of a product that are purely esthetic in principle—they are unrelated to any quality or durability aspects of the item. Style changes may occur without a change in the total cost to the firm. For example, when capital equipment wears out, the firm may replace it with a modified version that does not alter total cost, but does change the style of the product. Changes in packaging may often be effected without a change in total cost. Most style changes do, however, result in higher costs. The most typical example of the high cost of style changes relates to the automobile industry. In a classic study by Fisher, Griliches, and Kaysen, the researchers attempted to determine the cost of automobile model changes from 1949 to 1960.[66] Correcting for changes in true quality aspects, such as horsepower, length, and weight, the researchers attempted to determine the amount of resources that would have been saved had style remained the same from 1949 to 1960. They estimated that $454 per new car would have been saved had horsepower and size not changed during that time period. If optional equipment had not been added, $116 per car would have been saved. Finally, almost $100 per car would have been saved if auto manufacturers had not retooled each year in order to produce the new-style cars.

Fisher and his associates sought accurate estimates for automobiles. Few, if any, reliable estimates are available for other products. It can be argued, nonetheless, that frequent style changes render existing capital stocks ''artificially'' obsolete. After all, women's dresses and skirts are technically similar, even if the hemline varies by a few inches each year. It is difficult to measure any supposed social loss from style changes because we do not have an estimate of the social welfare function. Additionally, the measurement problem involved would be tremendous.

Planned Obsolescence

Style changes clearly have been associated with so-called planned obsolescence. The manufacturer of a durable good allegedly builds a reduction in serviceable life into the commodity. An automobile, for example, has a planned

---

[66] Franklin M. Fisher, Zvi Griliches, and Carl Kaysen, ''The Costs of Automobile Model Changes since 1949: Abstracts,'' *American Economic Reivew,* vol. 52 (May 1962), pp. 259–261, and ''The Costs of Automobile Model Changes since 1949,'' *Journal of Political Economy,* vol. 70 (October 1962), pp. 433–451.

reduction in resale value after approximately three years, attributable to the introduction of a different style that will render the old-style automobile model "obsolete," if only because it looks different.

Another notion of planned obsolescence involves designing the product so that it will become useless sooner than it would have otherwise. Implicit in this notion of planned obsolescence is the dubious assumption that the cost of having the product last longer is minimal to the manufacturer or, in the extreme case, zero.

Remember the formula for the present value of an asset, Eq. (9-9). Let's modify that formula slightly and assume that the resale or scrap value of the durable asset in question is 0 at the end of three years. The present value of the asset is therefore

$$PV = \frac{A_1}{(1 + r)} + \frac{A_2}{(1 + r)^2} + \frac{A_3}{(1 + r)^3} \tag{9-10}$$

Now consider what happens to the present value when planned obsolescence is effected by altering the production of the durable asset so that it lasts only two years. Present value is now

$$PV' = \frac{A_1}{(1 + r)} + \frac{A_2}{(1 + r)^2} + \frac{0}{(1 + r)^3} \tag{9-11}$$

But clearly PV > PV', assuming that A_1, A_2, and r remain the same. For a given nominal price of the durable good, the price per constant-quality unit will be higher in the second case than in the first case. If the good cost \$100 in both cases, its cost *per year of service* will certainly be higher when the good lasts only two years than when it lasts three years. If the unit of constant quality is one year of service, the price per constant-quality unit will have increased with planned obsolescence. Assuming the law of demand still holds, the services demanded of the durable asset that lasts two years will be less than the services demanded of a durable asset that will last three years. We can use the same arithmetic in the case of style changes. Style changes implicitly reduce the monetary value placed on the service flow per year. Thus A_1, A_2, and A_3 will be smaller. At any particular price, when the present value is smaller, the price per constant-quality unit will be larger and the quantity demanded will be less.

At this point, the most we can say about planned obsolescence is that a manufacturer engaging in this process will find the quantity demanded reduced at any given price.

Style Changes and the Elimination of Competition

It can be argued that style changes are a device used to eliminate competition. Menge, Selander, and Snell believe that style changes have been responsible for

the demise of all except the big four automobile firms.[67] Automobile manufacturers must use large, expensive dies in their metal-stamping presses. These
dies determine the particular style of automobile. They are indivisible because
of their minimum durability requirements. That is, to stamp even one automobile panel requires a die that may be good enough to stamp several hundred
thousand panels. In fact, McGee's study of the economies of size in the automobile industry found no examples of die replacement because dies were
''worn out.'' Some dies have produced several million parts.[68]

Firms producing a higher volume per unit time period have lower unit costs
per die than firms producing at a lower rate per unit time period. Thus, large
firms can frequently replace dies embodying a new style at a relatively small
cost per car. Smaller firms, in an attempt to follow suit, will incur higher die
costs per automobile produced because they will not be ready to change their
dies as quickly. Given any equilibrium price, a more rapid introduction of style
changes will drive smaller firms from the industry.

In order for the above argument to hold, style changes must be independent
of the level of the firm's output; thus they result in some economies of scale.
Another requirement is that smaller firms must introduce style changes at the
same rate as larger firms in order to maintain their share of the market. (Volkswagen is clearly a counter example.) Also, it must be true that restylized
automobiles are preferred by new car buyers. The evidence does seem to
suggest that new car buyers do prefer restyled cars, although some economists
contend that industry advertising has created the psychological ''need'' for
such newly designed cars.

THE MEASUREMENT OF PRODUCT DIFFERENTIATION

We cannot simply define product differentiation and measure it in such a way as
to derive an index. Even after we have determined what will be included in an
industry, we have no clearcut method to quantify actual physical differences.
Simply counting the number of different-flavored toothpastes or different-
scented hand soaps may not yield a satisfactory index of product differentiation. After all, product differentiation of such items is largely a subjective
concept; it is in the eyes of the beholder. Advertising may create more differentiated products than is indicated by simply counting the different flavors of
toothpaste. We have a hard time determining how different consumers evaluate

---

[67] John A. Menge, ''Style Change Costs as a Market Weapon,'' *Quarterly Journal of Econom-
ics*, vol. 76 (November 1962), pp. 632–647; Stephen E. Selander, ''Is Annual Style Change in the
Auto Industry an Unfair Method of Competition? A Rebuttal,'' *Yale Law Journal*, vol. 82 (March
1973), pp. 691–700; Bradford C. Snell, ''Annual Style Change in the Automobile Industry as an
Unfair Method of Competition,'' *Yale Law Journal*, vol. 80 (1971), pp. 567–613, and ''A Reply,''
Yale Law Journal, vol. 82 (March 1973), pp. 711–715.

[68] John S. McGee, ''Economies of Size in Auto Body Manufacture,'' *Journal of Law and
Economics*, vol. 16 (October 1973), pp. 239–273.

different products. We can say in some ordinal sense that products having physical characteristics in common are generally less well differentiated. We might also be able to say that products that are more heavily advertised will be more differentiated. Even so, we will have a hard time determining whether soaps, for example, are more differentiated than cigarettes.

Using Cross-Price Elasticity of Demand

One might be tempted to use cross-price elasticity of demand measures to determine the degree of product differentiation. Presumably, high cross-price elasticities of demand indicate low product differentiation and high substitutability. Nonetheless, these elasticities may still be consistent with a high degree of brand loyalty in the absence of any price changes by different sellers. Attempts to determine brand loyalty indexes fare no better, because they do not tell us the size of the cross-price elasticity dimension of product differentiation and the degree to which buyers will shift among sellers in response to changes in relative prices. Cross-price elasticity and brand loyalty concepts actually deal with different aspects of buyer behavior. Brand loyalty involves the behavior of consumers when confronted by a set of given items offered by a variety of sellers. Cross-price elasticity involves the changes in consumer behavior in response to changes in relative prices. Nonetheless, both of these concepts are aspects of product differentiation.

BRAND NAMES AND TRADEMARKS

It is possible to analyze brand names and trademarks as methods of reducing information costs to consumers. Brand names (including trademarks) allow buyers to determine which firm has made a given product. Imitation of brand names and trademarks does, nonetheless, fool some consumers, although given trademark laws, most buyers in most situations can believe that the information they are obtaining is correct. Brand names impart more than just information about the manufacturer. They can also indicate the quality and reliability of a product. Some consumers will be willing to pay a higher price for both quality and reliability. Higher reliability allows the consumer to obtain more regularly his or her optimum basket of goods. Thus it can be argued that consumers will be willing to pay for higher reliability. Although firms may be tempted to cheat, they know that through brand names and quality control, they may establish a valuable reputation for high reliability. At any point in time, they can reduce costs and reliability without reducing price or demand for their product in the short run. Profits in the short run will rise. The degree to which firms are tempted to cheat depends on the speed and ability of consumers to discover a change in reliability. The more costly it is to obtain this information and the more costly it is for buyers to switch to another brand, the greater the probability of cheating will be. The more a firm cheats, the faster it depreciates the present discounted value of its brand name. A typical example of cheating or depleting one's brand name capital refers to restaurants. How often has the reader observed a new restaurant serving superb food at a price equivalent to that charged by other restaurants serving food of a lesser quality? After a reputation (reliability) has been established, regular customers and those referred to the restaurant by regular customers may eventually witness a drop in quality. Clearly, the price per constant-quality unit is rising. The restaurant is "cheating" on its reputation and allowing its capital assets—reliability and reputation—to depreciate.

Seals of Approval

Several types of seals of approval appear on numerous products. Basically, they are designed to furnish consumers with information about product reliability, safety, and quality. Here we'll discuss two of the most well-known seals: the Underwriter's Laboratory, or UL, label and the Good Housekeeping Institute "Seal of Approval."

Underwriter's Laboratory.   Most household appliances display the UL label, and many manufacturers promote it in their advertising. The UL label, however, certifies only that the product or appliance does not have the potential of causing fire, electric shock, or accident under normal conditions. Underwriter's Laboratory does not evaluate the actual quality of any specific appliance. The UL label does not mean that the product has been compared to its competitors and been proved better than they are. Moreover, the only way the UL label can be obtained is by the manufacturer's either submitting the product and paying a fee or by agreeing to a specified control procedure. In order to keep the UL label, a fee must be paid every year. Some companies that decide not to pay that fee may have perfectly sound products.

Recently, the Underwriter's Laboratory has branched out into the testing of marine equipment (for example, life preservers), medical equipment (for example, adjustable hospital beds), and other equipment. UL has also entered the area of general safety hazards. For example, it might test a particular electric coffeepot to see if the lid falls off when the pot is tipped (this has nothing to do with the electrical part of the product). UL now requires manufacturers to include safety tips in the use-and-care manuals for products it approves.

Good Housekeeping Seal.   More than 35 years ago, the Federal Trade Commission required the Good Housekeeping Institute Laboratories to eliminate the term "seal of approval." Nonetheless, for many consumers, the seal does denote approval. Good Housekeeping does not test whether a product is good or bad. Presumably, it determines only whether a product or service submitted by a manufacturer who plans to advertise in *Good Housekeeping* magazine measures up to all the claims made for it in the advertisement.

In principle, if the Good Housekeeping seal is on a product, the manufacturer will give you a refund or replacement if the product or performance is defective. No product is tested by the Good Housekeeping Institute Laboratories in New York City unless there is a possibility of its being advertised in the magazine. Before a manufacturer can use this Good Housekeeping seal, it must guarantee to the magazine that the volume of advertising placed in *Good Housekeeping* is the same as that placed in other media (or at least two columns a year).

CHAPTER 10

PRICE DISCRIMINATION

In perfectly competitive markets, all buyers are charged the same price for a particular homogeneous product (price, of course, will reflect differential transportation charges). If we assume full knowledge on the part of all buyers, a difference in price per constant-quality unit cannot exist. Any seller of the product who tries to charge a higher price than the going market price will find that no one wants to purchase from him or her. However, in market structures other than perfect competition, it is conceivable for a nonuniform price to exist within a market area. The nonuniformity of prices may be due to an industry practice called price discrimination, which is designed to increase profits.

DEFINING PRICE DISCRIMINATION

The most common definition of **price discrimination** is the sale of technically similar goods at prices disproportional to their marginal cost, taking full account of manufacture, sale, delivery, and also risk and uncertainty. Otherwise stated, price discrimination exists when technologically similar goods are sold with a different markup, or

$$\frac{P_1}{MC_1} \neq \frac{P_2}{MC_2}$$

Just because we observe similar goods being sold at the same price by a supplier does not necessarily rule out the possibility of price discrimination. If indeed the goods are actually different, because of quality, amount of service offered, transportation charges, cost of sale, and so on, then charging the same price really indicates that the markup on the units is different. Hence, we are back into a situation of price discrimination.

Price Differentiation

It must be made clear at the outset that different prices may reflect differences in the costs of service. This is *not* price discrimination; it is price differentiation, or differences in prices that reflect differences in marginal costs. In fact, two different prices on seemingly like items often indicate two different commodities. After all, goods are differentiated by geographical location, by how they look, and by when they are sold. Indeed, it turns out that how we define a good often determines whether there is price discrimination. For example, two identical new cars might be sold by the same dealer at two different prices. If we define the commodity simply as a car, we would have to say that price discrimination exists. If, however, we include all other aspects of the transaction, such as credit terms, waiting time before delivery, trade-in allowance, and so on, we might find that, properly defined, the price per constant-quality unit is the same to the two individual buyers.

Necessary Conditions

Several conditions are necessary for the existence of price discrimination.

    1 The firm must face a downward-sloping demand curve.

    2 The two or more identifiable classes of buyers must be separable at a cost that does not exceed the monetary gains from separating them.

    3 The resale by those buyers who pay a low price to those who would be charged a higher price must be deterred.

    4 The price elasticity of demand for the product of two or more classes of buyers must be different and must be known by the firm, at least in an ordinal sense necessary for third-degree price discrimination.

Some economists have added to the above necessary requirements two further ones: (a) that there be control over existing sellers, and (b) that there be control over entry into the industry. To some extent, these two conditions seem overly restrictive. We will give examples of price discrimination in open monopolistically competitive markets where there is no control over existing sellers and no control over entry.

THE PROFIT-MAXIMIZING PRICE AND OUTPUT DECISION

To simplify our exposition, let's consider a monopolist who is able to price-discriminate between two classes of buyers, I and II; marginal costs are identical for both classes. For profit to be at a maximum, $MR_I = MR_{II} = MC$. It is as if the goods sold to class I and class II were two *different* goods having exactly the same marginal cost of production. To maximize total profits, the monopolist wants to set marginal revenue equal to marginal cost in all markets in which he or she is selling. If marginal revenue in either market exceeds marginal cost, profits could be increased by expanding sales (lowering price). On the other hand, if marginal revenue in either market were less than marginal cost, profit could be increased by reducing sales (raising price).

We show this situation in Figure 10-1. Class I buyers are presented in panel (*b*), class II buyers in panel (*a*). Note that in panel (*a*) the rate of sales to class II buyers gets larger as we move from right to left. We assume for simplicity's sake that the marginal cost for servicing both classes of consumers is both equal and constant. Marginal cost equals marginal revenue for class I at quantity Q_I. The price at which the quantity can be sold is P_I. On the other hand, for buyers in class II who have a more elastic demand curve (at any given P) than class I buyers, the intersection of marginal cost with MR_{II} is at quantity Q_{II}. The price

FIGURE 10-1
Price discrimination with constant marginal cost. Assume that the monopolist has been able to separate two classes of demanders, I and II. The profit-maximizing rate of output for each class will be given by the respective intersection of MR_I and MR_{II} with the common marginal cost MC. The output rate for class I demanders will be Q_I; the price charged will be P_I. For class II demanders the price will be lower, P_{II}. The demand curve for class II consumers is more elastic at any given P because it cuts the vertical axis closer to the origin.

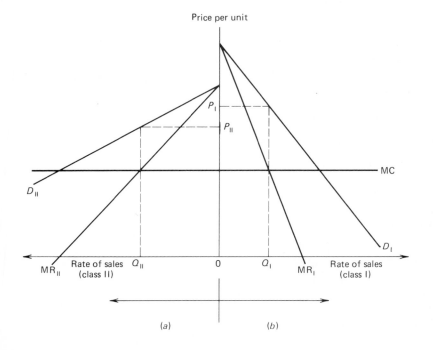

at which this quantity is sold is P_{II}, which is lower than P_I. In other words, the price-discriminating monopolist will sell the same product at a higher price to a class of buyers with a relatively less-elastic demand curve than that charged to the other class of buyers who have a relatively higher elasticity of demand.

This can be seen by using the formula in Eq. (10-1) and equating the two marginal revenues:

$$
\begin{aligned}
\text{MR}_I &= P_I\left(1 + \frac{1}{\eta_I}\right) \\
\text{MR}_{II} &= P_{II}\left(1 + \frac{1}{\eta_{II}}\right)
\end{aligned}
\tag{10-1}
$$

When we make these two equal (since $\text{MR}_I = \text{MR}_{II} = \text{MC}$), we get

$$
P_I\left(1 + \frac{1}{\eta_I}\right) + P_{II}\left(1 = \frac{1}{\eta_{II}}\right)
\tag{10-2}
$$

We know, however, that class I buyers have a market demand schedule that is more inelastic than that of Class II buyers. In order for the two sides of Eq. (10-1) to be equal, P_I must be greater than P_{II}.

The General Case

We can take a more general case with an upward-sloping marginal cost curve to show the profit-maximizing prices that a price-discriminating monopolist will charge to two identifiably different classes of buyers. In Figure 10-2, we have shown a demand curve for class I as D_ID_I. Its marginal revenue curve is labeled MR_I. Class II demanders have a demand curve represented by $D_{II}D_{II}$ and a marginal revenue curve of MR_{II}. In this case, the relative elasticity of demand is numerically greater for class II buyers than for class I buyers. (This is so even though $D_{II}D_{II}$ at first glance looks more inelastic than D_ID_I because it is steeper. We cannot, however, determine the elasticity of demand by the *slope* of the demand curve. Using the vertical axis formula for elasticity, whichever demand curve intersects the vertical axis closer to the origin will be the relatively more elastic at each price.)

We now derive the summed marginal revenue curve $\text{MR}_I = \text{MR}_{II}$ in Figure 10-2. Here we are horizontally summing the two separate marginal revenue curves. The horizontally summed marginal revenue curve intersects the common marginal cost curve at point E; thus, the profit-maximizing quantity to be produced and sold is Q_m. We now have a specific marginal cost labeled C_1 on the vertical axis. To satisfy the profit-maximization criterion, which requires that marginal revenue be equal to marginal cost, a monopolist will allocate quantity Q_I to class I and Q_{II} to class II, their sum being equal to Q_m. These quantities are given by the respective intersections of specific marginal cost C_1 with marginal revenue in each separate market. The prices that will be charged

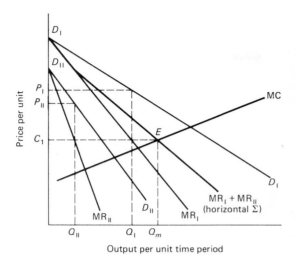

FIGURE 10-2
Price discrimination—the general case. We horizontally sum the marginal revenue curves to derive $MR_I + MR_{II}$. The summed marginal revenue curve intersects the common marginal cost curve at point E. The total output rate will be Q_m. It will be distributed between the two classes so that the first receives Q_I and the second receives Q_{II}. We find the prices that the monopolist can charge for those rates of output on their respective demand curves: class I buyers will pay a higher price P_I than the P_{II} charged class II buyers.

are P_I and P_{II}, or the price at which the profit-maximizing quantities can be sold in each individual market. As in the previous example, in the market with the more elastic demand curve, the price will be lower than in the market with the less elastic demand curve, that is, $P_{II} < P_I$.

CLASSIFICATION OF PRICE DISCRIMINATION BY DEGREE

Following the lead of A. C. Pigou, we can classify price discrimination into three types: first degree, second degree, and third degree.[1] Briefly, first-degree price discrimination is perfect in that each unit is sold to every consumer at its exact reservation price. Thus, every consumer pays the maximum amount he or she is willing to commit for the good in question instead of doing without it. No consumers' surplus is left. Second-degree price discrimination is a cruder method in which several prices approximate consumers' reservation prices. Third-degree price discrimination simply involves separating groups of consumers into two or more classes and charging a different price to each group depending on the relative price elasticity of demand. We will now discuss these types of discrimination in more detail.

First-Degree, or Perfect, Price Discrimination

We can visualize first-degree price discrimination with the help of Figure 10-3. The first-degree price discriminator is able to charge a different price for each unit of output, thus the shaded area that represents consumer surplus prior to

[1] Arthur C. Pigou, *The Economics of Welfare* (London: Macmillan, 1920), pp. 240–256. Also see Stephen Enke, ''Some Notes on Price Discrimination,'' *Canadian Journal of Economics and Political Science*, vol. 30 (February 1964), pp. 95–109.

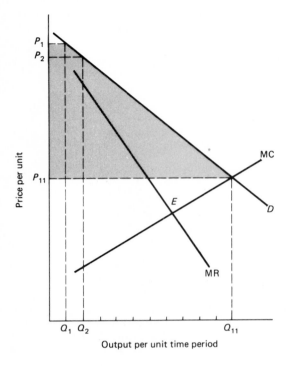

FIGURE 10-3
First-degree price discrimination. In first-degree price discrimination we find that the monopolist is able to charge the maximum price for each unit sold. Thus total revenue is $P_1 + P_2 + \cdots + P_{11}$.

the instigation of price discrimination for this monopolist is transferred to the monopolist and becomes monopoly rents.

Consider an example in which you are a gem purchaser. You go into a small room in which a sack of diamonds is presented to you. You are faced with the choice of "take it or leave it." If the seller of the diamonds can figure out exactly the shape of your demand curve, you can be charged a price that leaves you indifferent to buying or not buying the diamonds. You will then be the "victim" of perfect price discrimination.

Basically, perfect price discrimination allows the monopolist to extract every last bit of consumer surplus from each buyer. Remember that consumer surplus is defined as the difference between what the consumer would have paid for a particular quantity of a commodity rather than do without it and what the consumer actually paid. In the diamond case the difference is zero.

Second-Degree Price Discrimination

Second-degree price discrimination differs from first-degree price discrimination only in that it is cruder. We see in Figure 10-4 that the steps involved and the different prices charged (P_4 and P_8) are much further apart than those in Figure 10-3. The amount of consumer surplus extracted by the monopolist is equal to the shaded area, which will be smaller than the shaded area in Figure 10-3. It can be seen clearly that profits obtained under second-degree price

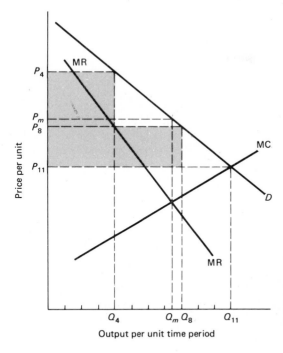

FIGURE 10-4
Second-degree price discrimination. In second-degree price discrimination the monopolist is not able to charge the maximum price for each unit sold. Here we observe that the revenue is equal to $P_4 \times Q_4 + P_8 \times Q_8$.

discrimination are greater than those obtained by the monopolist charging the pure monopoly price of P_m and selling the quantity Q_m.

Second-degree price discrimination occurs more often when there are many buyers within the market. A declining rate schedule embodying "quantity discounts" is an example of this type of discrimination. Some electric utilities charge lower prices for each additional block of electricity used. Anyone using a certain amount of electricity can buy the next block at a lower price. Second-degree price discrimination induces greater consumption by offering quantity discounts that are made in a stepladder fashion, also called multipart pricing, a topic we will discuss in Chapter 11.

Third-Degree Price Discrimination

Third-degree price discrimination occurs when a monopolist charges different prices in different markets for the same product. We have already illustrated the general case in Figures 10-1 and 10-2. There we saw two different markets for the product. A higher price is charged in the market with a less-elastic demand. Charging students a lower price than nonstudents for movies, magazines, and professional journals is a common example of third-degree price discrimination. Charging senior citizens a lower price than other buyers for transportation and spectator events is another common example.

Table 10-1 summarizes the various forms of price discrimination by degree.

TABLE 10-1
FORMS OF PRICE DISCRIMINATION

Type of price discrimination	Attributes	Examples
Third-degree	Different classes of buyers charged different prices for same product.	Student and senior citizen discounts at entertainment events and on public transportation.
Second-degree	Declining rate schedules; lower price per unit as larger quantities purchased.	Electricity pricing; quantity discounts at supermarkets.
First-degree (perfect)	Each buyer charged exactly that price which leaves him or her indifferent between buying and not buying.	Wholesale diamond sales; haggling over prices of souvenirs in "tourist traps."

EFFICIENCY CONSIDERATIONS

Price discrimination cannot be practiced in a perfectly competitive market structure. Therefore, it is associated with at least a minimum degree of monopoly or market power. Hence, price discrimination is often condemned as symptomatic of monopoly. Since monopoly output is less than what it would be under perfect competition, price discrimination is also associated with the misallocation of resources. We can show, however, that certain forms of price discrimination under certain conditions will not generate a misallocation of resources and indeed may actually increase output. In any event, in most cases, first- and second-degree price discrimination at least lead to a larger output than under a simple nondiscriminating monopoly situation. Going from simple monopoly to price discriminating monopoly can often actually improve the allocation of resources.

Perfect Price Discrimination

Go back and look at Figure 10-3. Here you see that each unit of output is sold at a separate price. Each marginal unit sold adds to revenue an amount equal to the price for which it is sold. Hence, the demand curve becomes the marginal revenue curve of the perfectly price-discriminating monopolist. Total output occurs where the marginal cost curve cuts the demand curve. Had the monopolist not perfectly price-discriminated, output would have been where the marginal cost curve intersects at the marginal revenue curve, or at point E.

Now if we wish to compare the perfectly discriminating monopolist with perfectly competitive industry, we must assume something about the cost curves in both cases. If we make the heroic assumption that the marginal cost curve in Figure 10-3 would be coincident with the summation of all the perfect competitors' cost curves, then it would represent the supply curve of the perfectly competitive industry. We would see that output would be exactly the same under perfect competition and perfectly discriminating monopoly. Thus, there would be no misallocation of resources. The only difference would be in who would receive the consumer surplus. Under perfect competition, it would be consumers; under perfectly discriminating monopoly, it would be the monopolist.

Second-Degree Discrimination

Second-degree discrimination is a cruder version of perfect discrimination to the extent that it approaches perfect discrimination. Thus, output will almost always be greater than for a simple monopoly. The closer second-degree discrimination approaches first-degree discrimination, the closer output will approach a perfectly competitive industry.

Third-Degree Discrimination

We can be less certain about the efficiency effects of third-degree price discrimination. If, as in Figure 10-3, all demand functions are linear, the total amounts produced under third-degree discrimination will be the same as under simple monopoly.[2] Under special conditions involving the shape of the demand curves, third-degree price discrimination can actually increase output when compared to the output associated with a single uniform monopoly price. Joan Robinson has shown that it will increase output in the two-market case whenever the more elastic demand is more convex to the origin than the less elastic demand curve.[3] Consider a recreation of her geometric proof in our Figure 10-5. There are two demand curves, d_1d_1 and d_2d_2. The total market demand curve is given by D_TD_T. The marginal revenue curve is given as MR_T in

---

[2] This result holds, ignoring income effects and assuming simply that the monopolist would have sold at least one unit in the more elastic market prior to discrimination.

[3] Joan Robinson, *The Economics of Imperfect Competition* (London: Macmillan, 1933), pp. 189–195.

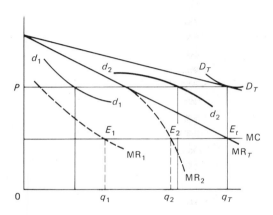

FIGURE 10-5
Comparative output under simple monopoly and third-degree price discrimination.
Source: Adopted from Joan Robinson, *The Economics of Imperfect Competition* (London: Macmillan, 1953), p. 191.

the absence of third-degree price discrimination. Marginal revenue intersects marginal cost at E_T and output is $0q_T$. If the two markets are separated, however, marginal revenue intersects marginal cost at E_1 and E_2, yielding output rates of $0q_1$ and $0q_2$. We observe that the output rate with third-degree price discrimination ($0q_1 + 0q_2$) is greater than the output rate with linear demand curves ($0q_T$). This is true merely because the more elastic market 1 has a demand curve that is more concave to the origin that is the less elastic demand curve (which we have drawn as convex).

Robinson argued that the real world might exhibit such "appropriate" variations in convexity so as to allow for an increase of output due to third-degree price discrimination. She maintained that consumers in the low-elasticity market will not change their buying habits much even with the higher price, but that those in the high-elasticity market will dramatically increase the quantities purchased.[4]

Full Utilization of Productive Capacity

Some argue that price discrimination can increase the efficiency of resource allocation when it allows for a fuller utilization of capacity. Electric utilities, for example, engage in price discrimination by giving commercial users, who could otherwise have an incentive to develop their own sources of power, lower rates than residential consumers. This policy allows utilities to increase total capacity and permits fuller utilization of that capacity. As long as the revenue received during the off-peak period covers variable costs plus some portion of fixed costs, price discrimination presumably improves resource allocation (assuming, of course, that prices have not been raised above what they were prior to peak-load pricing).

When Price Discrimination Is Required for the Existence of an Industry

Sometimes price discrimination is necessary if an industry is to continue to exist (or to begin in the first place). Consider the situation depicted in Figure 10-6. We have drawn the demand curves for two different classes of buyers of the product in question. Those curves are labeled D_1D_1 and D_2D_2. We know that demand curve D_2D_2 is relatively more price-elastic than D_1D_1 because it cuts the vertical axis closer to the origin. We now horizontally sum these two demand curves in order to derive the total or market demand curve that would face a monopolist in this industry. This demand curve is the heavily shaded line labeled D_1D_T. This market demand curve coincides with the demand curve D_1D_1 until the price at which D_2D_2 begins.

We have drawn in a long-run average cost curve, LAC, which is *everywhere* above the market demand curve D_1D_T. Thus, if a single price had to be charged

---

[4] Ibid., pp. 201–202.

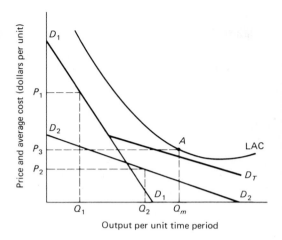

FIGURE 10-6
Price discrimination necessary for industry's existence. If the long-run average cost curve is everywhere above the market demand curve D_1D_T, the firm cannot exist without price discrimination. If, however, the monopolist is allowed to charge P_1 to those with less elastic demand and P_2 to those with more elastic demand, then in this example the weighted price P_3 would just equal long-run average cost at point A. The industry can and will exist.

in this market, no single price would allow the monopolist to cover long-run average costs. The industry would not exist.

Now consider the possibility of third-degree price discrimination. The profit-maximizing prices for the two different classes of demanders are given as P_1 and P_2. For the sake of simplicity, we have not drawn in the separate marginal revenue curve or the marginal cost curve. The profit-maximizing quantity that would be sold to class 1 demanders is given as Q_1 and to class 2 demanders as Q_2. The total quantity that the price-discriminating monopolist would provide is given as Q_m ($= Q_1 + Q_2$). It is sold at a (weighted) average price of P_3 that, in this particular example, is just equal to long-run average costs at rate of output Q_m, or point A. The weighted average is

$$P_3 = \frac{Q_1 P_1 + Q_2 P_2}{Q_m}$$

In this instance, unless price discrimination to obtain part or all of the consumer's surplus is both feasible and permitted, the industry will not exist, that is, the product will not be offered for sale.

RELAXING THE BASIC ASSUMPTIONS

Differing Costs

Typically, price discrimination occurs when different prices are charged to different groups of consumers. These prices are not in proportion to differences in marginal cost. In Figure 10-7 we show marginal cost for group A and marginal cost for group B. The demand curves are also different; they are drawn as $D_A D_A$ and $D_B D_B$. Marginal revenue is drawn accordingly as MR_A and MR_B. In our example we show a profit-maximizing price of $15 for group A and $12 for group B, but we see that marginal cost for A is $10 and marginal cost for B is

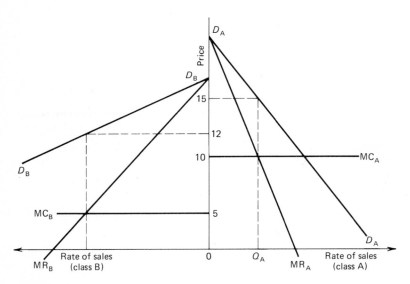

FIGURE 10-7
Price discrimination with different marginal costs.

only $5. Then, the ratio of price to cost is 1.5 for group A and 2.4 for group B. Clearly, group B is being discriminated against because its ratio of price to marginal cost is higher than group A's ratio.

Note, however, that if the monopolist in this situation chose to charge both groups the same price, that, too, would be a form of discrimination because the ratio of price to marginal cost would still be different for both groups.

Taking Account of Joint Costs   Common or joint overhead costs occur in a firm producing many products.[5] One piece of capital equipment may make two or more products. One building may house the production of many products. One management team may be responsible for many product lines. Some production processes yield by-products—producing petroleum often yields methane, for example. When joint costs occur, any allocation of such joint costs is purely arbitrary.[6] Firms will often justify price discrimination in legal cases by arbitrarily allocating joint costs. Ultimately, one finds that groups of demanders with low price elasticities end up paying a larger share of common costs. This has been shown to be the case in the pricing of postal services.[7]

---

[5] See William A. Lewis, *Overhead Costs* (London: Allen & Unwin, 1949), and John M. Clark, *Studies in the Economics of Overhead Costs* (Chicago: University of Chicago Press, 1923).
[6] See Alfred Marshall, *Principles of Economics,* 8th ed., Book V, Chap. 6, and Mathematical App. (New York: Macmillan, 1949).
[7] See Leonard Waverman, "Pricing Principles: How Should Postal Rates Be Set?" in Roger Sherman, ed., *Perspectives on Postal Service Issues* (Washington, D.C.: American Enterprise Institute, 1980), pp. 7–29.

The Multiproduct Firm

The notion of price discrimination can be extended to the pricing decisions that a multiproduct firm must face. Indeed, price discrimination is a special case of the general optimizing rule that a firm will maximize profits by always setting marginal revenue equal to marginal cost in every market for every product. In the case of pure price discrimination, the product sold in each market is the same, but the demand curves differ. When the demands are independent, the marginal revenue of any output sold in any market is simply equal to the price times (1 − 1/own price elasticity of demand). With identical products in markets with identical marginal costs, we have already seen that third-degree price discrimination dictates that the price charged is dependent only upon the relative price elasticity of demand in each market. On the other hand, when marginal costs differ, prices that proportionately reflect the difference in marginal cost merely indicate price differentiation, not price discrimination.

Physical Differentiation of Products.   Any physical differentiation of products may provide the multiproduct firm with the ability to separate the total market. The firm may then be able to practice price discrimination. A classic example has been presented by Clemens.[8] He considered firms selling fabrication services or other types of services such as printing, manufacturing of electrical apparatus, plastics, and machinery. These firms are selling manufacturing capacity at varying price-cost margins. According to Clemens, the "typical job shop" will survey market potential, define each market depending on the demand function, and then relate the potential price to be received to the percentage of the job shop's capacity that must be devoted to satisfying the demand in that market at that price. The job shop will satisfy markets with the relatively smallest price elasticities of demand, charging them the highest prices. The job shop will work down to more and more markets where demand is relatively more price elastic. It will stop when the next market will not contribute as much to revenues as to marginal cost. In other words, when the product is rearranged, the most profitable product is put on line first. The product here is job services, the manufacture of somebody else's product. The markup will be highest on the first jobs undertaken and lowest on the last. This is a form of price discrimination that allows the firm to utilize full capacity so that, at the margin, marginal cost will be equal to price.[9]

Substitutability and Complementarity.   We have been dealing with single-product markets that are independent. Now we look at multiple-product markets that are interdependent. Thus, an alteration in the price and quantity of

---

[8] Eli W. Clemens, "Price Discrimination and the Multiple-Product Firm," *Review of Economic Studies*, vol. 19 (January 1951), pp. 1–11. Also see Michael Spence, "Product Selection, Fixed Costs, and Monopolistic Competition," *Review of Economic Studies*, vol. 43 (June 1976), pp. 218–220, for a discussion of product variety and price discrimination.

[9] Of course, in job shops with little or no market power, such discrimination will not be possible.

one product will have effects on demand and cost conditions for other products and, hence, will have complicated effects on the firm's total revenues and total costs. Whenever there is interdependence between the demands for different products from a single firm, profit maximization by that firm requires prices that depend on its own price elasticity of demand for each product, as well as cross-price elasticity of demand between each product and all other products.

Whenever the substitute relationship between the good and other goods dominates, the profit-maximizing price of the product in question will be higher than it would be if no interdependence existed. Similarly, output will be lower. After all, marginal revenue associated with any rate of output is going to be lower, because the demand for other products of the firm will be reduced when the price of the product in question is reduced and output is increased. Conversely, if complementary relationships dominate, the profit-maximizing price of the good in question will be lower than it would be without interdependence, and output will be higher.

PRICE DISCRIMINATION CLASSIFIED BY LEGAL ACTIONS

Legislators as well as economists have taken an interest in price discrimination, because in many cases price discrimination has been deemed an unfair competitive practice. Most legal actions concern price discrimination in goods as opposed to services. First we will look at the principal statutes covering price discrimination, and then we will look at several important court cases.

The Statutes

The first statute that explicitly discussed price discrimination in the United States was the Clayton Act of 1914. Section 2 prohibited sellers of goods from discriminating in the prices charged different purchasers "where the effect of such discrimination may be to substantially lessen competition or tend to create a monopoly in any line of commerce." Some exceptions were allowed. For example, quantity discounts could be granted under certain circumstances. Also, even though sellers usually could not discriminate in prices charged to different buyers, they could refuse to make sales to any buyer at their discretion, as long as that refusal was not an attempt to create a monopoly or constituted unreasonable restraint of trade. The act stated that "nothing herein contained shall prevent persons engaged in selling goods . . . from selecting their own customers in bonafide transactions and not in restraint of trade." Price differentiation was allowed under section 2 because differentiation due to differences in quality grade or quantity sold was not deemed illegal.

Price discrimination was disallowed only when the effect was "to substantially lessen competition." The courts interpreted that clause to mean the lessening of competition between the seller and one or more competitors of the seller—not between customers of the seller. For some time other forms of price discrimination continued to be lawful. For example, if Ajax Company sold goods to buyer X at prices lower than those charged to buyer B, the mere fact that the discrimination lessened competition between X and B did not constitute a violation of this section.

The quantity discount loophole in section 2 of the Clayton Act proved to be the primary tool by which price discrimination was allowed. In court case after court case, discriminatory price structures were rationalized in terms of quantity price differences. Indeed, Congress found that many sellers were being pressured by large-scale buyers to grant them price reductions much larger than could be justified by cost savings alone.

The Robinson-Patman Act.   Because of Congress's supposed distress at the "loopholes" in the Clayton Act, section 2 was amended by section 2a of the Robinson-Patman Act in 1936. Basically, the Robinson-Patman Act makes it illegal to discriminate in price between different purchasers of commodities of like grade and quality where the effect of such discrimination may be to substantially lessen competition or tend to create a monopoly in any line of commerce. This section still allowed for price differentials based on actual differences in the cost of manufacture, sale, or delivery resulting from differing methods in which quantities were sold or delivered. A seller was still able to defend a price discrimination suit if he or she could prove that the price differences reflected differences in cost. The Robinson-Patman Act allowed for two additional escape routes: (1) when such discrimination was used "in good faith to meet an equally low price of a competitor," and (2) when it was used to dispose of obsolete goods, perishable goods, or goods offered in a bankruptcy sale.

The Robinson-Patman Act dealt with a number of industry practices that had developed despite section 2 of the Clayton Act. The act flatly prohibited attainment of brokerage commissions or any allowance or discount unless intermediaries actually performed services as independent brokers (section 2c). Further sections prohibited making payments to one customer for services or facilities rendered that were not made available to other customers.

One of the main changes effected by the Robinson-Patman amendment to the Clayton Act concerned the injury to competition between the buyer and the buyer's competitor rather than just among the seller's competitors. Remember, we pointed out that under the old Clayton Act, if the seller sold products or services for differing prices to two different buyers, no price discrimination existed, because competition among sellers was not affected, only among buyers. Under the Robinson-Patman amendment, if buyer X could unfairly compete with buyer Y because buyer X received a lower price from the seller, the seller had engaged in an unlawful act.

Even though the Robinson-Patman Act brought about certain clarifications to the law, it can by no means be said to have eliminated price discrimination. Considerable discriminatory pricing continues to exist in the real world of business. The Robinson-Patman Act has been enforced only sporadically. Recently it has come under attack because its actual effect has been to give undue protection to small, often inefficient, businesses. Additionally, there are extreme problems of statutory interpretation of the act. It has been difficult to prove that price discrimination in any given case has resulted in "a substantial lessening of competition."[10]

Robinson-Patman Court Cases

After the passage of the Robinson-Patman Act, the government brought a number of cases to define the limits of price discrimination. A principal case involved the Federal Trade Commission and Morton Salt Company, a salt producer that sold to wholesalers and large retailers, including major chain stores. The price schedule offered all parties after allowance rebate and discounts was:

Less-than-carload purchases	$1.60 per case
Carload purchases	$1.50 per case
5,000-case purchases in any consecutive 12 months	$1.40 per case
50,000-case purchases in any consecutive 12 months	$1.35 per case[11]

The Supreme Court found this discount price schedule discriminatory within the meaning of section 2a of the Robinson-Patman Act, even though the discounts were available to all on equal terms. The Court also rejected the company's argument that the Federal Trade Commission had failed to demonstrate that there was harm to competition in the industry. Morton Salt's argument was based on a proposition that the sale of salt was only one of many small items that retail grocers offer consumers, hence there was no harm to competition in the industry. The Court, however, found that "since a grocery store consists of many comparably small articles, there is no way to protect the grocer . . . except by applying the prohibitions of the Act to each end of article. . . ."[12]

The Court also made it explicit that the Robinson-Patman Act was specifically concerned with the protection of small businesses that were unable to purchase quantities in large lots. In addition, the burden of proof that differences in prices were attributable to costs continued to lie with the company, not with the Federal Trade Commission. Thus, unless price differentials can be explained by costs, they are deemed to be a violation of the law.

In recent years, there has been a growing recognition by economists, especially those in the Bureau of Economics at the Federal Trade Commission, that the Court's application of the Robinson-Patman Act may weaken rather than

---

[10] The future of the Robinson-Patman Act is uncertain. See "Recent Efforts to Amend or Repeal the Robinson-Patman Act," Hearings before the Ad Hoc Subcommittee on Antitrust . . . and Related Matters of the Committee on Small Business, U.S. Congress, House, 94th Cong. 1st Sess., 1975, pp. 282–312. See also, address by Paul Rand Dixon, "Robinson-Patman Is Not Dead, Merely Dormant," mimeographed (May 21, 1975).

[11] *Federal Trade Commission v. Morton Salt Company*, 334 U.S. 37 (1948).

[12] Ibid., p. 49.

strengthen competitive forces. The result of this insight has been a significant decrease in the number of Robinson-Patman price discrimination cases sought by the commission.

PRICING BELOW COST—PREDATORY PRICING

We have mentioned a special case in price discrimination where firms reduced price, sometimes below cost, in order to drive out a rival in a specific geographic area. In the models, predatory price cutting always involves a large firm with large financial resources. The reductions in price by the large firm are engaged in solely for the purpose of driving competitors out of business; they are not reflections of economies of scale or cost differences. When the predator sets price below cost, it will sustain losses. Presumably, the predator is able to sustain these losses longer than competitors because of his or her superior financial resources. Predatory pricing has also been called destructive competition and cutthroat competition.[13] Clearly, if the dominant firm prices below cost at any time period, the present value of the expected higher future profits must compensate for the present value of the losses absorbed during the price-cutting period.

Theoretical Problems with Predatory Pricing

Telser has pointed out certain subtle aspects of the predatory pricing argument that should be mentioned here.[14] He states that even if the predator is a large firm, sustaining losses is equivalent to borrowing to pay for those losses. Implicitly, then, the predator must face lower borrowing costs than its rivals face. If this is not the case, rivals should be able to borrow as much money as necessary to wait out the predator. Additionally, the predator must believe that the long-run rate of return by pricing below cost and incurring losses is greater than the market rate of interest. If this is not the case, it has no incentive to engage in predatory pricing, especially because the predator loses more from the larger sales volume that it attracts with its below-cost price. This is especially true when one recognizes that the predator normally will lose more revenue than its rivals. Assuming that the rivals reduce price to the level set by the predator, all the firms will suffer losses relative to their respective sales volumes. Since the predator's sales volume is typically larger than its rivals', the losses sustained by the predator will be proportionately larger.

Even if the two above conditions are satisfied, Telser points out that preda-

---

[13] See Phillip Areeda and Donald F. Turner, "Predatory Pricing and Related Practices under Section 2 of the Sherman Act," *Harvard Law Review*, vol. 88 (February 1975), pp. 697–733, and B. S. Yamey, "Predatory Price Cutting: Notes and Comments," *Journal of Law and Economics*, vol. 15 (April 1972), pp. 129–142.

[14] Lester G. Telser, "Cutthroat Competition and the Long Purse," *Journal of Law and Economics*, vol. 9 (October 1966), pp. 259–277.

tory pricing still may not make sense. During the time in which prices are being cut, consumers gain at the expense of all firms in the industry. Firms can avoid these losses in the short run if they merge. Therefore, we would expect that instead of engaging in predatory pricing, dominant firms would attempt mergers.

We may see predatory pricing, however, when:

1 Predatory pricing can be the result of very high costs of merger.

2 A merger is being negotiated and the dominant firm may engage in some price cutting in order to improve its bargaining position.

3 Entry costs are high and firms already in the industry may engage in price cutting together in order to retard further entry.

How to Judge Predatory Pricing

In order to judge predatory pricing correctly, it is important to compare the price charged with long-run marginal costs. Presumably, only when price is below long-run marginal cost does predatory pricing occur. The numerous complaints about predatory pricing often come from competitors who feel they are being squeezed out of the market by dominant firms. This may not be at all clear when one compares price with accurately measured long-run marginal cost.

The Standard Oil Example

The most famous case of predatory pricing involves the original Standard Oil Company. Between 1870 and 1899, the Standard Oil Trust headed by John D. Rockefeller obtained and maintained a share of over 90 percent of the petroleum-refining market. This large share of the market resulted from mergers and other practices, including, according to some researchers, obtaining discriminatory rail freight rates and rebates, physical destruction of competitors' capital equipment, price warfare, control of pipelines, and business espionage. Presumably, predatory pricing was a major tool in Rockefeller's hands. The oil trusts apparently cut prices in specific local markets where rivals existed and maintained prices at much higher levels in other markets that lacked rivals. When rivals realized they could not compete with Standard Oil, they were more receptive to a merger.

In a classic article, McGee attacked these allegations.[15] After reading the voluminous Standard Oil antitrust record, he found that there was little evidence to show that Standard Oil obtained its dominance in the market through predatory price cutting. McGee also pointed out that on a theoretical basis, predatory pricing may be irrational for wealth maximization because it often requires a sacrifice of current profits that are not worth future gains. He found,

---

[15] John S. McGee, "Predatory Price Cutting: The Standard Oil (N.J.) Case," *Journal of Law and Economics*, vol. 1 (October 1958), pp. 137–169.

for example, that competitors were purchased at prices attractive enough for several owners to sell out, purchase another company, then sell out again.[16]

Scherer disagreed with McGee's traditional criticism of the Standard Oil predatory price-cutting analysis. For example, Scherer points out that Rockefeller wrote to an associate:

> We want to watch and when our volume of business is to be cut down by the increase of competition to 50 percent, or less, it may be a very serious question whether we had not better make an important reduction, with a view of taking substantially all the business there is.[17]

Scherer's analysis, however, says nothing about the relationship of prices to costs. More important, the quote is consistent with greater competition, although an increased supply would yield a lower market price. Thus all firms would lower price even if they were close to price-taking conditions. Scherer, however, does recognize McGee's point—in its attempt to control the market, Standard Oil would have had to accept profit losses that were considerably larger than the losses that were inflicted upon smaller rivals.[18]

More recent examples also tend to support McGee's hypothesis. Kamerschen, Elzinga, and Zerbe generally found no systematic, successful predatory pricing in the ready-mix cement, gunpowder, and sugar-refining industries.[19] In addition, Koller found no evidence of positive returns from predatory pricing in an examination of 26 antitrust cases.[20]

---

[16] Ibid., p. 151. See also Roland H. Koller, II, "The Myth of Predatory Pricing," *Antitrust and Law and Economics Review*, vol. 4 (Summer 1971), pp. 105–123.

[17] Letter to A. Hutchins, quoted in Alan Nevins, *Study in Power: John D. Rockefeller, Industrialist and Philanthropist* (New York: Scribners, 1953), vol. 2, p. 65; referenced in Frederic M. Scherer, *Industrial Market Structure and Economic Performance* (Chicago: Rand McNally, 1980), p. 336.

[18] Scherer, *Industrial Market Structure and Economic Performance*, p. 336.

[19] David R. Kamerschen, "Predatory Pricing, Vertical Integration, and Market Foreclosure: The Case of Ready-Mix Cement in Memphis," *Industrial Organization Review*, vol. 2 (1974), pp. 143–168; Kenneth G. Elzinga, "Predatory Pricing: The Case of the Gunpowder Trust," *Journal of Law and Economics*, vol. 13 (April 1970), pp. 223–240; and Richard O. Zerbe, "The American Sugar Refinery Company, 1887–1914: The Story of a Monopoly," *Journal of Law and Economics*, vol. 12 (October 1969), pp. 339–375. Also see John S. McGee, "Predatory Pricing Revisted," *Journal of Law and Economics*, vol. 23 (October, 1980), pp. 289–330.

[20] Roland H. Koller, II, pp. 105–123, and "On the Definition of Predatory Pricing," *Antitrust Bulletin*, vol. 20 (Summer 1975), pp. 329–337, and "The Myth of Predatory Pricing."

CHAPTER 11

PRICE DISCRIMINATION: METHODS AND APPLICATIONS

In the last chapter, we presented the taxonomy of price discrimination, as well as the theory underlying the various forms of discrimination. In this chapter, we wish to look in more detail at the ways in which firms engage in the various practices of price discrimination. In the first section, we'll look briefly at Machlup's classification of price discrimination methods. Then we'll turn to a more detailed examination of traditional price discrimination, looking at movie theaters, telephone service, air fares, medical services, congressional information services, and college scholarships. In the next major section, we'll look at tie-in sales as a method of metering demand and charging accordingly. Next, we'll discuss multipart pricing by utilities and movie distributors. Finally, we'll examine the sale of hardback versus paperback books, different labels on physically similar items, sale of drugs, and trading stamps.

CLASSIFICATION BY TYPE

In the last chapter, we classified discrimination by degree—first, second, and third. Machlup has propounded a somewhat different set of discrimination classes: (1) personal, (2) group, and (3) product. Within each class of discrimination, he gives examples of many different actual types of discrimination. In Table 11-1, we recreate some of Machlup's categories.[1]

---

[1] Fritz Machlup, "Characteristics and Types of Price Discrimination," in *Business Concentration and Price Policy* (Princeton, N.J.: Princeton University Press, 1955), pp. 400–423; also, *The Political Economy of Monopoly* (Baltimore: Johns Hopkins Press, 1952).

TABLE 11-1
TYPES OF PRICE DISCRIMINATION

Personal discrimination

Size up customer's income
Customers are charged what the market will bear, depending on how wealthy the customer is. Presumably wealthier customers have inelastic demands and are charged a higher price. Examples—medical and legal services.

Give in if you must
Secret shaving off list prices is done when necessary to capture a sale.

Haggle every time
Each exchange is a separately negotiated transaction. Examples—bazaars in the Middle East, open-air markets in Latin America, and many private deals, such as purchases of used items through the classified sections of newspapers.

Measure the use
Those buyers who use the good or service more intensively are charged more, even if marginal costs of servicing are the same. Examples—Xerox machine rentals based on the number of copies made: the increased rental charge exceeds increased maintenance costs; IBM's rental of machines and sale of computer cards at above marginal cost per card.

Group discrimination

Dump the surplus
Sales are priced lower in foreign markets than in domestic markets in order not to depress the domestic price. Examples—drugs, TV sets, steel, free food for the U.S. Food for Peace program.

Absorb the freight
Freight is either absorbed or overcharged to customers who are located at varying distances from the production site.

Kill the rival
Prices are reduced only in markets served by a rival who, it is hoped, will be driven out of business; otherwise called predatory pricing. Examples—alleged practice of Standard Oil before 1900 and of American Tobacco.

Promote new customers
New customers are offered lower prices than old customers. The goal is to promote brand loyalty. Examples—magazine subscriptions.

Divide them by elasticity
Group discrimination exists whenever the group can be classified by occupation, age, or sex. Examples—children's versus adults' haircuts, student versus nonstudent rates at cinemas, professional discounts at motel chains and with national auto rental firms.

Protect the intermediary
Large retail buyers are charged the same price as small retail buyers who buy from wholesalers even though large retail firms do their own warehousing and distribution. This protects wholesalers from competition with retailers that might otherwise turn to vertical integration.

Favor the big ones
Large buyers are given price reductions that exceed cost savings normally associated with quantity sales.

Product discrimination

Pay for the label
Manufacturers distribute homogeneous products under various brands. Better-known brands have higher price tags. Examples—clothing, food, paint.

Appeal to the classes
Price differences are greater than differences in marginal cost when quality is upgraded. Examples—hardback versus paperback books, first-class versus tourist-class fares on airplanes.

Differing Demands

One specific type of price discrimination in Machlup's classification involves peak pricing where demand may shift during peak and off-peak periods. Consider Figure 11-1. Here we show a rising marginal cost curve and two demand curves, one for off-peak, DD, and the other for peak, $D'D'$. We see that marginal cost is low in slack periods and high during boom periods. It is not clear to what extent an increase in price from P to P' really is true price discrimination, because demand may be considered at different times for different products (hence we have not included price increase in Table 11-1).

Other Qualifications

Some of the forms of price discrimination listed in Table 11-1 are merely a statement of the conditions necessary for price discrimination. For example, under personal discrimination both "size up his income" and "give in if you must" may be translated into conditions necessary for identifying differing demand curves and recognizing the noninfinite elasticity of demand. In other cases, forms under product discrimination, such as "pay for the label" and "appeal to the classes," may create differential goods in the eyes of consumers. It is difficult to separate the differences in price attributable to the product from those caused by price discrimination.

METHODS OF PRICE DISCRIMINATION

Movie Theaters

Most movie theaters in the United States do not differentiate price on the basis of the seat in which one sits in the theater. On the other hand, most movie theaters do engage in an obvious form of price discrimination. There are usually

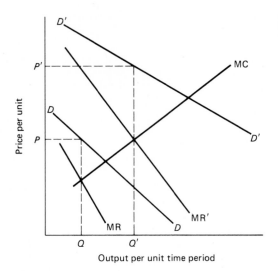

FIGURE 11-1
Peak pricing.

two and sometimes three or four different prices for the same movie at the same time. At a minimum, there is a higher price charged to adults than to children 11 and under. Presumably, the price elasticity of demand of children for movies is numerically higher than that of adults. It is basically costless to monitor the separation of the two groups because physical appearance will be roughly sufficient evidence of age. However, cheating clearly does occur when children who are 12 or older but look younger get in at the lower price.

Many movie theaters, particularly those around universities, offer special student prices upon presentation of either a student I.D. card or a specially obtained student pass issued by the movie theater or its chain. Again, monitoring of the two groups is relatively costless, although some cheating undoubtedly occurs. Many movie theaters price-discriminate in favor of senior citizens, presumably because they have a numerically higher price elasticity of demand. Upon presentation of proof of age or a special senior citizen pass similar to a student pass, those people age 65 and over enter the theater at a lower price than younger adults. We see in Table 11-2 a typical example of the varying rate schedule.

Changing Rates by Time of Day   Many movie theaters also engage in peak-load pricing that may constitute price discrimination, although more properly this pricing can be viewed as a means of exploiting unused capacity during off-peak hours. Movie theaters are rarely filled early in the day. In order to induce individuals to see a movie at off-peak times, theaters may reduce their rates to attract customers. We cannot consider this a form of pure price discrimination because the product being sold is clearly different. (A movie seen at a 7:30 P.M. showing is not exactly the same product as the same movie shown at 2:15 P.M.) Most people prefer movies in the evening, particularly since during the week fewer individuals have the leisure time available for daytime movie viewing. Price discrimination may be necessary for industry survival given film owners' exclusive copyright.

Telephone Services

Various rate schedules are utilized by the telephone company. In brief, they involve charging higher prices for business phones than for residential phones

TABLE 11-2
SAMPLE PRICES FOR MOVIES, OMNI THEATER,
SEPTEMBER 1980

	Matinee (2:00–5:00 P.M.)	Evening (after 5:00 P.M.)
Children (under 12)	$1.00	$1.50
Adults	2.50	3.50
Senior citizens	1.50	2.00

and higher prices for big-city users than for small-town users. In fact, telephone pricing has often followed a "value-of-service" format, attempting to discriminate on the basis of the value of the service or of the relative inelasticity of demand of some users. The ability to discriminate derives directly from the exclusive telephone franchise.

Business versus Residential Rates   Table 11-3 shows a typical rate schedule for business and residential phones. It can be argued that, although the higher price charged businesses is not fully reflective of just price discrimination, it may involve some price differentiation. Business people typically are more intensive phone users and thus they may impose higher marginal costs on the system than residential users do. If, however, high volume users create economies of scale, the opposite may be true. This is an empirical question that would have to be answered by looking at the degree to which business phone use actually causes the system to reach capacity sooner. Otherwise, the marginal cost for phone calls by businesses will be essentially zero.

In principle, peak-load pricing of local telephone calls could also be utilized. Currently many cities have flat-rate monthly charges, which essentially make the marginal price zero to the individual user no matter how many calls are made and no matter how long they last. Since it has been estimated that the peak cost per three-minute call is at least five times that of off-peak cost, peak loads involve relatively high capacity cost to the system. Flat monthly rates discriminate in favor of users who make frequent calls during business hours and against users who infrequently make calls or who frequently make calls after business hours.[2] Even in those cities where message rates are charged (for example, 5¢ or 10¢ per call) after a certain number of calls, the problem is not completely eliminated. Such a system of message rates still discriminates against off-peak callers. It is only when calls are charged by time of occurrence and by duration that such discrimination against off-peak calls can be eliminated.

Long-Distance Rates   Long-distance rates typically differ by time of day and day of week. Again, it is not clear to what extent such differential pricing is reflective of price discrimination or merely is similar to movie pricing at different times of the day—a system that expands the use of unutilized capacity at off-peak periods. We do know that the price elasticity of demand for telephone services is numerically quite low for calls during normal hours of business operations, as Table 11-4 shows.

Air Fares

Prior to the current era of deregulation, the United States airline industry was severely regulated by the Civil Aeronautics Board (CAB). Entry was typically

---

[2] Stephen C. Littlechild, "Peak-Load Pricing of Telephone Calls," *Bell Journal of Economics*, vol. 1 (Autumn 1970), pp. 191–210.

TABLE 11-3
SOUTHERN BELL TELEPHONE MONTHLY CHARGES,
DECEMBER 1980

	One private line, one phone	One private line, three phones
Private residence	$12.30	$15.40
Business phone	29.95	34.15

limited to one or two carriers between most cities. All passenger fares had to get CAB approval. Basically, airlines were not allowed to compete on the basis of fares, at least not in terms of first-class and regular coach fares. Competition, therefore, took on various forms, including preferred take-off and landing times and better service in the form of free champagne, free movies, bigger sandwiches, more hors d'oeuvres, and so on. Additionally, each airline sought to attract a larger clientele by lowering prices to special groups that had less elastic demand elasticities than other groups. The price elasticity of demand is certainly different for an expense account executive than for a student traveler who is deciding between an airplane flight and sharing driving expenses to go home for the summer. Given such differing demand elasticities, much price discrimination existed in airline travel until recently.[3] When we look at the

[3] Regulation by the CAB facilitated price discrimination since all interstate airlines were required to charge the same price on a particular route. See Richard E. Caves, *Air Transport and Its Regulators: An Industry Study* (Cambridge, Mass.: Harvard University Press, 1962), and George W. Douglas and James C. Miller, III, *Economic Regulation of Domestic Air Transport: Theory and Policy* (Washington, D.C.: Brookings Institution, 1974).

TABLE 11-4
INITIAL PRICE AND USAGE DATA

Route	Period	Initial price*	Initial usage†	Elasticity
Intra— Chicago	day	5	445	−0.1
	evening	5	486	−0.1
	night	5	210	−0.1
	after midnight	5	10	−0.1
Chicago— Peoria	day	65	73	−0.15
	evening	50	78	−0.37
	night	40	27	−0.36
	after midnight	40	3	−0.30
Chicago— New York	day	140	2570	−0.23
	evening	100	3873	−0.57
	night	70	1940	−0.57
	after midnight	70	148	−0.56

*In cents per three-minute call.
†Equivalent number of three-minute calls per hour on an average business day.
Intra-Chicago figures in thousands.
Source: Stephen C. Littlechild, "Peak-Load Pricing of Telephone Calls," *Bell Journal of Economics,* vol. 1 (Autumn 1970), p. 201.

typical fare schedule prior to deregulation, we find that the fare structure fits our ideas about relative price elasticities of demand. The difference between a first-class round trip between New York and Los Angeles and a travel group charter between those same two points was more than 50 percent. The businessperson paid the full fare, and the student vacationer, for example, took the steps necessary to obtain a lower fare. Not all the difference was due to price discrimination, because clearly the products are different. The first-class passenger, or even the full-fare coach passenger, need not reserve in advance or pay in advance, can change reservations quickly, is almost always guaranteed an available seat, and so on. Nonetheless, even accounting for differences in quality, it is probably true that the price per constant unit of quality is higher for the business traveler than for the student traveler.

Youth Fares Many airlines have offered youth fares at different periods. Passengers under a certain age, usually 22, were allowed to purchase youth fare tickets, particularly on flights to Europe. These tickets were lower than the price that adults had to pay for full-fare tickets. In the past, however, the youth-fare ticket holder was not guaranteed a seat on a particular flight. Rather, he or she had to accept seating on a standby basis, that is, arrive at the gate prior to the plane's departure and stand by until 10 minutes before flight time. If at that time empty seats were available, then the ticket was accepted and the youth could board the plane.

This is a form of third-degree price discrimination (although we are referring to different quality products, because youth fare tickets involve uncertainty). There is probably a difference in the relative elasticity of demand of young adults and that of adults and businesspeople. The demand of young adults is more elastic than the demand of businesspeople. However, the analysis does not end there. Young adults have more elastic demand curves because their time is usually less valuable than that of businesspeople. That is to say, the opportunity cost of waiting in a standby system is less for most young adults than for businesspeople. The total price of a trip by airplane is the money price of the ticket plus the opportunity cost of going to the airport, waiting in line, boarding the plane, sitting in the plane, and so on. Holding the number of hours constant, the lower the opportunity cost of time is, the greater the percentage of the total price of airplane travel is accounted for by the money price. Say that the money price of a plane flight is $85 and that the total time involved in waiting, boarding the plane, and flying is five hours. If a young person's opportunity cost is $3 per hour, then the total price to the young adult for the plane flight is $85 + (5 × $3) = $100. The money price of the plane flight expressed as a fraction of the total price is equal to $85/$100, or 85 percent. Thus, for those with a low opportunity cost, the observed demand curve for air travel in terms of the money price of the ticket may be more elastic. Hence, it makes sense to charge a lower price for youths than for adults. Their relative differences in opportunity cost lead to differences in the relative money price elasticities of demand.

Children's Fares   Children under the age of 12 have been eligible for special fares that in some periods are one-half the adult coach fare and currently are often two-thirds the adult coach fare. This is a form of price discrimination because the cost differences to the airline are nonexistent between the adult and the child. Further, the opportunity cost of a child is considerably less than that of an adult. A child occupies a full seat and is given a full meal and the same service that an adult is given.

Price Discrimination under Deregulation   In many respects, under the more flexible pricing rules in existence since 1977, more rather than less price disparities exist. In December 1980, for example, a typical round trip between Miami and London was as follows: first class, $2,372; economy (full-fare coach), $856 with 7–180 day stay and advanced purchase; excursion, $509; budget and standby fares, $197 (one way); and Laker Skytrain, $187 (one way).

Again, we are not comparing exactly similar products. First-class and economy seats are almost always available, so the purchaser is buying not only the air transportation, but also flexibility in his or her air travel scheduling. The 7–180 day fares require a predetermined stay. Advance purchase tickets require a definite date of departure and return, with a penalty assessed (usually to full fare) for every change. Standby fares require just that—standing by without absolute certainty of boarding on a given day. Laker's Skytrain fares are often obtained at the expense of long waits in ticket lines.

Medical Services

Since Kessel's seminal article on price discrimination in medicine, pricing of medical services has been used as a classic example of price discrimination.[4] Basically, doctors have been able to price discriminate in the past, not only because of restrictions on entry, but also because the American Medical Association was sometimes able to monitor and punish price cutters by banning them from hospitals. Physicians are able to charge different prices to different patients for the same medical services because individual patients are unable to resell services—separation of the markets is possible. Local medical associations that operate under the AMA have been known to impose sanctions on doctors that engage in price cutting. Further, since the AMA can influence the number of internships a hospital will receive, this association is in a position to impose costs on hospitals by restricting the availability of low-cost interns. Doctors who are members of their local medical societies are often given preferential treatment in hiring. Further, doctors who engage in price cutting have been expelled from local medical societies. On the other hand, where price cutting could have no appreciable effect on physicians' incomes, there have

---

[4] Reuben A. Kessel, "Price Discrimination in Medicine," *Journal of Law and Economics*, vol. 1 (October 1958), pp. 20-53. Also see Elton Rayack, *Professional Power and American Medicine* (Cleveland: World Press, 1967).

been no barriers. For this reason, and because of the possible savings in income taxes, physicians frequently do not charge one another for their services and sometimes offer such professional courtesy to members of other physicians' families.

Charging Price on the Basis of Income   Typically, wealthy individuals have been charged a higher price than poor people for similar medical services. There is, of course, some disagreement about whether poor people have received *exactly* the same medical care services, but let us assume for the moment that they have. Given that the marginal cost of servicing these two groups is the same, the price differences are indicative of third-degree price discrimination based on differing price elasticities of demand. In essence, we can apply our analysis given in the previous chapter in Figure 10-1. Simply substitute Group I and Group II for patient-group I and patient-group II. We now ask the question, Why do we expect wealthy individuals to have less elastic demand for medical services than poor individuals?

In the first place, the opportunity cost of being sick for a wealthy person is greater than for a poorer person, which translates into a higher demand for preventive medicine. Second, the time-cost analysis example that we presented for youth fares above also applies to medical services. Time costs, as a percentage of the total cost of medical care, are directly related to the wealth of an individual. As wealth increases, that portion of time costs attributable to total cost increases. Thus, any nominal price change will be a lower percentage change in total price (including time costs) for a richer person. For any given change in money price, the relative change in quantity demanded will be less for the richer person than for the poorer one. Hence, a rich person's price elasticity of demand for medical services will be numerically lower. Finally,

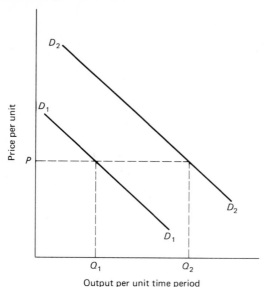

FIGURE 11-2
Rich versus poor people's demand curve for medical care.

because medical services are empirically a normal or superior good, higher income groups will demand more of them at each and every price. Look at Figure 11-2. Here we show demand curve for medical services to be D_1D_1 for poor people and D_2D_2 for rich people. At any price, the price elasticity of demand for medical services will be numerically less for the rich than for the poor since D_2D_2 intersects the vertical axis at a higher point than D_1D_1. [Alternatively, remember that at any price the price elasticity of demand is defined by the reciprocal of the slope of the demand curve times the quantity P/Q. Thus, at any price, since D_2D_2 is farther to the right than D_1D_1, the quantity P/Q will be lower for rich people than for poor people and, hence, the reciprocal of the slope times that quantity will be numerically smaller (if the slope is the same). Thus, a smaller numerical price elasticity of demand exists for rich people.]

Congressional Information Service

Information services often engage in a form of price discrimination based on the affiliation of the subscriber. We show an example in Figure 11-3 of the Congressional Information Service, which is an index to publications of the U.S. Con-

FIGURE 11-3
Sample order form—Congressional Information Service.

Order Form

We wish to subscribe to the CIS/Index for one year beginning with the ☐ January 1970 issue OR the _____ issue (please specify). Please ☐ do ☐ do not consider this a standing order, good until cancelled, with annual billing.

BASIC RATE

☐ Please enter our subscription at $320, the basic rate which applies to:
  • All offices and libraries maintained by corporations, associations, private law firms, and other private and semi-private organizations, and all other special libraries.
  • All academic, public, law or government libraries having annual book and periodical budgets in excess of $400,000.
  • All libraries in the U.S. and Canada which are maintained by foreign governments.
  • All libraries outside the U.S. and Canada **except** those maintained by the U.S. Government.
  NOTE: Foreign libraries should add $50 to this rate if Air Mail service is desired.
  Please ☐ do ☐ do not send via overseas airmail.

SPECIAL RATES

☐ We are eligible for a special rate, as indicated below.

Institutional Libraries
These rates apply only to academic, public, law and government libraries in the U.S. and Canada:

☐ $260 per year if the annual book and periodical budget of entire institution is between $200,000 and $400,000. Our budget is _____.

☐ $200 per year if the annual book and periodical budget of the entire institution is less than $200,000. Our budget is _____.

Small College and Public Libraries
These rates are reserved for small colleges and public libraries only. Libraries which are branches, divisions, or departments of larger institutions are not eligible for this rate:

☐ $140 per year if the annual book and periodical budget of the entire institution is between $30,000 and $75,000. Our budget is _____.

☐ $80 per year if the annual book and periodical budget of the **entire** institution is less than $30,000. Our budget is _____.

ADDITIONAL SUBSCRIPTIONS
Additional subscriptions are priced at $200 per year for all subscribers and may be entered at that rate only if the billing address is the same as on the original order. These additional subscriptions may be mailed to any address.

☐ Enter our order for_____additional subscriptions at $200 each.

ANNUAL BOUND VOLUMES
Each year Congressional Information Service cumulates both the abstracts and the indexes in two clothbound volumes. These permanent editions are offered to CIS/Index subscribers at the special price of $80 per set. The price for non-subscribers is $160.

☐ Please send us_____set(s) at the appropriate rate.
☐ Do not send bound volumes.

BINDERS
Monthly and quarterly issues of the CIS/Index measure 8½" x 11" and are hole-punched for convenient storage and use. A sturdy set of binders has been designed to hold a year's issues. Each binder is equipped with a spine pocket of clear acetate for cataloging purposes.

☐ Please send us_____set(s) of binders at $18, the set.
☐ Do not send binders.

CIS/MICROFICHE LIBRARY
☐ Please send information about the CIS/Microfiche Library.

Organization or Library

Address

City, State and Zip Code

Your Name and Title

gress. You will notice that in 1970 there was a basic rate of $320 per year, which applied to all private offices and libraries, all academic public law or government libraries that have a large enough budget (in this case an excess of $400,000), all libraries maintained by foreign governments, and all foreign libraries outside of the United States except those maintained by the U.S. government. Rates are lowered if the subscriber is a library with a small budget. The lowest rate, $80 per year, is given to small colleges and public libraries whose entire annual book and periodical budget is less than $30,000. In this case, the product is exactly the same, the cost of servicing each subscriber is presumably exactly the same, but the price charged is different.

Other information services such as microfilm copies of congressional reports have similar pricing structures.

Professional Journals Professional journals practice price discrimination in basically the same manner as the Congressional Information Service. We recreate a series of 1981 price schedules for the *American Economic Review* (Table 11-5) to show that there are different rates to libraries, students, and other parties. Of course, some cheating goes on. In order to obtain the student rate, the student usually has to have a note signed by a professor, a practice that will discourage some, but not all, from cheating.

College Scholarships and Fees Each year some eight and one-half million students go to colleges and universities throughout the United States. Most, if not all, colleges and universities do not and perhaps cannot charge different prices to different groups, except perhaps on the basis of residency in state-financed insitutions. It is possible, nonetheless, for colleges and universities to

TABLE 11-5
EXHIBIT OF 1981 PRICE SCHEDULES

• *THE AMERICAN ECONOMIC REVIEW* including four quarterly numbers, the *Proceedings* of the annual meetings, the Directory, and Supplements, is published by the American Economic Association and is sent to all members six times a year, in March, May, June, September, and semi-monthly in December.

Dues for 1981, which include a subscription to both the *American Economic Review* and the *Journal of Economic Literature,* are as follows:
$30.00 for regular members with rank of assistant professor or lower, or with annual income of $14,400 or less;
$36.00 for regular members with rank of associate professor, or with annual income of $14,400 to $24,000;
$42.00 for regular members with rank of full professor, or with annual income above $24,000;
$15.00 for junior members (registered students). Certification must be submitted yearly.
Subscriptions (libraries, institutions, or firms) are $100.00 a year. Only subscriptions to both publications will be accepted. Single copies of either journal may be purchased from the Secretary's office, Nashville, Tennessee.
In countries other than the United States, add $5.00 to cover extra postage.

Source: American Economic Review, vol. 71 (May 1981).

reduce the price to those students with numerically higher price elasticities of demand by awarding them grants, scholarships, and fellowships. For example, in many cases, financial aid decisions are made on the basis of ''need.'' In other words, colleges and universities price on the basis of wealth. The most financially impoverished individuals are offered the largest awards, while richer students get relatively little. We have already pointed out why price elasticity of demand is inversely related to income for medical services. At least one argument dealing with the fact that education is a normal or superior good still holds. Thus, it is rational for colleges and universities to attempt to charge more to wealthier students.

In Figure 11-4 we show a sample form from the Graduate and Professional School Financial Aid Service. It is a financial statement for students applying for financial aid. It collects information about the student's resources and liabilities, as well as those of the student's spouse or prospective spouse, in addition to the spouse's employment history, and financial information about the student's parents. Presumably, none of this information relates to the candidate's academic qualification, ability to perform in graduate school, or ability to succeed. One can surmise that the financial statement required by colleges and universities giving financial aid is merely a means of metering price elasticities of demand and making awards accordingly.

Trading Stamps

In the 1880s, Schuster's Department Store in Milwaukee, Wisconsin, began to issue stamps to its customers. Since then, we have seen the proliferation of approximately 250 trading stamp companies. Forty percent of the market is controlled by S&H (Sperry & Hutchinson) Green Stamps. Only about 5 percent of S&H Green Stamps and those of other large trading companies are unredeemed. Let's now try to answer the question of why stores give trading stamps.

The full price of the product includes not only the monetary price, but also the implicit opportunity cost of the time that went into searching out the product and purchasing it (and the time needed to consume it). We can assume that the higher one values time released from shopping, the less one will engage in seeking out lower-cost shopping arrangements. In other words, a person who values time more relative to money income will substitute more money income in order to save shopping time. That person will use less time to discover lower prices. Therefore, the person who values time highly will exhibit a less elastic demand curve in any given store than the person who does not value time so highly.

Charging More to the Richer Person   Let us assume that there is a strong correlation between the value of time and the relative wealth of a person. We are assuming that richer people place a higher value on time than do poorer people. It follows, therefore, that in a particular store, a richer person's relative

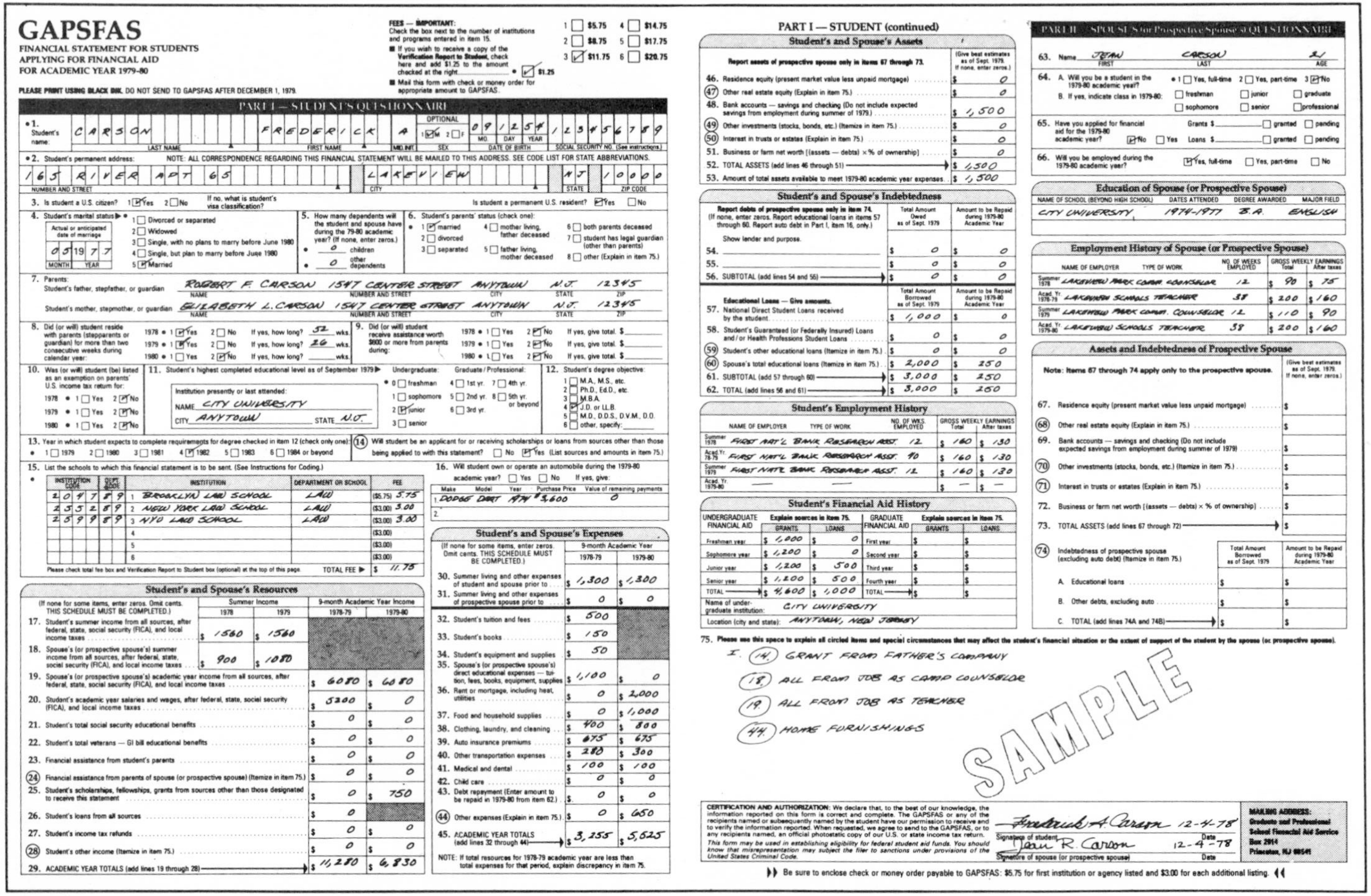

GAPSFAS
FINANCIAL STATEMENT FOR STUDENTS APPLYING FOR FINANCIAL AID FOR ACADEMIC YEAR 1979–80

PART I — STUDENT'S QUESTIONNAIRE

1. Student's name: CARSON, FREDERICK A. — SEX: M — DATE OF BIRTH: 09 12 54 — SOCIAL SECURITY NO.: 123456789
2. Student's permanent address: 165 RIVER APT 65, LAKEVIEW, NJ 10000
3. Is student a U.S. citizen? Yes
4. Student's marital status: Married (date of marriage 05 1977)
5. How many dependents will the student and spouse have during the 79-80 academic year? 0 children, 0 other dependents
6. Student's parents' status: married
7. Parents: ROBERT F. CARSON, 1547 CENTER STREET, ANYTOWN, N.J. 12345; ELIZABETH L. CARSON, 1547 CENTER STREET, ANYTOWN, N.J. 12345
8. Did (or will) student reside with parents for more than two consecutive weeks: 1978 Yes, 52 wks.; 1979 Yes, 26 wks.; 1980 No
9. Did (or will) student receive assistance worth $600 or more from parents: 1978 No; 1979 No; 1980 No
10. Was (or will) student (be) listed as an exemption on parents' U.S. income tax return: 1978 No; 1979 No; 1980 No
11. Institution presently or last attended: CITY UNIVERSITY, ANYTOWN, N.J. — junior
12. Student's degree objective: J.D. or LL.B.
13. Year in which student expects to complete requirements: 1982
14. Will student be an applicant for scholarships or loans from sources other than those being applied to with this statement? Yes
15. Schools: 20478 9 BROOKLYN LAW SCHOOL, LAW, 5.75; 23528 9 NEW YORK LAW SCHOOL, LAW, 3.00; 25998 9 NYU LAW SCHOOL, LAW, 3.00 — TOTAL FEE 11.75
16. Will student own or operate an automobile during the 1979-80 academic year? DODGE DART 1974 $3,600, 0

Student's and Spouse's Resources

	Summer 1978	Summer 1979	1978-79	1979-80
17. Student's summer income	1560	1560		
18. Spouse's summer income	900	1080		
19. Spouse's academic year income			6080	6080
20. Student's academic year salaries and wages			5200	0
21. Student's total social security educational benefits			0	0
22. Student's total veterans — GI bill educational benefits			0	0
23. Financial assistance from student's parents			0	0
24. Financial assistance from parents of spouse			0	0
25. Student's scholarships, fellowships, grants			0	750
26. Student's loans from all sources			0	
27. Student's income tax refunds			0	0
28. Student's other income			0	0
29. ACADEMIC YEAR TOTALS			11,280	6,830

Student's and Spouse's Expenses

	1978-79	1979-80
30. Summer living and other expenses of student and spouse	1,300	1,300
31. Summer living and other expenses of prospective spouse	0	0
32. Student's tuition and fees	500	
33. Student's books	150	
34. Student's equipment and supplies	50	
35. Spouse's direct educational expenses	1,100	0
36. Rent or mortgage	0	2,000
37. Food and household supplies	0	1,000
38. Clothing, laundry, and cleaning	400	800
39. Auto insurance premiums	675	675
40. Other transportation expenses	280	300
41. Medical and dental	100	100
42. Child care	0	0
43. Debt repayment	0	0
44. Other expenses	0	650
45. ACADEMIC YEAR TOTALS	3,255	5,525

PART I — STUDENT (continued)

Student's and Spouse's Assets: 46. Residence equity 0; 47. Other real estate equity 0; 48. Bank accounts 1,500; 49. Other investments 0; 50. Interest in trusts or estates 0; 51. Business or farm net worth 0; 52. TOTAL ASSETS 1,500; 53. Amount of total assets available 1,500

Student's and Spouse's Indebtedness: 54. 0, 0; 55. 0, 0; 56. SUBTOTAL 0, 0; 57. National Direct Student Loans 1,000, 0; 58. Guaranteed Loans 0, 0; 59. Other educational loans 0, 0; 60. Spouse's total educational loans 2,000, 250; 61. SUBTOTAL 3,000, 250; 62. TOTAL 3,000, 250

Student's Employment History

	Name of employer	Type of work	No. of wks.	Total	After taxes
Summer 1978	FIRST NAT'L BANK	RESEARCH ASST.	12	160	130
Acad. Yr. 78-79	FIRST NAT'L BANK	RESEARCH ASST.	40	160	130
Summer 1979	FIRST NAT'L BANK	RESEARCH ASST.	12	160	130
Acad. Yr. 1979-80	—	—		—	—

Student's Financial Aid History

	Grants	Loans
Freshman year	1,000	0
Sophomore year	1,200	0
Junior year	1,200	500
Senior year	1,200	500
TOTAL	4,600	1,000

Name of undergraduate institution: CITY UNIVERSITY; Location: ANYTOWN, NEW JERSEY

PART II — SPOUSE'S (or Prospective Spouse's) QUESTIONNAIRE

63. Name: JEAN CARSON, age 21
64. Will you be a student in the 1979-80 academic year? No
65. Have you applied for financial aid for the 1979-80 academic year? No
66. Will you be employed during the 1979-80 academic year? Yes, full-time

Education of Spouse: CITY UNIVERSITY, 1974–1977, B.A., ENGLISH

Employment History of Spouse

	Name of employer	Type of work	No. of weeks	Total	After taxes
Summer 1978	LAKEVIEW PARK COMM.	COUNSELOR	12	90	75
Acad. Yr. 1978-79	LAKEVIEW SCHOOLS	TEACHER	38	200	160
Summer 1979	LAKEVIEW PARK COMM.	COUNSELOR	12	110	90
Acad. Yr. 1979-80	LAKEVIEW SCHOOLS	TEACHER	38	200	160

Assets and Indebtedness of Prospective Spouse (items 67–74)

75. I. (14) GRANT FROM FATHER'S COMPANY
(18) ALL FROM JOB AS CAMP COUNSELOR
(19) ALL FROM JOB AS TEACHER
(44) HOME FURNISHINGS

SAMPLE

Signature of student: Frederick A. Carson 12-4-78
Signature of spouse: Jean R. Carson 12-4-78

MAILING ADDRESS: Graduate and Professional School Financial Aid Service, Box 2614, Princeton, NJ 08541

Be sure to enclose check or money order payable to GAPSFAS: $5.75 for first institution or agency listed and $3.00 for each additional listing.

FIGURE 11-4
Sample financial information request form.

price elasticity of demand will be less than a poorer person's. Now the retailer is confronted with two classes of consumers, those with relatively less elastic demands and those with relatively more elastic demands. The retailer's problem is to separate these two classes and charge the richer customers a higher price than the poorer customers. One way this is done is to offer a rebate only to those customers willing to incur a time cost to obtain that rebate. The rebate is in the form of real goods that are obtainable in exchange for blue, green, or gold trading stamps. However, the person who wants the rebate must collect the stamps, preserve them, and redeem them at a redemption station. All of these activities require time. Thus, poorer people, whom we are assuming can be used as a proxy for the relatively more elastic demanders, effectively pay a lower price for their food because they obtain goods when they redeem their trading stamps. The richer customers, with a relatively less elastic demand, refuse the stamps because of the time cost involved. They get no discount at all. Thus, the gross money price of groceries is the same to both classes of buyers, but the poor get a rebate equal to the value of the trading stamps' redemption exchange rate.

Some Implications   If the above trading stamp model is useful, it presents us with some testable implications.[5]

1 We predict that trading stamps will be used [by a seller] relatively less often in cases where the total value of a single purchase is large. In such instances, the receiver of the stamps from a large purchase incurs a small enough time cost in redeeming a large quantity of stamps to make the redemption worthwhile. In other words, not enough differential time costs are imposed to discourage relatively low elasticity demanders from collecting the stamps. This implication is consistent with the fact that trading stamps are used by grocery stores. One does not usually obtain them when purchasing an automobile or a home.

2 We predict that in cases where the commodity is personal service, relatively fewer trading stamps will be used. The differentiation of quality of services rendered is used as a substitute for the price discounting implicit in the trading stamp system. This implication is consistent with beauty shops and barbershops, which do not offer trading stamps.

3 We predict that owner-operated stores will use relatively fewer trading stamps than stores employing a large number of sales personnel. In the case of owner-operated stores, the owner can attempt to figure out relative price elasticities and alter the service given to the customers accordingly. Employees, on the other hand, have less incentive and less authority to figure out customer characteristics and therefore won't treat customers according to their relative price elasticities. Therefore, we predict more trading stamp use in large grocery stores than in small "mom and pop" stores. This use seems to be consistent with casual observation.

---

[5] Armen A. Alchian and Benjamin Klein, "Trading Stamps," mimeographed (Los Angeles: U.C.L.A., 1976).

MULTIPART PRICING

Multipart pricing involves charging successively lower prices for the marginal unit of a commodity as more of the commodity is purchased. Multipart pricing occurs, for example, in supermarkets when you are allowed to buy one can for 20¢ and two cans for 39¢. In other words, the first can is 20¢ and the marginal cost of the second can is 19¢. A uniform price of 19.5¢ is charged to all those who buy two cans, and so on.[6]

There is a difference between multipart pricing, which is second-degree price discrimination, and perfect, or first-degree, price discrimination. Multipart pricing is an imperfect way to extract as much consumer surplus as possible from each consumer. It is a way of dealing with broad, discrete intervals between quantities purchased and charging appropriate revenue-maximizing prices for each additional unit purchased, without ever selling any unit below MC.

We expect to observe second-degree price discrimination, or multipart pricing, rather than first-degree price discrimination because of the higher costs of negotiating, monitoring, and enforcing exchanges for the latter. It is difficult to determine what the actual price elasticity of demand is for different classes of buyers. It is even more difficult to prevent the resale of goods by buyers who bought the product at a lower price to those who would be charged a higher price if they purchased the product from the monopolist.

Sliding Scales for Public Utilities

It is often asserted that public utilities engage in price discrimination. It turns out that we can, indeed, analyze some of their pricing policies in terms of second-degree price discrimination. Public utilities do use multipart pricing, or what they call "declining block pricing."

Consider Figure 11-5. If the electrical utility wanted to sell the quantity Q_3, it could do so by charging the uniform price of P_3. Its total revenues would be represented by the rectangle OP_3CQ_3. However, if the utility engages in multipart pricing, or second-degree price discrimination, it might charge P_1 for the first Q_1 of kilowatts sold per month. It could charge P_2 for kilowatts sold between Q_1 and Q_2, and then finally it could charge P_3 for kilowatts sold between Q_2 and Q_3. The revenues it would receive would be the sum of the rectangle of OP_1AQ_1 plus Q_1DBQ_2 plus Q_2ECQ_3, or $OP_1ADBECQ_3$. The sum of these three rectangles exceeds the rectangle given by uniform pricing of P_3 times the quantity sold, Q_3. (Moreover, multipart pricing yields more revenue than charging the weighted average price.)[7]

[6] Some economists contend that multipart pricing in supermarkets is not a form of price discrimination, but rather a classic case of price *differentiation*. They point out that supermarkets are highly competitive and that multipart pricing is merely a method by which owners economize on transaction costs. For example, it takes less cashier time per unit sold when larger quantities are purchased. This saving in cashier time is, in essence, "passed on" to the consumer who buys in larger quantities.

[7] See Ralph K. Davidson, *Price Discrimination in Selling Gas and Electricity* (Baltimore: Johns Hopkins, 1955), and Hendrik S. Houthakker, "Electricity Tariffs in Theory and Practice," *Economic Journal*, vol. 61 (March 1951), pp. 1–25.

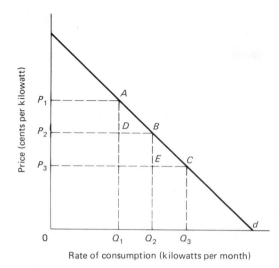

FIGURE 11-5
Declining block pricing. Public utilities often use declining block pricing in which separate "blocks" of electricity can be purchased at declining prices. If the electric utility charges a uniform price of P_3, its revenues will be $0P_3CQ_3$. If, however, it charges a price of P_1 for the first Q_1 kilowatts used and then P_2 for the next "block" used up to quantity Q_2 and then price P_3 for the next "block" up to Q_3, its total revenues will equal $0P_1AQ_1 + Q_1DBQ_2 + Q_2ECO_3 = 0P_1ADBECQ_3$.

Some Differences in Cost Not all the differences in electricity prices on the sliding scale constitute price discrimination. There are some differences in cost. Industrial customers consume power at higher voltage and on a more predictable basis. Also, there is usually a smaller connection cost. Basically, however, declining block pricing is a form of price discrimination. The reason that industrial users receive a lower price is because they have more elastic demand. Their options are greater than residential users' options are. If electricity reaches a high enough price, they can generate it themselves. Also, particularly for electric-intensive firms, users can decide to build a plant in a different location where electricity prices are lower. Since electricity prices constitute a larger fraction of their total operating budget, and the cost of alternative sources is relatively lower than that for individual households, industrial users are more price-sensitive to electricity costs than residential users are.

METERING DEMAND AND TIE-IN SALES

One industrial practice that has been associated with price discrimination involves tying contracts, or **tie-in sales**. A typical tie-in contractual arrangement requires that a buyer can either purchase or lease one product from the seller only on the condition that the buyer also agrees to purchase something else called the "tied good." Tie-in arrangements are normally illegal under section 3 of the Clayton Act if the effect "may be to substantially lessen competition or tend to create a monopoly in any line of commerce." However, the courts' usual understanding of tie-in arrangements and monopoly power has often been misguided. Under most circumstances, it is impossible to extend monopoly power by a tie-in agreement. Consider the following example. Xerox has a monopoly in the sale and lease of Xerox machines. It does not have a monopoly, however, in the sale of the paper used in the machines. Suppose the

XYZ firm rents the Xerox machines and purchases 1000 sheets of paper a month. The competitive price for the paper is $100. Now assume that the total value to the user of the Xerox machine (including the use of the paper) is $900. If Xerox required the tie-in arrangement whereby the rental of the machine was contingent upon purchase of the paper from Xerox, it could charge any combination for one month's rental and paper as long as it equaled $900. Thus, it could charge a competitive price for the paper of $100 plus $800 rental, or it could charge $600 rental and $300 for the 1000 sheets of paper. In all cases, Xerox would end up with the same profit. An $800 or other high rental fee, however, would preclude use by customers with low total demands for the machine.

Basically, if Xerox truly has monopoly power in the copying machine market and there is pure competition in the paper market, the supposed extension of Xerox's monopoly into the paper market will not alter its profits. The tie-in between the Xerox rental and the paper cannot be construed to *extend* Xerox's monopoly power. What is important here is looking at the combined price of the rental plus the paper to yield the price paid per constant quality unit of services, since the machine cannot be used without the paper. The same would be true if we analyzed a company that had monopoly power in selling cameras and decided to tie-in the film.[8]

Tying Arrangement as a Means of Metering Demand— The IBM Case[9]

International Business Machines Corporation has been the leader in the computer field since that industry began. For many years, IBM would only rent its computing and tabulating machines to users; it would not sell them. The rental agreement was generally expressed as a fee per shift per unit time period (one month, for example). Until the 1950s, IBM required that the users buy tabulating cards only from IBM. If the machines broke down and IBM's technicians found that the renting firms were using someone else's cards, IBM imposed a penalty by charging for repairs. This was the method the company used to police its requirement that no one else's cards be purchased.

We may not immediately understand why IBM required that its own cards

---

[8] There are diverse views on this subject, however. Ward S. Bowman, Jr., "Tying Arrangements and the Leverage Problem," *Yale Law Journal*, vol. 67 (November 1957), pp. 19–36, and William L. Baldwin and David McFarland, "Tying Arrangements in Law and Economics," *Antitrust Bulletin*, vol. 8 (September/October 1963), pp. 743–780. A new twist has been added in the case of *renting* a durable, as opposed to *selling*. Robert Ayanian, "The Economics of Tying and Leasing," forthcoming in *Economic Inquiry*. Ayanian points out that a higher-than-cost price on the tied good (for example, paper) attaches a positive marginal cost to use of the leased good and prevents its indiscriminate overuse at a fixed rental rate. How such tying arrangements are two-part tariffs (with the lease fee serving as the fixed fee and the price of the tied good serving as the variable charge) is examined. Ayanian also discusses these arrangements as an efficient method of financing machine use, allowing depreciation costs to be paid for through the payments on the tied good as the durable is *actually used*.

[9] *International Business Machines v. United States*, 298 U.S. 131 (1936).

be purchased and why it policed such an agreement. However, if we think of IBM in terms of a monopolist, then we arrive at a prediction from a price-discriminating monopoly model that is consistent with past IBM-pricing practices. We know from the theory in Chapter 10 that higher profits can be obtained by price discrimination; however, it is necessary to have information on the different price elasticities of demand for different classes of users. One way that IBM could approximate its users' consumer surplus was by *intensity of use*—those who used their machines more presumably had a relatively higher total consumer's surplus for computing services. One of the ways to monitor intensity of use is by knowing the number of tabulating cards used. That is exactly why IBM required that only its cards be used. The cards provided an index of use intensity and, hence, the size of consumer's surplus.

This argument would make little sense if IBM had not charged those who used more cards a higher price per unit of computing services than those who used fewer cards. The company did just that; it charged a price for cards that was in excess of their marginal cost. Its price per unit of computing services was effectively higher to those with the lower elasticity of demand, that is, those who used more cards.[10] IBM chose this method of price discrimination rather than charging a higher rental fee to different users. Perhaps this latter pricing technique was deemed too overt a form of price discrimination and was, therefore, subject to antitrust prosecution. In addition, higher rental fees would require ex ante determination of high and low demanders.

Nonetheless, various antitrust actions against IBM have resulted in the discontinuation of this particular pricing practice. Under Justice Department pressure, IBM agreed to ''cease and desist'' its dual practice of only renting hardware and of requiring the purchase of its own cards.

United Shoe Machinery

Another case of price discrimination using tie-in sales as a metering device involved United Shoe Machinery.[11] Prior to 1956, the company was convicted under the Sherman Act and its tie-in practices were forbidden. Customers of United Shoe Machinery Corporation (shoe manufacturers) had been required to use *only* United Shoe Machinery if they wanted to use any equipment made by that company. Actually, there were seven separate types of tie-ins. The most mentioned one involved the requirement that the lessees of United Shoe Machinery heel applicators were required to buy United Shoe Machinery staples.

We can use the same analysis presented above for IBM and IBM cards. If we assume that total consumer's surplus is directly related to intensity of use, which can be measured by the number of staples used per unit time period, then

---

[10] Computing services have been found to be highly correlated with the use of input data such as cards.

[11] *United Shoe Machinery Corp. v. United States*, 110 F.Supp 295 (1953).

United Shoe Machinery was able to meter demand. As long as it charged above marginal cost for the staples, it was able to effectively charge a higher machine price to low demanders than that charged to relatively high demanders.[12]

Cable TV Equipment

A cable TV system receives signals at one large antenna and then feeds them to subscriber households, usually by a network of underground wires. The first cable TV firm was started in 1951. It began by servicing remote small towns. By the early 1960s, cable had spread to larger towns and the industry was booming. The first firm in that industry was Jerrold Electronics. From the onset, Jerrold required all subscribers to install the entire Jerrold system plus purchase a five-year service contract. In other words, subscribers were not allowed to use non-Jerrold parts between the cable line and the TV set. This tie-in between the cable and the television set provided a way of metering demand. Presumably, the greater the number of television sets in the home, the more intensive the demand and thus the lower the price elasticity of demand. Provided that Jerrold charged above marginal cost for the connecting devices, it was practicing a form of price discrimination. Eventually, the Antitrust Division sued Jerrold for anticompetitive practices. In 1961, the courts declared that Jerrold could no longer require tie-ins.[13]

Other Reasons for Tie-In Sales

There are numerous other reasons why firms might engage in tie-in sales. We will discuss these other reasons in more detail in Chapter 12. Briefly, though, tie-in sales are used to avoid price controls, to take advantage of economies of scale, to protect goodwill by preventing cheating on brand names, to capture some consumer surplus, to reallocate risk bearing, and to create a barrier of entry because of increased capital requirements.

A VARIATION ON TIE-IN SALES—BLOCK BOOKING

One variation of tie-in sales that allows for price discrimination without overtly engaging in that practice is block booking. **Block booking** is an arrangement under which purchasers are forced to buy all of a firm's output each period or get none of it. In other words, block booking involves an all-or-none arrangement not dissimilar to the example we used in Chapter 10 concerning the purchase of diamonds at an option of all at the stated price or none at all.

---

[12] An important aspect of the United Shoe Machinery pricing scheme was the explicit recognition that a lower price would be charged on the machines that were exposed to competition from rivals relative to the pricing structure on those machines protected by United Shoe Machinery's patent portfolio.

[13] *United States v. Jerrold Electronics Corp.*, 187 F.Supp. 545 (1960), affirmed per curiam 365 U.S. 567 (1961).

In the famous Loew's case in 1962, the issue of block booking came up.[14] Six distributors were charged with violating section 1 of the Sherman Act. They made the sale of one or more feature films to television stations conditional on the purchase of other films. In order to get *The Treasure of Sierra Madre*, *Casablanca*, and several other winners, a Washington television station, WTOP, also had to purchase such greats as *Gorilla Man* and *Teargas Squad*.

In ruling on the case, the court found that the distributor's market power resulted from the copyright on the tied goods. The court further explained that given this monopoly power, the distributors had economic leverage sufficient to induce their customers to take the tied good along with the tying good. Speaking for the Supreme Court, Justice Goldberg considered each copyrighted film block a unique product, and thus block booking, according to Goldberg, had adverse effects on competition. Stations were forced to buy unwanted films and therefore denied access to films marketed by other distributors.

As with the IBM case, it is certainly not clear that the courts were correct in their interpretation. How could the tying arrangement allow the distributors to increase their monopoly power? The court was saying, in effect, that the block of movies was worth more than the value of each movie added together. Consider a simple example. Paramount Pictures has two movies, *Winner* and *Dog*. Clearly, they have a monopoly on these two movies because they own the copyright. The value of *Winner* to a prospective movie house is nebulous if the movie theater won't take the block. If both movies must be purchased, what does it matter to Paramount if it charges $500 for *Dog* or $600 for *Winner*, or $1,100, for *Dog* and $0 for *Winner*, or any combination? The most it can obtain is the maximum value of the block to the movie house.

Stigler has suggested that block booking, a form of tie-in sale, may be inspired by the desire to price-discriminate.[15]

A Numerical Example

In order to see how block booking allows for price discrimination, we will use a simple numerical example involving two movies that were indeed block booked by the distributor—*Star Wars* and *The Other Side of Midnight* (henceforth called *Midnight*). There are two theaters, X and Y. The maximum prices they will pay per week for the films are as follows:

$$\$12,000 = P^X_{Star\ Wars} \qquad \$\ 8,000 = P^Y_{Star\ Wars}$$
$$\$\ 3,000 = P^X_{Midnight} \qquad \$\ 4,000 = P^Y_{Midnight}$$

Therefore, we know that cinema X will pay more for *Star Wars* than cinema

---

[14] *United States v. Loew's, Inc.*, 371 U.S. 38 (1962).
[15] George J. Stigler, "A Note on Block Bookings," in Stigler, *The Organization of Industry* (Homewood, Ill.: Irwin, 1968), pp. 165–170.

Y will, but will pay less for *Midnight* than cinema Y. Consider the possibility of the distributor's simply selling each movie separately at a uniform price. He or she will have to charge the minimum price or $8,000 per week for *Star Wars* and $3,000 for *Midnight*. Thus, total revenues will equal 2 × $8,000 plus 2 × $3,000, or $22,000.[16]

Now consider the possibility of block booking. The distributor will charge a uniform price to both theaters, but they have to take both films. The maximum block-book price will equal the lowest combined valuation of each firm for the two films taken together times 2, or $12,000 × 2 = $24,000. Thus, with block booking the firm can capture $2,000 more a week in revenues, which translates into $2,000 higher profits assuming no additional reproduction costs in the block-book case. Also assumed is no reduction in the summed maximum values for the two movies due to the theater owners having their choice reduced under the block-booking arrangement.

Note that in order for block booking to result in price discrimination and higher profits, the relative value of the films must be different for different theaters. Also note that price discrimination arises only in the context of the implicit prices paid for each individual film. For example, from the $12,000 fee we know that cinema Y, with a higher demand for *Midnight*, is paying $4,000 for the rental of that film. This amount is $1,000 more than the maximum amount cinema X would pay for *Midnight*.

DIFFERENT GOODS

One common way of engaging in price discrimination involves selling physically different goods at prices that are not reflective of differences in marginal cost. In this section, we'll look at two examples: the sale of books and the sale of retail items with different labels.

Different Book Editions

Hardbacks are sold at a higher price than paperbacks. The difference in price does not, however, reflect simply a difference in production cost. On an industry average for trade books, the price of a hardback is only $5 to $8 more than the price of a paperback. In Table 11-6 we list a number of best sellers, giving their hardback price and their paperback price. Part of the difference in price reflects economies of scale in the mass production and perhaps in the distribution of paperbacks. Further, paperbacks are often associated with a lower risk because they may be established best sellers. Undoubtedly, though, a large part of the difference is due to price discrimination. Those who want to read best sellers as soon as they come out presumably have a numerically lower price elasticity of demand than all other readers. They end up paying the higher price for a hardback. Those who can wait for the softback to appear presumably have

---

[16] If each picture were sold for its maximum price, then total revenue would be $16,000 ($12,000 + $4,000).

TABLE 11-6
PRICES OF HARDBACK AND PAPERBACK BEST
SELLERS, FALL 1980

Title	Price	
	Hardback	Paperback
Smiley's People	$10.95	$3.50
Donahue	10.95	2.95
Portraits	11.95	3.50
Ordinary People	7.95	2.75
The Complete Scarsdale		
Medical Diet	7.95	2.95

a numerically higher price elasticity of demand. The increased price for the hardback does not dissuade large numbers of best seller readers, whereas the reduction in price to paperback readers increases quantity demanded greatly. Total profits will rise.

Library Editions

Price discrimination in book sales was clearly being practiced with so-called library editions. Library editions were specially bound books that presumably would last longer. The differences in price between the library edition and the regular hardback edition, however, were never equal to the differences in cost; the price difference was considerably greater than the cost difference.

Different Labels for the Same Product

Sometimes manufacturers will sell goods of similar grade and quality at different prices. In such cases, the major difference between the products arises from a brand name or label. In 1966, the Supreme Court ruled that Borden's practice of selling homogeneous canned evaporated milk at different prices, that is, charging a higher price for cans sold with the Borden label than for the cans to which other firms applied their own brand names, was price discrimination.[17]

PRESCRIPTION DRUGS

One famous case of price discrimination involves patented drugs. Patented drugs are a monopoly resource to drug companies for a period of 17 years. During that time, drug companies maximize profits by engaging in price dis-

---

[17] *Federal Trade Commission v. Borden Co.*, 383 U.S. 637 (1966). However, on remand an appellate court ruled that no injury to competition would result if the price differences between the premium and nonpremium brands reflect no more than consumer preferences for the premium brand. See *Borden Co. v. Federal Trade Commission*, 381 F.2d 175 (1967), esp. p. 181 of the opinion.

crimination. The largest bulk volume buyer, the Veterans Administration, receives the lowest prices. Prices increase as buyers move up toward the retail level where presumably individual customers have less elastic demand. In Table 11-7 we reproduce information from hearings by the U.S. Senate Select Committee on Small Business, Subcommittee on Monopoly.[18] We see a typical drug, Ritalin, sold for approximately 300 percent more to retail druggists than to the Veterans Administration. The drug companies contend that these price differences do not constitute price discrimination, but rather price differentiation. They point out that packaging and distribution costs are much lower for bulk orders for the Veterans Administration.

[18] *Report on Competitive Problems in the Drug Industry* (Washington, D.C.: U.S. Government Printing Office, 1971), part 20, p. 8181.

TABLE 11-7
PRICE DIFFERENCE TO GOVERNMENT AND RETAIL DRUGGISTS

	Price to Veterans Administration (1969)	Price quoted to other federal agencies (1970)	Price to retail druggists (1970)
Ritalin (Ciba) 10 mg. 1,000s	$17.34	$44.97	$ 54.51
Doriden (Ciba) 0.5 gm. 1,000s	18.04	32.01	40.01
Placidyl (Abbott) 500 mg. 100s	2.09	4.84	5.00
Mysoline (Ayerst) 0.25 gm. 1,000s	25.25	36.36	44.52
Griseofulvin (Ayerst) 250 mg. 500s	11.06	40.10	52.00
Macrodantin (Eaton) 50 mg. 1,000s	38.12	85.00	114.76
Ismelin (Ciba) 25 mg. 100s	5.75	7.84	9.50
Gelusil (Warner) 1,000s	7.60	12.04	14.50
Rio-Pan (Ayerst) 400 mg. 12 fl. oz.	.20	.88	1.02
Choledyl (Warner) 200 mg. 1,000s	21.26	26.89	32.40

Source: U.S. Congress, Senate Select Committee on Small Business Subcommittee on Monopoly, *Report on Competitive Problems in the Drug Industry* (Washington, D.C.: U.S. Government Printing Office, 1971), part 20, p. 8181.

PRICE DISCRIMINATION OR PRODUCT DIFFERENTIATION?

A review of the literature on price discrimination in this chapter, monopolistic competition in Chapter 7, and advertising and product differentiation in Chapter 9, shows that there is no clearcut definition of price discrimination relative to product differentiation. When we look at the courts' treatment of different cases, we find no further insights in solving this definitional problem. Thus, we conclude that the application of price discrimination or product differentiation theories will continue to reflect differences in the interpretation of the factual situations surrounding any particular pricing phenomenon.

CHAPTER 12

DELIVERED PRICE SYSTEMS, EXCLUSIVE AND RECIPROCAL BUYING

In this chapter, we will examine a number of industry practices that are often associated with some form of price discrimination. Included in these practices are delivered price systems, exclusive territories, exclusive dealing and requirement contracts, and reciprocal buying arrangements. First, we will examine various freight-pricing practices that arise in response to differences in geographic distance between the producer and its customers.

DELIVERED PRICING SYSTEMS

There are various forms of **delivered pricing systems** and thus various definitions. These include (1) spatial differentiation, (2) basing point, (3) phantom freight, and (4) freight absorption and freight advantage territory.

Spatial Differentiation

Differences in location will render even a perfectly homogeneous commodity heterogeneous. The ton of specialty steel produced in Pittsburgh is not the same to the potential consumer in Chicago as it is to the potential consumer in New Jersey. Clearly, the location of the producer is important to the consumer because the closer the producer is, the less freight charges will be. When producers are in different geographical locations, we say that their products are *spatially differentiated*.[1] Not only do pecuniary shipping costs differ among spatially differentiated products, but delivery time also differs. Spatial differentiation appears to be more important for commodities that have relatively low value, hence higher transportation costs per unit of weight. Products such as steel, cement, aluminum, and copper are subject to spatial differentiation. Economists are interested in spatial differentiation because they wish to assess the impact on competition of alternative pricing policies based on geographic location.

When spatial differentiation occurs, sellers can either quote a price at the point of origin, usually called f.o.b. (free on board), or at the point of destination, usually called a delivered price. Assume all firms in an industry are producing a strictly homogeneous product except for location. If all firms quoted f.o.b., then each firm would have a locational monopoly with nearby customers, who would pay the least amount of freight charges.[2] In essence, then, f.o.b. pricing would give each supplier a local sheltered market with size dependent on f.o.b. price, the nearness of other suppliers, and a distant impenetrable market. To the extent that sellers attempt to penetrate more distant segments of the market, a system of delivered pricing will often be used. The most attention has been given to basing-point price systems.

Basing-Point Pricing

A **basing-point price system** is a delivered pricing technique in which selling firms usually act in a concerted way. Under a single basing-point system, every seller will use the same point of origin in calculating freight charges to be added to the base or f.o.b. price. To the extent that all base prices are the same, then every seller's price at any location will be identical. For example, steel companies may use Pittsburgh as the base. When the calculated freight charge to any individual buyer is the same for all buyers, the delivered price quoted to any buyer will also be the same, provided that the base price for the individual buyer does not differ.

The effect of a basing-point price system is to eliminate the delivered price differentials that occur when each seller pursues independent pricing policy. As Machlup pointed out in his classic book on this subject, the basing-point pricing system allows a large number of sellers geographically located in different parts of the country to quote an "identically delivered price" going to any of the 60,000 or more possible destinations in the United States.[3]

---

[1] See Kenneth Boulding, *Economic Analysis*, vol. 1, 4th ed. (New York: Harper & Row, 1966), pp. 470–475.

[2] Often landowners will obtain the monopoly returns by increasing rents in this situation.

[3] Fritz Machlup, *The Basing-Point System; An Economic Analysis of a Controversial Pricing Practice* (Philadelphia, Pa.: Blakiston, 1949), p. 7.

Phantom Freight Pricing

The **phantom freight** price system quotes the same delivered price to all buyers and is closely related to the basing-point system. Under a pricing system with phantom freight, the quoted price includes an average freight charge to all buyers. Thus, those buyers located near the seller will pay more than the actual cost of transportation. If the quoted price is the same for all the selling companies, the delivered price will be the same for all buyers. Those customers that live far away from the producer are charged a phantom freight charge that is less than the actual transportation charges. They benefit from what is called **freight absorption** by the seller. This is a system which presumably discriminates in favor of more distant customers and against nearby customers. Variations on phantom freight and freight absorption involve the establishment of geographic zones in which a uniform delivered price is charged within each zone. Thus, within the zone, nearby customers still subsidize more distant customers. In some freight absorption situations, the supplier adds to a base price the freight from the competitor nearest to the customer, no matter where the actual shipping point is.

The careful reader will observe that basing-point pricing implies existence of phantom freight if the basing point and the production point differ. Thus, if the basing point is located in San Francisco, and the firm produces in New York and ships to New York, it receives phantom freight.

SOME THEORETICAL ASPECTS OF DELIVERED PRICING SYSTEMS

Delivered pricing systems divide sales among firms at a production center and also divide sales among production centers. We start with an industry in which transportation costs represent a significant fraction of delivered prices. In the industry, there are one or more production centers, and relatively few large firms operate at each production center. These firms desire to collude to maximize their profits. Any attempt at **covert collusion** will lead to rivalry that will be unprofitable from the industry's, and eventually the firm's, point of view. Thus, for effective collusion, the distribution of sales among firms at each production center must be determined by nonprice criteria. If the firms simply quote f.o.b. (factory) prices, then they can rely on nonprice competition to divide sales among them.[4] A delivered price system such as basing point will divide sales on a geographical basis within the production center.

Deciding how to divide sales among production centers presents an additional problem. Demand is geographically unstable because the proportion of national or regional sales in each consumption area (as opposed to production area) may fluctuate. Given unstable geographical patterns of demand, f.o.b.

---

[4] Stigler has pointed out that quotas or a joint sales agency plus quotas would be more efficient, albeit illegal. George J. Stigler, *The Organization of Industry* (Homewood, Ill.: Irwin, 1968), p. 151, footnote 9.

pricing would cause large variations in rates of output for all nonstorable products, thus increasing costs at times of less demand. Alternatively, for storable products, f.o.b. pricing would raise inventory costs at times of less demand. Both situations would cause some firms to lose income, while others would not. This difference in income would put a strain on any implicit agreement about sales distribution.

On the other hand, prices at the production center could fluctuate with demand changes. When demand was high in one production center, prices would rise and attract output from other centers. When demand was low, the reverse would occur. Such unpredictable alterations in f.o.b. prices would make any collusive agreement among firms at the production centers difficult to maintain; collusion among firms at many different production centers would be impossible to maintain. Thus, f.o.b. pricing would make collusion among firms difficult unless a joint sales agency could be established with sufficient policing powers. Because such agencies are illegal under our antitrust laws, this is not a viable solution.

Freight absorption, on the other hand, is a solution. At each point in the market, a single price exists at which price rivalry is eliminated. However, the fact that basing-point pricing eliminates competition is a point that even industry representatives seldom attempt to refute. For example, an official of the cement institute once said, "Ours is an industry that cannot stand free competition. . . ."[5] Since at times cement companies submit identical bids, no matter where they are located, one might presume that basing-point pricing does reduce competition. For example, Machlup reported that 11 cement companies submitted bids of $3.286854 per barrel to the state of New Mexico![6]

Efficiency Aspects of Basing-Point Price Systems

We now discuss several efficiency aspects of uniform delivered pricing systems, such as basing-point pricing. First of all, such uniform delivered price systems contribute to rigidity of relative prices. Changes in relative prices normally indicate changing relative scarcity of goods, services, and resources. Any contribution to more rigid price structuring impedes the movement of resources to locations where those resources are relatively more needed. Thus, the signalling aspect of the price system is reduced because of basing-point pricing systems.[7]

Second, uniform delivered pricing systems encourage customers to choose from suppliers in what would otherwise be economically inefficient locations. Customers will naturally gravitate toward a basing point. If production occurs elsewhere, the basing point's location will incur inefficient use of transportation

---

[5] Reported in Samuel Loescher, *Imperfect Collusion in the Cement Industry* (Cambridge, Mass.: Harvard University Press, 1959), p. 85.

[6] Machlup, *The Basing-Point System*, p. 99.

[7] This assumes that the f.o.b. price does not fluctuate as much as the delivered price.

resources. Another inefficient aspect of uniform delivered pricing systems involves **cross-hauling**. Consider a single basing-point system. Mills or factories located at the basing-point are unable to serve next-door customers any better or more cheaply than a distant rival because they charge the same price that the distant rival charges. Thus, we could expect some cross hauling from a distant plant to a nearby plant even though it would be economically more efficient for the nearby plant to service the customer. Cross hauling necessarily reduces the industry's profits because it increases cost. Perfectly colluding oligopolists would never choose a system that allowed for cross hauling. But, we have already indicated that uniform delivered pricing systems are also an imperfect way for oligopolists to collude.

Criticisms of the Theory

Not everyone agrees that uniform delivered pricing systems generate economic inefficiencies. For example, Alchian points out that so-called phantom freight charges may merely represent the payment for a superior resource called location. He uses the example of plywood shipped from Georgia to Florida with a basing point of Seattle. Rather than being a form of phantom freight, this supposed extra charge is merely the payment that the owner of the Georgia plant obtains for having a locational advantage over other plants. In a 1978 federal court case, a jury in New Orleans declared that the southeastern producers of plywood were collecting phantom freight on shipments to Florida because they were charging the Seattle price for plywood plus freight to Florida without actually shipping from Seattle.[8] The jury neglected to realize that the plywood produced in the southeast was produced with superior resources, that is, land close to the Florida market. Land nearer the market is worth a higher rent; it is the closest source of plywood to Florida. Its superiority of rental value reflects how much closer it is to Florida than the suppliers in Seattle are. The land and other resources for making plywood in the southeast will get a higher rent or payment because of that superiority (lower costs of supply). The difference is the freight saving due to the superior location of southeastern plywood production. Alchian points out that those who allege phantom freight and complain

are merely saying they have rights to that value of the superior land, not the landowners. The federal court jury, in asserting phantom freight was collected and that it should have been given to customers in Florida at a lower price, actually is saying Florida customers are the owners of those superior located resources of plywood. With that kind of reasoning, *all* land, no matter whether located in the center of the city or in the extreme margin distant from the city should all get the same rent—with the higher rental value of the city's center land being appropriated from the land owners and given to the lucky renters or buyers of the services of the land located closer to the consuming population. Those who allege phantom freight are alleging

---

[8] Armen A. Alchian, "Words: Musical or Meaningful?" (unpublished paper: U.C.L.A., 1978).

that all resources, no matter how different their productivity, should all get the same rent or wages.[9]

Stigler points out that a uniform delivered price system, or systematic freight absorption system, does not have to generate any more cross hauling than a competitive system.[10] After all, production center X sells in the area around production center Y only when Y cannot sell its share of the industry sales in its own area. At that time, Y will not be selling in X's territory. Nonetheless, we will see some cross hauling because of the difference between orders and deliveries, but this type of cross hauling exists under competition also.

EMPIRICAL EVIDENCE OF DELIVERED PRICING SYSTEMS

Studies have examined the actual application of delivered pricing systems. We examine several of these studies here, including those involving single basing point, multiple basing point, and cross hauling.

Single Basing Point

The issue of the price discriminating aspect of single basing-point delivered price systems has been examined in detail in a number of important antitrust cases. In *Corn Products* and *Staley Manufacturing*, section 2a of the Robinson-Patman Act was at issue as it applied to single basing-point pricing.[11] We will look at the Corn Products case in some detail now.

Corn Products Refining Company Case   Corn Products operated a plant in Chicago and opened another one in Kansas City, keeping Chicago as its basing point. Both plants sold anywhere in the United States at a uniform delivered price, adding to a base price at Chicago the transportation costs via railroad to the point of delivery. The Federal Trade Commission contended that users of glucose near Kansas City were paying phantom freight. Given that glucose customers in Kansas City competed with those in Chicago, the discrimination appeared to be *prima facie* unlawful.

According to the commission, the delivered prices from the Chicago plant were cost-justified, but those from the Kansas City plant were not. A customer located halfway between Chicago and Kansas City might receive glucose from the Kansas City plant. The delivered price would nonetheless include the Chicago base price plus freight transportation charges from Chicago. This delivered price, however, would actually be lower than the delivered price in Kansas City itself.

The facts were basically the same in the Staley Manufacturing Company,

[9] Ibid.

[10] Stigler, *The Organization of Industry*, pp. 153–154.

[11] *Corn Products Refining Company v. Federal Trade Commission*, 324 U.S. 726 (1945), and *Federal Trade Commission v. A. E. Staley Mfg. Co.*, 324 U.S. 746 (1945).

another glucose manufacturer that used the Chicago-plus basing-point system of Corn Products.

The Supreme Court declared the above outlined single basing-point system adopted by Corn Products and Staley Manufacturing illegal under section 2a of the Robinson-Patman Act. In deciding the case, the Court accepted the Federal Trade Commission's findings that users of glucose in Kansas City effectively competed with those in Chicago. These users were mainly candy manufacturers. According to the FTC, even slight differences in raw material costs were sufficient to divert business from one manufacturer to another. Competitive injury between candy manufacturers at the buyer level therefore resulted.

One can question this conclusion. A candy manufacturer in Kansas City attempting to sell candy in Chicago prior to Corn Products' building a plant in Kansas City presumably would have relocated to Chicago. If, on the other hand, the candy manufacturer wanted to service Kansas City, it had the choice of locating between Chicago and Kansas City or locating in Kansas City itself. It would have to balance the additional transportation charges of glucose from Chicago against the transportation costs saved by shipping finished candy a smaller distance.

Now consider what happens to the market structure after Corn Products builds the Kansas City plant. Are the candy manufacturers any worse off with the basing-point pricing system, using Chicago as a base? No. They are in exactly the same position as they were prior to the building of the Kansas City plant. On the other hand, if Corn Products decided to use an f.o.b. pricing system, then Kansas City candy manufacturers would clearly be able to get glucose at a lower price. This would allow them to increase the geographic area of their sales. They would certainly be able to meet Chicago competition more effectively. Alternatively, they could maintain the same price and sales volume as before and earn higher profits because glucose would be available at a lower price. In either case, it is not at all clear that Corn Products' decision to build a plant in Kansas City necessarily meant that Corn Products must enhance the profit position of Kansas City candy manufacturers. What comes into play here is Alchian's contention that phantom freight charges may not be anything of the kind. These charges are returned in the form of an economic rent that Corn Products earns because of its Kansas City plant's locational superiority.

Multiple Basing-Point Systems

Presumably, a multiple basing-point system reduces the purported incidents of phantom freight charges. More than one producing center is designed as a basing point. The delivered price quoted to any customer will be calculated according to the closest applicable basing point. In the extreme, every production location is a basing point. Each customer pays a delivered price equal to the base price charged by all producers, plus freight from the closest producer. This system has been called the **plenary basing-point system**, or **systematic freight equalization**. In such a system, there is never any phantom freight charge, and the seller charges actual freight to any customer within the seller's zone. Outside of the zone, the seller will meet the best price that any customer can obtain.

In more common multiple basing-point systems, two or three locations are designed as a base. For example, after 1924, there were several basing points for the steel industry, usually Pittsburgh, Birmingham, and Chicago. In 1937, the cement industry had 79 basing points reflecting freight costs.

Federal Trade Commission v. Cement Institute   In a relatively famous case, the Federal Trade Commission examined the industry-wide multiple basing-point system in the sale of cement. The industry was charged with unfair methods of competition under section 5 of the Federal Trade Commission Act, as well as with price discrimination under section 2a of the Robinson-Patman Act.[12] At the time of the suit, 74 companies and 21 associating individuals formed the membership of the Cement Institute.

The Court considered the FTC findings that members of the Cement Institute obtained different rates of return on sales to different customers. Rather than looking at simple price differences, the Court found that price discrimination existed because different rates of profit were made from different customers.[13] The Court also found that the Cement Institute engaged in a program of boycotts and reprisals when any member firm attempted to cheat on the delivered price system. Thus, the argument of unfair methods of competition was used because of the concurrent use of prices by competing companies, which included duress in the enforcement of a uniform delivered pricing system.

Cross Hauling   As we pointed out above, Stigler was not impressed with the arguments about the inefficiency of cross hauling. "One would not expect cross hauling to be a major waste under systematic freight absorption, however, and there is no empirical evidence that contradicts this expectation."[14] Some studies, nonetheless, have shown waste due to cross hauling. In the steel industry, it was estimated in February 1939 that freight absorption amounted to between 3 and 5 percent of delivered prices.[15] Presumably, with a multiple basing-point system, cross hauling will be prevalent. In the cement industry in 1927, cross hauling was estimated to be 15 percent of total revenue.[16] Most subsequent researchers believe that this figure is a gross overstatement by at least a factor of 2.

[12] *Federal Trade Commission v. Cement Institute*, 333 U.S. 683 (1948).

[13] By looking beyond simple price differences, the Court may indirectly take away firm incentives to find the lowest cost combination. When prices are identical, cement companies, like other firms, may have differential rates of returns attributable to the ownership of superior resources or more efficient methods of producing cement.

[14] Stigler, *The Organization of Industry*, p. 153.

[15] Machlup, *The Basing-Point System*, pp. 56–57.

[16] John M. Clark, "Basing Point Methods of Price Quoting," *Canadian Journal of Economics and Political Science*, vol. 4 (November 1938), p. 482.

THE COMPETITIVE ASPECTS OF UNIFORM DELIVERED PRICING SYSTEMS

Even though basing-point systems continue to be legal in many European countries, they have essentially been declared illegal in the United States through a number of Supreme Court decisions in the 1940s. It is believed that basing-point systems significantly reduce competition and allow for price discrimination.

Theoretically, one can argue that competition is impaired because uniform-delivered pricing reduces what would otherwise be a complicated pricing problem. Without basing-point pricing, competitors could attempt to undercut rivals by offering lower prices at certain locations. Retaliatory price cuts would ensue. Adhering to a basing-point formula reduces such competitive behavior and presumably brings about higher prices to consumers. Basing-point pricing eliminates all but secret, under-the-table price competition.

EXCLUSIVE TERRITORIES

Many producers will designate a specific wholesaler or retailer as the only one allowed to sell the producer's product in a specified territory. Under modified exclusive territory arrangements, another firm may make a sale in another territory, provided that the profit is shared with the exclusive territorial firm. A manufacturer may also attempt to restrict the customers to whom its dealers may sell. The purpose and effects of such a restriction are similar to those of territorial limitations.

Territorial Limitations—General Considerations

Territorial limitations basically insulate dealers from competition with each other. For example, a territorial limitation exists when a producer designates a dealer as the sole outlet for the producer's products within a distinct geographic area. As a result, the dealer will not engage in extensive competition with other dealers except at the borders of the designated area. Indeed, the greater the space separating the dealers, the greater is each dealer's freedom from other dealers carrying the same brand. Presumably, territorial exclusivity allows each dealer to devote his or her best efforts to serving and developing a particular territory rather than to looking at marketing opportunities in adjoining territories. In a typical territorial limitation situation, there is an agreement in which the dealer specifically indicates he or she will not solicit business outside the designated territory. In the most stringent case, the dealer agrees not to sell to buyers located elsewhere.

White Motor Company v. United States One of the most famous cases involving territorial limitation was the White Motor Company case. The territorial clause in the White Motor case stated,

Distributor is hereby granted the exclusive right, except as hereinafter provided, to sell during the life of this agreement, in the territory described below, White and Auto Car Trucks purchased from company hereunder. (The agreement went on to list the specific territory.) Distributor agrees to develop the aforementioned territory to the satisfaction of Company, and not to sell any trucks purchased hereunder except in accordance with this agreement, and not to sell such trucks except to individuals, firms, or corporations having a place of business and/or purchasing headquarters in said territory.[17]

White Motor argued before the Court that the territorial clauses were necessary for the company to compete with those who made other kinds of trucks. The territorial clauses were a substitute for White Motor Company having its own retail outlets. White Motor contended that the territorial clause was more efficient because it eliminated the costly and extensive sales organization that would be necessary if White undertook retailing itself. Further, according to the company, White's use of restricted territories was designed to induce distributors and dealers to compete effectively with larger companies.

In addition to the foregoing, the Supreme Court considered two other customer limitations imposed by White Motors: (1) distributors were prevented from selling to other dealers not approved by White, and (2) White prevented dealers from selling to the federal or local governments. The Court believed that White Motor was attempting to seek the best of both worlds—retaining a distribution system for the general customer while skimming off the cream of the trade for its own direct sales, mainly to federal and local governments where White's prices exceeded dealer cost. However, the Court was not ready to make a decision regarding the legality of the limitations imposed by White Motor. Instead, the Court remanded the case to the trial level for a determination of the effect of these limitations. The legality of the limitations would then be gleaned from this determination.

It is apparent from the Court's decision that any determination of a restraint of trade resulting from territorial or customer limitations should be made according to the facts of each individual case. Although three dissenters in White Motor called for a *per se* rule, the widespread effect of the decision was that a rule of reason approach to vertical limitations was adopted. Lower courts have subsequently used a rule of reason approach regarding territorial restrictions in which purpose, power, and effect are evaluated.[18]

The rule of reason approach to customers and territorial restrictions was short-lived, however. In 1969, the United States Supreme Court established what became known as the Schwinn rule.[19] The Schwinn case involved the famous bicycle manufacturer, which held about 25 percent of the market in the early 1950s. By the end of the decade, it had only 13 percent of the market, as

---

[17] *White Motor Company v. United States*, 372 U.S. 253 (1963).
[18] See, for example, *Sandura Company v. FTC*, 339 F.2d 847 (6th Cir. 1964).
[19] See *United States v. Arnold Schwinn & Co.*, 388 U.S. 365 (1969).

Sears and Montgomery Ward expanded sales. In order to combat the erosion of its market shares, Schwinn set up a complicated distribution system. It had 22 distributors to which it sold less than 50 percent of its bicycles. Each distributor was instructed to resell only within designated territories and only to retailers franchised by Schwinn. The remaining bikes were sold and shipped directly by Schwinn to its franchise retailers when so instructed by Schwinn distributors who had taken the orders. These distributors received a commission on the sales. Every dealer agreed not to resell to an unfranchised dealer. A lower court ruled that territorial restrictions imposed by Schwinn on its distributors were unlawful; it therefore enjoined these restrictions. When the case got to the Supreme Court, however, part of the decision was reversed. Schwinn was precluded from requiring distributors to sell only to franchise retailers. Also, Schwinn could not prohibit retailers from reselling to an unfranchised retailer.

In this case the Court revised the use of a rule of reason approach and mandated that producer-imposed territorial or customer restrictions on dealers regarding products purchased from the producers were *per se* violations of section 1 of the Sherman Act. Although seemingly inconsistent with this rule, the Court did allow the rule of reason approach to stand as applied to territorial and customer limitations on dealers with respect to goods *consigned* by the producer to the dealer.

The inconsistencies apparent in a distinction between goods sold and goods consigned resulted in a reversal of the Schwinn decision in 1977. In *Continental TV, Inc. v. GTE Sylvania, Inc.*,[20] the Supreme Court returned to the rule established in White Motor. Reasoning that territorial and customer restrictions could foster interbrand competition, the Court reestablished the rule of reason approach to such cases.[21]

Customer Limitations

A manufacturer may sell only to wholesalers but may still be concerned with the behavior of retailers. Manufacturers often limit the title of "authorized dealer" to those who are approved by the manufacturer. Nonetheless, those buyers dissatisfied with unapproved dealers will blame the manufacturer for defective products. It is conceivable that, under such circumstances, a manufacturer would want to require wholesalers to confine sales to approved retailers. The manufacturer can thereby assure that the product is handled only by competent dealers. Manufacturers may have a comparative advantage in deciding which retailers are "high quality." Section 1 of the Sherman Act can be

---

[20] *Continental TV, Inc. v. GTE Sylvania, Inc.*, 433 U.S. 36 (1977).
[21] Also see Kenneth W. Clarkson, Timothy J. Muris, and Donald L. Martin, eds. "Exclusionary Practices: Shopping Center Restrictive Covenants," in *The Federal Trade Commission Since 1970: Economic Regulation and Bureaucratic Behavior* (Cambridge, Mass.: Cambridge University Press, 1981), pp. 141–160, for further application of the rule of reason agreement.

applied to customer restrictions that prevent wholesalers from selling to other than approved retailers whenever such a practice is used in support of agreements to fix retail prices (see resale price maintenance in Chapter 13).[22] In Schwinn, the Court condemned customer limitations explicitly.

Allocating Customers among Dealers Some manufacturers attempt to allocate different customers to different dealers. As an example, a cosmetics producer may allow one wholesaler to sell only to beauty salons and another to sell only to drug stores. Presumably, this practice comes about for one or more of the following reasons: (1) to facilitate price discrimination, (2) to limit competition, and (3) to achieve efficient specialization.

Price Discrimination The manufacturer that has numerous wholesalers within each category may be attempting to practice customer restrictions to facilitate price discrimination. If the demand curve is relatively more elastic for beauty salons than for drug stores, the manufacturer would want to charge a lower price to wholesalers serving beauty salons than to wholesalers serving drug stores. As an alternative to using different wholesaling channels, the manufacturer may sell two different "brands" of the same product to discourage resale from beauty salons to drug stores. The manufacturer that uses different wholesaling channels, though, has to police the beauty salon wholesalers to prevent resales of the product to drug stores.

Limiting Competition Just as territorial restrictions limit intrabrand competition with respect to each geographic group of customers, allocation of customers among dealers will also limit intrabrand competition with respect to each customer class.

Efficient Specialization Different techniques of promotion, payment, and servicing may be required for different distribution outlets. Wholesalers may be specialized to such an extent that some can service drug stores more cost-effectively than they can service beauty salons and vice versa. To the extent that there are established specialists, the efficiency argument may hold as a reason for allocating customers among dealers. Courts have, in some cases, permitted customer restrictions when persuaded by this efficiency argument.[23]

Reserving Customers to the Manufacturer Some manufacturers preclude dealers from selling to specified customers that the manufacturer wishes to service directly. In some cases, this may be due to quantity efficiency by the manufacturer. That is to say, some customers may buy in such large quantities that the manufacturer can more efficiently handle them directly.

---

[22] *United States v. Bausch & Lomb Optical Company*, 321 U.S. 707 721 (1944). In this case, Soft-lite had arranged for Bausch & Lomb to make tinted lenses, which Soft-lite then sold to wholesalers, who sold them to retailers approved by Soft-lite. Retailers in turn agreed with Soft-lite to sell the lenses at locally prevailing prices and at a premium over untinted lenses. A similar situation arose in *Ethyl Gasoline Corporation v. United States*, 309 U.S. 436 (1940).

[23] See *Tripoli Company v. Wella Corp.*, 425 F.2d 932 (3d Cir. 1969), and *Paddington Corporation v. Major Brands, Inc.*, 359 Fed. Sup. 1244 (W.D. Oklahoma 1973).

Other Important Cases

United States v. Sealy, Inc.[24]   Sealy had been a manufacturer of mattresses and bedding products for 40 years when this case came to trial. In addition to a charge of price fixing, there was also a charge that Sealy allocated mutually exclusive territories among its manufacturer-licensees (firms that manufactured the Sealy mattresses and bedding products that were then sold under the Sealy name). The court trial did not conclude that the second claim was "in unreasonable restraint of trade in violation of section 1 of the Sherman Act." Each licensee was guaranteed that Sealy would not license any other person or firm to manufacture or sell in the designated area as long as the licensee agreed not to manufacture or sell "Sealy products" outside the designated area. Sealy did not deny this arrangement. The Supreme Court found that the territorial restraints were a part of the unlawful price fixing and policing policies of Sealy, even though Sealy contended that they were mere incidents of a lawful program of trademark licensing. Within each licensee's area, the trial court found that the licensee "zealously and effectively maintained resale prices, free from the danger of outside incursions." In summation, the Supreme Court found that the arrangements for territorial limitations were part of "an aggregation of trade restraints, including unlawful price fixing and policing," which are unlawful under section 1 of the Sherman Act.

Criticisms of the Case   The Court's opinion never mentioned the fact that Sealy, Inc., had a very small share of the mattress market. One wonders, then, how much control over prices the company actually had. In other words, if Sealy has only 2 or 3 percent of the market, it presumably must take the market price per constant quality unit as given, or very close to as given. This ruling shows the firm stand the Supreme Court has taken on the "intent" to fix prices. An aspiration to fix prices is certainly not the same thing as price fixing in practice and in reality.

Another interpretation of Sealy's territorial limitations was that there was an attempt to exploit the Sealy trademark. Consider an example. Thirty small manufacturers want to adopt a common trademark to obtain public visibility equivalent to that of a large manufacturer. Each of the 30 manufacturers hesitates, however, to commit his own resources to advertising the common trademark. He believes that others will make the commitment. In other words, he attempts to take a free ride on their advertising.[25]

If manufacturer X is in New Jersey and manufacturer Y is in New York, advertising for the common trademark by manufacturer X in New Jersey will generate benefits to the New York manufacturer. Manufacturer X, however, will choose a lower level of advertising when marginal costs equal its own

---

[24] *United States v. Sealy, Inc.*, 388 U.S. 350 (1967).

[25] Or, rather, a cheap ride. See George J. Stigler, "Free Riders and Collective Action: An Appendix to Theories of Economic Regulation," *The Bell Journal of Economics and Management Science*, vol. 5 (Autumn 1974), pp. 359–365.

marginal revenues and will be reluctant to advertise the common trademark. This may have been the situation for Sealy. In order to avoid the free rider problem, the 30 or so licensees agreed to allocate territories to each member of the group, forbidding each one to sell under the Sealy mark outside of that territory. Every member now has an incentive to advertise the Sealy mark within the assigned territory, knowing that other members will be unable to take a free ride on that advertising. (Admittedly, some cheating is likely to occur.)

Federal Trade Commission v. Coors   The Federal Trade Commission brought suit against Coors, a Colorado beer manufacturer, because of territorial restrictions on Coors distributors.[26] Additionally, the Court held that Coors attempted to fix wholesale and retail prices of the beer. Finally, the FTC objected to Coors' distribution contracts, which allowed the company to terminate the distributorship on five days' notice whenever the contract was violated. Like the Supreme Court's decision of the Sealy case, the Federal Trade Commission maintained that territorial restrictions are *per se* illegal when they are associated with price fixing.

In order to understand the territorial limitations that Coors invoked upon its distributors, one must know a little bit about Coors beer. Coors is different from other beers because it is not pasteurized. Thus, deterioration begins immediately after Coors is packaged. It must be moved to the consumer as quickly as possible and it must always be refrigerated. Coors could have been vertically integrated to perform the distribution and retailing functions itself. As a more economic substitute, it chose to have a distributorship system which would be a close substitute for vertical integration and which would provide quality control. The awarding of exclusive territories, according to Coors, was designed to create incentives to those distributors handling Coors beer to handle it the same way in which Coors would have if the firm had been vertically integrated.

Assume now that instead of establishing exclusive distributorships, Coors allowed a number of distributors to sell its beer in any particular geographical area. Each distributor is faced with constant refrigeration costs, inventory control costs, and the like. One or more distributors may attempt to cut costs by reducing the services. Consumers buying beer that had been improperly refrigerated, for example, would not be able to tell whether the fault was with the Coors manufacturing company, the distributor, or the retailer. The final result, nonetheless, would be the same—reduced consumption of Coors beer. Only a small part of the cost of reduced consumption would, however, be visited upon the perpetrator of the inferior Coors. We are in a free rider situa-

---

[26] *Federal Trade Commission v. Coors*, 83 FTC 32 (1973). For a more detailed description of this case, see Wesley J. Liebeler, "Bureau of Competition: Antitrust Activities," in Kenneth W. Clarkson and Timothy J. Muris, eds., *The Federal Trade Commission Since 1970: Economic Regulation and Bureaucratic Behavior* (Cambridge, Mass.: Cambridge University Press, 1981), pp. 79–84.

tion similar to the one described above in the Sealy case. Cheating distributors would attempt to take a free ride on the efforts of fellow distributors and Coors manufacturing company to provide beer drinkers with a high-quality product. This free ride possibility would reduce each distributor's incentive to achieve rapid distribution under refrigerated conditions of the unpasteurized beer.

In order to reduce such free riding, low-quality performance by distributors, Coors must engage in costly policing efforts. Policing costs rise (as well as the amount of potential cheating) with the number of distributors in any given area. Establishing exclusive territories alleviates this problem because the authorized distributor has a property right in all *future* sales of Coors. For the single distributor in an exclusive territory, the possibility of a free ride is very much lower. In essence, incentives to provide the optimal level of services (rapid refrigeration and inventory control) will coincide more with those of Coors manufacturing company if distributors are limited than if several distributors serve one area. Policing costs by Coors would also be greatly diminished. Viewed as such, territorial restrictions were an attempt by Coors to obtain more quality control and market penetration for a lower expenditure of resources. The Court rejected Coors' explanation and accepted the FTC's arguments.

Exclusive Auto Dealerships

The California Automobile Franchise Act provides that an auto manufacturer wishing to set up a new dealership in California or to relocate an existing one must notify the California New Motor Vehicle Board, as well as each of its existing franchise dealers handling the same make of auto located within 10 miles. Existing dealers are allowed 15 days to protest the new dealership. If one or more dealers protest, the new dealership cannot be set up until the board has held hearings and decided whether there is "good cause" for barring the competitor. Clearly, such a system is a modified form of territorial limitation. Basically, intrabrand competition is reduced, at least temporarily, because of the California act.

In California, two would-be dealers, along with General Motors, brought suit against the state and won. The decision was overturned by the Supreme Court, which ruled that the California law was constitutional. The Supreme Court indicated that the law was consistent with concern about the disparity in bargaining power between auto manufacturers and their dealers. Speaking for the Court, Justice William Brennan observed that the act's system of regulation was designed by the legislature "to displace unfettered business freedom in the matter of the establishment and relocation of automobile dealerships."

In the California automobile franchise case, we have a situation dissimilar to the ones already discussed. Here we find that the legislature is involved in helping manufacturers set up exclusive territories for distributors or retailers. Existing retailers use legal means to obtain territorial exclusivity by reducing or eliminating the competitive inroads of new dealers.

Exclusive Dealing and Requirements Contracts

Exclusive dealing contracts involve a commitment by a buyer to deal only with a particular user. Related to such contracts are requirements contracts, which normally entail a commitment by a buyer to take all he or she needs of a given product for a predetermined period from the seller. A requirements contract may also require a commitment by a seller to supply all of a buyer's needs. Some requirements contracts prevent the buyer from making purchases from any other seller. When the signatory to a requirements contract fails to follow the contract, the manufacturer will refuse to sell any further units of the product. Presumably, the aim of the manufacturer in such an agreement is to assure itself a share of the market. This type of agreement also increases the retailer's sales effort for the product. Both exclusive dealing and requirements contracts tend to foreclose a portion of the market from competition.

One of the benefits of an exclusive dealing or requirements contract is that the parties have a "planned" product flow spanning two vertical levels. Each party is thereby relieved of the uncertainties and expenses of going to the general market more frequently to purchase or sell perhaps only in smaller quantities.

Legal Status of Exclusive Dealing and Requirements Contracts

Requirement contracts are limited under section 3 of the Clayton Act, but their legal status is somewhat hazy. In cases where requirement contracts have involved a large share of a given market, the courts have typically invalidated them.[27] It should be noted that requirements contracts and exclusive dealing arrangements were upheld by common law and under the Sherman Act before the Clayton Act was passed.

Who Benefits from a Requirements Contract?

At first glance, it appears that only the manufacturer benefits from a requirements contract because it reduces uncertainty and forecloses a portion of the market from competition. If, however, only manufacturers benefited, few such agreements would probably exist. In order to attract signatories to a requirements contract, manufacturers often grant the retailer a franchise allowing the franchisee an exclusive territory. The franchisee obtains in exchange for signing a requirements contract the goodwill of the brand name and the known product—for example, Colonel Sanders restaurants—and selling techniques provided by the franchisor. As the data in Table 12-1 show, franchising is an important form of business organization. By 1979 there were more than 400,000

---

[27] *Standard Fashion Company v. Magrane-Houston Company*, 258 U.S. 346 (1922), where 40 percent of all retail dress pattern outlets were covered in a requirements contract, and *Standard Oil of California and Standard Stations, Inc. v. United States*, 337 U.S. 293 (1949), where 16 percent of the retail gas stations in the western United States were involved in requirements contracts.

TABLE 12-1

FRANCHISING IN THE ECONOMY: 1979*

Kinds of franchised business	Establishments (number) Total	Company-owned	Franchisee-owned	Percent changes 1978–1979 Estab.	Sales
Total—All franchising	492,379	89,367	403,012	5.4	8.8
Automobile and truck dealers	31,510	300	31,210	− 0.3	8.2
Automotive products and services	53,367	4,895	48,472	5.2	14.1
Business aids and services	46,622	5,860	40,762	20.0	24.1
Accounting, credit, collection agencies, and general business systems	4,638	66	4,572	11.4	18.5
Employment services	4,400	1,063	3,337	15.5	22.4
Printing and copying services	2,687	166	2,521	18.2	20.4
Tax preparation services	8,793	4,271	4,522	1.8	12.6
Real estate	22,045	154	21,891	33.8	27.3
Miscellaneous business services	4,059	140	3,919	16.3	20.0
Construction, home improvements, maintenance, and cleaning services	15,431	447	14,984	9.7	14.2
Convenience stores	16,268	10,553	5,715	7.0	10.7
Educational products and services	2,632	412	2,220	18.0	15.8
Fast-food restaurants (all types)	65,631	17,141	48,490	13.4	19.7
Gasoline service stations	171,000	32,490	138,510	− 0.8	5.5
Hotels and motels	5,833	979	4,854	7.2	11.7
Campgrounds	1,085	22	1,063	2.1	4.9
Laundry and drycleaning services	3,059	72	2,987	5.3	16.7
Recreation, entertainment, and travel	5,082	86	4,996	10.3	17.8
Rental services (auto-truck)	7,574	1,918	5,656	5.3	10.3
Rental services (equipment)	1,611	155	1,456	8.3	10.6
Retailing (non-food)	46,260	12,620	33,640	5.8	− 3.5
Retailing (food other than convenience stores)	15,339	1,011	14,328	8.5	12.1
Soft drink bottlers	2,025	70	1,955	− 3.4	11.8
Miscellaneous	2,050	336	1,714	16.3	19.2

*1979 data estimated by respondents.

Source: Franchising in the Economy, 1977–1979, U.S. Department of Commerce (Washington, D.C.: USGPO, 1979), p. 34.

franchisee-owned establishments with sales exceeding $254 billion. At the end of 1979 there was an increase of approximately 5.4 percent in the total number of franchisee-establishments.

The Barriers to Entry Question

Requirements contracts and franchises often force exclusive dealing upon a retail firm. The question arises as to what extent such agreements alter barriers to entry. It could be maintained that such agreements increase barriers for highly differentiated products that are well known. For example, McDonald's will not benefit by an unlimited number of franchises in a given market area. To that end, franchising agreements often contain specific provisions limiting the number of franchisees that will be allowed to operate within specified geographic limits around each franchise.

On the other hand, the success of franchises brings about increased entry into the particular industry, although not solely for the highly differentiated specific brand product. The successes of McDonald's and Burger King have fostered entry by Wendy's, Pizza Hut, and others.

Future Growth of Franchise Operations   Because requirement contracts in franchising ultimately benefit consumers, one should expect this form of contract to be used more extensively in the future. In any situation where the cost of acquiring information about the products or services provided is high, franchising is likely to continue.

Federal Trade Commission v. Great Lakes Carbon

The Federal Trade Commission attacked a series of requirements contracts generated by Great Lakes Carbon.[28] Great Lakes had agreed to purchase petroleum coke from various refineries. The initial terms of the contracts varied from 7 to 20 years and extensions were for minimum periods of five years. Although Great Lakes had effectively inaugurated the petroleum coke industry in 1932, by 1969 its share of the market had been reduced to 39 percent. Since 1945, 16 firms had entered the market.

Nonetheless, the FTC believed that Great Lakes had power to influence price and exclude competitors because of the long-term contracts that it had with petroleum coke suppliers. According to the FTC, these contracts excluded or foreclosed others from the processing market. The FTC concluded that reducing the length of these contracts would reduce Great Lakes' market power. Great Lakes, on the other hand, defended its requirements contracts "as a necessary protection from an unacceptable degree of 'risk' in (the) industry." In other words, Great Lakes did not want to invest in new plants unless satisfactory arrangements were made to obtain a constant supply of coke. The FTC was not swayed by this argument, for it believed that the cost of building the necessary plants could be recovered within five years.

Criticisms of the FTC Approach

The first criticism of the FTC case against Great Lakes concerns the 16 firms that entered the coke processing industry from 1945 to 1969. If requirements contracts were so effective at discouraging entry, why was there so much entry? Moreover, Great Lakes certainly wasn't very successful in maintaining its share of the market. It had almost 100 percent in 1945, but retained less than 39 percent in 1969. The second criticism involves the FTC's argument against the efficiency of vertical integration.

First, integrated end-users and other "buyers" would not have had an interest in barring entry into the unintegrated market. Yet these firms also used long-term requirements similar to those used by Great Lakes. Second, and more fundamentally, the commission failed to recognize that in many operations there exists a potential for opportunistic behavior when parties are under separate ownership.[29] Opportunistic behavior refers to those situations where individual parties attempt to obtain benefits or reduce costs at the expense of others. These situations amount to a zero sum game, since both parties will invest resources to detect and reduce potential opportunistic behavior by other parties. Requirements contracts reduce the basis for such investments.

RECIPROCAL BUYING AGREEMENTS

A reciprocal buying or dealing agreement involves one firm agreeing to buy from another on the condition that the second firm buys from the first firm. Firm X makes aluminum. Firm B makes machines and parts. Some of the machines and parts use aluminum, but also some of the machines are used in making aluminum. X may tell B that it will buy machines from B if B agrees to buy raw aluminum from X. This is a classical reciprocal buying arrangement. One would expect that the more conglomerate firms there are, the more room there is for reciprocal dealing arrangements. That is to say, the more individual firms that are operating in several unrelated markets, the greater their opportunity will be for reciprocity.

The courts and the Justice Department have often been disturbed about reciprocity agreements because they seem to be at odds with competitive market ideals. Presumably each market transaction must be made on its competitive merits. With reciprocity, foreclosure to competing sellers in a specific second market occurs. Additionally, reciprocity does not appear to involve integration efficiencies.

However, we can note at the onset that the effects of reciprocity are effectively negated when dealing with competitive markets. That is to say, a perfect competitor facing another perfect competitor cannot extract anything more

---

[28] *Federal Trade Commission v. Great Lakes Carbon*, 82 FTC 1529 (1973).

[29] Benjamin Klein, Robert Crawford, and Armen Alchian, "Vertical Integration, Appropriable Rents, and the Competitive Contracting Process," *Journal of Law and Economics*, vol. 21 (October 1978), pp. 297–326.

than the perfectly competitive price no matter what the arrangement. If firm X, the producer of aluminum, is selling in a perfectly competitive market, it cannot implicitly get more for its aluminum by forcing firm B, also a perfect competitor in selling machines, to buy its aluminum in exchange for firm X buying firm B's machines. Both markets are competitive, therefore both X and B can sell all they can profitably produce at the going market price. Under such circumstances, reciprocity must have some other desired result, such as convenience, reduction of risk, or commercial congeniality.

Now consider a situation in which a seller has substantial market power as a buyer (is a monopsonist). Presumably, reciprocity allows this monopsonist to improve his or her market position as a seller. Suppose that M is a mining firm and that R is the only refinery close enough to M's mine for the ore to be economically shipped. Additionally, suppose that R produces and sells mining equipment. R has monopsony power in the buying of ore from M's mine. In principle, R can use this power in either of two ways: (1) it can force M's price for ore down, or (2) it can require reciprocity in which R agrees to buy ore from M and M agrees to buy equipment at above competitive prices from R. In this manner, it can leverage its power as a monopsonistic buyer of ore into the mining equipment market in which it sells, thereby foreclosing M as a customer to competing makers of machinery.

What is strange about the foregoing argument is that it seems much "cleaner"—fewer transaction costs and monitoring costs—simply for R to exploit its monopsony power in the purchase of ore by paying the monopsony price rather than by requiring a reciprocity agreement. The monopsony position of R can be exploited using reciprocity, but why bother? The maximum amount of monopsonistic economic rents to be gained will not be increased and, depending on transactions and monitoring costs, may be diminished.

Reciprocal Buying in Practice

Industry surveys show that reciprocal buying is associated with (1) oligopolistic market structures in which the members prefer nonprice rivalry, (2) excess capacity (recessions rather than boom times), (3) asymmetry in the size of the firms involved (conglomerate giant over small rival seller), and (4) a two-way flow of transactions between industries in significant quantities.

Empirically, we have found that a number of reciprocal arrangements have been dealt with quite harshly by the Department of Justice. In 1963, for example, it sued General Motors because of GM's reciprocal dealing with respect to freight routings.[30] The Justice Department maintained that GM held its 80 percent share of the diesel locomotive market partly by agreeing to ship the output of its automobile divisions on railroads that bought General Motors locomotives. At the same time, GM would withhold or reduce shipments on

---

[30] *United States v. General Motors Corporation*, CCH *Trade Regulation Reporter*, ¶72,229. Complaint was issued in 1963 and abandoned in 1967 because of insufficient evidence.

railroads buying rival locomotives. The suit was never resolved because the Justice Department did not have sufficient evidence.

There are numerous other reported instances of reciprocity agreements. Du Pont allegedly used reciprocal agreements often.[31] When dealing with steel producers that were vertically integrated into iron-ore mining, Du Pont attempted to gain dynamite orders by indicating that it would place large steel purchases for many of its divisions with firms that bought its dynamite.

SUMMARY

The foregoing cases illustrate the courts' willingness to consider the nature of contracts between manufacturers and their purchasers. Although the different types of contracts may appear to lessen competition or discriminate in prices, the courts theoretically decide the cases on a consistent basis. If there is no rationale for the contested action, the discriminatory or anticompetitive provision is illegal; if there is a rationale, the court weighs the benefits against the costs and rules accordingly. Unfortunately, the court often fails to discover the efficiency rationale underlying the contract.

As seen earlier, basing-point systems are held to be illegal. In other words, the courts see no possible rationale for their use. They hold that prices and profits under basing-point systems are not based on actual cost; the effect is discriminatory. On the other hand, territorial and customer restrictions may be deemed legal. Here, although there may be an anticompetitive effect, it is possible that benefits derived from the restrictions may outweigh the costs. Therefore, a rule of reason approach has developed allowing the parties to the restrictive agreements to offer evidence that the benefits outweigh any barriers to competitive entry. However, these restrictions apply only to a party contracting with the manufacturer. The courts do not allow such restrictions to bar subsequent sales by the purchasers. Finally, requirements contracts and reciprocal buying agreements also may be held legal by the courts because of the benefits that may be derived. However, the courts appear to permit such agreements only to the point where they do not seem to restrict entry.

[31] George W. Stocking and Willard F. Mueller, "Business Reciprocity and the Size of Firms," *Journal of Business*, vol. 30 (April 1957), pp. 73–95.

CHAPTER 13

ADMINISTERED PRICES, PRICE RIGIDITY, AND RESALE PRICE MAINTENANCE

During the Great Depression, measured unemployment rates sometimes exceeded 30 percent of the work force. Corporate pricing policies came under fire from a number of observers, including Gardiner Means. He believed that each industry's output and employment were inversely related to changes in the prices in that industry. Thus, industries where prices did not drop significantly had less output and more unemployment. Means believed that the more monopolistic the industry was, the less prices would fall and hence the more unemployment would result. The price inflexibility due to monopolistic tendencies in industries was perceived to be detrimental to the economy. After all, simple microtheory predicts that relative prices will respond to changes in supply and demand.

Gardiner Means and Administered Prices

Means suggested that oligopolistic firms were administering prices. The term "**administered prices**" first emerged from Means' study of the behavior of industrial pricing during the period 1929 to 1932.[1] While examining price inflexibility, Means determined that it was associated with industry structure,

---

[1] Gardiner C. Means, *The Structure of the American Economy,* Part I, National Resources Committee (Washington, D.C.: 1939).

which later became known as administered price industries. Before we continue describing Means' study, we must distinguish between different but related terms that have been applied to the phenomenon of inflexible prices.

Defining Our Terms

We have already seen the term "administered prices." Additionally, "full cost prices" and "rigid prices" have been applied to price inflexibility. Administered pricing usually means a degree of discretion in price setting because of market power. Full cost indicates prices that are set to cover average costs. Finally, rigid price is the most general expression used to indicate inertia in pricing; it is typically the result of oligopolistic interdependence or relatively more stable supply and demand conditions.

Actually, even Means' term "administered price" does not mean the same thing for everyone studying the phenomenon of inflexible prices. Means originally defined the term as "a price which is set by administrative action and held constant for a period of time." Further, it arises "when a company maintains a posted price at which it will make sales or simply has its own price at which customers may purchase or not as they wish."[2]

The above definition is extremely broad. Unless a price is negotiated for an individual transaction, such as the purchase of a house, or the price is a result of auction-type markets, such as the stock exchange, it appears to be an administered price.

The Means Study

Means looked at 747 commodities in the Bureau of Labor Statistics wholesale price index. He then plotted a distribution giving the frequency of *recorded* price changes during the period 1926 to 1933. The curve was U-shaped, actually giving a bimodal distribution with one mode for items whose price index changed about every month and another mode for items whose price index changed less than once every 10 months. Viewing this bimodal distribution, Means concluded, "There were two different types of prices—administered, which change infrequently, and market prices, which change frequently.[3] A further point of interest was observed by Means. He found that the more frequently prices changed during the 1926–1933 period under study, the more they tended to fall during that period.

In summary, Means considered information from 37 manufacturing industries and 747 commodities between 1929 and 1932 and concluded that the more concentrated an industry was, the more the industry resisted pressures for price decreases during periods of extreme slack in demand. If Means' conclu-

---

[2] Means, "Industrial Prices and Their Relative Inflexibility," Senate Document 13 (Washington, D.C.), January 17, 1935.

[3] Means, *The Corporate Revolution in America* (New York: Crowell-Collier, 1962), p. 80.

sion is accepted, price inflexibility is therefore associated with more concentrated industries.

Means' Explanation and Analysis

Means never did set up an operationally meaningful definition of administrative action. From his explanation and definition of administered prices, we are unable to easily determine which prices are set through the interaction of buyers and sellers in the marketplace and which are set through administrative action. Even if we were able to classify industries strictly into administered and market-determined price categories on the basis of Means' observed price-change frequencies, we would still be left with the question of why the differences arise.

The Causes of Administered Prices   Means felt that administered prices were the result of market power, that is, the discretionary power over prices due to the fewness of sellers and other market imperfections. In essence, Means was relating conduct to market structure:

> The dominant factor making for depression, insensitivity of prices, is the administrative control over prices which results from the relatively small number of concerns dominating particular markets.[4]

In earlier statements Means pointed out instances where monopolized industries might have administered prices. He later stated that prices were administered by "a great many vigorously competitive industries in which the number of competitors is small."[5] Both the inconsistencies in Means' writing about the cause of administered prices and the vagueness of the definition of administrative actions resulted in a controversy in the economics profession, to which we now turn.

The Controversy

Means' findings generated controversy over the theoretical underpinnings and implications of the administered pricing model, as well as the validity of his empirical findings. For example, Neal found that industry price changes correlated with cost changes. He concluded that "evidence completed controverts Means' contention so far as the manufacturing industry is concerned."[6] Additionally, Thorp and Crowder found no measurable relationship between the amplitude of price changes and their measure of concentration.[7] The studies by

---

[4] Means, *The Structure of the American Economy*, Part I, p. 143.
[5] Means, *The Corporate Revolution in America*, p. 78.
[6] Alfred C. Neal, *Industrial Concentration and Price Inflexibility* (Washington, D.C.: American Council on Public Affairs, 1942), p. 124.
[7] Willard L. Thorp and Walter F. Crowder, *The Structure of Industry,* (Washington, D.C.: Temporary National Economic Committee, 1941).

Means, Neal, Thorp and Crowder have all been subjected to extensive criticism of the reliability of their data and of their methodology.[8] Kottke has surveyed several more recent studies and their methodological problems.[9]

Consider one methodological weakness in Means' research. What good is there in knowing the frequency of price changes without knowing the direction and the amplitude of those changes? For example, what good is knowing the event called a price change if that price change is in the opposite direction of what you believe to be appropriate to or consistent with shifts in supply and demand? What if the price change is trivial relative to shifts in supply and demand?

The Difference between Reported and Transaction Prices   A major objection to Means' study and many subsequent studies concerns the inaccuracy of the Bureau of Labor Statistics' wholesale price index. To the extent that the measured price index does not reflect secret price shading undertaken by oligopolists, a study such as Means' will be grossly inaccurate. We must know actual, as opposed to quoted, prices. The problem, of course, is that secret price cuts are difficult to discover simply because they *are* kept secret. Stigler and Kindahl attacked this problem by undertaking an independent examination of the behavior of industrial price indexes.[10] They point out that the physical variety of products produced in most industries is sometimes phenomenal. Hot-rolled carbon steel sheets can be bought with 12 different attributes leading to at least 135 million varieties. Additionally, the price per constant-quality unit of any good is also influenced by guarantees of performance, terms of credit, transportation charges, replacement facilities, promptness of delivery, and so on. The Bureau of Labor Statistics (BLS) is obviously unable to take account of even a small fraction of the possible attributes of any good. Thus, the BLS chooses to price a few well-defined, so-called typical products and transactions. It collects these prices directly from the seller.

Kindahl and Stigler went the other way. They asked buyers to tell the actual prices that they had been paying for a particular kind of product. The researchers combined the movements and the diverse prices into one index. Thus, in addition to obtaining actual prices charged, Stigler and Kindahl had about 1,300

    [8] John M. Blair, "Means, Thorp, and Neal on Price Inflexibility," *Review of Economics and Statistics,* vol. 38 (November 1956), pp. 427–435.

    [9] Frank J. Kottke, "Statistical Tests of the Administered Price Thesis: Little To Do About Little," *Southern Economic Journal,* vol. 44 (April 1978), pp. 873–882. Among the more important studies cited are Steven Lustgarten, "Administered Inflation: A Reappraisal," *Economic Inquiry,* vol. 13 (June 1975), pp. 191–206; P. David Qualls, "Market Structure and Price Behavior in U.S. Manufacturing, 1967–1972," *Quarterly Review of Economics and Business,* vol. 18 (Winter 1978), pp. 35–58; Philip Cagan, "Changes in Recession Behavior of Wholesale Prices in the 1920s and Post World War II," *Explorations in Economic Research,* vol. 2 (Winter 1975), pp. 54–104; and John M. Blair, "Administered Prices and Oligopolistic Inflation: A Reply," *The Journal of Business of the University of Chicago,* vol. 37 (January 1964), pp. 68–81.

    [10] George J. Stigler and James K. Kindahl, *The Behavior of Industrial Prices* (New York: National Bureau of Economic Research, Inc., 1970).

price reports for 70 different commodities, or an average of 17 reports per price series, as opposed to the BLS average of 3 (and often only 1 or 2) price reports. The researchers looked at commodities that figure prominently in the discussion of administered prices, including nonferrous metals, basic chemicals, steel, petroleum products, and ethical drugs.

Stigler and Kindahl's Main Findings   After looking at reported price histories over 10 years, Stigler and Kindahl found that their own index mirrored the trend in prices of the BLS for the first five years of the study. In the second five-year period, the BLS index rose about .7 percent a year relative to the Stigler-Kindahl index. Stigler and Kindahl's explanation for this difference was that price quotations are not revised immediately when market conditions and transaction prices change. This delay operates more strongly against reductions in price quotations than against increases.

Perhaps more interesting is their examination of the cyclical behavior of prices. Their own price indexes demonstrate no view of rigidity over the business cycle in the studied industries. They state:

> We find a predominate tendency of prices to move in response to the movement of general business. As a summary figure, in the four cycles we find prices moving in the same direction of business 56 percent of the time; remaining constant 17 percent of the time; and moving perversely 27 percent of the time. Since there is no reason on earth or in space why all prices should move in the same direction, especially during relatively mild expansions and contractions, we find no evidence here to suggest that price rigidity or "administration" is a significant phenomenon.[11]

More recent studies by Stigler and Weston provide additional support that factors other than concentration, such as cost, are more important in determining price changes.[12] Furthermore, their studies indicate that variations in prices across industries and over time are the simultaneous determination of many complex interactions, making identification of the single force difficult, if not impossible.

THE REVIVAL OF ADMINISTERED PRICES AND OLIGOPOLISTIC INFLATION

Although Gardiner Means' results were the subject of controversy during the 1930s, the subject of administered prices was left relatively in abeyance until the late 1950s. During a three-year period, administered prices and their relationship to inflation were the dominant theme of the Kefauver Committee.

---

[11] Ibid., p. 9.

[12] George J. Stigler and James K. Kindahl, "Industrial Prices as Administered by Dr. Means," *American Economic Review*, vol. 63 (September 1973), pp. 717–721; and J. Fred Weston, Steven H. Lustgarden, and Nanci Grottke, "The Administered Price Thesis Denied: Note," *American Economic Review,* vol. 64 (March 1973), pp. 232–234.

We'll look briefly at the revival of Means' doctrine of administered prices and the evidence presented.

Inflation in the 1950s

The Kefauver Committee maintained that since 1955, the main source of inflation had been the upward movement of administered prices. The committee asked Gardiner Means to produce some empirical evidence of the increase in amount of administered prices. The evidence Means presented showed 93 wholesale prices that changed 77 or more times during his original study period of 1926 to 1933, but which did not, on average, rise from May 1955 to May 1957. It also showed that 80 prices which changed less than eight times in his earlier period rose 6 to 7 percent from 1955 to 1957. Based on these original figures, Means presented a chart in January 1959 (reproduced in Figure 13-1), in which he showed that almost all price increases were in the administered price industries.

In Figure 13-1 we also show additional, more recent data that show the relationship between the percent weight in the wholesale price index and the percent change in the wholesale prices from 1953 to 1957. Means had divided the 15 Bureau of Labor Statistics' major wholesale pricing groups into three catergories: (1) "administration dominated"; (2) intermediate mixtures" of pricing systems where price administration plays some role; and (3) "highly competitive" industries. In the first classification we observe that in industries dominated by price administration, price changes were the greatest. The competitive industries actually show a decrease in prices for the 1953–1957 period. Virtually every price decrease was in the market-determined price industries.[13]

---

[13] Means' second chart covered the period 1953 to 1957, thus starting two years earlier than his first chart. He changed the beginning of administered price inflation simply by starting it two years earlier.

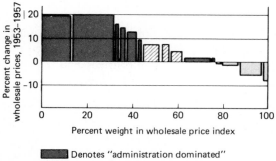

FIGURE 13-1
Gardiner C. Means' chart of wholesale price changes by product groups, 1953-1957. [*Source:* Jules Backman, "Do Administered Prices Create a Problem?" *Administered Prices: A Compendium on Public Policy,* Subcommittee on Antitrust and Monopoly, Committee on the Judiciary, U.S. Senate, 88th Cong., 1st Sess. (1963), p. 29.]

Percent change in wholesale prices, 1953-1957

Percent weight in wholesale price index

Denotes "administration dominated"
Denotes "intermediate mixtures"
Denotes "highly competitive"

Criticism of Means' Analysis   Again, Means' analysis generated critical reaction from segments of the economics profession. In particular, Stigler pointed out that:

1 The classification of price areas was highly subjective.

2 The criterion of frequency of price change was ambiguous.

3 Means' purposeful procedure yields no pattern after 1957.[14]

Concerning the first criticism, Stigler points out that Means' basic test of the presence of administered prices was a frequency of price changes. Nonetheless, he classified rubber products as administered, but textiles and apparel as market-dominated, even though they both had, on average, nine price changes from December 1953 to December 1956.

Backman provided some additional evidence supporting Stigler's third point.[15] His study took the percent changes in wholesale prices and the price index weights as classified by Means and contrasted them with a four-firm concentration ratio. This ratio measured the products for which the four largest firms accounted for 50 percent or more of industry shipments, shown in column 1 of Table 13-1. A quick reading of this table reveals no systematic relationship between concentration, which has been associated with price administration, and the percent change in wholesale prices.

Canadian Evidence

There have been a number of recent studies of administered pricing in Canada. The pattern and the results there are also mixed. Jones and Laudadio, for example, find a significant relationship between the ratio of prices in two successive years and the four-firm concentration rate.[16] Other authors studying the behavior of price changes on concentrated and unconcentrated industries find that the administered price hypothesis is not supported.[17]

ALTERNATIVE EXPLANATION FOR PRICE RIGIDITY

Gordon and Hynes have presented an alternative explanation of certain price rigidities.[18] Each firm is faced with a demand curve having a number of random

[14] George Stigler, *The Organization of Industry* (Homewood, Ill.: Irwin, 1968), pp. 236–237.

[15] Jules Backman, "Do Administered Prices Create a Problem?" in *Administered Prices: A Compendium on Public Policy,* Subcommittee on Antitrust and Monopoly, Committee on the Judiciary, United States Senate, 88th Cong., 1st Sess. (1963), pp. 25–43.

[16] J. C. H. Jones and Leonard Laudadio, "Concentration, Relative Price Flexibility, and 'Administered Prices': Some Canadian Experiences," *Antitrust Bulletin,* vol. 22 (Winter 1977), pp. 775–799.

[17] James J. McRae and Francis Tapon, "A New Test of the Administered Prices Hypothesis with Canadian Data," *Journal of Business,* vol. 52 (July 1979), pp. 409–427. The authors used a time series technique consistent with the market literature to study price changes.

[18] Donald F. Gordon and John A. Allan Hynes, "On the Theory of Price Dynamics" in E. S. Phelps, ed., *Microeconomic Foundations of Employment and Inflation Theory* (New York: Norton, 1970), pp. 369–393.

TABLE 13-1
RELATIONSHIP BETWEEN DEGREE OF CONCENTRATION (UNWEIGHTED INDEXES) IN 1954 AND CHANGES IN WHOLESALE PRICES, 1953–1957

Industry	Products for which Big Four account for 50 per-cent or more of shipments	Percent changes in wholesale prices 1953–57	Percent weights in wholesale price index, December 1954
Rubber and rubber products	75.0%	16%	1.8%
Tobacco manufactures and bottled beverages	75.0	9	2.4
Chemicals and allied products	53.8	4	6.5
Nonmetallic minerals	35.7	14	2.1
Fuel, power, and lighting materials	33.3	7	9.0
Metals and metal products	32.6	19	13.6
Machinery and motive products	32.5	19	17.1
Processed foods	29.3	1	13.7
Miscellaneous products	21.1	−8	2.8
Lumber and wood products	11.1	−1	2.7
Textile products and apparel	10.4	−2	8.3
Hides, skins, leather, and leather products	8.3	1	1.4
Pulp, paper, and allied products	8.3	12	3.7
Furniture and other household durables	6.7	7	4.1
Farm products		−6	10.8
Total			100.0

Source: Jules Backman, "Do Administered Prices Create a Problem?" in *Administered Prices: A Compendium on Public Policy,* Subcommittee on Antitrust and Monopoly, Committee on the Judiciary, United States Senate, 88th Cong., 1st Sess. (1963), p. 30.

components (a stochastic demand curve). The firm's estimate of demand is a function of, among other things, the price per unit of quantity and several random components, which are related to both the firm's demand and the aggregate industry demand. Assume that the random error term associated with aggregate demand is the same for two sellers. The two sellers differ, however, by the size of the variance of the random terms associated with changes in demand for the firm, which cannot be separated from industry variance. For any given shift in aggregate demand, the firm with the larger combination of internal and industry random error variances will take longer to detect the shift and will be slower in adjusting price. Thus a firm could potentially be faced with demand and cost functions that would imply a very small degree of monopoly power and yet be slow to adjust to a fundamental disequilibrium because of large variances in the firm's demand that the firm has come to regard as normal.

A different approach was taken by Kamerschen and Rubin, who looked at the differential changes in price and quantities or a change in cost.[19] In essence

[19] David R. Kamerschen and Paul H. Rubin, "The Differential Impact in Competition and Monopoly of a Change in Cost on Price and Quantity," *American Economist,* vol. 23 (Spring 1979), pp. 41–43.

their argument expands the traditional microeconomic theory implication that prices and quantities will change less in monopoly than in competition in response to a change in marginal cost. In general they find that the absolute price change will be less in monopoly markets. Furthermore, there will be an absolute smaller change in quantity demanded under price-making relative to price-taking conditions.

PRICE LEADERSHIP IN ADMINISTERED PRICES

Some economists have offered an explanation of price rigidity that relies on a price leader with long-run objectives.[20] The price leader attempts to develop a wide market for the industry's basic product. He or she reasons that the less erratic the prices for the industry's products are, the easier it will be for potential customers to plan ahead and compute potential cost economies for new uses of the product. The price leader may also take into account the long-run threat of potential entry, the attainment of a target rate of return on stockholders' equity, possible foreign competition, and so on. Further, the price leader may ultimately decide not to change prices when market conditions change, but rather to alter output and employment. One problem with this "theory" is that it lacks an explanation of why the price leader selects a particular price.

ADMINISTERED PRICING AND FIRM SIZE

In general, administered pricing is positively correlated with the size of firms. Kaplan, Dirlam, and Lanzillotti found administered pricing in one form or another in all firms in their sample of large U.S. businesses.[21] They also found that the mere length of production processes and communication problems with suppliers and distributors contributed to more stable quoted prices by the firm. Larger firms also have more potential effect on industry prices; they will therefore be more careful before making price changes. In some cases Kaplan and associates found that by keeping the price of raw materials relatively constant, producers were able to stabilize inventory values that both reduced their buyers' costs and permitted a higher average price.

INFLATION AND PRICE RIGIDITY

Some opponents of administered price models contend that, in addition to contributing to a higher average price, administered prices contribute to inflation. In 1972 Means hypothesized that administered prices moved countercyclically, which resulted in simultaneous inflation and recession.[22] Other

---

[20] See Chapter 8 for the price leadership models.

[21] A. D. H. Kaplan, Joel B. Dirlam, and Robert F. Lanzillotti, *Pricing in Big Business* (Washington D.C.: The Brookings Institution, 1958).

[22] Gardiner C. Means, "The Administered Price Thesis Reconfirmed," *American Economic Review*, vol. 62 (June 1972), pp. 292–306; and Daniel S. Hamermesh, "Market Power and Wage Inflation," *Southern Economic Journal*, vol. 39 (October 1972), pp. 204–212.

researchers such as Lustgarten and Wilder, et al., provide evidence that contradicts Means' thesis.[23] These studies show that there is no significant relationship between market power and inflation. However, Greer uses Hamermesh's data with a different methodology, yielding results "that product and labor market power substantially affect the overall rate of inflation in the U.S. economy at any given level of unemployment."[24]

International Evidence

Data from the United Kingdom tend to support the hypothesis that concentrated industries adjust prices faster and are allegedly the factor contributing to the inflationary problem in the United Kingdom.[25]

Public Concern

Congress and the administration have expressed concern over the relationship of market concentration and inflation. For example, the Senate Committee on Antitrust and Monopoly held a number of hearings that were critical of the steel industry's pricing practices. In addition, various presidents, including Eisenhower and Kennedy, have expressed strong vocal concerns or denouncements of price increases in the steel industry.[26]

FAIR TRADE LAWS OR RESALE PRICE MAINTENANCE

Another form of administered prices involves the establishment of an agreement between the manufacturer and retail outlets regarding the retail price of the manufacturer's item. Under **resale price maintenance**, prices are identically set for all establishments in a geographic market, usually the entire state.

Retail price maintenance, or fair trade laws, was legally enforceable in many states from 1937 to 1977. Fair trade laws are basically signed agreements preventing retailers from selling below a certain price. Resale price maintenance laws in some states even extended enforcement to retailers who had not signed agreements. In these states the no-signer clauses became part of the fair trade laws. Many familiar items were fair-traded from 1937 to 1977, including books, cameras, electrical appliances, scuba-diving equipment, and toiletries. Fair trade laws prohibited retailers from selling below the retail maintenance price. The power of the courts was used to back up these price-fixing agreements.

---

[23] Steven H. Lustgarten, "Administered Inflation: A Reappraisal," *Economic Inquiry*, vol. 13 (June 1975), pp. 191–206; and Ronald P. Wilder, C. Glyn Williams, and Davinder Singh, "The Price Equation: A Cross-Sectional Approach," *American Economic Review*, vol. 67 (September 1977), pp. 732–740.

[24] Douglas F. Greer, "Market Power and Wage Inflation: A Further Analysis," *Southern Economic Journal*, vol. 41 (January 1975), pp. 466–479.

[25] Simon Domberger, "Price Adjustment and Market Structure," *Economic Journal*, vol. 89 (March 1979), pp. 96–108.

[26] John M. Blair, *Economic Concentration: Structure, Behavior and Public Policy* (New York: Harcourt Brace Jovanovich, 1972).

The setting of a fair trade price by the manufacturer seems paradoxical. What interest does the manufacturer have in retailers' selling its products at some minimum price? At first blush, there seems to be no interest. Indeed, manufacturers would appear to gain by permitting retail outlets to compete by lowering prices and increasing total amount sold. Thus, the lower the retail price is (or markup over wholesale), the greater the quantity of products sold by the retailers and therefore by the manufacturers will be. Additionally, resale or retail price maintenance agreements require policing costs. The manufacturer must somehow check retail stores to make sure that no rebates are given, which often means that the manufacturer limits the expansion of retail outlets to avoid monitoring and enforcing costs.

Some Prior Explanations for Fair Trade Laws

As early as 1916, Taussig laid out his explanations for setting a fair trade price.[27] He believed that consumers associated price with quality. Thus, any reduction in retail price would reduce sales, because consumers would believe that the product quality had deteriorated. This explanation seems to assume some degree of ''irrational'' consumer behavior when information costs are low.

Silcock gave three reasons why manufacturers would endorse fair trade laws:[28]

1 A minimum retail price reduces customers' incentive to ''shop around,'' which might expose them to the temptation of buying another product.

2 With minimum prices, retailers may provide more services when they sell the good; the manufacturer may be better off because total sales will be greater with this additional service.

3 Resale price maintenance may lead to a wider distribution of the manufacturer's product.

It has also been alleged that resale price maintenance agreements had been forced on manufacturers by a retail cartel. Both Yamey and the Federal Trade Commission support this view.[29]

Any retail cartel that wished to prevent entry by price-cutting firms might successfully be able to do so if the manufacturer imposed resale price maintenance on the industry. Given that the extant members of the retail cartel have an interest in reporting infringements on the fair trade laws, the manufacturer will have lower policing costs in such a situation.

---

[27] Frank W. Taussig, ''Price Maintenance,'' *American Economic Review,* vol. 6 (March 1916), pp. 170–184.
[28] Thomas H. Silcock, ''Some Problems of Price Maintenance,'' *Economic Journal,* vol. 48 (March 1938), pp. 42–51.
[29] Basil S. Yamey, *Economics of Resale Price Maintenance* (London: Pitman, 1954); *Resale Price Maintenance,* symposium edited by Yamey, (Chicago: Aldine, 1966); and Federal Trade Commission, *1945 Report on Resale Price Maintenance.*

The Cartel Explanation

Telser offers two alternative reasons why resale price maintenance might be favored by a manufacturer.[30] The cartel argument involves a combination of manufacturers whose major sales are done via competing distributors to households. Telser points out that cartels are fragile organizations because of the divergent interests of their members. Thus, the cartel needs rules that quickly limit attempts to spoil the market for all. One such rule is a fair trade agreement. With resale price maintenance, a cartel member that gives the retailer a secret rebate does not put the retailer in the position to openly reduce price at the retail level and thereby increase sales. After all, the retailer has to abide by the fair trade law. Hence, a reduction in price by the manufacturer to the retailer for the purpose of increasing the retailer's purchases will not work. However, as long as there are competing manufacturers who are cartel members, any one manufacturer may induce a retailer to carry only his or her brand by secret price cutting. In order to prevent price cutting, the cartel members must agree that distributors can handle only a single brand. In essence, then, each distributor becomes an exclusive dealer of one brand, preventing any distributor from favoring one manufacturer at the expense of another. Thus, the necessary and sufficient conditions for effective collusion among manufacturers are resale price maintenance coupled with exclusive dealing arrangements. Then the only thing that the cartel members have to worry about is the shaving of price per constant-quality unit by dealers. This could be done by free delivery service, more favorable credit terms, and so on. Members of the cartel must agree on all quality dimensions of the product in order to prevent price cutting, and then, of course, they must police. Finally, in order to prevent any secret price concessions to win away retailers handling the product made by other members of the cartel, the cartel rules must specify that a retailer handling the brand of one cartel member may not drop it in order to replace it with the brand of another member.

Evidence of Cartels and Resale Price Maintenance

There have been numerous cartels where manufacturers have embodied price maintenance agreements. Some that have been involved in antitrust suits are producers of sanitary pottery, electrical fuses, gypsum wallboard, wrinkle finish varnish, enamel, and paint. Telser examined in detail the resale price maintenance of light bulbs and found that General Electric had established a system of exclusive dealerships with manufacturers' established retail prices. Telser concluded, "It is remarkable that the system (General Electric, Westinghouse, and others) device for distributing lightbulbs fits the cartel argument of the preceding section in every respect."[31]

---

[30] Lester Telser, "Why Should Manufacturers Want Fair Trade?" *Journal of Law and Economics,* vol. 3 (October 1960), pp. 86–105.

[31] Ibid., p. 99.

One of the key elements for the success of the cartel using resale price maintenance is that it really works only when there is a patent or some other closed market monopoly power condition. In the absence of a patent or other closed market monopoly power, resale price maintenance cannot raise the price above that of competing products, or it will risk the possibility of losing a significant market share.

The Joint Offer of Special Services and Resale Price Maintenance

Telser offers a second explanation of why resale price maintenance may be desirable from a manufacturer's point of view. He points out that a single manufacturer producing a differentiated product may find it advantageous to establish minimum retail prices, because the policy will induce retailers who handle the product to offer special services jointly with it, thereby increasing total sales. This argument applies to products that are unfamiliar to the mass of consumers, either because they are new (or embody new features) or because they are purchased infrequently by a small proportion of households.

Consider Figure 13-2. Demand curve DD is the demand curve for the product when the retailers offer S_1 of services. If they offer S_2 of services with S_2 greater than S_1, the demand curve will shift out to $D'D'$. At quantity Q_1, the increase in the equilibrium price from P to P' is the price per unit of product that consumers are willing to pay for an increase in services that are jointly provided with the product.

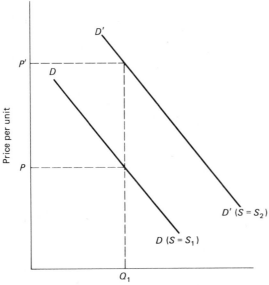

FIGURE 13-2
The Telser model.

D'

P'

D

Price per unit

P

$D'\ (S = S_2)$

$D\ (S = S_1)$

Q_1

Output with different service levels

Free Rider Problem In the absence of resale price maintenance, there may be a free rider problem. Let us presume that the only service the consumer is interested in is information about the way a product looks, its qualities, and so on. The consumer can obtain this information by visiting a retail outlet that is charging full list price. The consumer can look at the inventory, discuss performance with salespersons, read brochures, and so on. After finding out this valuable information, the consumer can then go to a so-called discount house and purchase the product at a lower price, having already obtained the information at zero monetary cost.

The coexistence of establishments offering the product and extensive information about it and discount houses supplying the product with little, if any, information, also acts somewhat like price discrimination. One must recognize, however, that individuals do not have zero opportunity costs of time. The full price of the commodity, that is, the transaction price plus opportunity costs of time multiplied by the individual's lost time, should be equal at the margin for all goods. For resale price maintenance to operate in this market, the goods necessarily have an informational content that requires time to acquire. Thus, stereos and other electronic equipment, cameras, microwave ovens, and other appliances are more likely to be fair-traded than are those goods where information is already known or is easily acquired.

Problems with Resale Price Maintenance

It is virtually impossible for manufacturers to fully police any resale price maintenance agreement. The ways in which retailers can cheat on the agreement are many, including, but not limited to: (1) giving higher trade-in prices, (2) giving discount stamps, (3) tying in the sale of complementary goods that are priced below retail. Indeed, the number of ways in which list prices can be shaved is so large that it is unknown.

CHAPTER 14

COLLUSION

Higher-than-normal rates of return can be created by the formation of a cartel or, less specifically, by collusion among an industry's members. In this chapter, we will discuss the desire on the part of individual firms to collude and also the reasons why collusive agreements often tend to break down.

When a collusive agreement is legal and open, it is generally called a **cartel**. However, economists often talk in terms of cartels even for illegal collusive agreements among firms in the same industry. A cartel can be thought of as a group of firms in the same industry that have banded together in order to increase the net worth position of their owners. This can be done by price fixing and restriction of output, as was accomplished by the Organization of Petroleum Exporting Countries (OPEC), by jointly expending resources on advertising (everybody needs milk), by getting legislation passed to prevent entry into the industry, and by policing the prevention of entry into the industry.

THE GAINS FROM COLLUSION

We can demonstrate the effects of cartelizing an industry on the rate of profit to each individual firm. In the simplest case, each firm in the industry has identical average and marginal cost curves. Otherwise stated, each firm is equally efficient.

To start the analysis, consider a competitive situation. Assume that there are

100 firms in the industry. Assume further that we are in a situation of perfect competition. Thus, the price at which each individual firm sells its output is equal to its marginal revenue. Each firm's output is the output at which $P = $ mc. This price P_c is set by the interaction of the industry supply curve, which is the horizontal summation of 100 mc curves, and the industry demand curve. The individual firm, of course, does not observe the industry demand curve; rather, it responds to its horizontal demand curve at price P_c. In any event, it will produce an output q_c, which is one one-hundredth of total industry output Q_c.

Now let's see what happens when the industry is cartelized. A cartel is formed with a central agency assigning production quotas. It assigns a production quota of one one-hundredth of the industry's total output to each individual firm. Assuming now that all firms obey these quotas, they will all produce the same output. Thus, we know that if each firm increases output by one unit, the industry will increase output by 100 units. It is no longer true that the individual firm can sell all it wants at the market-clearing price. Price now depends on the rate of output of the firms, because all the firms are acting in unison. We can now draw a demand curve ($= ^1/_{100}DD$) that faces the individual firm, which is labeled dd in Figure 14-1. Note that dd is based on two assumptions: (1) equal shares for each firm, and (2) no cheating, that is, costless monitoring and policing of the cartel agreement by the central agency. Since this demand curve is downward-sloping, we draw a marginal revenue curve mr ($= ^1/_{100}MR$) that is below dd.

The profit-maximizing rate of output for each firm is given by q_m and the profit-maximizing price for the firm and the industry is P_m. For the cartel, total industry output is 100 times q_m. The cartelized industry output is less than it was when the firms were in perfect competition; however, each individual firm

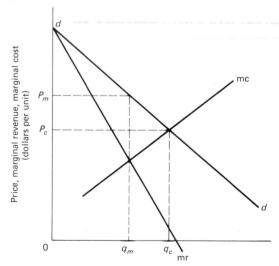

FIGURE 14-1
Increasing profits via perfect cartelization. We assume that all firms are of equal size and are equally efficient. The proportional demand curve facing each firm is given as dd. The curve marginal to it is mr. For the individual firm in this industry, if it is competitive, profit maximization will be at an output where price P_c will be equal to marginal cost mc. Each firm will produce q_c. If there are 100 firms in the industry, then total industry output will be 100 × q_c. Now assume that output is allocated by a single agency directing the entire industry. If there is no cheating, each firm will be assigned output q_m and will sell its output at price P_m. Profits will increase so that monopoly profits are being made.

Individual firm's output per unit time period

in the cartel is now making economic profits. In the competitive situation, price was equal to marginal cost; in the cartel situation, price exceeds marginal cost, and there is clearly a higher rate of profit for each firm.

Thus, we can see the incentives for cartelization of an industry. Cartelization does not have to be thought of as being desired for "evil" purposes, but rather as a natural phenomenon consistent with our profit-maximizing assumptions. These assumptions should hold throughout the analysis, and therefore, you should be skeptical about the long-run stability of the situation depicted in Figure 14-1. There will be forces preventing the successful formation of a cartel; and even if one is in fact initiated, there will be difficulty in the successful continuation of that cartel.

THE INCENTIVE TO CHEAT

The incentive to cheat in a cartel arrangement is great. The incentive not to join an existing cartel is also great, as we can see in Figure 14-2. In panel (*b*), the industry demand curve is *DD*. The curve marginal to that is MR. We assume a large number of equally efficient individual firms that are operated by a cartel manager. The summation of their individual marginal cost curves above their

FIGURE 14-2
The incentive to cheat in a cartel. The industry demand curve is *DD* in panel (*b*). Its marginal curve is MR. The summation of the individual firm's marginal cost curves is labeled ΣMC. A perfect cartel would set industry output at $Q_{industry}$. The cartel price would then be P_{cartel}. Assume that the individual firm's allotted output shown in panel (*a*) is q_{cartel}. It sells that output at P_{cartel}. Its average total costs are C_1; therefore, its profit is the diagonally lined area. However, if the individual firm believes that no one else will cheat, it will take P_{cartel} as given and therefore equal to marginal revenue. It will move out to point *E*, where mc = P_{cartel} = mr. It will produce at output rate q_1. If indeed no other firm does cheat on the cartel, this firm's profit will increase to the entire diagonally shaded and solidly shaded area, since its cost at output rate q_1 per unit will be C_2, but the price will remain the same as before.

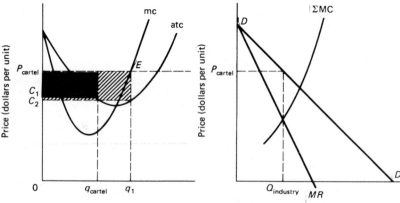

Individual firm's output per unit time period

(*a*)

Industry output per unit time period

(*b*)

average variable cost curves is labeled Σ MC in panel (b). The profit-maximizing rate of output for the cartel is $Q_{industry}$, and the profit-maximizing price is P_{cartel}.

The relevant curves concerning the individual firm are given in panel (a). Note that the horizontal axes in panels (a) and (b) use vastly different scales. In panel (b), the industry output is represented; in panel (a), the output of an individual firm is represented. We assume now that the cartel manager has assigned an equal share of total industry output to each of the firms; it is represented by q_{cartel} in panel (b). At that rate of output, the individual firm's average total cost is C_1. The profit that each firm in the cartel makes is therefore the difference between total revenues and total costs, or $(P_{cartel} \times q_{cartel})$ − $(C_1 \times q_{cartel})$.

If a disobedient firm attempts to cheat in the cartel, it might assume that the output rate of all other firms will remain constant. As a first approximation, it can take the cartel price as its demand curve and also as its marginal revenue curve. It will, therefore, profit-maximize by expanding output until marginal revenue equals marginal cost, or out to point E. At output rate q_1, it will make total revenues of $(P_{cartel} \times q_1)$. Its cost will be $(C_2 \times q_1)$ because at the new output rate q_1, the average total cost is equal to the vertical distance OC_2. Therefore, its profits will equal the sum of all the diagonally and shaded cross-hatched area in panel (a) of Figure 14-2. The increased profit either from not joining the cartel or from being a disobedient firm once in the cartel is equal to the diagonally shaded area.[1]

The Payoff Matrix

We can show the potential instability of collusive agreements in terms of a payoff matrix. Consider two firms, X and Y. We see from Table 14-1 that if both firms succeed in colluding, their profits will be $2,500 compared to both firms cheating, that is, competing against each other, where their profits will be $1,500 apiece. Additionally, we can see that if X cheats while Y does not cheat, X makes $3,000 and Y makes 0. Alternatively, if Y cheats while X continues to collude, X makes 0 and Y makes $3,000.[2]

Under such circumstances, the tendency will be for X to cheat because its payoff will increase by $500 over colluding. Additionally, if X cheats, it is protected against Y's cheating, for if X remained faithful to the collusive agreement and Y cheated, X would get nothing. Ultimately, we predict that X and Y will end up competing. This result, of course, is not absolutely certain. If the payoff from cheating (competing) is low or if cheating can be easily policed, then the collusive agreement may work. Our payoff matrix merely serves to demonstrate that there is potential instability in any collusive agreement.

---

[1] Strictly speaking, the cheater would have to lower the price only a slight amount to get the extra sales. So, we are probably overstating the potential increased profits from cheating.
[2] This is not a constant sum game, for if both cheat, the total payoff is $3,000, but if both collude, the total payoff is $5,000.

TABLE 14-1
PAYOFF MATRIX FOR X AND Y

		X	
		Collude	**Cheat**
Y	**Collude**	X = 2,500 Y = 2,500	X = 3,000 Y = 0
	Cheat	X = 0 Y = 3,000	X = 1,500 Y = 1,500

The Establishment of Collusive Organizations

Even in a world where perfect collusion—legal cartels—is allowed, the establishment of the collusive organization requires a clear definition of the competitors who will collude. In other words, one must be able to define an appropriate range of substitutes in order to determine which firms are necessary to constitute the collusive organization. For example, if one wished to cartelize the textbook industry effectively, the possible substitutes for textbooks include lecture notes, cassette learning systems, video learning systems, trade and general books, as well as certain how-to magazines. Would the cross-price elasticity of demand have to be calculated for all of these substitutes and then an arbitrary cutoff point decided upon? Perhaps, but even then the definition of potential competitors or potential substitutes will be difficult, if not impossible. Thus, one of the problems facing any collusive organization is defining all substitutes in order to recognize and determine potential competitors.

Once all potential competitors have been identified, then the potential collusive organization must somehow persuade them to join the cartel. To the extent that strong or numerous competitors are left out of the collusive organization, the effectiveness of that organization will be diminished. That is to say, when only a small percentage of the industry's productive capacity is included in the collusive organization, the included firms will be unable to capture above-normal rates of return, even if they collude perfectly.

Price and Output Determination

When we talked about the formation of a perfect cartel, we assumed that every firm faced a proportionate share of the total demand curve and that every firm had exactly the same marginal cost curve. When either of these two schedules facing the firms in the collusive organization differs, problems arise.

Different Firm Efficiencies   When we initially discussed the possibility of cartelization, we assumed that all firms were equally efficient. The quota for each firm would clearly be an aliquot share of industry's output. If firms have different cost curves, however, determining the appropriate quota for each firm becomes a problem.

The solution is similar to determining how a multiplant monopoly should operate. It should operate where marginal revenue = marginal cost of plant 1 = marginal cost of plant 2. The cartel should operate where industry marginal revenue = marginal cost of firm 1 = marginal cost of firm 2 = . . . = marginal cost of firm η, where there are η firms. Profit maximization for the industry cartel as a whole will often occur when quotas are inversely proportional to marginal costs. That is, those firms that are relatively less efficient will be given a quota that requires them to produce relatively less of the total industry output; the more efficient firms will be given larger quotas. We identify the former by the fact that they have higher marginal cost curves; the latter have relatively lower marginal cost curves.

Clearly, the less efficient firms may be unwilling to go along with industry profit maximization because it would mean reducing their output. Only if they can in some sense be "bribed" or if their reduced output can be compensated for by the more efficient firms that have higher output rates can we ever hope to see the collusive organization succeed for any period of time.

Demand Differences   In the real world, not all firms in an industry will face a demand curve similar to every other firm in the industry. Demand conditions change depending on location, weather, and a host of other variables. Further, how does the cartel deal with a firm whose demand curve has shifted in because of some unexpected natural disaster in the area? That firm will have an incentive to attract business from other areas by undercutting the collusive price agreement. Thus, for successful collusion to occur, firms facing inward shifts in their demand curves will have to be compensated.

Differing demand curves, and more important, shifting demands, significantly increase policing costs for the cartel. In some cases these costs may be sufficiently high that the cartel agreement cannot be maintained.

Cartels and Policing Costs

Throughout our discussion of the instability of cartels, the notion of policing or enforcement costs has been implicitly included. For any cartel to work, the cartel arrangement must be successfully policed. We could actually consider the entire cartel-collusion problem in terms of crime and punishment.[3] Any firm that violates a collusive agreement commits a "crime" against the cartel members. The cartel members, on the other hand, will try to detect and deter such crimes by punishing the "criminals." An "ideal," or "perfect," cartel results

---

[3] For examinations of economic analysis as applied to traditional meanings of "crime and punishment," see Gary S. Becker, "Crime and Punishment: An Economic Approach," *Journal of Political Economy*, vol. 76 (March/April 1968), pp. 169–217; and Simon Rottenberg, "The Clandestine Distribution of Heroin, Its Discovery and Suppression," *Journal of Political Economy*, vol. 76 (January/February 1968), pp. 78–90.

when the punishments are sufficient to deter *all* violations. On the other hand, an anarchistic competitive solution results when punishments and the cartel itself become ineffective.

The smaller the number of firms and customers in the industry, the lower the costs of policing any given collusive agreement will be. It is not surprising, then, that the degree of industry concentration is often used as a measure of the degree of monopoly power. However, the relationship is obviously inexact, and much must be inferred from industry data in order to come up with a notion of monopoly power using industry concentration ratios.

In markets where goods are not perfectly homogeneous, policing costs are higher. This is because firms may offer higher quality or additional services as a means of lowering the effective price of using their product. For this reason, most successful cartels effectively use the government to police their actions.

EXAMPLES OF TYPES OF COLLUSIVE ORGANIZATIONS

We have described some of the theoretical aspects of collusive organizations. We'll now look at some examples of different types of collusive organizations, including cartels, trade associations, and regulated industries.

Cartels

The formal definition of a cartel is an association of firms banded together with the express desire to limit output and increase industry profits. A typical cartel has written rules and penalties agreed to by its parties. The cartel will also have a staffed organization that polices these rules. Many cartels, such as the German steel cartel, have been arranged and enforced by the state itself. Alternatively, they can be sanctioned by several states in an international agreement. For example, the European Coal and Steel Community (ECSC), established by an international treaty signed by the foreign ministers of the participating nations, apparently worked as a cartel arrangement and continues to do so in its present form (as part of the European Community), despite pronouncements to the contrary.[4] In many countries cartels are supported by the courts as an enforceable contract. A full cartel will control virtually all aspects of the industry just as if a single monopoly firm were selling the output. Thus, the full cartel controls output, product mix, investment, pricing, quality, and profit pooling. Obviously information is of utmost importance to the full cartel in order to do all these things.

A less complete cartel is a marketing cartel. Germany had these for many years and called them the "syndicate." Sales and revenues are managed by the marketing cartel. Everything except investment and profit pooling is controlled by the cartel management.

---

[4] See Klaus Stegemann, *Price Competition and Output Adjustment in the European Steel Market* (Tübingen: Mohr, 1977).

The Organization of Petroleum Exporting Countries One of the most promi-
nent international cartels is the Organization of Petroleum Exporting Countries
(OPEC). In 1960, OPEC started as an organization designed to assist the oil-
exporting countries. By 1970, it included Abu Dhabi, Algeria, Indonesia, Iran,
Iraq, Kuwait, Libya, Nigeria, Qatar, Saudi Arabia, and Venezuela. Then a few
other countries, such as Ecuador, joined the group. During the 1960s, OPEC's
success was limited because an ever-expanding supply of oil kept just ahead of
demand. As demand grew, new discoveries expanded the supplies so fast that
nominal wellhead prices for crude oil actually fell slightly from 1960 to 1970.
Then in 1970 and 1971, the rate of growth of the demand for crude oil tapered
off. Also in 1970, Libya, which had become a major supplier of crude oil to
Western European markets, had a revolution. The successful regime cut output
sharply in a partly political move against the oil companies whose concessions
had been granted by the previous regime. Libya's cutback made sizable price
increases possible in 1971. These increases were ratified by the other members
in agreements drawn up in Tripoli and Teheran. Much of the success of this rise
in prices was due to OPEC, but some observers contend that Libya alone was
responsible and had no help from OPEC.

The main ingredient in OPEC's success was the outbreak of war in the
Middle East in 1973. In the wake of this war, Saudi Arabia, Kuwait, and a few
smaller Arab countries agreed to cut back their production of crude oil greatly,
thus allowing for large price increases. Remember that the only way to raise
prices when one is a pure monopolist is to cut back on production and sales.
Thus, the OPEC countries could have an effective cartel arrangement only if
some or all of them cut back on production and sales. Since Saudi Arabia,
which accounts for the bulk of the oil production in the Middle East, did cut
back greatly in 1973, the cartel arrangement worked as it had for several years.
The total profits for the oil-exporting countries were increased greatly as a
result.

The effect of OPEC cartelization activities on world oil prices was dramatic.
On January 1, 1973, one could buy Saudi Arabian crude oil at $2.59 a barrel.
Most of this amount—$1.99—was taken by the Saudi Arabian government.
Thus, only $.60 per barrel was left to cover private oil companies' costs of
operation and profit. Within one year, the price of crude oil had risen to $11.65
per barrel. Practically all this increase was taken by the Saudi Arabian
government—$11.05 per barrel. By 1975, the Saudi Arabian government was
taking $10.87 a barrel out of the $11.25 at which it was selling the crude oil. By
1981, the price had risen to $36.00.

Other international cartels have formed; many of them are involved with
internationally traded commodities. These cartels often state price stabilization
or producer-consumer coordination as their goal. For example, the International Bauxite Association (IBA) has attempted to control the price of bauxite
around the world, apparently with considerable success.[5] The International Tin

---

[5] See Robert S. Pindyck, "Cartel Pricing and the Structure of the World Bauxite Market," *Bell
Journal of Economics and Management Sciences*, vol. 8 (Autumn 1977), pp. 343–360.

Agreement has existed since before World War II. The Organization of Banana Exporting Countries has tried to duplicate OPEC's success. There are producer cartels in iron ore, mercury, tea, tropical timber, natural rubber, nickel, cobalt, tungsten, columbium, pepper, tantalum, and quinine. Not all of them are successful.[6] We now ask what the necessary ingredients are to a successful cartel arrangement.

A cartel must meet four basic requirements if it is to be successful:[7]

1 The cartel must control a large share of total actual output and potential. It must not face substantial competition from outsiders.

2 Available substitutes must be limited. More precisely, the price elasticity of demand for the product in question must be fairly low; that is, demand must be relatively (but not completely) inelastic. We can further make the distinction between the short and the long run. If there is the possibility of long-run substitution for the product, then the long-run price elasticity of demand will be relatively high and the cartel will be destroyed.

3 The demand for the cartel's product must be relatively stable, regardless of business conditions. If this is not the case, then the amount sold at any given price will be greater during economic expansions than during recessions, and the cartel will find it difficult to maintain any given price and output combination for very long. After all, it is harder to police a cartel in a changing world.

4 Producers must be willing and able to withhold sufficient amounts of their product to affect the market. Each member must resist the temptation to cheat. As a corollary, consumers must not have large stockpiles of the product on which to draw.

There are other conditions that would increase the probability of a cartel's success, but the above can be considered the basic ones.[8]

A major cause of cartel instability is cheating. When there are many firms or countries in a cartel arrangement, some will always be dissatisfied with the situation. Some will cheat by charging a slightly lower price than the one stipulated by the cartel. If there are geographical allocations for sales by each member firm in the cartel, any change in regional demand patterns will cause those cartel members who lose sales to be dissatisfied. These members may either require a bribe on the part of the satisfied members or cheat on the cartel by cutting prices and seeking customers outside their stipulated regions.

An individual cartel member is always tempted to cheat, to cut prices clandestinely. Any member who is producing a small percentage of the total output

---

[6] For example, CIPEC, the copper cartel, failed. For an explanation of why it did, see Robert S. Pindyck, "The Cartelization of World Commodity Markets," *American Economic Review*, vol. 69 (May 1979), pp. 154–158.

[7] This discussion is drawn from George J. Stigler, "A Theory of Oligopoly," *Journal of Political Economy*, vol. 72 (February 1964), pp. 44–61.

[8] For example, it is sometimes argued that the presence of sealed bidding makes policing less costly and so aids in cartel success. For a summary of the literature on this thesis and a confirming empirical examination, see Charles G. Geiss and John M. Kuhlman, "Estimating Price Lists, List Charges, and Market Shares from Sealed Bids," *Journal of Political Economy*, vol. 86 (April 1978), pp. 193–209.

of the cartel essentially faces a very elastic demand curve if he or she cheats and no one else does. A small drop in price by the cheater will result in a very large increase in total revenues. The best analogy is the extreme case of the firm in a competitive industry. It can increase output without affecting the market price, since it is a small part of the industry. The lure of such increases in revenues is too tempting for some cartel members to allow a cartel to last forever.

There will always be cartel members who figure that it will pay them to cut prices, to break away from the cartel. Each firm will consider this, thinking that the others will not do the same thing. Firms may cheat, figuring that other firms are going to cheat anyway, so why not be the first? Obviously, though, when a sufficient number of firms in the cartel tries to cheat, the cartel breaks up. We would expect, therefore, that as long as the cartel is not maintained by legislation, its very existence will be threatened. Its members will have a large incentive to price-cut. Once a couple of members do it, the rest might follow.

Consider, for example, the failure of the copper cartel known as the Intergovernmental Council of Copper Exporting Countries (Conseil Intergouvernemental des Pays Exportateurs de Cuivre, or CIPEC). It was founded in 1967 by Chile, Zambia, Zaire, and Peru. It still exists today, but it has never managed to show any strength in world markets. In 1974 the price of copper started falling. From April to the end of December, it dropped by 55 percent. CIPEC was powerless to bring the price back up. Why? Because most of the developing countries were unwilling to limit their output of copper. There isn't a Saudi Arabia of the copper world that is willing to cut back 50 percent on production so that the rest of the cartel can enjoy higher prices. Remember, the only way to keep prices up is to keep production down.

The coffee cartel hasn't fared much better. The price of coffee has vacillated constantly. Every time the price starts falling, powerful coffee producers, such as Colombia and Brazil, at the annual meeting of the Council of International Coffee Organization (ICO), urge other producing nations to cut back. However, ICO often finds out how great the price elasticity of demand for coffee really is. When the price has jumped, the quantity demanded has fallen, sometimes dramatically. In 1977, for example, the general manager of Colombia's coffee grower's federation thought that the 60¢ per pound increase in retail prices during the previous two years had caused consumption to drop by 15 percent. His suggestion to other coffee producers at that time? Lower prices. In other words, even a strong cartel cannot face up to the possibility of consumers cutting back on the consumption of the higher-priced good. Coffee consumers had apparently cut back on their intake of coffee, forgone consumption altogether, or shifted to substitutes, such as tea or hot chocolate.

Cartel instability, or lack of success, is not confined to business firms or even to nations engaging in international commodities selling. Have you ever noticed how short-lived a homemaker's boycott of supermarkets is? With so many members in that particular cartel, it is difficult for one of them not to "cheat" and actually go out and buy some food from the supermarket. It is impossible to police the large number of homemakers involved.

Consider a hypothetical example. In a class of 100 students who will be graded on a curve: (1) How easily could all of them get together and agree to each cut down study time? (2) Would this cartel be successful? The answers to both questions, of course, depends on each individual student's incentive to cheat. If only one student were to cheat and study longer than all the others, that student could get a higher grade than he or she would otherwise receive. But if enough students behave this way, the cartel will break down.

The Diamond Cartel   In terms of an actual cartel, the owners of diamond mines in South Africa have been successful for many years.

Every week 300 of the world's richest and most prestigious diamond dealers are invited to attend the "sights" in an office on Fleet Street in London. These sights are not typical; they are uncut diamonds being sold by the Central Selling Organization (CSO) in a nine-story office building in London popularly known as "the syndicate." Through its offices pass 85 percent of the supply of rough-cut diamonds in the world every year. The CSO is controlled by one organization—DeBeers, the famous diamond company, which in 1978 marketed $2.5 billion worth of gems, a 23 percent increase over 1977. It even markets diamonds mined in the Soviet Union's productive Siberian area. De-Beers also produces about 40 percent of the world's diamonds. The 300 diamond dealers who come in every week are shown the diamonds and told the price. Haggling is basically not allowed; in fact, it is rumored that if one haggles, one is not asked back. If DeBeers were simply the producer of 40 percent of the world's diamonds, it might not have such effective control over the market price of diamonds. However, it has also been successful in forming a very strong cartel-type arrangement in which it is the sole marketing agent of another 45 percent of the world's rough-cut diamonds. In this manner it becomes an effective monopoly; it controls the amount of sales that are offered to diamond dealers throughout the world. It can effectively police the number of diamonds that are offered for sale every year. DeBeers can do just what a monopolist wishes to do—restrict output and thereby raise price above what it would be in a perfectly competitive situation.

International Air Transport Association (IATA)   For many years, U.S. airlines have been an open participant (under the terms of the Webb-Pomerene Act) in the International Air Transport Association (IATA), a voluntary organization of airlines. IATA has as members virtually all the airlines that fly trans-Atlantic routes. For years IATA controlled traffic route schedules, financing, and, most important, fares. Conferences sponsored by IATA were typically devoted to discussing trans-Atlantic fares. Once participants agreed upon a given fare schedule, the schedule became binding upon all IATA members. Fines and penalties have been levied by IATA against member airlines that violated air agreements.

Airlines that wished to undercut IATA were often forced to use airports in countries that were not members of IATA. The most famous case was Icelandic

Airlines, which, until the era of deregulation, was virtually the only low-cost way to and from Europe from the United States. Icelandic priced its seats well below the cartel price and consequently achieved very high load factors relative to IATA airlines. However, Icelandic was forced to land in Luxembourg and Nassau (the Bahamas), which were not members of IATA. Eventually competition from Icelandic caused IATA members to introduce relatively cheaper flights and charter packages, in addition to excursion and youth fares. Progress was slow, however, until Freddie Laker's airline changed the entire trans-Atlantic pricing picture virtually overnight.

Regulatory Controls

One way to have partial cartelization of an industry is to have government impose regulatory controls. The most common type of controls in the United States are controls on entry. Standards may be set for all sellers in the market and the number of sellers may be limited. Numerous industries in the United States operate with at least partial control on entry.

Banking   For almost 70 years, entry into banking has been restricted by federal and state chartering. Many states have explicit laws against branch banking (more than one physical location per bank). Until recently, price controls have been set by law on the purchase of one of banking's inputs—demand deposits (checking account balances). In most cases, many firms in the industry were not allowed to pay higher than a zero percent rate of interest on that input, thus regulation served to uphold the monopsony power of the banks in the purchase of one of its major inputs.

It has been alleged that the Federal Deposit Insurance Corporation's power to insure new banks has also reduced the rate of entry into commercial banking by 60 percent.[9]

Taxicabs   Another case of effective collusion involves the regulation of taxicab services. In many, if not most, cities a license must be obtained in order to operate a taxi. In New York City, this license is called a medallion. Before 1937 in New York, the taxicab industry allowed free entry. The price of taxi medallions was near zero, since they were given to anyone who wanted to operate a taxi. Little by little, the city began to restrict its issuance of new medallions. Anyone wishing to buy a medallion from the initial owner had to pay a higher and higher price to purchase it. As the market price went up, those obtaining medallions at lower than the market price were treated to increases in their net worth. By the end of the 1960s, the market price of a medallion reached $30,000.

What does that price represent? It represents the fully discounted present

---

[9] Sam Peltzman, "Entry into Commercial Banking," *Journal of Law and Economics*, vol. 8 (October 1965), pp. 11–50.

value of the expected stream of monopoly profits that can be obtained by having a legal taxicab in New York City.

Taxicab drivers who purchased or received medallions in the late 1930s and early 1940s obtained monopoly profits. However, owners today receive no more than a competitive rate of return on their labor and capital if future changes in demand are fully anticipated. Why? Because they have typically paid the market price for their medallions, and this cost has been added to their other costs. An elimination of the restrictions on entry into the New York taxicab market would immediately subject all the present owners of medallions to a large loss. The emergence of ''gypsy'' cabs (whose owners don't have medallions) in New York City has already partially eroded the market value of medallions. Gypsies are cabs that have no *legal* right to pick up passengers for hire. Nonetheless, New York authorities have, for the most part, allowed these illegal cabs to operate in the city in recent years.

We can understand this situation by looking at Figure 14-3. Here we show that the city of New York has issued a fixed number of medallions equal to Q_1. The supply curve of medallions is thus completely price-inelastic at Q_1 and is represented by SS. As the city has grown and real income has increased, the demand curve for taxi services and hence, for medallions, has increased from DD to $D'D'$. The price of medallions has risen from P_1 to P_2. If free entry were allowed into the taxicab industry, the supply curve of medallions would shift to the right to intersect the demand curve at a price of zero. (This point is not lost on current owners!) In other words, the authorities would issue medallions to anyone who wanted them at a zero price. Whatever quantity was demanded at that zero price would equal the quantity supplied—it would merely mean printing up more pieces of paper that authorize the bearer to operate a taxi in New York City.

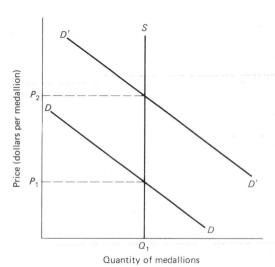

FIGURE 14-3
The rise in value of medallions. If the city of New York sets the number of medallions at Q_1, then the supply curve is vertical, SS. If the demand curve a number of years ago was DD, then the going price was P_1. As population and real incomes rise, however, the demand curve shifts outward to the right to $D'D'$. The price or value of a medallion rises to P_2 because the quantity supplied is fixed.

Price (dollars per medallion)

Quantity of medallions

Tobacco Farming More than three decades ago, owners of tobacco-producing land persuaded Congress to pass legislation that allotted to the half-million growers of tobacco the right to grow tobacco only on lands that were *then* in use. Since that time, there has been no new land put into tobacco production for a very good reason. Any tobacco that is grown on unlicensed land is taxed at 75 percent of its value. In the past, this tax has been prohibitive. No potential tobacco farmers could hope to make any money if they had to pay this tax, because they would be in competition with the tobacco growers who do not have to pay the tax. The market price is not sufficiently high to compensate growers for the additional expenses.

Who are the beneficiaries of restricting the supply of tobacco? Certainly not anyone who today purchases land that is licensed for tobacco growing. The price of licensed land was long ago bid up to levels that yielded new owners only a competitive rate of return. The ones who benefited from the monopoly position granted by Congress were the owners who had the land at the time the legislation was passed. To be more specific, only the owners who had the land at the time it was generally known that the legislation was going to be passed profited. They reaped monopoly profits of $1,500 to $3,000 an acre because they could sell their land for more than they could have prior to the acreage allotments.[10]

In addition to the restriction on acreage and tobacco growing, there are also tobacco price supports (that is, Commodity Credit Corporation nonrecourse loans). To ensure that not too much tobacco reaches the marketplace, marketing quotas keep output at a level consistent with price support objectives. The net results of the tobacco program have been:

1 A smaller supply of tobacco leaves than otherwise would have been grown

2 A higher price for tobacco than would have prevailed under an unrestricted market situation

3 A higher price for tobacco products than would otherwise have prevailed

Trade Associations

Trade associations promote cooperation among firms in an industry. Virtually every industry has at least one. In the United States, there are some 2,000 national associations, about 3,000 state and regional associations, and over 8,000 local associations. The Directory of National Associations of Businessmen (Washington, D.C.: U.S. Government Printing Office, issued occasionally) shows that about 70 trade associations have full-time staffs of over 400 employees. The extensive operations of some of the larger associations increase cooperation among firms in an industry. The most obvious industries in this regard are electrical equipment, aerospace, alcoholic beverages, textile

---

[10] See F. H. Maier, J. L. Hedrick, and W. L. Gibson, Jr., *The Sale of Flue-Cured Tobacco Allotments*, Agricultural Experiment Station, Virginia Polytechnic Institute Technical Bulletin No. 148 (April 1960).

products, lumber, transportation, and insurance. Interestingly, trade associations were actively promoted by the Federal Trade Commission in the 1920s, even though they increased cooperation among sellers and presumably reduced competition. At the very minimum, a trade association that provides members with extensive price information on other members can form the basis of a limitation on price cutting and often lobbies for or against specific legislation. Here we give some examples of trade associations.

The Tag Manufacturers Institute In 1949, the Federal Trade Commission filed suit against the Tag Manufacturers Institute under section 5 of the FTC Act, charging unfair methods of competition.[11] The institute's membership accounted for 95 percent of tag products sales. The institute's main function was to obtain list prices for each component of the product, such as wires, eyelets, and strings. Component part prices were necessary for price comparisons because most products were custom-made. Whenever the institute found that a firm was not complying with its reporting requirements, a fine was levied. The institute then freely publicized the firm's data. Even though the Court of Appeals absolved the institute of any illegal activities, holding that improved information will lead to more competitive outcomes, we note that the system of reporting all prices of all firms certainly would help to detect cheating on an implicit or even illegal price-fixing agreement among firms.

Retail Lumber One of the earliest trade association cases involved the Retail Lumber Dealers' Association.[12] The association circulated a list of wholesale lumber dealers who also sold to retail customers. If a member's name was included on the list, that particular wholesaler soon found that business dropped. In other words, a group boycott by retailers was effected by the publishing of the lists. Lumber retailers were able to punish wholesalers who were bypassing them in the market. The Supreme Court found it an unlawful agreement, because the conspiracy existed by inference from the behavior of the participants.

Today trade associations may represent business interests related to governmental activities. They may also engage in advertising and other promotions intended to reach potential customers. In many cases, trade association promotion avoids the free-rider problems, especially in advertisements that compare one industry to another. In some cases associations may also share information about product innovation and may engage in certain product standardization activities.

Limits of Trade Association Behavior As long as they are not associated with an anticompetitive purpose, trade association activities designed to pro-

---

[11] *Tag Manufacturers Institute, et al. v. Federal Trade Commission*, 174 F. 2d 452 (First Circuit, 1949).
[12] *Eastern States Retail Lumber Dealers' Association v. United States*, 234 U.S. 600 (1914).

mote a particular industry are legal. A list of legal activities includes industry publicity and promotion, plant safety programs, trade journals, new product development, education and training, and product research. Also acceptable is lobbying for industry interests before the legislative and executive branches of government. Unlawful activities include tampering with prices, restriction of output, allocation of customers or territories, and boycotts. Certain practices may or may not be unlawful, depending on their purpose and their effects on competition. Included in this category are certain reasons for membership in and expulsion from the association, certain forms of product standardization, certification and seals of approval, codes of conduct and customer credit policies, and exchange of statistical or price information.

Formal Agreements

Most collusive agreements generally have a price-fixing arrangement as their basis. Formal price-fixing agreements have occurred on numerous occasions in the U.S. economy, even though they are illegal. When they are discovered, the participants often claim that the agreements are necessary for orderly contracts or stable prices. In terms of price-fixing conspiracies during the 1960s alone, we find formal agreements in at least 22 industries, ranging from bedsprings to milk to wholesale baked goods to ready-mix concrete.[13] Price agreements can be reinforced by informal agreements such as market division. Virtually all successful cartels and collusive organizations have had some form of price agreement.

Electrical Equipment One of the most famous conspiracy cases in the antitrust field involved the electrical equipment companies in the 1960s. They had an extensive price-fixing ring consisting of virtually all large, heavy electrical equipment producers in the United States. The case tried in the early 1960s ultimately provoked almost 2,000 damage suits by electric utility firms that had bought electrical equipment. The conspiracies were in seven related markets covering billions of dollars of sales over a long period of time.

The conspiracies in the industry covered equipment such as circuit breakers, power transformers, and turbine generators. The cartel agreements were specifically designed to prevent price competition. This cartel had its greatest successes with electrical equipment that was sold to publicly owned electrical utilities, because public utilities purchased electrical equipment through "competitive" sealed bids. In such a process, potential suppliers of a particular piece of equipment submit sealed bids to the public utility. At a specified hour on a specified date, all the sealed bids are opened. Generally the lowest bidder is awarded the contract. The reason sealed bids are beneficial to any cartel is that all the sealed bids are opened and made available for public inspection at the

[13] See George A. Hay and Daniel Kelley, ''An Empirical Survey of Price-Fixing Conspiracies,'' *Journal of Law and Economics*, vol. 17 (April 1974), pp. 13–38.

same time. Late bids are disallowed. Thus, if a collusive agreement were reached beforehand and a particular firm in the cartel had been chosen to get the job, that firm would submit the lowest bid. All the other firms in the cartel would deliberately submit higher bids. If any one of them attempted to cheat, it would be known immediately because the sealed bid would be opened and the bid would become public knowledge.

We might point out that the electrical equipment cartel broke up because the individual firms engaged in implicit price "shaving" by discounting tied-in equipment in negotiations other than the sealed-bid type. In other words, although the cartel member firm would sell a particular piece of equipment that was covered by the cartel agreement at the stipulated cartel price, it would offer a discount separately on another piece of equipment that had to be used and was not covered by the cartel agreement. It might sell a switch at the cartel price and give (at zero price) a transformer to the buyer in order to take away business from some other cartel member.[14]

Tacit Controls and Conscious Parallelism

Since open collusion is illegal in the United States, numerous students of collusive activities believe that there are **tacit controls**, or what has become known as **conscious parallelism.** These activities may come about from the series of public statements about the need to raise prices from so-called price leadership or administered prices. It has been argued that tacit collusion has been supported by hidden conspiracies.

Movie Distribution One classic case of what later became known as conscious parallelism involved movie distribution. Under an implied conspiracy doctrine, the Supreme Court reaffirmed the lower court ruling against Interstate Circuit, Inc., a major chain of movie theaters in Texas.[15] Interstate sent identical letters to eight movie distributors, demanding that the distributors not deliver any first-run movies to theaters charging admission less than 25¢. Furthermore, it stipulated that no first-run movies should be distributed to theaters showing double features. If the distributors did not comply with Interstate Circuit's demands, Interstate would stop playing the distributor's films in first-run movie theaters. Every distributor complied with Interstate's demands. In other words, each movie distributor acted in an identical fashion; it placed the same restrictions on first-class films. Since every distributor knew that every other distributor received the same letter from Interstate, there was full knowledge of how other distributors might act. As the Court pointed out, "Acceptance by competitors, without previous agreement, of an invitation to partici-

---

[14] See J. G. Fuller, *The Gentlemen Conspirators: The Story of the Price-Fixers in the Electrical Industry* (New York: Grove Press, 1962); and John Herling, *The Great Conspiracy: The Story of the Antitrust Violations in the Electrical Industry* (Washington, D.C.: Luce, 1962).

[15] *Interstate Circuit, Inc., v. United States*, 306 U.S. 208 (1939).

pate in a plan, the necessary consequences of which . . . is restraint of interstate commerce, is sufficient to establish an unlawful conspiracy . . . ."[16]

Under the doctrine laid out by the Court in the Interstate Circuit case, proof of conspiracy was divorced from the question of overt or formal agreement. The Court held that circumstantial evidence was sufficient to demonstrate collusion.

Cigarettes   From 1923 to 1941, the three major cigarette sellers maintained virtually identical prices. Despite shifts in costs, prices appeared to be rigid over long periods. When price changes occurred, they occurred dramatically in one day for all firms at once. American, Liggett & Meyers, and R.J. Reynolds, as well as several company officials, were charged with violation of the Sherman Act, including conspiracy and restraint of trade, attempt to monopolize, conspiracy to monopolize, and actual monopolization. The trial court convicted the sellers on all counts. The Supreme Court reviewed the case and looked at all the evidence, including the price behavior mentioned above. For example, the Court found that the companies used the same kinds of tobacco in their regular brands, but avoided direct competition in purchasing. In other words, they never bid against each other for the same tobacco. As in the Interstate Circuit case, the Court found that no formal agreement was necessary to constitute an unlawful conspiracy. The Court went from performance backwards to infer a collusive structure in the industry.

The Paramount Case   The conscious parallelism doctrine was again applied in a case involving five major movie companies.[17] The Court found that the companies appeared to engage in parallel behavior in numerous aspects of their business over a long period of time. For example, they specified the same minimum admission prices to licensees of copyrighted films; they specified the same time period for the first run of a film and a subsequent run; and they also formally presented exhibitors with identical contract terms. Again the Supreme Court found that no express or formal agreement was necessary to constitute a conspiracy. The Court prohibited specific trade practices and by 1952, all major companies had agreed to divest themselves of theater interests.

Other Cases   Numerous other court cases involve tacit controls and agreements and the doctrine of conscious parallelism.[18] Unfortunately, without direct evidence, the courts may prohibit or severely limit policies of competitive

---

[16] Ibid., p. 227.

[17] *United States v. Paramount Pictures, Inc.*, 334 U.S. 131 (1948).

[18] See, for example, *Federal Trade Commission v. Cement Institute et al.*, 333 U.S. 683 (1948); *Triangle Conduit and Cable Company v. Federal Trade Commission*, F. 2d 175 7th Cir. (1948); *United States v. Griffith*, 334 U.S. 100 (1948); *Pevely Dairy Company v. United States*, 1978 F. 2d 363 8th Cir. (1949); *Milgram v. Loew's, Inc.*, 192 F. 2d 579 3d Cir. (1951); *C-O Two Fire Equipment Company v. United States*, 197 F. 2d 489 9th Cir. (1952); and *United States v. Container Corp. of America*, 393 U.S. 333 (1969).

firms, because competitive industries have more homogeneous product characteristics and similar, if not identical, prices.

COOPERATION OR PROBLEMS?

Now we'll look at certain aspects of an industry that will tell us whether collusion can exist and what problems will arise in attempting to obtain cooperation among competing firms.

The Number and Size Distribution of Sellers

The number and size distribution of sellers is a structural dimension that influences coordination. The more sellers there are in a market, the more difficult it will be to maintain prices above a competitive level. There are several reasons why this is so:

1 The larger the number of sellers is, the greater the probability is that there will be at least one "cheater" who will pursue an aggressive pricing policy. Depending on the price sensitivity of market shares, even one cheater, if large enough, will make it difficult for other firms to keep price above competitive levels.

2 The larger the number of sellers is, the greater the probability is that individual sellers will ignore the effect of their output and pricing decisions on rival actions.

3 The larger the number of sellers is, the greater is the probability of divergent cost and demand conditions facing each seller; thus, the larger the probability of divergent ideas about the most advantageous cartel price.

At least two economists have suggested that the costs of coordinating firms in an industry with the aim of raising prices will increase exponentially with the number of firms.[19] Without a central sales agency, each firm must communicate with every other firm (whether tacitly or overtly) on pricing. The number of two-way communications will be equal to $n(n - 1)/2$. Thus, with two sellers, the number of communication channels is 1, with four sellers, it is 6, and so on.

Product Heterogeneity

The more homogeneous the product is, the easier it will be to police the collusive agreement to fix prices. In fact, with perfect homogeneity, the only way in which to compete is by a change in price. The coordination task of joint profit-maximizing oligopolists therefore becomes less difficult because it is only along one dimension. To the extent that the good is heterogeneous, competition

---

[19] Oliver E. Williamson, "A Dynamic Theory of Inter-firm Behavior," *Quarterly Journal of Economics*, vol. 79 (November 1965), p. 600; and Almarin Phillips, *Market Structure, Organization, and Performance* (Cambridge, Mass.: Harvard University Press, 1962), p. 29.

can occur along many dimensions. Heterogeneity of the product can be a function of its quality, the location of the seller, the time it is produced and delivered, and the service given after delivery. Credit terms can also effect the price per constant-quality unit of the product.

In essence, then, the more heterogeneous the product is, the more collusive agreements will suffer from rivalrous behavior and cheating via nonprice competition, which is a substitute for price competition. A classic example involves airline service. The commodity sold—transportation from one point to another—involves numerous quality dimensions, including time of take off and landing, width of seats, number of bathrooms on the airplane, frequency of serving and quality of food, quality of movie shown, number of flight assistants, and so forth. The fact that the CAB-instituted cartel-maintained price was always effectively undercut by competition prior to deregulation is evidence enough that nonprice competition will exist in even the most closely regulated collusive organization.[20]

Size and Infrequency of Orders

It is conceivable that tacit collusive activities are more probable when orders are frequent, regular, and small. Although one might reason that effective collusion is less probable when the orders are infrequent and large, basically, the larger the orders are and the more infrequently they occur, the greater will be the profit from cheating on the collusive agreement. Members of the collusive agreement will presumably find it more difficult to police price shaving on infrequently ordered products. The amount of information each firm conveys to other members of the collusive organization increases with the number of transactions. The fewer the transactions, the less information will get out.

Phillips described the history of the cast iron pipe industry during the latter part of the 1800s in order to illustrate the application of the above theory.[21] Prior to the formation of a bidding cartel to restrain industrial price competition, the bids were submitted on large jobs at infrequent times. In the midwestern market, the number of sellers was 15. One order would keep an operation running for several weeks. Firms without orders would have tremendous excess capacity. A firm faced with excess capacity that was bidding on a large job would tend to cut prices down to cover variable costs plus a slight amount to cover fixed costs.

These conditions led to extensive price competition and several bankruptcies and contributed to the formation of a number of agreements among six of the leading producers of iron pipe. It was these agreements that the Court found illegal in its precedent-setting decision of 1898.[22]

[20] See, for example, George C. Eads, "Competition in the Domestic Trunk Airline Industry," in Almarin Phillips, ed., *Promoting Competition in Regulated Markets* (Washington, D.C.: Brookings Institution, 1975).

[21] Phillips, ed., *Promoting Competition in Regulated Markets*, p. 103.

[22] *United States v. Addyston Pipe and Steel Co. et al.*, 85 F. 271 (1898).

Cost Differences

The internal cost structure of different firms in the collusive organization may determine the probability of success in maintaining specified market shares, rates of output, and prices. Basically, the higher overhead costs are relative to operating costs, the more difficult coordination becomes. High overhead costs will make marginal costs relatively low. The lower marginal costs are, the higher the probability will be that a firm will wish to engage in price cutting in order to obtain a larger share of the market and use unused capacity. For any given reduction in demand, the greater the ratio of overhead to operating costs is, the smaller the profit-maximizing reduction in the rate of output will be and the greater the profit-maximizing price reduction will be. In other words, when demand falls below output levels that sustain plant capacity, the profit-maximizing firm with the higher ratio of overhead to operating costs will cut prices more than the firm with a lower ratio of overhead to operating costs.

We can conclude, therefore, that collusive organizations will be less stable in industries where the ratio of overhead to operating costs is relatively high (or where there is at least one large firm with a relatively high ratio of overhead to operating costs).

EVIDENCE OF THE EXTENT OF COLLUSIVE ORGANIZATION

Adam Smith once said:

> People of the same trade seldom meet together, even for merriment and diversion, but the conversation ends in a conspiracy against the public, or in some contrivance to raise prices. It is impossible indeed to prevent such meetings, by any law which either could be executed, or would be consistent with liberty and justice.[23]

It appears that Smith was correct. There is cooperation in price setting (although illegal) throughout much of the U.S. industrial structure. A *Business Week* article in 1975 quoted literally dozens of company executives who stated that "the overwhelming majority of businessmen discuss pricing with their competitors. It's just the way you do business." We reproduce some evidence on price-fixing conspiracies in U.S. industries for the 1960s in Table 14-2. Our data are modified from an appendix to a study by Hay and Kelley.[24]

As you can see from the table, trade associations are often involved in these conspiracies. The offense is usually price fixing; but sometimes customer allocation and other charges are involved.[25]

---

[23] Adam Smith, *The Wealth of Nations* (1776) rev. ed. (New York: Modern Library, 1937), book I, chap. 10, part 2, p. 128.

[24] Hay and Kelley, "An Empirical Survey of Price-Fixing Conspiracies," pp. 13–38.

[25] Similar results are found in Arthur G. Fraas and Douglas F. Greer, "Market Structure and Price Collusion: An Empirical Analysis," *Journal of Industrial Economics*, vol. 26 (September 1977), pp. 21–44. Fraas and Greer empirically substantiate the role played by the number of firms and the existence of trade associations in collusive agreements.

TABLE 14-2
SELECTED HORIZONTAL PRICE-FIXING CASES, 1961–1970

Product	Territorial scope	Concentration four-firm (percentage)	Conspirators		Number of firms in market	Nature of offense
			Number of firms	Percent of market		
Wrought-steel wheels	National	85	5	100	5	List price fixing; identical bidding
Bedsprings	National	<61	10		20	List price fixing
Metal library shelving	National	60	7	78	9	Complementary bidding; job allocation
Self-locking nuts	National	97	4	97	6	List price fixing; identical bidding
Liquefied petroleum gas delivery	Regional		5	100	5	List price fixing
Women's swimsuits	National	<69	9			Agreement on sale dates
Fabricated structural steel	Regional	91	6	99		Complementary bidding; job allocation
Commercial baking flour*	Regional	50	9	65		List price fixing
Stainless steel welding electrodes	National	77	7	87	8	List price fixing; identical bidding
Nonpremium beer*	Local		10		10	Elimination of discounts
Book matches (resale)*	National	77	10		10	List price fixing
Concrete pipe	Regional	100	4		4	Complementary bidding; job allocation
Linen supplies*	Local	49	31	90		Customer allocation
Class rings	Regional	<100	3	90	5	Bid rigging
Tickets	Regional	<78	9	<91	>10	Customer allocation
Brass plumbing fittings*	National	64	6		30	List price fixing
Baked goods (wholesale)	Regional	46	7		>8	List price fixing; elimination of discounts
Linen supply	Local	89	6	100	6	Allocation of customers
Dairy products	Regional	>95	3	95	13	List price fixing; bid rigging
Vending machines*	Local	93	6	100	6	Price fixing; customer allocation
Ready-mix concrete	Local	86	9	100	9	List price fixing
Automotive glass replacement parts	Local	75	8		11	Reduction of discounts

*Trade association was involved.

Source: Adapted from appendix in George Hay and Daniel Kelley, "An Empirical Survey of Price-Fixing Conspiracies," Journal of Law and Economics, vol. 17 (April 1974), pp. 29–38.

CHAPTER 15

MERGERS, VERTICAL INTEGRATION, AND DIVERSIFICATION

MERGERS

Vertical integration and conglomerate diversification are forms of **mergers**, which are simply defined as the joining of two or more firms under a single ownership or control. Vertical integration may be viewed as the merger of firms that are involved in various stages of the production of a single product or service. Conglomerate diversification is effected by the merging of firms that produce different final goods and services. Finally, horizontal integration, or horizontal merger, involves combination of, firms selling a similar commodity and takes place across a given commodity space. If two shoe manufacturing companies merge, that is horizontal integration. If a group of steel-producing firms merge into one, that also is horizontal integration. Most of the cartel and collusion analysis in the last chapter applies to horizontal integration. But none of the collusive enforcement costs are incurred where there is a single owner. Therefore, it might be stated that whatever monopoly power or monopoly profits can be obtained by way of collusion, they can better be obtained by merger, as long as this latter process is not *too* costly. A merger, or series of mergers, may increase concentration within a market. Thus, the possible consequences of mergers have elicited considerable antitrust legislation and prosecution to limit monopoly power available through merger activities.

A Brief History of Merger Movements

The first great merger movement in the United States began in 1979 *1879* with the formation of the original Standard Oil Trust. That movement ended in about

339

1892.[1] Clearly, any effort to classify movements as discrete is arbitrary. We note that some scholars believe the first merger movement began in 1890 and ran until 1904, with the second movement covering a period of 1920 to 1929. The third movement started about 1940 and continued through the 1960s.[2] Other scholars classify shorter movements: the first movement was from 1890 to 1892 or 1893, the second from 1897 to 1904, the third from 1920 to 1929, the fourth from 1940 to 1963, and the fifth, a conglomerate movement, from 1963 until recently.

The Changes in the Types of Mergers

The Federal Trade Commission classification and numeration of different types of mergers shows a definite trend in the last half-century. In the earliest periods, horizontal mergers were most prevalent, representing about three-fourths of all mergers from 1926 to 1930. In more recent years conglomerate mergers were most prevalent, accounting for about four-fifths of all mergers.

MERGER FORCES

We have discussed many of the forces that motivate firms to change their structure within the industry. One method that is used to change industry structure is merger. Prior to extensive government involvement in merger activity, the most common form of merger involved a combination of two firms in the same product market. The motivation for such activity may be either competitive, enabling the firms to utilize economies of scale and brand names, or anticompetitive, strengthening the merged firm's market position by reducing competition within the industry.[3]

Tax Avoidance

Existing tax laws and rules of accounting often create situations where mergers among firms with different tax liabilities may be profitable. For example, a firm in a declining industry with a series of losses may be acquired by a highly profitable firm in another industry. The acquisition permits the surviving firm to pool the profits in both firms, significantly reducing tax liabilities. Thus, mergers may be profitable purely on a tax basis.

---

[1] See David D. Martin, *Mergers and the Clayton Act* (Berkeley: University of California Press, 1959).

[2] See S. Chesterfield Oppenheim and J. Fred Weston, *Federal Antitrust Laws, Cases and Comments* (St. Paul, Minn.: West, 1967), pp. 317–323.

[3] See Jesse Markham, "Survey of the Evidence and Findings on Mergers," *Business Concentration and Price Policy* (Princeton, N.J.: Princeton University Press, 1955) pp. 141–212. After an extensive survey of the great merger movements in U.S. history, Professor Markham concluded that "contrary to what is perhaps the most frequently advanced explanation of merger, relatively few mergers appear to have had market monopolization as their goal." (p. 180)

Empire Building and Promoters' Returns

In some cases it is possible for the value of the combined firm to increase significantly over the sum of the firms prior to the merger. For example, if the acquiring firm has excellent management and a price-earnings ratio of 20 to 1 and the acquired firm has a price-earnings ratio of 5 to 1 prior to the merger, the implicit market value of the merged firms' equity may be significantly higher, reflecting the improved management and goodwill of the acquiring firm. In other cases mergers may be promoted by individuals for their own sake, if the agents who handle the merger are able to be compensated for their efforts. To this reason have been attributed J. P. Morgan's activities during the early merger periods in this country.

Growth

Mergers will increase the size of the acquired firm. If salaries or other benefits to managers are inherently tied with the size of the operation, any growth through natural phenomenon or merger will be desired by the managers of that organization. Managers in such conditions will be expected to engage in merger acquisition policies.[4]

Reid has determined that the relationship of mergers to variables is more likely to be related to managerial compensation than to stockholders' interest.[5] He tests his hypothesis with a sample of over 475 large industrial firms and examines their merger-acquisitions during the 1951 to 1961 period. Examination of the data found merger activity was positively related to managerial interests, such as increasing a firm's assets, sales, and employees, and sometimes merger activity was negatively related to profitability and stock prices. Reid accepted the hypothesis that mergers benefited managerial interests. On the other hand, some studies have shown that sales of newly merged firms are not significantly different from a sum of the expected sales of the individual merged firms.[6]

ANTITRUST MERGER GUIDELINES

In an attempt to limit the potential gains from monopolization through a merger, the Department of Justice has issued guidelines for situations that are likely to be challenged by the government. These guidelines, shown in Table

---

[4] Dennis C. Mueller, "A Theory of Conglomerate Mergers," *Quarterly Journal of Economics,* vol. 83 (November 1969), pp. 643–659. But compare with David R. Kamerschen, "A Theory of Conglomerate Mergers: Comment," *Quarterly Journal of Economics,* vol. 84 (November 1970), pp. 668–673, in which the opposite empirical conclusion is presented.

[5] See Samuel R. Reid, *Merger, Managers and the Economy* (Hightstown, N. J.: McGraw-Hill, 1968).

[6] See Thomas F. Hogarty, "Profits for Merger: The Evidence of 50 Years," *St. John's Law Review,* spec. ed. (Spring 1970), pp. 387–391.

15-1, are specified according to the type of merger, such as horizontal, vertical or conglomerate, and are structually oriented. Consequently, the burden of proof effectively shifts to the potentially merging firms as to whether there will be an increase or decrease in competitive outcomes. The advisability of these specific rules has been hotly debated.[7]

VERTICAL INTEGRATION

Vertical integration occurs when one firm merges with either a firm from which it purchases an input or a firm to which it sells its output. For example, a coal-using electrical utility purchases a coal-mining firm or a shoe manufacturer purchases a retail shoe outlet. When vertical integration occurs in the direction of factors of production or supplies, it is referred to as **backward integration**. When integration involves acquiring facilities for distribution, fabrication, or finishing, it is referred to as **forward integration**. Forward integration involves the acquisition of a stage of the productive process that is closer to the final consumer. Our general definition of **vertical integration** will simply be the performance by a firm of different successive stages in the production of a product. Now that we have defined vertical integration, we need to know why it occurs.

Trends in Vertical Integration

It is, perhaps, a popularly held conviction that firms become increasingly more vertically integrated over time. But studies indicate that there has been *no* discernible trend in vertical integration.[8]

THE REASONS AND DETERMINANTS OF VERTICAL INTEGRATION

Many reasons are proffered to explain why a firm may integrate vertically. The most common one involves supposedly increasing monopoly power.

Increasing Monopoly Power

There are few instances in which we can explain vertical integration in terms of increasing monopoly power. Consider the simplest case, where the purchaser of an input is a monopolist when selling the output but purchases its input in a competitive market.

---

[7] For a summary of the debate and a suggested modification to the rules, see James W. Meehan, "Rules v. Discretion: A Reevaluation of the Merger Guidelines for Horizontal Mergers," *Antitrust Bulletin,* vol. 23 (Winter 1978), pp. 769–795.

[8] Irwin B. Tucker and Ronald P. Wilder, "Trends in Vertical Integration in the U.S. Manufacturing Sector," *Journal of Industrial Economics,* vol. 26 (September 1977), pp. 81–94, and Arthur B. Laffer, "Vertical Integration by Corporations, 1929–1965," *Review of Economics and Statistics,* vol. 51 (February 1969), pp. 91–93.

TABLE 15-1
DEPARTMENT OF JUSTICE MERGER GUIDELINES

Horizontal mergers

---

1 When the sales of the four largest firms in a market amount to approximately 75% or more of industry sales, a merger will ordinarily be challenged between two firms with the following shares of the market:

Acquiring firm		Acquired firm
4% or more	and	4% or more
10% or more	and	2% or more
15% or more	and	1% or more

2 When the sales of the four largest firms in a market amount to less than approximately 75% of industry sales, a merger will ordinarily be challenged between two firms with the following shares of the market:

Acquiring firm		Acquired firm
5% or more	and	5% or more
10% or more	and	4% or more
15% or more	and	3% or more
20% or more	and	2% or more
25% or more	and	1% or more

3 Mergers occurring in a market in which there is a significant trend toward increased concentration are also likely to be challenged. The trend toward concentration is considered present when the market share of the eight largest firms in that market has increased by 7% or more within the 10 years prior to the merger. An acquisition by any of the eight largest firms of another firm that has a market share of approximately 2% or more will ordinarily be challenged.

Vertical mergers

---

1 When the supplying firm accounts for 10% or more of the sales in its market and the purchasing firm accounts for 6% or more of the total purchases in that market, the merger will ordinarily be challenged.

2 When the purchasing firm accounts for 6% or more of the total purchases in the market and the supplying firm accounts for 10% or more of the sales in the market, the merger will ordinarily be challenged.

3 In some situations, mergers outside the above limits may be challenged.

Conglomerate Mergers

---

1 When the acquired firm: (a) has approximately 25% or more of the market, (b) is one of the two largest firms in a market where the two largest firms have a market share of 50% or more, (c) is one of the four largest firms in a market where the eight largest firms have a market share of approximately 75% or more and the acquired firm has a 10% market share, or (d) is one of the market's eight largest firms that have a combined market share of approximately 75%, the merger will ordinarily be challenged.

2 When there is a danger that reciprocal buying might result, the merger will ordinarily be challenged.

3 When the acquisition might raise barriers to entry or increase the acquiring firm's market power, the merger will ordinarily be challenged.

Buying a Competitive Supplier   The price that the monopolist pays for its input has been, by assumption, competitive. The monopolist is but one of many firms purchasing the output of the supplier whose product is then used in the monopolist's product. The question arises of how much the monopolist will benefit by this "backward" integration. Assume that it purchases the input-supplying company. What is the appropriate internal transfer price that should be built into the cost of producing the final product and, hence, into the marginal cost curve for the monopolist? The internal transfer price of an input is the amount that is carried on the company's books when its costs of production are computed. From these costs, a marginal cost curve can be derived. If anything other than the full opportunity cost of the input is built into the monopolist's marginal cost curve, then a nonprofit-maximizing price and rate of output will result. In other words, it makes no difference to the monopolist whether the input supplier is independent or part of the firm. The price of the input will remain the same whether it be implicit or explicit. Consider the case where an automobile manufacturer purchases mufflers from an outside competitive supplier for $20 apiece. In that situation, the automobile firm considers the $20 a cost. Assume that the automobile manufacturer then purchases outright a supplier of mufflers. It will continue to charge itself $20 per muffler even though the muffler firm was making, say, $5 profit on each muffler. It would be a mistake to consider for cost calculations that the price of the muffler was only $15, just because the automobile manufacturer now owns that supplier. The opportunity cost of outside sales is still $20. This is exactly the same reasoning behind the incorrect notion that funds generated internally within the firm are less expensive than funds that must be borrowed or raised by selling additional shares in the company. Funds obtained by corporate saving (retained earnings and depreciation allowances) have an opportunity cost of whatever they could earn if they were loaned to someone else.[9] If the firm does not charge itself this opportunity cost (at least implicitly) in making its investment decisions, it will not be maximizing the net worth of the shareholders. That is to say, the firm might make more money for its shareholders if it sold some of its output at a higher price after taking account of the true higher opportunity cost of its inputs.

On Foreclosing the Market   American law discourages vertical integration.[10] Somehow it is assumed that such mergers "foreclose one part of the market for rivals." The purchase of retail tire outlets by a tire manufacturer is supposed to prevent rival tire manufacturers from being able to sell tires to these retail outlets. However, the ability of rivals to sell tires to consumers is impaired only if the *retail* chain of stores had monopolistic powers in the retail market when the tire manufacturer purchased them. And if this were true, we would know that the monopolistic chain of retail outlets would be sold to the

---

[9] Some economists do point out, however, that funds generated within a firm assure that firm a source of supply with first priority and without the transaction costs associated with searching for the best outside source of financing.

[10] *Brown Shoe v. United States*, 370 U.S. 294 (1962).

tire manufacturer at a price that capitalized the future stream of monopoly profits and that the tire manufacturer would not capture any of those profits.

The point to be made is that monopoly power at one particular place in the production and distribution chain in no way confers monopoly power to any other point in that chain. If you own the only supply of a critical raw material in the production of record albums, then all you need do to maximize profits is set the monopoly profit-maximizing price on what you own. You will only hope to make a competitive rate of return on the additional investment needed to purchase record manufacturing companies and/or retail record outlets. They will not yield any additional profits.[11] (However, integration will occur, just as a firm develops, whenever the benefits outweigh the cost of a larger collective unit, or in order to forestall monopolization by some other firm or firms.)

Cutthroat Competition, or The Squeeze Play In some instances, it is alleged that a powerful firm will be able to squeeze out independent and nonintegrated firms. Assume, for example, that the integrated firm has a monopoly at an early stage in the production of a final product. It is argued that the firm can raise the price it charges the nonintegrated firm for this input and use its position to lower the price of the final product at a later stage. The independent fabricator has to buy the unfinished input at the monopoly price but must sell at the relatively low price for final output. Independents can presumably be forced out of business by this "squeeze." As logical as this may seem, it is not a costless ploy on the part of a vertically integrated firm. The vertically integrated firm must forgo monopoly profits during the period in which the price of the final product is kept lower than it would be otherwise. This is sometimes known as cutthroat competition. Its rationality in terms of net worth maximization of the owners is certainly not without question. It can be shown that it's cheaper to buy rivals outright (but that may be illegal).[12]

Empirically, predation has been alleged to be a consequence of vertical integration in at least one legal case. Although the jury found predation in that case and awarded damages, a subsequent careful examination by an economist revealed that there was little evidence to support such a finding.[13]

Price Discrimination Vertical integration can sometimes allow a monopolist to practice more price discrimination than would be possible without such

---

[11] For a rigorous demonstration of this point, see Bruce T. Allen, "Vertical Integration and Market Foreclosure: The Case of Cement and Concrete," *Journal of Law and Economics,* vol. 14 (April 1971), pp. 251–274. Allen supports the theory that vertical integration does not increase profits by foreclosing markets with evidence from the mergers of cement and concrete firms. For a contrary view of both the theory and the evidence, see James W. Meehan, "Vertical Foreclosure in the Cement Industry: A Comment," *Journal of Law and Economics,* vol. 15 (October 1972), pp. 461–465.

[12] See Lester G. Telser, "Abusive Trade Practices: An Economic Analysis," *Law and Contemporary Problems,* vol. 30 (Summer 1965), pp. 488–505, and John S. McGee, "Predatory Price Cutting: The Standard Oil (N.J.) Case," *Journal of Law and Economics,* vol. 1 (October 1968), pp. 137–169.

[13] David R. Kamerschen, "Predatory Pricing, Vertical Integration, and Market Foreclosure: The Case of Ready-Mix Concrete in Memphis," *Industrial Organization Review,* vol. 2 (1974), pp. 143–168.

integration.[14] The fabricator of an intermediate product may perceive that the final product is being sold to classes of individuals who have different price elasticities of demand. Perhaps the manufacturer of the intermediate product can more easily exploit these differences if he or she also manufactures the final product. An example might be aluminum. The producer of aluminum cannot discriminate in the price of aluminum ingots for different final products, like pots, pans, and car grilles, unless that aluminum producer also produces those final products. In other words, the owner of the input supply can engage in third-degree price discrimination after vertical integration.

Barriers to Entry Vertical integration may be used to prevent entry into the industry. The manufacturer of aluminum products may prevent short-term entry into that industry by buying up one or more of the essential resources (for example, bauxite) that go into making aluminum.

The extent to which vertical integration may bar potential entry into the industry depends upon the degree of substitutability among inputs and factor markets, as well as upon substitutability at the output level. In the next chapter we'll focus more extensively on barriers to entry.

Avoiding Costs of Using the Market

Vertical integration may avoid certain costs of using the market. For example, a firm at an earlier stage of production may have been engaging in advertising or other promotional activities in order to increase sales. A vertically integrated firm now provides a certain market for the output of the combined firm's first stage, and these sales promotion costs can be reduced or eliminated altogether. Increased certainty of output from the first-stage firm after vertical integration may allow the integrated firm to reduce inventories previously purchased from the first-stage firm because of assured availability.

Transactions between Firms versus within the Firm We have already mentioned some of the transaction costs of going to the market. They involve searching for prices, closing contracts, collecting payments, communicating work specifications, and so on. Avoiding these costs is one of the main reasons for vertical integration.[15] Vertical integration essentially is the supersession of

[14] See Martin K. Perry, "Price Discrimination and Forward Integration," *Bell Journal of Economics,* vol. 9 (Spring 1978), pp. 209–217.

[15] See Ronald H. Coase, "The Nature of the Firm," *Economica,* vol. 4 (November 1937), pp. 386–405. Also see Oliver E. Williamson, *Markets and Hierarchies—Analysis and Antitrust Implications: A Study in the Economics of Internal Organization* (New York: The Free Press, 1975) for a complete discussion of this theory. This theory has been investigated as an explanation of vertical integration in the oil industry in David J. Teece, *Vertical Integration and Vertical Divestiture in the U.S. Oil Industry* (Stanford, Calif.: Stanford University Press, 1976). Teece concludes that this is the most appropriate motive to ascribe to the industry, and therefore that "vertical divestiture is an entirely inappropriate policy for improving competitive performance of the petroleum industry" (p. 121). But see Mark B. Schupack, "The Effect of Vertical Integration on Retail Gasoline Prices," Working Paper No. 79-17 (Brown University, Department of Economics, September 1979), in which the author shows that vertical integration caused higher gasoline prices (p. 6).

the price mechanism. On the other side, however, are the transaction costs of coordinating activities within a firm. Workers must be supervised; tasks must be assigned in an efficient manner to use workers and machines well. Indeed, the cheaper market transactions become, the more we would expect to see vertical disintegration, that is, specialization.

Certain information costs will also be saved by vertical integration. It is conceivable that the quality of the product at the early stages can be more closely monitored and that the service provided from the previous stages will be more even and certain.

Externalities Vertical integration can perhaps internalize certain externalities, perhaps by lowering transaction costs, that occur in the market. For example, contract revisions responding to outside events do not have to be undertaken continuously in the integrated firm. In addition, the creation of any good involves a substantial amount of exchange of information between successive stages of production. For example, parties may want to exchange information on conductive properties of particular alloys used in integrated computer circuits.

Opportunistic Behavior Problems Sometimes **opportunistic behavior** problems are created by divergence in the incentive structures among the various levels of production. General Motors' eventual purchase of Fisher Body, for example, occurred partially because of an inability of both firms to reduce undesirable behavior through contract clauses. The problem arose because the marginal cost of producing auto bodies from dies was small relative to total costs, and the costs of delayed production was high to the auto producer. Both parties had an incentive to renegotiate prices or related terms. Fisher Body could attempt to renegotiate for a higher auto body price through real or perceived production delays. Alternately, GM, which held the design patent, could attempt to renegotiate for a price closer to Fisher's marginal costs through real or perceived reductions in purchases of auto bodies that had value only to GM. Joint ownership of the design and production dies through vertical integration of the two firms solved many of these problems.[16]

Redistribution of Risk Bearing Vertical integration also permits a redistribution of risk bearing where the physical characteristics of the good between successive stages of production prohibit low-cost storage or other inventory adjustments. Thus, a producer of molten iron who wishes to operate on a low inventory policy will be able to integrate with a steel producer who uses the molten iron and is willing to bear the risk of carrying larger inventories.

Blair and Kaserman have shown that under conditions of stochastic final good demand and certain risk preferences, there is an incentive to vertically

---

[16] See Benjamin Klein, Robert G. Crawford, and Armen A. Alchian, "Vertical Integration, Appropriable Rents, and the Competitive Contracting Process," *Journal of Law and Economics,* vol. 21 (October 1978), pp. 297–326, and Timothy J. Muris, "Opportunistic Behavior and the Law of Contracts," *Minnesota Law Review,* vol. 65 (April 1981), pp. 521–590.

integrate, even when there are fixed proportions.[17] They conclude that vertical integrations undertaken for these motivations are socially efficient and therefore should not be discouraged.

Technological Economies The integration of a molten iron processor by a steel mill producer also facilitates transfer of primary iron products to processors to achieve technological economies. Through vertical integration, the molten iron producer may be able to locate next to the manufacturer of finished steel products, thereby avoiding reheating and transportation costs, and realizing other economies not available when primary iron and finished steel operations are geographically separate.

Inefficient Input Combinations In other cases, vertical integration may eliminate inefficient input combinations by processors. Suppose, for example, that a processor uses one input from a firm with a downward-sloping demand curve; all other inputs are purchased from competitive (or price-taking) industries. In this case, vertical integration would permit the processor to use more of the higher-priced input (since its price could be set at marginal cost), thereby lowering total cost production and hence the output price, since the marginal cost curve would shift downward to the right.[18]

Price Controls

Vertical integration may be a way to avoid price controls. Consider the example of an electric utility that is having trouble purchasing coal at the controlled price. The coal supplier finds that, at the controlled price, quantity demanded exceeds quantity supplied. The supplier institutes a system of allocation, or rationing, to various utilities and other customers. If one utility wishes to eliminate the problem of availability, presumably it could purchase the coal company and use the coal at a rate that reflects its true value. The purchase price of the coal mine might be allowed as part of the rate base on which the utility's electrical rates were computed.

Vertical integration may also permit the firm to choose resources in accordance with their true opportunity costs. In the presence of controls, some resources will be priced too low and their use will be encouraged beyond the optimal combination. If the electric utility purchases the coal company, it will be subjected to the true costs of production. Allocation of resources will then be based on the true costs rather than on the fixed controlled price.

[17] Roger D. Blair and David L. Kaserman, "Uncertainty and the Incentive for Vertical Integration," *Southern Economic Journal,* vol. 45 (July 1978), pp. 266–272. Also see David Flath, "The American Can Case," *Antitrust Bulletin,* vol. 25 (Spring 1980), pp. 169–193, for an application of risk bearing in the canning industry.

[18] See Meyer L. Burstein, "A Theory of Full-Line Forcing," *Northwestern University Law Review,* vol. 55 (March/April 1960), pp. 62–95. Also see Martin K. Perry, "Vertical Integration: The Monopsony Case," *American Economic Review,* vol. 68 (September 1978), pp. 561–570 for a discussion of the efficiency and distributional consequences of backward integration in monopsony markets.

In fact, vertical integration is an alternative for any market transaction that has been determined illegal.[19] Burstein and Hilton discuss how full-line enforcing can be viewed as a *de facto* method of obtaining vertical integration.[20] In particular, Burstein discusses how an input monopolist can increase his or her rent by preventing producers of noncompetitive complementary inputs from sharing in the generated rents.[21]

REASONS FOR VERTICAL DISINTEGRATION

We have just covered the reasons and determinants of vertical integration. Now we will look at why firms may wish to vertically disintegrate, or why we may expect to see specialization. Robinson describes the process of **vertical disintegration** as follows:

> Where some given process requires a scale of production considerably greater than the smaller firms in an industry can achieve, this process tends to be separated off from the main industry, and all the smaller firms get this particular process performed for them by an outside specialist firm. Thus the industry becomes broken up into two or more industries, and each is enabled to work at its most convenient scale of production. The specialist firm, working for a number of the smaller firms, is on a larger scale than any of the individual firms could have achieved for that particular process or product. Examples of this principle may be found in the finishing stages of the textile industries, and in the manufacture of various component parts, such as radiators, electrical equipment, body shells, and crankshafts and other forgings, in the motor industry.[22]

Basically, as an industry grows, more activities will be performed on a sufficient scale to permit firms to specialize in such activities full-time. Consider an example taken from Stigler.[23] From Figure 15-1 we see the average cost curves for a firm that has three stages of production. These are called ATC_1, ATC_2, and ATC_3. The combined average total cost is given as ATC_c. In order to show all of these processes on the same graph, we assume that the output of each process is proportional to the output of the final product. Process 1 shows decreasing returns; process 2, increasing returns; and process 3, first increasing and then decreasing returns.

Now consider several rates of output and several possibilities. If output rate is at q_1, average total cost will be at C_1. But assume that there were a significant number of firms similar to the one pictured in Figure 15-1. Process 2 could be undertaken by a specialized firm and sold, let us say, at price P_2 to all the firms

[19] See, for example, Chief Justice Douglas' opinion in *Standard Oil Co. of California v. United States,* 337 U.S. 293 (1949).

[20] See Burstein, "A Theory of Full-Line Forcing," and George W. Hilton, "Tying Sales and Full-Line Forcing," *Weltwirtschaftliches Archiv,* vol. 81 (1958), pp. 265–276.

[21] For a formal proof of this proposition, see Roger D. Blair and David L. Kaserman, "Vertical Integration, Tying, and Antitrust Policy," *American Economic Review,* vol. 68 (June 1978), pp. 397–402.

[22] Edward A. Robinson, *The Structure of Competitive Industry* (Chicago: University of Chicago Press, 1958), p. 20.

[23] George J. Stigler, *The Theory of Price,* 3d ed. (New York: Macmillan, 1966), p. 120.

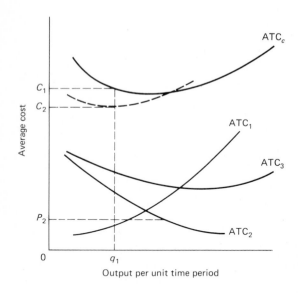

FIGURE 15-1
The effects of scale on specialization. [See George Stigler, *The Theory of Price,* 3d ed. (New York: Macmillan, 1966)].

in the industry. If this is the case, the average total cost curve to the representative firm will shift to the dashed line that eventually intersects ATC_c. The new average total cost to the representative firm will fall from C_1 to C_2. Thus, the process of vertical disintegration leads to a reduction in average total costs. With enough firms in the industry, the representative firm will engage only in process 1, which is subject to increasing costs. It will buy the remainder from independent firms.

THE PRICE AND OUTPUT EFFECTS OF VERTICAL INTEGRATION

We'll now examine the effects on price and output of the final product of combining two or more independent production processes, or stages.[24] Let's consider three examples, assuming for each that the cost conditions associated with every stage in the production process remain unchanged.

Case One—Vertical Integration of Two Purely Competitive Firms

This is the simplest case and the one in which neither output nor price will change due to vertical integration. Since the two firms are perfectly competitive, demand conditions will not change facing stage 1, nor will cost conditions change facing stage 2. If the vertically integrated firm wants to have an internal transfer price from stage 1 that is lower than it used to be, total profits will not change. Profits will merely be transferred from stage 1 to stage 2.

---

[24] Assuming no stochastic variation in final demand or other special market condition.

Case Two—Vertical Integration between a Monopolist and a Perfect Competitor with Fixed Factors of Production

As in the case of vertical integration between two perfect competitors, vertical integration between a monopolist and a perfect competitor will not change price and output for the final product. Basically, we have already explained the reasoning when we examined whether vertical integration could increase monopoly power. Let us assume that the monopolist engages in backward vertical integration. By assumption, it purchases its input at a competitive price. The internal transfer price that it uses from the newly purchased supplier will, if the monopolist wishes to profit-maximize, be the perfectly competitive price. If anything other than the full opportunity cost of the input is built into the monopolist's total marginal cost curve for the final output, then a non-profit-maximizing price and rate of output will result. In brief, a monopoly at any one of a number of successive stages in the production process will not change the level of output if factor proportions are fixed, because the monopoly already existing at one stage will have taken into account its position on output level and price. We see this monopoly in Figure 15-2. We have simplified Figure 15-2 so that one unit of the monopolist's output is associated with one unit of output at each of the competitive stages of production. Successive stages of production consequently modify only the characteristics of the output.

Case Three—Vertical Integration between a Monopolist at One Stage and All Other Firms in the Industry at a Perfectly Competitive Stage with Variable Factors of Production

With variable factors of production, competitive firms that purchase from previous stages which are organized under monopoly conditions will be able to substitute away from the higher-priced monopoly input. The ability to substitute lower-priced inputs implies that the cost curve associated with the subsequent producers will be lower than if the input were used in fixed proportions. This lower cost curve will result in a lower price of the final output and a higher level of output. This will happen because at the early stages a nonintegrated monopolist will not be able to obtain all the monopoly rents from the sale of the final product when factor substitution is possible.[25]

Changing Cost Conditions

Once we drop the assumption of no change in cost conditions, it is conceivable that if vertical integration reduces cost, price will be reduced and output will be increased. Even if cost conditions change, however, vertical integration may

---

[25] See Ronald L. Moomaw, "Vertical Integration and Monopoly: A Resolution of the Controversy," *Rivista Internazionale di Scienze Economiche e Commerciali* (January 1974), and Burstein, "A Theory of Full-Line Forcing." Also see F. R. Warren-Boulton, "Vertical Control with Variable Proportions," *Journal of Political Economy,* vol. 82 (August/September, 1974), pp. 783–802.

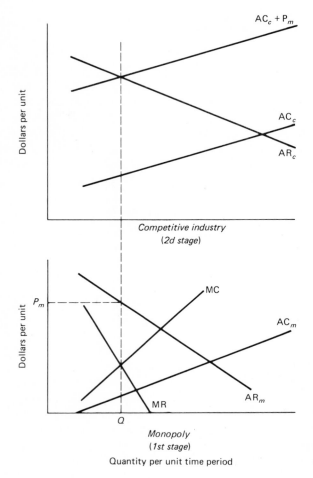

FIGURE 15-2
Vertical integration between monopolist and perfect competition.

not result in a change in the profit-maximizing rate of output if the slope of the total cost curve remains unchanged at every level of output. For this to occur, total cost has to be reduced by the same absolute amount at every rate of output; that is, the cost saving due to vertical integration must be independent of the rate of output.

Bilateral Monopoly

Vertical integration between a monopsonist and a monopolist can conceivably reduce price and increase output. We will demonstrate this possibility by considering a baseball player's union versus a cartel of team owners. This is a situation called **bilateral monopoly**. We show it in Figure 15-3. The marginal revenue product curve of the baseball team owners taken as a whole is represented by MRP. We draw a curve that is *marginal* to MRP and label it MR.

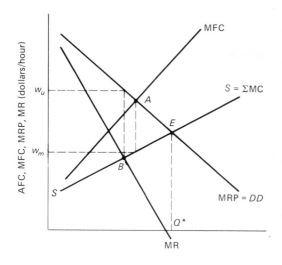

FIGURE 15-3
The players' union versus the team owners—bilateral monopoly in the factor market. Baseball team owners would like to set up a wage rate where MFC = MRP; this occurs at point A. They would, therefore, want to set wage rate w_m. However, if the baseball players form a union, they want to sell the quantity of their product where MR = MC. Marginal revenue is given by the curve that is marginal to the MRP curve. This curve is labeled MR. The intersection, then, of marginal revenue and marginal cost, or SS, is at point B. Because the supply curve SS represents the summation of the individual marginal cost curves of the individual players, the players' union would like to set a wage rate of w_u. Joint profit maximization would dictate that the team owners and team players' union get together to offer quantity Q^*.

MR is, in effect, a marginal revenue curve, when we consider that MRP is the demand curve for baseball players' services by monopoly team owners. Thus, MR is no different from any other marginal revenue curve in a monopoly situation. The union of baseball players has a supply curve of SS. The curve marginal to that curve is called marginal factor cost curve, or MFC. The baseball team owners would like to set a wage rate of w_m, because this is where the team owners could obtain the profit-maximizing number of players. The wage rate is determined by the intersection at point A of the marginal factor cost curve (MFC) and the marginal revenue product curve (MRP). The union, however, acting as the sole bargaining agent for all of the employees would, if it were maximizing the equivalent of monopoly profits, want to set a wage rate of w_u. We determine the maximizing wage rate w_u by considering that the union is acting as a monopolist. Every monopolist will set output where MR = MC. What is marginal revenue in this case? It is the curve labeled MR, which is marginal to the demand curve for baseball players (MRP) by monopoly team owners. What is marginal cost? It is given by the supply curve of baseball players, or SS. MR and SS intersect at point B. That amount of baseball players' services can be sold to the team owners at a price of w_u, given by the team owner's demand curve MRP. In a situation of bilateral monopoly, the agreed-upon wage rate will be in between w_m and w_u. If we were to assume that the union is proprietary or profit-seeking, we would state that the union would attempt to attain w_u because that is the wage rate which maximizes the difference between total wages paid to employed baseball players and the minimum amount of wages required to bring this quantity of labor into the baseball-playing market.

Joint Wealth Maximization

Actually, there is a determinant level of employment at which both the players and the team owners maximize their joint wealth. If we asume that transaction costs are zero, the two groups would agree to employ the number of players at which the supply curve intersects the marginal revenue product at point E. At this point the two groups are not attempting to exploit one another; rather, they are conspiring to exploit the spectators. There is a problem at point E, however. How should the wealth be split between the group of players and the group of team owners? If there is vertical integration between these two productive stages, there is no problem about how to split the wealth, because it is all under one ownership. Output will definitely increase and price will decrease.

THE MEASUREMENT OF THE DEGREE OF VERTICAL INTEGRATION

Here we discuss several possible ways to measure the degree of vertical integration.[26]

The Ratio of Value-Added to Sales

One possible index is equal to the ratio of value-added to sales revenues. **Value-added** is defined as sales revenues minus expenditures for fuel, power, and raw materials. In principle, the more successive stages that the firm performs in the production process, the greater will be the size of this ratio. There are defects in this theory, however.

Defects in the Ratio If input and output prices change at a different rate over time, the index will change even though the physical processes performed by the firm do not change. When comparing the degree of vertical integration of several firms, this index of integration may differ despite the same physical amount of integration being present. Such differences may be caused by one firm having higher profits than another firm, understanding that profits are part of value-added.

If we wish to compare firms in different industries, this particular index declines as we move closer to the final stage, even though all firms are, let us say, equally integrated. In this case, the index reflects the stage in the productive process, not the degree of vertical integration. Hence, we cannot use the index unless we are comparing different firms even in the same industry, unless they are at the same stage in the productive process.

The Ratio of Inventories to Sales

This index will be equal to the value of inventory/sales revenues. Implicitly we assume within this index that the greater the number of stages in the productive

[26] The following discussion draws heavily on Morris A. Adelman, "Concept and Statistical Measurement of Vertical Integration," in George J. Stigler, ed., *Business Concentration and Price Policy* (Princeton: Princeton University Press, 1955), pp. 281–322.

process performed by one firm are, the greater the level of the firm's inventories will be. To the extent that a firm benefits from vertical integration by economizing on inventories, this index will not be valid. Indeed, one could conceive of increased vertical integration leading to a smaller ratio of inventory to sales. Additionally, with the different rate of change in the prices of final output and inventories, the index can change without there being an actual change in the structure of the firm. Finally, given the differences across industries in cyclical patterns, one would expect quite different inventory patterns.

Interfirm Purchases—A Measure of Backward Integration

Take one particular stage of production. If we look at the following ratio

$$\frac{\text{Interfirm purchases of inputs at that stage}}{\text{Total value of inputs used at that stage}}$$

then we obtain a measure of backward vertical integration. This index or measure tells us the degree to which the firm must rely on the market to supply its inputs at any stage in the production process.

Interfirm Transfers of Output—A Measure of Forward Integration

If we look at the following ratio

$$\frac{\text{Interfirm transfers of output}}{\text{Total output}}$$

we can tell the degree of forward vertical integration at any particular stage of production. This ratio indicates the extent to which the firm depends on the market for disposing of its output at that stage.

The two ratios above are invariant to price level changes because the numerator and denominator use the same price. Additionally, one can use either quantity data or value data to estimate these ratios.

DIVERSIFICATION

A concept closely related to vertical integration is diversification. A diversified firm does not specialize in the production of a single product or service; it produces a number of different products or services. The definition of diversification depends critically on one's definition of a product. Since there are many ways in which products and markets can be defined, there are many definitions of diversification. This makes it difficult to discuss the determinants of diversification. If diversification is defined as the combination of one firm with one or more firms that sell different products, then vertical integration is a subset of diversification. So-called conglomerate mergers clearly fall within the definition of diversification because they occur when merged firms sell totally unrelated products.[27] The Federal Trade Commission categorizes conglomerate diversification under three rubrics: (1) product extension, (2) market extension, and (3) all others. For the first category, the FTC includes firms that produce products that do not compete directly with one another, but that are still related in either production or distribution. Classified under the market extension category are mergers of firms involved in producing the same products sold in different geographic markets. The third category is a catchall that involves all other types of conglomerate diversification.

Reasons for and Determinants of Diversification

Brand Names and Reliability   Consumer product reliability is often associated with brand names when individuals are unable to judge the reliability of other products produced by the firm. A brand name can enhance the sales promise of a new product by reducing search and evaluation costs. One possibility of diversification, particularly the conglomerate type, might have to do with the merging of a firm with an established brand name and a firm, particularly one with a new product line, that is unknown and lacks a brand name. To the extent that the firm with the established brand name does not attempt to free-ride on its past built-up goodwill, the acquisition of the unknown firm's product is a true information gain for a consumer. That is to say, consumers will be given accurate information about the reliability of the new product simply because of the merger. If the acquiring firm has established some monopoly power and attempts to free-ride in the short run on its established goodwill, then the diversification outlined here would be for the purpose of cashing in on that monopoly power in the short run.

Organizing Different Monopolies into One Firm When Their Products Are Interdependent   Conceptually, one can envision diversification, or the organization of separate monopolies, into one firm to enhance total profits if the products of those separate monopolists are interdependent. We are referring to a situation in which a change in the price of one product in one market shifts the demand curve in the other market. Consider two separate monopolists that sell substitutable products, that is, where the cross-price elasticity of demand is

---

[27] For an extensive cataloging of the many alleged motivations for conglomerate mergers, and a survey of the empirical evidence tending to support or refute the various theories, see Dennis C. Mueller, "The Effects of Conglomerate Mergers: A Survey of the Empirical Evidence," *Journal of Banking and Finance,* vol. 1 (1977), pp. 315–347.

positive. A conglomerate merger of the two firms selling A and B will increase profits. The combined firm will set the price of A somewhat higher than it would have had it ignored the effect of a change in the price of A on the demand for B, and similarly for product B. Slightly higher prices reduce profits on A, but they give a more than commensurate increase in profits on the larger quantity sold of B. We can state, then, that the diversified seller enjoying monopoly rights on both A and B will price each slightly higher than would be the case with two separate monopolists.

The opposite will occur if A and B are complements, that is, if the cross-price elasticity of demand is negative. The prices of A and B will be slightly below what they would be if two separate monopolists were producing A and B without taking account of the interdependence.

Spreading the Cost of Fixed Assets   One explanation for diversification involves the spreading of fixed costs over a larger range of output. This reduces average total costs for all the products involved. There are numerous problems with such an explanation of diversification.

1 The diversified firm must be using indivisible, or fixed, inputs that are not specialized. Typically, one cites financial, marketing, and managerial inputs as indivisible and capable of being applied equally well to many outputs. But to the extent that indivisible inputs are specific to a particular activity, any expanded level of activities by the diversified firm will require additional indivisible inputs.

2 The economics of diversification are not the same thing as economics of absolute size.[28] The idea of spreading fixed costs applies to the individual firm and is an argument for increasing the absolute scale of the firm rather than an argument in favor of increased diversification.

Cost of Investment Funds and Risk   It has been argued that investment funds may be more cheaply obtained by the diversified firm than by a group of identical specialized firms. Presumably, there is less risk attached to the diversified firm's operation. Some economists contend that the variance of the distribution of income from the diversified firm will be less than the variance of the individual firms. There is less probability of an extreme occurrence that will wipe out the entire firm when it is producing many products as opposed to a firm producing only one product. Indeed, the formula for variance of the sum of individual firms includes a covariance term that may indeed reduce the variance

---

[28] The economics of diversification most often concerns the direction of diversification once excess capacity occurs from a decline in the growth of the original activity of the firm. See Alfred Chandler, Jr., *Strategy and Structure: Chapters in the History of the American Industrial Enterprise* (Cambridge, Mass.: M.I.T. Press, 1962); Michael Gort, *Diversification and Integration in the American Industry* (Princeton: Princeton University Press, 1962); and Charles H. Berry, *Corporate Growth and Diversification* (Princeton: Princeton University Press, 1975).

of the anticipated earnings of the diversified firm (that is, var $[x + y]$ = var $[x]$ + var $[y]$ + 2 cov $[x + y]$).[29]

Tax Advantages   Sherman contends that certain tax reasons enable diversified firms to attract equity capital at a lower price than nondiversified firms.[30] Shareholders are, in effect, willing to pay more for a given expected gross earnings stream of the diversified firm because under some circumstances the diversified firm can reduce taxes paid, thereby increasing their investors' aftertax earnings stream.

Interest payments are a deductible expense for tax purposes. Therefore, the greater the use of debt as opposed to equity financing by a firm is, the lower the total taxable profits will be. Whenever a diversified firm can acquire other firms and in the process transfer the gross profit on a share into interest on debt, the total tax liability of the diversified firm falls. The remaining shareholders will have a tax saving and thus the aftertax return per share will rise. Since there is a larger pool of revenue to draw from, there is less risk of default on any one product line's debt. The proportion of debt that can be used to finance any given level of activity in a diversified firm is higher than an identical group of independent firms. Any given rate of return will therefore generate an increased supply of debt finance available, because more shareholders' equity will be available on which to draw to make up any financing problems.

Sherman also argues that the diversified firm can generate more capital gains relative to distributed dividends than individual specialized firms can. The diversified firm can shift investment funds internally from those activities that have low marginal returns to those with higher marginal returns. The shareholder who wishes to do the same thing with a set of identical specialized firms must sell out and pay taxes on the profits thereby gained, since taxes on shares of stock must be paid only upon liquidation.

Another tax advantage of the diversified firm is that it can shift losses to take full advantage of them rather than having to carry them forward and backward. In other words, the expected present value of tax offsets is higher with the diversified firm.

The Degree of Diversification

There are numerous ways to measure diversification, none of them completely satisfactory. If we wish to use the primary product specialization ratio given by

---

[29] This does not mean that, from the point of view of the lender, the diversified firm is less risky than a group of specialized firms. The lender can obtain the same amount of risk reduction (variance in anticipated yield) by allocating lending among the specialized firms that the diversified firms would buy up. In essence, then, risk reduction justifies a diversified lending portfolio but not a diversified firm from the point of view of the lenders. See Keith V. Smith and John C. Schreiner, "A Portfolio Analysis of Conglomerate Diversification," *Journal of Finance,* vol. 24 (June 1969), pp. 413–427.

[30] Roger Sherman, "How Tax Policy Induces Conglomerate Mergers," *National Tax Journal,* vol. 25 (December 1972), pp. 521–529.

the U.S. Census of Manufacturers (see pages 77–79), then we would be measuring diversification on the basis of the ratio of the firm's nonprimary activities to its total activity. This really doesn't tell us the degree of diversification unless we know the number of different products involved in the firm's nonprimary output. Two firms could have exactly the same primary product specialization ratio (see Chapter 3), but one firm could be much more diversified because its nonprimary output is divided among many more products than the other firm's.

A counting process might also give us an index of diversification. We simply count the number of different products in each firm. Such an index doesn't tell us much, though, because we have no idea of the weight to be given to each product. Perhaps a weighted index of the number of products would be more useful, where the weights were equal to the percentage of total output accounted for by each product; all the weights would add up to one. The index would be as follows:

$$D = \sum_{i=1}^{n} w_i q_i$$

where w_i is the percent of total sales accounted for by the ith product q_i.

A composite measure of diversification attempts to take account of both the percentage of total output accounted for by nonprimary activities and the total number of nonprimary activities. To obtain this composite index, we multiply the ratio of nonprimary to total output of the firm (or industry) by the total number of industries that account for a predetermined percentage of the total output of the firm.

CHAPTER 16

BARRIERS TO ENTRY

Firms are affected by various technological and cost factors that determine the efficient size and distribution of firms within industries. Through competition, including imitation, and entrepreneurship, the efficient industry structure evolves. Yet firms will attempt to develop strategies to counter entry by new firms that, if successful, could result in an inefficient industry structure. In the first part of this chapter we'll investigate the relationship of technology and cost conditions to industry structure, and then we will turn to a discussion of those factors that are traditionally identified as barriers to entry.

RETURNS TO SCALE

The law of diminishing marginal returns tells us that output grows at a decreasing rate when additional units of a variable factor are added to all other fixed units. But what happens when all inputs become variable and are changed in the same proportion? To answer this question, we must deal with **returns to scale**, a long-run concept applied to an individual firm (or plant) that has complete flexibility in its productive process.

There are three possibilities for the returns to scale. Output may increase by a larger proportion than each of the inputs; output may increase by the same proportion as each of the inputs; output may increase by a smaller proportion than each of the inputs. Accordingly, we talk about increasing, constant, and decreasing returns to scale. Remember that we are talking about altering all inputs by the same proportion. Thus, when we say a doubling of scale, we mean doubling all labor and all capital inputs, and all other inputs.

The Isoquant Approach

Assuming only two factors of production, increasing, constant, and decreasing returns to scale can be shown by using the isoquant approach.

Look at Figure 16-1, where we have three panels. Panel (a) represents increasing returns to scale; panel (b), constant returns to scale; and panel (c), decreasing returns to scale. We start off with a given rate of output, 1, in each of the three panels, and also with a given capital-labor ratio, K_1/L_1, which is the same in each of the three panels. Now the question arises of how much we have to increase capital and labor, while keeping their ratios constant, in order to increase the rate of output from 1 to 2. Isoquant 2 represents exactly twice the output of isoquant 1. We see in panel (a) that when there are increasing returns, the increase in capital and labor inputs is less in proportion to the increase in output. Look at the respective distances along the ray from the origin. The capital-labor ratio remains the same along any (straight line) ray from the origin in an input space. Since we are dealing with proportional changes in all inputs, we can look only at what happens along any given ray. The rays drawn in panels (a), (b), and (c) all have equal slopes. In any event, in panel (a), the length of the ray between zero and where it intersects the isoquant associated with the rate of output of 1 is less than the length of the portion of the ray between the isoquant labeled 1 and the isoquant labeled 2. Otherwise stated, a doubling of output is achieved by less than a doubling of input. The same experiment is even more persuasive when we increase output

FIGURE 16-1
Increasing, constant, and decreasing returns to scale. We wish to increase output by proportional changes in both capital and labor. Along any ray from the origin, the capital-labor ratio remains the same. In other words, K_1/L_1 will be equal along all the rays shown in panels (a), (b), and (c). In panel (a) we see increasing returns to scale. An increase in the output from 1 to 2 requires a less-than-proportional increase in capital and labor. In panel (b), we see constant returns to scale. An increase in output from 1 to 2 requires a proportional increase in both inputs. Finally, in panel (c), we show decreasing returns to scale. An increase in output from 1 to 2 requires a more-than-proportional increase in both inputs.

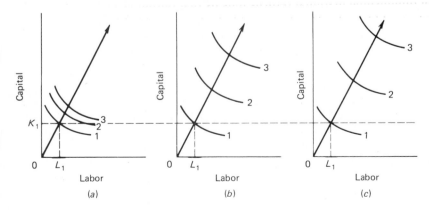

from a rate of 2 to a rate of 3, where isoquant 3 represents exactly three times the output of isoquant 1. (Thus the numbers 1, 2, and 3 are cardinal as opposed to ordinal.)

In panel (b), we show constant returns to scale. Here the length of the distance measured along the ray is the same between output rates of 0–1, 1–2, and 2–3. A doubling of input results in an exact doubling of output.

Finally, in panel (c), we show decreasing returns to scale. The distance between the isoquants gets larger for equal increments in output. Hence it requires more than proportionate increases in input to increase output. Otherwise stated, a doubling of output requires more than a doubling of input.

The Long-Run Average Cost Approach

If we assume constant input prices no matter what the scale of the firm is, then we can translate the results of panels (a), (b), and (c) in Figure 16-1 to long-run average cost curves. In Figure 16-2 we see panels (a), (b), and (c). In panel (a), the long-run average cost curve falls over the relevant range of outputs; in panel (b), it is horizontal, and in panel (c), it rises.

The Distinction between Returns to Scale and Economies of Scale

We have just referred to increasing, constant, and decreasing returns to scale. These phenomena are related to the technological relationship between a proportionate change in all input and the resultant change in output. In other words, returns to scale refer only to the *technological* phenomena that occur *within* a firm. The ability to combine input in a more efficient manner as the output rate increases would be an example of a technological phenomenon

FIGURE 16-2

Increasing, constant, and decreasing returns to scale with cost curves. The implication of Figure 16-1 is that long-run average costs will fall when there are increasing returns to scale [panel (a)], will be constant when there are constant returns to scale [panel (b)], and will rise when there are decreasing returns to scale [panel (c)].

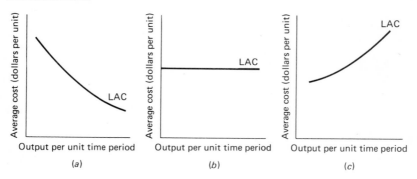

within a firm. When we consider the possibility of changes *exterior* to the firm, we are considering the possibility of changes in such things as the price of factors which are external to the firm. If all firms are expanding production and, therefore, demanding more factors of production at each and every price, the prices of those factors may change. When we allow for such external changes, we are considering what have been called external economies and **dis-economies of scale.** A firm may possibly enjoy the effects of external economies of scale because the industry is expanding; this leads to lower prices of input to *all* firms, since the input is now purchased in larger quantities by the industry. On the other hand, external diseconomies of scale might occur when input prices rise as the industry expands production.

Thus, economies of scale and increasing returns to scale are related but are not exactly the same. The latter is the technological basis for the former. However, economies of scale can come about solely from price effects on input. Hence, it is possible to have increasing returns to scale but no economies of scale if the firm must buy its input at a price that rises when the industry (or firm) expands production.

Increasing Returns to Scale   Here we list several reasons why a firm might be expected to experience increasing returns to scale:

1 *Specialization*   As a firm's scale of operation increases, the opportunities for specialization in the use of resource input also increases. This is sometimes called increased division of tasks, or operations. Gains from such division of labor or increased specialization are well known, as Adam Smith illustrated in his famous pin factory example.[1] When we consider managerial staffs, we also find that larger enterprises may be able to put together more highly specialized staffs. Larger enterprises may have the ability to tap managerial technology better.

2 *Dimensional factor*   Large-scale firms often use proportionately less input per unit of output simply because certain inputs do not have to be physically doubled in order to double the output. Consider the storage costs of, say, oil. The cost of storage is basically related to the cost of steel that goes into building the storage container; however, the amount of steel required goes up less in proportion to the volume of the container.

3 *Transportation factor*   The transportation cost per unit may fall as the market area increases. The market size increases by πr^2, which is the formula for the area of a circle where r is the radius. However, transportation distance from the center of the circle is equal to r. Thus, transportation distance only doubles when market area quadruples.

4 *Improved productive equipment*   The larger the scale of the enterprise is, the more it is able to take advantage of larger-volume types of machinery.

[1] Adam Smith, *The Wealth of Nations* (1776), rev. ed. (New York: Modern Library, 1937), book I, chap. 1, pp. 4–5.

Small-scale operations may not lend themselves to machines that require a large volume of output to be profitably used.

Decreasing Returns to Scale One of the basic reasons we can eventually expect to observe decreasing returns to scale at the firm level is that the efficient functioning of management does have limits. Moreover, as more workers are hired, a more than proportionate increase in managers may be needed, and this could cause increased costs per unit. For example, it might be possible to hire from 1 to 10 workers and give them each a shovel to dig ditches; however, as soon as 10 workers are hired, it may also be necessary to hire an overseer to coordinate their ditch-digging efforts. Thus, constant returns to scale will exist until 10 workers and 10 shovels are employed; then decreasing returns to scale may set in. As the layers of supervision grow, the cost of information and communication often grow more in proportion.

Returns to Scale at the Plant Level We have already talked about some of the implicit reasons why we might observe decreasing or increasing returns to scale at the plant level. Rather than go into detail here, we merely point out that at the plant level, increasing returns to scale are basically a result of production economies. A larger plant lends itself to greater specialization in the use of resource input and a greater subdivision of the productive tasks.

CONSTANT-, INCREASING-, AND DECREASING-COST INDUSTRIES

We have just referred to the individual firm; now let's look at the entire industry. When all firms increase output and the price of the product remains constant, we are dealing with a constant-cost industry. If, however, the average unit cost curve rises, we are dealing with an increasing-cost industry. Finally, if the unit cost curve falls when the industry expands output, we are dealing with a decreasing-cost industry. These three possibilities are shown by the slope of the long-run supply curve presented in panels (a), (b), and (c) in Figure 16-3.

We will work through the case in which constant costs prevail. We start out in panel (a) with demand curve DD and supply curve SS. The equilibrium price is P_e. There is a shift in market demand to $D'D'$. In the short run the supply curve remains stable. The equilibrium price rises to P'_e; this generates positive economic profits for those in the industry. Such economic profits induce capital to flow into the industry. The existing firms expand and/or new firms enter. The supply curve shifts out to $S'S'$. The new intersection with the new demand curve is at E''; the new equilibrium price is again P_e. The long-run supply curve is obtained by connecting the intersections of the various demand and supply curves E and E''; it is labeled $S_L S_L$. It is horizontal and its slope is zero. Long-run supply is perfectly elastic. Any shift in demand is eventually met by an equal shift in supply so that the long-run price is constant at P_e. This is a constant-cost industry.

An increasing-cost industry is shown by the upward-sloping supply curve

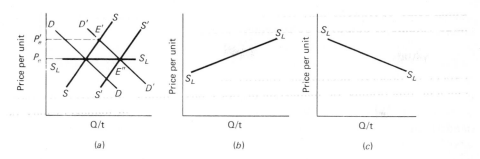

FIGURE 16-3
Constant, increasing, and decreasing cost industries. In panel (a) we show a
situation where the demand curve shifts from *DD* to *D'D'*. Price increases to P'_e;
however, in time the supply curve shifts out to *S'S'*, and the new equilibrium shifts
from *E'* to *E''*. The market-clearing price is, again, P_e. If we connect points such as *E*
and *E''*, we come up with the long-run supply curve $S_L S_L$. This is a constant-cost
industry. In panel (b) costs are increasing for the industry and, therefore, the supply
curve is upward-sloping; in panel (c) costs are decreasing for the industry as it
expands and, therefore, the supply curve is downward-sloping.

$S_L S_L$ in panel (b). A decreasing-cost industry is shown in panel (c). To test your
understanding of the derivation of $S_L S_L$, draw in the appropriate sets of short-
run market demand and industry supply curves in panels (b) and (c).

DISECONOMIES AND ECONOMIES OF SCALE

An industry can be other than a constant-cost industry when external
economies and diseconomies of scale are present. The former could generate
the long-run supply curve in panel (c) and the latter, the long-run supply curve
in panel (b) in Figure 16-3.

External Diseconomies of Scale

External diseconomies of scale are the factors that increase costs over which
the individual firm has no control. The most obvious external diseconomy of
scale is the impact of the industry's expanding production on resource prices.
When all firms expand production simultaneously and cause the price of one or
more inputs to rise, this is an increasing-cost industry. The external diseconomy to increasing output is not controllable by the individual firm and does
not occur within the firm itself. External diseconomy of scale may also be
caused by increased congestion in a manufacturing area, which results from an
expansion of all plants together.

External Economies of Scale

External economies of scale can occur when an increase in the output of the
entire industry allows suppliers to engage in increased specialization and to

lower their unit costs. This would cause the downward-sloping, long-run supply curve shown in panel (c) in Figure 16-3. Consider, for example, one or two firms that start business in a small residential area. They each need a photocopier, but not enough to justify the purchase or lease of one. They must send their originals elsewhere to be copied. If many firms move into the same area, it may become profitable for a photocopying firm to start a business nearby. There will at least be a reduction for the original two firms in the time cost of having their photocopying done at a more distant location. Additionally, it may turn out that larger and hence lower-per-unit-cost photocopying machines may be used by the photocopying firm and that the actual monetary price per unit of photocopying would fall. This would be another case of economies of scale which are external to the firm and over which the firm has no control.

Natural Monopoly

If scale economies are so great that the long-run average total cost curve is downward-sloping over the relevant range (determined by the demand curve), then only one firm can survive. The survivor will be the firm that expands output the most and hence enjoys the greatest decrease in average total cost. It is able to "undersell" rivals and eventually drive them out of business. This **natural monopoly** is depicted in Figure 16-4.

FIGURE 16-4
A natural monopoly. The long-run average cost curve LAC is downward-sloping over the entire relevant range of outputs. In a competitive solution, price is equal to long-run marginal cost. If this natural monopolist were forced to sell at price P_1 and to produce output rate Q_c, it would incur a loss per unit equal to the difference between C_1 and P_1. Unrestrained, the monopolist would produce where marginal revenue equals marginal cost, or at output rate Q_m. It would charge a price equal to P_m.

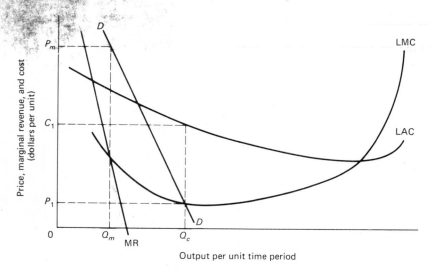

There we see that the LAC curve is downward-sloping over a relevant range of outputs. Now assume that the market demand curve is DD. The monopolist's profit-maximizing rate of output is where MR = LMC, or at output rate Q_m. The profit-maximizing monopolist would then charge price P_m. Clearly, a competitive solution to the price-output decision could not prevail in this industry. A competitive solution requires that price equal marginal cost, but if price were equal to marginal cost P_1, the firm in this industry (that is, the natural monopolist) would suffer a loss on every unit sold because the LAC curve is above the DD curve at the rate of output Q_c. The loss on each unit sold would be the vertical difference between C_1 and P_1 in Figure 16-4. Some theorists, in their desire to have price equal marginal cost, have suggested that a subsidy be given equal to the distance between C_1 and P_1 per unit of output sold in this natural monopoly situation. It may be true that with the subsidy, each consumer will pay a retail price for the product equal to long-run marginal cost. Taken together, however, consumers of the product do not pay a total equal to the true social opportunity cost of the total quantity of this commodity consumed; they are subsidized by the general taxpayers.

Multipart Pricing   Another approach can be used in the case of a natural monopoly. Conceivably, the natural monopolist who would otherwise suffer a loss if the uniform price of P_1 were charged could engage in multipart pricing. Those demanders of the product with relatively inelastic demand curves would pay prices higher than P_1. The revenues in excess of the marginal cost of providing the units of output to these demanders with relatively inelastic demand curves could be used to cover some or all of the fixed costs.

THE MEASUREMENT OF SCALE ECONOMIES

Schools of Thought

The existence or absence of scale economies rests on at least two theoretical foundations. According to Bain, initially there were two schools of thought, the British and the American. The British school, believing that scale economies are associated with firm size, particularly with large multiplant firms, argued that the mere existence of large firms and concentrated industries indicated scale economies.[2] From an efficiency point of view, this group recommended that public policy promote mergers and big firms.

The American school developed the opposite argument, led in the beginning by Knight and Simons.[3] This school argued that all scale economies could be

---

[2] See, for example, Edward A. Robinson, *The Structure of Competitive Industries* (Chicago: University of Chicago Press, 1958).

[3] Frank H. Knight, *Risk, Uncertainty, and Profit* (Chicago: University of Chicago Press, 1971); and Henry C. Simons, *Economic Policy for a Free Society* (Chicago: University of Chicago Press, 1948).

fully exploited within smaller firms. In other words, the American school argued that there is no substantial real or pecuniary economy of scale. Most current British and American economists fall into neither classification, however, and the debate has never been fully resolved.

Estimating Scale Economies

The Rate, Volume, and Time Effects   The rate, volume, and initial date of production are three dimensions of output that ultimately effect actual scale economies.[4] First, an increase in the rate of production, holding the volume and the starting date of production constant, increases total costs. Marginal and average costs also rise when rate and volume are both held constant and the starting date is moved closer to the present. Finally, increases in volume, holding rate of output and starting date constant, decrease marginal and average costs.

In actual production, all dimensions of output may change simultaneously so that isolating the effects becomes almost overwhelmingly difficult. Johnston, one of the premier researchers in this area, listed a number of necessary conditions that must hold if one wishes to estimate the long-run average cost curve. Without going into those conditions, we concur with his observation that the real world is seldom so kind to the researcher.[5] Nonetheless, many statistical studies on both sides of the Atlantic have purported to measure the extent of scale economies in America and Britain.[6]

Some Empirical Studies   The most famous statistical study was performed by Bain, who used questionnaires to obtain his data.[7] His results were in keeping with theories of the American School. He found virtually no scale economies at either the plant level or the firm level in most manufacturing industries. In spite of the fact that his sample included some relatively concentrated industries such as automobiles, basically he stated that the optimal scale of plant was less than 4 percent of the market's total productive capacity. He implied that many firms are larger than they need be to obtain maximum benefits from scale economies.

Criticism of Bain's Work   Although Bain's study has been considered important in the measurement of scale economies, it has nonetheless been

---

[4] See Armen A. Alchian, "Costs and Output," in Moses Abramovitz, et al., *The Allocation of Economic Resources: Essays in Honor of B. F. Haley* (Stanford, Calif.: Stanford University Press, 1959), pp. 23–40. An empirical estimate of these effects is found in Alchian, "Reliability of Progress Curves in Airframe Production," *Econometrica*, vol. 31 (October 1963), pp. 679–693. Also see John S. McGee, "Economies in Size in Auto Space Body Manufacture," *Journal of Law and Economics*, vol. 16 (October 1973), pp. 239–273.

[5] John Johnston, *Statistical Cost Analysis* (New York: McGraw-Hill, 1960), p. 26.

[6] See, for example, Roger D. Blair, Jerry R. Jackson, and Ronald J. Vogel, "Economies of Scale in the Administration of Health Insurance," *Review of Economics and Statistics*, vol. 57 (May 1975), pp. 185–189.

[7] Joe S. Bain, *Barriers to New Competition: Their Character and Consequences in Manufacturing Industries* (Cambridge, Mass.: Harvard University Press, 1956), chap. 3.

criticized. Many scientists question the efficacy of using subjective question-naire responses to determine optimal plant size. Imagine the predicament that the manager of a plant must find himself in when asked to determine whether his plant is an inefficient size. How many managers would respond in the affirmative to such a question? Given that probably very few did, there would be a bias in Bain's results in the sense that optimal plant sizes would be esti-mated to cover a very large range of plants due to the biased response of questionnaire respondents. Additionally, Bain obtained cost figures via these questionnaires. All plant and firm cost figures are suspect because of differ-ences in definitions of cost and differences in the method of allocating common costs. Additionally, long-run positive economic rents may be capitalized into the cost structure.[8]

Another pioneer in the estimation of empirical cost function is Joel Dean, who estimated cost functions for a number of firms in various industries, in-cluding a hosiery mill and a leather belt shop. In a study of the leather belt industry, Dean found a positive linear relationship between the total cost mea-sured in dollars and the output measured in both thousands of square feet and pounds.[9] He also found a linear relationship in a study of the hosiery mill, where total costs were found to be a function of output and time.[10] Since those studies, a large number of researchers have attempted to estimate long-run average cost functions. Many of these studies are summarized in Johnston's important book, *Statistical Cost Analysis*.[11] In recent years interest in estimat-ing cost functions has reduced dramatically, probably because of the absence of the conditions Johnston identified as being critical to estimating a cost curve. These conditions include:

1 The absence of exogenous changes affecting production or cost functions, such as a change in technology over time

2 A significant level of variation representing different costs and output levels

3 Proper identification of costs and output levels

Engineering Studies   A number of researchers have performed engineering studies of scale economies based on technological relationships. We have al-ready pointed out that the volume of a container increases more in proportion than the amount of steel necessary to build a larger container. Moore has examined a number of such engineering technological relationships.[12] He found that a number of productive processes exhibited scale economies. Many of

---

[8] See Caleb A. Smith, "Survey of the Empirical Evidence on Economies of Scale," in George J. Stigler, ed., *Business Concentration and Price Policy* (Princeton: Princeton University Press, 1955), pp. 213–230.

[9] Joel Dean, "The Relation of Cost to Output for a Leather Belt Shop" (New York: National Bureau of Economic Research, 1941), Technical Paper No. 2.

[10] Dean, *Statistical Cost Functions of a Hosiery Mill* (Chicago: University of Chicago Press, 1941).

[11] Johnston, *Statistical Cost Analysis*.

[12] Frederick T. Moore, "Economies of Scale: Some Statistical Evidence," *Quarterly Journal of Economics*, vol. 73 (May 1959), pp. 232–245.

them seem to result from the engineer's "Point 6 Rule." That rule describes a physical relationship between volume and output, where the increase in cost of machine capacity will be equal to the increase in capacity raised to the .6 power, or:

$$C_1 = C_o \left(\frac{q_1}{q_0}\right)^{.6}$$

where q_0 = capacity of existing machine
q_1 = capacity of larger machine
C_0 = cost of running existing machine
C_1 = cost of running larger machine

The Point 6 Rule shows the relationship between the surface and volume of a machine. The volume increases more in proportion than the surface if the volume represents the output capacity and the surface represents the cost. The Point 6 Rule will be valid so long as those representations are relatively accurate.

We note that in Moore's study of the Point 6 Rule, a single machine rather than a large group of machines is considered. The study did not relate to the purchase of new machines, but rather to the increased size or capacity of an existing machine.

Several other individuals have looked at the Point 6 Rule in more detail. For example, Haldi and Whitcomb modified the rule and applied it to almost 700 pieces of industrial equipment. They found that almost 95 percent of the individual pieces were subject to increasing returns to scale.[13]

Stigler's Survivor Technique   One technique for determining the existence of scale economies involves an examination of the size distribution of firms (or plants) over time. This has been called the "survivor principle" by Stigler, who pointed out that Mill suggested the technique during the nineteenth century.[14] The **survivor technique** involves a relatively simple calculation of the industry share of output coming from each class of firm by size over time. Presumably, if the share of a given class falls, that firm size is relatively inefficient; the more rapidly the share of the given class falls, the more inefficient that size is. Stigler is quick to point out that the survivor technique does not determine the socially optimum size of an enterprise.[15] Rather, the technique looks at the meaning of efficiency from the viewpoint of the enterprise. It attempts to see which size class of enterprises most successfully faces government regulation, unstable foreign markets, rapid innovation, and strained labor relations, as well as more common market forces. The survivor technique,

[13] John Haldi and David Whitcomb, "Economies of Scale in Industrial Plants," *Journal of Political Economy*, vol. 75 (August 1967), pp. 373–385.

[14] John S. Mill, *Principles of Political Economy*, William J. Ashley, ed. (New York: Longmans Green, 1929), p. 134.

[15] George J. Stigler, "The Economies of Scale," *Journal of Law and Economics*, vol. 1 (October 1958), pp. 54–71.

according to Stigler, will supersede any technological studies on costs or rates of return. For example, if a technological study shows that the optimum size of the firm is one that produces 1,000 units per day, but most of the existing firms that are three times as large are expanding their share of the market, then 1,000 units per day cannot be the optimum size. The experience of survivorship will be the final judge of the existence of economies of scale.

Stigler's Empirical Results   Table 16-1 shows Stigler's empirical results on the distribution of output of steel ingot capacity by relative size of company. He found a declining share of industry's capacity in firms with less than one-half of a percent of total capacity. The implication is that those size firms were not subject to substantial economies of scale. Firms with one-half to two-and-one-half percent of the industry capacity showed a moderate decline. They were subject to greater economies of scale. The one firm with more than 25 percent of industry capacity declined moderately over the 22–year period under study. It was less subject to economies of scale. Those firms that had 2½ − 25 percent of industry capacity grew or held their share. Stigler concluded that they constituted the range of optimum size. He translated Table 16-1 into a long-run average cost curve for the production of steel ingots, which we reproduce in Figure 16-5. Stigler concluded that there is no evidence of net economies or diseconomies of scale over time. His other studies confirmed the example given here. The survivor technique, therefore, questioned the importance of economies of scale. The technique has been applied by other economists to other industries as well.[16]

---

[16] See, for example, Harry E. Frech and Paul B. Ginsburg, "Optimal Scale in Medical Practice: A Survivor Analysis," *Journal of Business*, vol. 47 (January 1974), pp. 23–36; Roger D. Blair and Ronald J. Vogel, "A Survivor Analysis of Commercial Health Insurers," *Journal of Business*, vol. 51 (July 1978), pp. 521–529; and D. K. Round, "Optimal Plant Size in Australian Manufacturing Industries," *Australian Economic Papers*, vol. 14 (June 1975), pp. 14–34.

TABLE 16-1
DISTRIBUTION OF OUTPUT OF STEEL INGOT CAPACITY
BY RELATIVE SIZE OF COMPANY

Company size (percent of industry total)	Percent of industry capacity			Number of companies		
	1930	1938	1951	1930	1938	1951
Under ½	7.16	6.11	4.65	39	29	22
½ to 1	5.94	5.08	5.37	9	7	7
1 to 2½	13.17	8.30	9.07	9	6	6
2½ to 5	10.64	16.59	22.21	3	4	5
5 to 10	11.18	14.03	8.12	2	2	1
10 to 25	13.24	13.99	16.10	1	1	1
25 and over	38.67	35.91	34.50	1	1	1

Sources: Directory of Iron and Steel Works of the United States and Canada, 1930, 1938; Iron Age (January 3, 1952), in George J. Stigler, "The Economies of Scale," Journal of Law and Economics, vol 1 (October 1958), p. 60.

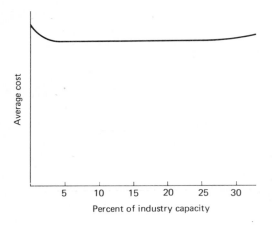

The relationship between average cost and firm size. [*Source:* George J. Stigler, *The Organization of Industry* (Homewood, Ill.: Richard D. Irwin, Inc., 1968), p. 76.]

Criticisms of the Survivor Technique A number of economists have criticized, some quite severely, the survivor technique.[17] For example, it has been pointed out that the underlying hypothesis of the survivor technique is that competition drives out inefficient firms. The characteristics of that competition are not very well specified, if at all. They could involve monopolization of inputs, predatory pricing, or any of a number of attempts to foreclose the market. But Stigler, as we pointed out above, explicitly stated he was measuring private, and not social, efficiency.

Another criticism is that the most efficient firms may be setting a high price umbrella in order to shelter the inefficient firms. The example of the post-World War I oil industry is given. In this case, the largest firms maintained a price umbrella over the market, allowing smaller, inefficient firms to survive. This may occur because of worries about potential antitrust investigations that might be triggered if a lower price were set that would drive out all the inefficient firms. In any case, if the price umbrella effect is at work, the survivor technique cannot discern which size firm is the most efficient, or optimum. Finally, the survivor technique has yielded conflicting estimates.

The Comanor and Wilson Measure Another method that has been used to determine scale economies which might act as an entry barrier is the "relative minimum-efficient scale" developed by Comanor and Wilson and modified by others.[18] The original measure was determined by taking the ratio of the average plant size of the largest plants representing half of the industry output to total output in the relevant market.[19] That method has been vigorously

[17] See, for example, William G. Shepherd, "What Does the Survivor Technique Show about Economies of Scale?" *Southern Economic Journal*, vol. 34 (July 1967), pp. 113–122.

[18] See Richard E. Caves, Javad Khalïlzadeh-Shirazi, and Michael Porter, "Scale Economies in Statistical Analyses of Market Power," *Review of Economics and Statistics*, vol. 57 (May 1975), pp. 133–140.

[19] William S. Comanor and Thomas A. Wilson, "Advertising Market Structure and Performance," *Review of Economics and Statistics*, vol. 49 (November 1967), pp. 423–440.

criticized in both its original and modified forms as poorly suited to the purpose for which it was designed.[20]

BARRIERS TO ENTRY

A concept often associated with economies of scale is barriers to entry. We define a **barrier to entry** as a production cost borne by firms seeking to enter an industry, but not borne by firms already in the industry. Barriers to entry are associated with monopoly power. For monopoly power to continue to exist in the long run, there must be some way in which the market is closed to entry. The conditions to entry tell us about potential rivals. Indeed, we can think of an industry's barriers to entry as being measured by the highest price that will just fail to tempt new firms into the industry. We present this measure of entry barriers in Figure 16-6. Here we show a monopolist with an average cost curve AC. In the short run, the profit-maximizing rate of output would be Q_1 sold at a price of P_1. Compare this to the competitive price P_c that would occur at the intersection of the marginal cost curve and the demand curve, which is also the minimum point on the average cost curve. If the potential entrant faced zero barriers to entry, then the monopolist would be forced to charge a price of P_c.[21] The degree to which barriers to entry exist can therefore be measured (ordinally) by the premium above the competitive price that the monopolist can charge in the long run. Thus, barriers to entry depend upon the elasticity of

---

[20] See Brian C. Brush, "On the Large-Scale Measurement of Plant Scale Economics," *Industrial Organization Review*, vol. 4 (1976), pp. 134–141.

[21] Paul A. Samuelson, *Foundations of Economic Analysis* (New York: Atheneum, 1965), p. 79.

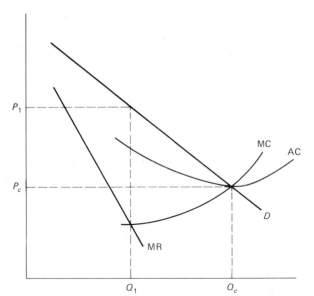

FIGURE 16-6
A measure of the degree of barriers to entry.

demand. If there are "absolute" barriers to entry, then the monopolist could charge P_1.

The presence or absence of entry barriers, then, might be tested indirectly by examining whether firms that earn supranormal profits maintain those profits.[22]

We now look at various potential sources of barriers to entry, including (1) substantial economies of scale, (2) capital requirements, (3) ownership of a vital resource, (4) patents and licensing, (5) advertising, (6) product differentiation and style changes, and (7) excess capacity.

Substantial Economies of Scale

Sometimes it is not profitable for more than one or two firms to exist in an industry.[23] This occurs when the industry demand curve's relation to the long-run average cost curve is such that several firms sharing the market cannot each individually cover average total costs. Only when one or two firms engage in the production of the product can they take advantage of the economies of scale and cover average total costs.

Consider the situation depicted in Figure 16-7. Here the industry demand curve is DD, and the long-run average total cost curve is LATC. Notice that average total costs are falling over a wide range of outputs. Indeed, over the entire range of output for which the average total cost curve lies below the

---

[22] See Dennis C. Mueller, "The Persistence of Profits above the Norm," *Economica*, vol. 44 (November 1977), pp. 369–380.

[23] Donald Dewey, "Industrial Concentration and the Rate of Profit: Some Neglected Theory," *Journal of Law and Economics*, vol. 19 (April 1976), pp. 67–78.

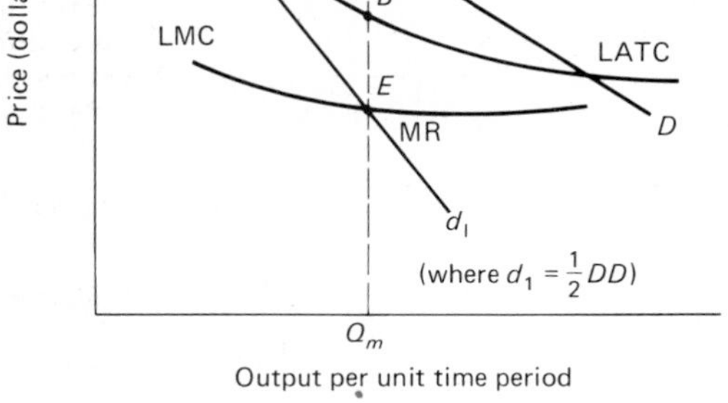

FIGURE 16-7
Economies of scale and monopoly. Assume that the industry demand curve is DD. A single monopolist has a long-run average total cost curve LATC. It produces where long-run marginal cost LMC intersects marginal revenue MR, or at point E, which is quantity Q_m. It can sell this quantity at price P_m. It makes a profit per unit of the vertical distance between points A and B. Now, if two firms enter the industry and each shares the market equally, each firm's demand curve would be equal to d_1, which is equal to $\frac{1}{2} DD$. d_1 coincides with the original marginal revenue curve facing the monopolist. However, with two firms in the industry, each would suffer economic losses because the average total cost curve ATC is everywhere above the proportionate demand curve facing each of the two firms in that industry. Only one firm will survive.

industry demand curve, average total costs are falling. One firm can success-fully operate in this industry at a rate of output of Q_m and make a profit per unit equal to the vertical distance between points A and B. The profit-maximizing output rate Q_m is determined by the intersection of the monopolist's marginal cost curve LMC and its marginal revenue curve MR. That intersection occurs at point E. Now consider what would happen if the industry were split evenly between firm 1 and firm 2. Each firm's demand curve would look like the demand curve d_1.[24] (Demand curve d_1 is identical to the single monopolist's marginal revenue curve MR.) Notice that the duopolist's demand curve, or average revenue curve, is always below the average total cost curve. It would not be profitable for even a second firm to enter this industry and share the sales. Thus, we have a situation where economies of scale are so great that the long-run average total cost curve falls over such a large range that only one firm can successfully exist in this market. This is called the natural monopoly, which we have already discussed on page 366.

Empirical Evidence Several researchers have estimated the barriers to entry due to scale economies in selected American industries.[25] We reproduce some of their results in Table 16-2. The first column gives us the industry, the second column is the output of the most efficient firm as a percentage of na-tional market, and the third column gives cost disadvantage of a plant that is one-half the optimum size firm. Their results take into account the economies of operating more than one plant under the ownership of a single enterprise. In the aircraft, rubber, and cement industries, the cost advantage due to economies of scale seems "significant."

Criticisms of the Argument Some economists criticize the argument that economies of scale represent a barrier to entry. Stigler, for example, uses a definition of a barrier to entry that deals with a cost of potential entrants not borne by firms already in the industry. Thus, the expansion of output by exist-ing firms does not constitute entry using Stigler's framework. Consequently, when discussing the example presented in Figure 16-7, showing how only one firm can exist in a declining cost industry, Stigler responds,

> Some economists will say that the economies of scale are a barrier to entry, meaning that such economies explain why no additional firms enter. It would be equally possible to say that inadequate demand is a barrier to entry. If we define a barrier as a differentially higher cost of new firms, there is no barrier and the firm size is governed by economies of scale and demand conditions.[26]

In other words, Stigler believes that economies of scale do not cause a

---

[24] They both have identical price elasticities of demand at any given price because they intersect the vertical axis at the same point.

[25] See Bain, *Barriers to New Competition: Their Character and Consequences in Manufactur-ing Industries*, pp. 80 and 86, for an earlier classification of scale economies as barriers to entry.

[26] George J. Stigler, *The Organization of Industry* (Homewood, Ill.: Irwin, 1968), p. 67.

TABLE 16-2
MINIMUM-EFFICIENT SCALE PLANTS, COSTS OF
SUBOPTIMAL PLANTS, 1967

Industry	MES as a percentage of U.S. 1967 output	Increase in unit cost at 1/2 MES (%)
Refrigerators	13.0	7
Home laundry equipment	11.2	8
Manufactured fiber	11.1	5
Aircraft (commercial)	10.0	20
Synthetic rubber	7.2	15
Cigarettes	6.6	2.2
Transformers	4.9	7.9
Paperboard	4.4	8
Tires and inner tubes	3.8	5
Blast furnaces and steel	2.7	10
Detergents	2.4	2.5
Storage batteries	1.9	4.6
Petroleum refining	1.8	4.0
Cement	1.7	13
Glass containers	1.5	11
Ball and roller bearings	1.4	8
Paints, varnishes	1.4	4.4
Beer	1.1	10
Flour mills	0.7	3
Machine tools	0.3	5
Cotton textiles	0.2	5
Shoes	0.2	1.5

Sources: F. M. Scherer et al., *The Economics of Multi-Plant Operation* (Cambridge, Mass.: Harvard University Press, 1975), chap. 3; C. F. Pratton, *Economies of Scale in Manufacturing Industries* (New York: Cambridge University Press, 1971); and L. W. Weiss, "Optimal Plant Size and the Extent of Suboptimal Capacity," in R. T. Masson and P. D. Qualls, eds., *Essays on Industrial Organization in Honor of Joe S. Bain* (Cambridge, Mass.: Ballinger, 1976), pp. 123–141.

barrier of entry because the existing firm (or firms) faces exactly the same cost conditions as any potential firm. Scale economies are equally available to all firms and therefore, according to Stigler, they are not a barrier to entry of new firms.

Bain disagrees. He asks a much more pragmatic question, "Do existing economies of scale deter the entry of new firms into the market?" If economies of scale do deter entry, then they are a barrier to entry. Stigler contends merely that economies of scale determine firm size rather than act as barriers to entry.

Capital Requirements

It is often contended that certain industries require a large initial capital investment and that the firms already in the industry can obtain monopoly profits in the long run because no competitors can raise the large amount of capital needed to enter the industry. This is the so-called imperfect capital market argument employed to explain long-run, relatively high rates of return in certain industries where large fixed costs must be incurred in order to start production. These fixed costs generally are for expensive machines necessary in the production process.

Certainly, it is more difficult for any given level of risk to raise a larger amount of capital than a smaller amount of capital. But a sufficiently high-risk premium can presumably be added to the anticipated rate of return from investing in the risky industry to enable a newcomer to raise the needed capital. It may be, of course, that the anticipated rate of return offered to investors in such an industry would have to be so high that it would not be profitable for an entrepreneur to undertake entry into the industry. It is not clear why such a situation is called an imperfect capital market or why it should be considered a barrier to entry any more than any other higher-risk venture, but it often is.

Moreover, one must realize that it is not necessary to purchase all the capital equipment required to enter an industry. Equipment can be leased, and numerous parts of the commodity to be sold can be purchased from outside suppliers. A few years ago, the Bricklin two-seater sports car venture did just that. Many of the components of the automobile were purchased from other automobile manufacturers. The company ultimately went into receivership after only a few thousand Bricklins were sold. Nonetheless, it had been able to raise sufficient amounts of capital to enter the industry but, as it turned out, not enough to sustain the initial production year's losses.

The Debate Again Stigler defines a barrier to entry as a cost differential applying to firms outside the industry. He claims that capital requirements are

TABLE 16-3
THE 500 LARGEST INDUSTRIAL CORPORATIONS, 1979

Company	Assets		
	($000)	Rank	Sales Rank
Exxon (New York)	$49,489,964	1	1
General Motors (Detroit)	32,215,800	2	2
Mobil (New York)	27,505,756	3	3
International Business Machines (Armonk, N.Y.)	24,529,974	4	8
Ford Motor (Dearborn, Mich.)	23,524,600	5	4
Texaco (Harrison, N.Y.)	22,991,955	6	5
Standard Oil of California (San Francisco)	18,102,632	7	6
Gulf Oil (Pittsburgh)	17,265,500	8	7
Standard Oil (Indiana and Chicago)	17,149,899	9	10
General Electric (Fairfield, Conn.)	16,644,500	10	9

Source: Fortune (May 5, 1980), p. 299.

TABLE 16-4
CLASSIFICATION OF INDUSTRIES ACCORDING TO CAPITAL REQUIREMENTS FOR A SINGLE OPTIMAL PLANT, AND RELATED INFORMATION

(1) Industry	(2) Capital requirement for one plant of minimum optimal scale (millions of dollars)	(3) Percentage of largest submarket supplied by one optimal plant	(4) Estimated shape of plant scale curve at suboptimal scales	(5) Existence of production economies of multiplant firms	(6) Incidence of economies of large-scale sales promotion
I. Industries with very large capital requirements per plant (generally above $100 million)					
Steel	265–665‡	2½–6¼	Moderately sloped	Yes	Negligible
Automobiles	250–500*	10–20	Moderately sloped	No estimate	Promotional economies up to size of optimal plant
Petroleum refining	225–250†	4⅓	Relatively flat	No	Promotional economies up to size of optimal plant
Tractors	125	10–15	Relatively flat	No estimate	Promotional economies up to size of optimal plant
Cigarettes	125–150	5–6	Relatively flat	Yes	Promotional economies of multiplant firms possible
II. Industries with large capital requirements per plant (generally $10 to $50 million)					
Rayon	50–75‡ 90–135§	4–6	Relatively steep	No estimate	Negligible
Liquor	30–25	1¼–1¾	Relatively flat	No estimate	Promotional economies of multiplant firms possible
Cement	20–25	4–5	Relatively steep	Yes	Negligible
Tires and tubes	15–30	1⅜–2¾	Moderately sloped	No estimate	Promotional economies of multiplant firms possible
Soap	13–20¶	4–6	Moderately sloped	No	Promotional economies of multiplant firms possible
Meat packing (diversified)	10–20	8–10	Relatively flat		Negligible

III. Industries with moderate capital requirements per plant (generally $2.5 to $10 million)

Industry					
Fountain pens	6	10–15	No estimate	No	Promotional economies up to size of optimal plant for "quality" pens
Metal containers	5–20	2–12	No estimate	No estimate	Promotional economies of multiplant firms possible
Gypsum products	4–6	8–12	No estimate	Yes	Negligible
Canned fruits and vegetables	2½–3	2½–5	Moderately sloped	No	Negligible for standard items; multiplant economies for specialties

IV. Industries with small capital requirements per plant (generally under $2 million)

Industry					
Flour	$7/10$–3½	$1/3$–1½	No estimate	No estimate	Negligible for promotional economies for commercial and private-label sales; multiplant economies for miller's-brand sales
Shoes	½–2	$3/5$–1$1/5$	Moderately sloped	Yes	Negligible for most lines; multiplant economies for high-priced men's or specialties
Meat packing (fresh)	Under 1	$1/10$	Relatively flat	No	Negligible

V. Nonclassified industries (capital requirements not estimated)

Industry					
Typewriters	No estimate	10–30	Relatively steep	No	Promotional economies up to size of optimal plant
Farm machinery	No estimate	4–8	Moderately sloped	No estimate	Promotional economies of multiplant firms probable
Copper	No estimate	10	No estimate	No	Negligible

*Supposes integration of bodies and engines, but not of maximum range of components.
†Includes crude-oil transport facilities (average requirement).
‡Acetate rayon.
§Viscose rayon.
¶Excludes working capital.
Source: Reprinted by permission of the publishers from Joe S. Bain, *Barriers to New Competition* (Cambridge, Mass.: Harvard University Press, 1956).

therefore not a barrier to entry since existing firms had to meet those requirements. They are a determinant of economies of scale—the shape of the long-
run average cost curve. Bain and others point out simply that the higher the
capital requirement is, the fewer the number of truly qualified entrepreneurs
who can obtain the needed amount of capital will be. The amount of capital in
terms of assets is sometimes phenomenal. We look at the 10 highest-ranked
companies in terms of total assets from the Fortune 500 list for 1979 in Table
16-3 on page 377. Firms with the largest sales volume also tend to have the
largest assets. In other words, the size of the firm is positively correlated with
its assets. It is, according to Bain and others, these large capital requirements
that discourage entry of new firms.

Empirical Estimates   Bain used questionnaire data to obtain an estimate of
what he considered to be a capital requirements barrier in 20 manufacturing
markets.[27] Table 16-4 is a summary of his results. He found that capital requirements barriers were the highest in cigarettes, automobiles, steel, petroleum refining, and tractor production.[28] We note, however, that using the survivor technique elicits different results. The range of optimal-size plants and
firms in terms of the amount of capital required is usually estimated at only a
fraction of Bain's estimated capital requirement for an optimal-size plant or
firm.

Some researchers have attempted to show a positive correlation between the
size of minimum capital requirements and industry profit rates. Hall and Weiss,
for example, concluded that firm profit rates were about 20 percent higher in
markets where the minimum optimal size of the plant required about $500
million worth of capital.[29] Koch and Fenili found that average profit margins
(markups) were strongly correlated with the capital intensity of the market
studied.[30]

Ownership of a Vital Resource without Close Substitutes

Preventing a newcomer from entering an industry is often difficult. Indeed,
some economists contend that no monopoly acting without government support has been able to prevent entry into the industry unless that monopoly had
the control of some "essential" natural resource. Consider the possibility of
one firm owning the entire supply of raw material essential in the production of
a particular commodity. The exclusive ownership of a vital resource serves as a
barrier to entry until an alternative source of, or substitute for, the raw material

[27] Bain, *Barriers to New Competition*.
[28] Ibid., pp. 158–159.
[29] Marshall Hall and Leonard Weiss, "Firm Size and Profitability," *Review of Economics and Statistics*, vol. 49 (August 1967), pp. 319–331.
[30] James V. Koch and Robert N. Fenili, "The Influence of Industry Market Structure upon Industry Price-Cost Margins," *Rivista Internazionale di Scienze Economiche e Commerciali*, vol. 18 (November 1971), pp. 1037–1045.

is found or an alternative technology not requiring the raw material in question is developed.[31]

The resource essential for the successful production process need not be a raw material; it can be a person such as a manager. A manager with a superior talent for directing a firm may enable the firm to obtain long-run monopoly profits. The monopoly, however, is not in the selling of the commodity, but rather in the possession by the manager of the superior talents. The manager will be paid according to his or her superior ability. Further, if someone were to take over that firm without the services of that manager, no more than the normal rate of return would be available.

A Case History—The Aluminum Company of America   A case in which a monopoly was maintained because a firm owned an essential raw material is found in the history of the Aluminum Company of America (Alcoa). Alcoa was the sole manufacturer of aluminum ingots in the United States from the late nineteenth century until World War II. The monopoly position of the firm was at first maintained by the many patents that it had obtained for the different phases of the aluminum ingot production process. For example, the first person who discovered a process by which oxygen could be eliminated from bauxite assigned the patent to Alcoa. However, this patent expired on April 2, 1906. Another process was invented that permitted smelting to be carried on without the use of external heat. This patent was assigned to Alcoa in 1903 but expired on February 2, 1909. Essentially, Alcoa held either a monopoly on the manufacture of virgin aluminum ingot or a monopoly on the cheapest production process, eliminating all competition. After 1909, one of the major ways in which Alcoa kept its monopoly position was by cornering sources of the raw material bauxite. It signed long-term contracts with the companies owning rights to bauxite; the contracts specified that those companies could not sell the essential ore to any other company. As early as 1895, Alcoa obtained electric energy from three power companies and signed contracts with each of them prohibiting these companies from selling or leasing power to anyone else for the manufacture of aluminum. Unfortunately for Alcoa, in 1912 the courts invalidated these agreements.

In order to maintain its market position in the industry after 1912, Alcoa expanded its productive capacity as fast as necessary to meet the increase in demand at the going price for aluminum. In its defense against an antitrust suit, Alcoa contended that its dominance in the "virgin" ingot market in the United States did not give it a monopoly in that market. Alcoa claimed that it was subject to the competition of the imported virgin ingot market and to the competition of the secondary ingot market, which is scrap aluminum. Since aluminum does not deteriorate very quickly, over time the supply of secondary

---

[31] For a theory of how a cartel should price an *exhaustible* natural resource, see Robert S. Pindyck, "Gains to Producers from the Cartelization of Exhaustible Resources," *Review of Economics and Statistics*, vol. 60 (May 1978), pp. 238–251.

aluminum will become sufficiently large to provide competition for virgin aluminum, Alcoa contended. The Court rejected this analysis.[32]

Control over a Scarce Resource, Vertical Integration, and Capital Requirements One could consider control over a vital resource a special case in the larger problem of vertical integration and entry barriers. Consider the more general case where there are two stages of production. Firm 1 has neither complete control over the primary stage nor the secondary stage in which the primary stage involves an essential raw material. One firm or a number of firms become fully integrated. If the integrated firms control the entire stage 1 output and refuse to sell to a new entrant at stage 2, then the unintegrated entrant at stage 2 will be compelled to begin operations at both stages. Thus, the new entrant is faced with an increase in the capital requirements for double-stage entry as compared to single-stage entry. If one believes that increased capital requirements increase barriers to entry, then backward vertical integration (and forward, too) can be said to lead to increased barriers to entry.

Licenses and Patents

It is illegal to enter many industries without a government-provided license, a "certificate of convenience and public necessity." Specifically, you could not form an electrical utility to compete with the electrical utility already operating in your area without first obtaining a certificate of convenience and public necessity from the appropriate authority, which is usually the state's public utility commission. However, public utility commissions rarely, if ever, issue a certificate to a group of investors who want to compete directly in the same geographic area with an existing electrical utility. Hence, entry into the industry in a particular geographic area is prohibited, and long-run monopoly profits could conceivably be earned by the electrical utility already serving the area.

In order to enter interstate (and also many intrastate) markets for pipelines, airlines, trucking, television and radio signals, the production of natural gas, and so on, it is necessary to obtain the equivalent of a certificate of convenience and public necessity. Since these franchises or licenses aren't given very often, long-run monopoly profits might be earned by those firms already in the industry. The logic behind issuing few certificates of convenience has to do with supposed large economies of scale in the industries where certificates are required. Allowing a large number of firms to compete would, it is reasoned, prevent consumers from benefiting from one firm's being able to sell a large output with significantly reduced average costs.

Patents Closely related to the franchise required for entry is a patent. A patent is issued to an inventor to protect him or her from having the invention copied for a period of 17 years. Suppose I discover a new film for super-8 movie

---

[32] *United States v. Aluminum Co. of America et al.*, 148 F. 2d 416 (1945). For a recent examination of the effects of secondary aluminum on price, see Peter Swan, "Alcoa: The Influence of Recycling on Monopoly Power," *Journal of Political Economy*, vol. 88 (February 1980), pp. 76–99.

cameras that develops itself instantaneously so that the roll is ready for projection as soon as it is exposed. If I am successful (or my attorneys are) in obtaining a patent on this discovery, I can prevent other individuals from copying me. Note, however, that I must expend resources to prevent them from imitating me even if I do have a watertight patent. Many resources are devoted to enforcing the exclusive right of patent owners. Indeed, I can have a patent on a particular commodity or production process and end up having no monopoly profits at all, because the costs of policing are so high that I don't bother to protect my patent or, if I do, I end up spending so much on policing costs that I eat up all my monopoly profits.

It is contended that patents are necessary for defining and enforcing property rights in ideas. However, there is little theoretical justification for a patent to extend to precisely 17 years. Why not 10, 20, or 50 years, or infinity? Economists don't have any generally accepted answers. There is a trade-off involved when the patent extends longer than 17 years. The longer an individual can anticipate having a property right or monopoly in a specific invention, the more resources will presumably go into inventing patentable items or patentable substitutes. However, the longer a patent exists, the longer the monopoly exists and presumably the longer the price will remain at a monopoly level rather than a competitive one. To find the socially optimal length of a patent, we must weigh the benefits of inducing more research and creative efforts into patentable products against the higher price tags that those products will carry during the greater length of the patent. Some economists believe that the optimal length of patent rights should be 0 years!

Advertising, Trademarks, and Promotional Expenses

We have already discussed advertising and product differentiation, along with trademarks and brand names, in Chapter 9. Some have argued that all are sources of barriers to entry.

Advertising   Because advertising is subject to economies of scale, it represents a capital cost and has long-lasting effects. Some argue that advertising deters entry.[33] For example, Palda argues that the effects of advertising are lagged and carry over several periods.[34] Because it may take several ads before a purchaser is persuaded to buy, current period advertising may not be directly linked to increased current sales.

In early 1972, the Federal Trade Commission argued that excessive advertising expenditures by the major manufacturers of ready-to-eat cereals created high barriers to the entry of new firms, resulting in prices that were 20 to 25 percent above the competitive levels. The commission argued that the four

---

[33] William S. Comanor and Thomas A. Wilson, "Advertising Market Structure and Performance," in *Advertising and Market Power* (Cambridge, Mass.: Harvard University Press, 1974), chap. 4.

[34] Kristian S. Palda, *The Measurement of Cumulative Advertising Effects* (Englewood Cliffs, N.J.: Prentice-Hall, 1964).

largest cereal producers were participants in a "shared monopoly" and filed an antitrust suit against them in April 1972.[35] The shared monopoly concept is novel and may have implications for other manufacturing industries. Although the FTC's theory has changed over time, each theory has been identified with a concept of shared monopoly. Despite the fact that the case has not yet been decided, it has been subject to numerous criticisms.[36]

Product Differentiation and Brand Names   Product differentiation, particularly through the establishment of name brands, is sometimes said to lead to barriers to entry. Even after doing the necessary research and development to establish a new product, potential entrants must convince people that their product is as good or better than existing brand name products. It appears, then, that the newcomer has to spend more on advertising and sales promotion than existing firms, causing its average selling cost per unit sold to be higher at all sales rates than the existing firms' are. It can be argued, therefore, that more capital is necessary to start the firm because of these increased advertising costs. Thus, if capital requirements are a problem, the problem will be exacerbated and a barrier to entry will be raised.[37]

Empirical Evidence   Many studies relate advertising expenditures to profit rates, but very few actually relate advertising to entry barriers.[38] We do not know whether the purported positive correlation between advertising intensity and profitability is attributed to advertising as entry barrier or, rather, to the incorrect measurement of both profitability and advertising expenditures.[39]

Style Changes

Firms attempt to influence the position of the demand curve for their products by style changes. Some researchers further argue that the use of style changes has been aimed at foreclosing the market.[40]

[35] Federal Trade Commission Docket No. 8883, April 26, 1972. For an analysis of this case see Richard L. Schmalensee, "Entry Deterrence in the Ready-to-Eat Breakfast Cereal Industry," *Bell Journal of Economics*, vol. 9 (Autumn 1978), pp. 305–327.

[36] See, for example, Walter Kiechel, III, "The Soggy Case against the Cereal Industry," *Fortune*, vol. 97 (April 10, 1978), pp. 49–51.

[37] See Oliver E. Williamson, "Selling Expense or a Barrier to Entry," *Quarterly Journal of Economics*, vol. 77 (February 1963), pp. 112–128, and also Dennis C. Mueller and John E. Tilton, "Research & Development Costs as a Barrier to Entry," *Canadian Journal of Economics*, vol. 2 (November 1969), pp. 570–579.

[38] However, at least one study claims to demonstrate empirically that advertising expenditures are correlated with reduced amounts of entry. See Larry L. Duetsch, "Structure, Performance, and the Net Rate of Entry into Manufacturing Industries," *Southern Economic Journal*, vol. 41 (January 1975), pp. 450–456.

[39] See pp. 97–103.

[40] See Stephen E. Selander, "Is Annual Style Change in the Automobile Industry an Unfair Method of Competition? A Rebuttal," *Yale Law Journal*, vol. 82 (March 1973), pp. 691–710; Bradford C. Snell, "Annual Style Change in the Automobile Industry as an Unfair Method of Competition," *Yale Law Journal*, vol. 80 (1971), pp. 567–613; "Reply," *Yale Law Journal*, vol. 82 (March 1973), pp. 711–715; and John A. Menge, "Style Change Costs as a Market Weapon," *Quarterly Journal of Economics*, vol. 76 (November 1962), pp. 632–647.

Basically, the argument is as follows: There is a minimum level of durability for a particular type of "fixed" input into many production processes. An automobile manufacturer's dies necessary for body-stamping machines must be made of certain minimum quality, but this minimum quality may be sufficient for half a million bodies. Thus, a die will last a certain physical life, that is, a certain number of stampings. A firm that produces many millions of cars will use the dies up more often than a smaller firm whose output may not even use the die up completely in the first instance. A large firm can replace dies with those embodying a new style. If the smaller firm attempts to do likewise, the die cost per automobile will be higher for those firms producing at smaller rates of output. In other words, the style change will be more expensive for the smaller firm. In principle, therefore, accelerated style changes will drive small firms from the industry.

For this argument to have any validity, smaller firms must have to follow suit in order to remain competitive in the industry. The long-lasting success of certain European imports such as the Volkswagen Beetle gives some evidence to the contrary, that is, not all cars have to change body styles every one, two, or three years in order to remain competitive.

Excess Capacity

Excess capacity in an industry can sometimes be an effective barrier to the entry of new firms. Assume that there are a large number of firms making, for example, quadrophonic high-fidelity equipment. Rave reviews have come out telling all who are interested about the virtues of switching from stereo to "quad." The existing number of firms start tooling up for an anticipated boom in the quad industry. They purchase new plants, buy new machinery to make components, and generally expand in all dimensions. A year later, however, the public has not reacted with as much enthusiasm as was originally anticipated. The rate of sales of quad equipment is not what the firms expected it would be. Everyone in the industry is faced with excess capacity, since no one finds it profitable to continue the high rates of production used in the past.

Now all firms in the industry are in a position to cut price dramatically should would-be competitors attempt to enter the industry. The existing firms are sitting with large amounts of capital equipment specialized to the product that they are selling. Much of that capital equipment represents a sunk cost. The existing firms are therefore in a position to lower prices to meet any and all new competition. Thus, they can effectively keep out new entrants for some time.

Limit Pricing as a Barrier to Entry

A model in which existing firms in the industry set prices in an attempt to discourage or prevent entry is called a **limit-pricing oligopoly model**. In all such models, the industry firms set prices so as to maximize the present value of their profit stream by retarding the entry of new firms; thus, a price is chosen that still allows some monopoly profits but not enough to attract new entrants.

The firm contemplating entry into a new market has to consider at least two possibilities: (1) entry will depress the market price if existing firms maintain their outputs, and (2) if the new firm contracts its output so as to reduce the price depression caused by its additional output, then this new firm may encounter higher average costs if it moves leftward and up its long-run average cost curve.

In Figure 16-8, we draw a hypothetical long-run average cost curve LAC and assume it is the same for all firms. The industry price is set at P_1; each firm's output is q_1. Assume further that existing firms will attempt to maintain that rate of output even with entry. Now consider the possibility that a new firm enters. According to the law of demand, price must fall if this additional output is to be sold. Its additional output causes price to fall from P_1 to P_2. Clearly, all firms will now have losses that are equal to the distance between the long-run average cost curve LAC and the price P_2, or the distance between E and F in Figure 16-8.

Now we know that the price-depressing effect of a new firm is directly related to its rate of output. If it reduces its rate of output, there will be a smaller reduction in the market price, but the firm will still suffer losses. Consider the possibility of the new entrant reducing output from q_1 to q_2. The market price will now fall only to P_3 rather than P_2. However, the new firm will not be able to enjoy the lower per-unit cost that the existing firms already enjoy, because they will continue to produce at the same rate. The new firm's cost will rise to G. It will make a loss per unit of output equal to the vertical difference between G and H. Other firms will incur a smaller loss per unit of output.

In this simplified example, any rate of output that a new entrant can produce

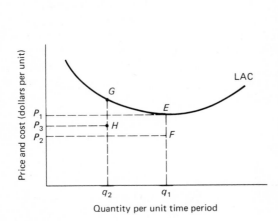

FIGURE 16-8
Pricing and entry. Assume that each existing firm produces at output rate q_1, and that each firm enjoys such cost advantages of large-scale production so that their average total costs are equal to q_1E. Assume that price is P_1. If one firm enters with the same lowest-cost scale of operations and all other firms maintain their rate of output, the price will fall perhaps to P_2. Each firm that was in the industry will now suffer losses per unit of output equal to the vertical distance between E and F. If, on the other hand, the entering firm does not attempt to produce as much as the other firms, but adopts the scale of production q_2, price will fall less, perhaps to P_3. The firms already in the industry will have smaller losses; but, the entering firm will not be able to enjoy minimum average costs. It will suffer a greater loss, equal to the vertical distance between point H and point G.

will cause the market price to drop below the new entrant's long-run average cost. Entry is said to be blocked. If existing firms realize this, they may choose to raise prices above their long-run average cost. The degree to which they can raise their price above their minimum long-run average cost per unit depends on (1) the cost disadvantage the entrant realizes if it enters at a scale where LAC per unit is greater than that experienced by the existing firms, and (2) the price-depressing effect caused by the new entrant's output.[41]

Sylos Postulate

The theory on entry is often based on an assumption that potential entrants act as if they expected existing establishments to maintain their output at the pre-entry level. This assumption has been referred to as the **Sylos postulate**.[42] The Sylos postulate is similar to Cournot's assumption that firms expect rivals to maintain their output at an unchanged level (see page 138). Given the Sylos postulate, any potential entrant is confronted by a sloping demand curve, which is only that part of the industry demand curve left after the existing firms have produced their pre-entry quantity. The potential entrant decides whether to enter the industry by comparing that segment of the industry demand curve that is left to him with his own cost conditions. Entry will occur only if the price established in the industry exceeds the average total cost in existing firms by more than the difference in average total cost between the potential entrants and the existing firms. Assuming that entry occurs, under the Sylos postulate established firms will have to lower price to maintain existing quantity sold. In this model, the greater the difference is in absolute cost of existing firms in the industry and that of the potential entrant, the greater will be the amount by which industry price can reasonably exceed average costs of existing firms without inducing entry. Indeed, the difference is a measure of so-called absolute cost entry barriers given the Sylos postulate.

If we complicate the model slightly by introducing scale economies, the size of the market will determine how much price will be greater than average costs without inducing entries, again given the Sylos postulate. Additionally, we have to look at the price elasticity of industry demand, the rate of output at which economies of scale are exhausted.

Under the Sylos postulate, the optimal level of a potential producer's output is related to the pre-entry price and output policy of the existing firms in the industry. The greater the excess of the pre-entry price over the entry-deterring price is, the greater will be the scale of entry.

---

[41] See Joe S. Bain, ''Pricing in Monopoly and Oligopoly,'' *American Economic Review*, vol. 39 (March 1949), pp. 448–464. Also see Darius W. Gaskins, Jr., ''Dynamic Limit Pricing: Optimal Pricing under Threat of Entry,'' *Journal of Economic Theory*, vol. 3 (September 1971), pp. 306–322; and A. Michael Spence,''Entry, Capacity, Investment and Oligopolistic Pricing, '' *Bell Journal of Economics*, vol. 8 (Autumn 1977), pp. 534–544.

[42] Paolo Sylos-Labini, *Oligopoly and Technical Progress* (Cambridge, Mass.: Harvard University Press, 1969).

Criticisms   A number of researchers, including Wenders, Pashigian, Osborne, and Stigler, have criticized the above theory quite severely.[43] It is clear that the shape of the long-run average cost curve facing the typical or representative firm is of crucial importance in a limit-pricing model. If the typical firm faces a long-run average cost curve that declines only briefly and is flat thereafter, the scale economies barrier is going to be minimal because there is little cost disadvantage to any entrant. This constitutes a significant scale economies barrier in the eyes of the entry limit-pricing theorist.

One also might wish to question the collusive nature of the oligopolisitc industry. The amount of collusion necessary for a limit entry-pricing model seems more than is often observed in American industries. It is not surprising that the empirical evidence used to test entry limit-pricing models is sparse.[44]

Wenders has also demonstrated that the assumption of output maintenance when entry occurs is not consistent with a profit-maximization strategy.[45] A further criticism involves an implication arising from a constant long-run average cost curve. If there are constant average costs beyond the minimum output, why doesn't pure monopoly occur? One firm could have practiced limiting-entry pricing from the very beginning, eliminating the possibility of any entry at all. In other words, why do we find oligopoly instead of pure monopoly? Finally, why should a potential entrant believe the threat?

REGULATION AS A BARRIER TO ENTRY

Recently we have seen increasing amounts and forms of government regulation in the American economy. The forms in which we are interested concern safety and quality regulation. For example, pharmaceutical quality control regulation administered by the Food and Drug Administration may require that each pharmaceutical company install a $2 million computer/testing machine that requires elaborate monitoring and maintenance because of its complex nature. Presumably, this large fixed cost can be allocated over a larger number of units of output by larger firms than by smaller firms, thereby putting the smaller firm at a competitive disadvantage. It will also deter entry to the extent that the scale of operation of a potential entrant must be sufficiently large to cover the fixed costs of the piece of testing equipment. We refer the reader to Chapter 20 for a more detailed look at regulation.

---

[43] John T. Wenders, "Collusion and Entry," *Journal of Political Economy*, vol. 79 (November/December 1971), pp. 1258–1277; B. Peter Pashigian, "Limit Price and the Market Share of the Leading Firm," *Journal of Industrial Economics*, vol. 16 (July 1968), pp. 165–177; Dale K. Osborne, "The Role of Entry in Oligopoly Theory," *Journal of Political Economy*, vol. 72 (August 1964), pp. 396–402; and George J. Stigler, *The Organization of Industry*, pp. 67–70.

[44] But see Roger D. Blackwell, "Price Levels in the Funeral Industry," *Quarterly Review of Economics and Business*, vol. 7 (Winter 1967), pp. 75–84; and Bernard J. McCarney, "Oligopoly Theory and Intermodel Transport Price Competition: Some Empirical Findings," *Land Economics*, vol. 46 (November 1970), pp. 474–478.

[45] John T. Wenders, "Collusion and Entry."

CHAPTER 17

TECHNOLOGICAL INNOVATION, PATENTS, AND COPYRIGHTS

This chapter deals with technological change, patents, and copyrights and with their effects on market structure.

A MICROECONOMIC REVIEW OF TECHNOLOGICAL CHANGE

Technological change consists of discovering alternative methods of producing old products, developing alternative products, and introducing techniques of marketing, organization, and management. Technological change is synonymous with a change in the production function. (In this section, we are assuming that factor prices remain constant.) Technological change is motivated by the desire either to produce the same quantity at a lower average cost through changes in production methods or to introduce new products. We can examine technological change by using the isoquant technique that we have used already. The examination will involve three types of technological change: neutral, labor-saving, and capital-saving.

Neutral Technological Change

An improvement in technology that allows for the production of the same amount of output as before, but permits proportionate reductions in both capital and labor inputs is termed **neutral technological change**. Panel (*a*) in Figure 17-1 depicts a situation of neutral technological change. We start off on the isoquant labeled $Q = 1$. The rate of output per unit time period is 1. As a result of technological change to obtain the same output, we now have to use less of both labor and capital. We move from the isoquant labeled $Q = 1$ to the lower

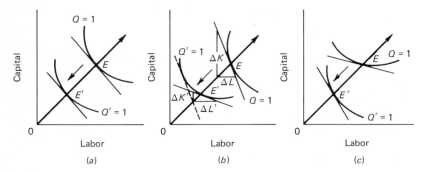

Figure 17-1
Technological change. In panel (a), we show neutral technological change. Output
equal to 1 can be attained using less capital and less labor. This is shown by
movement from isoquant Q to isoquant Q', both of which have an output rate equal
to 1. The reduction in capital and labor is proportionate as we move from point E to
point E'. In panel (b) we show labor-saving technological change. There is a
movement similar to the one in panel (a) from isoquant Q = 1 to isoquant Q' = 1;
however, with constant factor prices, the firm would not stay at point E' because at
that point $\Delta K/\Delta L$ = MPP$_K$/MPP$_L$ is no longer equal to the ratio of the price of capital to the price of labor. The firm would have to use more capital and less labor. In
panel (c), we show a capital-saving technological change.

isoquant labeled $Q' = 1$. The tangency along a particular ray drawn from the
origin, which has the same slope as the rays drawn from the origin in panels (b)
and (c), is given at points E and E'. The slope of the tangents along that ray is
equal. The marginal rate of technical substitution (MRTS) is constant before
and after technological change. The ratio of the marginal physical product of
labor and the marginal physical product of capital have not changed since
MRTS = MPP$_L$/MPP$_K$. Because the technological change does not induce the
firm to change the capital-labor ratio, it is considered neutral. The ratio of the
marginal physical products and the marginal rate of technical substitution have
not changed.

Labor-Saving Technological Change

Panel (b) in Figure 17-1 represents **labor-saving technological change**, which
occurs when less labor is used per unit of output than before. The original
position is given by the isoquant labeled $Q = 1$, where output is at the rate of 1
per unit time period. Now technological change takes place. The isoquant shifts
downward so that an output of 1 per unit time period can be obtained with less
labor and less capital. However, there is a difference between what has happened in this situation and what happened in the previous situation. Look at the
respective slopes of the tangents drawn at point E and point E'. The slope is
much steeper at point E than it is at point E'. This means that for any given ratio
of capital to labor, such as the one represented along the line drawn from the
origin in panel (b), the marginal rate of technical substitution has changed; or

otherwise stated, the ratio of the marginal physical product of labor to the marginal physical product of capital has changed. In fact, in this situation it is clear that the marginal physical product of capital has risen relative to the marginal physical product of labor. Thus, given the relative price of labor and capital, w/r, less labor will be used per unit of output than before. In this sense, technological change is labor-saving.

If, for example, E were an optimum position, then E' is *not* an optimum position for the firm if factor prices are constant. Given constant-factor prices, the optimum position will require that less labor be used and more capital be used. Why? Because of the law of diminishing marginal physical returns. At point E', the marginal product of capital has increased relative to the marginal product of labor. At firm optimum, however, we know that the ratio of the two marginal physical products must be equal to the ratio of their respective prices. However, with the price of capital and labor given, the only way to decrease the marginal physical product of capital is to increase the amount of capital used relative to labor. Conversely, the only way to increase the marginal physical product of labor is to decrease the amount of labor used relative to capital. Hence, this is why the technological change depicted in panel (*b*) is called labor-saving change. It could also be called capital-using.

Capital-Saving Technological Change

Capital-saving technological change, as depicted in panel (*c*) of Figure 17-1, occurs when the marginal physical product of labor increases relative to capital. Hence, less capital need be used per unit of output with a given quantity of labor. The only way to get to the firm optimum will be to increase the amount of labor used and to decrease the amount of capital required, thereby affecting their relative marginal physical products. This is why it is called capital-saving. (It could also be called a labor-using technological change.)

THE IMPORTANCE OF TECHNOLOGICAL CHANGE

Smith and Ricardo discussed the economics of technological change about two hundred years ago. It wasn't until relatively recently, however, that economists devoted much research to the topic. The study of technological change may be considered essential to industrial organization in order to have a full understanding of how competition takes place. After all, the introduction of new products or processes forms the basis of much of the competition that we see around us. Technological change also may account for a significant amount of economic growth in the United States. One estimate by Solow had technological change accounting for between 80 and 90 percent of the economic growth in the United States.[1]

---

[1] Robert M. Solow, "Technological Change and the Aggregate Production Function," *Review of Economics and Statistics,* vol. 39 (August 1957), pp. 312–320.

While economists generally agree that technological change leads to increased competition, they are certainly less in agreement about how market structure affects either the incentive to engage in technological change or the speed with which technological advances are diffused throughout the economy. Industrial organization specialists, therefore, wish to study which market structures are more conducive to technological change and its diffusion.

The Process of Invention, Innovation, and Imitation of Technological Change

Technological change is most often associated with research and development, or is best seen as the result of research and development. The process by which technological change becomes part of the economy's productive process has been outlined by several writers, the most famous of whom was Schumpeter. The three steps of technological change according to him were: (1) invention, (2) innovation, and (3) diffusion (or imitation from the firm's viewpoint).

Invention—Research and Development The invention stage of technological change is basically equivalent to what we think of when we talk about research and development, or R&D.[2] Schumpeter believed invention to be the act of conceiving a new product or process and of solving the associated technical problems.

Innovation The innovation stage occurs when knowledge is applied for the first time and results in a product or productive process. Thus, innovation involves entrepreneurial functions that take the raw invention and put it into practice for the first time. Some of the phases involved in innovation are raising capital, doing market research, identifying markets in which a new product will sell, and so on.

Imitation The imitation, or diffusion, stage of technological change occurs when the new product or productive process becomes widely used. One manufacturer after another follows the innovating firm's first market forays with the new process or product.

An Alternative Scheme for Describing Technological Change

Scherer believes that Schumpeter's trichotomization of the process of technological change is deficient because it ignores many of the technical activities that form the basis of modern research and development programs. Scherer uses a four-stage description of technological change: (1) invention, (2) entrepreneurship, (3) investment, and (4) development.[3] For Scherer, invention is

---

[2] Joseph A. Schumpeter, *The Theory of Economic Development: An Inquiry into Profits, Capital, Interest, and the Business Cycle* (Cambridge, Mass.: Harvard University Press, 1934).

[3] Frederic M. Scherer, "Invention and Innovation in the Watt-Boulton Steam-Engine Venture," *Technology and Culture*, vol. 6 (Spring 1965), pp. 165–187.

the "act of insight" by which a new technological advance is recognized and worked out in its most rudimentary form. The entrepreneurial function involves at least one person's decision to go forward with the effort necessary to develop the project and to obtain financial support. Investment is the act of risking the funds for the venture, and development is the final detailed technical activities necessary to bring the original concept to commercial fruition.

The actual form of research and development is described by Scherer through two real-world examples—the development of the steam engine and of the Xerox copier.[4] The steam engine was invented in 1765 by James Watt. However, for some time Watt was unable to find the support that he needed to develop his invention. It was not until Matthew Boulton provided the financial support and the entrepreneurial medium needed for development that the engine became commercially practical. As a result, the steam engine was finally developed in 1776—11 years after its invention.

Although a more recent development, Xerography suffered similar problems. The invention was conceived by Chester Carlson in 1938. However, it took 21 years and over $20 million before the invention was finally developed by Xerox Corporation for commercial use.

By raising these examples, Scherer points out the difficulties in actual development. Of primary importance is the fact that the initial invention is inexpensive and easily conceived relative to the expenditures in time and money required for final commercial development. After the initial invention is conceived, a great deal of ingenuity and luck are needed to perceive the problem accurately and to conceptualize a viable solution. (Although thousands may perceive a problem, only a few may have the ingenuity and luck to solve the problem.) Next, financial and entrepreneurial support may be required before production is possible. Once this support is available, a decision must be made regarding the actual feasibility of marketing the invention. Finally, after all the preliminary problems have been encountered, the largest expenditure of capital is necessary to develop the concept to a commercially acceptable form. At this point in the development the risk involved is at its highest level, and final development will not be considered unless all the preliminary steps have been satisfactorily resolved. The decision to continue with development involves committing relatively substantial amounts of resources in the face of possible technological uncertainties.

R&D Expenditures

The data on R&D expenditures is usually broken down into three types: (1) basic research, (2) applied research, and (3) development. In Table 17-1 we show what has happened to the amount of resources used in these three categories through time. We also show that there has been an increase in the

---

[4] Scherer, "Invention and Innovation in the Watt-Boulton Steam-Engine Venture," and John Jewkes, D. Sawers, R. Stillerman, *The Sources of Invention*, 2d ed. (New York: W. W. Norton, 1969), pp. 321–333. Also see Scherer, *Industrial Market Structure and Economic Performance*, 2d ed. (Chicago: Rand McNally, 1980), pp. 411 and 412.

TABLE 17-1
RESEARCH AND DEVELOPMENT FUNDS, BY PERFORMANCE SECTOR AND SOURCE:
1960 TO 1979 (millions of dollars)

Performance sector and source of funds	1960	1965	1970	1975	1978 (est.)	1979 (est.)
Research and Development Expenditures						
Totals*	13,523	20,044	25,905	35,200	47,295	51,630
In 1972 dollars	19,693	26,970	28,355	27,684	31,136	31,772
Percent Federal						
as source	64.6	64.9	56.6	51.6	50.4	49.8
Basic and Applied Research Expenditures						
Federal government	1,726	3,093	3,855	5,397	6,565	6,940
Industry	10,509	14,185	18,062	24,164	33,250	36,750
Federal funds	6,081	7,740	7,779	8,605	11,750	13,000
Industry funds	4,428	6,445	10,283	15,559	21,500	23,750
Total research, basic and applied	4,217	6,891	9,226	12,474	16,770	18,450
In 1972 dollars	6,141	9,276	10,099	9,811	11,041	11,354
Percent Federal						
as source	31.1	40.6	40.9	39.3	38.6	(NA)
Basic Research Expenditures						
Federal government	755	1,354	1,862	2,499	3,260	(NA)
Industry	2,405	3,250	4,028	5,295	7,225	(NA)
Federal funds	912	1,224	1,207	1,287	1,725	(NA)
Industry funds	1,493	2,026	2,821	4,008	5,500	(NA)
Total basic research	1,197	2,555	3,513	4,527	6,045	6,700
In 1972 dollars	1,743	3,438	3,845	3,561	3,940	4,123
Percent of total research and development	8.9	12.7	13.6	12.9	12.8	13.0
Percent Federal						
as source	13.4	14.2	15.4	15.1	16.1	(NA)

NA: not available
*Basic research, applied research, and development.
Source: U.S. National Science Foundation, *National Patterns of R&D Resources–Funds and Personnel in the United States, 1960–79.*

amount of basic research expenditures from 8.9 percent in 1960 to about 13 percent in 1979. Finally, there has been a shift in terms of the mix between publicly and privately provided R&D expenditures, with more basic research funded by federal dollars.

R&D and Profitability

R&D is carried out (at least in the private sector) because it is hoped that R&D will lead to a higher rate of return in the use of resources than if those resources were used elsewhere. We have very little evidence on the actual profitability of R&D expenditures. Mansfield, however, has done some work in the area.[5] In one study he examined five petroleum firms and five chemical firms. The marginal rates of return on R&D expenditures in the petroleum firms ranged from 40 to 60 percent and in the chemical firms from 7 to 30 percent.[6] He found an inverse relationship between profitability of R&D expenditures and firm size in the petroleum industry and a direct relationship in the chemical industry. When examining manufacturing markets, he found R&D expenditures had rates of return exceeding 15 percent in apparel, furniture, and food markets.[7] The rates of return indicated by Mansfield seem to be quite high and indicative of an underinvestment in R&D by numerous manufacturing firms. Mansfield cautioned his readers about the possible large sampling errors in his data, as well as the lags in relationship between R&D expenditures and their profitability.

The Distribution of R&D Effort

Large amounts of research and development funds have been supplied by the government over the years. Table 17-1 shows that more than $25 billion of government funds were allocated for research and development in 1979. Although when expressed as a percentage of GNP, this amount has gone down, it does represent a real increase of 61 percent since 1960.

Defense and space R&D comprise the largest share of government research expenditures. However, other areas are finding increased government support. As a percentage of government R&D expenditures, defense spending dropped from 52 percent in 1960 to 25 percent in 1979; space funding dropped from a high of 21 percent of federal R&D funds in 1965 to 8 percent in 1979. On the other hand, research in such areas as basic sciences (research without immediate government or commercial application), energy, health, environment, transportation, communication, natural resources, and agriculture have all received increased shares of government funding.[8]

One explanation behind government-financed research and development is that private incentives for research in certain areas may be lacking. The social benefits from research in these areas may be greater than the return that may be recovered privately. For example, expenditures for environmental and health research may result in large benefits for society in general, yet the benefits to any one firm in the private sector would not be high enough to foster investing in such research and development activities. Further, entry cost may be prohibitive to those in private business. The risk may be so great and the capital requirements so high that those investors in the private sector are effectively

[5] Edwin Mansfield, *Industrial Research and Technological Innovation* (New York: W. W. Norton, 1968).

[6] Ibid., p. 70.

[7] Ibid., p. 71.

[8] National Science Foundation, *National Patterns of R&D Resources—Funds and Personnel in the U.S., 1960–1979* (Washington, D.C.: U.S. Government Printing Office, 1980).

excluded from getting involved. However, even though no one firm may be willing to invest billions of dollars in a risk-laden project with questionable returns, the social benefits and needs for such a project may be deemed worthy enough that such a project should be initiated. In such cases, the government often finances the research and development.

Small versus Large Firms   The minimum-size firm with some R&D activity usually has from 500 to 1,000 workers. In 1967, small firms carried out a very small percentage of total R&D effort. For example, only 4 percent of R&D was executed by firms that employed 1,000 employees or less. Many small companies did not even undertake R&D.[9] Those firms that had more than 10,000 employees accounted for almost 85 percent of all industrial R&D efforts. In the early 1960s, the top 20 industrial R&D firms undertook more than half of all R&D effort.[10]

We have to be careful about our estimates here, because they are in terms of percentages of total R&D efforts. If we express R&D efforts as a percentage of firm sales or investment, it is not at all clear that a positive correlation exists between intensity of R&D effort and firm size. Worley, for example, found that in six out of eight 2-digit S.I.C. industries, the percentage of R&D personnel expressed relative to total personnel declined as firm size grew. Thus, only two of the eight industries studied showed a positive correlation between intensity of R&D efforts and firm size.[11]

In a similar study, Comanor concluded that little, if any, relationship occurs between intensity of R&D effort and firm size.[12] Furthermore, in a study of R&D personnel in Fortune 500 firms, Rosenberg found a significant negative relationship between the employment of R&D personnel and market share.[13] These conflicting results may also reflect the condition that technological opportunities are not the same in all markets. In fact, roughly 84 percent of all R&D activities in 1977 were accounted for by six industries.[14]

One final point should be mentioned here concerning the relationship between inputs and outputs. Intensity of R&D activity, as measured by the number of personnel or even the dollars spent, may not tell us much about the efficiency of the use of those resources. Does R&D input correlate one-to-one or almost so with R&D output? If it does, then we can substitute inputs for

[9] Richard E. Caves, *American Industry: Structure, Conduct, Performance,* 2d ed. (Englewood Cliffs, N.J.: Prentice-Hall, 1967), pp. 100–104.

[10] Daniel Hamberg, *R&D: Essays on the Economics of Research and Development* (New York: Random House, 1966), p. 6.

[11] James S. Worley, "Industrial Research and the New Competition," *Journal of Political Economy,* vol. 69 (April 1961), pp. 183–186.

[12] William S. Comanor, "Market Structure, Product Differentiation, and Industrial Research," *Quarterly Journal of Economics,* vol. 81 (November 1967), pp. 639–657.

[13] Joel B. Rosenberg, "Research and Market Share: A Reappraisal of the Schumpeter Hypothesis," *Journal of Industrial Economics,* vol. 25 (December 1976), pp. 101–112.

[14] National Science Foundation, *Research and Development in Industry Funds, Scientists and Engineers* (Washington, D.C., National Science Foundation, 1979).

outputs. If it doesn't, we cannot make this substitution, and therefore less can be said about the relationship between R&D results and intensity of R&D expenditures and firm size.

MARKET STRUCTURE AND TECHNOLOGICAL CHANGE

The Schumpeterian Model

Schumpeter argued that technological change required the existence of large firms.[15] He further stated that the intensity of innovation and its rate of diffusion will be positively correlated with short-run protection and market power. Although he was not arguing for monopoly itself, Schumpeter clearly felt that innovation should be protected legally to give short-run market power, at a minimum. Schumpeter felt that perfect competition was not efficient because the small firms required for this type of organization were incapable of optimal expenditures for research and development. Therefore, Schumpeter argued in favor of large firms, which he believed were more capable of maximizing technological innovation. Underlying this argument was Schumpeter's belief that technological change is itself an element of competition. As such, competition is not destroyed by the introduction of larger firms; it is enhanced by efforts toward technological change. Furthermore, he indicates that everyone benefits because of optimal expenditures for research and development.

The Galbraithian View

Following in Schumpeter's footsteps, Galbraith has argued that large firms are "an almost perfect instrument for inducing technological change,"[16] and are the most efficient originators and transmitters of technological change. His conclusion follows from some relatively straightforward reasoning. R&D expenditures may be too costly for small firms to engage in because it is a time-consuming process. Small firms perhaps cannot wait for deferred rewards because they do not have sufficient financing.[17] Additionally, there may be economies of scale in R&D so that large, necessary R&D efforts cannot be financed or justified in small firms. Furthermore, since R&D expenditures are risky, only large firms may be able to spread this risk over a sufficiently large number of projects. Finally, perhaps only large firms can fully exploit the results of R&D expenditures.

[15] Joseph A. Schumpeter, *Capitalism, Socialism, and Democracy* (New York: Harper & Row, 1942).

[16] John Kenneth Galbraith, *American Capitalism: The Concept of Countervailing Power* (Boston: Houghton-Mifflin, 1956), p. 86.

[17] For a contrary view, see Morton I. Kamien and Nancy L. Schwartz, "Self-Financing of an R&D Project," *American Economic Review,* vol. 68 (June 1978), pp. 252–261. Kamien and Schwartz's analysis shows that "a cash constraint will not impede development at all for a large class of R&D projects by established firms," and that where the incentive to innovate is not "defensive," "no project would be bypassed because of financial limitations" (p. 260).

Monopoly Power and Innovation

We will now look at the theoretical issue relating research and development under competition with that under monopoly. We will assume that the gains from an innovation are captured because of a legal patent system that enforces the innovator's rights (see pp. 403–406). Our first example of an innovation will be a cost-reducing one. The innovation reduces constant average costs by a fixed amount.

There are two major competing views on the relationship of monopoly power to the amount of innovative activity. Arrow's analysis of the relationship between market power and R&D led him to believe that a competitive economy will underinvest in inventive activities because competitive firms are (1) less willing to take risk, (2) less able to appropriate returns, and (3) unable to capture the gains from increasing returns to the use of inventions.[18] This analysis also implies that there will be greater underinvestment for basic research in a competitive industry. First, risk-bearing is not distributed optimally in competitive markets since the equivalent of commodity option markets to redistribute risk-bearing does not exist. Thus any unwillingness to bear risk would result in a nonoptimal allocation of resources.[19]

Second, Arrow also finds that since the theft of knowledge is relatively easy and competitive firms will be less able to establish property rights in information, there will be an underproduction of research and development.[20]

Third, if appropriability is possible, the public good characteristic of research and development will tend to be underutilized in competitive firms since individual competitive firms will have a smaller market share than a comparable monopolist in the same industry.

Demsetz argues that each of these conditions is not necessarily characteristic of market equilibrium and concludes that competition may produce *greater* research and innovative activity.[21] Demsetz's attack on Arrow's conditions relies on the comparison of ideal situations with actual institutional arrangements. Risk reduction, he argues, is not achievable at zero cost, so there is never a complete shifting of risk.

Second, Demsetz questions the relative appropriability of property rights under competitive and monopoly conditions. Appropriability, he argues, stems from legal arrangements that are exogenous to the firm's structure. Finally, Demsetz argues that indivisibilities and the use of knowledge become important only when the costs of contracting are relatively large. In the absence of high

[18] Kenneth J. Arrow, "Economic Welfare and the Allocation of Resources for Invention," in *The Rate and Direction of Inventive Activity* (Princeton, N.J.: National Bureau of Economic Research, Princeton University Press, 1962), pp. 609–625.

[19] Ibid., pp. 610–611.

[20] Ibid., p. 615.

[21] Harold Demsetz, "Information and Efficiency: Another Viewpoint," *Journal of Law and Economics,* vol. 12 (April 1969), pp. 1–22.

contracting costs, firms may diffuse information to competitors through contractual arrangements.[22]

Firm Size and Innovation

There are many reasons that would explain why research and development expenditures would be taken on by larger firms and, therefore, why technological change would be found in larger firms. We list several of the possible reasons here.

1 *Risk spreading*   Research and development projects are risky. Small firms would be undertaking too much risk if they put all their resources in one single innovative project. The larger firm can maintain a "balanced" portfolio of research and development projects.

2 *Cost*   The cost of technological innovation may be so great that it can be borne only by large corporations. This is an argument that Galbraith has used repeatedly.[23] He states that most simple and cheap inventions have already been made. Although small companies or individuals may conceptualize the problems, development of solutions is far more costly. Therefore, it follows from this argument that development can be carried on only by a firm that has substantial resources. Furthermore, decreased rivalry between large firms would predictably result in larger profits, which, in turn, would supply the funds for riskier investments. Reduced rivalry would be likely to result in greater protection of new inventions, which, because of the fact that ideas would not be stolen, would add incentive for increased expenditures for research and development.

3 *Economies of scale*   There may be economies of scale in research and development. A larger firm can engage in specialization that a smaller firm cannot engage in. The larger firm can justify specialized equipment that the smaller firm cannot justify. Also, a large firm may be able to wait longer for the pay-off on technological innovations.

4 *Process innovations*   Large firms apparently have an advantage in making process innovations. Any process that they invent which will reduce cost by a given percentage leads to a larger absolute reduction in cost and therefore justifies a larger absolute expenditure in research and development in a given area. This advantage is offset by the ability of small firms to sell or buy the rights to use processes.

5 *Diversification*   Large diversified firms may derive larger benefits from research and development due to the inherent uncertainty in such investments.

---

[22] Also see Morton I. Kamien and Nancy L. Schwartz, "Market Structure, Elasticity of Demand and Incentive To Invent," *Journal of Law and Economics*, vol. 13 (April 1970), pp. 241–252. They argue that where *industry* demand curves are *equally elastic*, the monopoly will have the greater incentive to invest.

[23] See, for example, Galbraith, *American Capitalism*, p. 87.

Richard R. Nelson believes that research may end in various different results so that speculative research in one area may result in a discovery in another area. Therefore, the incentive for such speculative research is higher in large diversified firms.[24] Also, an unexpected result may cause further diversification in a firm large enough to fund such an enterprise. Risk is effectively reduced due to diversification and possible expansion.

Regulation of Monopoly Profits

One could argue that the regulation of profits reduces or indeed eliminates completely the possibility of a regulated firm incurring a high-risk R&D venture. The electric utility industry, for example, supports relatively little research and development. Thus, regulation does cut off the upper end of the profit possibility distribution that the firm faces. On the other hand, a regulated firm is often protected against the risk of loss inherent in technological progress, because the regulating agencies will usually permit prices to increase to reach the allowable rate of return. In other words, regulation tends to cut off the lower end of the profit possibility distribution a firm faces. This is a reason for the regulated firm to engage in more research and development than it otherwise would. The net effect of the two offsetting influences just discussed is unclear.

Barriers to Entry

One can argue that barriers to entry protect regulated firms from aggressive new firms that might enter the industry on the basis of cost-reducing innovation. Such barriers to entry reduce incentive for investment in research and development. On the other hand, one might expect that, once any innovation is introduced, it will be rapidly diffused throughout the industry since there is little interfirm competition in regulated industries and less effort would be expended to avoid technological diffusion.[25]

An examination of the Interstate Commerce Commission would, nonetheless, probably reveal that the ICC has impeded rather than encouraged technological progress in transportation. The commission has never developed procedures to compensate the railroads that lost traffic to motor carriers offering better service. The commission continues to be reluctant to approve new service made possible by improved equipment. A classic case is the ICC's "heel dragging" in allowing the introduction of piggybacking in freight transport. In brief, the commission has never wanted to allow changes that threaten existing operators.

---

[24] Richard R. Nelson, "The Simple Economics of Basic Scientific Research," *Journal of Political Economy*, vol. 67 (June 1959), pp. 297–306.

[25] Of course, regulated firms do compete, but presumably less so than if they were unregulated and if there were no barriers to entry.

THE EMPIRICAL EVIDENCE

In this section, we will comment briefly on some of the more important studies trying to relate firm size to research and development.[26] We'll first look at studies that explore R&D differences among various industries.

Differences within Industries

Using 1955–1956 data, Worley classified 198 very large firms among eight S.I.C. 2-digit industry groups.[27] Worley found in his inquiry of the relationship between firm size and R&D expenditures that "the evidence calls for a more convincing case for bigness than has so far been marshalled." His research results, however, do not inspire much confidence in his conclusion. Only for electrical machinery and petroleum do his statistical tests suggest such a strong relationship. First of all, he was looking at the amount of R&D employment relative to total firm employment. Although R&D employment may be a good proxy for total expenditures on R&D and total employment may be a proxy for firm size, his study does not clearly demonstrate the relationship.

Hamberg uses the same technique with data from 1953 to 1960.[28] He looked at 340 firms classified into seventeen 2- and 3-digit industry groups. He then looked at the relationship between R&D employment and firm size measured both by total employment and assets. He found "no solid evidence" in 15 industries that research intensity increases with the size of firm or with the degree of concentration in an industry. "In any case it seems clear that increased concentration of industry beyond certain limits cannot be counted upon, in most cases, to act as a spur to the conduct of R&D."[29]

Comanor looked at data from 1955 to 1960 to find out intraindustry R&D differences.[30] He found that in many industries, smaller firms undertake larger proportionate levels of research. He was not referring to truly small firms but rather to relatively smaller firms within a group of large firms. Comanor recognizes that research personnel are not all alike and that quality differences may be systematic among types and sizes of firms. Therefore, a measure of total R&D employment may bias results. Additionally, even if we were able to measure R&D inputs correctly, they do not necessarily translate into R&D results.

Mansfield looked at detailed data from three chemical and five petroleum-

---

[26] For a more complete survey, see Morton I. Kamien and Nancy L. Schwartz, "Market Structure and Innovation: A Survey," *Journal of Economic Literature,* vol. 13 (March 1975), pp. 1–37.

[27] James S. Worley, "Industrial Research and the New Competition," *Journal of Political Economy,* vol. 69 (April 1961), pp. 183–186.

[28] Daniel Hamberg, "Size of Firm, Oligopoly, and Research: The Evidence," *The Canadian Journal of Economics and Political Science,* vol. 30 (February 1964), pp. 62–75.

[29] Ibid., p. 74.

[30] William S. Comanor, "Market Structure, Product Differentiation, and Industrial Research," *Quarterly Journal of Economics,* vol. 81 (November 1967), pp. 639–657.

refining firms. He concluded that, except for the chemical industry, there was no evidence that the largest firms spent more on research and development relative to sales than did somewhat smaller firms. Indeed, in petroleum, glass industries, and drugs, the largest firms spent significantly less relative to sales than the smaller firms.[31] However, Mansfield's sample included only large firms, so this may have biased his results.

Differences in Technological Change among Industries

Now we'll look at studies showing differences in technological change among various industries rather than among firms within an industry.

Williamson took Mansfield's sample of firms in petroleum, bituminous coal, and steel in order to analyze the statistical relationship between innovation and industry concentration. He used four-firm concentration ratios as a measure of "monopoly."[32] He concluded that the relative share of innovations contributed by the largest firms in an industry *decreases* as monopoly power increases. He found that the four largest firms in an industry contributed less than their proportionate share of innovations when concentration ratios exceeded 50 percent.

Scherer looked at data on the number of patents related to the R&D employment from leading industrial firms. He found that corporate patenting tended to increase less than proportionately with rising sales, except in the cases of a few giant firms. Thus, his evidence did not support the hypothesis that large corporations are favorable to high inventive output. In 1955, he found that firms with sales below $500,000 generated more inventions relative to their size than did most giant firms. Finally, he found little correlation between structural market power and the output of patented inventions.

In a later study, Scherer revised the above findings somewhat.[33] He withdrew his conclusion that the relationship between industrial inventive effort measured by patents and industry concentration did not exist. He stated that he believed that there was evidence of a modest positive correlation between the employment of scientists and engineers and industry concentration.

Criticisms of Empirical Evidence

There have been many criticisms of the studies purporting to show the relationship between firm size and inventive activity or output. The critic Jesse Markham stated:

---

[31] Edwin Mansfield, *Industrial Research and Technological Innovation: An Econometric Analysis* and *The Economics of Technological Change* (New York: W. W. Norton, 1968).

[32] Oliver E. Williamson, "Innovation and Market Structure," *Journal of Political Economy,* vol. 73 (February 1965), pp. 67–75.

[33] See Frederic M. Scherer, "Firm Size, Market Structure, Opportunity, and the Output of Patented Inventions," *American Economic Review,* vol. 55 (December 1965), pp. 1097–1125.

Any answers to how inventive and innovative efforts are affected by firm size hang on an extraordinarily slender reed that may alternatively bend upward or droop downward, depending on the species of statistical zephyrs blowing at the time. Similarly, we are equally unsure about the precise relationship between market power and inventive and innovative effort.[34]

On a more theoretical basis, if the studies are correct that the disadvantages of large firms are such that less R&D intensity occurs in them, it would seem that a natural deconcentration would occur. It does not, however, and therefore, as McGee has put it,

"It is not only arrogant for economists to argue, against the market, that large firms are inefficient and unprogressive; it is also somewhat inconsistent with their creed: if economists know better than the whole pool of actual and potential entrepreneurs and investors, it would pay them—or those they teach—to enter or invest. If they do not, they must be unwilling to take their own diagnosis seriously, or are betraying their social trust."[35]

PATENTS

Article I, section 8 of the Constitution reads as follows:

The Congress shall have power . . . to promote the progress of science and useful arts, by securing for limited times to authors and inventors the exclusive right to their respective writings and discoveries.

This provision provides the foundation for our patent and copyright statutes. In this section, we will examine briefly the history of patents and look at some of their economic aspects.

Patentable Subject Matter

Patent law protects for 17 years inventions that seem to promise a new and useful process, machine, articles of manufacture, or composition of matter. Generally, unless an invention falls within one of these four classes, a patent will not be granted. Further, design patents are granted for original and ornamental designs for articles of manufacture and may include designs for furniture, fabrics, vehicles, and industrial equipment, as well as jewelry.

1 *Process*   The term "process" is synonymous with method. Examples of process-type inventions are chemical processes such as the treating of metals and the manufacture of drugs. Examples of mechanical processes are electrical processes and the forming of articles.

---

[34] Jesse W. Markham, "Market Structure, Business Conduct, and Innovation," *American Economic Review,* vol. 55 (May 1965), p. 330.

[35] John S. McGee, *In Defense of Industrial Concentration* (New York: Praeger, 1971), p. 122.

2 *Machines*   All machines such as typewriters and lathes are patentable. The general definition of a machine is a mechanism with moving parts.

3 *Articles of manufacture*   Manufactured articles include clothing, simple tools lacking moving parts, and furniture.

4 *Composition of matter*   The term "composition of matter" includes pure chemical compounds and mixtures of chemicals.

Usefulness

A patent will not be issued unless the invention is useful, although the standards of usefulness applied by the Patent Office are not very strict. If they were, the first telephone or radio tube would have faced a strong barrier. Nonetheless, inventions that are frivolous or immoral cannot be patented because they lack utility. Basically, the test for utility is that there must be the barest suggestion that something practical might ensue from the patented invention.

Novelty and Obviousness

In order to obtain a patent, the inventor must show that the invention is new and not obvious. The obvious aspect of the test for patentability involves an inquiry into the state of knowledge of the pertinent field of technology. The basic rule is that the invention is not patentable if "the subject matter as a whole would have been obvious at the time the invention was made to a person having ordinary skill in the art."[36] But the person having ordinary skill is a mythical being who is presumed to know everything relating to the invention that was either previously patented or described in any prior printed publication.

Operativeness   Patents can be refused if the invention is inoperative. The Patent Office can require that a working model or some physical exhibit be submitted to prove that the invention is operative. This requirement is rarely encountered. The apparent ease with which patent rights are granted by the U.S. Patent Office is not the whole story, however. Patents may be challenged in court, and the courts are not as lenient in allowing such rights. For example, between 1966 and 1971, 69 percent of the patents brought before federal courts of appeal were invalidated.[37]

Who May Ask for a Patent

The United States patent system requires that the patent application be filed only by the inventor. (There are exceptions—for example, when the inventor is

---

[36] 35 U.S.C. 103.
[37] Robert G. Hummerstone, "How the Patent System Mousetraps Inventors," *Fortune,* vol. 87 (May 1973), p. 262.

dead, insane, or incapacitated, or when the inventor is a joint inventor or has assigned his or her patent rights to another and refuses to sign the patent application, or when the inventor cannot be found.) Each patent applicant must take an oath verifying that he or she believes himself or herself to be the original, first, and sole inventor. Patents are generally issued to individuals or corporations and not to partnerships, or to fictitious legal entities.

The Purpose of the Patent Grant

The conventional view of the patent grant is that it is used to promote inventions. A second purported purpose of the patent system is to promote investment. A third purported purpose is to encourage disclosure, because the patent protection allows inventors to make public what they might otherwise keep secret.[38] Finally, Western societies often create property rights for individuals' ideas as an extension of natural law principles.

TECHNOLOGICAL INNOVATION VERSUS LOST CONSUMER-PRODUCER SURPLUS

We have outlined some of the potential benefits of the patent system by examining the reward view of patents and the prospect view of the patent system. Here we will look at the social costs of the patent system. Presumably, a social cost is due to resource misallocation because of monopolistic pricing of the patented invention. Innovators holding patent rights may recover monopoly profits through exclusive use of the patent, or by granting licenses to other firms, collecting royalties that could amount to the equivalent of monopoly profits. Still society may recover net gains through savings in resources that may be allocated elsewhere. Society gains from the new products or new and more efficient production processes. However, resource misallocation due to monopoly pricing may overcome the gains from a particular patented innovation if the good would eventually become available on the market. If no suitable substitutes are available or consumers have no knowledge of possible substitutes, patent holders may reduce outputs below those outputs and raise prices above those prices that would be dictated under competition. Also, greater and extended monopoly profits may be obtained by patenting improvements for the initial patent. As a result, the cost of the patent system may be far higher than the benefits gained. In order to properly complete a cost-benefit analysis of the

---

[38] See Carole E. Kitti and Charles L. Trozzo, "The Effects of Patent and Antitrust Laws, Regulations, and Practices on Innovation," Paper P-1075 of the Institute for Defense Analyses Program, Analysis Division, available from the National Technical Information Service, Reporter #PB252860, PB252861, and PB 252862; and Fritz Machlup, "An Economic Review of the Patent System," Study #15 of the Subcommittee on Patents, Trademarks, and Copyrights of the Senate Judiciary Committee, 85th Cong. 2d Sess. (Washington, D.C.: U.S. Government Printing Office, 1958), pp. 3–5. Also see less comprehensive summaries in Ward S. Bowman, Jr., *Patent and Antitrust Law: A Legal and Economic Appraisal* (Chicago: University of Chicago Press, 1973).

patent system , we would have to add up the benefits discussed above and then subtract the cost of any resource misallocation, including the suppression pursuant to the patent system of inventions from which the public might otherwise benefit. Presumably, the patent system exists because in some instances the gains derived from a particularly innovative development outweigh the costs produced as a result of the patent. However, the patent system may exist simply because no suitable alternative system is available.

Trade Secrets

The standards of patentability in recent years have risen considerably. The result has been a wholesale invalidation of patents by many courts. At the same time, a counter-phenomenon, or reaction, by the courts has occurred in the field of trade secrets. There has been an extensive modern development in the law relating to trade secrets. It is now recognized by most courts that the misappropriation of a confidential disclosure of an invention is against the law. The doctrine of the protection of trade secrets rests on the principles of unjust enrichment. Courts will not allow individuals to profit from acts of unfair competition or from violations of business ethics in respect to confidential information. The courts have protected such trade secrets as methods of treating chemicals, chemical formulas, credit ratings, architectural plans, and advertising slogans. Well-known as a trade secret is the formula for Coca-Cola. Another is the formula for Smith's black cough drops, reportedly over 100 years old and not yet "cracked." The 17 years of protection given by a patent appear quite short in comparison to the protection offered a trade secret. The secret metallurgical process used to make the metals employed in the best grade musical cymbals is centuries old. It has been kept in the same family throughout that entire period.

Nonetheless, one who retains information in the form of a trade secret (rather than a patent) runs the risk that the secret will be lost or that it will become publicly known.

Patent Protection—Is the Optimal Time 17 Years?

Our patent system extends over 17 years. This is a compromise between England's 14- and 21-year possibilities. Other countries allow their patents to extend from 15 to 20 years. Certain countries have two or three different periods of protection depending on the type of invention. There is a trade-off involved when patent protection is extended. The longer an individual can anticipate having a property right or monopoly in a specific invention, the more resources will presumably go into inventing patentable items. However, the longer a patent exists, the longer the monopoly exists and presumably the longer the price will remain at a monopoly level rather than a competitive one. To find the socially optimal length of a patent, we must weigh the benefits of inducing more research and more creative efforts for patentable products against the higher price tags that those products will carry during the length of a patent.

PUBLIC POLICY

CHAPTER 18

LEGAL VIEWS OF COMPETITION AND MONOPOLY

This chapter provides an overview of the legislative and judicial views of competition and monopoly. In the preceding chapters we have looked more intensely at various aspects of the courts' treatment of monopoly behavior. Thus, the topics discussed have represented a blend of industrial organization theories and empirical findings with legal treatment of these activities. Recent developments in antitrust, public policy, and regulation are deferred to the next chapter.

A review of earlier chapters, especially Chapter 3, The Measure of Market Structure, will reveal that there is no single theoretical base on which to establish a clear and consistent public policy toward business behavior. Nor does the existing collection of empirical evidence yield a concise guideline for public policy. For example, due to differing economies of scale, lower levels of concentration may be beneficial in some industries and harmful in others. Further, differences in production functions, information, resources, and other variables that determine market structure also imply that no single model for industry behavior is always applicable for public policy analysis. Thus, economic theory does not provide a uniform or consistent ideal against which various public policies may be measured. For this reason and because of the fact that judicial decisions often create incentives different from those arising from market forces, we turn our attention to the court's interpretation of competition and monopoly.

EARLY PUBLIC POLICY

Current public policy toward restraints of trade began in the late nineteenth century. Prior to the enactment of a series of federal antitrust laws that started in 1890, restraints of trade were governed by the common law that was borrowed from England. For our purposes, **common law** will refer to judicial action that is formed outside of legislative action. Common law is also the medium by which statutory law is given its ultimate meaning. The public policy governing restraints of trade had its origin in the common law governing private property in contracts.

Ancillary Clauses

Public policy toward restraints of trade evident in contract law focused on **ancillary clauses** or contracts that supplemented another contract. During the fifteenth century in England, ancillary contracts in restraint of trade were unenforceable due to the then-existing low level of mobility of the population. Many ancillary contracts and agreements prohibited any competition by the seller of the business with the buyers. A seller's inability to move would effectively result in a loss of his or her livelihood. The first recorded common law case dealing with restraint of trade involved a clause ancillary to a contract for the sale of a business owned by John Dyer.[1] Dyer agreed not to "use his art of a dyer's craft within the town . . . for half a year." The court denied the plaintiff the ability to collect on a bond for Dyer's breach of his agreement. The agreement was restraining trade, according to the common law. At that time, the notion of a restraint in trade was that which went against "fair" commercial activity.

Later, when markets became larger and the mobility of goods and services became greater, the common law dictated enforcement of ancillary contracts if (1) they specified a certain time period (for example, five years) and area, and (2) if they were "reasonable."[2]

The change to enforcement of ancillary clauses is evident in the celebrated 1711 case known as *Mitchel v. Reynolds*.[3] In this case, the plaintiff, Mitchel, leased a baking shop from the defendant, Reynolds, subject to the condition that Reynolds, who was also a baker, would not practice the baking art in the immediate area for the term of the lease. Thus, the plaintiff was actually buying the use of a baking shop *and* the trade that went with it. The court rejected Reynolds' ancillary clause argument and Mitchel won the case. The reason this case is so celebrated is that the court systematically classified trade restraints as "good" and "bad." Lord Parker, who rendered the opinion, distinguished between *general* and *particular* restraints, the former being invalid and the latter being valid. He pointed out that general restraints were used for the

---

[1] This case has become known as *Dyer's Case*, Y. B. Pasch. 2 Hen. 5 f. 5, PL. 26 (1414).

[2] In the law, reasonableness is not a specifically designed concept. For example, in the past the courts have defined the reasonableness of a contract from the point of view of (1) the seller, (2) the buyer, and (3) the public. Thus, what might be reasonable for one person may be unreasonable for another. If, on the other hand, reasonableness is defined as some gross sense of economic efficiency, then a consistent definition may be found. There is some evidence that the courts have moved toward an efficiency view of reasonableness.

[3] *Mitchel v. Reynolds*, 1 P. WMS. 181, 24 ENG. REP 347 (1711).

purpose of limiting competition. On the other hand, certain particular restraints that were supported by "good consideration" were acceptable. These *partial*, or *ancillary restraints* were generally upheld if limited in time and restricted to a geographical place. Thus, *Mitchel v. Reynolds* stands for the formulation of the so-called **rule of reason** (the court must ask whether the restraint is reasonable).

By the eighteenth century, ancillary contracts were legal; late in the century the courts dropped the "particular requirements" and began to look solely at the reasonableness of the restraint. Since then, the rule of reason has also played an important role in the antitrust litigation in this country. In order to find out whether a partial restraint was "good," the courts would inquire about the purpose for which it was imposed and the effect that would result.

Explicit Contracts

The second type of contract in restraint of trade involved those whose primary purpose was to fix prices or engage in other monopoly tactics. This type of contract typically requires a collusive agreement among firms in an industry to set industry-wide prices, production limits, quality levels, or other uniform practices that lessen competition in the industry. Such practices can effectively create a monopoly in the market or industry for those firms involved. Common law treatment of this second type of contract was not consistent.

English Common Law

As laissez-faire became the overriding philosophy in England, the courts granted many exceptions to the rule of reason outlined above. For example, courts would suggest that what was reasonable could best be judged by those involved in the contract, not an outsider. The presumption was, then, that the terms had to be reasonable and therefore not against the public interest. Ultimately, the rule became the exception and the exceptions became the rule in England. Price-fixing agreements were enforced. The House of Lords even upheld a worldwide covenant not to compete.[4]

Common Law in the United States

Common law in the United States was not so receptive to restraints in trade, as evidenced by interpretations of it in various cases. In *United States v. Addyston Pipe & Steel Company*,[5] an early Sherman Act case, Circuit Judge William Howard Taft concluded that apart from "reasonable" ancillary (partial) restraints, the common law condemned all other restraints of trade. Thus, contrary to the English rule, American courts did not apply a reasonableness test to price fixing, territorial divisions, or concerted refusals to deal. The courts de-

---

[4] See *Mogul Steamship Company v. McGregor Gow & Company* (1892) A.C. 25 (1891).
[5] *United States v. Addyston Pipe & Steel Company*, 85 FED 271 (6th Circuit, 1898), modified and affirmed 175 U.S. 211 (1899).

clared that all contracts in constraint of trade were *per se* unlawful and could not be enforced. The purpose of the contract made no difference; if a firm obtained a monopoly through methods other than by being the lowest-cost producer, it was treated as an unlawful act. This view formed the basis for section 1 of the Sherman Act, the mainstay of American antitrust law, and the Supreme Court adopted this view in its first interpretations of the act.

In other situations, contracts in restraint of trade were still subject to a reasonable determination. These contracts were enforced as long as they involved a relatively small minority of the industries' firms and if the total market for the good was generally not affected.[6] In addition, a contract in restraint of trade would be enforced if it were reasonable with respect to the agreement's objective. If the parties involved did not abuse the privilege and if prices were not unduly raised, such a contract would often be enforced. To a certain extent, sections 2 and 5 of the Clayton Antitrust Act also incorporate this concept.

ORIGINS OF U.S. ANTITRUST LAW

With the growth of national markets following the close of the Civil War, a number of large companies were formed from combinations of several small companies, and they started to engage in what was considered monopolistic practices. Reported abusive practices by corporate giants in the second half of the nineteenth century finally led to legislation restricting the power of these so-called trusts. The initial response was the passage of the Interstate Commerce Act of 1887. In 1890, the Sherman Act was passed. These acts were designed to prevent trusts from acting against the public interest.

The Formation of Trusts

Interestingly, **trusts** were a legal innovation that was first used extensively by Rockefeller's Standard Oil Company. Standard's attorneys established an arrangement whereby owners of stock in several companies transferred their stock to a set of trustees. In return, the owners received consideration in the form of certificates entitling them to a specified share in the pooled earnings of the jointly managed companies. In the late 1800s the term "trust" was randomly applied to all forms of suspect business combinations. There were trusts in oil, sugar, cotton, whiskey, and other industries. The trusts seemed to absorb new enterprises at an expanding rate. Furthermore it was felt that the process of consolidation was achieved by *predatory* tactics. In fact, the Standard Oil Company is given as the prime example of such tactics. It was determined by the courts that kerosene was sold by Standard Oil at a price below its cost. The court felt that lower prices forced many competitors to sell out to

---

[6] See, for example, *Appalachian Coals, Inc. v. United States,* 288 U.S. 344 (1933). This case involved a majority of the coal producers in its region.

their competitors or close down. By reducing output, Standard Oil could raise the price and presumably obtain monopoly power.[7] The 1890 Sherman Act [26 Stat 209 (1890)] as amended [15 U.S.C. § 1–7] was the response to this activity. The public policy behind this act was to promote competition within the American economy. Senator Sherman, the author of the legislation, told Congress that the Sherman Act "does not announce a new principle of law, but applies old and well-recognized principles of the common law."[8] But, as we have seen above, the common law was not very clear and, indeed, it was certainly not very familiar to the legislators of the 51st Congress of the United States. Actually, it appears that the Sherman Act was an attempt by Congress to get the federal courts to create a common law of federal antitrust.

PRINCIPAL STATUTES

In 1890 Congress enacted the first of a long series of explicit statutes designed to curb restraints of trade and monopolization. An investigation of these statutes reveals that the Congress has attacked the monopolization problem in a three-pronged manner. There are, for example, statutes such as section 2 of the Sherman Act that focus on structural factors which monopolize industries. In addition, a number of statutes, including sections 2 and 3 of the Clayton Act, directly attack monopolistic behavior. Finally, a number of statutes focus directly on performance, such as the Economic Stabilization Act of 1970. Table 18-1 lists the important federal trade regulation statutes designed to counteract restraints of trade.

Structural

Three statute sections attempt to eliminate monopoly by regulating the structure of industries.

Section 2 of the original antitrust statute, the Sherman Act of 1890, prohibits monopoly behavior in the following broad language:

> . . . every person who shall monopolize or attempt to monopolize, or combine or conspire with any other person or persons, to monopolize any part of the trade or commerce among the several States, or with foreign nations, shall be deemed guilty of a misdemeanor, and, on conviction thereof, shall be punished by fine not exceeding fifty thousand dollars, or by imprisonment not exceeding one year, or by both said punishments, in the discretion of the court.

Because of the Supreme Court's *interpretation* of the broad statutory language and the murky legislative history of section 2 of the Sherman Act in the

---

[7] Not everyone agrees with this rendition of the facts. See, for example, John S. McGee, "Predatory Price Cutting: The Standard Oil (N.J.) Case," *Journal of Law and Economics*, vol. 1 (October 1958), pp. 137–169.

[8] 21 Congressional Record 2456 (1890).

TABLE 18-1
IMPORTANT FEDERAL TRADE REGULATION STATUTES

Structure-oriented statutes	Behavior-oriented statutes	Performance-oriented statutes
Sherman Act (1890) sec.2* prohibits monopolies and attempts or conspiracies to monopolize. **Clayton Act** (1914) sec. 7 prohibits mergers, when the effect may be to substantially lessen competition or to create a monopoly. Amended (1950)—Celler-Kefauver Act clarified application of Section 7 to acquisition of assets. **Clayton Act** (1914) sec. 8 prohibits interlocking directorates.	**Sherman Act** (1890) sec. 1* prohibits combinations and conspiracies in restraint of trade including vertical and horizontal price fixing, group boycotts, division of markets, and other practices. **Clayton Act** (1914) sec. 2 prohibits price discriminations, substantially lessening sellers' competition (primary violations). Amended (1936)—Robinson-Patman Act prohibits price discriminations, substantially lessening buyers' competition (secondary violation). **Clayton Act** (1914) sec. 3 prohibits exclusive dealing and tying arrangements where the effect may be to substantially lessen competition. **Federal Trade Commission Act** (1914) sec. 5† prohibits unfair methods of competition; established and defined powers of FTC. Amended (1938)—Wheeler-Lea Act prohibits unfair trade practices and false advertising. Amended (1976)—Hart-Scott-Rodino Act increases merger-reporting requirements.	**Emergency Price Control Act of 1942** set up the Office of Price Administration to control prices and rents during World War II. **Defense Production Act of 1950** was passed to control prices during the Korean War. **Economic Stabilization Act of 1970** gave the president the power to control prices during a period of high inflation.

*Amended in 1974 and 1976 to increase penalties and broaden enforcement.
†Amended in 1973 and 1975 to increase penalties and grant industry-wide, rule-making power.

Standard Oil case,[9] in 1914 Congress passed the Clayton Act to provide more specific criteria for the regulation of industry structures.[10]

[9] *Standard Oil Co. of New Jersey v. United States,* 221 U.S. 1 (1911).

[10] As we will see in Chapter 19, there is debate over the extent to which section 2 can be applied to structure without evidence of monopolistic behavior.

Section 7 of the Clayton Act outlawed mergers that would cause the structure of an industry to change so that competition would substantially decrease.

That no corporation engaged in commerce shall acquire, directly or indirectly, the whole or any part of the stock or other share capital and no corporation subject to the jurisdiction of the Federal Trade Commission shall acquire the whole or any part of the assets of one or more corporations engaged in commerce, where in any line of commerce in any section of the country, the effect of such acquisition . . . may be substantially to lessen competition, or to tend to create a monopoly.

The original section 7 banned only anticompetitive mergers that resulted from the purchase of stock, leaving several loopholes. In 1950 the section was amended by the Celler-Kefauver Act to include mergers accomplished through the purchase of assets. Finally, section 8 of the Clayton Act banned interlocking directorates for corporations with assets larger than $1 million.

Behavioral

The Sherman, Clayton, and Federal Trade Commission Acts all have sections aimed at preventing certain types of business behavior that have anticompetitive effects.

Section 1 of the Sherman Act states that "every contract, combination in the form of trust or otherwise, or conspiracy, in restraint of trade or commerce among the several states, or with foreign nations, is hereby declared to be illegal." This broad language has been interpreted by the courts to prohibit such practices as vertical and horizontal price fixing, group boycotts, and division of markets.

Section 2 of the Clayton Act, as amended by the Robinson-Patman Act in 1938, is aimed at preventing price discrimination. The basic rule laid down by the Congress is stated in section 2(a).

That it shall be unlawful for any person engaged in commerce, in the course of such commerce, either directly or indirectly, to discriminate in price between different purchasers of commodities of like grade and quality, where either or any of the purchases involved in such discrimination are in commerce, . . . where the effect of such discrimination may be substantially to lessen competition or tend to create a monopoly in any line of commerce, or to injure, destroy, or prevent competition with any person who either grants or knowingly receives the benefit of such discrimination, or with customers of either of them: *Provided,* that nothing herein contained shall prevent differentials which make only due allowance for differences in the cost of manufacture, sale, or delivery resulting from the differing methods or quantities in which such commodities are to such purchasers sold or delivered.

The original section 2 was primarily aimed at preventing the anticompetitive effects of price discrimination, which might be seen as lessening competition among sellers. The Robinson-Patman Act, however, was the result of complaints by small businesses that larger competitors were using their power to induce suppliers to give them discriminatory, lower prices. The language of section 2(f) is evidence of Congressional intent to stop such practices.

> That it shall be unlawful for any person engaged in commerce, in the course of such commerce, knowingly to induce or receive a discrimination in price which is prohibited by this section

Section 3 of the Clayton Act prohibits exclusive dealing contracts and tying arrangements where the effect would be to substantially lessen competition.

> That it shall be unlawful for any person engaged in commerce, in the course of such commerce, to lease or make a sale of contract for sale of goods, wares, merchandise, machinery, supplies or other commodities, whether patented or unpatented, for use, consumption or resale within the United States . . . or discount from or rebate upon, such price, on the condition, agreement or understanding that the lessee or purchaser thereof shall not use or deal in the goods, wares, merchandise, machinery, supplies, or other commodities of a competitor or competitors of the lessor or seller, where the effect of such lease, sale, or contract for sale or such condition, agreement or understanding may be to substantially lessen competition or tend to create a monopoly in any line of commerce.

Section 5 of the Federal Trade Commission Act states that "unfair methods of competition in or affecting commerce and unfair or deceptive acts or practices in or affecting commerce are hereby declared illegal." The Federal Trade Commission is given the power to enforce section 5. The original Act banned only "unfair methods of competition"; however, the ban on unfair or deceptive acts or practices was added in 1938 by the Wheeler-Lea Act.

Section 5 originally prohibited the stated acts "in commerce"; however, section 201 of the Magnuson-Moss Warranty Federal Trade Commission Improvement Act of 1975 expanded the reach of section 5 to "in or affecting commerce." That act also officially gave the commission the power to issue industry-wide rules having the effect of law to prohibit unfair or deceptive acts or practices and unfair methods of competition.

The Hart-Scott-Rodino Antitrust Improvements Act of 1976 amended section 7 of the Clayton Act to require advance notification to the Justice Department and FTC of mergers between companies of a certain size.

Performance-Oriented Statutes

In addition to the statutes affecting the structure and behavior of business, Congress has in the past implemented laws that attempt to control market outcomes more directly. These statutes traditionally have taken the form of wage and price stabilization programs that existed during times of war and more recently during a period of rising inflation.

During World War II, Congress passed the Emergency Price Control Act of 1942. The act's purpose was stated as follows:

> The purposes of this Act are, to stabilize prices and to prevent speculative, unwarranted, and abnormal increases in prices and rents; to eliminate and prevent profiteer-

ing, hoarding, manipulation, speculation, and other disruptive practices resulting from abnormal market conditions or scarcities caused by or contributing to the national emergency. . . ."[11]

The act set up the Office of Price Administration, which regulated prices and rents during the war.

During the Korean conflict, Congress passed the Defense Production Act of 1950. That act authorized the president to establish price and rental ceilings to stabilize the national economy during the time of war.

During a period of high inflation when the country was not engaged in a declared war, Congress passed the Economic Stabilization Act of 1970, an amendment to the Defense Production Act of 1950. That act again authorized the president to stabilize wages, prices, and rents. In a series of executive orders, President Nixon used the power delegated to him under the act to institute wage and price controls.

Other Important Aspects of Antitrust Enforcement

Proscriptive Nature   Antitrust decisions do not tell business people how they should act. Rather, they tell them how they should *not* act. In this sense, antitrust is *proscriptive* rather than *prescriptive*. It follows that antitrust is not the basis for the regulation of business conduct.

Jurisdiction   Antitrust statutes apply only to restraints that have a "significant" impact on interstate commerce. The Commerce Clause of the U.S. Constitution, as interpreted by the Supreme Court, limits congressional regulation to activities affecting interstate commerce.[12] In principle, only commerce clothed with some interstate aspect may be regulated. However, the courts have more and more broadly construed the meaning of "interstate" to apply to cases involving a significant effect on commerce. Furthermore, state regulation of anticompetitive practices covers local restraints of trade.

Actually, some statutes such as the Sherman Act extend to American nationals abroad who are engaged in activities that will affect this country's foreign commerce. The Sherman Act was applied, for example, in *Continental Ore Company v. Union Carbide and Carbon Corporation* [370 U.S. 690 (1962)]. In that case, the defendants tried to monopolize the vanadium market in Canada. They did this by having their Canadian subsidiary initiate political action that closed off the plaintiff from Canadian markets.

Remedies and Sanctions   Antitrust statutes usually carry explicit penalties. The Sherman Act, for example, indicates that any person found guilty of violating either section 1 or section 2 can be subjected to criminal prosecution for a felony. Currently, upon conviction a person can be fined up to $100,000 or

---

[11] 56 Stat. 23, 24 (1942).
[12] U.S. Constitution, Art. 1, sec. 8, par. 3.

imprisoned for three years, or both. A corporation can be fined $1 million. The Department of Justice can simultaneously institute civil proceedings to restrain the conduct that is in violation of the act. The various remedies for which the Justice Department has asked the court include divestiture, dissolution, and divorcement, or making a company give up one of its operating functions. A group of meat packers may be forced to divorce themselves from controlling or owning butcher shops, for example.

One of the unique features of the Sherman Antitrust Act is that it allows any person injured as a result of violations of the act to bring suit for treble damages against defendants in addition to reasonable attorneys' fees. In the 1960s General Electric Company, along with other major electrical equipment manufacturers, paid over $200 million in treble damage claims. Some corporate officers were fined and some of them even went to jail.

Who Has the Right to Sue?   The Department of Justice and the Federal Trade Commission are not the only entities that may file suit under the antitrust laws. For example, private parties can also sue for damages or other remedies for violations of the Sherman Act. The courts have determined that the test of the right to sue depends on the directness of the injury suffered by the purported plaintiff. Thus, if you wish to sue under the Sherman Act, you must prove that (1) the injury that you suffered was directly caused by the antitrust violation, or the violation was at least a substantial factor in causing the injury, and (2) the unlawful actions of the purported defendant affected business activities of the plaintiff that were intended to be protected by the antitrust laws.

EXEMPTIONS FROM ANTITRUST LAWS

In a sense, Congress' attention to the antitrust laws after the Clayton Act has focused primarily on writing exceptions to the coverage of the Sherman Act. The Clayton Act sought unsuccessfully to exempt unions from the antitrust law. The National Labor Relations Act of 1935, however, did protect unions from antitrust legislation. Today, therefore, unions can lawfully engage in actions that are normally prohibited as long as they do not conspire or join with nonlabor groups to accomplish their goals.

The Miller-Tydings Act

The Miller-Tydings Act was passed in 1937 as an amendment to section 1 of the Sherman Act; it allowed fair-trade agreements. A **fair-trade agreement** occurs when a manufacturer can specify to all the people who sell his or her product that they cannot sell it below a listed, or fair-trade, price. This is also called **resale price maintenance**. This type of fair-trade agreement would seem to violate antitrust laws aimed at preventing price fixing. Nonetheless, the Miller-Tydings Act made this type of price fixing legal.

On March 13, 1976, Congress repealed the Miller-Tydings Act. It had become clear by then that a major result of this exemption to the Sherman Act was the stifling of price competition among retailers.

Small Businesses

Small businesses are allowed to engage in certain concerted activities without violating the antitrust laws. This legislation started with the Small Business Act of 1953.

Labor and Agriculture

Labor and agricultural organizations are exempted from the Sherman Antitrust Act by section 6 of the Clayton Act. Agriculture's exemption from antitrust legislation is further extended by the Capper-Volstead Act (1922), the Cooperative Marketing Act (1926), and certain provisions of the Robinson-Patman Act. Labor's exemption was strengthened by the Norris-La Guardia Act of 1932.

Sports

Most commercial activities are subject to the antitrust laws, but there are exceptions. For example, baseball remains untouched by the antitrust laws; it was not thought to be commerce in the Sherman Act's original thinking and is thus not treated as commerce today. Baseball's exemption is anomalous, since no other professional sport receives such treatment.

Professionals

A current controversial topic in antitrust law is the regulation of professionals, such as lawyers and doctors. Professional organizations are no longer exempt from antitrust enforcement. They cannot establish minimum fee schedules or prohibit competitive bidding in any way. The traditional incantations about the maintenance of high quality no longer shield professionals from the antitrust laws.

Insurance

The McCarran-Ferguson Act exempts from the antitrust laws all activities that are in the "business of insurance." The primary element of the insurance business is the spreading and underwriting of policyholder risk. Thus, such activities that are regulated by state laws may be exempt from the antitrust laws because of the McCarran-Ferguson Act.

Some government actions that hinder competition are exempt from antitrust laws. In *Parker v. Brown,* the Supreme Court upheld the activities of a California agency that fixed raisin production and prices, even though this was done at the request of and with the concurrence of a majority of growers.[13] The state regulation was not a burden on interstate commerce since it coincided with federal agricultural policy. Moreover, the Sherman Act's prohibition of contracts in restraint of trade by ''any person'' applied to private businesses, not government agencies. Since *Parker v. Brown,* the state action exception has been narrowed by the courts. Today bold attempts by states to engage in price fixing are within the jurisdiction of the Sherman Act.

Foreign Trade

Sometimes the choice to exempt certain activities from antitrust actions is based upon a decision that certain goals can be better achieved through cartelization. For example, the Webb-Pomerene Act exempts acts or agreements made in the course of export trade by associations of producers formed solely for the purpose of engaging in export trade.

Public Utilities Industries

It has been argued that free competition of electricity and natural gas would lead to undesirable results. Basically, the natural monopoly outline on pages 366–367 has been the basis for this agrument. Rather than recreate the diagram from page 366, we simply mention here that regulated industries are ones in which the rate of return is supposed to be kept fair by government actions. In order to fully regulate the industry, entry is virtually completely blocked and the existing firms are not subject to antitrust prosecution for the monopoly they hold.

Banking

As with public utilities, antitrust issues have arisen in banking. Control over the services and rates that banks provide is not so pervasive as that of the public utility commissions; no antitrust challenges on the day-to-day operations of the banking industry have been made. Questions about mergers and antitrust policy have, nonetheless, arisen. Bank mergers are susceptible to prosecution under section 7 of the Clayton Act.

MAJOR CASES

In the previous chapters, many industrial organization concepts were analyzed in the context of a particular case. The purpose of this section is to identify the general legal principles and boundaries of court actions having impacts on industrial structure, behavior, and performance.

---

[13] *Parker v. Brown,* 317 U.S. 341 (1943).

Structure

Section 2 of the Sherman Act makes it an offense to monopolize. It should be noted that the act makes it illegal to monopolize, not to *be* a monopolist. Thus, when a monopoly is discovered, the court must determine if the monopolist came by his or her position by monopolizing activities. The courts, however, have extensively focused on various structural elements in determining whether monopolization has occurred.

An illegal monopolistic position has been defined by one court as overwhelming market share, the preclusion of actual and potential competition by market strength that is not attributed solely to economies of scale, research, natural advantages, and adaptation to inevitable economic laws.[14] Once a firm has such a position, it may not do anything in terms of pricing or output changes to maintain its position, even under the guise of meeting competition and even if the practice does not violate section 1 of the Sherman Act.

A firm may defend its position only if it has a **natural monopoly**, one which is thrust upon the firm or which results from superior skill or foresight.[15]

As was previously noted, section 7 of the Clayton Act usually applies to horizontal mergers, those most likely to raise competitive concerns. With limited exceptions, section 7 forbids the acquisition by one corporation in commerce of the stock or assets of another corporation in commerce when the effect might be to lessen competition substantially or to create a monopoly in any section of the country. The adverse competitive effects must occur in a defined product or geographic market. It must be shown that the acquiring and acquired firms actually or potentially compete and that the merger alters structure in a way that threatens competition throughout the market to an unacceptable degree. Of all these factors the most difficult to deal with and measure are the competitive effects and market definition.

In a series of cases the Supreme Court has searched for a workable standard to apply to mergers under section 7.[16] To establish a *prima facie* case, the government must show certain factors. There must be a trend toward concentration in the industry; the proposed merger must cause an increase in concentration; the merged firm must have an undue market share; and there must be difficult entry into the market.

Possible defenses to a section 7 action include (1) an increase in efficiency caused by the merger (although this defense is not widely accepted), and (2) what is known as the failing company defense. In *General Dynamics Corp.*, two leading coal producers merged, significantly increasing the concentration in the relevant geographic markets.[17] The Court looked beyond the raw concentration figures and determined that the acquired firm was not a viable com-

---

[14] *United States v. United Shoe Machinery Corp.*, 110 F. Supp 295, *aff'd* 347 U.S. 521 (1953).
[15] *United States v. Aluminum Co. of America*, 148 F.2d 416 (1945).
[16] See *Brown Shoe Co. v. United States*, 370 U.S. 294 (1962); *United States v. Philadelphia National Bank*, 374 U.S. 321 (1963); and *United States v. Von's Grocery Co.*, 384 U.S. 270 (1966).
[17] *United States v. General Dynamics Corp.*, 94 S.Ct. 1186 (1974).

petitor; therefore, because of the failing company doctrine, the merger was allowed. The Department of Justice publishes merger guidelines (discussed in Chapter 15), which put companies on notice that mergers taking place in certain markets involving certain-sized competitors will be challenged.

A problem with section 7 (and other structural monopoly) cases involves defining the relative product market. In *Brown Shoe Co.,* the Court defined the product market as follows:

> The outer boundaries of a product market are determined by the reasonable inter-changeability of use or the cross elasticity of demand between the product itself and substitutes for it. However, within this broad market well-defined submarkets may exist which, in themselves, constitute product markets for antitrust purposes.

Another problem with horizontal mergers under section 7 is whether the companies actually are competitors. While the question is easily answered when the two companies are in the same product line, it becomes more difficult when the merger is challenged on the grounds that the acquiring firm was a potential entrant into the market on a *de novo* basis. Generally in such cases the court has looked at the concentration level in the market, the number of potential entrants, and the history of the industry, among other things.[18]

The creation of monopoly through vertical integration can be accomplished in two ways. First, a company can vertically integrate by merging with one of its suppliers or customers. Second, a company can enter into contractual arrangements such as requirements or output contracts. The result of either of these actions can be foreclosure or the denial of markets to competitors. These contracts are generally challenged under Sherman section 1 and/or Clayton section 3 (see *Standard Oil of California*), while mergers are covered by Clayton section 7 (see *Brown Shoe Co.*).[19]

In analyzing vertical mergers or exclusive contracts, the court will look at the amount of the market foreclosed. In order to do this, the relevant market and product must be defined. The court will next look at the nature and purpose of the agreement or merger and whether it results in efficiency increases or tends to reduce the risk of supply or demand variations. Another factor that is considered is a trend in the industry toward concentration and vertical integration that would result in barriers to entry or forcing out competitors.

It should be pointed out that this is a rule-of-reason (as opposed to *per se* illegality) approach to the law; the court will look at the reasons behind a merger or contract.

Behavior

It is illegal *per se* under section 1 of the Sherman Act for competitors to agree to limit rivalry among themselves by fixing prices.

---

[18] See *United States v. Penn-Olin Chemical Co.,* 378 U.S. 158 (1964), and *United States v. El Paso Natural Gas Co.,* 376 U.S. 651 (1964).

[19] *Standard Oil of California v. United States,* 337 U.S. 293 (1949), and *Brown Shoe v. United States,* 370 U.S. 294 (1962).

In *Addyston Pipe & Steel Co.*, members of a trade association rigged their bids to decide who would get certain jobs.[20] In defense of its action, the association argued that the rigged prices were reasonable; the price fixing was necessary to prevent ruinous competition; and it would have been legal at common law. In the Court's opinion, Judge Taft announced his famous rule-of-reason approach. According to Taft, if a price restraint is ancillary to a main agreement with a legitimate cause, then it should be examined under a rule-of-reason standard. That is, the court should consider whether the restraint is justified by the beneficial effects of the main agreement. However, when a restraint is naked, or not ancillary to another agreement, then it should be per se illegal. In this case, since the primary purpose of the agreement was to fix prices, the restraint is *per se* illegal.[21]

Forty-two years later, in *Socony Vacuum Oil Co.*, the Supreme Court more clearly enunciated the *per se* rule in the famous footnote 59 of the opinion.[22] Major oil companies agreed to buy up excess oil that had flooded the market in order to keep the market price of oil high enough to avoid "ruinously low prices." The Court held that any conspiracy to fix prices was a violation of section 1 of the Sherman Act regardless of the parties' ability to carry out the plan, the reasonableness of the prices, the quantity or quality of the injury or the market power of the parties. The majority of the Court endorsed the Taft naked ancillary distinction, where, after finding a naked restraint, the only inquiry the Court has to make is whether the contract combination or conspiracy existed. Generally price-fixing cases involve a search for documents and testimony showing the *intent* of the defendants to fix prices, or meetings where prices were discussed. The mere showing that competitors consciously paralleled each other's behavior, however, is normally not sufficient to prove that an agreement existed. See *Theatre Enterprises, Inc.*[23]

The advantage of the strict *per se* rule is that it makes law enforcement much easier by easing problems of proof and by acting as a deterrent to illegal activity.

If we assume that there is a contract combination or conspiracy, the question becomes whether the effect is to restrain trade or competition. One form of agreement that frequently occurs is the development of a trade association for the purpose of exchanging information. The question resolves, then, on when an exchange of information becomes a violation of section 1.

In *American Column & Lumber Co.*, a trade association of lumber manufacturers controlling one-third of U.S. production instituted a plan of information exchange for current price information by name of company and names of buyers.[24] The association had monthly meetings and audited its members. One

---

[20] *United States v. Addyston Pipe & Steel Co.*, 85 FED 271 (6th Circuit, 1898).

[21] The rule of reason was further enunciated in *Standard Oil Company of New Jersey v. United States*, 221 U.S. 1 (1911). The *per se* rule was really formulated in *United States v. Trenton Potteries Co. et al.*, 273 U.S. 392 (1927).

[22] *United States v. Socony Vacuum Oil Co.*, 310 U.S. 150 (1940).

[23] *Theatre Enterprises, Inc. v. Paramount Film Distributing Corp.*, 346 U.S. 537 (1954).

[24] *American Column & Lumber Co. v. United States*, 257 U.S. 377 (1921).

of the goals of the program was to prevent overproduction; however, during the time the plan was in effect, prices rose significantly. The Court found a violation of section 1 because of the extent of disclosure among competitors.

Four years later, in *Maple Floorings*, the Court was faced with an association of wood-flooring producers representing 70 percent of the nation's production.[25] The association's plan of information exchange involved *past* pricing information in the form of composite industry statistics. The Court found no violation of section 1 because individual competitors' prices were not disclosed, so no pressure could be brought to bear on nonconforming members of the association.

In a more recent case, *Container Corporation of America,* an association of 18 firms of container manufacturers representing 90 percent of shipments from the southeast provided information on individual competitors' recent prices, but no agreement to adhere to prices existed.[26] The Court found a *per se* violation of section 1 and applied footnote 59 of *Socony Vacuum,* finding that such an information exchange leads to price uniformity and a reduction in competition.

With regard to information exchange, the Court appears to use a modified *per se* approach. The Court will look at the types of information exchanged (present versus past, aggregate versus individual) as well as structural elements of the market, such as concentration and ease of entry. In applying this less stringent standard, the Court recognizes that certain types of information exchange can be beneficial in allowing a market to function more efficiently.

A *per se* rule applies to market division arrangements regardless of whether they are linked to price fixing or other restraints and apparently without a need for a specific showing of significant power or discernible competitive effects.

In *Topco,* small- and medium-sized regional supermarket chains formed a co-op for the purchase and the development of a private brand label to compete with the private labels of large chain stores.[27] There was an agreement that the stores would not use the private brand to compete with other members of the agreement. The Court found a *per se* violation of section 1 even though the agreement among the competitors would diminish only intrabrand competition and would enhance interbrand competition. The Court said it does not have the tools to balance the two types of competition.

In *Colgate & Co.,* Colgate told its retailers that if they did not follow suggested retail prices, they would be cut off from all dealings with the company.[28] The Court found no violation of the Sherman Act since Colgate's actions were purely unilateral and there was no agreement between Colgate and the retailers. A company can deal with whomever it pleases on whatever terms as long as there is no intent to create a monopoly.

The *Colgate* doctrine was greatly narrowed by *Albrecht,* where the Herald

---

[25] *Maple Floorings Mfgs. Ass'n v. United States,* 268 U.S. 563 (1925).
[26] *United States v. Container Corporation of America,* 393 U.S. 333 (1969).
[27] *United States v. Topco Associates, Inc.,* 405 U.S. 596 (1972).
[28] *United States v. Colgate & Co.,* 250 U.S. 300 (1919).

newspaper told one of its distributors that if the distributor did not stop raising prices, the company would take over the route.[29] The Herald then used an outside service to solicit the distributor's customers to receive their papers directly from the company. Cutting back on *Colgate*, the Court found a combination, not between the distributor and Herald, but between Herald and its solicitor. According to the Court, this link was sufficient to constitute a combination to fix prices under section 1 of the Sherman Act. Little is left of the *Colgate* doctrine after this case because a purely unilateral action is difficult to accomplish.

Vertical territorial restrictions, in which a manufacturer grants a retailer or distributor an exclusive territorial franchise, have also been subject to attack under section 1. In *Arnold Schwinn & Co.,* the Court found vertical territorial allocations to be *per se* illegal.[30] In a landmark decision, however, the Court overruled *Schwinn* and applied a rule-of-reason test to vertical territorial allocations.[31] The Court stated that the *per se* rule should be used only when a practice has a pernicious effect on competition and lacks redeeming value. The Court recognized that legitimate economic justifications for vertical restrictions do exist and that the decrease in intrabrand competition must be weighed against the increase in interbrand competition. While such a ruling might seem to overrule a case such as *Topco,* the Court specifically saved that case and did not extend the rule-of-reason analysis to vertical price restraints.

Boycotts generally occur when members of an industry, in an attempt to encourage or require certain types of behavior, refuse to deal with those who do not comply with the standards set up by the group. Since such boycotts represent a combination contract or conspiracy, they are subject to attack under section 1 of the Sherman Act as restraints of trade.

The Supreme Court has consistently found any boycott to be a *per se* violation of the Sherman Act.[32] Even if the industry is trying to police practices that are not legitimate, the Court will still find a boycott *per se* illegal because it is adverse to any extra governmental bodies attempting to police markets.

If industry self-regulation tends to have the effects of a boycott, the Court will make more of an inquiry into the reasons behind the practice. Self-regulation generally occurs when industry standards are set for safety, quality control, or other reasons. The Court will look at the objectivity of and the motives behind the standards.[33]

Section 3 of the Clayton Act prohibits sellers from tying the purchase of one product to that of another where the effect would be to substantially lessen competition or to create a monopoly. Such arrangements may also be attacked

---

[29] *Albrecht v. Herald Co.,* 390 U.S. 145 (1968).
[30] *United States v. Arnold Schwinn & Co.,* 388 U.S. 365 (1967).
[31] *Continental TV Inc. v. GTE Sylvania, Inc.,* 433 U.S. 36 (1977).
[32] See *Eastern States Retail Lumber Dealer's Ass'n v. United States,* 234 U.S. 600 (1914); *Fashion Originator's Guild of America v. FTC,* 312 U.S. 457 (1971); and *United States v. General Motors Corp.,* 384 U.S. 127 (1966).
[33] See *Radiant Burners, Inc. v. Peoples Gas Light & Coke Co.,* 364 U.S. 656 (1961).

under section 1 of the Sherman Act. The question that has had to be resolved by the Court is when tying arrangements should be tolerated.

In *IBM Corp.*, IBM tied the leasing of its tabulators to the sale of cards used in the tabulators.[34] In other words, IBM required all lessees of its tabulating machines to use only IBM-manufactured tabulating cards in those machines. IBM defended against the government's section 3 Clayton attack on the grounds that the machines would not function properly with inferior cards, so the arrangement was needed to guard against loss of goodwill because of machine breakdowns. The company also said that since the patent on the machine already gave it a monopoly, the tying arrangement was not an attempt to extend monopoly power. However, the Court found a section 3 violation because there was a substantial effect on the card industry and because there was a less restrictive alternative for the protection of the company's goodwill through the publishing of required specifications for the cards.

In a series of cases following *IBM*, the Court wrestled with what standard should be used to invalidate tying arrangements under Sherman section 1 and Clayton section 3. In *Times-Picayune Pub. Co.*, the court articulated separate standards for each of the two sections.[35] For a Sherman section 1 violation, the Court said that the act is violated only if the defendant has substantial (monopoly) power in the tying product *and* if substantial volume of commerce in the tied product is restrained. The test for a section 3 violation was less exacting in that a violation occurred if the seller had monopoly power in the tying product *or* if a substantial amount of commerce in the tied product is constrained.

Since *Times-Picayune*, however, the distinction between section 1 and section 3 violations has become blurred. However, the following general principles can be abstracted from the case law.

For a violation to be proven, two conditions must exist. Sufficient power must be shown in the tying product to give the seller the ability to get a higher-than-normal price for the product. Such power may be inferred from a patent or trademark or some other unique factor such as cost advantage. The amount of commerce affected by the tied product must also be "not insubstantial."

The protection of goodwill will be a justification for tying only when no less restrictive alternative is available. This usually occurs when the tied product is unique. For example, a franchisor of a fast-food fried chicken chain could require franchisees to purchase a secret recipe, which is necessary to protect the goodwill of the trademark. The franchisor could not, however, require the franchisee to purchase napkins from him or her since napkins are not a unique product.

Section 2(a) of the Clayton Act, known as the Robinson-Patman Act, prohibits price discrimination. A *prima facie* case under the act has five elements:

---

[34] *IBM Corp. v. United States*, 293 U.S. 131 (1936).
[35] *Times-Picayune Pub. Co. v. United States*, 345 U.S. 594 (1953).

1 Different prices must be charged to different purchasers of the same product.

2 The difference in price must involve a commodity; services are not covered by the act.

3 Commodities that are priced differently must be of like grade and quality.

4 Either of the purchasers has to be involved in interstate commerce.

5 The effect of the pricing must be to lessen competition substantially.

Defenses to a Robinson-Patman action include an attempt to meet competition in good faith and provision of cost-justified price variations. For practical purposes, the latter defense is not very useful.

Robinson-Patman cases involve two types of injury to competition. Primary-line injury refers to harm to competitors of the firm doing the discriminating. Secondary-line discrimination, on the other hand, refers to harm to the competitors of the favored buyer.

The Robinson-Patman Act has not been actively enforced in recent years because it is widely believed to be anticompetitive.[36]

Section 5 of the Federal Trade Commission Act prohibits unfair methods of competition in or affecting commerce. The broad language of the statute was intended to allow the commission to enumerate specific restraints by its interpretation.

To show a violation of section 5, the FTC does not have to prove the elements of a Clayton or Sherman Act violation. The purpose of the section is to allow the FTC to stop anticompetitive practices in their incipiency, or, in other words, *before* they become Sherman or Clayton violations.[37] The commission has been given broad power by the Supreme Court to define what constitutes a violation of section 5.

Performance

Unlike the structure and behavior statutes, the performance statutes did not have broad language needing a great deal of interpretation by the courts. The important litigation dealing with the performance statutes involved challenges to its constitutionality. Since the statutes basically authorized the president to do whatever was needed to stabilize prices, wages, and rents, they had to be challenged on the ground that the delegation of such power by Congress to the president violated the separation of powers principle of the Constitution.

Despite the strong argument of delegation of too much authority to the president, the Emergency Price Control Act of 1942 was upheld in *Yakus* as necessary during the wartime emergency.[38]

---

[36] See, for example, *House Committee on Small Business: Recent Efforts to Amend or Repeal the Robinson-Patman Act*, 94th Cong., 1st Sess. (1975), and Paul Rand Dixon, "Robinson-Patman Is Not Dead—Merely Dormant" (mimeographed address, May 21, 1975).

[37] See, for example, *FTC v. Brown Shoe Co.*, 384 U.S. 316 (1966), and *FTC v. Motion Picture Advertising Co.*, 344 U.S. 392 (1953).

[38] *Yakus v. United States*, 321 U.S. 414 (1944).

The Economic Stabilization Act of 1970 also withstood constitutional challenge in *Amalgamated Meat Cutters,* despite the lack of a wartime emergency.[39]

ECONOMIC THEORY IN LEGAL DECISIONS

In this chapter we have explored the legal meaning of monopoly and competition. We found that in general the statutory language is very broad, creating difficulties for the courts in defining social policies toward industry and firm practices. In fact there are many cases where the economic distinction between competition and monopoly differs substantially from that defined by the law. This occurs most often when the courts are more concerned with wealth transfers than with economic efficiency, such as the dead-weight loss attributable to monopoly pricing. Furthermore, the courts often seek political, as opposed to economic, goals in their decisions. Thus, the courts may prohibit firms from offering lower prices to consumers in hopes of helping small businesses.

In Chapter 19 on antitrust, we will examine the theory and effects of various business practices. Often the examination will arise in the context of a legal action initiated by the government (or a private party under section 4 of the Clayton Act). Finally, in Chapter 20, we will examine current trends and public policy toward regulation by administrative agencies and other governmental bodies.

APPENDIX: Legal Research

Much of the material that constitutes the field of industrial organization involves an analysis of the cases and rules that form the constraints facing decision makers in industrial firms. Unfortunately, it is impossible to identify all legal materials relevant to the field of industrial organization. Nevertheless, unlike economics, legal materials are conveniently indexed and are relatively easy to find.

In addition, the student of industrial organization will also find a large number of similar situations that apply to the same economic problem. An important advantage in legal research is the ability to find similar economic conditions. Furthermore, materials are indexed and organized in such a fashion that one can quickly determine the most recent rule in a particular field. For example, if one is investigating price discrimination in the distribution of movie films, one can easily find other cases on (1) the particular form of price discrimination used, and on (2) price discrimination in the movie industry. For the purposes of industrial organization, we can confine the legal research to two main areas: the treatment of economic activity by the courts and by administrative agencies.

ACCESS TO JUDICIAL REPORTS

In order to understand case law and the impact of court decisions, students must first have a basic understanding of the organization of the court system. The federal courts

---

[39] *Amalgamated Meat Cutters v. Connally,* 337 F.Supp. 237 D.D.C. (1971).

are structured in three tiers: the district courts, the courts of appeals, and the Supreme Court. The district courts are the lowest-ranking federal courts, while the Supreme Court is the highest-ranking court in the country; its decisions are binding on all federal courts in the nation.

Each state also has its own court system, which is usually structured in three tiers. The lowest level is the trial court, then the appellate courts, with the state Supreme Court being the highest court in the state. Decisions by a state Supreme Court are binding on all the courts in that particular state.

Some cases are limited to state jurisdictions. For example, fair-trade laws are state-created-and-enforced statutes; they are not treated uniformly throughout the country. On the other hand, more important decisions involving constraints on managerial decision making and industry stem from decisions in the federal courts, particularly the appellate courts and the Supreme Court. In addition, other specialized courts deal with subjects such as customs, tax, and administrative agencies. In Figure A18-1, the hierarchy of the federal court system is presented.

The decisions of the courts in both the state and federal systems are listed in reports. Each of the various levels of the courts has its own reporting system. The official report of the United States Supreme Court is *U.S. Reports*. In addition, two privately published editions of the Supreme Court's decisions, the West's *Supreme Court Reporter*,

FIGURE A18-1
The organization of the federal court system.

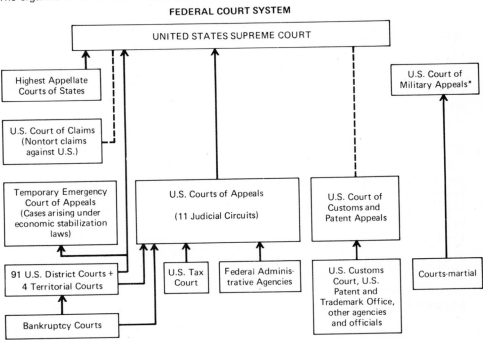

FEDERAL COURT SYSTEM

*Appeal to higher federal courts solely via defendant's petition for a writ of habeas corpus.

———— Appeal as a matter of right, available for some or all cases. Review of some cases may be at option of higher court, via writ of certiorari.

– – – – Review at option of higher court, via writ of certiorari.

and the Lawyer's Edition of the *U.S. Supreme Court Reports,* provide special research aids and supplementary material not in the official edition. All decisions in the U.S. Court of Appeals are published in West's *Federal Reporter.* Selected U.S. District Court decisions are recorded in West's *Federal Supplement.* The coverage of special federal courts has varied over the years but is presently reported in the *Federal Reporter.*

Generally decisions in the state courts are published in two forms. Most states publish official reports, which are important to a researcher because they are authoritative and must be cited in legal reports. However, two unofficial reporting systems—the West Publishing Company's comprehensive *National Reporter System* and Lawyers Co-operative Publishing Company's selective *American Law Reports*—are widely used because they provide superior research aids and excellent notes on cases.

Most of the decisions of the state appellate courts and all of the state Supreme Court decisions are published in West's *National Reporter System.* This system publishes seven regional reporters: *Atlantic, Northeastern, Southeastern, Southern, Southwestern, Northwestern,* and *Pacific.* In addition, West publishes the *New York Supplement* and *California Reporter,* which include not only appellate and state Supreme Court decisions, but also include selected lower-court decisions.

The greatest asset in using the West *Reports* is that they provide a summary of each case followed by a listing of the important points of the decisions, which are indexed in what is called a key-numbering system. The synopsis and key numbers are known as the headnotes; they provide the researcher with the necessary information to find additional related cases. Once a researcher has found the key number concerning the specific topic of interest, he or she can use the *Digest* published by West to find all the cases related to that topic.

The *American Law Reports* is not as exhaustive as the West system, but provides the researcher with another perspective. The *A.L.R.* is an annotated reporter that publishes only selected cases which significantly affect the development of the law. The *A.L.R.* often provides easier access to the leading decisions.

Finding Cases

Various digests and indexes facilitate the search for cases. West publishes a digest for every state, which lists the various topics alphabetically. Under each topic in the law, concise abstracts of cases are listed according to the key numbers. A digest is also published for the federal courts. The student can quickly find all the relevant cases listed next to the appropriate key number. The *American Law Reports* provides a similar but not as comprehensive index system.

If a student is unsure exactly what legal topic he or she is looking for, West publishes a multivolume publication that lists in alphabetical arrangement thousands of key words and phrases that are followed by abstracts of judicial decisions which have interpreted and defined them. For example, the student of industrial organization may focus on a phrase such as "price discrimination" and look in the index to find all the relevant cases.

Once the student has found a case, it is important that he or she verify it in the *Shepard's Citations,* which provides a listing of every place the case is reported, describes other decisions that have cited the case, and tells whether the case is still applicable. For instance, let's assume that the researcher has found a restraint of trade case such as *FTC v. Morton Salt Company.* The official citation in the *U.S. Reports* is 334 U.S. 37. Hence, the student can find the case in volume 334 on page 37 of *U.S.*

Reports. By looking in the *Shepard's United States Citations* the student can discover other places the case is listed, such as West's *Supreme Court Reporter* and all the other decisions that have cited this case. Figure A18-2 presents how *FTC v. Morton* would be listed in the citator. Under the number for page 37 are listed the citations for the Lawyer's Edition, followed by West's *Supreme Court Reporter*. The rest of the decisions listed are cases that have cited the *FTC v. Morton* opinion. The small letters beside the cases are abbreviations as to whether the *Morton* decision was distinguished, over-

FIGURE A18-2
A sample listing from Shepard's United States Citations.

Conn	343US⁷474	264F2d¹288	165FS⁷56	60FTC1815	–62–
174A2d688	344US⁸20	d265F2d³676	172FS¹226	60FTC1897	(92LE1212)
D C	j344US⁷214	269F2d⁶957	177FS⁸323	61FTC649	(68SC972)
60A2d926	j344US³402	282F2d³597	187FS²353	61FTC682	s198Ok1350
63A2d652	345US⁶621	288F2d⁷259	199FS³347	61FTC819	Okla
100A2d451	346US³75	289F2d⁴843	206FS³154	61FTC1183	s180P2d1009
Ill	j346US⁹85	291F2d⁷838	210FS858	62FTC170	336US¹351
224NE798	360US⁶63	294F2d⁷628	241FS⁴487	62FTC904	j360US¹259
240NE608	363US²544	298F2d⁷440	d242FS³605	63FTC19	369US¹125
Iowa	f363US⁶552	301F2d⁴539	259FS⁴183	63FTC44	370US¹306
60NW115	368US⁷366	317F2d³55	261FS⁶950	63FTC79	371US¹552
78NW500	368US⁷368	323F2d⁴46	262FS388	63FTC1326	j371US¹574
Mass	370US²312	d325F2d⁸106	267FS502	63FTC1341	j375US¹82
124NE235	370US²414	329F2d⁴702	284FS531	63FTC1728	j377US¹397
Mich	370US³467	332F2d⁷356	287FS³763	63FTC2095	384US¹222
52NW162	j383US⁷660	333F2d209	306FS²83	64FTC556	j390US487
116NW368	j384US⁴286	334F2d⁷925	20FRD⁶474	64FTC577	177F2d¹28
144NW625	386US³366	335F2d⁴51	34FRD230	64FTC597	181F2d¹779
157NW221	386US³694	335F2d⁴53	17FCC370	64FTC603	229F2d¹434
157NW230	390US⁷357	335F2d⁶53	45FTC328	64FTC626	232F2d¹368
Mo	173F2d⁴216	338F2d³782	46FTC641	64FTC1444	239F2d¹338
225SW128	176F2d³7	L339F2d⁹57	46FTC896	65FTC28	288F2d¹603
N J	176F2d¹9	347F2d²788	49FTC155	65FTC249	j416F2d¹1020
59A2d841	j182F2d⁸45	348F2d⁶679	49FTC1170	65FTC350	123FS¹211
106A2d363	185F2d745	349F2d⁴148	50FTC563	65FTC707	147FS¹643
Ohio	187F2d¹923	350F2d⁴622	50FTC887	65FTC950	155FS¹733
83NE87	189F2d⁸515	359F2d³365	50FTC902	65FTC958	282FS756
136NE349	189F2d³895	j376F2d204	51FTC166	337ICC77	140CCl73
205NE367	189F2d⁷896	d381F2d¹177	51FTC940	103MCC546	138Ct372
Okla	d191F2d⁶58	381F2d⁴178	51FTC952	105MCC235	203Okl40
237P2d1020	j191F2d²61	f384F2d⁶250	51FTC967	7McA64	203Okl51
Ore	191F2d⁴792	384F2d³251	51FTC987	346Mch680	203Okl53
204P2d578	194F2d³438	395F2d⁸522	51FTC1004	364Mch513	Conn
Pa	194F2d⁶685	398F2d³529	51FTC1123	197Md454	84A2d682
127A2d316	200F2d⁴821	405F2d	51FTC1153	259Min220	Okla
Wis	203F2d¹797	[⁸1059]	52FTC198	95NH177	220P2d284
179NW790	206F2d⁶425	407F2d³7	52FTC1172	157OS446	220P2d294
–28–	d208F2d⁶779	427F2d²336	52FTC1518	Md	220P2d296
428F2d²460	215F2d⁷759	d78FS⁴860	52FTC1670	79A2d528	–100–
–37–	227F2d⁶835	87FS⁴488	54FTC824	Mich	(92LE1236)
(92LE1196)	228F2d⁷445	87FS³489	55FTC962	78NW575	(68SC941)
(68SC822)	d231F2d⁵368	87FS⁵489	55FTC976	111NW799	s68FS180
(1Æ260)	237F2d³14	87FS⁶489	57FTC783	151NW184	s94FS747
s332US850	238F2d²49	87FS¹495	57FTC788	Minn	cc334US110
s162F2d949	238F2d⁴51	87FS²495	60FTC129	106NW904	cc208F2d316
s39FTC35	239F2d⁴154	87FS⁶497	60FTC579	N H	cc216F2d920
s45FTC328	239F2d⁷254	87FS¹988	60FTC582	59A2d473	334US¹155
334US⁴522	245F2d⁴282	112FS³239	60FTC1147	Ohio	334US¹171
337US⁴300	248F2d³326	117FS²694	60FTC1171	105NE877	334US¹173
340US³246	258F2d⁴678	142FS³235	60FTC1222	41ABA185	
343US⁷473	258F2d³682	142FS⁷235	60FTC1806	47ABA347	

ruled, criticized, and so on. Table A18-1 explains the meanings of the abbreviations. Since no case listed has overruled or reversed the *Morton* decision, the researcher can be confident that *FTC v. Morton* is still applicable today.

In recent years, computerized legal research has also become available. Although access to computerized research systems is still limited, the systems provide a remarkably fast method of finding cases. Lexis and West Law are two systems that offer electronic access to the most important cases.

Lexis is a computer system that enables the researcher to search for key words in the full text of recent cases and statutes at the federal level and from a selected number of states.[40] Citations, abstracts, and the entire text may be displayed on the screen and may be recorded on paper copy. There are also specialized libraries of materials on trade regulation.[41]

ADMINISTRATIVE AGENCIES

The most important administrative agencies that have an impact on industrial organization are the Antitrust Division of the Department of Justice and the Federal Trade Commission. In recent years, however, organizations such as the Occupational Health and Safety Administration, the Food and Drug Administration, and the Consumer Product Safety Administration, are playing an increasingly large role in the regulation of industrial activity.

Finding Federal Statutes

A researcher in administrative law will often want a preliminary understanding of the function and structure of the agency under consideration. The most comprehensive single source for such information is the *United States Government Manual,* an annual directory of general information about the federal government with emphasis upon regulatory agencies. The manual may save the researcher considerable time because it provides descriptions of the agencies and their functions, organizational charts, citations to relevant statutes affecting the agency, and sources of information available from the agency.

Since 1935 all executive orders and administrative regulations have been published in the *Federal Register.* The register provides a chronological source and the only complete history of the regulations with the text of all changes. Because of the great bulk of the register, more and more libraries carry its microfilm edition.

A companion publication to the *Federal Register* is the *Code of Federal Regulations.* The advantage to the code is that it is arranged not chronologically but by subject matter, and it has a general index volume providing access to its contents by agency

---

[40] West Law utilizes a different approach, containing materials from West digest system rather than the full text of original documents.

[41] These materials include Federal Trade Commission decisions on (1) commissioners' opinions beginning in 1950, (2) administrative law judges' initial decisions beginning in 1950, (3) administrative law judges' procedural orders beginning in 1976, and (4) consent and interlocutory orders beginning in 1970. They also include (1) trade regulation cases decided in the Supreme Court beginning in 1890, (2) trade regulation cases decided in the courts of appeals beginning in 1945, and (3) trade regulation cases decided in the district courts beginning in 1950.

TABLE A18-1
ABBREVIATIONS—ANALYSIS

	History of Case	
a	(affirmed)	Same case affirmed on appeal.
cc	(connected case)	Different case from case cited but arising out of same subject matter or intimately connected therewith.
D	(dismissed)	Appeal from same case dismissed.
m	(modified)	Same case modified on appeal.
r	(reversed)	Same case reversed on appeal.
s	(same case)	Same case as case cited.
S	(superseded)	Substitution for former opinion.
v	(vacated)	Same case vacated.
US cert den		Certiorari denied by U. S. Supreme Court.
US cert dis		Certiorari dismissed by U. S. Supreme Court.
US reh den		Rehearing denied by U. S. Supreme Court.
US reh dis		Rehearing dismissed by U. S. Supreme Court.

	Treatment of Case	
c	(criticized)	Soundness of decision or reasoning in cited case criticized for reasons given.
d	(distinguished)	Case at bar different either in law or fact from case cited for reasons given.
e	(explained)	Statement of import of decision in cited case. Not merely a restatement of the facts.
f	(followed)	Cited as controlling.
h	(harmonized)	Apparent inconsistency explained and shown not to exist.
j	(dissenting opinion)	Citation in dissenting opinion.
L	(limited)	Refusal to extend decision of cited case beyond precise issues involved.
o	(overruled)	Ruling in cited case expressly overruled.
p	(parallel)	Citing case substantially alike or on all fours with cited case in its law or facts.
q	(questioned)	Soundness of decision or reasoning in cited case questioned.

name and subject. The code provides the easiest way to find a statute since only it provides the current text with subject access. Another source of administrative regulations is the *U.S. Code Congressional & Administrative News,* which gives a legislative history of some federal laws.

In addition to these sources, many looseleaf services publish decisions of administrative agencies in their subject fields. Decisions of the Federal Trade Commission are published in the *Trade Regulation Reporter.* Another important publication for the student of industrial organization is the *FTC Watch.*

Finding State Statutes

As a general rule, publication of state agency rules and decisions is far less systematic than that of the federal government. Finding regulations may be a more difficult proposition. Only 15 states issue compilations of their administrative regulations. For states without an up-to-date compilation, the researcher may have to apply to the secretary of the state or to a particular agency for a copy of a specific regulation. However, one helpful source to the researcher is the *Monthly Checklist of State Publications* issued by the Library of Congress, which lists all state documents received. The documents are arranged by state and agency and a comprehensive index provides easy access.

CHAPTER 19

ANTITRUST AND THE COURTS TODAY

Antitrust laws have been legislated and enforced in order to keep business behavior and markets competitive. In this chapter, we will look at the current purpose, practice, and direction of antitrust laws in this country. The materials in this chapter have been organized along traditional legal classifications as a means of giving the student an overall view of present antitrust activities and court decisions. In this overview of antitrust laws we have also deemphasized the economic arguments in the various legal disputes. In fact, this chapter provides a good test of the student's understanding of the materials in previous chapters as they apply to current antitrust laws. It is impossible to consider all the ramifications of such laws. We'll look at statutes enforced by the Department of Justice and the Federal Trade Commission. Indeed, many of the antitrust and trade regulation statutes apply to both the antitrust activities administered by the Department of Justice and to the Federal Trade Commission. While there is some overlap, the activities of the FTC do, in general, differ from those of the Antitrust Division of the Justice Department. But first let us take a look at recent developments in the construction of antitrust laws by the courts.

Statutory Reforms

In 1974 Congress passed legislation which considerably strengthened criminal antitrust penalties.[1] Formerly a section 1 violation of the Sherman Act was a misdemeanor punishable by up to one-year imprisonment. It is now a felony

---

[1] *Antitrust Procedures and Penalties Act*, Public Law 93-528, 88 Stat. 1706, 93rd Cong., 2d Sess. (1974).

that calls for imprisonment of up to three years. Additionally, former sanctions called for individual and corporation fines up to $50,000. Now fines up to $100,000 may be imposed for individuals and up to $1,000,000 for corporations. Of course the promulgation of new penalties does not necessarily mean that courts will impose tougher sentences. In fact, fines have historically been very low in antitrust cases, and imprisonment has seldom been imposed.[2] Furthermore, the effect of corporate fines is diminished somewhat due to current tax laws. One-third of a judicial award, or a settlement after a judicial determination, may be deductible if there is a settlement without a judicial adjudication. However, the congressional action establishing tougher antitrust penalties may be seen by the courts as a mandate for the imposition of stiffer penalties.

CURRENT ANTITRUST GUIDELINES

The Justice Department currently focuses on eliminating devices that facilitate monopoly behavior. This focus is based on the belief that firms operating in concentrated industries are able to increase prices and reduce output without entering into overt price-fixing arrangements. By focusing on mechanisms that facilitate the achievement of price fixing or other monopoly behavior, the costs of proof may be lower. This is because the traditional antitrust approach requires focusing on the existence of an agreement that is implied by price patterns.[3] Enforcement costs are also lowered by the ability to use injunctions against identified unlawful practices. However, current guidelines necessarily reject the former view that it may be rational, and therefore nonculpable, for firms in concentrated industries to consider the reaction of the other firms to any shift in their output or price.

The Shared Monopoly Approach

As early as 1978, in a memorandum to his chief officials of the Antitrust Division, Assistant Attorney General John H. Shenefield wrote that he was "vitally concerned with the 'shared monopoly' problem" and wanted this matter placed as a "highest priority."[4] Shenefield proceeded to outline an approach for effective use of section 1 of the Sherman Act to prevent or eliminate covert price-setting practices in concentrated industries. A Sherman Act section 2 approach was supposed to follow; however, it apparently never got off the ground.

The Antitrust Division's approach was based on the notion of two essential prerequisites for the effective achievement of the "shared monopoly" or collusive outcome. First, a consensus on a noncompetitive price structure must be

---

[2] Roger D. Blair, "Antitrust Penalties: Deterrence and Compensation," Center for the Study of American Business, Working Paper 31 (May 1978), pp. 3–4. For a contrary opinion regarding sanctions since 1974, see S. S. Arkon, "Too Many Executives Are Going to Jail," *Fortune* (December 17, 1979), p. 113.

[3] John H. Shenefield, "Memorandum on Identification and Challenge of Parallel Pricing Practices in Concentrated Industries," Antitrust Division, Department of Justice (May 26, 1978).

[4] Ibid., p. 223.

met. Second, the probability that individual firms act independently and undercut prices to increase profits must be low. In this context, the existence of only a few firms in an industry is critical since higher levels of concentration facilitate the detection of firms departing from the agreement. If firms are to achieve returns above the competitive rate, they must adopt mechanisms or devices to facilitate this outcome because the courts have reduced the availability of more efficient means such as covert price fixing, output allocation, or exclusive territories.

We now look at the potential mechanisms facilitating shared monopoly.

Information Exchange   One of the more important devices for the detection of nonconformity among firms is the existence of information exchange systems, which reduce the number of factors that rival firms must monitor.

Standardization Systems   Another approach is to standardize the product. With more homogeneous products, nonprice deviations are more easily detectable. Standardization includes the use of standard freight rates, price formulas, price books, bidding systems, and the definition of the product.

Automatic Policing Devices   An alternative to lowering the costs of detecting deviations is to institute mechanisms that automatically encourage compliance with shared monopoly pricing. For example, in greater Los Angeles there were compensation requirements for competitors in the provision of solid waste management.[5]

Antitrust Case Selection   The final determination of whether a practice is a facilitating device involves weighing the business justification against the competitive effect. The competitive effect must overcome business justification. Once a facilitating device is found, it must be demonstrated that its use unreasonably restrains trade.

The Antitrust Division uses a four-step approach to determine if the use of a facilitating device violates section 1:

1 A parallel course of conduct by firms in a concentrated industry with respect to the adoption of, or adherence to, a business practice that may be used as a facilitating mechanism

2 An awareness by each firm that its rivals are following a parallel course with respect to the suspect practice

3 An anticompetitive benefit derived by each firm from this parallel course of conduct

4 Action contradictory to the independent self-interest of each firm, in that a single firm would not have adopted the practice unless it was also adopted by its major rivals

[5] *United States v. Greater L.A. Solid Wastes Management*, 1974-1 Trade Cases ¶ 74, 994 (C.D. Cal. 1974).

In order to prove section 1 violation, the Antitrust Division must provide evidence for all four of the above steps.[6]

Possible Decline of Shared Monopoly In early 1981, the newly appointed head of the Justice Department Antitrust Division, William Baxter, announced that the antitrust laws should seek solely to promote economic efficiency, and that antitrust attorneys will be judged on their economic expertise.[7]

The Allocation of Antitrust Resources

It is difficult to judge the effectiveness of antitrust laws, particularly the effectiveness of their enforcement. Posner has concluded that cases have not been brought in industries that are the most concentrated or ones for which antitrust prosecution would enhance economic welfare the most.

A careful study of antitrust cases by Posner and others reveals that their enforcement has not been directly aimed at correcting the welfare loss or any other measure of economic inefficiency.[8] Nonetheless, we can see some clues to the effectiveness of antitrust policy.

A Change in Corporate Mergers Antitrust laws seem to have had some impact on the merger policies of firms. The 1950 amendment of section 7 of the Clayton Act and its subsequent enforcement seem to have caused firms to shift away from horizontal acquisitions toward conglomerate mergers. Apparently the trend toward conglomerate acquisitions has kept concentration levels in specific industries below those that would have prevailed in the absence of antitrust legislation and enforcement.

ANTITRUST IN THE LATE 1970s

The Reach of the Antitrust Laws

In a series of cases since 1977, the Supreme Court has given the antitrust laws a broader reach by narrowly construing antitrust exemptions.

In *Bates v. State Bar of Arizona* the Court refused to strike down the

---

[6] Shenefield, "Memorandum on Identification and Challenge of Parallel Pricing Practices in Concentrated Industries." For a proposed alternative set of case selection standards in shared monopoly cases, see Wesley J. Liebeler, "Market Power and Competitive Superiority in Concentrated Industries," *UCLA Law Review*, vol. 25 (August 1978), pp. 1231–1300, esp. pp. 1275 ff.

[7] *The Wall Street Journal* (May 15, 1981), p. 1. Also, the FTC lost its shared monopoly case against the three largest cereal firms. *The Wall Street Journal* (September 11, 1981), p. 5.

[8] Richard A. Posner, "A Statistical Study of Antitrust Enforcement," *Journal of Law and Economics*, vol. 13 (October 1970), pp. 365–420. See, for example, William F. Long, Richard Schramm, and Robert Tollison, "The Economic Determinants of Antitrust Activity," *Journal of Law and Economics*, vol. 16 (October 1973), pp. 351–364. Compare Roger Blair and David Kaserman, "Market Structure and Costs: An Explanation of the Behavior of the Antitrust Authorities," *Antitrust Bulletin*, vol. 21 (Winter 1976), pp. 691–702. Blair and Kaserman reach the opposite conclusion after adjusting the Long, Schramm, and Tollison profit data to include advertising expenditures, which they view as dissipating oligopoly profits.

Arizona bar's ban on lawyer advertising on the grounds that it violated the Sherman Act.[9] Citing *Parker v. Brown,* the court reaffirmed the principle that certain types of state action, such as the bar's ban on advertising, are exempt from antitrust laws.[10] Although the advertising ban survived the Sherman Act attack, it was struck down on First Amendment commercial speech grounds.

The *Parker v. Brown* state action exemption was construed narrowly in *City of Lafayette v. Louisiana Power & Light Co.*[11] The city, which owned and operated electric utility companies, sued a privately owned power company for alleged antitrust violations. The private company then counterclaimed against the city on antitrust grounds. The city urged that the counterclaim should be dismissed because, as a government entity, the city was immune from antitrust suits under the *Parker v. Brown* state action exemption. The Supreme Court held that *Parker* does not automatically exempt from antitrust laws all government entities merely because of their status as such. It exempts only anticompetitive conduct engaged in as an act of government by the state as sovereign or by its subdivisions pursuant to state policy to displace competition with monopoly public service or regulation.

In two recent cases the Supreme Court has narrowly construed the antitrust exemption given to state-regulated insurance businesses under the McCarran-Ferguson Act. According to the Court's opinion in *St. Paul Fire & Marine Insurance Company v. Barry,* section 3(b) of the Sherman Act was meant to prohibit *any* boycott, including that by insurance companies against policyholders.[12] Insurance companies refused to deal with the policyholders of another company as a means of compelling them to submit to new ground rules imposed by that company.

In the 1979 case of *Group Life & Health Insurance Co. v. Royal Drug Co., Inc.* the Court held that an agreement between Blue Shield and a group of Texas pharmacies, whereby the latter would supply drugs to Blue Shield's policyholders for two dollars with the remainder of the cost to be paid by Blue Shield, was not the business of insurance and therefore not exempt from antitrust attack under the McCarran-Ferguson Act.[13] The business of insurance, the Court held, involved the underwriting or spreading of risk, which this arrangement lacked.

The jurisdiction of the Sherman Act was given an expanded reading in *McLain v. Real Estate Board of New Orleans, Inc.,* where a suit was brought against real estate brokers in the New Orleans area who had agreed to abide by fixed commission rates.[14] The Court rejected the brokers' argument that the Sherman Act did not reach the agreement because it was purely local in nature and did not substantially affect interstate commerce. According to the Court

[9] *Bates v. State Bar of Arizona,* 97 S.Ct. 2691 (1977).
[10] *Parker v. Brown,* 317 U.S. 341 (1943).
[11] *City of Lafayette v. Louisiana Power & Light Co.,* 98 S.Ct. 1123 (1978).
[12] *St. Paul Fire & Marine Insurance Company v. Barry,* 98 S.Ct. 2923 (1978).
[13] *Group Health & Life Insurance Co. v. Royal Drug Co., Inc.,* 98 S.Ct. 1448 (1978).
[14] *McLain v. Real Estate Board of New Orleans, Inc.,* 49 U.S.L.W. 4063 (1980).

the brokerage activity did affect an appreciable amount of interstate commerce through its financing of property and its title insurance. The agreement was therefore subject to attack under the Sherman Act.

Standing to Sue

In three recent cases the Supreme Court has taken the opportunity to better define who has standing, i.e., the right to sue for antitrust violations.

In *Illinois Brick Co. v. Illinois*, several government entities sued for treble damages (three times the court-awarded damages) under section 4 of the Clayton Act, alleging that concrete block manufacturers engaged in price fixing and that the increased prices were passed on to the plaintiffs by general contractors who built buildings for the plaintiffs.[15] The Court refused to grant these indirect purchasers standing to sue on the grounds that to do so would open the door for suits with problems of massive evidence and complicated theories.

In another standing suit, the Third Circuit Court of Appeals ruled that a person purchasing directly from a nonconspiring competitor of the defendants in an antitrust suit could not sue the defendants for damages caused by higher than competitive industry prices that resulted from the conspiracy. The court did state, however, that indirect purchasers such as those in *Illinois Brick* do have standing to seek injunctive relief against the anticompetitive conduct.

Another significant Supreme Court decision related to the right to sue under the antitrust laws is *Reiter v. Sonotone Corp.*[16] In that case a consumer brought a class action suit against a hearing aid manufacturer for treble damages under section 4 of the Clayton Act. The plaintiff alleged that she and other members of the class were forced to pay illegally fixed higher prices because of antitrust violations. The defendant argued that section 4, which allows recovery for any person injured in his or her business or property by antitrust violation, applies only to property of a commercial or business nature and not to consumers. The Court ruled that consumers who suffer monetary loss because of antitrust violations may sue under section 4.

In another case interpreting section 4 of the Clayton Act, *Pfizer, Inc. v. Government of India*, the Court ruled that a foreign government is a "person" for purposes of a treble damage action under that section.[17] Thus a foreign government may sue for injuries resulting from antitrust violations.

Mergers

The most recent substantive merger case decided by the Court under section 7 of the Clayton Act was *Brunswick Corp. v. Pueblo Bowl-O-Mat, Inc.*[18] Brunswick, one of the largest manufacturers of bowling equipment and the

---

[15] *Illinois Brick Co. v. Illinois*, 97 S.Ct. 2061 (1977).
[16] *Reiter v. Sonotone Corp.*, 99 S. Ct. 2326 (1979).
[17] *Pfizer, Inc. v. Government of India*, 98 S.Ct. 584 (1978).
[18] *Brunswick Corp. v. Pueblo Bowl-O-Mat, Inc.*, 97 S.Ct. 690 (1977).

largest operator of bowling centers, often acquired bowling centers that defaulted in payments for equipment sold to them by Brunswick. Bowling centers not owned by Brunswick and operating in three different markets brought suit for treble damages, alleging that the acquisition of the defaulted bowling centers by Brunswick might substantially lessen competition or tend to create a monopoly in violation of section 7 of the Clayton Act. To establish their damages, the plaintiffs attempted to show that had Brunswick allowed the defaulting centers to close, the plaintiffs would have had increased profits. The Supreme Court held that in order to recover, the plaintiffs must show that their loss was causally linked to illegal activities engaged in by Brunswick. Even if the acquisitions by Brunswick constituted section 7 violations, this violation did not automatically entitle the plaintiffs to their claimed damages. The Court stated that if the plaintiffs' damages were caused by the failure of the defaulting centers to go out of business, they would have suffered the same damages had these centers been acquired by a smaller company, whose acquisition would not be a section 7 violation. The damage award of the lower court was therefore vacated.

In another significant merger case, *BOC International Limited v. FTC*, the Second Circuit Court of Appeals refused to accept the Federal Trade Commission's version of the actual potential entrant theory.[19] BOC, the world's second-largest supplier of industrial gases, sought review of an FTC order requiring BOC to divest itself of its interest in a recently acquired American company that was the country's third-largest producer of industrial gases. The court of appeals rejected the FTC's holding that, because there was a reasonable probability that BOC would eventually enter the American market on its own, the acquisition violated section 7 of the Clayton Act. The "eventual entry" standard was based on "ephemeral possibilities" according to the Court, and it therefore was not justified by the statute. The proper standard was said to be whether there was a reasonable probability that the company would enter the market in the near future.

Vertical Restraints

Perhaps the most significant and far-reaching antitrust case in recent years deals with a vertical market decision. GTE, the defendant in *Continental TV, Inc. v. GTE Sylvania Corp.*, was sued by one of its franchisees on the grounds that a restriction which allowed a franchisee to sell only from the franchised location violated section 1 of the Sherman Act (see the earlier discussion on page 425).[20] Continental relied on the Court's decision in *U.S. v. Arnold Schwinn & Co.*, which held similar restrictions to be *per se* violations of the Sherman Act.[21] On the basis of *Schwinn*, the district court instructed the jury that the *per se* test was applicable. The result was a verdict in favor of Conti-

---

[19] *BOC International Limited v. FTC*, 557 F.2d 24 (2d Cir. 1977).
[20] *Continental TV, Inc. v. GTE Sylvania Corp.*, 97 S.Ct. 2549 (1977).
[21] *United States v. Arnold Schwinn & Co.*, 388 U.S. 365 (1967).

nental. The Ninth Circuit Court of Appeals reversed, distinguishing *Schwinn* and ruling that the restrictions should be judged by the rule of reason.

In a 6-2 decision the Supreme Court affirmed the court of appeals application of the rule of reason but overruled *Schwinn*, finding that case to be indistinguishable from *GTE Sylvania*. In its opinion, the Court recognized that there are legitimate economic justifications for vertical territorial restrictions, and that the possible decrease in intrabrand competition they may cause must be weighed against the resulting increase in interbrand competition. Significantly the Court stated that the departure from the rule of reason must "be based upon demonstrable economic effect rather than — as in *Schwinn* — upon formalistic line drawing." The Court further said that the *per se* rule should be used only when a practice has a pernicious effect on competition and lacks redeeming value.

While some commentators have said that the *GTE Sylvania* reasoning should be applied to all vertical restrictions, the Court limited its holding to nonprice vertical restrictions. Vertical price restrictions, therefore, remain in the *per se* illegal category.

A post-*GTE Sylvania* case, *Eastern Scientific Co. v. Wild Heerbrugg Instrument, Inc.*, presented an interesting mix of vertical price maintenance and market division.[22] In that case, an importer of scientific instruments enforced its territorial market divisions by price maintenance. The importer allowed its dealers freedom to price as they wished within their territories, but prohibited them from selling below list price outside their territories. The First Circuit Court of Appeals upheld the restrictions under the rule-of-reason approach required under *GTE Sylvania*. Under *GTE Sylvania* extraterritorial sales could have been banned completely; consequently, the Court reasoned that the price restrictions would not have a greater anticompetitive effect than such a ban.

Tying Arrangements

United States Steel Corp. v. Fortner Enterprises, Inc.[23] reached the Supreme Court in 1977 for the second time. In exchange for a real estate developer's promise to purchase prefabricated houses from U.S. Steel's Home Division, Credit Corp., a wholly owned subsidiary of U.S. Steel, agreed to finance the developer's cost of acquiring and developing the land. The financing offered by Credit Corp. was unusually favorable in that it covered 100 percent of the acquisition and development costs.

Problems arose between the companies, resulting in a treble damage action against U.S. Steel by the developer, who alleged that the transaction was a tying arrangement in violation of the Sherman Act because the competition for prefabricated houses (the tied product) was restrained by U.S. Steel's power

---

[22] *Eastern Scientific Co. v. Wild Heerbrugg Instrument, Inc.*, 572 F.2d 883 (1st Cir. 1978) *cert. denied* 99 S.Ct. 112 (1978).

[23] *United States Steel Corp. v. Fortner Enterprises, Inc.*, 97 S.Ct. 861 (1977).

over credit (the tying product). In the case's first appearance before the Supreme Court, the Court reversed a summary judgment in favor of U.S. Steel, finding that the agreement affected a "not insubstantial" amount of commerce in the tied product and that Fortner should have the opportunity to prove U.S. Steel had appreciable economic power in the tying product market. Upon remand the district court found that U.S. Steel had sufficient power in the credit market to make the tying arrangement illegal. The court of appeals affirmed.

The basis of Fortner's argument and the lower court's findings was that because the credit offered by U.S. Steel was so favorable, it was a unique product from which market power in the credit business could be inferred. An important factor in this finding was the size of U.S. Steel, which backed its credit company. The Supreme Court, however, held that the favorable credit terms were used merely to sell houses that were higher-priced than the average prefabricated house on the market. The Court stated that the mere showing that credit terms are unique, because the seller was willing to accept a lesser profit or incur more risks than its competitors, does not establish the existence of any power in the credit market.

Another significant tying case, *Heatransfer Corp. v. Volkswagen-Werk*, involved the sale of air conditioners for a type of foreign car.[24] The plaintiff in the case manufactured and sold air-conditioning units for the cars in competition with the only manufacturer approved by the U.S. importer of the cars. When the plaintiff began to make serious inroads into the market share of approved air-conditioner manufacturers, the U.S. importer acquired the approved manufacturer as well as the largest U.S. distributor of the cars, to whom the plaintiff had been selling its units. Eventually the plaintiff's relationship with this distributor was terminated. After various efforts to capture other markets, the plaintiff later closed the business.

The plaintiff sued for treble damages alleging *inter alia* that there was an illegal tie-in because of a clause in the franchise contracts, which required distributors and dealers to carry factory-approved parts and to use their best efforts to promote the sale of approved parts. The Fifth Circuit Court of Appeals held that, standing alone, the best-efforts clause did not constitute a *per se* illegal tie-in. When it was considered in light of the other actions taken by the U.S. importer to foreclose competition, it was considered an illegal tying arrangement.

Price Fixing

In *United States v. U.S. Gypsum Co.*, the Supreme Court set forth the standard of what intent must be shown for a defendant to be convicted of criminal price fixing.[25] One of the actions taken by the defendants in this price-fixing case was telephone price verification, whereby the competing gypsum manufacturers

---

[24] *Heatransfer Corp. v. Volkswagen-Werk*, 553 F.2d 964 (5th Cir. 1977) *cert. denied* 98 S.Ct. 1282 (1978).

[25] *United States v. U.S. Gypsum Co.*, 98 S.Ct. 2864 (1978).

would call one another to determine the price currently offered on gypsum board to a particular customer. The defendants said that the purpose of the price information exchange was to take advantage of the meeting-competition defense in section 2(b) of the Robinson-Patman Act, which allows a seller to rebut a *prima facie* price discrimination charge by showing that the lower price was offered to meet a competitor's lower price.

The trial court had instructed the jury that, if the effect of the price verification action was to fix prices, then the parties were presumed as a matter of law to have intended that result. The court of appeals reversed, holding that verification of price with competitors for the sole purpose of taking advantage of the Robinson-Patman meeting-competition defense constituted a controlling circumstance precluding liability under section 1 of the Sherman Act.

The Supreme Court held that the trial judge erred in his instruction to the jury because price fixing under the Sherman Act is not a strict liability crime and thus requires the showing of intent. The Court did say, however, that showing an action was undertaken with the knowledge of its probable consequences and having the requisite anticompetitive effects can be sufficient to impose criminal liability. The Court went on to say that exchanges of price information, even for purposes of Robinson-Patman compliance, must be subject to close scrutiny under the Sherman Act. The court of appeals, therefore, was wrong in treating the interseller price verification as a controlling circumstance exception precluding Sherman Act liability.

In *National Society of Professional Engineers v. U.S.*, the government attacked a part of the Society's Canon of Ethics, which prohibited the discussion of price with potential customers until after the customer chose an engineer.[26] The purpose and effect of the canon was to eliminate the submission of competitive bids by engineers. The government alleged that the ban on competitive bidding was a violation of section 1 of the Sherman Act. The society defended the restriction on the grounds that it was justified under the rule of reason because it minimized the risk that competition would produce inferior engineering work, resulting in a danger to the public.

The Supreme Court rejected the society's justification for the ban on competitive bidding and held that the canon on its face restrains trade. While recognizing that the canon was not outright price fixing, the Court stated that the ban on competitive bidding was "nothing less than a frontal assault on the basic policy of the Sherman Act."

The application of the rule of reason was the subject of another recent Supreme Court case, *Broadcast Music, Inc. v. CBS, Inc.*[27] CBS sued BMI and the American Society of Composers, Authors, and Publishers (ASCAP), alleging that the issuance of blanket licenses by ASCAP and BMI to copyrighted musical compositions was price fixing and *per se* illegal under the Sherman Act. The blanket licenses gave the purchasers the right to perform any of the com-

---

[26] *National Society of Professional Engineers v. United States*, 98 S.Ct. 1355 (1978).
[27] *Broadcast Music, Inc. v. CBS, Inc.*, 99 S.Ct. 1551 (1979).

positions owned by members or affiliates of ASCAP or BMI. CBS claimed that the issuance of such licenses was horizontal price fixing because it was unable to negotiate with the individual artists for the use of their compositions.

The Supreme Court ruled that, because the licenses were not naked restraints of trade with no purpose except to stifle competition, they should be judged under the rule of reason. The purposes and effects of the licensing arrangement, according to the Court, show that it has developed over the years as the most effective method of integrating sales—monitoring and enforcing against unauthorized copyright use. Such activities would be difficult and expensive for individual copyright owners to conduct. The practice therefore should be judged by the rule of reason.

Price Discrimination and Predation

In *Great Atlantic & Pacific Tea Co., Inc. v. FTC*, the Federal Trade Commission charged A&P with violating section 2(f) of the Robinson-Patman Act, which makes it unlawful to knowingly induce or receive a discrimination in price prohibited by the act.[28] Having decided to sell private-brand milk, A&P solicited a bid from its long-time supplier, Borden Co. A&P rejected Borden's original bid and solicited offers from other companies, resulting in a lower bid by one of Borden's competitors. A&P then told Borden that its bid was ''not even in the ball park'' and stated that at least a $50,000 reduction was needed. The result was a bid by Borden that was much lower than the competitors'. The lower courts agreed with the FTC and held that A&P violated section 2(f) despite its defense that the Borden offer was made to meet competition.

The Supreme Court reversed, saying that a buyer who has done no more than accept the lower of two bids competitively offered cannot be guilty of a section 2(f) violation, provided the seller has a meeting-competition defense. Therefore the Court interpreted the act as saying that a firm cannot be guilty of inducing or receiving a discriminatory price that violates the act if the price given is not prohibited because of the meeting-competition defense. The Court rejected as anticompetitive any duty of disclosure by a buyer to a seller that the latter's bid had beaten competition.

In two cases involving instances of alleged attempted monopolization by predatory pricing in violation of section 2 of the Sherman Act, courts in the ninth circuit used relatively sophisticated economic analysis to determine whether predatory pricing had occurred. In *Janich Bros., Inc. v. American Distilling Co.*, the plaintiff Janich sued American Distilling for treble damages on the grounds that the latter had attempted to monopolize the sale of private-label vodka and gin in California through discriminatory and predatory pric-

---

[28] *Great Atlantic & Pacific Tea Co., Inc. v. FTC*, 99 S.Ct. 925 (1979). It is likely that Robinson-Patman cases will become less important since the head of the Justice Department antitrust division has stated there will be limited resources for price discrimination enforcement. See *Trade Regulation Reports*, vol. 485 (April 13, 1981), p. 5.

ing.[29] The Ninth Circuit Court of Appeals held that predatory pricing exists only when a firm sells below marginal cost. Since marginal cost can be difficult to ascertain, the court followed the theory of Areeda and Turner that, since average variable cost can approximate marginal cost, it can be used as evidence of marginal cost. Since Janich did not produce evidence that American priced below average variable cost, the court held that Janich did not meet its burden of showing predatory pricing.

The U.S. District Court for the Northern District of California added a further refinement to the *Janich* predatory pricing test in *William Inglis & Sons v. ITT Continental Baking Co., Inc.*[30] That case again involved alleged predatory pricing. Inglis claimed that Continental sold bread below cost in order to injure competition. Relying on the *Janich* holding, which said that average variable cost *may* be used as a substitute for marginal cost, Inglis produced a study to show that Continental was selling its bread below average variable cost. The court, however, rejected the proof of below average variable cost selling as establishing predatory pricing, stating that in this case average variable cost did not closely approximate short-run marginal cost, which is the true cutoff level for predatory pricing. According to the court, excess capacity in the wholesale bakery business at the time meant that average variable cost was substantially higher than marginal cost, because the former would include costs of using otherwise idle ovens when wages were already being paid and excess space in delivery trucks was shown. Marginal cost would not include these costs. The court rejected Inglis' use of Areeda and Turner's argument that average variable cost should be used as a proxy for marginal cost, even when the two are known to diverge. *Janich* was therefore interpreted as holding that average variable cost cannot always be used in place of marginal cost.

Monopolization

While the Supreme Court has not decided a monopolization case in recent years, three recent lower-court decisions are worthy of note.

In *Memorex Corp. v. IBM Corp.*, Memorex charged that IBM monopolized or attempted to monopolize four markets in the computer industry by making certain price cuts and product changes.[31] The District Court for the Northern District of California granted IBM a directed verdict on several grounds. First, Memorex failed to establish specifically enough the four relevant markets by drawing their bounds too narrowly. According to the court, Memorex failed to include within the markets certain substitutes for IBM computers.

In judging IBM's alleged price cuts, the court used the marginal cost-average variable cost standard and ruled that Memorex failed to prove that IBM priced

---

[29] *Janich Bros., Inc. v. American Distilling Co.*, 570 F.2d 848 (9th Cir. 1977) *cert. denied* 99 S.Ct. 103 (1978).

[30] *William Inglis & Sons v. ITT Continental Baking Co., Inc.*, 461 F.Supp. 410, N.D. Cal. (1978).

[31] *Memorex Corp. v. IBM Corp.*, 458 F.Supp. 423, N.D. Cal. (1978).

below either of these costs. The court however did note one exception to the marginal cost-average variable cost standard. That exception is that if barriers to entry are high, pricing above marginal or average variable cost but below the short-run profit maximizing price is predatory.

The court also refused to accept Memorex's argument that IBM should be forced to disclose new product information upon introduction rather than after first shipment, as was its usual practice. To do so, the court stated, would destroy IBM's incentive to innovate since it would lose the lead time needed to recover development costs. The court summarized by saying that IBM's product innovations and price cuts substantially benefited purchasers of the computers and that Memorex was merely using the antitrust law in an attempt to preserve its own profitable position.

IBM was again sued for monopolization in *Greyhound Computer Corporation, Inc. v. IBM Corp.*[32] Greyhound, a computer-leasing company, brought suit alleging that IBM had a monopoly in the computer-leasing market and that IBM had used anticompetitive practices to maintain that monopoly. Greyhound was both a customer and a competitor of IBM in that it purchased computers from IBM, then leased them to others in competition with IBM's leasing and sale of computers.

IBM had a predominant but gradually declining market share of the computer-leasing business. In order to maintain its dominant position in the computer industry, IBM took what Greyhound alleged to be anticompetitive steps to make the purchase of IBM computers for lease unattractive. These steps included cutting the discount in sale price on used computers, which were often purchased by leasing companies. IBM also raised the "multiplier" or ratio describing the relationship between IBM's sales price and IBM's monthly rental charge. A rise in the multiplier significantly affects leasing companies' ability to compete with IBM.

IBM defended first on the grounds that its market power rested on superior technology and business activity. Second, IBM contended that Greyhound's failure to show that IBM had monopoly power in the purchase and sale of computers was fatal to Greyhound's case since the latter complained of IBM's practices, making it more difficult for leasing companies to purchase computers at a price that would make their leasing competitively viable.

In reversing a directed verdict in favor of IBM, the Ninth Circuit Court of Appeals held that there was sufficient evidence for a jury to find that IBM had attempted through anticompetitive practices to monopolize the computer-leasing market. The court also said that Greyhound's failure to establish that IBM had monopoly power in the sales market was not a legal bar to finding that IBM had used exclusionary sales practices to maintain its monopoly in the lease market.

A third major monopolization case, *Berkey Photo, Inc. v. Eastman Kodak*

---

[32] *Greyhound Computer Corporation, Inc. v. IBM Corp.*, 559 F.2d 488, 9th Cir. (1977) *cert. denied* 98 S.Ct. 782 (1978).

Co.[33], was based on the allegation that Kodak illegally used its monopoly power in the film market to enhance its position in the camera market. When Kodak introduced new types of film, rival camera makers were foreclosed from a substantial part of the market until they were able to manufacture cameras that could use the new film. Berkey contended that Kodak should be required to predisclose film innovations to its camera-manufacturing competitors so that they would have the opportunity to manufacture cameras to be ready for the film's introduction.

The Second Circuit Court of Appeals held that Kodak should not be required to predisclose film and camera innovations since even a monopolist should have the right to the lead time such innovations produce. The court held that Kodak's development of the new camera-film system was a benefit of integration, not a use of Kodak's power in the film market to gain a competitive advantage in cameras. The court did state, however, that once the competing camera makers developed their own cameras, Kodak, as a film monopolist, could not refuse to sell film to them.

Berkey also objected to Kodak's agreement with Sylvania and General Electric to develop new flash systems jointly and to keep them off the market until Kodak's new camera system was ready for introduction. The court agreed with Berkey that such an agreement between two or more companies may be illegal. The court distinguished such an agreement from Kodak's actions involving its new film production because in the latter case Kodak acted alone and not in concert with other companies. While the agreement should not be *per se* illegal, the court stated, it could be the basis for a jury finding that Kodak as a monopolist unreasonably restrained trade.

NEW DEVELOPMENTS

No-Fault Monopoly

In the late 1970s, there was extensive discussion on a new rule for use in antitrust cases in which conduct will no longer be needed for a finding of guilt. The phrase "no-fault monopoly" seems to have originated with the late Senator Philip Hart of Michigan. The term was repeatedly used in numerous hearings on antitrust presided over by Senator Edward M. Kennedy, and in *National Law Journal* articles. In addition, Robert Pitofsky, a commissioner of the Federal Trade Commission, gave a speech entitled "In Defense of 'No-Fault Monopoly' Proposals." The idea of no-fault monopoly is to eliminate the necessity of proving intent in demonstrating that corporations have actually violated sections 1 and 2 of the Sherman Antitrust Act. In other words, using the concept of no-fault monopoly, the Justice Department or the Federal Trade Commission need not prove that a corporation intended to monopolize markets

---

[33] *Berkey Photo, Inc. v. Eastman Kodak Co.*, 603 F.2d 263 (2d Cir. 1979) *cert. filed* 48 U.S.L.W. 3310 (1979).

or that it was actually doing something in furtherance of that intent. Under the no-fault concept, nothing is required to prove monopolistic intent. Companies would be viewed as monopolists and could be prevented from effecting mergers on the basis of their size. However, there would be limits in the use of this rule. For example, corporations with $500 million in sales and $250 billion of assets might not be able to merge unless they were able to show that economic efficiencies would result. Consequently, violations of the Sherman Act could be established through a showing of size alone.

Recent actions by government agencies lead one to question whether they would be properly serving competitive ideals in their role as antitrust enforcers. Antitrust laws were enacted to promote competition in the interest of efficient allocation of resources, so that prices would remain at a competitive level and output would be optimal. No attempt to reduce efficiency or technological innovation may be inferred from these laws. Yet recently the Federal Trade Commission served a complaint on Du Pont, ostensibly because Du Pont had increased its market share of 90 percent in the production of titanium dioxide pigments. Du Pont captured this market share primarily because it had developed a low-cost method for providing this pigment. As a result, Du Pont was able to pass the savings on to consumers, resulting in an increased market share.[34] In bringing an antitrust action against Du Pont, the FTC apparently was expanding the reach of antitrust laws to be brought on the grounds of size alone. The fact that market share increases due to efficiency or technological innovation is immaterial. The FTC apparently wants to prohibit large size itself. The consequences of such actions are considerable. Efficiency could no longer be rewarded by increased market share. Du Pont, for example, would have to restrict its output rather than expand to market-derived levels. If the new antitrust guidelines are practiced, this trend will be reversed.

Private Treble-Damage Actions

In the *Illinois Brick* case referred to earlier in this chapter, the Supreme Court held that only direct purchasers have standing to sue in antitrust matters. In response, a bill was introduced in Congress in 1979 to overturn this decision.[35] This legislation would allow indirect purchasers to bring private treble-damage actions against those accused of anticompetitive practices. In turn, this legislation may limit the damages that could be awarded to the direct purchasers. If a direct purchaser passes on its added costs to customers, damages may be reduced by this amount because the direct purchaser has mitigated damages. A criticism of this bill is that it offsets any attempts to expedite antitrust matters.

---

[34] See Yale Brozen, "The Antitrust Witch Hunt," *National Review*, vol. 30 (November 24, 1978), p. 1470.

[35] S.300, 96th Cong., 1st Sess. (1979). Concerning the question of treble damage, see William Breit and Kenneth Elzinga, *The Antitrust Penalties: A Study in Law and Economics* (New Haven: Yale University Press, 1976).

The additional complaints that would arise and the complicated calculations of damages could flood the courts.[36]

Conglomerate Mergers

Another bill, presented by Senator Edward Kennedy in 1979, has been termed the "Small and Independent Business Protection Act."[37] If this legislation is passed, companies with $2 billion in sales or assets would not be allowed to merge even if their respective businesses were entirely unrelated. Second, companies with $350 million in sales or assets would be prohibited from merging with any firm holding 20 percent of this industry's market share. Inherent in the framework of this bill is the idea that mergers of companies, even if unrelated in business, will be prohibited based upon their size. The only alternative for large companies wishing to enter another market would be the much more difficult task of forming an enterprise from the ground up.

Social and Environmental Issues

In the late 1970s, the chairman of the FTC and the assistant attorney general of the Antitrust Division redefined the goals of antitrust enforcement. Instead of targeting the traditional goal of fostering competition, the government would primarily seek to foster social and environmental development. In other words, the Antitrust Division would no longer emphasize the economic analysis of business practices; it would consider human values.[38] It is difficult to conceive how far this approach will extend. For example, it is difficult to imagine how such an approach will affect interpretations of the wording of current antitrust laws. However, section 5 of the Clayton Act has been construed in the past to prohibit business practices that violate public policy. Therefore, these policies could open many doors to future antitrust action. The appointment of William Baxter and others who influence antitrust and trade regulation policy will likely end this approach in the immediate future.

Law and Economic Theory

As judges are becoming more aware of the economic repercussions of their decisions, they are increasingly requiring that arguments be supported by sophisticated economic theory. Their own awareness of these theories is being reflected in their determinations. For example, in *William Inglis & Sons Baking Co. v. ITT Continental Baking Co.,* Judge Spencer Williams found that, even

---

[36] See Orrin G. Hatch, "Report from the United States Senate," *Antitrust Law Journal*, vol. 48 (April 1976), pp. 619–621.

[37] S.600, 96th Cong., 1st Sess. (1979).

[38] See Ernest Gellhorn, "The New Gibberish at the FTC," *Regulation* (May/June 1978), pp. 37–42.

when viewed in a light most favorable for the plaintiff, the evidence was not sufficient to find the defendant guilty of predatory pricing.[39] Despite a jury verdict awarding the plaintiff $5,048,000, the judge entered a judgment notwithstanding the verdict in favor of the defendant. In support of his ruling, Judge Williams included in his decision average variable cost and marginal cost curves, along with a discussion of their relevance to a determination of predatory pricing practices. It might be expected that as economics is more widely understood, legal decisions relying on economic theory will become more widespread.

[39] *William Inglis & Sons Baking Co. v. ITT Continental Baking Co.*, 461 F.Supp. 410 (1978).

CHAPTER 20

REGULATORY AGENCIES

Until the last decade or so, it was thought that the major rules and regulations affecting businesses and other participants in the market arose from the evolution of the common law and from judicial interpretation of statutory regulations. Furthermore, the functions and authority of many government agencies were primarily ministerial, so their actions were generally limited to carrying out specific activities mandated by legislatures. Thus, Social Security offices gave information and advice to individuals filing for benefits, but possessed relatively little discretionary power. Starting in the late 1960s, an increasing number of new rules and regulations were established along with new federal regulatory agencies. It is likely that the current constraints placed on business transactions by regulatory authorities are more economically important than those that stem from the common law and the courts. For example, seven new regulatory agencies, including the Occupational Safety and Health Agency (OSHA), the Consumer Product Safety Commission (CPSC), and the Environmental Protection Agency (EPA), were created in the early 1970s. The first four years of the 1970s saw a doubling of the number of pages in the *Federal Register*, the primary document for notification of federal rules and regulations.

INCREASING REGULATIONS

The new wave of regulation also has an expanded scope surpassing the traditional judicial regulation of commerce, transportation, health, and financial markets. For example, the Clean Air Act amendments of 1970 provide for setting air quality standards, and the Consumer Product Safety Commission Act of 1972 establishes a commission with the power to set safety standards for consumer products and to ban products with undue risk of injury. The early 1970s also saw the emergence of extensive controls over petroleum manufacturers with the Emergency Petroleum Allocation Act of 1973. Existing agencies have also expanded activities in the promulgation of rules affecting commercial transactions. For example, Table 20-1 shows that since 1971, the administrative costs in real dollars of 57 regulatory agencies more than doubled by fiscal year (FY) 1979. In FY 1971 the administrative costs when expressed in 1970 dollars for these agencies was $1.2 billion; it was $3.0 billion in FY 1979. The administrative costs, however, are but a small portion when compared to the compliance costs of business. For example, in 1976, the estimated total cost of federal regulation was approximately $65.5 billion; administrative costs represented only $3.2 billion, or less than 5 percent of the total costs.

Another indication of the overall activity of administrative agencies can be obtained by examining the number of employees assigned to those agencies. In 1979 we find that for the 57 regulatory agencies, the overall employment was approximately 87,500, almost three times as large as in 1971.

The percent of gross national product subject to regulation has also been increasing over time. MacAvoy, for example, estimates that between 1965 and 1975, the percent of GNP in the regulated sector of the economy composed of

TABLE 20-1
GROWTH OF FIFTY-SEVEN FEDERAL REGULATORY AGENCIES
Selected Fiscal Years, 1971–81

Area	1971	1977	1978	1979	1980 (est.)	1981 (est.)
	Expenditures ($ billions)					
Social regulation						
Consumer safety and health	$ .6	1.8	2.3	2.5	2.6	2.9
Job safety and other working conditions	$ .1	.5	.5	.6	.7	.8
Energy and the environment	$ .1	1.0	1.3	1.5	1.7	2.2
	$ .8	3.3	4.1	4.6	5.0	5.9
Economic regulation						
Finance and banking	$ .1	.2	.3	.3	.3	.3
Other industry-specific	$ .2	.3	.3	.3	.4	.4
General business	$ .1	.2	.2	.3	.3	.3
	$ .4	.7	.8	.9	1.0	1.0
Total	$1.2	4.0	4.9	5.5	6.0	6.9
Total in 1970 dollars*	$1.2	2.6	3.0	3.0	3.1	3.2
	Permanent full-time positions (thousands)					
Social regulation		10.8	58.4	61.9	63.6	65.4	66.2
Economic regulation		18.3	23.6	24.3	23.9	24.5	24.6
Total		29.1	82.0	86.2	87.5	89.9	90.8

*Adjusted by GNP deflator (actual and, for 1980–81, estimated in 1981 budget).
Source: Center for the Study of American Business, Washington University.

regulations governing price, financial markets, and health and safety rose from 8.2 percent to 23.7 percent.[1] During that decade, price regulation for railroads, motor freight, air, communications, utilities, and petroleum rose from 5.5 percent to 8.8 percent. The greatest growth occurred for health and safety regulation in mining, construction, paper products, chemicals, primary metals, vehicles, and other manufacturing, which increased to 11.9 percent of GNP in 1975 from almost nothing in 1965.

The 1980 election of President Ronald Reagan may have some impact on the growth of federal rules and regulations. During the first few months of 1981, the number of pages in the *Federal Register* decreased by 60 percent (January 1981 to March 1981), reflecting a decline of 54 percent in the number of proposed rules.

Another important distinction between regulations created formally by government agencies and regulations established informally through the judicial system arises in the creation, promulgation, and enforcement of these regulations. Administrative agencies contain a mixture of legislative and judicial authority as well as executive powers. In addition, procedural differences combined with the broader discretionary authority given governmental agencies yield regulations that often differ significantly from those created in the legislative-judicial process.[2] In this chapter we'll investigate the general scope of regulatory actions and the activities that are subject to their control. In addition, some emphasis is given to regulatory powers and procedures, including a review of the regulation process.

ADMINISTRATIVE AGENCIES

The primary interpreters and enforcers of many legislative statutes that focus on business regulation are administrative agencies. Sometimes these agencies are part of a traditional administrative branch of the government. For example, the Justice Department enforces the Sherman Act, the Clayton Act, and other antitrust laws. The National Highway Traffic Safety Administration and the Department of Transportation enforce regulations regarding safety, emission controls, and fuel economy of automobiles. In other cases, administrative agencies have been established independent of the executive branch. For example, the Interstate Commerce Commission regulates service transportation within the United States and foreign countries to the extent that commerce takes place within the boundaries of the United States. Other independent agencies include the Civil Aeronautics Board, Commodity Futures Trading Commission, Equal Employment Opportunity Commission, Export-Import Bank of the United States, Federal Communications Commission, Federal

---

[1] Paul W. MacAvoy, *The Regulation Industries and the Economy* (New York: W. W. Norton, 1979), p. 25.

[2] Murray Weidenbaum, "On Estimating Regulatory Costs," *Regulation* (May/June 1978), pp. 14–17.

Energy Administration, Federal Home Loan Bank Board, Federal Maritime Commission, Federal Power Commission, Federal Trade Commission, International Trade Commission, National Labor Relations Board, Security and Exchange Commission, and Small Business Administration.

Uniqueness

Administrative agencies are unique in their structure, combining duties and responsibilities of the judicial, executive, and legislative branches of the government. Heads of administrative agencies are generally appointed by the president of the United States with the consent of two-thirds of the Congress. The agencies also effectively combine the legislative and judicial powers that are traditionally separated under the Constitution. Thus, agencies are able to promulgate rules, to police them for compliance, and to judge whether there have been violations. If violations have occurred, the agency is empowered to impose penalties or remedies as prescribed by law. Administrative decisions may be appealed to the courts, but since the subject matter is generally very specialized or technical in nature (and the agency has been given broad discretionary powers initially), the courts will not generally reverse agency actions unless those decisions can be identified as being arbitrary and capricious.

Procedure

Initially administrative agencies are generally given a wide range of discretion for establishing particular rules governing the activity that they are to regulate. Regulations may come in the form of complaints to a particular situation, or responses to complaints, or establishment of a rule that applies to a specified activity or industry classification.

Complaints

Complaints may be issued by private parties including individuals or corporations, or they may be initiated by an employee of the administrative agency. After the complaint is served to the alleged wrongdoer, the party is given an opportunity to answer the complaint. Eventually the complaint is heard by an administrator appointed by the agency. The administrator makes a final decision and enters an order directing the party to cease (or engage) in certain acts if the administrator finds that the party has engaged in misconduct. Otherwise the complaint is dismissed. Compliance with the order is usually enforced by a separate division of the administrative agency; failure to comply can result in fines and other penalties. After the final hearing, the affected party may appeal to the courts. In some cases the party can engage in an informal settlement process or agree to a consent decree.

Adjudication

The best-known and most frequent function for most administrative agencies having direct impacts on industry is adjudication. In most cases the agency performs activities in the same manner as courts. Both the Administrative Procedure Act and the legal background of participants help form the investigation, complaint, hearing, and final-order procedures. Sometimes, however, commissioners will stop proceedings, usually prior to costly hearings.

Most investigations do not result in a hearing. They are either closed or result in a cease and desist order. Cease and desist orders avoid a costly hearing process and protect respondent firms, since an admission of guilt is not made.

Rule Making

In recent years rule making has become a more important method for regulating business behavior than case-by-case administrative action. Rule making is similar to the enactment of law except that the regulation or rule is subject to greater scrutiny in the courts. The enactment of a regulation involves formation, announcement, comment, hearings, revision, and potential legislation, as well as judicial review. Unlike antitrust litigation, rule making applies to all firms in the industry, which often makes the promulgation of the rule difficult.[3]

SCOPE OF REGULATORY ACTIONS

Regulatory authorities and their actions impact virtually every form of economic activity, including profits, prices, outputs, standards, and other mechanisms for altering the use of resources or techniques for producing them. In some cases, the regulations originate in a large number of independent authorities that have overlapping jurisdiction. Such cases often make final determination of the precise rules difficult to follow, if not impossible to interpret. In Table 20-2 we see that more than a dozen agencies have jurisdiction regarding the use of energy. In each case, some of the more important activities are listed along with their estimated expenditures in FY 1979. One learns from this table, for example, that the interstate transportation of petroleum is governed by regulations of the Department of Energy, the Department of the Interior, the Interstate Commerce Commission, and several other agencies, including the Internal Revenue Service.

Profits

One of the most important forms of regulation concerns the government agencies' direct or indirect control of profits. Traditionally, profits were generally

---

[3] See, for example, the rule-making history of the FTC rule for funeral homes in Kenneth W. Clarkson, "Legislative Constraints," in K. W. Clarkson and T. J. Muris, eds., *The Federal Trade Commission since 1970: Economic Regulation and Bureaucratic Behavior* (New York: Cambridge University Press, 1981), esp. pp. 24–26.

TABLE 20-2

AGENCIES HAVING JURISDICTION OVER THE USE OF ENERGY

Agency	Function	Estimated FY 1979 expenditures (millions of dollars)
Department of Energy	Energy information, regulation, and policy.	$990.0
Federal Energy Regulatory Commission	Regulation of interstate gas pipeline and electricity rates and gas field prices; new conventional power plant licensing.	44.0
Department of the Interior	Leasing of offshore oil and gas and public land leasing for oil, gas, and coal fields.	402.1
Interstate Commerce Commission	Regulation of oil and coal slurry pipeline rates and routes.	54.5
Environmental Protection Agency	Standards for vehicle and smokestack emission levels.	712.8
Materials Transportation Bureau (Department of Transportation)	Pipeline safety standards.	24.4
Nuclear Regulatory Commission	Licensing of nuclear energy plants and control of nuclear fuel export.	46.0
Department of Commerce	Control of tanker construction and safety; establishment of marine sanctuaries.	112.5
U.S. Coast Guard (Department of Transportation)	Inspection and monitoring of tankers and LNG carriers.	20.5
National Highway Traffic Safety Administration (Department of Transportation)	Establishment of safety regulations affecting vehicle weight and fuel consumption.	18.44
Occupational Safety and Health Administration (Department of Labor)	Regulation of safe levels for benzene and other energy-related substances in working areas.	118.5
Consumer Product Safety Commission	Control of safety of home insulation and other energy-saving materials.	23.3
Federal Trade Commission	Litigation involving energy industry.	NA
Department of Justice	Antitrust regulation.	46.4
Internal Revenue Service (Department of the Treasury)	Tax regulations affecting energy users and producers.	NA
Internal Trade Commission	Relief from import injury and relief, including tariffs and/or quotas on energy imports.	NA

Source: Abstracted from Executive Office of the President, *Budget of the U.S. Government,* Fiscal Year 1979, Appendix.

NA: not available.

unregulated, and it was not until the middle of the nineteenth century that the "laissez-faire" doctrine was challenged. Today we find the most important profit regulations arise in situations where the state has granted exclusive rights to produce the commodity. Most electric and water public utilities (discussed later in this chapter) fall into this category. In such situations, the regulatory form usually chosen is rate making. Rather than directly regulate profits, regulatory commissions or their equivalent set an acceptable rate of return on capital.

Price Regulation

A closely related form of regulation controls the actual prices that sellers can offer. Price regulation may take the form of a maximum, minimum, or uniform price. New York City, for example, establishes the maximum price that certain apartment owners may charge their tenants. The interstate movement of natural gas is also subject to a maximum price based on geographic location. Minimum prices are often established as floors for certain agricultural products such as wheat. Price regulations can often have substantial effects on the number of units sold, the quality of goods or associated services, and other terms of business transactions. For example, a producer who finds that his or her profit rate on a price-controlled product is too low may decide not to produce such a product any longer. Instead, he or she will sell existing supplies, then cut out that particular line of production from the business.

CAB and the Regulation of Domestic Airlines   One of the most striking examples of price regulation is the CAB regulation of airfares during the last decade. A comparison of airfares in the California intrastate market with fares for similar routes in the East Coast interstate market reveals significant differences in fares of regulated and unregulated firms. Since air carriers operating wholly within a state are not subject to CAB regulation, the relatively unregulated airlines operating in the intrastate markets of California and Texas provide some evidence as to the airfares that might have prevailed in the absence of CAB regulation. In Table 20-3, William Jordan shows that in July 1970, airfares in the California intrastate market were about 40 percent less than fares in similar East Coast interstate markets, which were subject to CAB regulation. The recent deregulation of interstate airline fares also provides evidence of the consequence of price regulation.

Ophthalmic Goods   Prior to May 1978, some states and localities prohibited the advertising of eyeglasses and eye examinations, and the absence of such advertising was linked with significantly higher prices for ophthalmic goods and services.[4] In 1978 the Federal Trade Commission issued regulations which

---

[4] Lee Benham, "The Effect of Advertising on the Price of Eyeglasses," *Journal of Law and Economics,* vol. 15 (October 1972), pp. 337–352.

TABLE 20-3

COMPARISON OF AIRFARES IN CALIFORNIA INTRASTATE MARKETS WITH FARES IN
SIMILAR EAST COAST INTERSTATE MARKETS, JULY 1970

Market	Distance (miles)	Annual passengers*	Coach fare† (dollars)	Fare per mile (cents)
California				
Los Angeles– San Francisco	340	3,023,341	16.20	4.76
San Diego– San Francisco	449	359,025	22.63	5.04
San Diego– Los Angeles	109	637,447	7.97	7.31
East Coast				
Boston–New York	186	1,985,680	21.60	11.61
Boston–Washington	413	435,920	35.64	8.63
New York– Washington	228	1,663,850	23.76	10.42

Sources: William A. Jordan, *Airline Regulation in America: Effects and Imperfections* (Johns Hopkins Press, 1970), p. 105; and *Official Airline Guide: Quick Reference, North American Edition* (Reuben H. Donnelly, July 1, 1970).

*On-line origin-and-destination passengers, 1965. These data show where passengers originate and terminate their journeys on individual carriers. Passengers using two or more carriers are counted in two or more city-pairs—one for each carrier.

†Including tax.

stated that it is an unfair practice for states to enforce restrictions against advertising except for the purpose of preventing unfairness or deception. Unfairness involved a two-pronged test involving whether the practices (i.e., prohibitions against advertising) cause substantial harm to consumers and whether they offend public policy. In the Eyeglass Rule, the commission found harm to consumers in the form of higher prices and lower rates of consumption, especially for the poor and elderly. In addition, the Supreme Court's ruling that the First Amendment establishes the consumer's right to receive price information was sufficient to satisfy the second criteria.[5]

Lee Benham estimated a range of the possible effects of prohibitions on advertising restriction. In Table 20-4 there are two estimates for individuals in states with no restrictions on advertising (column 2) in states with prohibition on advertising (column 3) in 1963. The second category compares prices in Texas and the District of Columbia (column 2), which classified as the most open market states relative to North Carolina (column 3), which had a long history of extensive restrictions on advertising for a considerable period of time. For eyeglasses alone, the difference in price ranged from $6.70 to $19.50, and for eyeglasses and eye examinations the range was $3.86 to $20.76, with the

[5] *Virginia Pharmacy Board v. Virginia Consumer Council* 425 U.S. 748 (1976). The Eyeglass Rule may encourage selective administrative deregulation of state and local regulations. The commission recognized that prohibition and certain required affirmative disclosures regulating commercial speech may be detrimental to consumer welfare.

TABLE 20-4

MEAN COST OF EYEGLASSES AND MEAN COMBINED COST OF EYE EXAMINATION PLUS EYEGLASSES IN 1963 AS A FUNCTION OF RESTRICTIONS ON ADVERTISING IN STATES

Population group	States with complete advertising restrictions		States with no advertising restrictions		Difference in Means
	Mean $(\bar{X}_1)$	N^*	Mean $(\bar{X}_2)$	N^*	$(\bar{X}_1 - \bar{X}_2)$
Eyeglasses alone					
All individuals†	$33.04	50	$26.34	127	$ 6.70
All individuals in Texas, North Carolina, and the District of Columbia	$37.48	21	$17.98	27	$19.50
Eyeglasses and eye examinations combined					
All individuals†	$40.96	121	$37.10	261	$ 3.86
All individuals in Texas, North Carolina, and the District of Columbia	$50.73	37	$29.97	72	$20.76

*Number of observations.

†States classified as having no restrictions on advertising in 1963 are Alabama, the District of Columbia, Georgia, Illinois, Indiana, Kansas, Maryland, Michigan, Minnesota, Missouri, Texas, and Utah. States classified as having total prohibition of (eyeglass) advertising are Arkansas, Massachusetts, North Carolina, North Dakota, Oklahoma, and South Carolina.

Source: Lee Benham, "The Effect of Advertising on the Price of Eyeglasses," *Journal of Law and Economics,* vol. 15 (October 1972), p. 342.

higher prices in states with restrictions on advertising. Note the prices in North Carolina, where such advertising was completely prohibited.

Price Controls

Since their initial appearance in Egypt 5,000 years ago, price controls have been imposed in countries across the world.[6] Although some of these controls may have been considered successful in the short run, no evidence supports their success in the long run. Still, between 1971 and 1979, price controls were imposed in the United States. They had been moderately successful in the United States during World War II, probably due to the use of rationing and the patriotic sentiment that prevailed at that time.[7] Actually, results of these post-war controls and 1970s price controls were apparently entirely consistent with other such occurrences throughout recent history. For example, during the 1971–1974 period of price controls, the Wholesale Price Index and the Con-

[6] See Robert L. Schuettinger and Eamonn F. Butler, *Forty Centuries of Wage and Price Controls* (Washington, D.C.: Caroline House Publishers, 1979).

[7] Ibid., p. 83.

sumer Price Index were considerably higher than their respective annual rates during the 12 months prior to the imposition of controls. Obviously, the controls were not a success; even so, during recent inflationary times people like consumerist Ralph Nader and economist John Kenneth Galbraith have once again begun advocating the use of price controls.[8] Price control theory and its recent use are therefore worthy of some discussion here.

Theoretically price controls are capable of producing positive results. For example, assume a monopoly situation with a downward-sloping demand curve. The monopolist in Figure 20-1 is operating at a price P_m with an output of Q_m. Now assume that the government imposes a lower price at P_c. At the controlled price, the marginal revenue curve between O and Q_c is effectively replaced by the line from P_c to its intersection with the demand curve. There is now an equilibrium point where P_c = MR = MC. Further, at this point, output has increased to Q_c. By imposing a lower price on this monopolist where P_c = MR = MC, not only has price been lowered, but also output has increased. Obviously price controls produce positive results in this type of situation.

The problem, however, is setting this optimal price. Even if the government is capable of determining the price P_c, many people are not going to be satisfied with that price, considering the fact that the monopolist is still making above-normal profits. Further, it will be most difficult to determine the equilibrium price P_c. If the price is set too low, MR will be below MC, and the monopolist

[8] Ralph Nader, *The Washington Star*, June 17, 1978, p. B2; and Tom Wicker's column, *The New York Times*, July 4, 1978, p. 17.

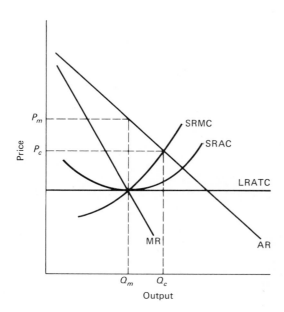

FIGURE 20-1
Output changes with price control. With no price control the monopolist produces Q_m at P_m. With a maximum price control below a monopoly price, shown as P_c, output increases to Q_c.

will reduce output. At the same time, because price has decreased, quantity demanded will increase. As a result, inventories will be used up, and shortages will occur.

U.S. Price Controls: 1971–1974

From 1971 to 1974, the United States operated under several phases of different price controls. Initially, on August 15, 1971, President Nixon imposed a 90-day surprise price freeze to control price increases. This government-imposed zero rate of increase required relatively little bureaucratic action and resulted in a decrease from the 40 percent annual rate of increase in the Consumer Price Index to a rate of 1.6 percent. However, the actual impact is somewhat questionable due to the fact that there was a large decrease in the Wholesale Price Index and some wage indexes.

On November 14, 1971, Phase 2 of the wage and price controls was imposed. With it came large increases in both wage and price indexes. Phase 2 limited price increases to the percentage increase in costs of production. For calculation purposes a base period was established on January 1, 1971, or on a firm-by-firm basis at the last price increase if more recent than January 1, 1971. Additionally, profits could not exceed the best two out of three years preceding August 15, 1971. Wage increases were also limited to 6.2 percent annually: the average rate of productivity increase (3.0 percent), plus the government's goals for price inflation (2.5 percent), plus added fringe benefits (.7 percent). There were also prenotification and reporting requirements based on firms' total sales and the size of their respective collective-bargaining units. Although the Cost of Living Council held primary authority over these controls, the Price Commission and the Pay Board were also established to monitor prices and wages.

Phase 2 should have been somewhat more successful than the initial controls, because it was less constraining. However, because of significant difficulties in interpreting the rules and regulations, traditional bureaucracy problems developed, including delayed and inconsistent rulings. Also, it was impossible to monitor all activities adequately. For example, foreign producers could not be controlled, so lumber companies in the Northwest shipped lumber to Canada and then reimported the woods at substantially higher prices.[9] Because prices could be increased based on added services, unnecessary services were performed by producers to increase prices. At any rate, given these and other problems, Phase 2 price and wage controls were only minimally successful, if at all. It appears that wage controls were even less successful than price controls.[10]

---

[9] William Poole, "Wage-Price Controls: Where Do We Go from Here?" Brookings Papers on Economic Activity, No. 1 (1973), p. 292.

[10] See Samuel Brittan and Peter Likey, *The Delusion of Incomes Policy* (New York: Holmes & Meier, 1977), pp. 146–150.

On January 11, 1973, Phase 3 of the wage and price controls was implemented. Essentially, this phase was meant to continue the basic ideas of Phase 2 on a voluntary basis. Prenotification and reporting requirements, as well as the Price Commission and the Pay Board, were abolished. The result was an increase in the Wholesale Price Index to an annual rate of 22.3 percent and an increase in the Consumer Price Index to an annual rate of 8.0 percent.

As you might expect, Phase 3 did not last long. On June 13, 1973, it was superseded by another mandatory wage and price freeze that lasted until August 12, 1973. At this time Phase 4 was implemented. Like Phase 2, Phase 4 allowed price increases based on increases in cost. However, under Phase 4 price increases were based on absolute dollar levels of increase in cost. In other words, if cost increased one dollar per unit produced, price could be increased by one dollar per unit. As a result, no added percentage for return was included in the price increases. Since producers were not receiving a proportional return on their investments when costs increased, they reduced domestic output and shortages appeared. Phase 4 was dropped on April 30, 1974. At that time prices were increasing three times faster than they were when Phase 2 was implemented.

The problems referred to above seem inherent in the methods used by the United States in imposing wage-price controls. However, there are additional problems that not only were apparent in the U.S. controls but also will prevail in nearly all attempts to control wages and price. Of primary importance is the fact that many exogenous variables will cause distortions and inefficiencies in any wage and price control program. For example, while controls were in effect in the United States, large agricultural setbacks and a large industrial boom occurred throughout the world. Further, it was during this time that OPEC increased oil prices dramatically. The result, a major shortage of food and raw materials, drove prices for those commodities very high. This price increase had a direct effect on costs of production of items utilizing these materials. Remember, if prices do not keep pace with production costs, shortages and inefficiencies will necessarily occur. Second, blanket price controls have adverse effects on firms operating in competitive markets with elastic demand curves. In such markets firms will be unable to maintain output levels with increasing costs if prices do not rise. Finally, controls will nearly always create incentives to operate outside the regulated market. As a result, black markets form, products are redefined, and quality and output are reduced.

Licensing and Allocating Rights

One of the more common forms of regulation involves the licensing of producers who wish to sell products in the market. State licensing of medical personnel, attorneys, and other professionals is found throughout the country, as is licensing of other trades, such as plumbers and beauticians. Sometimes licensing is indirect, as when rights are allocated to engage in a particular activity.

For example, the Civil Aeronautics Board grants certificates that permit air carriers to transport passengers from one point to another. These certificates are generally not transferable to other parties nor can they be applied to other routes. Yet we have seen they have value.

Sometimes the value of the rights to engage in a service can be seen directly by observing sales of certificates or licenses. For example, in 1978 the value of the right to drive a taxi in New York City legally was $50,000, and in Boston was $40,000. This compares with $40,000 in Canberra, the capital city of Australia.[11] By contrast, in Washington, D.C., licenses are only about $2,000.[12]

Motor Carriers   By the Motor Carriers Act of 1935, the Interstate Commerce Commission was given control over entry into the trucking industry through the creation of operating rights.[13] At the time of the act, existing motor carrier routes were "grandfathered," that is, routes established before the act were automatically allowed to remain in the industry. Additional routes may be authorized and each "certificate of public convenience and necessity" specifies classes of goods as well as particular routes.

The operating rights are considered valuable assets by trucking firms as well as by bankers. Estimation of the value of rights varies and may represent as much as 15 to 20 percent of the annual revenues associated with the rights. Kafoglis has determined the rates of return earned on operating rights sold between 1967 and 1972; they are shown in Table 20-5.

In addition, operating rights increase in value over time, sometimes at rates in excess of the cost of capital. This increase has been attributed to increases in efficiency resulting from sales and purchases of rights among alternative trucking operations.

Standard Setting

Another form of regulation involves standard setting. The U.S. Department of Agriculture establishes a large number of standards for food products. For example, the department grades beef and issues standards for other meat and poultry products. Such grading often helps consumers in evaluating alternative selections of meat. Other labeling standards regulate the content of various food products. For example, food products that are labeled "beef with gravy" must contain at least 50 percent cooked beef, but if the ingredients are reversed

---

[11] Peter L. Swan, *On Buying a Job: The Regulation of Taxi Cabs in Canberra* (Turramurra, Australia: The Centre for Independent Studies, 1979).

[12] For an explanation of the different incentives and associated consequences of independent regulatory agencies (political appointments) and government bureaus (civil servants), see Ross D. Eckert, "On the Incentives of Regulators: The Case of Taxicabs," *Public Choice*, vol. 14 (Spring 1973), pp. 83–100.

[13] See Paul W. MacAvoy and John W. Snow, eds., *Regulation of Entry and Pricing in Truck Transportation* (Washington, D.C.: American Enterprise Institute, 1977), and Milton Kafoglis, "A Paradox of Regulated Trucking: Valuable Operating Rights in a 'Competitive' Industry," *Regulation*, vol. 1 (Sept./Oct. 1977), pp. 27–32.

TABLE 20-5
RATES OF RETURN EARNED ON 43 TRANSACTIONS IN OPERATING RIGHTS,
1967–1971

	Purchase price (thousands of dollars)	Sale price (thousands of dollars)	Compound annual rates of return
Current dollars:*	776.8	3,844.1	17%
Constant (1972) dollars:*	1,163.1	4,181.4	13
Mean percent return (unweighted), 1972 dollars:			78
1 year			298
0–5 years†			203
5–10 years			15
10–20 years			11
Over 20 years			3

*Average life is 10.1 years
†Includes 1-year rights
Source: Milton Kafoglis, "A Paradox of Regulated Trucking," *Regulation* (Sept./Oct., 1977), p. 30.

so that the label reads "gravy with beef," only 35 percent of the contents are required to be beef.

Disclosure Requirements

In recent years regulatory authorities have instituted a number of measures that require sellers to disclose certain information to consumers prior to completion of the sale. In some cases, disclosures must be made in alternative forms. For example, if Martin Pontiac advertises on a local television that a 1981 Pontiac may be paid for over the next 36 months, the down payment, amount of monthly payment, and annual percentage rate of interest must also be specified in the ad. When other attributes of the product are well known, such disclosures may lower search costs to consumers. If other attributes of the good are not known, search costs may actually increase or at best remain constant. This problem is evident in the proposal for disclosure of the nature and type of repairs performed on all used cars prior to resale.

Materials and Process Regulations

Regulatory agencies may also specify the type of material that may be used in a product. The Occupational Safety and Health Administration, for example, regulates the design and materials for ladders.[14] In other cases, regulatory

---

[14] *Federal Register*, vol. 37 (October 18, 1972), esp. pp. 22105–22106.

action may also specify the form of manufacturing or prohibit certain processes. For example, the Food and Drug Administration issues regulations that prohibit the use of U-shaped assembly lines in the manufacturing of pharmaceutical products. Firms must use an assembly line that follows a perfectly straight line.[15]

Taxes and Subsidies

In many cases, taxes are imposed as a means of raising revenue for the government. However, in some cases they have been imposed as a means of changing economic behavior. If taxes are imposed on some inputs, for example, firms that use those inputs will find them more costly than substitute lower-cost alternatives. Taxes on the final product will also cause consumers to switch purchases to lower-cost alternatives. In other cases, subsidies may be used to encourage the use of a particular input or the consumption of a commodity. While such forms of regulation may not be as constraining as previously mentioned, behavior is often altered. An example of a particular subsidy is the investment tax credit that applies to capital equipment with a service life of three years or more. The investment tax credit is given to purchasers of capital equipment and effectively reduces their taxes owed. This is equivalent to lowering the price of the capital equipment purchased and therefore encourages the purchase of more such capital equipment eligible for the investment tax credit.

REGULATED ACTIVITIES

A large number of activities are regulated by government agencies. We see in Table 20-6 the amount and percent of national income originating in regulated sectors in the economy in 1978. In fact, virtually every economic activity is subject to some regulation at one stage in the process of manufacture, wholesaling, and retailing. A small sample of those activities is discussed below.

Transportation

Virtually all forms of transportation—surface, air, and water—are subject to a multitude of governmental regulations. The commerce clause of the Constitution grants the government the basic right to regulate commerce and interstate trade, and transportation is a likely category to be subject to this clause. For this reason it is not surprising that the first major forms of regulation applied to the transportation industries.

The Interstate Commerce Commission The Interstate Commerce Commission (ICC), created by the Act to Regulate Commerce in 1887, has regulated freight service transportation throughout the United States since that time.

---

[15] *Code of Federal Regulations*, Title 21, section 211.42(a).

TABLE 20-6
AMOUNT AND PERCENT OF NATIONAL INCOME ORIGINATING IN
REGULATED SECTORS OF THE ECONOMY, 1978

Sector	Portion of national income, 1978 (billions)	Percent of national income, 1978
Transportation*	$68.2	3.86%
Railroads	14.2	.80
Local & interurban passenger	3.8	.22
Trucking & warehousing	28.5	1.61
Water transportation	4.7	0.27
Air transportation	12.1	.68
Communications	40.5	2.29
Electric, gas, sanitary services	34.9	1.98
Total, regulated sectors	$206.9	11.71%

*Includes items not shown separately.
  Source: U.S. Department of Commerce, *Statistical Abstract of the United States*
(Washington, D.C.: U.S. Government Printing Office, 1979), p. 442.

The ICC was established in reaction to the purported monopoly position of
the railroads, as well as to their discriminatory pricing structure. After the
establishment of the ICC, the railroads were pressured into setting a more
uniform pricing tariff. They were no longer able to engage in price wars. Apparently the railroads were not necessarily against regulation by the ICC. Kolko
has interpreted the history of the late 1800s as showing that the railroads secret-
ly welcomed regulations as a means of eliminating price competition. Additionally, Kolko believes that the ICC has protected the railroads from themselves by reducing price competition in a way that the railroads could never
have achieved.[16]

The major form of regulation by the ICC concerns the rates that may be
charged for different commodities as well as the rates for distance traveled.[17] In
addition to rate regulation the ICC prohibits carriers from carrying freight on
back hauls (return trips) in a number of situations. Such prohibitions have the
effect of decreasing options to shippers and generating higher prices for all
shipping.

The ICC also regulates the lease rates on railroad freight cars and other
rolling stock. In recent years the price has not been permitted to rise; some
individual firms have found that rail cars have become a cheaper means of
storing merchandise than renting a warehouse. A significant shortage of railroad cars has been the main result of this regulation.

[16] Gabriel Kolko, *Railroads and Regulation* (Princeton: Princeton University Press, 1970).
[17] Thomas Gail Moore, *Freight Transportation Regulation: Surface Freight and the Interstate
Commerce Commission* (Washington, D.C.: American Enterprise Institute for Public Policy Research, 1972).

In some cases the ICC's regulatory powers may exceed those of other governmental agencies. For example, in *United States v. Interstate Commerce Commission*, the Justice Department attempted to block the commission's approval of the merger of Great Northern Railway Company and the Northern Pacific Railway Company.[18] The department argued that the ICC failed to give sufficient weight to the diminution of competition between the lines. Thus, it argued, the commission did not properly balance antitrust objections and national transportation goals. By supporting the commission, the Court gave the ICC the right to approve mergers when the cost savings outweigh the anticompetitive consequences of the merger.

National Highway and Traffic Safety Administration

Beginning in the mid-1960s, Congress imposed regulations to protect the environment, improve automobile safety, and meet other national goals. The most important of these regulations were introduced in the mid-1970s to improve fuel economy.

Compliance with the regulations involves fixed or common costs and marginal costs. In Table 20-7 we show the Bureau of Labor Statistics' estimated costs for new models attributable to mandated regulations excluding, as the BLS does, changes from car resizing to comply with fuel economy standards. Both current dollar and constant 1980 dollar estimates are presented.

Safety   The effects of safety regulations are somewhat difficult to determine. Peltzman, for example, provides evidence that increased negligence is one driver response to improved safety in vehicles that produces negligible changes in automobile safety.[19] Other evidence associated with the combined emission, safety, and fuel economy regulations implies that overall safety will likely deteriorate, because fatalities and injuries increase when occupants ride in smaller cars that are less able to absorb the shock of collision. However, the only way automobile manufacturers have found to satisfy all the regulations simultaneously is to significantly reduce the size of automobiles. Howard Bunch has estimated that the number of fatalities and injuries will increase by approximately 6 percent by 1995 when compared to the accident rate implied in the 1975 fleet mix.[20] Other researchers have estimated that the risk of death and serious injury will increase by approximately 25 percent as a direct result of the reduction in the average weight of passenger vehicles between 1977 and 1985.[21]

[18] *United States v. Interstate Commerce Commission*, 396 U.S. 491 (1970).

[19] Sam Peltzman, "The Regulation of Automobile Safety," in Henry G. Manne and Roger L. Miller, eds., *Auto Safety Regulations: The Cure or the Problem?* (New Jersey: Thomas Horton, 1976), pp. 1–52.

[20] Howard M. Bunch, "The Small Car May Be Dangerous to Your Health: The Consequences of Downsizing" (Ph.D. dissertation, Harvard Business School, 1978).

[21] Lawrence Goldsmutz, "The Public Interest in Auto Fuel Economy" (Paper, Economics and Science Planning, Inc., 1978).

TABLE 20-7

NEW MODEL PRICE INCREASES FROM MANDATED REGULATIONS EXCLUDING
CHANGES FROM CAR RESIZING
(1968–1980 Model Years)

Model year	Safety	Emissions*	Other	Total* Current dollars	Total* Constant 1980 dollars†
1968	$11.51	$16.00		$27.51	$65.45
69	25.45			25.45	57.46
70	4.35	5.50	$7.85‡	17.70	37.73
1971		19.00		19.00	38.83
72	22.25	7.00		29.25	57.87
73	91.60			91.60	170.61
74	107.60	1.40		109.00	182.95
75	10.70	119.20		129.90	199.77
1976	13.40	7.60		21.00	30.53
77	6.95	14.30	37.90§	59.15	80.79
78		9.99	40.13§	50.12	63.59
79	5.75	12.10	28.50§	46.35	52.78
80	13.29	118.04	110.18§	241.51	241.51
Total					$1,279.85

*Excludes amounts for resizing automobiles to meet fuel economy standards.

†Based on consumer price index (urban wage earners and clerical workers) for 1980 as projected by the Carter Administration at the end of March 1980.

‡Theft protection.

§Engine and chassis changes for fuel economy and corrosion protection.

Sources: Bureau of Labor Statistics (1968–73) and (1974–80); Joint Economic Committee, Subcommittee on Economic Growth and Stabilization, 95th Cong., 2nd Sess., *The Costs of Government Regulation of Business* (Committee Print, 1978).

Energy Consumption   Although reducing gasoline consumption over the life of the vehicle creates a savings to individuals from the higher fuel economy standards, these savings have a cost. Comparing the present value of gasoline savings with the cost estimates of research and development expenditures and with the costs of acquiring property, plant equipment, and special dies necessary for downsizing, reveals that the costs far exceed the savings for reduced gasoline consumption. For example, if we assume that the real price of gasoline in December 1979 is increased by 3 percent each year, the total costs of the mandated safety emissions and fuel economy standards will offset the savings in gasoline by more than $300 when reduced to present values over the life of the car.[22]

Impact on Automobile Firms   The cost of complying with the mandated regulations per year from 1978 through 1985 are approximately $800 million for

---

[22] For details see Kenneth W. Clarkson, Charles W. Kadlec, and Arthur B. Laffer, *The Impact of Government Regulations on Competition in the U.S. Automobile Industry* (Boston: H. C. Wainwright, May 1979).

Chrysler, $1,000 million for Ford, and $2,000 million for General Motors. As Table 20-8 shows, for each car this compliance costs approximately $550 for Chrysler, $340 for Ford, and $345 for General Motors. Assuming that total revenues do not change for each firm and there is no increase in the variable costs of manufacturing, one can estimate impact of the regulations on the rates of return for Chrysler, Ford, and General Motors. In Figure 20-2 economic rates of return are calculated for the period 1970–1977 and then recalculated assuming impacts of regulations for the period of 1978–1985.[23]

Shipping Household Goods

The movement of household goods from one state to another is subject to regulations of the Interstate Commerce Commission. In most states a public service commission or its equivalent regulates intrastate movement of household goods. There are exceptions, however, and Maryland is one of the largest geographic areas whose market for the movement of household goods within the state is unregulated. In the early 1970s, approximately 175 firms participated in the movement of household goods to various locations within the state of Maryland. These include firms whose sole service was intrastate, firms that

---

[23] For details on the difference between economic and accounting rates of return, see pages 97–103.

TABLE 20-8
SALES, PROFITS, AND ESTIMATED REGULATION-MANDATED
COSTS FOR THE BIG THREE AUTO MANUFACTURERS

	Chrysler	**Ford**	**General Motors**
Cost of regulation (millions)*	$800	$1,000	$2,000
Cost as percent of sales	7.0	4.2	4.6
Cost as percent of aftertax profits	496.9	112.7	68.5
Cost per car produced	$550	$340	$345
Net sales (millions)†	$11,390	$23,969	$43,430
Aftertax profits (millions)†	$161	$887	$2,918
Number of cars produced (thousands)†	1,451	2,933	5,782

*Average for 1978–85
†Figures are for 1977 North American operations.

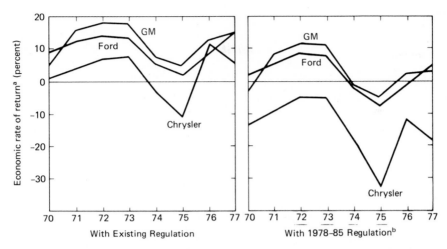

^aEconomic rates of return were calculated from Securities and Exchange Commission 10-K data for the firm's world-wide operations, using the procedure detailed in Kenneth W. Clarkson, *Intangible Capital and Rates of Return* (American Enterprise Institute, 1977).

^bAdjusted to include estimated regulation-induced costs of $800 million a year for Chrysler, $1 billion for Ford, and $2 billion for General Motors.

FIGURE 20-2
The effects of regulation on economic rates of return for major automobile producers, 1970–1977. In the left panel, economic rates of return with then-existing regulation are given for General Motors, Ford, and Chrysler. The right panel shows what the rates of return would have been with 1978–85 regulation.

also served as agents for the large interstate carriers, and firms that held interstate ICC authorizations.

Moving rates for intrastate service are established by each company, while the rates charged by ICC-regulated carriers in interstate service are the result of legalized collusion. Breen's study of the Maryland market showed that interstate rates ranged from one-third to two-thirds higher than intrastate rates for the same weight-and-distance move.[24] These differences were computed for a 7,000-pound shipment for a distance of 125 miles. In Table 20-9 the rates from Baltimore and Maryland suburbs of Washington, D.C., to Cumberland are shown both for all movers and for interstate movers only. Breen estimates that the cost of moving is likely to exceed $240 million more each year as a result of ICC regulations than it would without them.

Communications

The FCC, established in 1934, grants only a limited number of licenses. Each recipient has the right to utilize only a particular portion of the radio spectrum. Once obtained, the license for most recipients can be held in perpetuity unless

[24] See Denis A. Breen, "Regulation and Household Moving Costs," *Regulation* (Sept./Oct. 1978), pp. 51–54.

TABLE 20-9
INTRASTATE AND INTERSTATE MOVING COSTS FOR 7,000-POUND
125-MILE SHIPMENT

	Intrastate rates* (averages)	Interstate rates	Difference
All movers			
From Baltimore—			
September 1973	$319	$461	+44.5%
March 1974	382	533	+39.5
From Maryland suburbs of Washington, D.C.—			
September 1973	351	552	+57.3
March 1974	381	637	+67.2
Interstate movers only			
From Baltimore—			
September 1973	$325	$461	+41.8
March 1974	421	533	+26.6
From Maryland suburbs of Washington, D.C.—			
September 1973	395	552	+39.7
March 1974	468	637	+36.1

at renewal, the FCC or intervenors can show that such renewal will lead to deleterious results. In effect, then, licenses have been a semipermanent monopoly grant. The opening up of markets for cable television and pay television has seriously weakened the monopoly position of the three major networks.

Consumer Products

Ultimately consumer products are subject to a large number of regulations, since virtually every regulation has its final impact on the price of the commodity on the market. Some regulations, however, are more direct. The Consumer Product Safety Commission (CPSC) has jurisdiction over more than 10,000 products. The agency has been given the authority to establish mandatory safety standards, to require warnings by manufacturers, to require producers to give rebates to consumers, and to ban or recall products without a court hearing. In addition, it can impose criminal penalties so that executives in violating firms may face jail sentences.[25]

During its first three years of operation, the Consumer Product Safety Commission promulgated regulations for over 80 products. Linneman has found in his study of the 1973 Mattress Flammability Standard that consumer safety was increased by an amount somewhere between $1 million to $106 million, depend-

---

[25] Consumer Product Safety Act, Public Law 92-573 (1972).

ing upon the parametric assumptions chosen.[26] Estimated costs of complying with the standard range from $5 million to $66 million. The study also revealed that the flammability standard created significant wealth redistributions from small producers to large ones, and further evidence suggests noticeable income transfers from more careful to less careful consumers.

Health and Safety

In 1970 the Congress created the Occupational Safety and Health Administration (OSHA). OSHA has been one of the more severely criticized regulatory agencies, a consequence partially of its hurried initial promulgation of rules, overlapping levels of regulation, and lack of any single overriding criterion for evaluating its rules. For example, in the initial promulgation of a rule OSHA often deleted references to circumstances where the standard would be applied. This led to the creation of rules that, though appropriate in limited situations, were applied to all situations. For example, when OSHA rule makers neglected to describe the circumstances surrounding the prohibition of using pond ice in drinks for workers who were cutting ice in ponds, the stated general rule, if enforced, would have prohibited *all* employees from putting ice in drinking water. Thus, a reasonable rule that would have reduced the possibility of contaminated pond ice being consumed by ice cutters became an unreasonable rule.

The separate levels of regulation also contribute to OSHA's difficulties. For example, one level is a general duty clause that requires employers to provide a work place which is "free from recognized hazards that are causing or are likely to cause death or serious physical harm" to employees.[27] The next level of regulation is also general but applies to a specific category of situations such as protective shields for machines.[28] The third level is more rigid and mandates particular performance requirements for individual machines or work situations. The fourth and most complex level involves detailed specifications involving, for example, the exact distances between moving parts of machines and shields, the number of fasteners involved, and other technical input specifications.

When these regulations are superimposed on each other, they often create new hazards while eliminating an old one. For example, a work rest intended to help support a tool must be placed one-eighth of an inch from a grinding wheel. However, when large objects are being ground, a work rest close to the wheel may interfere with proper operation and actually decrease safety. In such cases an adjustable work rest would be an improvement, yet OSHA has condemned thousands of violations of the one-eighth-of-an-inch rule.

---

[26] Peter Linneman, "A Case Study of the Impacts of Consumer Safety Standards: In the 1973 Mattress Flammability Standard," (Working paper, University of Chicago, Center for Study of the Economy and the State, 1979).

[27] Public Law 92-573, section 5.

[28] See, for example, *Code of Federal Regulations*, vol. 29, section 1910.212(a).

A Brighter Future?   In 1978 a circuit court in *American Petroleum Institute* found invalid the OSHA regulation that limited Benzene exposure in the work place.[29] OSHA had promulgated regulations reducing the permissible exposure by 90 percent from the 1971 standard. In 1977 these regulations were based primarily on the results of a number of studies that showed an increased risk of leukemia in workers who had been exposed to Benzene levels in excess of 100 times the permissible levels.[30] The 1978 court of appeals interpreted the "reasonably necessary" language of the Occupational Safety and Health Act to include an estimate of the expected costs of compliance, as well as the benefits of the regulation "in order to determine whether the benefits bear a reasonable relationship to the standard's demonstrably high costs."[31]

Airline Safety   The Federal Aviation Administration is responsible for establishing and enforcing regulations governing the safety of airlines, including airport procedures, facilities and equipment, and traffic control, as well as other air service operations. The FAA has published violations in "Air Carrier Enforcement History, Jan. 1974–Jan. 1979." In Table 20-10 we reproduce total violations for the 1974–1978 period as well as results adjusted for revenue passenger miles. An examination of this table reveals significant differences in safety across airlines as measured by FAA violations.

Industrial Production

In addition to health and safety, government regulations may also specify the type of process, inventories, or other factors that affect the production of goods and services. For example, the Energy Policy and Conservation Act of 1975 specified that oil refineries must establish certain stockpiles of crude oil suitable for use in emergency situations. In other cases the actual production process is often subject to regulations. For example, the Food and Drug Administration requires that all storage facilities used in the production of pharmaceutical products, including refrigerators, maintain at least two-feet clearance between walls and stored items. In addition, various production processes must be isolated from one another by walls with double doors. These regulations all have obvious compliance costs that seem not to have been considered at the time they were promulgated.

Employment

A number of regulations govern the salary that employers may pay employees, as well as hiring practices, pensions, and other conditions of employment. In

---

[29] *The American Petroleum Institute v. Occupational Safety and Health Administration*, 581 F.2d 493 (1978).

[30] Ibid., pp. 498–499, and footnote 13.

[31] Ibid., pp. 504–505. OSHA appealed to the Supreme Court and the lower-court holding was affirmed, 100 S. Ct. 2844 (1980).

TABLE 20-10
AIRLINE SAFETY RULE VIOLATIONS

Airline	FAA violation reports (1974–78)	1978 revenue passenger miles (RPM billions)	Reports per billion RPM
1. National	19	7.90	2.41
2. United	109	41.44	2.63
2. Continental	29	8.77	3.31
4. TWA	106	28.21	3.76
5. Pan Am	90	23.66	3.80
6. Delta	90	23.50	3.83
7. Eastern	109	25.23	4.32
8. Western	46	10.63	4.33
9. American	171	29.41	5.82
10. Braniff	60	9.43	6.36
11. Northwest	57	7.22	7.90
12. Alaska	7	0.80	8.76
13. Air West	24	2.72	8.82
14. Allegheny	52	4.24	12.26
15. Air California	12	0.81	14.76
16. Southern	23	1.44	15.98
17. Aloha	6	0.36	16.48
18. Frontier	43	2.38	18.05
19. Ozark	34	1.64	20.80
20. PSA	52	2.50	20.84
21. Southwest	27	1.05	25.74
22. Texas International	51	1.69	30.21
23. Piedmont	45	1.47	30.63
24. Air Florida	6	0.18	33.15
25. North Central	84	1.92	43.64
26. Hawaiian	25	0.48	51.87
27. Wien Air Alaska	30	0.24	125.00
28. Air New England	28	0.07	388.89

Source: "Which Airlines Violate Safety Rules," Reason (December 1979), p. 16.

most industries employers are constrained to pay a minimum wage specified by Congress in the Fair Labor Standards Act. In 1980 the minimum wage was $3.36 per hour. The act prohibits the employment of children under the age of 14 years. Employers must make a number of mandatory payments on behalf of the employee, including payments to Social Security for retirement (OASI), disability income (DI), unemployment compensation funds, and workmen's compensation (for work-related accidents).

A number of additional regulations also govern hiring, promotion, and labor-management dispute procedures. For example, employers cannot discriminate against individuals because of age, race, sex, color, national origin, or religious beliefs. Since 1964, under Title 7 of the Civil Rights Act the courts have increasingly defined the limits of employment discrimination.

Innovation

A large number of federal regulations indirectly affect investment and innovation. In some industries, however, the regulations are more closely applied to innovative actions such as the research and developmental process. For example, the 1962 Kefauver-Harris amendments to the Food, Drug, and Cosmetic Act effectively eliminated the time constraint of the Food and Drug Administration in denying approval of a new drug application. After 1962 the FDA could withhold the drug from the market indefinitely until the agency was satisfied the drug was both safe and effective for its intended use. As a consequence, the average approval time for new drugs has gone from six months to more than six years.

Energy

As noted earlier in this chapter, energy is regulated by a large number of independent agencies, each of which promulgates numerous rules and regulations. More important, numerous studies have shown that these organizations have been extremely effective in altering economic activity in energy and related industries. For example, the Federal Power Commission (FPC) has regulated the price of natural gas for many years. The FPC uses a geographic area rate-regulation procedure that is based on average regional accounting costs for establishing maximum prices. Initial price ceilings were set close to market prices in the 1960s so there was little or no immediate effect from the regulation. In its determination to hold the line against increases in natural gas prices throughout the 1960s, the Federal Power Commission failed to increase regional maximum prices to reflect real increases in demand and inflationary pressures. As a consequence, shortages appeared and in some cases represented extreme problems by the 1970s.[32]

THE REGULATION OF PUBLIC UTILITIES

Public utilities have attained a position known as a natural monopoly. In other words, it is commonly thought that due to economies of scale, public utilities are most effective as the sole distributor of their commodities in their individual regions. Consequently, they are allowed to operate in their respective regions free from any antitrust action. However, given this monopoly power, they have the ability to capture monopoly profits. It is for this reason that public utilities are monitored and controlled by government agencies. Most of the regulation imposed by these agencies takes the form of rate-of-return regulation. By setting rates of return, the government agencies attempt to lower the price that would otherwise be set by these natural monopolies, and thereby increase output as well.

---

[32] Paul MacAvoy, "The Regulation Induced Shortage of Natural Gas," *Journal of Law and Economics*, vol. 14 (April 1971), pp. 167–200.

Scope of Regulation

Because of the specific regulatory nature of public utilities, local and state governments have various provisions regulating electric power services, water services, natural gas, and phone service. In addition to setting the maximum rates that utilities can charge, regulatory commissions have instituted requirements to serve new customers. Such commissions may even prohibit individuals from purchasing private or additional services. For example, in Santa Barbara, California, the local government placed a moratorium on new construction by prohibiting water and sewer hookups for new homes.

We'll look at several types of regulation of public utilities.

Cost-of-Service Regulation

One type of regulation involves a regulatory commission attempting to ascertain what the cost of service is for the provision of some commodity, say, electricity. Cost-of-service regulation requires detailed knowledge of the costs of production and of distribution of the commodity in question. Moreover, in many instances cost-of-service regulation requires that common costs be allocated to specific products. For example, the U.S. Postal Service has a truck that it uses to haul first-, second-, and third-class mail to various addresses. The cost of the truck constitutes a common cost for mail delivery. In what way can such a common cost be allocated? As we have seen earlier, there is no way other than arbitrarily. Thus, cost-of-service regulation faces the problem of arbitrarily allocating common costs.[33]

Moreover, cost-of-service regulation has to grapple with the problem of distinguishing between historical costs and opportunity costs. This distinction is particularly relevant in the inflationary setting of the last decade. The historical cost of a steam generator may be very much lower than its opportunity cost because of inflation. Price based on this lower historical cost will not cover current opportunity costs.

Additionally, prices based on all costs rolled in together ignore the long-run marginal cost that may be many times greater than current average cost. Again, this distinction is particularly true in an inflationary setting. An electric utility that must expand in order to satisfy the demand at the current regulated price may have to incur costs that are many times greater than what it had to pay in the past for capital equipment. This is due in part to inflation and also in part to increased pollution-abatement equipment that must be purchased along with the "productive" capital equipment. In some instances, it has been shown that the long-run marginal cost of electricity is 5 to 10 times the price charged for it. If electricity consumers are not charged a price that reflects true, long-run marginal costs of providing additional generations of that type of energy, then the quantity demanded by consumers will be greater than it would be other-

---

[33] See Alfred Marshall, *Principles of Economics*, 8th ed., book 5, chap. 6, and mathematical appendix (New York: Macmillan, 1954).

wise. Thus, not allowing electrical utilities to "pass on" increased costs of expanding output leads to consumers *not* being faced with the true social opportunity cost of the electricity that they use. This causes an economically inefficient use of resources and potential problems with excess quantities of electricity demanded at regulated prices.

Rate-of-Return Regulation

Rate-of-return regulation involves a public utility commission, or some other commission, that establishes a price which allows a "fair" rate of return on investors' equity in the regulated industry. Presumably, rate-of-return regulation prevents the monopoly, whether it be an electrical utility or telephone company, from reaping monopoly profits. In the simplest model of regulatory process, the company in question produces one output and uses two inputs, labor and capital, each of which is available in unlimited quantities at market-determined prices. The decisions of the firm are affected by regulation in only one way. No more than some fixed percentage of the value of its capital is allowed to be earned in any year. This fixed percentage is the fair rate of return computed on its so-called rate base, which is its capital stock. In the simplest of regulatory models, the management of the regulated firm is allowed to pursue its objective of maximizing profits exactly as it would in the absence of regulation, except for the establishment of prices. And for the model to make any sense, the fair rate of return and, therefore, the product price allowed by the regulatory agency are less than the rate of return that would be earned without constraints. In equation form, the regulated firm maximizes total profits subject to a regulatory constraint, or it maximizes

$$\text{Profit} = Pq - wL - rK \tag{20-1}$$

where P = output price
$\quad q$ = output
$\quad L$ = labor
$\quad w$ = wage rate
$\quad K$ = capital stock
$\quad r$ = unit cost of capital (implicit rental rate/unit)

subject to

$$\frac{Pq - wL}{K} \leq z \tag{20-2}$$

where $z = r + v$ = rate of return allowed by regulation and above the
$\qquad\qquad$ unit cost of capital with $v \geq 0$

The regulated firm is allowed to have a rate of return at least equal to the implicit rental value of the capital stock. The rate of return may be greater than r and depends on what v is. The regulators decide on v and hence on z. Presumably, z is less than the profit-maximizing rate of return since the regulators do not want to allow monopoly profits.

We know that the way in which the profit-maximizing firm will act in a constrained situation will be different from its action in an unconstrained situation. Employing the simplified assumptions of the model above, it can be shown that the firm will overinvest in capital.

The Averch-Johnson Effect

In their 1962 seminal paper, Averch and Johnson presented the thesis that regulation biases firms toward developing and using more capital-intensive production processes than they would in the absence of regulation. This capital-intensive bias has been called the Averch-Johnson effect. The overinvestment occurs because when the allowed rate of return on investment is fixed at z and is less than the profit-maximizing rate, the regulated companies will have an incentive to overinvest. The objective is to maximize total profits. If the rate of profit that can be earned on an investment is fixed, then why not increase capital investment to get higher absolute profits? The ratio of capital to labor in regulated industries is going to be higher than it would be without regulation at the chosen output level. This expansion of the rate base is inefficient.[34]

Problems with Regulation

Even in principle regulation is not seen as an easy job. In reality, it has proven to be extremely complicated. Below we'll examine a few of the problems associated with regulation.

Quality of Service   For regulation to be effective, the price per constant-quality unit must be regulated. If only the nominal price per nominal-quality unit is regulated, then a change in the quality of the commodity in question will alter the *real* price. So long as regulators are unable to regulate the quality of the commodity sold, the difficulty of effective regulation becomes relatively greater.

Consider regulating the price of a constant-quality unit of telephone service. Look at the many facets of the quality of this service. Getting a dial tone, hearing other voices clearly, getting the operator to answer quickly, having out-of-order telephones repaired rapidly, and putting through a long-distance call quickly are some of those facets. Regulation of the telephone company

---

[34] When the model becomes more complicated, however, it is not clear that the A-J effect works the way it is supposed to work. See, for example, William J. Baumol and Alvin K. Klevorick, "Input Choices and Rate-of-Return Regulation: An Overview of the Discussion," *Bell Journal of Economics and Management Science*, vol. 1 (Autumn 1970), pp. 162–190.

usually deals with the prices charged for telephone service. Regulators are concerned with the quality of service, but they can regulate only some of the dimensions of quality. If the telephone company wants to raise the price per constant-quality unit and the regulatory agency refuses a nominal price increase, the phone company can cut down on the quality of the service and thereby implicitly raise the price per constant-quality unit. In many areas of the country, telephone companies are not allowed to charge a significantly higher service price to out-of-the-way rural areas than the price charged for service to dense urban areas. In order to raise the price per constant-quality unit in the rural areas, telephone companies lower the quality of the service. In some rural communities, it may take months or even years before a private line can be obtained; in the city, obtaining a private line is easy. Obviously, if all parties are charged a fee of $20 a month for phone service, whether or not they have a private line, it is better to have your private line than to have three other people sharing your party line. You have to wait to call if someone else has engaged your party line; you're constantly interrupted by others lifting up their phones in order to make calls when you are on the line; and in some cases, each party's special ring is audible on your phone.

Pricing Policies and "Excess" Profits Regulatory commissions are presumably in the business of preventing higher-than-fair rates of return. It is not surprising, therefore, that regulatory agencies are reluctant to allow long-run marginal cost pricing or peak-load pricing. The former often results in higher-than-fair profits if long-run marginal costs exceed average costs by a great amount. LMC does exceed SAC for electricity in many areas of the country because of the increased costs of building plants, adding pollution equipment, and financing capital expenditures. Prices based on average costs, therefore, are much lower than prices based on long-run marginal costs. A regulatory agency presumably does not like the idea of allowing a firm to charge long-run marginal costs, even if that is the most efficient pricing solution, because excess profits may result.

Peak-load pricing involves the same problem. There are peaks in the demand for electricity during different times of the day and different times of the year, and storage is too costly. Regulatory agencies have been reluctant to require, or to allow when requested, electrical utilities to charge higher rates for peak-load times than for non-peak-load times. If higher rates were charged for peak-load times, electrical utilities would again find themselves with excess profits, and this would presumably serve as an embarrassment to the regulatory commissioners. Even though peak-load pricing leads to an allocation of scarce resources in such a way that requires those who purchase the scarce resources to pay the full social opportunity cost, we have seen very little peak-load pricing in regulated industries. The Environmental Defense Fund (EDF) developed the arguments and the records that led to an order by the Wisconsin Public Service Commission in 1974 to the Madison Gas & Electric Company to inaugurate a system for peak-load pricing. Higher rates were set for summer months when air conditioning puts greater stress on the system. In addition to calling for a winter-summer price differential, the company was directed to differentiate between daytime and nighttime rates for large industrial users. However, it seemed that the cost of metering was too high to institute a time-of-day pricing system for all users.

In 1975 an experiment was started in the state of Vermont by the Central Vermont Public Service Corporation. From 8 A.M. to 11 A.M. and from 5 P.M. to 9 P.M., the families in the experiment were charged a higher rate for electricity; the rest of the day they were charged a lower rate. Some families started running the dishwasher and cooking their dinners before 5 P.M. Others did their laundry before 8 A.M. in order to save on electrical bills.

Regulation and Technological Change

Some investigators claim that regulation has had an adverse effect on technological change in some industries studied. This view does not square with other empirical studies, which show that regulated industries have enjoyed long-term productivity increases above the national average. Theoretically it has already been shown in the discussion on the Averch-Johnson effect that regulated firms may actually have an incentive to expend resources on research and development based on the manner in which rates are set. Additionally, there may be another reason for regulated firms to search for new technological innovations. Regulatory agencies typically review a firm's rate of return only periodically. As a result, there is a lag period between times when the price is established, pursuant of course, to a set rate of return. Until the next determination of price, the management of the firm is free to operate in relative freedom, meaning that they may earn profits above the regulatory agency's mandated rate of return. In other words, although price is set outside the firm, there are incentives to improve efficiency because the above-authorized returns may be captured.

Retroactive Rate Making   Recent developments, however, have limited this occurrence. Lately, regulatory commissions have been implementing retroactive rate-making procedures that effectively reduce or eliminate the regulatory lag. Prices are based not only on costs, revenue, and rate of return, but also take into consideration excess profits received over and above the set rate of return. These profits are returned to the consumer in the form of reduced prices. The effect, however, is to reduce incentives for research and development because of the elimination of the regulatory lag. Additional effects of retroactive rate making that may be expected are larger costs involved in rate making, reduced product quality, and a transfer of the role of monitoring managerial activities from investors to the regulatory agency.

Property Rights and Public Utilities

Economic theory has traditionally incorporated certain assumptions that eliminated constitutional constraints in studies on resource allocation. It has been assumed that resources are allocated, held, and exchanged at zero information and transaction (negotiating, contracting, and policing) costs. This method was eventually criticized due to the fact that differences in information and transaction costs as perceived by managers and decision makers may result in differing firm or managerial behavior. By considering property rights as concepts associated with the firms or institutions involved, predictions may be made regarding the behavior in those firms and institutions.[35]

In considering the economics of property rights, it is assumed that every decision maker maximizes his or her own utility. For further prediction it is necessary to identify the goods in the manager's utility function and to specify any change of circumstances that affects the relative scarcity of these goods. Although a hired manager is expected to maximize utility in the acquisition of inputs, it is assumed that he or she will react less frequently to changes in input prices than will managers who have a proprietary interest in the firm.

Differences in property rights associated with a firm will result in differences in its operation. Decision makers will be presented with a set of costs and rewards associated with the property rights which characterize the individual firm. In turn, these costs and rewards obviously affect the decisions of management. For example, in an owner-operated firm the management of the firm is rewarded for proper decisions and assessed the costs of production. Decisions will be directly related to the proximity of ownership to management. Prices, risks, and accounting procedures will be done with a perspective of ownership. The fact that owners are in management control may mean lower transaction and information costs because the welfare of the owner is directly associated with management decisions.

A public utility may assume one of two forms of property rights. It may be regulated but privately owned, or it may be wholly government owned. The property rights aspects of these two structural forms provide considerable insight into the management functions of public utilities.

Because public utilities are considered natural monopolies, they are basically given a monopoly grant in their individual territories. They would be able to capture monopoly profits but for the intervention of the government, which establishes prices for the utilities based on the utilities' costs and revenues and the allowed rate of return. This structural form implies a constraint on profits and a reduction in the control held by owners. This loss of control also implies that managers may have increased discretionary opportunities to increase their own pecuniary and nonpecuniary sources of utility.[36] In contrast, govern-

---

[35] See Armen A. Alchian, "The Basis of Some Recent Advances in the Theory of Management of the Firm," *Journal of Industrial Economics*, vol. 14 (November 1965), pp. 30–41; Alchian, "Some Economics of Property Rights," *Il Politico*, vol. 32 (December 1965), pp. 816–829; Ronald H. Coase, "The Problem of Social Cost," *Journal of Law and Economics*, vol. 3 (October 1960), pp. 1–44; Harold Demsetz, "The Exchange and Enforcement of Property Rights," *Journal of Law and Economics*, vol. 7 (October 1964), pp. 11–26; and Louis De Alessi, "Private Ownership and Limits to Retroactive Ratemaking," LEC Working Paper, Law and Economics Center, University of Miami, June 1981.

[36] Louis De Alessi, "An Economic Analysis of Government Ownership and Regulation: Theory and the Evidence from the Electric Power Industry," *Public Choice*, vol. 19 (Fall 1974), pp. 1–42.

ment-owned public utilities also have a constraint on profits but have considerably less owner control. Owner control is effectively nonexistent because there is no transferability of ownership control (owners must move out of the voting district to change ownership).

Several comments can now be made on the operation of regulated privately owned and government-owned public utilities based on property rights inherent in each. First, wealth can be increased by investment in more capital if the regulated privately owned organization's set rate of return is above the opportunity cost of any capital.[37] Second, because ownership in government-owned public utilities is removed from managerial functions, there will be less incentive to seek a wealth-maximizing rate structure. Managers may set prices according to simple rate structures at levels below those that would provide profit maximization.[38] Third, there would probably be increased risk aversion under both sets of property rights due to the fact that errors of commission are more noticeable than errors of omission. Finally, earnings are probably the lowest in government-owned public utilities due to lack of the monitoring that occurs in privately owned, government-regulated firms.

ESTIMATING REGULATORY COSTS

In 1977 the Business Roundtable conducted a study of 48 of its members to estimate the cost of regulation by the Environmental Protection Agency, the Occupational and Health Administration, the Department of Energy, and the Federal Trade Commission. In addition the costs of complying with the Employment Retirement Income Security Act and Equal Employment Opportunity programs were included.[39] Each firm was asked to estimate the costs of actions that they would have taken in the absence of regulations from these agencies and programs, thus estimating the costs associated with responding to all other forces such as interest group pressures, changes in market conditions, and other nonregulatory factors.

Estimation of Incremental Costs The actual calculations of the costs of regulatory compliance were prepared by identifying actions that the company would not have taken in the absence of the regulation and estimating their associated costs. Next the firm determined what actions would otherwise have been taken and estimated their associated costs. Incremental cost of the regulatory action was calculated by the difference between the costs of the actions taken to comply with the regulation less costs of the alternative nonregulatory actions. For example, suppose a firm was required to install an air pollution system to remove 98 percent of the pollutants subject to federal regulations.

[37] William J. Baumol and Alvin K. Klevorick, "Input Choices and Rate-of-Return Regulation."

[38] Sam Peltzman, "Pricing in Public and Private Enterprises: Electric Utilities in the United States," *Journal of Law and Economics*, vol. 14 (April 1971), pp. 109–147.

[39] The 48 companies that participated in the study represented more than 20 industries and accounted for 8 percent of U.S. industry sales, 5 percent of civilian nonagricultural employment, and approximately 19 percent of private sector expenditures of plant and equipment.

Suppose that in the absence of the regulations the firm would have installed equipment that would have removed 90 percent of the pollutants. If the first action would cost $2 million and the alternative, $1 million, the incremental cost would be $1 million. Table 20-11 shows the costs incurred for the 48 companies in 1977. The total of $2.6 billion represents the regulatory costs for these companies and is equivalent to approximately 43 percent of research and development expenditures, 10 percent of total capital expenditures, and roughly 16 percent of aftertax profits for 1977.

REGULATORY REFORMS

In recent years recognition of the broad discretionary powers given to administrative agencies has grown. In response Congress and the administration have attempted to impose new constraints on agencies as a means of limiting the number of ineffective or potentially harmful rules. In 1973, for example, Congress held hearings focusing solely on the burden of federal paperwork. Table 20-12 describes the compliance forms for a typical firm subject to governmental regulations. In late 1974 President Ford established through executive order a requirement that each agency prepare an inflation impact statement in order to provide each "relevant agency with analyses of the inflation implications of specific government regulation and legislative actions." Four years later, in 1978, the president issued an order requiring agencies to determine the possible economic impacts of regulations that have substantial economic effects. The order required agencies that wished to promulgate rules which would have major consequences to prepare a clear statement of problems requiring action, to analyze the economic consequences of the proposed regulation, and to offer alternative solutions to the problem. In 1981, more stringent controls were placed on many regulatory actions by President Reagan's executive order requiring certain federal agencies to choose the most cost-effective options in seeking regulatory goals.

TABLE 20-11
INCREMENTAL COSTS
(millions of dollars)

Area	Operating & admin.	Capital	Product	R&D	Total
EPA	623	765	555	75	2,018
EEO	209	8	—	—	217
OSHA	103	68	2	11	184
DOE	70	28	10	8	116
ERISA	61	—	—	—	61
FTC	23	1	—	2	26
Total	1,089	870	567	96	2,622

Source: Michael Simon, "What We Did," *Regulation* (July/Aug. 1979), p. 21.

TABLE 20-12
GOVERNMENT FORMS REQUIRED OF GRAYMILLS CORPORATION

Agency	Form or subdivision	Form number	Time to fill out form
Federal			
Department of Commerce	Census of Manufacturers	MC-35M	8.0 hours
Office of Equal Employment Opportunity	Employer Information Report EEO-I	265-41	0.5
Federal Trade Commission	Division of Financial Statistics	MG-1	0.8
Department of Labor	Log of Occupational Injuries and Illnesses	100	1.0
Department of Labor	Supplementary Record of Occupational Injuries and Illnesses	101	0.5
Department of Labor	Summary—Occupational Injuries and Illnesses	102	1.0
Department of Labor	Wage Developments in Manufacturing	BLS 2675b	0.5
Department of Labor	Employee Welfare or Pension Benefit Plan Description	D1	1.0
Department of Labor	Employee Welfare or Pension Benefit Plan Description Amendment	D-1A	1.0
Department of Labor	Employee Welfare or Pension Benefit Plan Annual Report	D-2	8.0
Department of Labor	Information on Employee Welfare or Pension Benefit Plan Covering Fewer than 100 Participants	D-3	—[a]
Department of the Treasury	Federal Tax Deposits—Withheld Income and FICA Taxes	501	104.0
Department of the Treasury	Unemployment Taxes	508	12.0
Department of the Treasury	Employer's Annual Federal Unemployment Tax Return	940	3.0
Department of the Treasury	Employee's Withholding Exemption Certificate	W-4	—[b]
Department of the Treasury	Reconciliation of Income Tax Withheld from Wages	W-3	24.0
Department of the Treasury	Report of Wages Payable under the Federal Insurance Contributions Act	941a	64.0
Department of the Treasury	Return of Employee's Trust Exempt from Tax	990-P	1.0
Department of the Treasury	U.S. Information Return for the Calendar Year 1971	1099	3.0

[a] Not available.
[b] 5 minutes per form.

TABLE 20-12 *(continued)*

Agency	Form or subdivision	Form number	Time to fill out form
State of Illinois			
Industrial Commission	Application for Adjustment of Claim—Notice of Disputed Claims and Memorandum of Names and Addresses	None	—c
Industrial Commission	Employer's Report of Compensable Injury	None	—c
Industrial Commission	Memorandum of Names and Addresses for Service of Notices	None	—c
Industrial Commission	Notice of Filing Claim	77	—c
Employment Service	DOL-BES Form	None	—d
Division of Unemployment Compensation	Notice of Possible Ineligibility	UC (Ill.) Ben-22	—e
Division of Unemployment Compensation	Employer's Contribution Report	UC-3D	64.0
Department of Revenue	Retailers' Occupation Tax, Use Tax, County, Municipal Service Occupation and Service Use Tax Return	RR-1A	2.0
Department of Revenue	Employee's Illinois Withholding Exemption Certificate	Il-W-4	—b
Department of Revenue	Monthly State Income Tax Payment Form	Il-501	1.0
Department of Revenue	Application for Renewal of Resale Certificate Number	RR-490H	—f
State of California			
Department of Business Taxes	State, Local, and District Sales and Use Tax Return	BT 401C	2.0
State of New Jersey			
Division of Taxation	Resale Certificate	SF-3	—f
Division of Taxation	Blanket Exemption Certificate	1786 AC	—f
City of Chicago			
Commission on Human Relations	Contractor Employment Practices Report	None	1.0
Metropolitan Sanitary District	Industrial Waste Surcharge Certified Statement	FI-235	2.0
Metropolitan Sanitary District	Report of Exemption Claim or Estimate of Liability for Surcharge	FI-236	1.0
Metropolitan Sanitary District	Computation of Initial Estimate of Liability for Surcharge	FI-236A	2.0

TABLE 20-12 *(continued)*

Agency	Form or subdivision	Form number	Time to fill out form
City of Los Angeles			
Department of Building and Safety	Application and Agreement for Testing Electrical Equipment	B&S E-147	1.0
Department of Building and Safety	Application for Approval Labels	B&S R9	1.0

*b*5 minutes per form.
*c*½ hour each.
*d*15 minutes per form.
*e*15 minutes per form.
*f*1 hour each.
Source: U.S. Senate, Hearings, Subcommittee on Government Regulation, *The Federal Paperwork Burden*, 92d Cong., Part 1, pp. 124–128.

Inflation Impact Statement

For two years beginning in March 1975, 61 inflation impact statements were prepared. Fifty-three statements proposed regulations and eight statements proposed legislation. Most analyses were prepared by the U.S. Department of Agriculture, the Environmental Protection Agency, and the Occupational Safety and Health Administration, reflecting in part the importance of those agencies in promulgating new regulations and the commitment of governmental resources to generate analyses.[40]

Public Participation

Another alternative to reforming regulation was to include interested non-government experts and witnesses in the decision-making process. In 1975 the Congress authorized the Federal Trade Commission to compensate individuals for their expenses in participating in rule-making proceedings, provided that the particular interest of these individuals would not otherwise be adequately represented. This participation was thought necessary for a fair determination of the rule-making proceeding, and financial compensation was considered necessary to insure its success.

Subsequently, in 1976 the General Accounting Office ruled that other regulatory agencies had authority to reimburse other individuals for participating in a proceeding. In 1978 a number of bills were passed concerning the compen-

---

[40] Few resources for regulatory analyses have been allocated by agencies such as the Food and Drug Administration. The quality of the analyses varies widely, and in general the estimates of cost are considerably better than those associated with benefits. Overall there appears to be little effect of these analyses on decision making and program alternatives.

sation of participants in rule-making procedures.[41] In late 1979 and early 1980, it became increasingly apparent that agencies were choosing individuals who would generally support agency regulations and that so-called public participation was coming under increasing attack by the Congress.[42]

The Regulatory Calendar

In 1979 the administration began to issue a semiannual regulatory calendar (published in November and May each year), listing federal regulatory activities that have economic impacts estimated to exceed $100 million a year. Independent agencies, such as executive branch agencies and other regulatory commissions, are not required to submit data concerning their projects, however.[43]

The Calendar of Federal Regulations is the first comprehensive and continuously updated catalog of important federal regulations under development. Each entry in the calendar describes:

1 The problem which the agency developing the regulation intends to address

2 The major alternatives that the agency has identified while developing the regulation

3 The benefits and costs that could result from the proposal

4 The sectors affected by the action

5 The major related regulations

6 Any collaboration that occurred while developing the proposal between the issuing agency, other agencies, and state and local governments

7 The estimated timetable for agency action[44]

---

[41] See, for example, S.720 sponsored by Senator Edward Kennedy that would have created a government-wide program for compensating persons participating in all types of regulatory proceedings, including rule making, rate making, licensing, adjudication, and judicial review of agency decisions.

[42] See, for example, Public Law 96-252, Section 12, where the Congress cut public participation funds from the Federal Trade Commission's budget.

[43] Executive branch agencies include Administrative Conference of the United States; Department of Agriculture; Department of Commerce; Department of Energy; Department of Health and Human Services; Department of Education; Department of Housing and Urban Development; Department of the Interior; Department of Justice; Department of Labor; Department of Transportation; Department of the Treasury; Environmental Protection Agency; Equal Employment Opportunity Commission; General Services Administration; National Credit Union Administration; Small Business Administration; United States International Trade Commission; and Veterans Administration. Independent regulatory agencies include Civil Aeronautics Board; Commodity Futures Trading Commission; Consumer Product Safety Commission; Federal Communications Commission; Federal Deposit Insurance Corporation; Federal Election Commission; Federal Energy Regulatory Commission; Federal Home Loan Bank Board; Federal Maritime Commission; Federal Mine Safety and Health Review Commission; Federal Reserve System; Federal Trade Commission; Interstate Commerce Commission; National Labor Relations Board; Nuclear Regulatory Commission; Occupational Safety and Health Review Commission; Postal Rate Commission; and Securities and Exchange Commission.

[44] U.S. Regulatory Council, *Calendar of Federal Regulations*, November 1979 (Washington, D.C.: U.S. Government Printing Office, 1979), p. 2.

The calendar also includes appendices on sector impacts, public participation, publication dates of regulatory agendas, and status of individual regulation proposals.

Regulatory Budget

The recognition that regulation involves extensive costs has stimulated a call for proposals to introduce a regulatory budget.[45] The regulatory budget would operate by establishing an upper boundary on the total costs of regulatory activities in each year. It would also apportion the total sum among the most likely individual regulatory agencies through a process involving the OMB, the administration, and Congress, similar to the existing budgetary process. In most proposals, the regulatory budget would include a report of the total costs of all past, present, and future regulations. Excess costs would require supplemental appropriations.

Lacking control over private expenditure compliance, the regulatory budget will not automatically improve outcomes. Further cost measures without associated estimates of benefits may not be particularly useful. More important, agencies would find that regulations involving less observable costs would become easier to promulgate. These costs often take the form of forgone benefits. For example, many argue that the most important costs of drug regulation originate from the delayed and sometimes absolute prohibition of the introduction of new pharmaceutical products.

SUMMARY

In this chapter we have seen that economic regulation has become an increasingly important constraint on the behavior of industrial decision makers. Early evidence seems to point to the conclusion that many regulations have had unintentionally harmful effects on society in general. In this book we have attempted to provide the reader with a better understanding of both the determinants of industrial organization and the likely consequences of modifying those constraints on industrial organization and operation.

[45] Council of Economic Advisors, *Annual Report*, 1980.

AUTHOR INDEX

COMPANY INDEX

LEGAL CASE INDEX

SUBJECT INDEX